Technologies for Constructing Intelligent Systems 2

Studies in Fuzziness and Soft Computing

Editor-in-chief
Prof. Janusz Kacprzyk
Systems Research Institute
Polish Academy of Sciences
ul. Newelska 6
01-447 Warsaw, Poland
E-mail: kacprzyk@ibspan.waw.pl
http://www.springer.de/cgi-bin/search_book.pl?series=2941

Further volumes of this series can be found at our homepage.

Vol. 68. A. Kandel, M. Last and H. Bunke (Eds.)
Data Mining and Computational Intelligence, 2001
ISBN 3-7908-1371-0

Vol. 69. A. Piegat
Fuzzy Modeling and Control, 2001
ISBN 3-7908-1385-0

Vol. 70. W. Pedrycz (Ed.)
Granular Computing, 2001
ISBN 3-7908-1387-7

Vol. 71. K. Leiviskä (Ed.)
Industrial Applications of Soft Computing, 2001
ISBN 3-7908-1388-5

Vol. 72. M. Mareš
Fuzzy Cooperative Games, 2001
ISBN 3-7908-1392-3

Vol. 73. Y. Yoshida (Ed.)
Dynamical Aspects in Fuzzy Decision, 2001
ISBN 3-7908-1397-4

Vol. 74. H.-N. Teodorescu, L.C. Jain and A. Kandel (Eds.)
Hardware Implementation of Intelligent Systems, 2001
ISBN 3-7908-1399-0

Vol. 75. V. Loia and S. Sessa (Eds.)
Soft Computing Agents, 2001
ISBN 3-7908-1404-0

Vol. 76. D. Ruan, J. Kacprzyk and M. Fedrizzi (Eds.)
Soft Computing for Risk Evaluation and Management, 2001
ISBN 3-7908-1406-7

Vol. 77. W. Liu
Propositional, Probabilistic and Evidential Reasoning, 2001
ISBN 3-7908-1414-8

Vol. 78. U. Seiffert and L.C. Jain (Eds.)
Self-Organizing Neural Networks, 2002
ISBN 3-7908-1417-2

Vol. 79. A. Osyczka
Evolutionary Algorithms for Single and Multicriteria Design Optimization, 2002
ISBN 3-7908-1418-0

Vol. 80. P. Wong, F. Aminzadeh and M. Nikravesh (Eds.)
Soft Computing for Reservoir Characterization and Modeling, 2002
ISBN 3-7908-1421-0

Vol. 81. V. Dimitrov and V. Korotkich (Eds.)
Fuzzy Logic, 2002
ISBN 3-7908-1425-3

Vol. 82. Ch. Carlsson and R. Fullér
Fuzzy Reasoning in Decision Making and Optimization, 2002
ISBN 3-7908-1428-8

Vol. 83. S. Barro and R. Marín (Eds.)
Fuzzy Logic in Medicine, 2002
ISBN 3-7908-1429-6

Vol. 84. L.C. Jain and J. Kacprzyk (Eds.)
New Learning Paradigms in Soft Computing, 2002
ISBN 3-7908-1436-9

Vol. 85. D. Rutkowska
Neuro-Fuzzy Architectures and Hybrid Learning, 2002
ISBN 3-7908-1438-5

Vol. 86. M.B. Gorzałczany
Computational Intelligence Systems and Applications, 2002
ISBN 3-7908-1439-3

Vol. 87. C. Bertoluzza, M.Á. Gil and D.A. Ralescu (Eds.)
Statistical Modeling, Analysis and Management of Fuzzy Data, 2002
ISBN 3-7908-1440-7

Vol. 88. R.P. Srivastava and T.J. Mock (Eds.)
Belief Functions in Business Decisions, 2002
ISBN 3-7908-1451-2

Vol. 89. B. Bouchon-Meunier, J. Gutiérrez-Ríos, L. Magdalena and R.R. Yager (Eds.)
Technologies for Constructing Intelligent Systems 1, 2002
ISBN 3-7908-1454-7

Bernadette Bouchon-Meunier
Julio Gutiérrez-Ríos
Luis Magdalena · Ronald R. Yager
Editors

Technologies for Constructing Intelligent Systems 2

Tools

With 61 Figures
and 24 Tables

Springer-Verlag Berlin Heidelberg GmbH

Professor Bernadette Bouchon-Meunier
Université Paris VI
CNRS, LIP6
8 rue du Capitaine Scott
75015 Paris
France
Bernadette.Bouchon-Meunier@lip6.fr

Professor Julio Gutiérrez-Ríos
Universidad Politécnica de Madrid
Facultad de Informática
Campus de Montegancedo
28660 Boadilla del Monte, Madrid
Spain
jgr@fi.upm.es

Dr. Luis Magdalena
Universidad Politécnica de Madrid
Escuela Técnica Superior de Ingenieros
de Telecomunicación
Ciudad Universitaria s/n
28040 Madrid
Spain
llayos@mat.upm.es

Professor Ronald R. Yager
Iona College
Machine Intelligence Institute
New Rochelle, NY 10801
USA
yager@panix.com

ISSN 1434-9922
ISBN 978-3-7908-2504-6 ISBN 978-3-7908-1796-6 (eBook)
DOI 10.1007/978-3-7908-1796-6

Cataloging-in-Publication Data applied for
Die Deutsche Bibliothek – CIP-Einheitsaufnahme
Technologies for constructing intelligent systems / Bernadette Bouchon-Meunier ... (ed.). –
Springer-Verlag Berlin Heidelberg 2002
2. Tools: with 24 tables. – 2002
(Studies in fuzziness and soft computing; Vol. 90)

Originally published by Physica-Verlag Heidelberg in 2002
Softcover reprint of the hardcover 1st edition 2002

Hardcover Design: Erich Kirchner, Heidelberg

Preface

At the beginning of this new century, Intelligent Systems represent a cutting edge of applied artificial intelligence. Most of the applications of Intelligent Systems are based upon an amalgamation of different techniques and methods. An Intelligent System resembles an ensemble rather than a soloist. Each attempt at constructing an intelligent system or improving the intelligence of a pre-existing system, has to deal with different aspects of information processing and uncertainty management. In the light of this situation the representation of uncertain information, the definition of suitable aggregation operators, the modelling of decisions and preferences, and the integration of learning capabilities become core technologies.

These technologies are the pieces of the ensemble, it is necessary to have them available when constructing intelligent systems. The focus of the International Conference on Information Processing and Management of Uncertainty in Knowledge Based Systems (IPMU) is on the development of intelligent systems and the allied technologies. The eighth IPMU conference, held in Madrid and organized by the Universidad Politécnica de Madrid in July 2000, brought together some of the worlds leading experts in these technologies. In these two companion volumes, Technologies for Constructing Intelligent Systems: Volume I Tasks and Volume II Tools, we have collected a selection of papers from this conference. The topics included in these volumes range from fundamental issues in uncertainty, information aggregation and preference modelling through technologies for effective decision making to applied research on pattern recognition for text classification or texture detection.

The first volume begins with a paper by Lotfi A. Zadeh presenting the new paradigm he proposes for the construction of intelligent systems, a Computational Theory of Perceptions. This new theory provides a machinery for computing and reasoning with perceptions described in a natural language. It provides an additional tool to help with decision making in problems where the available information is perceptual in nature. This of course, corresponds to many of the situations found in the real world.

Zadeh's paper makes clear a general concern underlying the content of these two volumes: the need for both theories and methodologies to help provide a computational solution to difficult problems in which the available knowledge and data may be imprecise, incomplete, linguistic and subjective. Various methodologies exist to manage such information in probabilistic, possibilistic, fuzzy, logical, evidential, and network-based frameworks. The purpose of these volumes is not to consider these methodologies separately, but rather to address key subjects in which they may be involved.

The first section of volume one is devoted to the issue of computing with words. This subject being an extension and generalization of the idea of using perceptions provides an important technique for enhancing the ability to have user friendly human–machine interactions and develop knowledge-based systems. Concepts such as linguistic modifiers, quantifiers and granulation of information are considered here. The following parts of this volume are concerned with subjects covering some of the important fields of intelligent systems. Decision making is the first domain covered. The notions of consensus, utility and preference are major items discussed in this part. Classification and clustering as well as example-based learning is the next domain considered. Another domain considered here, one which has great importance for the internet, concerns information retrieval and flexible queries in databases.

Volume two begins with a section devoted to fundamental issues of uncertainty. The concepts of independence and conditioning are discussed in different frameworks and this part is introduced in a paper by Richard Jeffrey proposing a "radical probabilism" in which probabilistic judgments are used instead of objective probabilities, and which also discusses the problem of probability updating.

Next issues related to aggregation, a necessary step in all aspects of intelligent systems construction, are discussed in great detail and several kinds of aggregation operators are presented.

The rest of this second volume deals with specific approaches underlying the development of intelligent systems. Fuzzy set theory is first addressed. Properties of basic tools in this field such as, fuzzy measures, fuzzy control, fuzzy relations and fuzzy temporal knowledge are discussed. Several of the papers in this volume are related to causal networks and neural networks. Finally, methods based on logics describe links between logic and the management of uncertain information.

In summary, these two companion volumes overview the various methods and domains involved in the construction of intelligent systems and provides a broad view of research in the field.

Bernadette Bouchon-Meunier
Julio Gutiérrez-Ríos
Luis Magdalena
Ronald R. Yager

Table of Contents

Fundamental Issues in Uncertainty

Epistemology Probabilized

Richard Jeffrey
Department of Philosophy
Princeton University
Princeton, NJ 08544
USA
dickjeff@princeton.edu

Abstract

Here is a framework for judgment in terms of a continuum of "subjective" probabilities, a framework in which probabilistic judgments need not stand on a foundation of certainties. In place of propositional data bases, this *radical* probabilism ("probabilities all the way down to the roots") envisages full or partial probability assignments to probability spaces, together with protocols for revising those assignments and their interconnections in the light of fresh empirical or logico-mathematical input. This input need not be of the limiting 0-or-1 sort. Updating by ordinary conditioning is generalized (sec. **2.2**) to *probability kinematics,* where an observation on a random variable X need not single out one value, but may prompt a new probability distribution Q over all values of X.

The effect of an observation itself, apart from the influence of prior probabilities (sec. **3**), is given by the ("Bayes") factors $\frac{new\ odds}{old\ odds}$ by which the observer's odds between hypotheses are updated. We are not generally interested in adopting an observer's new odds as our own, for those are influenced by the observer's old odds, not ours. It is rather the observer's Bayes's factors that we need in order to use that observation in our own judgments. An account of collaborative updating is presented in these terms.

Jon Dorling's bayesian solution of the Duhem-Quine "holism" problem is sketched in sec. **4**.

We finish with a brief look at the historical setting of radical probabilism (sec. **5**), and an indication of how "real" probabilities can be accomodated in subjectivistic terms (sec. **6**).

1 Judgmental ("Subjective") Probability

Your "subjective" probability is not something fetched out of the sky on a whim; it is your actual judgment, normally representing what you think your judgment *should* be, even if you do not regard it as a judgment that everyone must share on pain of being wrong in one sense or another.

1.1 Probabilities from Statistics: Minimalism

Where do probabilistic judgments come from? Statistical data are a prime source; that is the truth in frequentism. But that truth must be understood in the light of certain features of judgmental probabilizing, e.g., persistence, as you learn the relative frequency of truths in a sequence of propositions, of your judgment that they all have the same probability. That is an application of the following theorem of the probability calculus.[1]

> **Law of Little Numbers.** In a finite sequence of propositions that you view as equiprobable, if you are sure that the relative frequency of truths is p, then your probability for each is p.

Then if, judging a sequence of propositions to be equiprobable, you learn the relative frequency of truths *in a way that does not change your judgment of equiprobability,* your probability for each proposition will agree with the relative frequency.[2]

The law of little numbers can be generalized to random variables:

> **Law of Short Run Averages.** In a finite sequence of magnitudes for which your expections are equal, if you know only their arithmetical mean, then that is your expectation of each.

Then if, while requiring your final expectations for a sequence of magnitudes to be equal, you learn their mean value in a way that does not lead you to change that requirement, your expectation of each will agree with that mean.[3]

Example: Guessing Weight. Needing to estimate the weight of someone on the other side of a chain link fence, you select ten people on your side whom you estimate to have the same weight as that eleventh, persuade them to congregate on a platform scale, and read their total weight. If the scale reads

---

[1]See Jeffrey (1992) pp. 59-64. The name "Law of Little Numbers" is a joke, but I know of no generally understood name for the theorem. That theorem, like the next (the "Law of Short Run", another joke) is quite trivial; both are immediate consequences of the linearity of the expectation operator. Chapter 2 of de Fineti (1937) is devoted to them. In chapter 3 he goes on to a mathematically deeper way of understanding the truth in frequentism, in terms of "exchangeability" of random variables (sec. **1.3**, below).

[2]To appreciate the importance of the italicized caveat, note that if you learn the relative frequency of truths by learning which propositions in the sequence are true, and which false, and as you form your probabilities for those propositions you remember what you have learned, then those probabilities will be zeros and ones instead of average of those zeros and ones.

[3]If you learn the individual values and calculate the mean as their average without forgetting the various values, you have violated the caveat (unless it happens that all the values were the same), for what you learned will have shown you that they are not equal.

1080 lb., your estimate of the eleventh person's weight will be 108 lb.—if nothing in that process has made you revise your judgment that the eleven weights are equal.[4]

This is a frequentism in which judgmental probabilities are seen as judgmental *expectations* of frequencies, and in which the Law of Little Numbers guides the recycling of observed frequencies as probabilities of unobserved instances. It is to be distinguished both from the intelligible but untenable finite frequentism that simply identifies probabilities with actual frequencies (generally, unknown) when there are only finitely many instances overall, and from the unintellible long-run frequentism that would see the observed instances as a finite fragment of an infinite sequence in which the infinitely long run inflates expectations into certainties that sweep judgmental probabilities under the endless carpet.[5]

1.2 Probabilities from Statistics: Exchangeability[6]

On the hypotheses of (a) equiprobability and (b) certainty that the relative frequency of truths is r, the the Law of Little Numbers identified the probability as $=r$. Stronger conclusions follow from the stronger hypothesis of EXCHANGEABILITY:

> You regard a set of propositions as exchangeable when, for any two disjoint subsets, your probability that those in the first are all true and those in the second are all false depends only on the sizes, t, f, of the two sets.[7]

Here, again, as in sec. **1.1**, probabilities will be seen to come from statistics—but, again, only under probabilistic hypotheses.

In the presence of exchangeability of a set $\{H_1, \ldots H_n\}$, your probabilities for all $2^{(2^n)}$ of their Boolean compounds are determined by your probabilities for the following $n+1$ of those compounds:

$$H_t^n =_{df} \text{the number of truths among } H_1, \ldots, H_n \text{ is } t\ (= 0, \ldots, n).$$

[4]Note that turning statistics into probabilities or expectations in this way requires neither conditioning nor Bayes's theorem, nor does it require you to have formed particular judgmental probabilities for the propositions or particular estimates for the random variables prior to learning the relative frequency or mean.

[5]See Jeffrey (1992) chapter 11.

[6]See chapters 3 and 5 of Finetti (1937), (1980).

[7]This comes to the same thing as invariance of your probabilities for Boolean compounds of finite numbers of the H_i under all finite permutations of the positive integers, e.g., $P(H_1 \wedge (H_2 \vee \neg H_3)) = P(H_{100} \wedge (H_2 \vee \neg H_7))$.

DE FINETTI'S RULE OF SUCCESSION.[8]

If you regard $\{H_1, \ldots, H_{n+1}\}$ as exchangeable, your probability for truth of H_{n+1}, given a conjunction ("H") of a particular t of them with the denials of the $f = n - t$ others will be

$$P(H_{n+1}|H) = \frac{(t+1)\,P(H_{t+1}^{n+1})}{(n+1)\,P(H_t^n)} = \frac{t+1}{n+2+(f+1)(\frac{P(H_t^{n+1})}{P(H_{t+1}^{n+1})}-1)}$$

EXAMPLE: THE UNIFORM DISTRIBUTION, $P(H_0^{n+1}) = \ldots = P(H_{n+1}^{n+1})$. In this ("Bayes-Laplace-Johnson-Carnap") case, the denominator at the end of de Finetti's rule reduges to $n+2$, and we have $P(H_{n+1}|H) = \frac{t+1}{n+2}$.

2 Updating on Your Own Observations

In this section we determine the conditions of applicability of certain maps $P \mapsto Q$ that update your prior probability function P to a posterior probability function Q. The maps are:

$\overset{A,1}{\longmapsto}$, Conditioning on a data proposition A for which $Q(A) = 1$, and

$\overset{\vec{A},\vec{q}}{\longmapsto}$, Generalized Conditioning (or "Probability Kinematics") on a partition $A_1, \ldots, A_n$ on which you have new probabilities $Q(A_i) = q_i$.

The discussion addresses "you," a medical oncologist who is also a histopathologist. The A_i are diagnoses, whose probabilities have been driven to new values q_i by your observations. The B_s are prognoses, "s-year survival". Your problem is to determine your new probabilities for them.

On the basis of a microscopic examination of cells wiped from your patient's bronchial tumor you have updated your probabilities on a set of mutually exclusive, collectively exhaustive diagnoses A_i:

A_1, Benign; A_2, Adeno ca; A_3, Small cell ca.; A_4, none of the foregoing.

How are you to extend the map, $P(A_i) \mapsto Q(A_i)$ on the diagnoses to a map $P(B_s) \mapsto Q(B_s)$ on the prognoses? There is no general answer, but there are answers in the two special cases defined above: $\overset{A,1}{\longmapsto}$ and $\overset{\vec{A},\vec{q}}{\longmapsto}$.

2.1 A Special Case: Conditioning

Suppose an observation drives your probability for some diagnosis (say, A_2) all the way to 1:

$Q(A_2) = 1$, CERTAINTY.

Question. When is it appropriate to update by conditioning on A_2?

$P(B_s) \mapsto Q(B_s) = P(B_s|A_2)$, CONDITIONING.

[8]de Finetti, "Foresight," pp. 104-5. The best thing to read on this is Zabell (1989).

Answer. When the change $P(A_2) \mapsto Q(A_2) = 1$ leaves conditional probability given truth of A_2 invariant:[9]

$$Q(B_s|A_2) = P(B_s|A_2), \text{ INVARIANCE.}$$

The invariance condition is equivalent to uniformity of expansion within A_2, i.e., constancy of odds between propositions $C, D \subseteq A_2$: $\frac{P(C)}{P(D)} = \frac{Q(C)}{Q(D)}$, or

$$P(C)Q(D) = P(D)Q(C) \text{ for all } C, D \subseteq A_2, \text{ UNIFORMITY.}$$

Certainty alone is not enough to license conditioning, for one observation will generally yield many new certainties, on which conditioning would lead to different updated probability functions.

EXAMPLE. Drawing a card from a well-shuffled deck, you see that it is a heart. Conditioning on that certainty yields $P(\text{Queen of hearts}|\text{heart}) = \frac{1}{13}$. But in seeing that the card is a heart, you have also seen that it is red, and conditioning on *that* certainty yields $P(\text{Queen of hearts}|\text{red}) = \frac{1}{26}$.

2.2 A Less Special Case: Probability Kinematics

Suppose an observation changes your probability distribution over a partition of diagnoses $A_1, \ldots, A_n$, without necessarily changing any of the $P(A_i)$ to $Q(A_i) = 1$.

Question. When is it appropriate to update by "probability kinematics"?

$$Q(B) = \sum_{i=1}^{n} Q(A_i)P(B|A_i), \text{ PROBABILITY KINEMATICS}$$

Answer. When the invariance condition holds for each of the A_i's:

$$Q(B|A_i) = P(B|A_i) \text{ for } i = 1, \ldots, n, \text{ INVARIANCE}$$

Notes:

- By the law of total probability in the form $Q(B) = \sum_i Q(A_i)Q(B|A_i)$, invariance relative to all the A_i is *equivalent* to probability kinematics.
- Conditioning is the special case in which some $Q(A_i) = 1$.
- On the native ground of probability kinematics, you are your own probability meter. In the context of *your* prior judgments, *your* new observations urges new probabilities $Q(A_i) = q_i$ upon *you.* In the most highly prized cases, you are able to explain these urges in terms of considerations which would weigh with other experts as well. But the urge is there, nudging the needle of your inner probability meter, even in the absence of such an explanation.

[9]It is easy to verify that conditioning is equivalent to invariance together with certainty.

3 Collaborative Updating

We now move outside the native ground of probability kinematics into a region where your new $Q(A_i)$'s are based on other people's observations. You are unlikely to simply adopt such alien probabilities as your own, for they are a confusion of the bare alien observation, which you would like to use, with the alien prior judgmental state, for which you may prefer to substitute your own.

We continue in the medical setting. You are a clinical oncologist, but no longer a histopathologist. You want to make the best use you can of the observations of a histopathologist whom you have consulted.

3.1 Adopt the Expert's New Probabilities?

P and Q : Your probabilities *before* and *after* the histopathologist's observation has replaced her prior probabilities $P'(A_i)$ for the diagnoses by her posterior values $Q'(A_i)$.

Will you simply adopt her new probabilities for the diagnoses, setting your $Q(A_i)$'s = her $Q'(A_i)$'s? If so, you can update by probability kinematics even if you had no prior diagnostic opinions $P(A_i)$ of your own; all you need are *her* new $Q'(A_i)$'s and *your* invariant conditional prognoses $P(B|A_i)$.

Note that she may have conditional prognoses $P'(B|A_i)$ different from yours and invariant as yours. No matter. What concern you are her diagnoses, not her prognoses.

3.2 Dissecting out the Purely Observational Part

But suppose you have priors $P(A_i)$ which you take to be well-founded, and although you have high regard for the histopathologist's ability to interpret histographic slides, you view her prior probabilities for the various diagnoses as arbitrary and uninformed. (Perhaps she has told you that she had no prior judgment in the matter, but for the purpose of formulating her report adopted convenient flat priors, $P'(A_i) = \frac{1}{n}$ for all i.)

Here you would like to dissect out of the histopathologist's report the components that represent what she has actually seen, and combine them with your own priors. These components will be her BAYES FACTORS,[10]

$$\beta'_{i1} = \frac{\text{her old odds on } A_i \text{ against } A_1}{\text{her new odds on } A_i \text{ against } A_1}.$$

In general, the factor $\beta(A : B)$ updates your odds on hypothesis A against hypothesis B:

$$\beta(A : B) =_{df} \frac{Q(A)}{Q(B)} / \frac{P(A)}{P(B)}.$$

[10]The choice of A_1 as a reference point is arbitrary, since the ratios $\beta'_{i,k} : \beta'_{j,k}$ are the same for all choices of k from 1 to n. See Schwartz et al. (1981).

Where the hypotheses are diagnoses A_i, A_j, we abbreviate

$$\beta_{i,j} =_{df} \beta(A_i : A_j) = \frac{Q(A_i)}{Q(A_j)} / \frac{P(A_i)}{P(A_1)}.$$

Note that if we write your PROBABILITY FACTOR on A_i as

$$\pi_i =_{df} \frac{Q(A_i)}{P(A_i)},$$

your Bayes factor on A_i against A_j can be written

$$\beta_{i,j} = \frac{\pi_i}{\pi_j}.$$

The histopathologist's probabilities and factors will be written P', Q', β', π'.

According to Bayesian lore it is the histopathologist's β''s that tell you what she has learned from the observation itself, with her prior probabilities factored out.

Now you can simply multiply your prior odds on A_i against A_1 by her Bayes factors $\beta'_{i,1}$ to get your posterior odds in the light of her observations. It is straightforward to verify that you can then update your probability for a prognosis B by using the formula for probability kinematics in sec. **2.2**, but with your $Q(A_i)$'s computed as follows from her β''s and your $P(A_i)$'s:

$$Q(A_i) = \frac{P(A_i)\beta'_{i1}}{\sum_i P(A_i)\beta'_{i1}}, \text{ so that } Q(B) = \frac{\sum_i \beta'_{i1} P(B \wedge A_i)}{\sum_i P(A_i)\beta'_{i1}}.$$

Here the choice of A_1 as anchor for the Bayes factors is arbitrary; any A_j would do as well, to the same effect.

Finally, note that these equations can also be written equivalently (and more simply) in terms of unanchored probability factors:

$$\boxed{Q(A_i) = \frac{P(A_i)\pi'_i}{\sum_i P(A_i)\pi'_i}, \text{ so that } Q(B) = \frac{\sum_i \pi'_i P(B \wedge A_i)}{\sum_i P(A_i)\pi'_i}.}$$

3.3 Updating Twice: Commutativity

Here we consider the outcome of successive updating on the reports of two different experts—say, a histopathologist and a radiologist.

If you update twice, should order be irrelevant?

$$\text{Should } \overset{1}{\mapsto}\overset{2}{\mapsto} \;=\; \overset{2}{\mapsto}\overset{1}{\mapsto}\ ?$$

The answer depends on particulars of

(1) the partitions on which $\overset{1}{\mapsto}$ and $\overset{2}{\mapsto}$ are defined;
(2) the mode of updating (by probabilities? Bayes factors?); and
(3) your starting point, P.

3.3.1 Updating on New Probabilities for Diagnoses

A propos of (2), suppose you accept two new *probability* assignments to the same partition—first one, then another.

- Can order matter?

Certainly. Since the second assignment simply replaces the first, the result of accepting first one and then the other is the same as the result that just accepting the second would have had, by itself.

- When is order immaterial?

When there are two partitions, and updating on the second leaves probabilities of all elements of the first unchanged. This happens when the two partitions are independent relative to P.[11]

3.3.2 Updating on Factors for Diagnoses

In updating by Bayes factors, order never matters.[12]

Example 1: One partition. Adopting both a pathologist's Bayes factors β_i^1 and a radiologist's Bayes factors β_i^2 on the same partition as your own—in either order—you come to the same result: your overall Bayes factors will be products $\beta_{i1}^1\beta_{i1}^2 = \frac{\pi_i^1\pi_i^2}{\pi_1^1\pi_1^2}$. Your final probabilities for the diagnoses will be

$$Q(A_i) = \frac{P(A_i)\beta_{i1}^1\beta_{i1}^2}{\sum_i P(A_i)\beta_{i1}^1\beta_{i1}^2} = \frac{P(A_i)\pi_i^1\pi_i^2}{\sum_i P(A_i)\pi_i^1\pi_i^2}.$$

Example 2: Two updates:[13] $\overset{1}{\longmapsto}$, with partition $\{A_i^1\}$ and factors π_i^1 $(i = 1, \ldots, m)$, and $\overset{2}{\longmapsto}$, with partition $\{A_j^2\}$ and factors π_j^2 $(j = 1, \ldots, n)$. These must commute, being equivalent, in either order, to a single mapping, $\overset{3}{\longmapsto}$, with partition $\{A_i^1 \wedge A_j^2 : P(A_i^1 \wedge A_j^2) > 0\}$ and factors $\pi_i^1\pi_j^2$. Now

$$Q(A_i \wedge A_j) = \frac{P(A_i \wedge A_j)\pi_i^1\pi_j^2}{\sum_{ij}\pi_i^1\pi_j^2}, Q(B) = \frac{\sum_{i,j}\pi_i^1\pi_j^2 P(B \wedge A_i^1 \wedge A_j^2)}{\sum_{i,j}\pi_i^1\pi_j^2 P(A_i^1 \wedge A_j^2)}$$

4 Dorling on the Duhem-Quine Problem

Skeptical conclusions about the possibility of scientific hypothesis-testing have been drawn from the presumed arbitrariness of answers to the question of which to give up—a theory (e.g., in **4.2** below, general relativity), or an auxiliary hypothesis ('The equipment was in working order')—when they jointly contradict empirical data. The problem, posed by Pierre Duhem

[11] For more about this, see Diaconis and Zabell (1982), esp. 825-6.

[12] Proofs are straightforward. See my Petrus Hispanus Lectures, II: 'Radical Probabilism', *Actas da Sociedade Portuguesa da Filosofia* (forthcoming; and currently available in http://www.princeton.edu/ bayesway/pu/Lisbon.pdf).

[13] Adapted from Field (1978) 361-7.

in the first years of the 20th century, was reanimated by W.V. Quine in mid-century.[14] But the holistic conclusion depends on the assumption that deductive logic is our *only* tool for confronting theories with empirical data. That would leave things pretty much as Descartes saw them, just before the mid-17th century emergence of the probabilistic ("Bayesian") methodology that Jon Dorling has brought to bear on various episodes in the history of science. Here is an introduction to Dorling's work, using extracts from his important but still unpublished 1982 paper[15]

4.1 Setting the Stage

Were, as in Dorling's analysis, updating is by conditioning on a data statement D, the Bayes factor for a theory T against an alternative theory S equals the likelihood ratio,

$$\beta(T:S) = \frac{P(D|T)}{P(D|S)}.$$

The empirical result D is not generally deducible or refutable by T alone, or by S alone, but in interesting cases of scientific hypothesis testing D is deducible or refutable on the basis of the theory and an auxiliary hypothesis A (e.g., the hypothesis that the equipment is in good working order). To simplify the analysis, Dorling makes an assumption, prior independence, that can generally be justified by appropriate formulation of A:

$$P(A \wedge T) = P(A)P(T), \quad P(A \wedge S) = P(A)P(S),$$

Generally speaking, S is not simply the denial of T, but a definite scientific theory in its own right, or a disjunction of such theories, all of which agree on the phenomenon of interest, so that, as an explanation of that phenomenon, S is a rival to T. In any case Dorling uses the independence assumption to expand the right-hand side of the Bayes Factor = Likelihood Ratio equation:

$$\beta(T:S) = \frac{P(D|T \wedge A)P(A) + P(D|T \wedge \neg A)P(\neg A)}{P(D|S \wedge A)P(A) + P(D|S \wedge \neg A)P(\neg A)}$$

To study the effect of D on A, he also expands $\beta(A:\neg A)$ with respect to T (and similarly with respect to S, although we do not show that here):

$$\beta(A:\neg A) = \frac{P(D|A \wedge T)P(T) + P(D|A \wedge \neg T)P(\neg T)}{P(D|\neg A \wedge T)P(T) + P(D|\neg A \wedge \neg T)P(\neg T)}$$

[14]Quine (1953), p. 41: 'our statements about the external world face the tribunal of sense experience not individually but as a corporate body.'

[15]This section is based on Dorling (1982). His work is also discussed in Howson and Urbach (1993). See also Dorling (1979) and Redhead (1980).

4.2 Einstein/Newton, 1919

In these terms Dorling analyzes two famous tests that were duplicated, with apparatus differing in seemingly unimportant ways, with conflicting results: one of the duplicates confirmed T against S, the other confirmed S against T. Nevertheless, the scientific experts took the experiments to clearly confirm one of the rivals against the other. Dorling explains why the experts were right:

"In the solar eclipse experiments of 1919, the telescopic observations were made in two locations, but only in one location was the weather good enough to obtain easily interpretable results. Here, at Sobral, there were two telescopes: one, the one we hear about, confirmed Einstein; the other, in fact the slightly larger one, confirmed Newton. Conclusion: Einstein was vindicated, and the results with the larger telescope were rejected." (1982, sec. 4)

NOTATION

T: Einstein: light-bending effect of the sun

S: Newton: no light-bending effect of the sun

A: Both telescopes are working correctly

D: The conflicting data from both telescopes

In the Bayes factor $\beta(T:S)$ above, $P(D|T \wedge A) = P(D|S \wedge A) = 0$ since if both telescopes were working correctly they would not have given contradictory results. Then the first terms of the sums in numerator and denominator vanish, so that the factors $P(\neg A)$ cancel and we have

$$\beta(T,S) = \frac{P(D|T \wedge \neg A)}{P(D|S \wedge \neg A)}$$

Dorling continues: "Now the experimenters argued that one way in which A might easily be false was if the mirror of one or the other of the telescopes had distorted in the heat, and this was much more likely to have happened with the larger mirror belonging to the telescope which confirmed S than with the smaller mirror belonging to the telescope which confirmed T. Now the effect of mirror distortion of the kind envisaged would be to shift the recorded images of the stars from the positions predicted by T to or beyond those predicted by S. Hence $P(D|T \wedge \neg A)$ was regarded as having an appreciable value, while, since it was very hard to think of any similar effect which could have shifted the positions of the stars in the other telescope from those predicted by S to those predicted by T, $P(D|S \wedge \neg A)$ was regarded as negligibly small, hence the result as overall a decisive confirmation of T and refutation of S." Thus the Bayes factor $\beta(T,S)$ is very much greater than 1.

5 Radical Probabilism

Descartes sought to refute skepticism about experience by proving the existence of a God ($=_{df}$ the perfect being) who surely does not deceive us. On this "dogmatic" foundation of certainty he would build empirical science.

Shortly after Descartes's death, probabilistic thinking—in much the same form in which we know it today—emerged from a famous correspondence between Fermat and Pascal. It was given the place of honor at the end of the best-selling "How to Think" book known as "The Port-Royal Logic" (Arnauld, 1662):

> "To judge what one must do to obtain a good or avoid an evil, it is necessary to consider not only the good and the evil in itself, but also the probability that it happens or does not happen; and to view geometrically the proportion that all these things have together."

But a quasi-Cartesian dogmatism figured prominently in 20th century thought about the foundations of probabilistic thinking. Here is an example from the pragmatist–empiricist philosopher C. I. Lewis (1946, p. 186):

> "If anything is to be probable, then something must be certain. The data which themselves support a genuine probability, must themselves be certainties. We do have such absolute certainties, in the sense data initiating belief and in those passages of experience which later may confirm it."

What I call "radical probabilism" denies this claim. The claim itself seems to be based on the thought that conditioning on certainties is the only way to update probabilities. That basis for dogmatic probabilism is undermined by the existence of a generalized conditioning—probability kinematics—as a way of updating on mere probabilities.

Radical probabilism offers Bayes factors as a surrogate for Lewis's absolute certainties. Lewis held that these certainties cannot

> "be phrased in the language of objective statement — because what can be so phrased can never be more than probable. Our sense certainties can only be formulated by the expressive use of language, in which what is signified is a content of experience and what is asserted is the givenness of this content."

In radical probabilism the Bayes factors β_{ij} do the job of your ineffable sense certainties. Like those ineffables, your Bayes factors lie outside the Boolean algebra of objective statements on which your P and Q are defined. But where Lewis can give no intelligible account of your sense certainities, radical probabilism can identify the β's as ratios of your new to old odds between items that *are* expresible in the language of objective statement.

6 Real Subjectivism

Radical probabilism gets along without objective probabilities, real chances ("R"). The thought is that these are nothing but projections of judgmental probabilities P out into the world, whence we hear them clamoring to be let back in. The following equation ("Miller's Principle") could be their return ticket:[16]

$$P[H|R(H) = r] = r, \text{ where '}r\text{' is a purely mathematical designator.}$$

(If you know the real chance, that will be your judgmental probability.) But they don't need a return ticket; they never really left.

There certainly *are* numbers "out there"—numbers like the fraction of 70-year-olds who live to be 80—and it may well be that if you knew that number you would adopt it as your judgmental probability that your 70-year-old uncle, Bob, will live to be 80. But maybe not. Maybe you know that Bob comes from remarkably long-lived stock, in which case your probability for his reaching 80 might be higher than the statistics on 70-year-olds would suggest. (But maybe you also know that Bob has pancreatic cancer, so that your probability is below the statistical average for 70-year-olds.) This is the famous reference-class problem. According to radical probabilism, this problem can be solved by putting the horse before the cart, using your probabilistic judgments to choose among the various numbers out there. But the point is that there are enough familiar numbers out there—statistics, fractions of green balls in urns, etc.—to do the jobs that objectivists send "real probabilities" out there to do.

Once such numbers have been chosen, formulas that look rather like the return ticket may come into play:

$$P(H|X = x) = x, \text{ where } X \text{ is an ordinary random variable}$$

EXAMPLE. P(A green ball will be drawn|70% are green)=70% if you think the balls are well mixed, etc.

To hypostasize $R(H)$ as a physical magnitude is to sweep the subjective element in "objective" probability under the carpet. We do better to identify the parameter X case by case, as the fraction of green balls in the urn, or of septuagenerian men who live to be 80, or whatever. In all of these quests for a suitable X the great clue, the sticky subjective core, is that, whatever X turns out to be, it must satisfy the equation $P(H|X = x) = x$.

[16]Here, 'r' might be '.7' or '$1/\pi$', but not '1/(my mass in Kg)', and not '$R(H)$'. The thought is that you must be able to tell what number 'r' denotes without recourse to any empirical facts. The need for this restriction is seen when we put '$R(H)$' for 'r'. We then have $P[H|R(H) = R(H)] = R(H)$, which is equivalent to $P(H) = R(H)$. Unrestricted, Miller's Principle thus implies that your subjective probabilities always agree with the objective probabilities. In effect, Miller (1966) rejected the restriction and welcomed the result as a reductio ad absurdum of the concept of judgmental probability. (Note that since 'R' means real chance, not future probability, van Fraassen's (1984) reflection principle is only formally identical with Miller's principle.)

References

Arnauld, Antoine (1662, 1964) *Logic, or, the Art of Thinking* ("The Port-Royal Logic") tr. J. Dickoff and P. James, Bobbs-Merril, Indianapolis.

Bayes, Thomas (1763) An essay towards solving a problem in the doctrine of chances, *Philosophical Transactions of the Royal Society* **53**, 370-418.

Carnap, R. (1950), *Logical Foundations of Probability*, Chicago: University of Chicago Press. (2nd ed., 1962)

de Finetti, Bruno (1937, 1980) La prévision, ses lois logiques, ses sources subjectives, *Annales de l'institut Henri Poincaré* **7**, 1-68. Translation ("Foresight ...") in *Studies in Subjective Probability,"* Henry Kyburg, Jr. and Howard Smokler (eds.), Krieger, New York, 53-118.

Diaconis, Persi and Sandy Zabell (1989) Updating Subjective Probability, *Journal of the American Statistical Society* **77**, 822-30.

Dorling, Jon (1979) Bayesian personalism, the methodology of research programmes, and Duhem's problem, *Studies in History and Philosophy of Science* **10**, 177-87.

Dorling, Jon (1982) Further illustrations of the Bayesian solution of Duhem's problem (29 pp., photocopied); see *http* : *www.princeton.edu*\ ~*bayesway*

Duhem, Pierre (1906, 1914. 1954) *La Théorie Physique: Son Object, Sa Structure*, Paris. Translation, *The Aim and Structure of Physical Theory.* Princeton University Press.

Field, Hartry (1978) A Note on Jeffrey Conditionalization, *Philosophy of Science* **45**, 361-7.

Howson, Colin and Peter Urbach (1993) *Scientific Reasoning: the Bayesian approach,* Open Court, La Salle, Illinois, 2nd ed.

Jeffrey, Richard (1970) [untitled review of Miller (1966) and other papers] *Journal of Symbolic Logic* **35**, 124-127.

Jeffrey, Richard (1992) *Probability and the Art of Judgment,* Cambridge U. P.

Lewis, C. I. (1946) *An Analysis of Knowledge and Valuation,* Open Court.

Miller, David (1966) A Paradox of Information, *British Journal for the Philosophy of Science* **17**, 59-61.

Neurath, Otto (1932), Protokollsätze, *Erkenntnis* **3**, 204-214. Translated in his *Philosophical Papers 1913-1946*, Dordrecht: Reidel.

Quine, Willard van Orman (1951. 1953) Two Dogmas of Empiricism, *Philosophical Review* **60**, 20-43. Reprinted in *From a Logical Point of View,* Harvard University Press.

Redhead, Michael (1980) A Bayesian reconstruction of the methodology of scientific research programmes. *Studies in History and Philosophy of Science* **11**, 341-7.

Schwartz, W.B., Wolfe, H.J., and Pauker, S.G. (1981) Pathology and Probabilies: A New Approach to Interpreting and Reporting Biopsies, *The New England Journal of Medicine* **305**, 917-23.

van Fraassen, Bas (1984) Belief and the will, *J. Philosophy* **65**, 243-60.

Zabell, Sandy (1989) The Rule of Succession. *Erkenntnis* **31**, 283-321.

Stochastic Independence for Upper and Lower Probabilities in a Coherent Setting

Giulianella Coletti[1] and **Romano Scozzafava**[2]

[1] Dipartimento di Matematica, Università di Perugia,
Via Vanvitelli, 1 – 06100 PERUGIA (Italy)
coletti@dipmat.unipg.it

[2] Dipartimento Metodi e Modelli Matematici, Università "La Sapienza",
Via Scarpa, 16 – 00161 ROMA (Italy)
romscozz@dmmm.uniroma1.it

Abstract. In this paper we extend to upper and lower probabilities our approach to independence, based solely on *conditional* probability (in a coherent setting). Most difficulties arise (when this notion is put forward in the classical framework) either from the introduction of marginals for upper and lower probabilities (often improperly called, in the relevant literature, "imprecise" probabilities) when trying to extend to them the "product rule", or from the different ways of introducing conditioning for upper and lower probabilities. Our approach to conditioning in the context of "imprecise" probabilities is instead the most natural: in fact its starting point refers to a *direct* definition (through coherence) of the "enveloping" *conditional* "precise" probabilities. The discussion of some critical examples seems to suggest that the intuitive aspects of independence are better captured by referring to *just one* (precise) probability than to a *family* (such as that one singling-out a lower or upper probability).

1 Introduction

Given an *arbitrary* family $\mathcal{C}$ of conditional events, we can define on $\mathcal{C}$ a function $P(\cdot|\cdot)$, bound to *satisfy the requirement of coherence*: an assessment $P(\cdot|\cdot)$ on $\mathcal{C}$ is *coherent* if, given $\mathcal{C}' \supset \mathcal{C}$, with $\mathcal{C}' = \mathcal{G} \times \mathcal{H}^o$ (where $\mathcal{G}$ is a Boolean algebra and $\mathcal{H} \subseteq \mathcal{G}$ an *additive* set, with $\mathcal{H}^o = \mathcal{H} \setminus \{\emptyset\}$), it can be extended from $\mathcal{C}$ to $\mathcal{C}'$ as a *conditional probability*, according to the following definition (de Finetti [10], Rényi [13], Krauss [12], Dubins [11]). A function $P(\cdot|\cdot)$ is said a *conditional probability* on $\mathcal{G} \times \mathcal{H}^o$ if

(a) for any given $H \in \mathcal{H}^o$ and n mutually exclusive events $A_1, ..., A_n \in \mathcal{G}$, the function $P(\cdot|H)$, defined on $\mathcal{G}$, satisfies

$$P((\bigvee_{k=1}^{n} A_k)|H) = \sum_{k=1}^{n} P(A_k|H) \quad , \quad P(\Omega|H) = 1\,;$$

(b) $P(H|H) = 1$ for any $H \in \mathcal{H}^o$;

(c) given $E, A \in \mathcal{G}$, $H, E \wedge H \in \mathcal{H}^o$, then

$$P(E \wedge A|H) = P(E|H)P(A|E \wedge H).$$

Notice that *(c)* reduces, when $H = \Omega$, to the classic "compound probability theorem" for probability. So, in the particular case that the probability $P_o = P(\cdot|\Omega)$ is *everywhere positive* on $\mathcal{H}^o$, a conditional probability can be derived by means of this *unique* probability. Otherwise – to get a similar "kolmogorovian" representation – we need to resort (see Section 2) to a *family* of probabilities.

So the knowledge (or the assessment) of the "joint" and the "marginal" probabilities $P(E \wedge H)$ and $P(H)$ is not required; moreover, $P(E|H)$ makes sense for any $H \neq \emptyset$, including those such that $P(H) = 0$.

As far as stochastic independence (for "precise" probabilities) is concerned, in [3] we pointed out the lack of the classical definition, which gives rise to counterintuitive situations. For example, we are able to avoid situations where *logical* dependence – in the framework of the classical definition – does not (contrary to intuition) imply *stochastic* dependence. Our results have been extended to *families* of events and to *conditional* independence in [15].

In this paper we extend to upper and lower probabilities (often called, in the relevant literature, "imprecise" probabilities: see our discussion in [5]) our approach to independence, based solely on *conditional* probability.

The difficulties that arise when trying to introduce this notion in the classical framework, are well known (see, for example, [9], [8]). Most of these difficulties arise from the introduction of marginals for "imprecise" probabilities, when one tries to extend the "product rule"

$$P(A \wedge B) = P(A)P(B). \tag{1}$$

In fact, considering for example the lower probability $\underline{P}$, we may have

$$\underline{P}(A \wedge B) = \underline{P}(A)\underline{P}(B), \tag{2}$$

while there is no element P of the class of dominating "precise" probabilities (see Section 4) such that (1) holds. Conversely, we may have classes of probabilities such that each element P of the class satisfies (1), but (2) does not hold for the corresponding lower probability.

Other formulations, such as

$$P(A|B) = P(A),$$

give rise to similar difficulties. In fact, even when conditional probability is used, the usual "kolmogorovian" definition of the latter requires anyway resorting to marginals. But problems come also (in the usual approaches) from the different ways of introducing conditioning for upper and lower probabilities, while our approach to conditioning in this context is the most natural. In fact its starting point refers to the *direct* definition (through coherence) of the "enveloping" *conditional* "precise" probabilities: this avoids the (quite usual) assumption $\underline{P}(B) > 0$, where B is the conditioning event, that is a very strong one.

2 Coherent Conditional Probability

Let $P = P_o$ be a coherent probability on an arbitrary set $\mathcal{E}$ of events (*i.e.* P_o can be extended as a ***finitely additive probability*** to the set $\mathcal{A}$ of atoms generated by the events of $\mathcal{E}$). Consider the set $\mathcal{E}_1 \subset \mathcal{E}$ of events $E \in \mathcal{E}$ such that $P_o(E) = 0$ (notice that ***classical*** conditioning is possible only on $\mathcal{E} \setminus \mathcal{E}_1$): we can define a new coherent probability P_1 on $\mathcal{E}_1$ (*i.e.* P_1 can be extended to the set $\mathcal{A}_1 \subset \mathcal{A}$ of atoms generated by the events of $\mathcal{E}_1$) and consider the set $\mathcal{E}_2 \subset \mathcal{E}_1$ such that $P_1(E) = 0$ for $E \in \mathcal{E}_2$, then define in the same way on $\mathcal{E}_2$ a new coherent probability P_2, and so on. It is clear that in this process, given $\beta > \alpha$, the assignment of the probability P_β is in no way bound by the probability P_α (except for the relevant domain). Any such family $\{\mathcal{E}_\alpha\}$ will be called a *supporting family* of $\mathcal{E}$.

So, starting from a class $\mathcal{P} = \{P_\alpha\}$ of probabilities as the previous ones, we can build a function $P(\cdot|\cdot)$ on $\mathcal{E} \times \mathcal{E}^o$ by putting, for any $E|H \in \mathcal{E} \times \mathcal{E}^o$,

$$P(E|H) = \frac{P_\alpha(E \wedge H)}{P_\alpha(H)}, \tag{3}$$

where α is the index such that $P_\alpha(H) > 0$. We showed – for a direct proof, see [4] – that this function is a coherent *conditional* probability on $\mathcal{E} \times \mathcal{E}^o$.

Consider now the reverse procedure: we proved (see, e.g., [1], [4]) that, starting from a conditional probability assessment $P(E_i|H_i)$ on an arbitrary family

$$\mathcal{C} = \mathcal{E} \times \mathcal{F}^o = \{E_1|H_1, ..., E_n|H_n\}$$

(with $\mathcal{F} \subseteq \mathcal{E}$) of conditional events, it can be suitably built (at least) a relevant family $\mathcal{P} = \{P_\alpha\}$ that allows a representation such as (3). Every value $P(E_i|H_i)$ constitutes a constraint in the building of the probabilities P_α ($\alpha = 0, 1, ...$); in fact, given the set $\mathcal{A}_o$ of atoms generated by $E_1, ..., E_n, H_1, ..., H_n$, and its subsets $\mathcal{A}_\alpha$ such that $A_r \in \mathcal{A}_\alpha$ if $P_\beta(A_r) = 0$ for any $\beta < \alpha$, each P_α must satisfy the following system with unknowns $P_\alpha(A_r) \geq 0$, $A_r \in \mathcal{A}_\alpha$,

$$(S_\alpha) \qquad \begin{cases} \sum_{r \atop A_r \subseteq E_i \wedge H_i} P_\alpha(A_r) = P(E_i|H_i) \sum_{r \atop A_r \subseteq H_i} P_\alpha(A_r), \quad [\text{if } P_{\alpha-1}(H_i) = 0] \\[2ex] \sum_{r \atop A_r \subseteq H_0^\alpha} P_\alpha(A_r) = 1 \end{cases}$$

where $P_{-1}(H_i) = 0$ for all H_i's, and H_o^α denotes, for $\alpha \geq 0$, the union of the H_i's such that $P_{\alpha-1}(H_i) = 0$; so, in particular, $H_o^o = H_o = H_1 \vee \ldots \vee H_n$.

The previous considerations can be summarized in a theorem, reported below in the form given in [4].

Theorem 1 - Let $\mathcal{C}$ be an arbitrary finite family of conditional events and let $\mathcal{A}_o$ denote the relevant set of atoms. For a real function P on $\mathcal{C}$, the following two statements are equivalent:

(i) P is a coherent conditional probability on $\mathcal{C}$;

(ii) there exists (at least) a class of probabilities $\{P_o, P_1, \ldots\}$, each probability P_α being defined on a suitable subset $\mathcal{A}_\alpha \subseteq \mathcal{A}_o$, such that for any $E_i|H_i \in \mathcal{C}$ there is a unique P_α with

$$(4) \qquad \sum_{A_r \subseteq H_i}{}_r \; P_\alpha(A_r) > 0$$

and

$$(5) \qquad P(E_i|H_i) = \frac{\sum_{A_r \subseteq E_i \wedge H_i}{}_r \quad P_\alpha(A_r)}{\sum_{A_r \subseteq H_i}{}_r \; P_\alpha(A_r)} \; ;$$

moreover $\mathcal{A}_{\alpha'} \subset \mathcal{A}_{\alpha"}$ for $\alpha' > \alpha"$ and $P_{\alpha"}(A_r) = 0$ if $A_r \in \mathcal{A}_{\alpha'}$.

A class $\{P_\alpha\}$ *agreeing with a conditional probability* $P(\cdot|\cdot)$ is any class such as that singled–out by the above condition *(ii)*. Notice that in general there are infinite classes of probabilities $\{P_\alpha\}$; in particular we have only one class in the case that $\mathcal{C}$ is a product of Boolean algebras.

The probabilities $P_\alpha(A_r)$ are precisely the solutions of the systems (S_α).

We recall now the concept of *zero–layer* given in [3].

Definition 1 - For any event E of a family $\mathcal{E}$, we call *zero-layer* of E, with respect to a class of coherent probabilities $\mathcal{P} = \{P_\alpha\}$ (defined on a supporting family $\mathcal{E}_\alpha$ of $\mathcal{E}$), the number α such that $P_\alpha(E) > 0$: in symbols, $\circ(E) = \alpha$.

Obviously, for the certain event Ω and for any event E with positive probability, we have $\circ(\Omega) = \circ(E) = 0$ (so that, if the class $\mathcal{P}$ contains only an *everywhere positive* probability P_o, there is only one (trivial) zero-layer with $\alpha = 0$), while the zero-layer $\circ(\emptyset)$, where $\emptyset$ denotes the impossible event, is greater than that of any possible event (so that we put $\circ(\emptyset) = +\infty$).

Definition 2 - Let $\mathcal{C}$ be a family of conditional events and P a coherent conditional probability on $\mathcal{C}$. For any conditional event $E|H \in \mathcal{C}$, we call *zero-layer* of $E|H$, with respect to a class $\mathcal{P} = \{P_\alpha\}$ of probabilities agreeing with P, the (nonnegative) number

$$\circ(E|H) = \circ(E \wedge H) - \circ(H)\,.$$

We note that $P(E|H) > 0$ if and only if $\circ(E \wedge H) = \circ(H)$, *i.e.* $\circ(E|H) = 0$.

For the connections of zero-layers to Spohn's ranking functions [14], see [7].

3 Stochastic Independence for "Precise" Probabilities

It is well known that the classical definition of stochastic independence of two events A, B, *i.e.*

$$P(A \wedge B) = P(A)P(B)\,,$$

gives rise to counterintuitive situations, in particular when the given events have probability 0 or 1. For example, an event A with $P(A) = 0$ or 1 is stochastically independent of itself, while it is natural (due to the intuitive meaning of independence, a concept that should catch the idea that being A independent of B entails that assuming the occurrence of B would not change the probability of A) to require for *any* event E to be *dependent* on itself.

Other formulations of the classical definition are

$$P(A|B) = P(A)$$

and

$$P(A|B) = P(A|B^c),$$

that are equivalent to the previous one for events of probability different from 0 and 1: actually, without this assumption these two formulations *may even lack meaning*, due to the usual "kolmogorovian" *definition* of conditional probability.

We recall now the main results from [3].

Definition 3 - Given a set $\mathcal{E}$ of events containing A, B, A^c, B^c, with $B \neq \Omega$, $B \neq \emptyset$, and a *coherent* conditional probability P, defined on a family $\mathcal{C} \subset \mathcal{E} \times \mathcal{E}^0$ and containing $\mathcal{D} = \{A|B, A|B^c, A^c|B, A^c|B^c\}$, we say that A is *stochastically independent* of B with respect to P (in symbols $A * B$) if *both* the following conditions hold:

(i) $P(A|B) = P(A|B^c)$;

(ii) there exists a class $\mathcal{P} = \{P_\alpha\}$ of probabilities agreeing with the restriction of P to the family $\mathcal{D}$, such that

$$\circ(A|B) = \circ(A|B^c) \quad \text{and} \quad \circ(A^c|B) = \circ(A^c|B^c).$$

Remark 1 - Note that if $0 < P(A|B) < 1$ (these inequalities imply also $0 < P(A^c|B) < 1$) and if condition *(i)* holds (so that also $0 < P(A|B^c) < 1$ and $0 < P(A^c|B^c) < 1$), then both equalities in condition *(ii)* are trivially (as $0 = 0$) satisfied. Therefore in this case condition $A * B$ *should* coincide with the classic one: nevertheless notice that the latter would require the assumption $0 < P(B) < 1$, so that our approach actually covers a wider framework, since (as recalled in the Introduction) *to give sense to the two probabilities under (i) the aforementioned assumption is not needed.*

If condition *(i)* holds with $P(A|B) = 0$, then the second equality under *(ii)* is trivially satisfied, so that stochastic independence is ruled by the first one (in other words, equality *(i)* is not enough to assure independence when both sides are null: *it needs to be "reinforced" by the requirement that also their zero-layers must be equal*). Analogously, if condition *(i)* holds with $P(A|B) = 1$ (so that $P(A^c|B) = 0$), independence is ruled by the second equality under *(ii)*.

Since $P(A|A) = 1$ and $P(A|A^c) = 0$ for any (possible) event A (even if $P(A) = 0$ or $P(A) = 1$), we have the following

Proposition 1 - For any coherent P and for any possible event A, one has $\neg(A * A)$, *i.e.* the relation $*$ is *irreflexive.*

Proposition 2 - For any coherent P and for any possible event B, one has $\Omega * B$ and $\emptyset * B$.

Remark 2 - The conclusion of the previous Proposition is very natural, since the probabilities of Ω and $\emptyset$ cannot be changed by assuming the occurrence of any other event B. Conversely, we recall that Definition 4 of $A * B$ requires $B \neq \Omega$ and $B \neq \emptyset$ (since a *conditioning* event cannot be impossible): in fact Ω and $\emptyset$ correspond to a situation of complete information and so it does not make sense asking whether they could "influence" the probability of any other event

A. We point out that this is a first instance (even if in a limiting case) of a *lack of symmetry* in the concept of independence (see also the following Theorem 6).

Proposition 3 - Let P be a coherent conditional probability, and A, B two possible events. If $A * B$, then $A^c * B$, $A * B^c$, and $A^c * B^c$.

The following two theorems (for the proofs, see the quoted paper) study the connections between our definition of stochastic independence and others known in the literature:

Theorem 2 - If $A * B$, then $P(A|B) = P(A)$. Conversely, assuming that $P(B) < 1$ and $0 < P(A) < 1$, if $P(A|B) = P(A)$, then $A * B$.

Remark 3 - When $P(B) = 1$, so that, trivially, $P(A|B) = P(A)$, the relation $A*B$ may not hold. In fact it can be proved that, when $P(B) = 1$, the probability $P(A|B^c)$ can take any value of the interval [0,1].

Theorem 3 - If $A * B$, then $P(A \wedge B) = P(A)P(B)$. Conversely, assuming that $0 < P(A) < 1$ and $0 < P(B) < 1$, if $P(A \wedge B) = P(A)P(B)$, then $A * B$.

Remark 4 - When $P(B) = 0$, the equality $P(A \wedge B) = P(A)P(B)$ holds for any $P(A)$, but this does not imply $A * B$. If $P(B) = 1$, both equalities $P(A \wedge B) = P(A)P(B)$ and $P(A|B) = P(A)$ hold for any A, but (as it has been already noticed in Remark 3) this does not imply $A * B$. If $P(A) = 0$, the product rule is satisfied for any B, and we may have also $P(A|B) = P(A|B^c) = 0$, but it does not follow $A * B$, since condition $\circ(A|B) = \circ(A|B^c)$ may not hold. Finally, if $P(A) = 1$, both equalities hold, but it is not necessarily true that $\circ(A^c|B) = \circ(A^c|B^c)$.

The next theorem gives the fundamental connection to *logical* independence:

Theorem 4 - Let A, B two possible events. If $A * B$, then A and B are *logically independent* (*i.e.*, none of the four relevant atoms is impossible).

The following Theorem 5 characterizes stochastic independence of two logically independent events A and B in terms of the probabilities $P(B)$, $P(B|A)$ and $P(B|A^c)$, *giving up any direct reference to the zero-layers.*

Theorem 5 - Let A and B be two *logically independent* events. If P is a *coherent* conditional probability such that $P(A|B) = P(A|B^c)$, then $A*B$ if and only if one (and only one) of the following *(a), (b), (c)* holds:

(a) $0 < P(A|B) < 1$;

(b) $P(A|B) = 0$ and the extension of P to B and $B|A$ satisfies one of the three following conditions:

1. $P(B) = 0\,, \quad P(B|A) = 0\,,$
2. $P(B) = 1\,, \quad P(B|A) = 1\,,$
3. $0 < P(B) < 1\,, \quad 0 < P(B|A) < 1\,,$

(c) $P(A|B) = 1$ and the extension of P to B and $B|A^c$ satisfies one of the three following conditions:

1. $P(B) = 0\,, \quad P(B|A^c) = 0\,,$
2. $P(B) = 1\,, \quad P(B|A^c) = 1\,,$
3. $0 < P(B) < 1\,, \quad 0 < P(B|A^c) < 1\,,$

Concerning the possible symmetry of the independence relation, we have the following result:

Theorem 6 - Let $A * B$. We have:

(i) if $P(B) = 0$ then $B * A$;

(ii) if $P(B) = 1$ then $B * A$;

(iii) if $0 < P(B) < 1$ and $0 < P(A|B) < 1$, then $B * A$.

Remark 5 - We note that if $0 < P(B) < 1$ and $P(A|B) = P(A|B^c) = 0$ (and so $P(A) = 0$), then $A * B$ does not assure that $B * A$. In fact, by condition 3. under *(b)* of Theorem 5, we have $0 < P(B|A) < 1$, but $P(B|A)$ not necessarily equals $P(B|A^c) = P(B)$: see Example 3 of [3].

This lack of symmetry is *not* counterintuitive: the validity of $A * B$ means (roughly speaking) that the occurrence of the event B with *positive* probability does not "influence" the probability of A; but this circumstance would not necessarily entail, conversely, that the occurrence of the "unexpected" (*i.e.*, zero probability) event A should not "influence" the (positive) probability of B.

4 Upper and Lower Coherent Conditional Probabilities

A typical situation where we need to consider the coherence of probability evaluations possibly involving both "precise" and "imprecise" assessments occurs when we get – as coherent updating of an initial assessment – a not necessarily unique value, but a set of values constituting *a real interval bounded by a lower and an upper probability.* In particular, we may obtain a lower probability equal to zero, so that assuming instead its positivity (as it is usually done in many approaches to conditioning for "imprecise" probabilities) is a very crucial step. For a thorough discussion of these aspects, see [5].

We will refer - here and in the sequel - only to *lower* conditional probabilities $\underline{P}$: clearly, we can get corresponding results concerning *upper* probabilities.

Given an *arbitrary* set $\mathcal{C}$ of conditional events, a *coherent lower conditional probability* on $\mathcal{C}$ is a nonnegative function $\underline{P}$ such that there exists a non-empty family $\mathcal{P} = \{P(\cdot|\cdot)\}$ of coherent conditional probabilities on $\mathcal{C}$ (*dominating family*) whose lower envelope is $\underline{P}$, that is, for any $E|H \in \mathcal{C}$,

$$\underline{P}(E|H) = \inf_{\mathcal{P}} P(E|H).$$

When $\mathcal{C}$ is finite, if $\underline{P}$ is a coherent lower conditional probability, then there exists a *dominating family* $\mathcal{P}' \supseteq \mathcal{P}$ such that

$$\underline{P}(E|H) = \min_{\mathcal{P}'} P(E|H).$$

The following relevant theorem has been given in [2]; see also [5].

Theorem 7 - Let $\mathcal{C}$ be an arbitrary finite family of conditional events $F_i|K_i$, and denote by $\mathcal{A}_o$ the relevant set of atoms. For a real function $\underline{P}$ on $\mathcal{C}$ the following two statements are equivalent:

(i) the function $\underline{P}$ is a coherent *lower* conditional probability on $\mathcal{C}$;

(ii) there exists, for any $F_i|K_i \in \mathcal{C}$ (at least) a class of probabilities $\Pi^i = \{P^i_o, P^i_1, \ldots\}$ (each probability P^i_α being defined on a suitable subset $\mathcal{A}^i_\alpha \subseteq \mathcal{A}_0$) such that for any $F_j|K_j \in \mathcal{C}$ there is a unique P^i_α with

$$\sum_{A_r \subseteq K_j}^{r} P^i_\alpha(A_r) > 0$$

and

$$\underline{P}(F_j|K_j) \leq \frac{\sum_{A_r \subseteq F_j \wedge K_j}^{r} P^i_\alpha(A_r)}{\sum_{A_r \subseteq K_j}^{r} P^i_\alpha(A_r)} \qquad \text{if} \qquad j \neq i$$

$$\underline{P}(F_j|K_j) = \frac{\sum_{A_r \subseteq F_j \wedge K_j}^{r} P^i_\alpha(A_r)}{\sum_{A_r \subseteq K_j}^{r} P^i_\alpha(A_r)} \qquad \text{if} \qquad j = i$$

and, moreover, $\mathcal{A}^i_{\alpha'} \subset \mathcal{A}^i_{\alpha''}$ for $\alpha' > \alpha''$, while $P^i_{\alpha''}(A_r) = 0$ if $A_r \in \mathcal{A}^i_{\alpha'}$.

Actually, it is possible to build the classes $\{P^i_\alpha\}$ as solutions of sequences of systems (one for each conditional event $F_i|K_i \in \mathcal{C}$) like the following one:

$$(\mathcal{S}^i_\alpha) \begin{cases} \sum_{A_r \subseteq F_i \wedge K_i}^{r} P^i_\alpha(A_r) = \underline{P}(F_i|K_i) \sum_{A_r \subseteq K_i}^{r} P^i_\alpha(A_r) \quad \left[\text{if } P^i_{\alpha-1}(K_i) = 0\right], \\ \sum_{A_r \subseteq F_j \wedge K_j}^{r} P^i_\alpha(A_r) \geq \underline{P}(F_j|K_j) \sum_{A_r \subseteq K_i}^{r} P^i_\alpha(A_r) \left[\text{if } P^i_{\alpha-1}(K_j) = 0\,, j \neq i\right], \\ \sum_{A_r \subseteq K^\alpha_{o,i}}^{r} P^i_\alpha(A_r) = 1 \end{cases}$$

where $K^\alpha_{o,i}$ is, for $\alpha \geq 0$, the union of the K_i's such that $P^i_{\alpha-1}(K_i) = 0$ (and $P^i_{-1}(K_i) = 0$ for all K_i's).

This procedure suggests, as in the case of probabilities, an actual algorithm to prove the consistency (coherence) of a *lower* probability assessment on a finite set of events.

Definition 4 - Given a coherent lower conditional probability $\underline{P}$ on $\mathcal{C}$ and any conditional event $F_i|K_i \in \mathcal{C}$, the element P of the dominant family $\mathcal{P}$ such that $P(F_i|K_i) = \underline{P}(F_i|K_i)$ will be called *i–minimal probability*, and the relevant class $\Pi^i = \{P^i_o, P^i_1, \ldots\}$ (see statement *(ii)* of the previous Theorem) will be called *i–minimal class*.

5 Two Critical Examples

In this Section we discuss the role, in the definition of stochastic independence, of the product rules (1) – for "precise" probabilities – and (2) – for lower probabilities – recalled in the Introduction. In fact, considering the lower probability $\underline{P}$, we may have that (2) holds, while there is no element P of the class of dominating "precise" probabilities such that (1) holds. Conversely, we may have classes of probabilities such that each element P of the class satisfies (1), but (2) does not hold for the corresponding lower probability.

Example 1 - Given two (logically independent) events A and B, consider the following assessment

$$\underline{P}(A) = \underline{P}(B) = \frac{1}{4} ,$$

$$\underline{P}(A \wedge B) = \frac{1}{16} , \qquad \underline{P}(A \vee B) = \frac{3}{4} .$$

To prove that $\underline{P}$ is a lower probability, we resort to Theorem 7 of Section 4: so we need writing down four systems, one for each event; the unknowns are the probabilities of the atoms

$$A_1 = A \wedge B , \qquad A_2 = A \wedge B^c ,$$
$$A_3 = A^c \wedge B , \qquad A_4 = A^c \wedge B^c .$$

For the sake of brevity, we show only the system referring to the event A, denoting by x_i the relevant unknowns:

$$\begin{cases} x_1 + x_2 = \frac{1}{4} \\ x_1 + x_3 \geq \frac{1}{4} \\ x_1 \geq \frac{1}{16} \\ x_1 + x_2 + x_3 \geq \frac{3}{4} \\ x_1 + x_2 + x_3 + x_4 = 1 \\ x_i \geq 0 \end{cases}$$

A solution is

$$x_1 = x_2 = \frac{1}{8} , \qquad x_3 = \frac{1}{2} , \qquad x_4 = \frac{1}{4} .$$

Solutions of the other systems are the following : that corresponding to B is

$$y_1 = y_3 = \frac{1}{8} , \qquad y_2 = \frac{1}{2} , \qquad y_4 = \frac{1}{4} ,$$

that corresponding to $A \wedge B$ is

$$z_1 = \frac{1}{16} , \qquad z_2 = \frac{1}{4} , \qquad z_3 = \frac{1}{2} , \qquad z_4 = \frac{3}{16} ,$$

that corresponding to $A \vee B$ is

$$u_1 = \frac{1}{16} , \qquad u_2 = \frac{3}{16} , \qquad u_3 = \frac{1}{2} , \qquad u_4 = \frac{1}{4} .$$

Now, notice that

$$\underline{P}(A \wedge B) = \underline{P}(A)\underline{P}(B) ;$$

nevertheless, *there is no dominating class $\mathcal{P}$ such that the product rule holds for all probabilities $P \in \mathcal{P}$*. In fact, consider (for instance) the system corresponding to the event $A \wedge B$, that we write in the form (for $a, b, c \geq 0$)

$$\begin{cases} z_1 + z_2 = \frac{1}{4} + a \\ z_1 + z_3 = \frac{1}{4} + b \\ z_1 = \frac{1}{16} \\ z_1 + z_2 + z_3 = \frac{3}{4} + c \\ z_1 + z_2 + z_3 + z_4 = 1 \\ z_i \geq 0 \end{cases}$$

and assume that the corresponding "minimal" probability satisfies the product rule, that is

$$\left(\frac{1}{4} + a\right)\left(\frac{1}{4} + b\right) = \frac{1}{16} .$$

Since the latter equation holds only for $a = b = 0$, it follows easily the contradiction

$$z_1 + z_2 + z_3 < \frac{3}{4}$$

Remark 6 - Actually, lower probabilities (and probabilities, too) are (usually) defined on a family *containing* the events A, B and $A \wedge B$ (in particular, in the classic approach this family is a Boolean algebra), and *not* only on these three events. This is the essential reason why a "local" condition as that of independence is not necessarily inherited by an enveloping class of probabilities. So it should be clear that what inhibits the existence of a family of probabilities satisfying the product rule, is the presence of the event $A \vee B$: obviously, this would not be the case if the only involved events were A, B and $A \wedge B$.

The following example shows that we may have families of probabilities such that *each element P satisfies the product rule, but the latter does not hold for the dominated lower probability.*

Example 2 - Take the simple family with two elements P_1 and P_2

$$P_1(A) = \frac{1}{4}, \qquad P_1(B) = \frac{1}{2}, \qquad P_1(A \wedge B) = \frac{1}{8},$$

$$P_2(A) = \frac{1}{2}, \qquad P_2(B) = \frac{1}{4}, \qquad P_2(A \wedge B) = \frac{1}{8}.$$

These two probabilities satisfy the product rule, while the corresponding lower probability

$$\underline{P}(A) = \underline{P}(B) = \frac{1}{4}, \qquad \underline{P}(A \wedge B) = \frac{1}{8}$$

does not.

6 Stochastic Independence for Upper and Lower Probabilities

We introduce now a definition of *stochastic independence for lower probabilities* that avoids (as can be easily checked) the situations pointed out in Examples

1 and 2: we recall that in these examples, given a lower probability and an enveloping class, the independence property may hold for the former but not for the latter, or conversely.

Definition 5 - Given a set $\mathcal{E}$ of events containing A, B, A^c, B^c, with $B \neq \Omega$, $B \neq \emptyset$, and a *coherent* lower conditional probability $\underline{P}$, defined on a family $\mathcal{C} \subset \mathcal{E} \times \mathcal{E}^o$, with $\mathcal{C}$ containing $\mathcal{D} = \{A|B, A|B^c, A^c|B, A^c|B^c\}$, we say that A is ***stochastically independent*** of B with respect to $\underline{P}$ (in symbols $A \underline{*} B$) if there exists a dominating class $\mathcal{P}$ such that, for every $P \in \mathcal{P}$, one has $A * B$.

Notice that the latter requirement of Definition 5 can be limited only to *i–minimal* probabilities, for any $F_i|K_i \in \mathcal{C}$.

Remark 7 - According to our definition, the events A, B of Example 1 are *not* stochastically independent: in fact, if they were independent, by Theorem 3 the product rule would hold for a dominating class, while we proved that such a class does not exist. The events of Example 2 *are* independent, as can be easily checked by expressing the relevant conditional probabilities by means of the given (unconditional, with values strictly greater than 0 and less than 1) probabilities of A, B and $A \wedge B$.

Definition 6 - Let $\mathcal{C}$ be a family of conditional events and $\underline{P}$ a coherent lower conditional probability on $\mathcal{C}$. For any conditional event $F_i|K_i \in \mathcal{C}$, we call *zero-layer* of $F_i|K_i$, with respect to a set $\Pi = \{P_i^r\}$ of minimal classes, the (nonnegative) number

$$\underline{\circ}(F_i|K_i) = \circ_i(F_i|K_i)\,,$$

where $\circ_i(F_i|K_i)$ is the zero layer $\circ(F_i|K_i)$ (see Definition 2 in Section 2) with respect to the i–minimal class P_i^i .

The following Proposition is an easy consequence of the properties of stochastic independence for "precise" probabilities:

Proposition 4 - If $A \underline{*} B$, then *both* the following conditions hold:

(i) $\underline{P}(A|B) = \underline{P}(A|B^c) = \underline{P}(A)$;

(ii) there exists a class $\Pi = \{P_i^r\}$ as those of Definition 6, such that

$$\underline{\circ}(A|B) = \underline{\circ}(A|B^c) \quad \text{and} \quad \underline{\circ}(A^c|B) = \underline{\circ}(A^c|B^c)\,.$$

Remark 8 - Clearly, stochastic independence implies logical independence: the conclusion follows easily from Theorem 4 by referring to just one of the dominating probabilities.

From the "necessary" part of Theorem 5 it follows:

Proposition 5 - Let A and B be two *logically independent* events. If $A \underline{*} B$, then $\underline{P}(A|B) = \underline{P}(A|B^c)$ and one (and only one) of the following *(a), (b), (c)* holds:

(a) $0 < \underline{P}(A|B) < 1$;

(b) $\underline{P}(A|B) = 0$ and the extension of $\underline{P}$ to B and $B|A$ satisfies one of the three following conditions:

1. $\underline{P}(B) = 0\,, \quad \underline{P}(B|A) = 0\,,$
2. $\underline{P}(B) = 1\,, \quad \underline{P}(B|A) = 1\,,$
3. $0 < \underline{P}(B) < 1\,, \quad 0 < \underline{P}(B|A) < 1\,,$

(c) $\underline{P}(A|B) = 1$ and the extension of $\underline{P}$ to B and $B|A^c$ satisfies one of the three following conditions:

1. $\underline{P}(B) = 0\,, \quad \underline{P}(B|A^c) = 0\,,$
2. $\underline{P}(B) = 1\,, \quad \underline{P}(B|A^c) = 1\,,$
3. $0 < \underline{P}(B) < 1\,, \quad 0 < \underline{P}(B|A^c) < 1\,,$

Differently from the case of conditional (precise) probability, here the converse is not true. In fact, for *(a), (b), (c)* to imply independence it is necessary (and sufficient) that the restriction of the imprecise conditional probability to the relevant events be a *precise* conditional probability, as stated in the following

Theorem 8 - Let $\mathcal{E}$ be a set of events containing A, B, A^c, B^c, with $B \neq \Omega$, $B \neq \emptyset$, and $\underline{P}$ a *coherent* lower conditional probability, defined on $\mathcal{C} \subset \mathcal{E} \times \mathcal{E}^o$, with $\mathcal{C}$ containing $\mathcal{D} = \{A|B, A|B^c, B|A, B|A^c\}$. Suppose $\underline{P}(A|B) = \underline{P}(A|B^c)$: if A and B are logically independent and $\underline{P}$ satisfies one of the conditions *(a), (b)* or *(c)* of Proposition 5, then $A \,\underline{*}\, B$ if and only if the restriction of $\underline{P}$ to $\mathcal{D}' = \mathcal{D} \cup \{A, B\}$ is a coherent conditional ***probability***.

Proof - Put $F_1|K_1 = A|\Omega$, $F_2|K_2 = B|\Omega$, $F_3|K_3 = A|B$, $F_4|K_4 = A|B^c$, $F_5|K_5 = B|A$, $F_6|K_6 = B|A^c$.

Suppose that the restriction of $\underline{P}$ to $\mathcal{D}'$ is a coherent conditional (precise) probability P and consider the case *(a)*, *i.e.* $0 < \underline{P}(A|B) < 1$.

Consider the relevant system (S_o^1) of Theorem 7 (for the details, see [6]), which has a solution satisfying (as equalities) the inequalities related to the events $F_i|K_i$, with $i \leq 6$. Then this solution gives rise to i–minimal coherent conditional probabilities P_i for every $i \leq 6$. Moreover P_i satisfies the condition of independence $A * B$. It is also easy to prove that it is possible to find i–minimal probabilities for $i > 6$. For the cases *(b)* and *(c)* the proof is similar.

Conversely, suppose now that $A \,\underline{*}\, B$; then there exists an i–minimal class $\{P_i\}$ such that $A * B$ for any i (that is $P_i(A|B) = P_i(A|B^c) = P_i(A)$ and one of the above conditions *(a), (b), (c)* of Theorem 4 holds). Therefore such a P_i, for $i = 1$, is necessarily a solution of the system $(\mathcal{S}_o^1)$ that satisfies (as equalities) the inequalities related to $F_i|K_i$, with $i \leq 6$. Then it follows that all the i–minimal probabilities with $i \leq 6$ coincide, and this ends the proof.

Remark 9 - When the *restriction* of $\underline{P}$ on the relevant events is a probability P, the sufficiency of the conditions *(a), (b), (c)* of Proposition 5 for the stochastic independence of A and B – a property that involves all the probabilities of a dominating class – is not (as it could appear) a trivial consequence of Theorem 5: see the discussion in Remark 6. What is more, for other usual definitions (based on the product rule) a similar result *does not hold.* Consider in fact Example 1: even if the restriction of $\underline{P}$ to $\{A, B, A \wedge B\}$ is a coherent ***probability*** and (2) holds, nevertheless this form of independence does not imply the existence of a class of dominating ***probabilities*** satisfying the product rule.

7 Conclusions

Concerning "imprecise" probabilities, in the literature there are several different definitions of independence that give rise to many difficulties and inconsistencies. Often the latter are due also to the ambiguity concerning the information "carried" by the upper and lower probabilities, which should be clearly distinguished from the concept of independence. For example, in [8] the authors discuss the phenomenon called *dilation* as if it were counterintuitive. The fact that a "precise" probability $P(A)$ may give rise – under conditioning with respect to B – to an interval whose extremes are a lower and an upper probability, is well known in Bayesian statistics and it is not at all strange in terms of coherence. We prefer to rely more on the *syntactic* aspects than on the *semantic* ones, so avoiding any deepening of vague statements such as "losing" or "carrying" information, which are not clearly and unambiguously interpretable, especially in the framework of "imprecise" probabilities. For example, does it carry more information a *precise* assessment p, with $p = .5$, or an *imprecise* one (p', p''), with $p' = .8$ and $p'' = .95$? If this question had any essential significance, we would prefer – in this case – an "imprecise" conclusion (since it looks more "informative").

Our opinion is that dilation looks as counterintuitive since what is usually emphasized in the literature – when a conditional probability $P(A|B)$ is taken into account – is only the fact that $P(\cdot|B)$ *is a probability for any given* B: this is a very restrictive (and misleading) view of conditional probability, corresponding trivially to just a modification of the "world" Ω. It is instead essential to regard the conditioning event B as a "variable", *i.e.* the "status" of B in $A|B$ is not just that of something representing a given *fact*, but that of an (uncertain) *event* (like A) for which the knowledge of its truth value may not be required: so $P(B|A)$, which plays an essential role – through Bayes' theorem – in the updating $P(A|B)$ of $P(A)$, may be naturally "imprecise" (for example, consider two urns with N balls – one of them, U, being of unknown composition – and take A=*an urn chosen at random out of the two is* U, and B=*a ball drawn from the selected urn is white*).

Going back to independence, although it might seem obvious that, given a measure of uncertainty (as a lower probability) involving *a family* of (precise) probabilities, a "natural" definition of stochastic independence should require the independence condition *for each element* of a class of probabilities (for example, a dominating class, as in Definition 5), we had better *be careful in other contexts*. In other words, while a concept of independence for a lower probability not referring to a dominating family might be not significant (see Examples 1 and 2), on the other hand the conclusion of Theorem 8 may suggest that the intuitive aspects of stochastic independence (*i.e.*, a new "information" on the event B should not change our belief in the event A) are better captured by referring to *just one* probability.

For example, convex combinations of probabilities do not inherit stochastic independence relations that hold for *all* the element of a relevant family. An urn of unknown composition supplies (by referring to successive drawings with replacements) a natural (and classic) example of *not* independent (even if *ex-*

changeable) events E_i =*white ball at the i-th drawing* (since at each drawing we learn "something"). Nevertheless all the probabilities corresponding to the different compositions (*i.e.*, conditionally to H_r=*the number of white balls is* r, with $r = 0, 1, 2, ..., N$, if N is the total number of balls in the urn) satisfy the condition of independence. It is not difficult to prove that this is not true for the convex combination

$$P(E_i \wedge E_j) = \sum_{r=1}^{N} P(H_r)P(E_i \wedge E_j|H_r) \neq P(E_i)P(E_j).$$

References

1. Coletti, G., Scozzafava, R. (1996) Characterization of Coherent Conditional Probabilities as a Tool for their Assessment and Extension. International Journal of Uncertainty, Fuzziness and Knowledge-Based System **4**, 103–127.
2. Coletti, G., Scozzafava, R. (1998) Conditional measures: old and new. In: Proc. of "New Trends in Fuzzy Systems", Napoli 1996 (eds. D.Mancini, M.Squillante, and A.Ventre), World Scientific, 107–120.
3. Coletti, G., Scozzafava, R. (2000) Zero Probabilities in Stochastical Independence. In Information, Uncertainty, Fusion (Eds. B. Bouchon-Meunier, R. R. Yager, and L. A. Zadeh), Kluwer, Dordrecht, 185–196. (Selected papers from IPMU '98, Paris)
4. Coletti, G., Scozzafava, R. (1999) Conditioning and Inference in Intelligent Systems. Soft Computing **3**, 118–130
5. Coletti, G., Scozzafava, R. (2000) The Role of Coherence in Eliciting and Handling Imprecise Probabilities and its Application to Medical Diagnosis. Information Sciences **130**, 41–65
6. Coletti, G., Scozzafava, R. (2001) Stochastic Independence in a Coherent Setting. Annals of Mathematics and Artificial Intelligence (Special Issue on "Partial Knowledge and Uncertainty: Independence, Conditioning, Inference"), to appear
7. Coletti, G., Scozzafava, R., Vantaggi, B. (2001) Probabilistic Reasoning as a General Inferential Tool, ECSQARU 2001, submitted.
8. Couso, I., Moral, S., Walley, P. (1999) Examples of independence for imprecise probabilities. In: Int. Symp. on Imprecise Probabilities and their applications (ISIPTA '99), Ghent, Belgium, 121–130
9. De Campos, L.M., Moral, S. (1995) Independence concepts for convex sets of probabilities. In: Uncertainty in Artificial Intelligence (UAI '95), Morgan & Kaufmann, San Mateo, 108–115
10. de Finetti, B. (1949) Sull'Impostazione Assiomatica del Calcolo delle Probabilità. Annali Univ. Trieste **19**, 3–55. (Engl. transl.: Ch.5 in Probability, Induction, Statistics, Wiley, London, 1972)
11. Dubins, L.E. (1975) Finitely Additive Conditional Probabilities, Conglomerability and Disintegration. Annals of Probability **3**, 89–99
12. Krauss, P.H. (1968) Representation of Conditional Probability Measures on Boolean Algebras. Acta Math. Acad. Scient. Hungar. 19, 229–241
13. Rényi, A. (1956) On Conditional Probability Spaces Generated by a Dimensionally Ordered Set of Measures. Theory of Probability and its Applications **1**, 61–71
14. Spohn, W. (1999) Ranking Functions, AGM Style. Research Group "Logic in Philosophy" Preprint **28**
15. Vantaggi, B. (2001) Conditional Independence in a Finite Coherent Setting. Annals of Mathematics and Artificial Intelligence, to appear

Qualitative Possibilistic Independence Based on Plausibility Relations

Nahla Ben Amor[1], Salem Benferhat[2], and Khaled Mellouli[1]

[1] Institut Supérieur de Gestion de Tunis
{nahla.benamor, khaled.mellouli}@ihec.rnu.tn
[2] Institut de Recherche en Informatique de Toulouse (I.R.I.T)
benferhat@irit.fr

Abstract. Independence is very important in many fields of Artificial Intelligence. It is particularly well studied in Bayesian networks. This paper analysis the notion of independence in the possibility theory framework. More precisely, we propose new definitions of possibilistic independence that we call qualitative independence, which only exploits the plausibility relation induced by a possibility distribution. A comparative study between existing (quantitative) possibilistic independence with qualitative independence is given. Lastly, results on graphoid properties of qualitative independence relations are provided.

1 Introduction

We can distinguish two forms of independence : the *decompositional independence* allowing the decomposition of a joint distribution pertaining to tuples of variables into local distributions on smaller subsets of variables, and the *causal independence* for expressing the lack of causality. The link between these two kinds of independence relations is not always obvious. Ideally, a good definition of independence should be *causal* in order to be easily expressed by experts and also *decomposable* for calculus considerations.

In the probabilistic framework, the causal independence defined by $Pr(B \mid A) = Pr(A)$ is equivalent to the decompositional independence defined by $Pr(A \wedge B) = Pr(A) * Pr(B)$.

In possibility theory, the situation is different since causal and decompositional independence are not always equivalent. This paper proposes new forms of independence obtained by only considering the plausibility relation induced by a possibility distribution.

In Section 2, we give a brief background on possibility theory then in Section 3 we present the existing independence relations relative to the this framework. In Section 4, we propose several definitions of qualitative independence relations, namely those based on well known ordering functions like Pareto ordering, and refinement of it such that leximin and leximax orderings. In the Section 5, we provide a comparative study between existing possibilistic independence and proposed qualitative independence. Lastly, in Section 6 we study the graphoid properties of the different independence relations presented in this paper.

2 Background on possibility theory

We first introduce some notations. Let $U = \{A, B, C, ...\}$ be the set of all variables. The set $D_A = \{a_1, ..., a_n\}$ represents the domain of the variable A. By a we denote any instance of A.
$X, Y, Z, ...$ denote disjoint subsets of variables in U, and $D_X = \{x_1, x_2, ..., x_m\}$ the Cartesian product of variables' domains in X i.e., $D_X = \times_{A \in X} D_A$,. By x we denote any instance of X. Ω denotes the universe of discourse, which is the Cartesian product of all variables' domains in U. Each element of Ω is called situation or state of the world. ϕ, ψ denote the subsets of Ω, called events and $\neg\phi$ denotes the complementary set of ϕ i.e. $\neg\phi = \Omega - \phi$.
In the following, we only give a brief recalling on possibility theory, for more details see [7].

2.1 Possibility distribution and possibility measure

The basic concept in possibility theory is the notion of *possibility distribution.* It is a mapping from Ω to the scale [0, 1] usually denoted by π. Possibility distribution aims at encoding our knowledge about ill-known situation : $\pi(\omega) = 1$ means that ω is completely possible and $\pi(\omega) = 0$ means that ω is impossible as being the real situation. A possibility distribution π is said to be *normalized* if there exists at least one situation ω which is totally possible.
Given a possibility distribution π, the uncertainty of any event $\phi \subseteq \Omega$ is estimated by means of two dual measures:

- The **possibility measure** of ϕ:

$$\Pi(\phi) = max_{\omega \in \phi} \pi(\omega). \tag{1}$$

  The measure $\Pi(\phi)$ evaluates at which level ϕ is **consistent** with our knowledge represented by a possibility distribution π.

- The **necessity measure**, associated with Π by duality:

$$N(\phi) = 1 - \Pi(\neg\phi) = min_{\omega \notin \phi}(1 - \pi(\omega)). \tag{2}$$

  The measure $N(\phi)$ evaluates at which level ϕ is **certainly** implied by our knowledge (represented by a possibility distribution π).

2.2 Possibilistic conditioning

Conditioning is a crucial notion in studying independence relations. In the possibilistic setting conditioning consists in modifying our initial knowledge, encoded by a possibility distribution π by the arrival of a new *sure* piece of information $\phi \subseteq \Omega$. The initial distribution π is then transformed into a new one denoted by $\pi' = \pi(. \mid \phi)$. The possibility theory offers two major definitions of conditioning depending on whether we are in a qualitative or in a numerical setting [9]. In the first case the conditioning is based on the minimum operator and is defined by:

$$\Pi(\psi \mid_m \phi) = \begin{cases} 1 & if\ \Pi(\psi \wedge \phi) = \Pi(\phi) \\ \Pi(\psi \wedge \phi) & \text{otherwise (i.e } \Pi(\psi \wedge \phi) < \Pi(\phi)) \end{cases} \tag{3}$$

while in the second case the conditioning is based on the product-operator and is defined by:

$$\Pi(\psi \mid_* \phi) = \begin{cases} \frac{\Pi(\psi \wedge \phi)}{\Pi(\phi)} & \text{if } \Pi(\phi) \neq 0 \\ 0 & otherwise \end{cases} \tag{4}$$

Each of these two definitions satisfies an equation close to the Bayesian rule, of the form:

$$\forall \omega,\ \pi(\omega) = \pi(\omega \mid \phi) \otimes \Pi(\phi) \tag{5}$$

respectively for $\otimes$ are the **min** and the **product** operators. The min-based conditioning corresponds to the least specific solution of Equation 5 proposed by Hisdal [12]. The existence of these two conditioning definitions explains why in possibility theory there are two definitions of independence based on conditioning as shown in Section 3.2.

3 Existing possibilistic independence relations

We briefly recall the existing independence relations proposed in the possibilistic framework.

3.1 Possibilistic Non-interactivity independence

The well known decompositional possibilistic independence relation between X and Y in the context Z is represented by the **Non-interactivity** [15] defined by:

$$\Pi(x \wedge y \mid_m z) = min(\Pi(x \mid_m z), \Pi(y \mid_m z)), \forall x, y, z \tag{6}$$

This form of independence denoted I_{NI} is clearly symmetric.

3.2 Possibilistic causal independence

The possibilistic causal independence relation is based on the possibilistic conditioning. The idea is that X is considered as independent from Y in the context Z if for any instance z, the possibility degree of any x remains unchanged for any value y. More formally :

$$\Pi(x \mid y \wedge z) = \Pi(x \mid z), \forall x, y, z. \tag{7}$$

Since possibility theory has two kinds of conditioning, this leads to two definitions of causal possibilistic independence :

- **Min-based independence relation** obtained by using $|_m$ in Equation 7. This form of independence called I_M is not symmetric [10] as shown by the following counter-example.

  Counter-example 1 *Let us consider three binary variables A, B and C with the following possibility distribution:*

  Table 1. Lack of symmetry property for I_M

a	b	c	$\pi(a \wedge b \wedge c)$
a_1	-	-	0.6
a_2	b_1	c_1	0.7
a_2	b_1	c_2	0.8
a_2	b_2	c_1	0.9
a_2	b_2	c_2	1

  we can check that $\pi(a \mid b \wedge c) = \pi(a \mid c), \forall a, b, c$ *but,* $\pi(b_1 \mid a_1 \wedge c_1) = 1 \neq \pi(b_1 \mid c_1) = 0.7$.

  Let I_{MS} be the symmetric version of I_H defined by [10] :

  $$\textbf{(i) } \Pi(x \mid_m y \wedge z) = \Pi(x \mid_m z) \text{ and}$$

  $$\textbf{(ii) } \Pi(y \mid_m x \wedge z) = \Pi(y \mid_m z), \forall x, y, z. \tag{8}$$

  I_{MS} is a very strong relation since the MS-independence between two sets of variables X and Y implies the ignorance of one of them [5] i.e $\pi(x) = 1, \forall x$ or $\pi(y) = 1, \forall y$.

- **Product independence relation** denoted I_{Prod}, this relation is based on the product and obtained by using $|_*$ in Equation 7.

4 Qualitative independence

In this section, we propose several new definitions of possibilistic independence (causal and decomposable) defined from the plausibility relations induced from possibility distributions.

4.1 Causal Ordinal independence

The idea of the Causal Ordinal independence is that two variable sets X and Y are independent in the context of Z, if for all z, the preferential ordering between the different values of X is preserved after the revision by any value y of Y (and vice versa). More formally:

Definition 1 *Let X, Y and Z be three disjoint subsets of U. The variable set X is said to be CO-independent (CO for Causal Ordinal) of Y in the context Z, denoted $I_{CO}(X, Z, Y)$, if $\forall z \in D_Z, \forall y \in D_Y$:*

$$\forall x_i, x_j \in D_X, \Pi(x_i \wedge z) > \Pi(x_j \wedge z) \textit{ iff } \Pi(x_i \wedge y \wedge z) > \Pi(x_j \wedge y \wedge z) \quad (9)$$

Note that this relation is not symmetric as shown by the following counter-example:

Counter-example 2 *Let us consider two binary variables A and B with the following possibility distribution:*

Table 2. Lack of symmetry property for I_{CO}

a	b	$\pi(a \wedge b)$
a_1	b_1	1
a_1	b_2	0.8
a_2	b_1	0.5
a_2	b_2	0.7

we can check that the local possibility distribution relative to B is $\Pi(b_1) = 1 > \Pi(b_2) = 0.8$. However, in the context a_2, we have $\Pi(b_2) = 0.7 > \Pi(b_1) = 0.5$, thus, the relation $I_{CO}(B, \emptyset, A)$ is false contrary to $I_{CO}(A, \emptyset, B)$

We denote I_{COS} the symmetric version of I_{CO}; i.e. X is said to be COS-independent of Y in the context Z if $\forall z \in D_Z, y \in D_Y, x \in D_X$:

(i) $\forall x_i, x_j \in D_X, \Pi(x_i \wedge z) > \Pi(x_j \wedge z)$ iff $\Pi(x_i \wedge y \wedge z) > \Pi(x_j \wedge y \wedge z)$, and

(ii) $\forall y_k, y_l \in D_Y, \Pi(y_k \wedge z) > \Pi(y_l \wedge z)$ iff $\Pi(y_k \wedge x \wedge z) > \Pi(y_l \wedge x \wedge z)$. (10)

4.2 Decompositional qualitative independence

In the following we define decompositional independence relations based on well known orderings used in the qualitative setting namely the *Pareto-ordering*, and refinements of it like *leximin* and *leximax* orderings that we briefly present now.

1. A possibility relation π is said to be **Pareto-ordered** on X and Y in the context Z, if $\forall z \in D_Z, \forall x_i, x_j \in D_X, \forall y_k, y_l \in D_Y$, we have:
$\Pi(x_i \wedge y_k \wedge z) \geq \Pi(x_j \wedge y_l \wedge z)$ iff
$\Pi(x_i \wedge z) \geq \Pi(x_j \wedge z)$ and $\Pi(y_k \wedge z) \geq \Pi(y_l \wedge z)$

   Remark : We can give a stronger definition of Pareto by:
$\Pi(x_i \wedge y_k \wedge z) > \Pi(x_j \wedge y_l \wedge z)$ iff :
$[\Pi(x_i \wedge z) \geq \Pi(x_j \wedge z)$ and $\Pi(y_k \wedge z) \geq \Pi(y_l \wedge z)]$ and
$[\Pi(x_i \wedge z) > \Pi(x_j \wedge z)$ or $\Pi(y_k \wedge z) > \Pi(y_l \wedge z)]$.

   The first definition of Pareto implies this one, but the converse in not true as shown by this counter-example:

   Counter-example 3 *We can check that the possibility distribution π given in Table 3 is ordered w.r.t the second definition but not w.r.t the first one since $\pi(a_1 \wedge b_2) \geq \pi(a_2 \wedge b_1)$ while $\Pi(b_2) < \Pi(b_1)$.*

Table 3. Pareto-ordered distribution

a	b	$\pi(a \wedge b)$
a_1	b_1	1
a_1	b_2	0.8
a_2	b_1	0.8
a_2	b_2	0.4

2. A possibility relation π is said to be **leximin-ordered** on X and Y in the context Z, if $\forall z \in D_Z, \forall x_i, x_j \in D_X, \forall y_k, y_l \in D_Y$, we have :
$\Pi(x_i \wedge y_k \wedge z) > \Pi(x_j \wedge y_l \wedge z)$ iff :
(i) $min(\Pi(x_i \wedge z), \Pi(y_k \wedge z)) > min(\Pi(x_j \wedge z), \Pi(y_l \wedge z))$ or
(ii) $min(\Pi(x_i \wedge z), \Pi(y_k \wedge z)) = min(\Pi(x_j \wedge z), \Pi(y_l \wedge z))$ and
$max(\Pi(x_i \wedge z), \Pi(y_k \wedge z)) > max(\Pi(x_j \wedge z), \Pi(y_l \wedge z))$.

3. A possibility relation π is said to be **leximax-ordered** on X and Y in the context Z, if $\forall z \in D_Z, \forall x_i, x_j \in D_X, \forall y_k, y_l \in D_Y$, we have :
$\Pi(x_i \wedge y_k \wedge z) > \Pi(x_j \wedge y_l \wedge z)$ iff :
(i) $max(\Pi(x_i \wedge z), \Pi(y_k \wedge z)) > max(\Pi(x_j \wedge z), \Pi(y_l \wedge z))$ or
(ii) $max(\Pi(x_i \wedge z), \Pi(y_k \wedge z)) = max(\Pi(x_j \wedge z), \Pi(y_l \wedge z))$ and
$min(\Pi(x_i \wedge z), \Pi(y_k \wedge z)) > min(\Pi(x_j \wedge z), \Pi(y_l \wedge z))$.

Definition 2 *Two variable sets X and Y are said **Pareto-independent** (resp. **leximin-independent, leximax-independent**) in the context Z if the possibility distribution π is Pareto-ordered (resp. leximin-ordered, leximax-ordered) on X and Y in the context Z.*

Example 1 *Let us consider the possibility distributions given in Table 4. We can check that A and B are Pareto-independent in* π_1. *Moreover, these two variables are leximax-independent in* π_2 *and leximin-independent in* π_3. *Indeed, in* π_3 *we have* $\forall a_i, a_j \in \{a_1, a_2\}, \forall b_k, b_l \in \{b_1, b_2, b_3\}$,
$\Pi(a_i \wedge b_k) > \Pi(a_j \wedge b_l)$ *iff* : *(i)* $min(\Pi(a_i), \Pi(b_k)) > min(\Pi(a_j), \Pi(b_l))$ *or* *(ii)* $min(\Pi(a_i), \Pi(b_k)) = min(\Pi(a_j), \Pi(b_l))$ *and* $max(\Pi(a_i), \Pi(b_k)) > max(\Pi(a_j), \Pi(b_l))$.
For instance, $\Pi(a_1 \wedge b_2) = 0.9 > \Pi(a_2 \wedge b_3) = 0.5$ *and we have* $min(\Pi(a_1), \Pi(b_2)) = min(1, 0.9) > min(\Pi(a_2), \Pi(b_3)) = min(0.8, 0.6)$.

Table 4. Pareto, leximax and leximin ordered distributions

a	b	$\pi_1(a \wedge b)$	a	b	$\pi_2(a \wedge b)$	a	b	$\pi_3(a \wedge b)$
a_1	b_1	1	a_1	b_1	1	a_1	b_1	1
a_2	b_1	1	a_1	b_2	0.9	a_1	b_2	0.9
a_1	b_2	0.4	a_2	b_1	0.8	a_2	b_1	0.8
a_2	b_2	0.4	a_1	b_3	0.7	a_2	b_2	0.7
a_1	b_3	0.3	a_2	b_2	0.6	a_1	b_3	0.6
a_2	b_3	0.3	a_2	b_3	0.5	a_2	b_3	0.5

5 Comparative study

In this section, we provide a comparative study between the different independence relations introduced in this paper. First we give a proposition to solve the equivalence between MS and Pareto independence.

Proposition 1 *If a possibility distribution* π *is Pareto-ordered on* X *and* Y *then one of the local distributions on* X *or* Y *should be* uniform[1].

Proof 1 *Suppose that this proposition is false*
$\Rightarrow \exists x, x', \exists y, y'$, *s.t.* $\Pi(x) > \Pi(x')$ *and* $\Pi(y) > \Pi(y')$.
Since the joint distribution π *encodes a total-preorder, two situations can occur :*

- $\Pi(x \wedge y') \geq \Pi(x' \wedge y)$ *but this relation contradicts the Pareto-ordering since* $\Pi(y') \ngeq \Pi(y)$.
- $\Pi(x' \wedge y) \geq \Pi(x \wedge y')$ *but this relation again contradicts the Pareto-ordering since* $\Pi(x') \ngeq \Pi(x)$.

Proposition 2 *Let* X, Y, Z *three disjoint sets of* U. *Then* X *and* Y *are MS-independent in the context of* Z *if and only if they are Pareto-independent in this context.*

[1] π is said to be uniform on X, if for all $x \in D_x$, $\pi(x) = 1$

Proof 2 *For the sake of simplicity, we give the proof without context.*
We firstly prove that $I_{Pareto}(X, \emptyset, Y) \Rightarrow I_{MS}(X, \emptyset, Y)$.
Suppose that this relation is false $\Rightarrow \exists x \in D_X, \exists y \in D_Y$, *such that :*
$\Pi(x \mid y) \neq \Pi(x)$. *Then two cases can appear :*

- case 1 : $\Pi(x) = 1 \Rightarrow \Pi(x \mid y) < 1$
  $\Rightarrow \Pi(x \wedge y) < \Pi(x)$ *and* $\Pi(x \wedge y) < \Pi(y)$
  $\Rightarrow \exists x', \exists y', s.t. \Pi(x \wedge y) < \Pi(x \wedge y')$ *and* $\Pi(x \wedge y) < \Pi(x' \wedge y)$.
  Since $I_{Pareto}(X, \emptyset, Y)$ *is true* $\Pi(y) < \Pi(y')$ *and* $\Pi(x) < \Pi(x')$ *which contradicts Proposition 1.*

- case 2 : $\Pi(x) < 1$
  - $\Pi(x \mid y) = 1 \Rightarrow \Pi(x \wedge y) = \Pi(y)$
    $\Rightarrow \forall x', \Pi(x \wedge y) \geq \Pi(x' \wedge y)$.
    Since $I_{Pareto}(X, \emptyset, Y)$ *is respected we have* $\forall x', \Pi(x) \geq \Pi(x')$ *which contradicts* $\Pi(x) < 1$.
  - $\Pi(x \mid y) \neq 1 \Rightarrow \Pi(x \wedge y) < \Pi(y)$ *and* $\Pi(x \wedge y) < \Pi(x) \Rightarrow \exists x', \exists y'$, *s.t.* $\Pi(x \wedge y) < \Pi(x \wedge y')$ *and* $\Pi(x \wedge y) < \Pi(x' \wedge y)$. *From* $I_{Pareto}(X, \emptyset, Y)$ *we have* $\Pi(y) < \Pi(y')$ *and* $\Pi(x) < \Pi(x')$ *which contradicts Proposition 1.*

We prove now that $I_{MS}(X, \emptyset, Y) \Rightarrow I_{Pareto}(X, \emptyset, Y)$.
Suppose that this relation is false
$\Rightarrow$ *(a)* $\exists x, y, \exists x', y'$ *s.t.* $\Pi(x \wedge y) \geq \Pi(x' \wedge y')$ *but* $\Pi(x) < \Pi(x')$.

Since $I_{MS}(X, \emptyset, Y)$ *is true, we have:* $\Pi(x \mid y) = \Pi(x)$ *and* $\Pi(x \mid y') = \Pi(x)$. *Moreover, from (a) we deduce that* $\Pi(x) < 1$ *(otherwise* $\Pi(x') > 1$ *which is impossible), thus:*
(i) $\Pi(x \mid y) = \Pi(x) < 1$ *and (ii)* $\Pi(x \mid y') = \Pi(x) < 1$.
Moreover:

- $\Pi(x \wedge y) < \Pi(y)$, *indeed we have by definition* $\Pi(x \wedge y) \leq \Pi(y)$ *but if* $\Pi(x \wedge y) = \Pi(y)$ *then* $\Pi(x \mid y) = 1$ *which contradicts (i).*
- $\Pi(x \wedge y') < \Pi(y')$, *indeed we have by definition* $\Pi(x \wedge y') \leq \Pi(y')$ *but if* $\Pi(x \wedge y') = \Pi(y')$ *then* $\Pi(x \mid y') = 1$ *which contradicts (ii).*

$$\textit{Thus (b):} \begin{cases} \Pi(x \wedge y) = \Pi(x) < 1 \text{ and } \Pi(x \wedge y) < \Pi(y) \text{ and} \\ \Pi(x \wedge y') = \Pi(x) < 1 \text{ and } \Pi(x \wedge y') < \Pi(y') \end{cases}$$

(a) + (b) $\Rightarrow$ *(c):*
$min(\Pi(y), \Pi(y')) > \Pi(x \wedge y') = \Pi(x \wedge y) = \Pi(x) \geq \Pi(x' \wedge y')$.
Moreover we have $\Pi(x' \mid y') = \Pi(x')$ *(From MS) and* $\Pi(x' \wedge y') < \Pi(y')$ *(From (c)). Then we can deduce that* $\Pi(x' \wedge y') = \Pi(x')$. *If we use this relation in (c) we obtain* $\Pi(x) \geq \Pi(x')$ *which contradicts (a).*

The following proposition relates existing independence relations in possibility theory.

Proposition 3 *If X and Y are MS-independent in the context Z, then they are NI-independent and Prod-independent but the converse is not true. However, the NI and the Prod independence are incomparable.*

Proposition 4 relates proposed qualitative independence relations.

Proposition 4 *If X and Y are Pareto-independent in the context Z, then they are leximin-independent and leximax-independent but the converse is not true.*

The leximin and the leximax independence relations are incomparable. Moreover, all of these relations imply the COS-independence but the converse in not true.

However, there are particular cases where the independence relations COS, leximin and leximax are equivalent. For instance in the case of two-level distributions as stated by the following proposition:

Proposition 5 *If X and Y are two-level distributions, then X is COS-independent of Y in the context of Z if and only if they are leximin-independent and if and only if they are leximax-independent.*

Propositions 6 and 7 relate the Product and the NI independence relations to the qualitative independence relations, namely the leximin, leximax and COS independencies.

Proposition 6 *In the general case, the Product independence is incomparable with the leximin and leximax independence relations. However, the Product independence implies the COS-independence but the converse in not true.*

Proposition 7 *The Pareto independence implies the NI-independence relation (since Pareto is equivalent to MS). However, the NI-independence relation is incomparable with the other qualitative independence relations, namely the leximin, leximax and COS independencies.*

We give now some counter-examples (due to the lack of space) relative to non-existent links between different relations.

Counter-example 4 *Let us consider two variables A and B,*

- *with the possibility distributions given in Table 4, we can check that in π_2 A and B are leximax-independent but neither leximin-independent since $\pi_1(a_1 \wedge b_3) > \pi_2(a_2 \wedge b_2)$ while $min(\Pi_2(a_2), \Pi_2(b_2)) > min(\Pi_2(a_1), \Pi_2(b_3))$, nor Pareto-independent since $\pi_2(a_1 \wedge b_3) > \pi_2(a_2 \wedge b_2)$ while $\Pi_2(b_2) > \Pi_2(b_3)$.*
  Moreover, in π_3 we can check that A and B are leximin-independent but neither leximax-independent since $\pi_3(a_2 \wedge b_2) > \pi_3(a_1 \wedge b_3)$ while $max(\Pi_3(a_1), \Pi_3(b_3)) > max(\Pi_3(a_2), \Pi_3(b_2))$, nor Pareto-independent since $\pi_3(a_2 \wedge b_2) > \pi_3(a_1 \wedge b_3)$ while $\Pi_3(a_1) > \Pi_3(a_2)$

- *with the possibility distributions given in Table 4, we can check that in π_2 A is COS-independent of B but that these two variables are not leximin-independent since $\pi_2(a_1 \wedge b_3) > \pi_2(a_2 \wedge b_2)$ while $min(\Pi_2(a_2), \Pi_2(b_2)) > min(\Pi_2(a_1), \Pi_2(b_3))$.*
  Moreover, in π_3 we can check that A is COS-independent of B but these two variables are not leximax-independent since $\pi_3(a_2 \wedge b_2) > \pi_3(a_1 \wedge b_3)$ while $max(\Pi_3(a_1), \Pi_3(b_3)) > max(\Pi_3(a_2), \Pi_3(b_2))$.

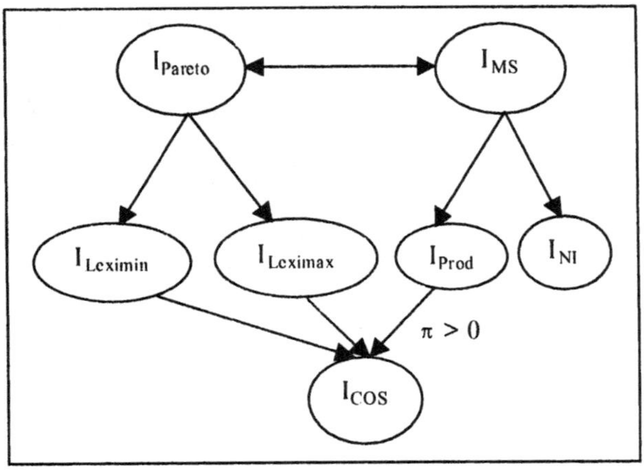

Fig. 1. Links between symmetric independence relations

Figure 1 illustrates the existing links between the different independence relations. The arrows show the inclusion of independence relations. Note that the I_{MS} and I_{Pareto} are the strongest independence relations since the MS or the Pareto independence between two sets of variables implies the ignorance of one of them. However, I_{COS} is the weakest one. Finally, note that I_{NI} is implied by I_{MS} but it is incomparable with the other independence relations.

6 Graphoid properties

The independence relations can be characterized by some properties which have been initially established for probabilistic conditional independence [4] [14], and which offer another base for comparing independence relations. In addition, these properties can be considered as a rules' set useful to infer new independence relations from an initial set. They are also important when we need a graphical representation of dependencies. Such properties are:

- *P1: Symmetry* : $I(X, Z, Y) \Rightarrow I(Y, Z, X)$
  This relation asserts that in any state of knowledge Z, if Y tells us nothing new about Y, then X tells us nothing new about Y.

- *P2: Decomposition*: $I(X, Z, Y \cup W) \Rightarrow I(X, Z, Y)$ and $I(X, Z, W)$
  This relation asserts that if (Y and W) are irrelevant to X then Y (resp. W) is irrelevant to X.
- *P3: Weak union*: $I(X, Z, Y \cup W) \Rightarrow I(X, Z \cup Y, W)$
  This relation asserts that the learning of an irrelevant information W, cannot transform an irrelevant information Y into a pertinent one for X.
- *P4: Contraction*: $I(X, Z \cup Y, W)$ and $I(X, Z, Y) \Rightarrow I(X, Z, Y \cup W)$
  This relation asserts that if W is irrelevant to X after receiving irrelevant information Y, then W should be also irrelevant to X knowing Y. Together, the weak union and this property state that irrelevant information should not modify the relevance of other propositions.
- *P5: Intersection*: $I(X, Z \cup W, Y)$ and $I(X, Z \cup Y, W) \Rightarrow I(X, Z, Y \cup W)$
  This relation states that if Y is irrelevant to X when W is known and if W is irrelevant to X when Y is known, then neither W, nor Y, nor their combination is relevant to X.

Any independence structure that satisfies the properties P1-P4 is called a *semi-graphoid.* If it also satisfies property P5 it is said to be a *graphoid.* It has been shown that the probabilistic independence relation is a *semi-graphoid,* and it is a *graphoid* if the considered probability distribution is strictly positive (P>0) [14].
The graphoid properties of independence relations introduced in this paper are specified by the following propositions.

Proposition 8 *The I_{NI} and I_{Prod} relations are semi-graphoids. Indeed I_{NI} does not satisfy the intersection, while I_{Prod} satisfies this property only if we consider strictly positive distributions.*
The proofs can be found in [11].

Proposition 9 *The I_H and I_{CO} relations satisfy all graphoid properties except the symmetry as already shown by Counter-examples 1 and 2.*

Proposition 10 *The I_{MS} independence relation satisfies all graphoid properties [11].*

This implies that I_{Pareto} is a graphoid too since these two relations are equivalent as stated by Proposition 2.

Proposition 11 *The I_{COS} relation is not a semi-graphoid, since it satisfies the symmetry (by definition), the decomposition and the weak union but not the contraction and the intersection properties as shown by Counter-examples 5 and 6.*

Note the unexpected result : the addition of symmetry to I_{CO} leads to the loss of contraction and intersection properties as it is shown by the following counter-example.

Table 5. Lack of contraction and intersection properties for I_{COS}

a	b	c	$\pi(a \wedge b \wedge c)$	a	b	c	$\pi(a \wedge b \wedge c)$
a_2	b_2	c_1	1	a_1	b_2	c_1	0.6
a_2	b_2	c_2	0.9	a_1	b_1	c_1	0.5
a_2	b_1	c_1	0.8	a_1	b_2	c_2	0.4
a_2	b_1	c_2	0.7	a_1	b_1	c_2	0.3

Counter-example 5 : LACK OF CONTRACTION PROPERTY FOR I_{COS}
Consider three binary variables A, B and C with the possibility distribution given in Table 5. It can be checked that $I_{COS}(A, B, C)$ and $I_{COS}(A, \emptyset, B)$ are true contrary to $I_{COS}(A, \emptyset, B \cup C)$. Indeed, $\Pi(b_1 \wedge c_1) < \Pi(b_2 \wedge c_2)$ while in the context a_1, we have $\Pi(b_1 \wedge c_1) > \Pi(b_2 \wedge c_2)$.

Counter-example 6 : LACK OF INTERSECTION PROPERTY FOR I_{COS}
Let us consider the possibility distribution given in Table 5, it can be checked that $I_{COS}(A, C, B)$ and $I_{COS}(A, B, C)$ are true contrary to $I_{COS}(A, \emptyset, B \cup C)$. Indeed, $\Pi(b_1 \wedge c_1) < \Pi(b_2 \wedge c_2)$ while in the context a_1, we have $\Pi(b_1 \wedge c_1) > \Pi(b_2 \wedge c_2)$.

Proposition 12 *The $I_{leximax}$ relation only satisfies the symmetry and the decomposition but not the other graphoid properties i.e the weak union, contraction and intersection as shown by Counter-examples 7, 8 and 9.*

Some properties may be recovered in particular cases. For instance in the case of two-level distributions, the $I_{leximax}$ and $I_{leximin}$ satisfy the weak union since they are equivalent to the I_{COS} (see Proposition5).

Counter-example 7 : LACK OF WEAK UNION PROPERTY FOR $I_{leximax}$

Table 6. Lack of weak union property for $I_{leximax}$

a	b	c	$\pi(a \wedge b \wedge c)$	a	b	c	$\pi(a \wedge b \wedge c)$
a_1	b_1	c_1	1	a_2	b_2	c_2	0.5
a_2	b_1	c_1	0.9	a_2	b_1	c_2	0.4
a_1	b_2	c_2	0.8	a_2	b_2	c_1	0.3
a_3	b_1	c_1	0.7	a_3	b_2	c_2	0.2
a_1	b_1	c_2	0.7	a_3	b_1	c_2	0.1
a_1	b_2	c_1	0.6	a_3	b_2	c_1	0.05

Consider three variables A, B and C with the possibility distribution given in Table 6. It can be checked that $I_{leximax}(A, \emptyset, B \cup C)$ is true contrary to $I_{leximax}(A, B, C)$. Indeed, $\Pi(a_2 \wedge b_2 \wedge c_1) > \Pi(a_3 \wedge b_2 \wedge c_2)$ but $max(\Pi(a_3 \wedge b_2), \Pi(b_2 \wedge c_2)) > max(\Pi(a_2 \wedge b_2), \Pi(b_2 \wedge c_1))$

Counter-example 8 *: Lack of contraction property for $I_{leximax}$*

Table 7. Lack of contraction property for $I_{leximax}$

a	b	c	$\pi(a \wedge b \wedge c)$	a	b	c	$\pi(a \wedge b \wedge c)$
a_1	b_2	c_1	1	a_1	b_1	c_2	0.7
a_1	b_2	c_2	0.9	a_1	b_1	c_1	0.6
a_2	b_2	c_1	0.9	a_2	b_1	c_2	0.6
a_2	b_2	c_2	0.8	a_2	b_1	c_1	0.5

Consider three binary variables A, B and C with the following possibility distribution. It can be checked that $I_{leximax}(A, \emptyset, B)$ *and* $I_{leximax}(A, B, C)$ *are true contrary to* $I_{leximax}(A, \emptyset, B \cup C)$*. Indeed,* $\Pi(a_2 \wedge b_1 \wedge c_2) > \Pi(a_1 \wedge b_1 \wedge c_1)$ *but* $max(\Pi(a_1), \Pi(b_1 \wedge c_1)) > max(\Pi(a_2), \Pi(b_1 \wedge c_2))$.

Counter-example 9 *: Lack of intersection property for $I_{leximax}$*

Table 8. Lack of intersection property for $I_{leximax}$

a	b	c	$\pi(a \wedge b \wedge c)$	a	b	c	$\pi(a \wedge b \wedge c)$
a_1	b_1	c_1	0.9	a_2	b_2	c_2	0.6
a_1	b_2	c_2	0.9	a_2	b_1	c_1	0.5
a_1	b_2	c_1	0.8	a_2	b_2	c_1	0.4
a_1	b_1	c_2	0.7	a_2	b_1	c_2	0.3

Consider three binary variables A, B and C with the possibility distribution given in Table 8. It can be checked that $I_{leximax}(A, C, B)$ *and* $I_{leximax}(A, B, C)$ *are true contrary to* $I_{leximax}(A, \emptyset, B \cup C)$*. Indeed,* $\Pi(a_2 \wedge b_2 \wedge c_2) > \Pi(a_2 \wedge b_1 \wedge c_2)$ *but* $max(\Pi(a_2), \Pi(b_2 \wedge c_2)) = max(\Pi(a_2), \Pi(b_1 \wedge c_2))$ *and* $min(\Pi(a_2), \Pi(b_2 \wedge c_2)) = min(\Pi(a_2), \Pi(b_1 \wedge c_2))$.

7 Conclusion

This paper has studied independence relation in possibility theory framework, from qualitative and quantitative points of view. Independence relations considered in this paper are compared and an analysis of their graphoid properties is provided. One result of this comparison is that the well known causal possibilistic independence (i.e I_{MS}) is equivalent to a decomopositional qualitative independence based on Pareto principle.
The main advantage in defining independence relations based on qualitative orderings in the possibilistic framework (or any other ranking function) is that all the orderings are defined on the same scale i.e. [0, 1]. This solves the

commensurability problem which is very important in the recomposition of joint distributions from marginal ones. Namely, in a purely qualitative setting even a plausibility relation is leximin or leximax ordered, it cannot be decomposable without loss of information [1].

References

1. N. Ben Amor, S. Benferhat, D. Dubois, H. Geffner and H. Prade, Independence in Qualitative Uncertainty Frameworks. Procs. of KR'2000, 2000.
2. S. Benferhat, D.Dubois and H. Prade, Expressing Independence in possibilistic framework and its application to default reasoning, ECAI'94, 150-153, 1994.
3. C. Boutilier, R. I. Brafman, H. H. Hoos and D. Poole, Reasoning with conditional Ceteris Paribus preference statements, UIA'99, 1999.
4. A. D. Dawid, Conditional independence in statistical theory, Journal of the Royal Statistical Society, B 41, 1-31, 1979.
5. L.M de Campos and J. F. Huete, Independence concepts in possibility theory, Fuzzy Sets and Systems, 1998.
6. D. Dubois, Belief structures, possibility theory and decomposable confidence measures on finite sets, Computers and Artificial Intelligence (Bratislava), 5, 403-416, 1986.
7. D. Dubois and H. Prade, Possibility theory : An approach to computerized, Processing of uncertainty, Plenium Press, New York, 1988.
8. D. Dubois, L. Farinas del Cerro, A. Herzig, H. Prade, Qualitative relevance and independence: a roadmap, IJCAI'97, 62-67, 1997.
9. D. Dubois, H. Prade, An introductory survey of possibility theory and its recent developments, Journal of Japan Society for Fuzzy Theory and Systems, Vol.10, 1, 21-42, 1998.
10. P. Fonck, Conditional independence in possibility theory, Uncertainty in Artificial Intelligence, 221-226, 1994.
11. P. Fonck, Rseaux d'infrence pour le raisonnement possibiliste. PhD thesis, Universit de Lige, 1994.
12. E. Hisdal, Conditional possibilities independence and non interaction, Fuzzy sets end Systems, Vol. 1, 1978
13. D. Lehmann, what does a conditional knowledge base entail ?, Proc. of 1st Inter. Conf. on Principles of Knowledge Represntation and Reasoning (KR'89), 357-367, 1989
14. J. Pearl, Probabilistic Reasoning in intelligent systems: networks of plausible inference, Morgan Kaufmman , Los Altos, CA, 1988.
15. L. A. Zadeh, Fuzzy sets as a basis for a theory of possibility, Fuzzy Sets and Systems, 1, 3-28, 1978

Independence Concepts for Belief Functions

Boutheina Ben Yaghlane[1], Philippe Smets[2], and Khaled Mellouli[1]

[1] AMID, Université de Tunis, IHEC Carthage Présidence 2016 Tunisia
[2] IRIDIA, Université Libre de Bruxelles 50 av. F. Roosevelt, CP 194/6 1050 Bruxelles Belgium

Abstract. In this paper, we try to study the independence concept for belief functions theory, as applied to one interpretation of this theory called the *transferable belief model* (TBM). In this context, two new results are given in this paper : first, the concept of belief function independence has different intuitive meaning which are non-interactivity, irrelevance and doxastic independence, second, the concepts of non-interactivity and independence are identical under a new property called *irrelevance preservation under Dempster's rule of combination.*

Keywords: Independence, Irrelevance, Non-interactivity, Belief functions, Transferable Belief Model.

1 Introduction

For managing uncertainty reasoning systems, a main requirement is to specify the conditions under which one item of information is considered dependent (or independent) from another, given what we already know, and to represent knowledge in structures that display these conditions. In the probabilistic framework, these conditions are identified with the notion of *independence*, also called *irrelevance* or *informational irrelevance* [14].

In addition to the obvious theoretical reasons for the study of independence, there are also practical interests. Indeed, thanks to independence, many computational tasks can be simplified. Complex evidential problem can be modularized into simpler components in such a way that we only treat the pieces of information having relevance to the question we are interested in. So, in order to get an efficient performance, reasoning systems must take into account independence considerations.

There are two main approaches to define independence :

1. Irrelevance approach : Two variables are said to be *independent* if no piece of information that can be learned about one of them can change our state of knowledge about the other. This form of independence is called *irrelevance.* It can be expressed by experts.

2. Decomposition approach : Two variables are said to be *independent* if the global information about the two variables can be expressed as a combination of two pieces of knowledge, one for each variable. This form of independence is called here *non-interactivity.* It permits an efficient computation by local calculus without loosing any information.

In the case of probability theory, both approaches are equivalent. However, these approaches do not have identical meaning in belief functions theory.

In this paper, we try to clarify the notion of independence between variables when uncertainty is expressed under the form of belief functions. Some other researches studying this topic are (Shafer [15], and Studeny [19]). We focus on belief functions in the context of the transferable belief model (Smets and Kennes [17]), a model to represent quantified beliefs where the beliefs are represented by belief functions. In order to avoid possible confusion, we insist on the fact that the TBM is unrelated to lower probability models. We concentrate on the intuitive meaning of each definition of independence and we discuss the possible links between them. In this paper, we consider only the marginal case, and for the full proofs of the different theorems, the reader is referred to (Ben Yaghlane *et al.* [2]).

The rest of this paper is organized as follows: in section 2, we briefly review the basic elements of belief functions theory based on the transferable belief model. Next, in section 3, we present some useful notations needed for belief function context. In section 4, the different definitions of the belief function independence concepts have been discussed. We first recall two definitions proposed by Shafer [15] called cognitive independence (section 4.1) and evidential independence (section 4.2). After this, we define the concepts of marginal non-interactivity (section 4.3), irrelevance (section 4.4) and independence (section 4.5) for belief functions, making clear the links between them. Finally, in section 5, we give a brief summary.

2 Belief Function Theory and Transferable Belief Model

The theory of belief functions, also known as Dempster-Shafer theory and theory of evidence, aims to model someone's degree of belief. It is regarded as a generalization of the Bayesian approach. Since this theory was developed by Shafer [15], many interpretations have been proposed. Among them, we can distinguish:

- **a lower probability model** where beliefs are represented by families of probability functions and the belief functions are the lower envelop of these families (Jaffray [10]). This model is considered as a special case of imprecise probabilities (Walley [21]).
- **Dempster's model** derived from probability theory where a probability space is mapped by a one-to-many mapping on another space. It is represented by hints theory (Kohlas and Monney [11]).
- **The transferable belief model (TBM)** where beliefs are represented by belief functions. This model is introduced by Smets [17] in order to justify the use of belief functions. The TBM is unrelated to probability models whereas the other two are the generalization of them.

In this paper, we are only concerned with the TBM, so we will use the concepts based on this model.

Definition 1 *Let Ω be a finite set of elements, called the frame of discernment. The mapping $bel : 2^{\Omega} \rightarrow [0,1]$ is an (unnormalized) belief function iff there exists a basic belief assignment (bba) $m : 2^{\Omega} \rightarrow [0,1]$ such that:*

$$(i)\ \sum_{A \subseteq \Omega} m(A) = 1,$$

$$(ii)\ bel(A) = \sum_{\emptyset \neq B \subseteq A} m(B),$$

$$(iii)\ bel(\emptyset) = 0.$$

The value $m(A)$ represents the degree of belief that is exactly committed to A. Due to the lack of information, $m(A)$ cannot support any more specific event. The value $bel(A)$ quantifies the strength of the belief that the event A occurs. A subset A such that $m(A) > 0$ is called a *focal element* of *bel*. *bel* is *vacuous* if the only focal element is Ω. In the TBM, we accept that $m(\emptyset)$ can be positive (open-world assumptions, [17]).

Given a belief function *bel*, we can define a *plausibility function pl*: $2^{\Omega} \rightarrow$ [0,1] and a *commonality function q*: $2^{\Omega} \rightarrow$ [0,1] as follows: for $A \subseteq \Omega$,

$$pl(A) = bel(\Omega) - bel(\overline{A}) = \sum_{B \cap A \neq \emptyset} m(B),$$

$$pl(\emptyset) = 0,$$

$$q(A) = \sum_{A \subseteq B \subseteq \Omega} m(B).$$

The value $pl(A)$ quantifies the maximum amount of potential specific support that could be given to A. The commonality function $q(A)$ represents a measure of uncertainty in the context where A holds and it is useful for simplifying some computations. It is proved that m, *bel*, *pl* and q are in one-to-one correspondence with each other (Shafer [15]).

3 Notations

In this section, we give some notations which are convenient when belief functions are used.

Variables. Let U $= \{X, Y, Z, ...\}$ be a set of finite variables, $\Theta_X = \{x_1, ..., x_n\}$ be the domain relative to the variable X (with a finite cardinality n), and x represents any instance of X. For simplicity sake, we denote Θ_X by X, Θ_Y by Y... Let Ω be a frame of discernment (Shafer [15]). It is the Cartesian product of the domains of the variables in U. For example, $X \times Y$ represents the product space of variables X and Y, and when there is no ambiguity, it is simply denoted by XY. The elements of X (Y...) are represented by indexed variables x_i (y_j...) whereas x (y...) denote subsets of X (Y...). For $x \subseteq X$ and $y \subseteq Y$, (x, y) is defined by $(x, y) = \{(x_i, y_j) : x_i \in x, y_j \in y\}$.

While studying marginal independence, all we need is two disjoint subsets of variables in U. We can as well redefine two new variables X and Y which domains are the Cartesian product of those variables considered in each set, respectively. This simplifies the notation as we may consider only two variables X and Y, and $\Omega = XY$.

We also often use the set $Rect_{XY}$ which is the set of subsets of XY that can be represented as (x, y) for some $x \subseteq X$ and some $y \subseteq Y$.

Belief functions. Let BK denotes the background knowledge that holds and that underlies the beliefs. In BK, we find the classical conditioning events. We introduce the following notations and their related properties:

- $bel^{\Omega\downarrow X}$ is the marginal of bel^{Ω} on X. The Ω superscript will not be mentioned when there is no risk of confusion. In particular, we have:

$$bel^{XY\downarrow X}(x) = bel^{XY}(x, Y),$$

$$pl^{XY\downarrow X}(x) = pl^{XY}(x, Y).$$

- $bel^{\Omega}[BK]$ denotes the belief function on Ω when BK holds. It can be seen as a vector in a $2^{|\Omega|}$ dimensional space. Classically, it was denoted as $bel^{\Omega}(. \mid BK)$, but the bracket notation turns out to be more convenient.
- $bel^{\Omega}[BK](A)$ denotes the value of $bel^{\Omega}[BK]$ at $A \subseteq \Omega$. When BK is the proposition that states that the actual value of Ω belongs to $B \subseteq \Omega$, its value is given by :

$$\begin{aligned} bel^{\Omega}[B](A) &= bel^{\Omega}(A \cup \overline{B}) - bel^{\Omega}(\overline{B}) \\ pl^{\Omega}[B](A) &= pl^{\Omega}(A \cap B) \\ q^{\Omega}[B](A) &= q^{\Omega}(A) \text{ if } A \subseteq B, \\ &= 0 \text{ otherwise.} \end{aligned}$$

  These are the so called Dempster's rule of conditioning (except for the normalization factor).
- The (conjunctive) combination of two distinct bba's m_1 and m_2, both defined on Ω, results in a new bba m_{12} on Ω with, $\forall A \subseteq \Omega$:

$$m_{12}(A) = \sum_{B,C: B \cap C = A} m_1(B) m_2(C),$$

$$q_{12}(A) = q_1(A) q_2(A).$$

  This rule is Dempster's rule of combination (except for the normalization factor). It is denoted here by the classical $\oplus$ symbol. So $m_{12} = m_1 \oplus m_2$.

- Note that conditioning and marginalization do not commute, so the order of the symbols is important. $bel^{XY}[y]^{\downarrow X}$ is the belief function obtained by conditioning bel^{XY} on y and the result is then marginalized on X.

In order to distinguish between normalized belief functions as those defined by Shafer and the unnormalized ones used in the transferable belief model, we use the following convention. Normalized functions have their first letter in upper-cases, whereas the unnormalized ones have theirs in lower cases. So M, Bel, Pl and Q denote the normalized forms, whereas m, bel, pl and q denote the unnormalized forms. To get the normalized forms, one just divide the unnormalized ones by the factor $1 - m(\emptyset)$ (putting $M(\emptyset) = 0$) or identically by $bel(\Omega)$ or $pl(\Omega)$.

We next present two useful lemmas.

Lemma 1 *For any plausibility function pl^{XY} defined on XY, we have*

$$pl^{XY}[y]^{\downarrow X}(x) = pl^{XY}(x, y), \ \forall x \subseteq X, \forall y \subseteq Y$$

Lemma 2 *For any plausibility function pl^{XY} defined on XY, we have*

$$pl^{XY \downarrow X}(x) = pl^{XY}(x, Y)$$

4 Belief Function Independence

The notion of informational irrelevance has been extensively studied in probability theory (Dawid [6], [7], Lauritzen *et al.* [13], Pearl [14]), where it is identified with independence or more specifically conditional independence. The concept of independence has also been studied in non-probabilistic frameworks such that Spohn's theory of ordinal conditional functions (Spohn [18]), Zadeh's possibility theory (Benferhat *et al.* [1], deCampos *et al.* [8], Fonck [9], Vejnarova [20], Zadeh [22]), upper and lower probabilities theory (Couso *et al.* [4], Cozman [5]), and in abstract framework that unifies different calculi called valuation-based system (Shenoy [16]). However, the concept of independence for variables has not been widely treated in belief functions theory.

The aim of this section is to investigate some ways to define independence relationships between variables when uncertainty is expressed by belief functions. We concentrate on the intuitive meaning on each definition and we discuss the possible links between them. In this section, we consider two variables X and Y defined on the space $\Omega = \Theta_X \times \Theta_Y$ (denoted as $\Omega = XY$).

Previously, we recall the definition of probabilistic independence. We say that two random variables X and Y are (*marginally*) *independent* with respect to a distribution P on the space XY, denoted by $X \perp\!\!\!\perp_P Y$, if and only if one of the following conditions is satisfied: for all $x \subseteq X$, all $y \subseteq Y$,

- $P^{XY}(x,y) = P^{XY\downarrow X}(x)P^{XY\downarrow Y}(y)$
  where $P^{XY\downarrow X}$ and $P^{XY\downarrow Y}$ are the marginal probabilities of P^{XY} on X and Y, respectively.
- $P^{XY}[y]^{\downarrow X}(x) = P^{XY\downarrow X}(x)$
  where $P^{XY}[y]^{\downarrow X}$ is the conditional probability on X given y.

Remark. Our notation is more cumbersome than the usual one (i.e. such as in Dawid [7] and Pearl [14]), but it helps when belief functions are involved.

The first definition of independence is presented in terms of the *factorization* of the joint probability distribution through its marginal distributions on X and Y, respectively (a mathematical property). It is also called *separability* or *non-interactivity* [22]. We will use the last name (see section 4.3). However, the second definition can be interpreted in terms of *irrelevance*, it means that any information about Y is irrelevant to the uncertainty about X (an epistemic property). In probability context, irrelevance and independence imply each other, hence the distinction is usually not considered.

To extend these definitions of independence to the case of belief functions, Shafer ([15], page 147 *et seq.*) proposes two definitions of independence. After recalling these definitions, we introduce our definitions of marginal non-interactivity, irrelevance and doxastic independence for variables.

4.1 Cognitive Independence : Weak Independence

Following Shafer [15], two variables are "*cognitively independent*" with respect to a belief function if new evidence that bears on only one of them does not change the degree of belief for propositions discerned by the other. The formal definition of "cognitive independence" is the following :

Definition 2 *(Shafer [15], page 149) : The variables X and Y are "cognitively independent" with respect to M^{XY} iff: for all $x \subseteq X$, all $y \subseteq Y$,*

$$Pl^{XY}(x,y) = Pl^{XY\downarrow X}(x)\ Pl^{XY\downarrow Y}(y) \tag{1}$$

4.2 Evidential Independence : Strong Independence

The definition of "cognitive independence" is very weak. Shafer [15] proposed another notion of independence called "*evidential independence*" [1]: two variables are "*evidentially independent*" if their joint belief function is represented by the combination of their marginals using Dempster's rule of combination. The formal definition of evidential independence is as follows.

Definition 3 *(Shafer [15], page 147) : The variables X and Y are "evidentially independent" with respect to M^{XY} iff: for all $x \subseteq X$, all $y \subseteq Y$,*

$$Pl^{XY}(x,y) = Pl^{XY\downarrow X}(x)\ Pl^{XY\downarrow Y}(y) \tag{2}$$

$$Bel^{XY}(x,y) = Bel^{XY\downarrow X}(x)\ Bel^{XY\downarrow Y}(y) \tag{3}$$

[1] It is also called *strong independence* in [12].

Based on the definition of "evidential independence", let us state the following theorems:

Theorem 1 *The variables X and Y are "evidentially independent" with respect to M^{XY} if and only if:*

$$M^{XY}(w) = M^{XY\downarrow X}(x)\ M^{XY\downarrow Y}(y),\ \ if\ w = (x,y) \tag{4}$$
$$= 0,\ otherwise.$$

where x is the projection of w on X, and y is the projection of w on Y.

This theorem just states that the focal elements of M^{XY}, i.e., those subsets w of XY where $M^{XY}(w) > 0$, belong to $Rect_{XY}$.

Theorem 2 *The variables X and Y are "evidentially independent" with respect to M^{XY} if and only if:*

$$Q^{XY}(w) = Q^{XY\downarrow X}(x)\ Q^{XY\downarrow Y}(y),\ \forall w \subseteq XY \tag{5}$$

where x is the projection of w on X, and y is the projection of w on Y.

Remarks.

- All definitions by Shafer and Kong assume normalized belief functions.
- Shafer [15] does not explain the signification of the two adjectives : cognitive and evidential.
- Shafer speaks of "independence" but we will prefer the expression 'non-interactivity' as this definition is essentially a mathematical one and we keep the word 'independence' for the common sense property.
- "Cognitive independence" may hold whereas "evidential independence" fails, as shown in the following example.

Example. Let G and S be two variables representing Gender and Smoking and taking their values in Θ_G = {Male, Female} and Θ_S = {Yes, No}, respectively. Let Ω = {(Male,Yes), (Female,Yes), (Male,No), (Female,No)} be the frame of discernment representing the product space $\Theta_G \times \Theta_S$.

Define the refining $\omega_1 : 2^{\Theta_G} \to 2^{\Omega}$ by:

ω_1({Male}) = {(Male,Yes), (Male,No)} ≡ M,

ω_1({Female}) = {(Female,Yes), (Female,No)} ≡ F,

and define the refining $\omega_2 : 2^{\Theta_S} \to 2^{\Omega}$ by:

ω_2({Yes}) = {(Male,Yes), (Female,Yes)} ≡ Y,

ω_2({No}) = {(Male,No), (Female,No)} ≡ N,

Suppose that we have the following basic belief assignment (bba) over the product space Ω:

m{(Male,Yes)} = 0.5

m{(Male,Yes), (Female,Yes), (Male,No)} = 0.25

m{Ω} = 0.25

The corresponding plausibility functions are:
pl(M) = pl({(Male,Yes), (Male,No)}) = 1
pl(F) = pl({(Female,Yes), (Female,No)}) = 0.5
pl(Y) = pl({(Male,Yes), (Female,Yes)}) = 1
pl(N) = pl({(Male,No), (Female,No)}) = 0.5
Then, we can easily verify that :
pl({(Male,Yes)} = pl(M,Y) = pl(M) pl(Y) = 1
pl({(Female,Yes)} = pl(F,Y) = pl(F) pl(Y) = 0.5
pl({(Male,No)} = pl(M,N) = pl(M) pl(N) = 0.5
pl({(Female,No)} = pl(F,N) = pl(F) pl(N) = 0.25
But bel({(Male,Yes)} = bel(M,Y) = 0.5 is not equal to bel(M) . bel(Y) = $0.5 \times 0.5 = 0.25$. So, we conclude that G and S are cognitively independent. But, they are not evidentially independent.

4.3 Belief Function Non-Interactivity

In this section, we propose the definition of decompositional independence for belief functions. In possibility theory, there is an analogous definition introduced by Zadeh [22] where the decompositional independence between two variables is represented by the **non-interactivity** relation. We use this last terminology. The non-interactivity is a mathematical property useful for computations considerations when propagating beliefs in evidential networks.

Intuitively, the *non-interactivity* of two variables X and Y with respect to m^{XY} means that the joint mass can be reconstructed from its marginals. The purpose is that for any functions $f \in \{m, bel, pl, q\}$, we have that f^{XY} is some function of f^X and f^Y. As far as once it is true for m, it is true for all of them, we propose the following definition of non-interactivity.

Definition 4 ***Non-interactivity.*** *Given two variables X and Y, and $m = m^{XY}$ on XY. X and Y are non-interactive with respect to m, denoted by $X \perp_m Y$, if and only if :*

$$pl^{XY}(X,Y)\, m^{XY} = m^{XY\downarrow X} \oplus m^{XY\downarrow Y} \tag{6}$$

The scalar $pl^{XY}(X,Y)$ is introduced because we tolerate unnormalized belief functions. We could (almost) identically propose the definition as:

$$M^{XY} = M^{XY\downarrow X} \oplus M^{XY\downarrow Y}$$

which is equal to:

$$\frac{m^{XY}}{pl^{XY}(X,Y)} = \frac{m^{XY\downarrow X}}{pl^{XY\downarrow X}(X)} \oplus \frac{m^{XY\downarrow Y}}{pl^{XY\downarrow Y}(Y)}$$

These definitions are all equal once $pl^{XY}(X,Y) > 0$. The 'almost' qualification covers the highly degenerated case where $pl^{XY}(X,Y) = 0$, relation (6) being still valid, whereas the others become undefined.

Theorem 3 *Let m^{XY} be a bba on XY and $X \perp_{m^{XY}} Y$. Then the focal elements of m^{XY} belong to $Rect_{XY}$.*

From theorem 1, non-interactivity and Shafer's evidential independence definitions are equivalent when we consider normalized belief functions. Thus relations (2) and (3) can be directly generalized into:

$$pl^{XY}(X,Y)\ pl^{XY}(x,y) = pl^{XY\downarrow X}(x)\ pl^{XY\downarrow Y}(y) \tag{7}$$

$$pl^{XY}(X,Y)\ pl^{XY}(x,y) = pl^{XY}(x,Y)\ pl^{XY}(X,y) \tag{8}$$

$$pl^{XY}(X,Y)\ bel^{XY}(x,y) = bel^{XY\downarrow X}(x)\ bel^{XY\downarrow Y}(y) \tag{9}$$

where relation (8) is obtained from relation (7) and lemma 2.

Non-interactive belief functions can easily be build by using any pair of belief functions, one being defined on X, the other on Y, provided they give the same bba to the empty set.

Theorem 4 *Let m^X and m^Y be two bba defined on X and Y where X and Y are independent coarsenings of Ω with $m^X(\emptyset) = m^Y(\emptyset) = \alpha$ with $\alpha \in [0,1]$. Then the bba m^{XY} defined on XY by:*

$$(1-\alpha)\ m^{XY} = m^X \oplus m^Y$$

with $m^{XY}(\emptyset) = 1$ if $\alpha = 1$, satisfies non-interactivity: $X \perp_{m^{XY}} Y$.

4.4 Belief Function Irrelevance

In probability theory, the notion of independence can be defined in term of **irrelevance**. This kind of independence is based on *conditioning*. The intuitive meaning of irrelevance is that knowing the value y_j of Y does not affect belief on X. In belief functions theory, the formal definition of irrelevance is the following:

Definition 5 ***Irrelevance.*** *Given two variables X and Y, and $m = m^{XY}$ on XY, Y is irrelevant to X with respect to m, denoted by $IR_m(X,Y)$, if and only if :*
$\forall y \subseteq Y$ such that $pl^{XY}(X,y) > 0$

$$m^{XY}[y]^{\downarrow X}(x) \propto m^{XY\downarrow X}(x),\ \forall x \subseteq X, x \neq \emptyset \tag{10}$$

and $\forall y \subseteq Y$ such that $pl^{XY}(X,y) = 0$

$$m^{XY}[y]^{\downarrow X}(x) = 0,\ \forall x \subseteq X, x \neq \emptyset,\ \text{and}\ m^{XY}[y]^{\downarrow X}(\emptyset) = 1.$$

In relation (10), we need $\propto$ because in the TBM context we do not normalize when applying Dempster's rule of conditioning. Under normalization, proportionality becomes equality.

Theorem 5 *Given two variables* X *and* Y, *and* $m= m^{XY}$ *on* XY, $IR_m(X,Y)$ *if and only if* $pl^{XY}[y]^{\downarrow X} = \alpha_y\ pl^{XY\downarrow X}$, $\forall y \subseteq Y$, *where*

$$\alpha_y = \frac{pl^{XY}(X,y)}{pl^{XY}(X,Y)}.$$

Based on the definition of irrelevance, we can deduce the following consequences.

Theorem 6 *Given two variables* X *and* Y, *and* $m= m^{XY}$ *on* XY, *the following assertions are equivalent:*

1. $IR_m(X,Y)$
2. $pl^{XY}[y']^{\downarrow X} = \beta\ pl^{XY}[y'']^{\downarrow X}$ (11)

   $$where\ \beta = \frac{pl^{XY}(X,y')}{pl^{XY}(X,y'')},\ (\beta\ independent\ of\ x)$$
3. $$pl^{XY}(x,y) = \frac{pl^{XY}(x,Y)\ pl^{XY}(X,y)}{pl^{XY}(X,Y)} \quad (12)$$

Furthermore,

$$IR_m(X,Y) = IR_m(Y,X) \quad (13)$$

The third item of theorem 6 implies that IR is equivalent to Shafer's cognitive independence when belief functions are normalized.

In the following example, we show that irrelevance does not imply non-interactivity between variables.

Example. Suppose $X = \{x_1, x_2\}$ and $Y = \{y_1, y_2\}$ and let $\Omega = X \times Y = \{a, b, c, d\}$ where $a = (x_1, y_1), b = (x_2, y_1), c = (x_1, y_2), d = (x_2, y_2)$. We present in table 1 a bba m^Ω such that $IR_{m^\Omega}(X,Y)$ even though we do not have $X \perp_{m^\Omega} Y$.

We start with m^Ω, compute its related pl^Ω (table 1). Then we present in table 2 (3) the values of the bba and their related plausibility functions on X (Y) after conditioning on y_1, y_2, and Y (x_1, x_2 and X).

Using the marginals on X and on Y, that is $m^{\Omega\downarrow X}$ and $m^{\Omega\downarrow Y}$, which are given in the rightmost columns of the tables 2 and 3, we compute $m^{\Omega\downarrow X} \oplus m^{\Omega\downarrow Y}$ which result is given in table 1, fourth column. It can be seen that $m^\Omega \neq m^{\Omega\downarrow X} \oplus m^{\Omega\downarrow Y}$.

Nevertheless X and Y are irrelevant to each other with respect to m^Ω. Indeed, we can see that the conditional bba's on X (Y) table 2 (3) satisfy the proportionality requirement of the IR definition. Identically, we show that pl^Ω and $pl^{\Omega\downarrow X} \oplus pl^{\Omega\downarrow Y}$ are equal on those subsets of Ω where such equality is required by the IR definition, that is those indicated by a $\surd$ symbol in the 'Required' column of table 1.

Ω	m^Ω	pl^Ω	M	PL	Required
$\emptyset$	.0000	0	0	.0000	√
a	.1275	.3000	.13	.3000	√
b	.17	.3500	.17	.3500	√
ab	.1025	.5000	.10	.5000	√
c	.16	.3600	.16	.3600	√
ac	.0125	.6000	.01	.6000	√
bc	0	.6550	.00	.6800	
abc	.0075	.7925	.01	.8000	
d	.2075	.4200	.21	.4200	√
ad	.01	.6700	.01	.6900	
bd	.0225	.7000	.02	.7000	√
abd	0	.8400	.00	.8500	
cd	.1325	.6000	.13	.6000	√
acd	0	.8300	.00	.8400	
bcd	.0075	.8725	.01	.8800	
abcd	.04	1.0000	.04	1.0000	√

Table 1. For each subset of $\Omega = X \times Y$, listed in column 1, the columns 2 and 3 present the value of m^Ω and of its related pl^Ω. The column 4 presents the values of $\mathrm{M} = m^X \oplus m^Y$ where $m^X = m^{\Omega\downarrow X}$ and $m^Y = m^{\Omega\downarrow Y}$. Column 5 presents the plausibility function $\mathrm{PL} = pl^{\Omega\downarrow X} \oplus pl^{\Omega\downarrow Y}$ related to the bba of column 4. Column 6 indicates by √ those subsets of Ω where the equality for the plausibility functions is required.

X	$m^\Omega[ab]^{\downarrow X}$	$pl^\Omega[ab]^{\downarrow X}$	X	$m^\Omega[cd]^{\downarrow X}$	$pl^\Omega[cd]^{\downarrow X}$
$\emptyset$	.50	0	$\emptyset$	.40	0
a	.15	.30	c	.18	.36
b	.20	.35	d	.24	.42
ab	.15	.50	cd	.18	.60

X	$m^{\Omega\downarrow X}$	$pl^{\Omega\downarrow X}$
$\emptyset$	0	0
ac	.30	.60
bd	.40	.70
abcd	.30	1.00

Table 2. Bba and plausibility after marginalization on X of the bba obtained by the conditioning of m^Ω on the values of Y.

But irrelevance seems to weak and does not imply what we feel should be the definition of "independence". In particular, our definition of irrelevance does not imply "non-interactivity". Nevertheless, we feel the next property should also be satisfied by irrelevance, in which case non-interactivity and irrelevance become equal.

Let A_1 and A_2 denote two agents whose beliefs are considered. The idea is when the first agent A_1 claim that Y is irrelevant to X and produce his beliefs and the second A_2 tell me that Y is irrelevant to X and produce his

Y	$m^{\Omega}[ac]^{\downarrow Y}$	$pl^{\Omega}[ac]^{\downarrow Y}$	Y	$m^{\Omega}[bd]^{\downarrow Y}$	$pl^{\Omega}[bd]^{\downarrow Y}$
∅	.40	0	∅	.30	0
a	.24	.30	b	.28	.36
c	.30	.36	d	.35	.42
ac	.06	.60	bd	.07	.60

Y	$m^{\Omega\downarrow Y}$	$pl^{\Omega\downarrow Y}$
∅	0	0
ab	.40	.50
cd	.50	.60
abcd	.10	1.00

Table 3. Bba and plausibility after marginalization on Y of the bba obtained by the conditioning of m^{Ω} on the values of X.

own beliefs, then I want that Y is still irrelevant to X for me and my belief will be equal to the combination of agents' beliefs. This idea can be explicitly formulate by the next property called **Irrelevance Preservation under Dempster' rule of combination**, denoted by IRP$\oplus$.

Definition 6 *: Irrelevance Preservation under Dempster' rule of combination. If* $IR_{m_1}(X,Y)$ *and* $IR_{m_2}(X,Y)$ *then* $IR_{m_1 \oplus m_2}(X,Y)$

We can state the main theorem of this work proving that $IR_m(X,Y)$ & $IRP\oplus$ implies non-interactivity (i.e. $X \perp_m Y$).

Theorem 7 *Let* $\Omega = XY$ *and* $m = m^{XY}$. *If* $IR_m(X,Y)$ *and if for all* m' *defined on* XY *such that* $IR_{m'}(X,Y)$, *we have* $IR_{m \oplus m'}(X,Y)$, *then* $X \perp_m Y$

This theorem means that when Y is irrelevant to X with respect to m and this irrelevance is preserved under Dempster' rule of combination with any other m' such that Y is also irrelevant to X with respect to m', then X and Y are non-interactive with respect to m. We also show the reverse.

Theorem 8 $X \perp_m Y \Rightarrow IR_m(X,Y)$.

Theorem 9 $X \perp_m Y \Rightarrow IRP\oplus$.

4.5 Doxastic Independence

The most obvious difference between probabilistic independence and belief function independence is that irrelevance and independence have not identical meaning in the belief function framework. This distinction is not commonly considered in probabilistic framework where authors like Pearl [14] and Dawid [7] use the words irrelevance and independence interchangeably.

In order to enhance this distinction, we use the expression **doxastic independence** for belief function independence. In Greek, 'doxein' means 'to believe'. The formal definition of doxastic independence is as follows :

Definition 7 ***Doxastic Independence.*** *Given two variables X and Y, and a bba m on XY. Variables X and Y are doxastically independent with respect to m, denoted by* $X \perp\!\!\!\perp_m Y$*, if and only if m satisfies:*

- $IR_m(X,Y)$
- $\forall m_0$ *on* $XY : IR_{m_0}(X,Y) \Rightarrow IR_{m \oplus m_0}(X,Y)$

The intuitive meaning of this definition is that two variables are considered as doxastically independent only when they are irrelevant and this irrelevance is preserved under Dempster's rule of combination.

Theorem 10 *Doxastic independence preservation under* $\oplus$.
If $X \perp\!\!\!\perp_{m_1} Y$ *and* $X \perp\!\!\!\perp_{m_2} Y$ *then* $X \perp\!\!\!\perp_{m_1 \oplus m_2} Y$

The link between doxastic independence and non-interactivity is given by the next theorem :

Theorem 11 *Given two variables X and Y, and a bba m on XY. The variables X and Y are doxastically independent with respect to m if and only if X and Y are non-interactive with respect to m:*

$$X \perp\!\!\!\perp_m Y \Leftrightarrow X \perp_m Y$$

5 Conclusion

In this paper, we have studied different concepts of independence for belief functions. Of special interest for us is to clarify the relationships between the concepts of non-interactivity, irrelevance and doxastic independence when uncertainty is expressed under the form of belief functions. These concepts of marginal independence for belief functions can be extended to conditional case which successfully depict our intuition about how dependencies should update in response to new pieces of information. In fact, the study of *conditional independence* in the framework of belief functions theory was not sufficiently developed. More detailed research of conditional belief function independence is under way (see for instance Ben Yaghlane *et al.* [3]). It will be usefull for the practical use of belief functions in Artificial Intelligence.

References

1. S. Benferhat, D. Dubois and H. Prade (1994), *Expressing Independence in Possibilistic Framework and its application to default reasoning*, European Conference on Artificial Intelligence (ECAI'84), 150-153.
2. B. Ben Yaghlane, Ph. Smets and K. Mellouli (2000a), *Belief Function Independence: I. The Marginal Case*, Technical Report TR/IRIDIA/2000-13, Institut de Recherches Interdisciplinaires et de Développements en Intelligence Artificielle, Université Libre de Bruxelles.

3. B. Ben Yaghlane, Ph. Smets and K. Mellouli (2000b), *On Conditional Belief Function Independence*, In Workshop on Partial Knowledge and Uncertainty: Independence, Conditioning, Inference, (Eds. R. Scozzafava and B. Vantaggi), Rome.
4. I. Couso, S. Moral and P. Walley (1999), *Examples of Independence for Imprecise Probabilities*, 1st International Symposium on Imprecise Probabilities and Their Applications ISIPTA'99, Ghent, 121-130.
5. F.G. Cozman (1999), *Irrelevance and Independence Axioms in Quasi-Bayesian Theory*, ECSQARU'99, London, Lecture Notes in AI 1638, A.Hunter and S. Parsons (Eds), Springer-Verlag, 128-136.
6. A.P. Dawid (1979), *Conditional Independence in Statistical Theory*, Journal of the Royal Statistical Society, Series B, Vol. 41, 1-31.
7. A. P. Dawid (1999), *Conditional Independence*, In Encyclopedia of Statistical Science (Update) Volume 3, Wiley, New York.
8. L.M. deCampos, Huete J.F. and S. Moral (1995), *Possibilistic Independence*, Third European Congress on Intelligent Techniques and Soft Computing EUFIT'95, Germany, vol. 1, 69-73.
9. P. Fonck (1994), *Conditional Independence in Possibility Theory*, Uncertainty in Artificial Intelligence, 221-226.
10. J.Y. Jaffray (1989), *Linear Utility Theory for Belief Functions*, Operations Research Letters, 8, 107-112.
11. J. Kohlas and P.A. Monney (1995), *A Mathematical Theory of Hints. An Approach to Dempster-Shafer Theory of Evidence*, Lecture Notes in Economics and Mathematical Systems No. 425, Springer-Verlag.
12. C.T.A. Kong (1988), *A Belief Function Generalization of Gibbs Ensemble*, Joint Technical Report, S-122 Harvard University and N239 University of Chicago, Departments of Statistics.
13. S. L. Lauritzen, A.P. Dawid, B.N. Larsen and H.G. Leimer (1990), *Independence Properties of Directed Markov Fields*, Networks, 20(5), 491-505.
14. J. Pearl (1988), *Probabilistic Reasoning in Intelligent Systems: Networks of Plausible Inference*, Morgan Kaufmman, Los Altos, CA.
15. G. Shafer (1976), *Mathematical Theory of Evidence*, Princeton University Press, Princeton.
16. P.P. Shenoy (1994), *Conditional Independence in Valuation-Based Systems*, International Journal of Approximate Reasoning, 10, 203-234.
17. P. Smets and R. Kennes (1994), *The Transferable Belief Model*, Artificial Intelligence, 66, 191-234.
18. W. Spohn (1988), *Ordinal Conditional Functions : A Dynamic Theory of Epistemic States*, Causation in decision, belief changes and statistics, W. Harper and B. Skyrms (Eds), 105-134.
19. M. Studeny (1993), *Formal Properties of Conditional Independence in Different Calculi of Artificial Intelligence*, ECSQARU'93, K. Clarke K., R. Kruse and S. Moral (Eds), Springer-Verlag, 341-348.
20. J. Vejnarova (1999), *Conditional Independence Relations in Possibility Theory*, 1st International Symposium on Imprecise Probabilities and Their Applications ISIPTA'99, Ghent, 343-351.
21. P. Walley (1991), *Statistical Reasoning with Imprecise Probabilities*, Chapman and Hall, London.
22. L.A. Zadeh (1978), *Fuzzy Sets as a Basis for Theory of Possibility*, Fuzzy Sets and Systems, 1:3-28.

Conditional Possibility and Necessity

Bernadette Bouchon-Meunier[1], Giulianella Coletti[2*], and Christophe Marsala[1]

[1] LIP6, Université Paris VI, 8 rue du Capitaine Scott, 75015 Paris, France
[2] Università di Perugia, Dipartimento di Matematica e Informatica, via Vanvitelli, 1, 06123 Perugia, Italy

Abstract. We introduce the definition of a conditional possibility (and a conditional necessity by duality) as a primitive concept, *ie* a function whose domain is a set of conditional events. The starting point is a definition of conditional event $E|H$ which differs from many seemingly "similar" ones adopted in the relevant literature, which makes the third value depending on $E|H$. It turns out that this function $t(E|H)$ can be taken as a conditional possibility by requiring "natural" property of closure of truth-values of the conditional events with respect to max and min. We show that other definitions of conditional possibility measures, present in the literature, are particular cases of the one proposed here. Moreover, we introduce a concept of coherence for conditional possibility and a relevant characterization theorem, given in terms of a class of unconditional possibility measures.

1 Introduction

There is clearly not a unique definition of a conditional possibility distribution since the concept of conditioning is complex and has first been studied in probability theory. It has first been introduced through the idea of conditional probability, deduced from joint and marginal probabilities. Conditioning has further been considered for non-probabilistic structures, for instance in possibility theory [1,10,22,26,32]. These seminal works have given rise to various definitions of conditional possibility (see for instance [8,15,16,18,31]), by analogy with the probabilistic case or by extending it. All these definitions have in common the fact that the conditional possibility is obtained as a derived concept from joint and marginal possibility distributions or measures.

In this paper we introduce conditional possibility as a primitive concept. More precisely we present an approach where conditional possibility is *directly* introduced as a function whose domain is a set of conditional events; so the knowledge (or the assessment) of the "joint" possibility $\Pi(E \wedge H)$ (where $\wedge$ denotes the logical product) and the "marginal" one $\Pi(H)$ is not required; moreover, $\Pi(E|H)$ makes sense for any $H \neq \emptyset$, where $\emptyset$ is the impossible event.

Following the line adopted in [7], our starting point is a "logical" one, in the sense that we consider a family $\mathcal{T}$ of *conditional events* $E|H$, each one

* The work of this author was conducted during her visit at the Université Paris VI as an invited professor.

being represented by a suitable *three–valued random variable* whose values are $1, 0, t(E|H)$, the latter turning out to be the relevant conditional possibility $\Pi(\cdot|\cdot)$.

We recall that in the literature many different definitions of conditional events have been introduced starting with de Finetti ([12]) and much later by several authors (see for instance [4,20,21,25,30]). The definition adopted here (formally introduced in [7]) differs from the one given by de Finetti and many other authors, for the choice of the third value of $E|H$: in fact it is not just an undetermined *common value* for all ordered pairs (E, H) (sometimes $u \in [0, 1]$, sometimes $u = 1$), but it suitably depends on the given pair.

In fact, considering the operations max and min, we suitably define corresponding operations among the random variables of the set $\mathcal{T}$. We obtain as a "result" a random variable, but it does not belong to $\mathcal{T}$ in general. If we consider only those elements of $\mathcal{T}^2$ such that the range of each operation is $\mathcal{T}$, we get "in a natural way" conditions on $t(E|H)$ that can be taken as the axioms for a conditional possibility measure. This definition of conditional possibility is a generalization of the classical ones present in the literature.

We introduce also a concept of "coherence" for conditional possibility assessment in terms of compatibility of a possibility measure. Moreover we characterize coherent possibility assessments in the sense that they can be represented in terms of *classes* of unconditional possibility measures.

2 Conditional events

An *event* can be singled-out by a (nonambiguous) *proposition* E, that is a statement that can be either *true* or *false* (corresponding to the two "values" 1 or 0). Since in general it is not known whether E is true or not, we are *uncertain* on E.

In general, it is not enough to direct attention just toward an event E in order to assess "convincingly" its measure of uncertainty f, but it is also essential to take into account *other* events which may possibly contribute in determining the "information" on E. Then the fundamental tool must be a *conditional measure of uncertainty*, since the true problem is not assessing $f(E)$, but rather assessing $f(E|H)$, taking into account all the relevant "information" carried by some other event H.

Dealing with conditional measures requires the introduction of *conditional* events $E|H$, with $H \neq \emptyset$.

A conditional event can be defined through its *truth-value* $T(E|H)$ – recall that, for an (unconditional) event E, this is just its *indicator* $|E| = T(E|\Omega)$, equal to 1 or 0 according to whether E is respectively true or false – that is 1 if E and H are true, 0 if E^c and H are true and $t(E|H)$ if H is false, where t is a function with values in $[0, 1]$.

We note that a conditional event induces a (unique) partition of certain event Ω; viceversa, given a triple $(E \wedge H, E^c \wedge H, H^c)$, it can be induced only by the event $E|H$. Therefore the function t can be seen as a function defined on the triples $\{(E \wedge H, E^c \wedge H, H^c)\}$. A useful representation of $T(E|H)$ can be given through a discrete random variable $Y = \sum_{k=1}^{\nu} y_k |E_k|$, with $\nu = 2$, $E_1 = EH$, $E_2 = H^c$, and $y_1 = 1$, $y_2 = t(E|H)$:

$$T(E|H) = 1 \cdot |E \wedge H| + 0 \cdot |E^c \wedge H| + t(E|H) \cdot |H^c|,$$

that is (by an elementary property of indicators)

$$(1) \qquad T(E|H) = |E||H| + t(E|H)|H^c|,$$

To simplify the notation, from now on we will use the same symbol for a (conditional) event and its truth–value. So (1) will be written as

$$(2) \qquad E|H = EH + t(E|H)H^c.$$

Suppose now that we have a set $\mathcal{C}$ of conditional events $E_i|H_i$ and suppose that the set $\mathcal{E} = \{E_i\}$ is a boolean algebra, $\mathcal{H} = \{H_i\}$ is an additive set (that is closed with respect to finite logical sums $\vee$) contained in $\mathcal{E}$ and such that $\emptyset \notin \mathcal{H}$. Consider the relevant set $\mathcal{T}$ of random variables $T(E_i|H_i)$.

First of all, notice that it is immediate to see that for any $E|H \in \mathcal{C}$, one has

$$(3) \qquad T(E|H) = T[(E \wedge H)|H].$$

since these two conditional events give rise to the same partition of Ω, and then also to the same value of t, that is

$$(3') \qquad t(E|H) = t(E \wedge H|H).$$

If $\otimes$ is any operation from $\mathbb{R} \times \mathbb{R}$ to $\mathbb{R}$, and $X = \sum_{k=1}^{\nu_1} x_k |E_k|$ and $Y = \sum_{h=1}^{\nu_2} y_h |F_h|$ are two discrete random variables we can define $X \otimes Y$ as the random variable $Z = \sum_{h,k} z_{hk} |G_{hk}|$, where $G_{hk} = E_k \wedge F_h$ and $z_{hk} = x_k \otimes y_h$. Therefore to define an operation among random variables it is sufficient to define the relevant operation among real numbers.

Let us consider now two commutative, associative and monotone operations from $[0,1] \times [0,1]$ to $[0,1]$, $\oplus$ and $\odot$ having respectively 0 and 1 as neutral element, and let us use the same symbols for the relevant operations on $\mathcal{T} \times \mathcal{T}$. If we operate between two elements of $\mathcal{T}$, in general we do not obtain an element of $\mathcal{T}$. We have in fact, by (2), for any $E|H$, $A|K \in \mathcal{C}$:

$$\begin{aligned}(4)\ E|H \oplus A|K = {} & [1 \oplus 1]EHAK + EHA^cK + E^cHAK + [1 \oplus t(A|K)]EHK^c \\ & + t(A|K)E^cHK^c + [1 \oplus t(E|H)]AKH^c \\ & + t(E|H)A^cKH^c + [t(E|H) \oplus t(A|K)]H^cK^c,\end{aligned}$$

and

$$\begin{aligned}(5)\ (E|H) \odot (A|K) = {} & EHAK + t(E|H)H^cAK \\ & + t(A|K)K^cEH + \big(t(E|H) \odot t(A|K)\big)H^cK^c\end{aligned}$$

Nevertheless we notice that in the case $H = K$ and $E \wedge A \wedge H = \emptyset$ we get by (4)

$$E|H \oplus A|H = (E \vee A)H + \big(t(E|H) \oplus t(A|H)\big)H^c\,.$$

Therefore, since the family $\mathcal{T}$ containing $E|H$ and $A|H$, contains also $(E \vee A)|H$ (for the boolean properties of $\mathcal{C}$), we have necessarily as its "third" value

$$\text{(6)} \qquad t\big((E \vee A)|H\big) = t(E|H) \oplus t(A|H)\,.$$

Consider now the operation $E|H \odot A|K$ in the particular case $K = E \wedge H$. For these events we obtain, by (5):

$$\begin{aligned}(E|H) \odot \big(A|(E \wedge H)\big) &= EAH + t(E|H) \odot t\big(A|E \wedge H\big)(EH)^c H^c \\ &= EAH + t(E|H) \odot t\big(A|E \wedge H\big)H^c\end{aligned}$$

Therefore, since the family $\mathcal{T}$ containing conditional $E|H$ and $A|E \wedge H$, contains also $(E \wedge A)|H$ (for the boolean properties of $\mathcal{C}$), we have necessarily as its "third" value

$$\text{(7)} \qquad t\big(E \wedge A|H\big) = t(E|H) \odot t\big(A|E \wedge H\big)\,.$$

If $A = E$, we obtain in particular

$$\text{(7')} \qquad t(E|H) = t(E|H) \odot t(E|E \wedge H)\,,$$

while in the case $A \wedge E \wedge H = \emptyset$, taking into account condition (3′), we have

$$\text{(7'')} \qquad t(\emptyset|H) = t(E|H) \odot t(\emptyset|E \wedge H)\,.$$

In [7] the above procedure was considered in the specific case where $\oplus$, and $\odot$ are the usual sum and product, respectively.

In this case, if the family $\mathcal{C} = \mathcal{E} \times \mathcal{H}$ of conditional events satisfies the above boolean properties with respect to $\mathcal{E}$ and $\mathcal{H}$, then the third value $t(\cdot|\cdot)$ satisfies the following "familiar" rules:

(i) $t(E|H) = t\big(E \wedge H|H\big)$, for every $E \in \mathcal{E}$ and $H \in \mathcal{H}$
(ii) $t(\cdot|H)$ is a (finitely additive) probability on $\mathcal{E}$ for any given $H \in \mathcal{H}$
(iii) $t\big(E \wedge A|H\big) = t(E|H) \cdot t\big(A|(E \wedge H)\big)$, for every $A \in \mathcal{E}$ and E, $H \in \mathcal{H}$, $E \wedge H \neq \emptyset$

Condition (i) can be replaced by the following

(i') $t(H|H) = 1$, for every $H \in \mathcal{H}$

Recall that the above conditions (i'), (ii) and (iii) are exactly the axioms given by [11,14,23] to define a *conditional probability*. Properties (i') and (iii) are also in the definition of "generalized conditional probability" by [29], where condition (ii) is replaced by the stronger one of σ-additivity (obviously, all definitions are equivalent if the algebra $\mathcal{E}$ is *finite*).

Following the same procedure, we analyze here the case where $\oplus$ and $\odot$ coincide with *max* and *min* respectively.

Supposing $\mathcal{C} = \mathcal{E} \times \mathcal{H}$ as above, the third value satisfies the following rules:

(u) $t(E|H) = t(E \wedge H|H)$, for every $E \in \mathcal{E}$ and $H \in \mathcal{H}$
(uu) $t(E \vee A|H) = \max\{t(E|H), t(A|H)\}$ for any given $E, A, \in \mathcal{A}$, $H \in \mathcal{H}$
(uuu) $t(E \wedge A|H) = \min\{t(E|H), t(A|E \wedge H)\}$, for every $A \in \mathcal{E}$ and $E, H, E \wedge H \in \mathcal{H}$.

Moreover, taking into account that relation (7′) and (7″) hold for every pair of events $H, K \in \mathcal{H}$, $H \subseteq K$:

$$t(H|H) = \max\{t(H|K), t(H|H)\}$$

while by relation (7″) we have, for every $E|H$: $t(\emptyset|H) = \min\{t(\emptyset|H), t(E|H)\}$

3 Conditional possibility

Taking into account the above remark, it seems natural to give the following definition of conditional possibility:

Definition 1. Let $\mathcal{E}$ be a boolean algebra, $\mathcal{H}$ an additive set, with $\mathcal{H} \subseteq \mathcal{E}$ and $\emptyset \notin \mathcal{H}$. A real-valued function Π defined on $\mathcal{C} = \mathcal{E} \times \mathcal{H}$ is a *conditional possibility* if the following conditions hold:

(I) $\Pi(E|H) = \Pi(E \wedge H|H)$, for every $E \in \mathcal{E}$ and $H \in \mathcal{H}$
(II) $\Pi(\cdot|H)$ is a possibility measure, for any given $H \in \mathcal{H}$
(III) $\Pi(E \wedge A|H) = \min\{\Pi(E|H), \Pi(A|E \wedge H)\}$, for every $A \in \mathcal{E}$ and $E, H, E \wedge H \in \mathcal{H}$.

Given a conditional possibility, it is easy to deduce a particular *conditional necessity* [17].

Definition 2. Let Π be a conditional possibility. The *conditional dual function* N of Π is defined by: $N(E|H) = 1 - \Pi(E^c|H)$ for every $H \in \mathcal{H}$.

If N is the conditional dual function of Π, then we have:

- from condition (II), $\Pi(.|H)$ is a possibility measure, for any given $H \in \mathcal{H}$. It is easy to prove that $N(.|H)$ is a necessity measure. We have $\Pi(\emptyset|H) = 0$ thus $N(H|H) = 1$, and from $\Pi(H|H) = 1$, we have $N(\emptyset|H) = 0$. We have also $\Pi(A \vee E|H) = \max(\Pi(A|H), \Pi(E|H))$ for any $A, E \in \mathcal{E}$, thus $1 - N((A \vee E)^c|H) = \max(1 - N(A^c|H), 1 - N(E^c|H))$, and finally we have $N(A^c \wedge E^c|H) = \min(N(A^c|H), N(E^c|H))$, for any given $A, E \in \mathcal{E}$ and $H \in \mathcal{H}$, and we prove that $N(.|H)$ is a necessity measure.

- from condition (III), we have $\Pi(A \wedge E) = \min(\Pi(E|H), \Pi(A|E \wedge H))$ for every $A \in \mathcal{E}$ and E, $H \in \mathcal{H}$, $E \wedge H \neq \emptyset$. Thus, we have $N((E \wedge A)^c|H) = 1 - \min(\Pi(E|H), \Pi(A|E \wedge H)) = \max(1 - \Pi(E|H), 1 - \Pi(A|E \wedge H)) = \max(N(E^c|H), N(A^c|E \wedge H))$, and thus, for every $A \in \mathcal{E}$ and E, $H \in \mathcal{H}$, $E^c \wedge H \neq \emptyset$, we have $N(E \vee A|H) = \max(N(E|H), N(A|E^c \wedge H))$.
- moreover, we have $N(E \wedge H|H) = 1 - \Pi(E^c \vee H^c|H)$ for any $E \in \mathcal{E}$ and $H \in \mathcal{H}$. Thus, we have $N(E \wedge H|H) = 1 - \max(\Pi(E^c|H), \Pi(H^c|H)) = 1 - \max(\Pi(E^c|H), 0) = 1 - \Pi(E^c|H) = N(E|H)$, which is a result equivalent to condition (I).

This gives rise to the following definition of conditional necessity:

Definition 3. Let $\mathcal{E}$ be a boolean algebra, $\mathcal{H}$ an additive set, with $\mathcal{H} \subseteq \mathcal{E}$ and $\emptyset \notin \mathcal{H}$. A real-valued function N defined on $\mathcal{C} = \mathcal{E} \times \mathcal{H}$, is a *conditional necessity* if the following conditions hold:

(I') $N(E|H) = N(E \wedge H|H)$, for every $E \in \mathcal{E}$ and $H \in \mathcal{H}$
(II') $N(\cdot|H)$ is a necessity measure, for any given $H \in \mathcal{H}$
(III') $N(E \vee A|H) = \max\left(N(E|H), N(A|E^c \wedge H)\right)$, for every $A, E \in \mathcal{E}$ and H, $E^c \wedge H \in \mathcal{H}$.

Particular cases

The concept of conditional possibility has been introduced in several ways in 1978 [22,26,32]. Because each of the definitions has its own drawbacks, many papers have studied this concept, providing states of the art, extending some of the previous results, or proposing new definitions [15,18,28], and more recently [9,10,31]. We show here that these definitions are compatible with the definition of conditional possibility we propose.

We first remark that, in the case where Ω itself belongs to $\mathcal{H}$, we obtain as a particular case for the conditional possibility the following equality:
(IV) $\Pi(E \wedge A|\Omega) = \min\{\Pi(E|\Omega), \Pi(A|E)\}$, for every $A \in \mathcal{E}$ and $E \in \mathcal{H}$.
Because of condition (II), $\Pi(\cdot|\Omega)$ is a possibility measure.

Let X, Y, Z be random variables whose domains are respectively C_X, C_Y and C_Z. We denote simply by x the event $\{X = x\}$ for any $x \in C_X$(and similarly for y and z) and by $\Pi(x|z)$ the possibility measure of x given z; moreover we denote by (x, y) the conjunction $x \wedge y$. Moreover, if C_X is the range of X and $A \subseteq C_X$, we denote by A the event $\{X \subseteq A\}$.

Let $A \subseteq C_X$ and $E \subseteq C_Y$. Then $\Pi_X(A) = \Pi(A|\Omega)$ is the possibility that X takes the values in A, and it can be considered as a marginal possibility measure. Finally we can also consider $\Pi_{XY}(A, E) = \Pi(E \wedge A|\Omega)$ the joint possibility of X and Y, or the possibility that X takes the values in A and Y in E. Then condition (III) becomes: $\Pi_{XY}(A, E) = \min\{\Pi_Y(E), \Pi(A|E)\}$, for every value $A \in C_X$ and $E \in C_Y$ which has been very frequently considered as a basis for the definition of conditional possibility measures [9,22,26].

Zadeh's conditioning Let us consider Zadeh's [32] concept of conditional possibility measure, defined as:

$$\Pi_z(A|E) = \Pi_{XY}(A, E)$$

Thus, it is easy to check the following:

Proposition 1. *Zadeh's Π_z satisfies properties (I) and (III).*

Proof. In the sequel, we drop the indices X, Y, Z for the sake of simplicity. Let us consider Zadeh's definition. Then for every $A \subseteq C_X$ and $E \subseteq C_Y$ we have $\Pi_z(A \wedge E|E) = \Pi(E, A, E) = \Pi(E, A) = \Pi_z(A|E)$ and (I) is satisfied. Now, let us check property (III). For arbitrary $A \subseteq C_X$, $E \subseteq C_Y$, $H \subseteq C_Z$ we have:

$$\begin{aligned} &\Pi_z(A \wedge E|H) = \Pi(A, E, H), \\ &\Pi_z(A|E \wedge H) = \Pi(A, E, H), \\ &\Pi_z(E|H) = \Pi(E, H). \end{aligned}$$

and we have $\Pi(E, H) = \max(\Pi(A, E, H), \Pi(A^c, E, H))$ because Π is a possibility measure and thus $\Pi(E, H) \geq \Pi(A, E, H)$. Thus $\min(\Pi_z(A|E \wedge H), \Pi_z(E|H)) = \Pi_z(A \wedge E|H)$ and (III) is satisfied. And the proposition is proved.

We must remark that $\Pi_z(.|H)$ is not a possibility measure for any H.

Hisdal's conditioning Let us consider Hisdal's [22] concept of conditional possibility measure, defined as:

$$\Pi_h(A|E) = \begin{cases} \Pi_{XY}(E, A) & \text{if } \Pi_{XY}(E, A) < \Pi_Y(E) \\ 1 & \text{if } \Pi_{XY}(E, A) = \Pi_Y(E) \end{cases}$$

Thus, it is easy to check the following:

Proposition 2. *Hisdal's Π_h is a particular case of conditional possibility.*

Proof. Let us consider Hisdal's definition. Then for every $A \subseteq C_X$ and $E \subseteq C_Y$ we have $\Pi_h(A \wedge E|E) = \Pi_h(A|E)$ and (I) is satisfied. Moreover $\Pi_h(.|E)$ is a possibility measure as soon as $\Pi_Y(E) \neq 0$ for any $E \neq \emptyset$ and (II) is satisfied. Now, let us check property (III). For arbitrary $A \subseteq C_X, E \subseteq C_Y, H \subseteq C_Z$ we have:

$$\Pi_h(A \wedge E|H) = \begin{cases} \Pi(A, E, H) & \text{if } \Pi(A, E, H) < \Pi(H) \\ 1 & \text{if } \Pi(A, E, H) = \Pi(H) \end{cases},$$

$$\Pi_h(A|E \wedge H) = \begin{cases} \Pi(A, E, H) & \text{if } \Pi(A, E, H) < \Pi(E, H) \\ 1 & \text{if } \Pi(A, E, H) = \Pi(E, H) \end{cases},$$

$$\Pi_h(E|H) = \begin{cases} \Pi(E, H) & \text{if } \Pi(E, H) < \Pi(H) \\ 1 & \text{if } \Pi(E, H) = \Pi(H) \end{cases}.$$

Thus $\min(\Pi_h(A|E \wedge H), \Pi_h(E|H)) = \Pi_h(A \wedge E|H)$ and (III) is satisfied. Then the proposition is proved.

4 Coherent conditional possibilities

An uncertainty measure is usually defined by using both conditions on the set of events (Boolean conditions) and on the function of reference (additivity, sub-additivity, monotonicity and so on). We notice that the second ones are not sufficient to define the measure if the set of events is an arbitrary set.

The concept of coherence is essentially a rule of compatibility of a (possibly partial) assessment on an arbitrary family of events with an uncertainty measure.

This concept is well known relatively to the framework of probability, starting from de Finetti (see [12]). In this context many equivalent conditions of coherence are given, both for unconditional and conditional probability, in terms of betting scheme and penalty (see for instance [12],[13], [24], [19]). For conditional probabilities also a condition involving a family of unconditional probabilities ([5],[6]), agreeing with the assessment, is given.

Recently, conditions of coherence for different measure in terms of betting scheme have been given (see for instance [27] for decomposable measures with an archimedean t-conorm).

We introduce now a concept of coherence for conditional possibility.

Definition 4. Let $\mathcal{C}$ be an arbitrary finite family of conditional events, and Π a real-valued function defined on $\mathcal{C}$. We call Π a *coherent conditional possibility* if for every $\mathcal{C}' \supseteq \mathcal{C}$, where $\mathcal{C}' = \mathcal{E} \times \mathcal{H}$, with $\mathcal{E}$ a boolean algebra, $\mathcal{H}$ an additive set, $\mathcal{H} \subseteq \mathcal{E}$ and $\emptyset \notin \mathcal{H}$, there exists a conditional possibility defined on $\mathcal{C}'$ extending Π.

In the literature (see [23], [5–7]) the representability of a conditional probability P is known in terms of a family of (unconditional) probabilities $\{P_\alpha\}$, such that for any event $E|H$ there exists an element $P_{\alpha'}$ of this class, with a conditional probability $P(E|H)$ equal to the ratio of $P_{\alpha'}(E \wedge H)$ and $P_{\alpha'}(H)$. Notice that the family $\{P_\alpha\}$ contains a unique element only in the case where $P(H|\Omega) > 0$ for every H and the class is unique only in the case where the set of events is a product of Boolean algebras.
A similar result for conditional possibilities is proved in the following theorem.

Theorem 1. *Let $\mathcal{C} = \{E_i|H_i\}_{i=1,\cdot,n}$ be an arbitrary finite family of conditional events and $\mathcal{A} = \{A_r\}$ denote the set of atoms generated by $\{E_i, H_i\}_{i=1,\cdot,n}$. For a real-valued function Π on $\mathcal{C}$, the following two statements are equivalent:*

(a) *Π is a coherent conditional possibility on $\mathcal{C}$;*
(b) *there exists a class $\{\mathcal{A}_\alpha\}$, with $\mathcal{A}_{\alpha'} \subset \mathcal{A}_{\alpha''}$, for $\alpha' > \alpha''$, $\mathcal{A}_0 = \mathcal{A}$, and a relevant class of possibility measures $\{\Pi_0, \Pi_1, \ldots\}$, $\Pi_\alpha : \mathcal{A} \to I\!R$, such that for any $E_i|H_i \in \mathcal{C}$, $\Pi(E_i|H_i)$ is solution of the following equation for every α, such that $H_i \subseteq \mathcal{A}_\alpha$:*

$$\Pi_\alpha(E_i \wedge H_i) = \min\{x, \Pi_\alpha(H_i)\}\,; \tag{8}$$

and there exists a unique α' such that $x = \Pi(E_i|H_i)$ is the unique solution of equation (8).
Moreover an atom A_r belongs to $\mathcal{A}_{\alpha'}$ ($\alpha' \geq 1$) if and only if there exists $E_i|H_i \in \mathcal{C}$, with $A_r \subseteq H_i$ and $\Pi_\alpha(E_i \wedge H_i) = \Pi_\alpha(H_i) < \Pi(E_i|H_i)$ for every $\alpha < \alpha'$.

Proof. We prove implication $(b) \rightarrow (a)$.

First consider the function $\Pi(\cdot|\cdot)$, defined on $\mathcal{E} \times \mathcal{H}$, where $\mathcal{E}$ is the algebra spanned by $\mathcal{A}$ and $\mathcal{H}$ is the additive set obtained by the closure of the set $\{H_i\}_{i=1,\cdot,n}$ with respect to the logical sum, by putting for every $E|H \in \mathcal{E} \times \mathcal{H}$:

$$\max_{A_r \subseteq E_i \wedge H_i} \Pi_0(A_r) = \min\{\Pi(E_i|H_i), \max_{A_r \subseteq H_i} \Pi_0(A_r)\},$$

where α is the index such that the equation

$$\max_{A_r \subseteq E_i \wedge H_i} \Pi_0(A_r) = \min\{x, \max_{A_r \subseteq H_i} \Pi_0(A_r)\}$$

admits a unique solution.

Obviously Π is an enlargement of the given possibilistic assessment, we are going to prove that Π is a conditional possibility.

To prove condition (I) it is sufficient to note that $\Pi(E|H)$ and $\Pi(E \wedge H|H)$ are solutions of the same equation.

To prove condition (II) consider in advance that, for any event $E|H$, equation (8) admits a unique solution if and only if either condition holds:

$$\Pi_\alpha(E \wedge H) < \Pi_\alpha(H) \text{ or } \qquad \Pi_\alpha(E \wedge H) = \Pi_\alpha(H) = 1$$

So, in the first case we have $\Pi(E|H) = \Pi_\alpha(E \wedge H)$ and in the second one $\Pi(E|H) = 1$.

Therefore, since for every H the equality $\Pi_\alpha(\Omega \wedge H) = \Pi_\alpha(H)$ (trivially) holds for any α, then there exists an α' such that $\Pi_{\alpha'}(H) = 1$ and so $\Pi(\Omega|H) = 1$.

To prove that

$$\Pi(E \vee F|H) = \max\{\Pi(E|H), \Pi(F|H)\},$$

recall that, by condition (I), we have

$$\Pi_\alpha(E \vee F|H) = \Pi_\alpha((E \wedge H) \vee (F \wedge H)\,|H).$$

By condition (b), there exists an α such that $\Pi_\alpha((E \wedge H) \vee (F \wedge H)) = \Pi(E \vee F|H)$. Then, since for every α the function Π_α is a possibility measure, we have

$$\begin{aligned} \Pi(E \vee F|H) &= \Pi_\alpha((E \wedge H) \vee (F \wedge H)) \\ &= \max\{\Pi_\alpha(E \wedge H), \Pi_\alpha(F \wedge H)\}. \end{aligned}$$

On the other hand, if $\Pi(E \vee F|H) = 1$, then we have $\Pi_\alpha((E \wedge H) \vee (F \wedge H)) = \Pi(H) = 1$ and so either $\Pi_\alpha(E \wedge H) = \Pi_\alpha(H) = 1$, or $\Pi_\alpha(F \wedge H) = \Pi_\alpha(H) = 1$.

Therefore $\Pi_\alpha(H) = 1$, or $\Pi(F|H) = 1$.

If $\Pi_\alpha(E \vee F|H) < 1$, then both inequalities $\Pi_\alpha(E \wedge H) < \Pi_\alpha(H)$, and $\Pi_\alpha(F \wedge H) < \Pi_\alpha(H)$ hold, and so we have $\Pi_\alpha(E \wedge H) = \Pi(E|H)$ and $\Pi_\alpha(F \wedge H) = \Pi(F|H)$.

Now let us prove that $\Pi(\emptyset|H) = 0$. For this, let us consider that for every α we have:

$$0 = \Pi_\alpha(\emptyset) = \min(x, \Pi_\alpha(H)). \tag{9}$$

Therefore

(s1) if $\Pi_\alpha(H) > 0$, then the unique solution for (9) is $\Pi(\emptyset|H) = 0$.
(s2) if $\Pi_\alpha(H) = 0$, then equation (9) does not admit a unique solution and then it is necessary to proceed and calculate Π_β, $\beta > \alpha$, until we have situation (s1).

To prove condition (III), consider the events $E \wedge F|H$, $E|F \wedge H$, $F|H$.

If $\Pi(E \wedge F|H) = 1$, then there exists a possibility measure $\Pi_{\alpha''}$ such that $\Pi_{\alpha''}(E \wedge F \wedge H) = \Pi_{\alpha''}(H) = 1$ (and $\Pi_{\alpha'}(E \wedge F \wedge H) = \Pi_{\alpha'}(H)$, for any $\alpha' < \alpha''$). This implies $\Pi_{\alpha''}(E \wedge F \wedge H) = \Pi_{\alpha''}(F \wedge H) = \Pi_{\alpha''}(H) = 1$ (and $\Pi_{\alpha'}(E \wedge F \wedge H) = \Pi_{\alpha'}(F \wedge H) = \Pi_{\alpha'}(H)$, for $\alpha' < \alpha''$) and then necessarily $\Pi(E|F \wedge H) = \Pi(F|H) = 1$.

Now consider $\Pi(E \wedge F|H) < 1$.

In this case there exists a possibility measure $\Pi_{\alpha''}$ such that $\Pi_{\alpha''}(E \wedge F \wedge H) < \Pi_{\alpha''}(H)$ (and $\Pi_{\alpha'}(E \wedge F \wedge H) = \Pi_{\alpha'}(H)$).

Therefore by monotonocity of possibility measures Π_α, we have $\Pi_{\alpha'}(E \wedge F \wedge H) = \Pi_{\alpha'}(F \wedge H) = \Pi_{\alpha'}(H)$, and $\Pi_{\alpha''}(E \wedge F \wedge H) \leq \Pi_{\alpha''}(F \wedge H) \leq \Pi_{\alpha''}(H)$, with at least one equality.

Then either

$$\Pi(E \wedge F|H) = \Pi(E|F \wedge H) = \Pi_{\alpha''}(E \wedge F \wedge H) \leq \Pi(F|H)$$

or

$$\Pi(E \wedge F|H) = \Pi(F|H) = \Pi_{\alpha''}(E \wedge F \wedge H) \leq \Pi(E|F \wedge H).$$

We now prove implication $(a) \to (b)$. For this purpose put $\mathcal{A}_0 = \mathcal{A}$ and consider the following system (S_0) with unknowns $\Pi_0(A_r) \geq 0$, $A_r \in \mathcal{A}_0$,

$$(S_0)\begin{cases} \max_{A_r \subseteq E_i \wedge H_i} \Pi_0(A_r) = \min\{\Pi(E_i|H_i), \max_{A_r \subseteq H_i} \Pi_0(A_r)\}, \\ \qquad\qquad\qquad\qquad [\text{for } E_i|H_i \in \mathcal{C}] \\ \max_{A_r \subseteq H_0^0} \Pi_0(A_r) = 1 \end{cases}$$

where $H_0^0 = \bigvee_{H_i \in \mathcal{H}} H_i$.

Since $\Pi(\cdot|\cdot)$ is a conditional possibility (so conditions I–III hold), then (S_0) has a solution $\Pi_0(A_r) = \Pi(A_r|H_0^0)$. In fact, by (I) we must have

$$\max_{A_r \subseteq E_i \wedge H_i} \Pi_0(A_r) = \Pi(E_i \wedge H_i|H_0^0)$$

and

$$\max_{A_r \subseteq H_i} \Pi_0(A_r) = \Pi(H_i|H_0^0);$$

by (III), $\Pi(E_i|H_i)$ is solution for the equation

$$\Pi(E_i \wedge H_i|H_0^0) = \min\{x, \Pi(H_i|H_0^0)\}.$$

But the above equation can be satisfied either if

$$\Pi(E_i \wedge H_i|H_0^0) < \Pi(H_i|H_0^0))\}$$

or if

$$\Pi(E_i \wedge H_i|H_0^0) = \Pi(H_i|H_0^0) < \Pi(E_i|H_i).$$

In this second case we have no constraint for $\Pi(E_i|H_i)$ and then it is not the unique solution of the equation.

Let $\mathcal{C}_1 \in \mathcal{C}$ be the set of conditional events $E_i|H_i$ such that $\Pi(E_i \wedge H_i|H_0^0) = \Pi(H_i|H_0^0) < \Pi(E_i|H_i)$ and let $\mathcal{A}_1 \in \mathcal{A}_0$ be the set of atoms contained on $H_0^1 = \bigvee_{E_i|H_i \in C_1} H_i$. Consider the following system (S_1), with unknowns $\Pi_1(A_r)$, $A_r \in \mathcal{A}_1$ and whose equations are only those related to the events of $\mathcal{C}_1$:

$$(S_1)\begin{cases} \max_{A_r \subseteq E_i \wedge H_i} \Pi_1(A_r) = \min\{\Pi(E_i|H_i), \max_{A_r \subseteq H_i} \Pi_1(A_r)\}, \\ \qquad\qquad\qquad\qquad\qquad\qquad [\text{for } E_i|H_i \in \mathcal{C}_1] \\ \max_{A_r \subseteq H_0^1} \Pi_0(A_r) = 1 \end{cases}$$

This system has a solution $\Pi_1(A_s) = \Pi(A_s|H_0^1)$.

If this is the unique solution, the procedure stops (and the proof is complete), on the contrary we build $\mathcal{A}_2$, by proceeding as above, and so on.

It is easy to prove that the family $\Pi_\alpha = \Pi(H_0^\alpha)$ satisfies the properties of condition (b).

Remark We notice that the class $\{\Pi_\alpha\}$ of Theorem 1 contains a unique element only when there exists no conditional event $E|H$, such that $\Pi(H|\Omega) = \Pi(E \wedge H|\Omega) < \Pi(E|H)$.

Moreover the class $\{\Pi_\alpha\}$ is unique only if $\mathcal{C} = \mathcal{E} \times H$, for an algebra $\mathcal{E}$ and an additive set $\mathcal{H}$.

5 Conclusion

We have introduced an intrinsic definition of conditional possibility, not requiring the definition of joint or marginal possibility measures. We show that it generalizes classically used definitions of conditional possibilities. Then, a definition of conditional necessity has been deduced by duality. Moreover, we have introduced a concept of coherent conditional possibilities able to handle possibilistic assessments and finally, we have characterized coherent conditional possibilities in terms of a class of unconditional possibility measures. This definition of conditional possibility can be used to define a new concept of possibilistic independence [2,3].

References

1. B. Bouchon-Meunier. Fuzzy inference and conditional possibility distributions. *Fuzzy Sets and Systems*, 23: 23-41, 1987.
2. B. Bouchon-Meunier, G. Coletti and C. Marsala. Independence and Possibilistic Conditioning. *Workshop on Conference Partial Knowledge and Uncertainty: Independence, Conditioning, Inference*, Roma, Italy, May 2000.
3. B. Bouchon-Meunier, G. Coletti and C. Marsala. Independence and Possibilistic Conditioning. in *Journal of Mathematical Analysis, to appear.*
4. P. Calabrese. An algebraic synthesis of the foundations of logic and probability, *Information Sciences* 42, 187-237, 1987.
5. G. Coletti. Coherent numerical and ordinal probabilistic assessments. *IEEE Transactions on Systems, Man, and Cybernetics*, 24:1747–1754, 1994.
6. G. Coletti and R. Scozzafava. Characterization of coherent conditional probabilities as a tool for their assessment and extension. *International Journal of Uncertainty, Fuzziness and Knowledge-Based Systems*, 4:103–127, 1996.
7. G. Coletti and R. Scozzafava. Conditioning and Inference in Intelligent Systems. *Soft Computing*, 3 (3): 118–130, 1999
8. L.M. De Campos, J.F. Huete, S. Moral. Possibilistic independence, in *Proceeding of EUFIT 95*, Verlag Mainz and Wisseschaftverlag, Aachen,1: 69-73, 1995
9. L.M. de Campos, J.F. Huete. Independence concepts in possibility theory, *Fuzzy sets and Systems 103*, part I, pp. 127-152, part II, pp. 487-505, 1999.
10. G. de Cooman. Possibility Theory II: Conditional possibility, *Int. J.General System*, 25:325-351, 1997.
11. B. de Finetti. Sull'impostazione assiomatica del calcolo delle probabilità. *Annali Univ. Trieste*, 19:3–55, 1949. – *Engl. transl.*: Ch.5 in *Probability, Induction, Statistics*, Wiley, London, 1972.
12. B. de Finetti. Sul significato soggettivo della probabilità. *Fundamenta Mathematicae*, 17(1931) 298–329 - *Engl.transl.*: in *Induction and Probability* (Eds. P. Monari, D.Cocchi), CLUEB, Bologna: 291–321, 1993.
13. B. de Finetti. *Teoria delle Probabilità*. Einaudi Torino, 1970. (English translation: *Theory of Probability*, London, Wiley 1975).
14. L.E. Dubins. Finitely additive conditional probabilities, conglomerability and disintegration. *Ann. Probab.*, 3:89–99, 1975.
15. D. Dubois, H. Prade. Conditioning in possibility and evidence theories - a logical viewpoint, in *Uncertainty and Intelligent Systems* (B. Bouchon, L. Saitta, R.R. Yager, eds.), Lecture Notes in Computer Science vol. 313,401-408, 1988.
16. D. Dubois, H. Prade. *Possibility theory.* Plenum Press, New York, 1998.
17. D. Dubois, H. Prade. *Basic notions of possibility theory.* in the Handbook of Fuzzy Computation, E.H. Ruspini, P.P. Bonnissone and W. Pedrycz eds, 1998.

18. P. Fonck. Conditional independence in possibility theory, in: *Proceeding of 10th Conference UAI* (R.L.de Mantaras, P.Poole eds.), 221-226, Morgan Kaufman, San Francisco, 1994.
19. A. Gilio. Criterio di penalizzazione e condizioni di coherenza nella valutazione soggettiva della probabilità. it Boll. Un. Mat. Ital., (7) 4-B: 645–660, 1990.
20. I.R. Goodman, H.T. Nguyen. Conditional objects and the modeling of uncertainties, in *Fuzzy computing* (M.M. Gupta, T. Yamakawa, eds.), North Holland, 1988.
21. I.R. Goodman, H.T. Nguyen, E.A. Walker. *Conditional inference and logic for intelligent systems: a theory of measure-free conditioning*, North Holland, Amsterdam, 1991
22. E. Hisdal. Conditional possibilities independence and noninteraction, *Fuzzy Sets and Systems*,1: 299-309, 1978.
23. P.H. Krauss. Representation of conditional probability measures on Boolean algebras. *Acta Math. Acad. Scient. Hungar.*, 19:229–241, 1968.
24. R. S. Lehman. On confirmation and rational betting. *The Jour. of Symbolic Logic*, 20:251–262, 1955.
25. D. Lewis. Probabilities of conditionals and conditional probabilities, *Phil. Rev.* 85, 297-315, 1976.
26. H.T. Nguyen. On conditional possibility distributions. *Fuzzy Sets and Systems*, 1: 299–309, 1978.
27. H.T. Nguyen, E. A. Walker. *A First Course in Fuzzy Logic*, CRC Press, Boca Raton, New York, London, Tokyo, 1997.
28. A. Ramer. Conditional possibility measures.in *Readings in Fuzzy Sets for Intelligent Systems*, D. Dubois, H. Prade and R.R. Yager eds, Morgan Kaufmann
29. A. Rényi. On conditional probability spaces generated by a dimensionally ordered set of measures. *Theor. Probab. Appl.*, 1:61–71, 1956.
30. G. Schay. An algebra of conditional events, *J. Math. Analysis and Applications*, 24: 334-344, 1968.
31. J. Vejnarova. Conditional independance relations in possiblity theory. *1st International Symposium on Imprecise Probabilities and their applications*, Ghent: 343-351, 1999.
32. L.A. Zadeh. Fuzzy sets as a basis for theory of possibility *Fuzzy sets and Systems*,1: 3-28, 1978.

The Membership Problem for Probabilistic and Data Dependencies

S.K.M. Wong[1] and C.J. Butz[2]

[1] Department of Computer Science, University of Regina, Regina, Canada, S4S 0A2

[2] School of Information Technology & Engineering, University of Ottawa, Ottawa, Canada, K1N 6N5

It has been suggested that Bayesian networks and relational databases are *different* because the membership problems for probabilistic conditional independence and embedded multivalued dependency do not always coincide. The present study indicates that the membership problems coincide on *solvable* classes of dependencies and differ on *unsolvable* classes. We therefore maintain that Bayesian networks and relational databases are the *same* in a practical sense, since only *solvable* classes of dependencies are useful in the design and implementation of both knowledge systems.

1. Introduction

The *relational database model* [3] is well established as the basis for developing database systems. The lossless decomposition of a relation into two projections (smaller relations) is based upon the notion of *embedded multivalued dependency* (EMVD). On the other hand, *Bayesian networks* [6] have become a proven framework for uncertainty management. In this approach, *probabilistic conditional independence* is used to factorize a probability distribution into two smaller distributions. It has been suggested [9] that Bayesian networks and relational databases are *different* because the membership problems for probabilistic conditional independence and EMVD do not always coincide. This remark, however, does not take into consideration the important issue of the *solvability* of the membership problem.

Our Bayesian database model [11, 12, 13] provides a *unified* framework for modeling both Bayesian network and relational database applications. We extend the standard relation by adding a column to store the probability values. We introduce *Bayesian embedded multivalued dependency* (BEMVD) as the necessary and sufficient condition for the lossless decomposition of a probabilistic relation into two smaller probabilistic relations. It is important to realize that BEMVD is simply probabilistic conditional independence expressed as a database dependency. Moreover, EMVD is a necessary but not a sufficient condition for BEMVD. Therefore, our Bayesian model offers a convenient tool to present a comprehensive study of the implication of BEMVDs and EMVDs.

The *membership problem* [1, 2, 6, 7, 9, 10, 12, 14] is to determine whether a set $\sum$ of dependencies *logically implies* another dependency σ. We say $\sum$ logically implies σ, written $\sum \models \sigma$, if every relation which satisfies $\sum$ also satisfies σ. That is, there is no counter-example relation such that all of the dependencies in $\sum$ are satisfied but σ is not. We would like to know:

Do the membership problems coincide in these two database models?

That is, we would like to know whether the following proposition holds:

$$\mathbf{C} \models \mathbf{c} \iff C \models c, \tag{1.1}$$

where $\mathbf{C}$ and $\mathbf{c}$ are *probabilistic* dependencies in our Bayesian database model, and C and c are the corresponding *data* dependencies in the relational database model. In this paper, we study whether Proposition (1.1) holds in the following four pairs of dependencies: (BMVD,MVD), (conflict-free BMVD, conflict-free MVD), (conflict-free BEMVD,conflict-free EMVD), and (BEMVD,EMVD), as illustrated in Figure 1.1. We will show that the only pair for which the membership problems do *not* coincide is (BEMVD,EMVD). This is an important observation since the BEMVD class does *not* have a finite complete axiomatization [9, 14]. Similarly, the EMVD class does *not* have a finite complete axiomatization [5, 7]. On the contrary, each of the classes in the former three pairs *do* indeed have a finite complete axiomatization. These results suggest that the membership problems coincide on the *solvable* classes of dependencies and differ on the *unsolvable* classes, as depicted in Figure 1.2. We therefore maintain that Bayesian networks and relational databases are the *same* in a practical sense, since only *solvable* classes of dependencies are useful in the design and implementation of both knowledge systems.

This paper is organized as follows. In Section 2, we review the notions of embedded multivalued dependency (EMVD) and Bayesian embedded multivalued dependency (BEMVD), i.e., probabilistic conditional independence. We define three subclasses of BEMVD in Section 3. In Section 4, we use the membership problem to study the relationship between the relational database model and the Bayesian database model. In Section 5, we examine the role solvability plays in this relationship. The conclusion is presented in Section 6.

2. Embedded Multivalued Dependency and Bayesian Embedded Multivalued Dependency

Before introducing our Bayesian database model [11, 12, 13], we briefly review the notions of *relation* and *embedded multivalued dependency* (EMVD) in the standard relational database model [3].

A *relation scheme* $R = \{A_1, A_2, \ldots, A_m\}$ is a finite set of *attributes*. Corresponding to each attribute A_i is a nonempty finite set D_{A_i}, $1 \leq i \leq m$,

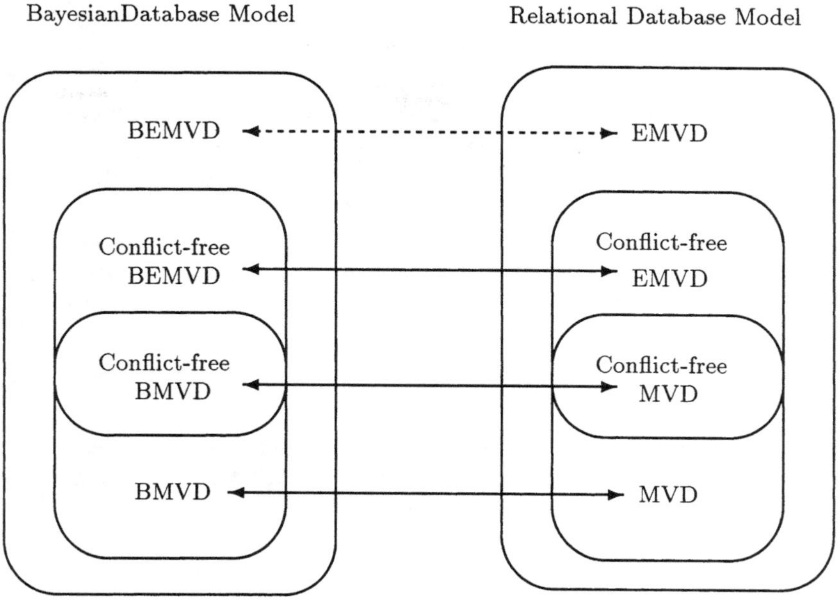

Fig. 1.1. The four classes of *generalized* dependencies in the Bayesian database model and the corresponding class of *data* dependencies in the standard relational database model. A double solid arrow means that Proposition (1.1) holds, while a double dashed arrow indicates that Proposition (1.1) does *not* hold.

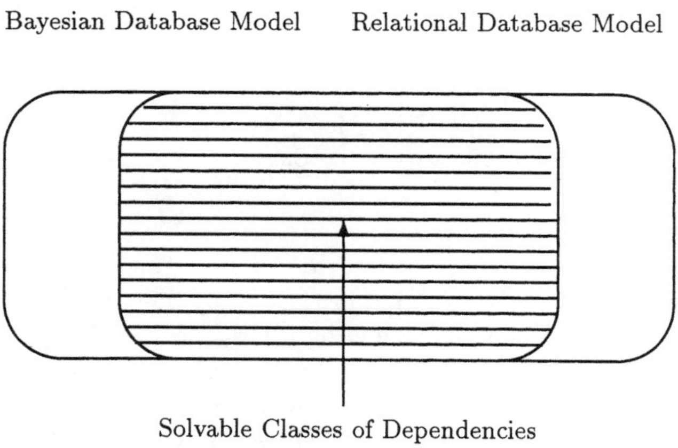

Fig. 1.2. The membership problems coincide on the *solvable* classes of dependencies.

called the *domain* of A_i. Let $D = D_{A_1} \cup D_{A_2} \ldots \cup D_{A_m}$. A *relation* r on the relation scheme R, written $r(R)$, is a finite set of mappings $\{t_1, t_2, \ldots, t_s\}$ from R to D with the restriction that for each mapping $t \in r$, $t(A_i)$ must be in D_{A_i}, $1 \leq i \leq m$, where $t(A_i)$ denotes the value obtained by restricting the mapping to A_i. The mappings are called *tuples* and $t(A)$ is called the A-value of t. To simplify the notation, we will simply write a relation r on R as $r(A_1 A_2 \ldots A_m)$.

Let X, Y, Z, W be pairwise disjoint subsets of attributes of scheme $R = XYZW$. We say relation $r(XYZW)$ satisfies the *embedded multivalued dependency* (EMVD) $X \rightarrow\rightarrow Y|Z$ in the context XYZ, if the projection $\pi_{XYZ}(r)$ of $r(XYZW)$ satisfies the condition:

$$\pi_{XYZ}(r) \quad = \quad \pi_{XY}(r) \bowtie \pi_{XZ}(r), \tag{2.1}$$

where π and $\bowtie$ are the *projection* and *natural join* operators, respectively. For example, relation $r(ABCD)$ on the top of Figure 2.1 satisfies the EMVD $B \rightarrow\rightarrow A|C$, since $\pi_{ABC}(r) = \pi_{AB}(r) \bowtie \pi_{BC}(r)$.

$r(ABCD) =$

A	B	C	D
0	0	0	0
0	0	0	1
0	0	1	1
1	0	0	0
1	0	1	0
1	1	1	1

$\pi_{ABC}(r) =$

A	B	C
0	0	0
0	0	1
1	0	0
1	0	1
1	1	1

$=$

A	B
0	0
1	0
1	1

$\bowtie$

B	C
0	0
0	1
1	1

Fig. 2.1. Relation $r(ABCD)$ satisfies the EMVD $B \rightarrow\rightarrow A|C$, since $\pi_{ABC}(r) = \pi_{AB}(r) \bowtie \pi_{BC}(r)$.

We *generalize* a traditional relation $r(R)$ by adding an additional column A_p. A *probabilistic* relation is denoted by $\mathbf{r}(RA_p)$, where the column labelled by A_p stores the probability values. Note that $\mathbf{t}(A_p) > 0$, for all $\mathbf{t} \in \mathbf{r}(RA_p)$, namely, tuples with zero probability are *not* stored in relation $\mathbf{r}(R)$. For convenience, we will write $\mathbf{r}(RA_p)$ as $\mathbf{r}(R)$ and say relation $\mathbf{r}$ is on R with the attribute A_p understood by context. That is, relations denoted by boldface represent probabilistic relations.

Let $\mathbf{r}(R)$ be a relation and X be a subset of R. The *marginalization of* $\mathbf{r}$ *onto* X, written $\tau_X(\mathbf{r})$, is:

$$\tau_X(\mathbf{r}) = \{ \mathbf{t}(XA_{p(X)}) \mid \mathbf{t}(X) \in \pi_X(\mathbf{r}) \text{ and } \mathbf{t}(A_{p(X)}) = \sum_{\mathbf{t}' \in \mathbf{r}, \mathbf{t}'(X) = \mathbf{t}(X)} \mathbf{t}'(A_p) \}.$$

In the literature [6], the relation $\tau_X(\mathbf{r})$ is called the *marginal distribution* $p(X)$ of $p(R)$ onto X.

The *product join* of two relations $\mathbf{r}_1(X)$ and $\mathbf{r}_2(Y)$, written $\mathbf{r}_1(X) \times \mathbf{r}_2(Y)$, is defined as

$$\mathbf{r}_1(X) \times \mathbf{r}_2(Y) = \{\mathbf{t}(XYA_{p(X) \cdot p(Y)}) \mid \mathbf{t}(XY) \in \pi_X(\mathbf{r}_1) \bowtie \pi_Y(\mathbf{r}_2) \text{ and } \mathbf{t}(A_{p(X) \cdot p(Y)}) = \mathbf{t}(A_{p(X)}) \cdot \mathbf{t}(A_{p(Y)})\}.$$

Thus, $\mathbf{r}_1(X) \times \mathbf{r}_2(Y)$ denotes the product $p(X) \cdot p(Y)$ of the two distributions $p(X)$ and $p(Y)$.

Let X, Y, Z, W be pairwise disjoint subsets of attributes of scheme $R = XYZW$. A probabilistic relation $\mathbf{r}(XYZW)$ satisfies the *Bayesian embedded multivalued dependency* (BEMVD), $X \Rightarrow\Rightarrow Y|Z$, if

$$\tau_{XYZ}(\mathbf{r}) = \tau_{XY}(\mathbf{r}) \times \tau_{XZ}(\mathbf{r}) \times \tau_X(\mathbf{r})^{-1}, \tag{2.2}$$

where the inverse relation $\tau_X(\mathbf{r})^{-1}$ is defined using $\tau_X(\mathbf{r})$ as follows:

$$\tau_X(\mathbf{r})^{-1} = \{\mathbf{t}(XA_{1/p(X)}) \mid \mathbf{t}(X) = \mathbf{t}'(X) \in \tau_X(\mathbf{r}) \text{ and } \mathbf{t}(A_{1/p(X)}) = 1/\mathbf{t}'(A_{p(X)})\}.$$

Note that this relation $\tau_X(\mathbf{r})^{-1}$ is well defined because by definition $\tau_X(\mathbf{r})$ does not contain any tuples with zero probability. By introducing a binary operator $\otimes$ called *Markov join*, we say that a relation $\mathbf{r}(XYZ)$ satisfies the BEMVD $X \Rightarrow\Rightarrow Y|Z$, if

$$\begin{aligned} \tau_{XYZ}(\mathbf{r}) &\equiv \tau_{XY}(\mathbf{r}) \otimes \tau_{XZ}(\mathbf{r}) \\ &= \tau_{XY}(\mathbf{r}) \times \tau_{XZ}(\mathbf{r}) \times \tau_X(\mathbf{r})^{-1}. \end{aligned}$$

For example, relation $\mathbf{r}(ABCD)$ on the top of Figure 2.2 satisfies the BEMVD $B \Rightarrow\Rightarrow A|C$, since the marginal $\tau_{ABC}(\mathbf{r})$ can be written as $\tau_{ABC}(\mathbf{r}) = \tau_{AB}(\mathbf{r}) \otimes \tau_{BC}(\mathbf{r})$.

Two important remarks need to made. First, EMVD is a *necessary* but not a sufficient condition for BEMVD [11]. It is straightforward to construct a probabilistic relation $\mathbf{r}(R)$ which does *not* satisfy a given BEMVD $X \Rightarrow\Rightarrow Y|Z$, yet the traditional relation $r(R)$ (obtained by striking out the column A_p) does indeed satisfy the corresponding EMVD $X \rightarrow\rightarrow Y|Z$. Second, we say that Y and Z are *conditionally independent* given X in a probability distribution $p(XYZW)$, written $I(Y, X, Z)$, if

$$p(XYZ) = \frac{p(XY) \cdot p(XZ)}{p(X)}, \tag{2.3}$$

$\mathbf{r}(ABCD) =$

A	B	C	D	$A_{p(ABCD)}$
0	0	0	0	0.1
0	0	0	1	0.1
0	0	1	1	0.2
1	0	0	0	0.1
1	0	1	0	0.1
1	1	1	1	0.4

$\tau_{ABC}(\mathbf{r}) =$

A	B	C	$A_{p(ABC)}$
0	0	0	0.2
0	0	1	0.2
1	0	0	0.1
1	0	1	0.1
1	1	1	0.4

$=$

A	B	$A_{p(AB)}$
0	0	0.4
1	0	0.2
1	1	0.4

$\otimes$

B	C	$A_{p(BC)}$
0	0	0.3
0	1	0.3
1	1	0.4

$=$

A	B	C	$A_{\frac{p(AB)p(BC)}{p(B)}}$
0	0	0	$(0.4)(0.3)/(0.6) = 0.2$
0	0	1	$(0.4)(0.3)/(0.6) = 0.2$
1	0	0	$(0.2)(0.3)/(0.6) = 0.1$
1	0	1	$(0.2)(0.3)/(0.6) = 0.1$
1	1	1	$(0.4)(0.4)/(0.4) = 0.4$

Fig. 2.2. Relation $\mathbf{r}(ABCD)$ satisfies the BEMVD $B \Rightarrow\Rightarrow A|C$, since $\tau_{ABC}(\mathbf{r}) = \tau_{AB}(\mathbf{r}) \otimes \tau_{BC}(\mathbf{r})$.

where X, Y, Z, W are pairwise disjoint. By comparing Equations (2.2) and (2.3), it can be easily seen that BEMVD is simply *probabilistic conditional independence* expressed as a database dependency. Let $\mathbf{r}(XYZW)$ be the probabilistic relation representing the probability distribution $p(XYZW)$. Saying that $\mathbf{r}(XYZW)$ satisfies the BEMVD $X \Rightarrow\Rightarrow Y|Z$ is the same as saying that Y and Z are *conditionally independent* given X in $p(XYZW)$, namely,

$$X \Rightarrow\Rightarrow Y|Z \iff I(Y, X, Z). \tag{2.4}$$

Thus, we use the terms BEMVD and probabilistic conditional independency interchangeably.

3. Subclasses of Bayesian Embedded Multivalued Dependency

Here we define three special subclasses of BEMVD. The corresponding classes of *data* dependencies are defined by replacing the notion of BEMVD with EMVD.

In the special case when the BEMVD $X \Rightarrow\Rightarrow Y|Z$ involves all the attributes in a relation scheme R, i.e., $R = XYZ$, we call $X \Rightarrow\Rightarrow Y|Z$ a *full* BEMVD, or simply *Bayesian multivalued dependency* (BMVD). We write the BMVD $X \Rightarrow\Rightarrow Y|Z$ as $X \Rightarrow\Rightarrow Y$, if the context is understood.

A graphical structure $\mathcal{G}$ is called a *perfect-map* [2, 6] of a set $\sum$ of dependencies, if every dependency logically implied by $\sum$ can be inferred from $\mathcal{G}$, and every dependency inferred from $\mathcal{G}$ is logically implied by $\sum$. We can use the *separation* method [2] to infer BMVDs from an acyclic hypergraph. We say that a BMVD $X \Rightarrow\Rightarrow Y$ is inferred from an acyclic hypergraph $\mathcal{R}$, if and only if Y is the union of some disconnected components of $\mathcal{R}$ with the set X of nodes deleted. (For example, consider the acyclic hypergraph $\mathcal{R} = \{R_1 = AB, R_2 = BCD, R_3 = DE, R_4 = DFG, R_5 = DFH\}$ on the set $R = ABCDEFGH$ of attributes. The disconnected components obtained by deleting node D in $\mathcal{R}$ are $S_1 = ABC$, $S_2 = E$, and $S_3 = FGH$. By definition, the BMVDs $D \Rightarrow\Rightarrow ABC$, $D \Rightarrow\Rightarrow E$, $D \Rightarrow\Rightarrow FGH$, and $D \Rightarrow\Rightarrow ABCE$ can be inferred from $\mathcal{R}$. On the other hand, the BMVD $D \Rightarrow\Rightarrow BC$ is *not* inferred from $\mathcal{R}$ since BC is not equal to the union of some of the sets in $\{S_1, S_2, S_3\}$.)

In general, not every set of BMVDs can be faithfully represented by a single acyclic hypergraph. For example, there is no single acyclic hypergraph that can simultaneously encode the set $\mathbf{C} = \{A_1 \Rightarrow\Rightarrow A_2,\ A_3 \Rightarrow\Rightarrow A_2\}$ of BMVDs on $R = A_1A_2A_3$. The *conflict-free BMVD* [2] class contains every set of BMVDs which has a perfect-map in the form of an acyclic hypergraph.

We now introduce a new subclass within BEMVD called *conflict-free BEMVD*. The *d-separation* [6] method for inferring BEMVDs from a *directed acyclic graph* (DAG) in a manner similar to using the *separation* method for inferring BMVDs from an acyclic hypergraph. Just as there are some sets of BMVDs which cannot be faithfully represented by a single acyclic hypergraph, there are some sets of BEMVDs which cannot be faithfully represented by a single DAG. For example, there is no *single* DAG that can simultaneously encode the set $\mathbf{C} = \{A_2 \Rightarrow\Rightarrow A_1|A_3,\ A_3 \Rightarrow\Rightarrow A_1|A_2,\ A_3 \Rightarrow\Rightarrow A_1A_2|A_4\}$ of BEMVDs on $R = A_1A_2A_3A_4$. The *conflict-free BEMVD* class is defined as those sets of BEMVDs which have a perfect-map in the form of a DAG.

4. Comparing the Bayesian and Relational Database Models

In this section, we show that the membership problems in the Bayesian database model and the relational database model coincide on those classes of dependencies with a finite complete axiomatization. We remind the reader that $\mathbf{C}$ and C denote corresponding sets of BEMVDs and EMVDs, respectively. That is, $C = \{X \rightarrow\rightarrow Y|Z \mid X \Rightarrow\Rightarrow Y|Z \in \mathbf{C}\}$. Similarly, c denotes the EMVD corresponding to the BEMVD $\mathbf{c}$. We begin our analysis with the pair (BMVD,MVD).

The following three inference axioms (M0), (M1) and (M2) are both minimal [4] and *complete* [1] for the MVD class:

(M0) If $Y \cap Z \subseteq X$, then $X \rightarrow\rightarrow Y$ iff $X \rightarrow\rightarrow Z$,
(M1) If $Y \subseteq X$, then $X \rightarrow\rightarrow Y$,
(M2) If $X \rightarrow\rightarrow Y$ and $Y \rightarrow\rightarrow Z$, then $X \rightarrow\rightarrow Z - Y$.

Since the corresponding inference axioms (B0), (B1) and (B2) are *sound* [12] for the BMVD class:

(B0) If $Y \cap Z \subseteq X$, then $X \Rightarrow\Rightarrow Y$ iff $X \Rightarrow\Rightarrow Z$,
(B1) If $Y \subseteq X$, then $X \Rightarrow\Rightarrow Y$,
(B2) If $X \Rightarrow\Rightarrow Y$ and $Y \Rightarrow\Rightarrow Z$, then $X \Rightarrow\Rightarrow Z - Y$,

it immediately follows that the membership problems coincide in the pair (BMVD, MVD).

Theorem 4.1. $\mathbf{C} \models \mathbf{c} \iff C \models c$ in the pair (BMVD,MVD).

Proof: ($\Rightarrow$) $\mathbf{C} \models \mathbf{c} \implies C \models c$ is a *tautology* in the pair (BMVD,MVD) [11].

($\Leftarrow$) Let $C \models c$. Since the MVD class has a complete axiomatization, $C \models c$ implies that $C \vdash c$. That is, there exists a derivation sequence s of the MVD c by applying the MVD inference axioms (M0)-(M2) to the MVDs in C. This means there exists a derivation sequence $\mathbf{s}$ of the BMVD $\mathbf{c}$ using the BMVDs inference axioms (B0)-(B2) on the BMVDs in $\mathbf{C}$, which parallels the derivation sequence s of the MVD c. That is, $\mathbf{C} \vdash \mathbf{c}$. Since these BMVD axioms are sound, $\mathbf{C} \vdash \mathbf{c}$ implies that $\mathbf{C} \models \mathbf{c}$. □

Obviously the membership problems coincide in the pair (conflict-free BMVD, conflict-free MVD), as this pair is a subclass of the pair (BMVD,MVD).

Theorem 4.2. $\mathbf{C} \models \mathbf{c} \iff C \models c$ in the pair (conflict-free BMVD, conflict-free MVD).

This concludes our brief discussion of *full* (nonembedded) dependencies.

We now consider *embedded* dependencies. The special classes of conflict-free BEMVD and conflict-free EMVD both have a finite *complete* axiomatization [6].

Theorem 4.3. [6] $\mathbf{C} \models \mathbf{c} \iff C \models c$ in the pair (conflict-free BEMVD, conflict-free EMVD).

Theorems 4.1, 4.2, and 4.3 are significant since they indicate that testing the implication of *probabilistic* dependencies is the *same* as testing the implication of *data* dependencies. An immediate consequence is that the *chase* [3] algorithm can be directly applied as a *nonaxiomatic* method to test the implication of BMVDs [10, 12].

5. The Role of Solvability

In the last section, it was shown that the membership problems coincide for some classes of dependencies. However, Studeny [9] pointed out that the membership problems for EMVD and BEMVD do *not* always coincide.

Example 5.1. Consider the set $\mathbf{C} = \{A_3A_4 \Rightarrow\Rightarrow A_1|A_2,\ A_1 \Rightarrow\Rightarrow A_3|A_4,\ A_2 \Rightarrow\Rightarrow A_3|A_4,\ \emptyset \Rightarrow\Rightarrow A_1|A_2\}$ of BEMVDs, and $\mathbf{c}$ the single BEMVD $\emptyset \Rightarrow\Rightarrow A_3|A_4$. In [8], Studeny showed that $\mathbf{C} \models \mathbf{c}$. Now consider the set $C = \{X \rightarrow\rightarrow Y|Z \mid X \Rightarrow\Rightarrow Y|Z \in \mathbf{C}\}$ of EMVDs corresponding to the set $\mathbf{C}$ of BEMVDs, and the single EMVD $\emptyset \rightarrow\rightarrow A_3|A_4$ corresponding to the BEMVD $\mathbf{c}$. Consider the relation $r(A_1A_2A_3A_4)$ in Figure 5.1. It can be verified that $r(A_1A_2A_3A_4)$ satisfies all of the EMVDs in C but does not satisfy the EMVD c. That is, $C \not\models c$. □

Example (5.1) indicates that

$$\mathbf{C} \models \mathbf{c} \not\Rightarrow C \models c. \tag{5.1}$$

$r(A_1A_2A_3A_4)$ =

A_1	A_2	A_3	A_4
0	0	0	0
0	0	0	1
0	1	0	0
1	0	0	0
1	1	0	0
1	1	1	0

Fig. 5.1. Relation r satisfies all of the EMVDs in C but does not satisfy the EMVD c, where C and c are defined in Example 5.1. Therefore, $C \not\models c$.

Example 5.2. Consider the set $C = \{A_1 \rightarrow\rightarrow A_3|A_4,\ A_2 \rightarrow\rightarrow A_3|A_4,\ A_3A_4 \rightarrow\rightarrow A_1|A_2\}$ of EMVDs, and let c be the single EMVD $A_1A_2 \rightarrow\rightarrow A_3$. It can be shown [12] that $C \models c$. Now consider the corresponding set of BEMVDs $\mathbf{C} = \{A_1 \Rightarrow\Rightarrow A_3|A_4,\ A_2 \Rightarrow\Rightarrow A_3|A_4,\ A_3A_4 \Rightarrow\Rightarrow A_1|A_2\}$ and $\mathbf{c}$ is the BMVD $A_1A_2 \Rightarrow\Rightarrow A_3$. It is easily verified that relation $\mathbf{r}(A_1A_2A_3A_4)$ in Figure 5.2 satisfies all of the BEMVDs in $\mathbf{C}$ but does not satisfy the BEMVD $\mathbf{c}$. Therefore, $\mathbf{C} \not\models \mathbf{c}$. □

Example 5.2 indicates that

$$\mathbf{C} \models \mathbf{c} \not\Leftarrow C \models c. \tag{5.2}$$

$\mathbf{r}(A_1A_2A_3A_4) =$

A_1	A_2	A_3	A_4	A_p
0	0	0	0	0.2
0	0	0	1	0.2
0	0	1	0	0.2
0	0	1	1	0.1
0	1	1	1	0.1
1	0	1	1	0.1
1	1	1	1	0.1

Fig. 5.2. Relation $\mathbf{r}$ satisfies all of the BEMVDs in $\mathbf{C}$ but does not the BEMVD $\mathbf{c}$, where $\mathbf{C}$ and $\mathbf{c}$ are defined in Example 5.2. Therefore, $\mathbf{C} \not\models \mathbf{c}$.

Based on Equations (5.1) and (5.2), Studeny [9] argued that the Bayesian database model and the relational database model are *different*. This remark, however, does not take into consideration one important issue. The question naturally arises as to why the membership problem coincides for some classes of dependencies but not for others. The answer lies in the *solvability* of the membership problem.

There is *no* single DAG which can faithfully represent all of the BEMVDs in the set $\mathbf{C}$ of BEMVDs in Example 5.1. This means that set $\mathbf{C}$ of BEMVDs belongs to the *general* BEMVD class. Similarly, there is *no* single DAG which can faithfully represent all the EMVDs in the set C of EMVDs in Example 5.2. This means that the set C of EMVDs belongs to the *general* EMVD class. This means that Studeny's argument that Bayesian networks and standard relational databases are *different* was based on the analysis of the membership problems in the general pair (BEMVD,EMVD). This is an important observation since the general BEMVD class does *not* have a finite complete axiomatization [9, 14], contrary to Pearl's [6] conjecture. Similarly, the general EMVD class does *not* have a finite complete axiomatization [5, 7]. This supports our argument that there is no *real* difference between Bayesian networks and standard relational databases in a practical sense, since only *solvable* classes of dependencies are useful in the design and implementation of both knowledge systems.

6. Conclusion

It has been suggested in [9] that Bayesian networks are *different* from relational databases since the membership problems of probabilistic conditional independence and embedded multivalued dependency do not always coincide. In this paper, we reviewed the fact that our *Bayesian database model* [11, 12, 13] serves as a *unified* model for both Bayesian networks and relational databases. In particular, probabilistic conditional independence can be expressed as *Bayesian embedded multivalued dependency* (BEMVD). We pointed out that Studeny's observation [9] was based on an analysis of the *general* pair (BEMVD,EMVD). This is important since both the general EMVD class [5, 7] and the general BEMVD class [9, 14] do *not* have a finite complete axiomatization. This means that there is no *real* difference between Bayesian networks and standard relational databases in a practical sense, since only *solvable* classes of dependencies are useful in the design and implementation of both knowledge systems.

References

1. C. Beeri, R. Fagin, and J.H. Howard. A complete axiomatization for functional and multivalued dependencies in database relations. In *Proceedings of ACM-SIGMOD International Conference on Management of Data*, pages 47–61, 1977.
2. C. Beeri, R. Fagin, D. Maier, and M. Yannakakis. On the desirability of acyclic database schemes. *Journal of the ACM*, 30(3):479–513, July 1983.
3. D. Maier. *The Theory of Relational Databases*. Principles of Computer Science. Computer Science Press, Rockville, Maryland, 1983.
4. A. Mendelzon. On axiomatizing multivalued dependencies in relational databases. *Journal of the ACM*, 26(1):37–44, 1979.
5. D. Parker and K. Parsaye-Ghomi. Inference involving embedded multivalued dependencies and transitive dependencies. In *Proceedings of ACM-SIGMOD International Conference on Management of Data*, pages 52–57, 1980.
6. J. Pearl. *Probabilistic Reasoning in Intelligent Systems: Networks of Plausible Inference*. Morgan Kaufmann Publishers, San Francisco, California, 1988.
7. Y. Sagiv and F. Walecka. Subset dependencies and a complete result for a subclass of embedded multivalued dependencies. *Journal of the ACM*, 20(1):103–117, 1982.
8. M. Studeny. Multiinformation and the problem of characterization of conditional-independence relations. *Problems of Control and Information Theory*, 18(1):3–16, 1989.
9. M. Studeny. Conditional independence relations have no finite complete characterization. In *Eleventh Prague Conference on Information Theory, Statistical Decision Foundation and Random Processes*, pages 377–396. Kluwer, 1990.
10. S.K.M. Wong. Testing implication of probabilistic dependencies. In *Twelfth Conference on Uncertainty in Artificial Intelligence*, pages 545–553. Morgan Kaufmann Publishers, 1996.
11. S.K.M. Wong. An extended relational data model for probabilistic reasoning. *Journal of Intelligent Information Systems*, 9:181–202, 1997.

12. S.K.M. Wong, C.J. Butz, and D. Wu. On the implication problem for probabilistic conditional independency. *IEEE Transactions on Systems, Man, and Cybernetics*, Vol. 30, Part A, No. 6, 785–805, 2000.
13. S.K.M. Wong, C.J. Butz, and Y. Xiang. A method for implementing a probabilistic model as a relational database. In *Eleventh Conference on Uncertainty in Artificial Intelligence*, pages 556–564. Morgan Kaufmann Publishers, 1995.
14. S.K.M. Wong and Z.W. Wang. On axiomatization of probabilistic conditional independence. In *Tenth Conference on Uncertainty in Artificial Intelligence*, pages 591–597. Morgan Kaufmann Publishers, 1994.

Belief Functions Induced by Randomized Communication Channels

Ivan Kramosil

Institute of Computer Science
Academy of Sciences of the Czech Republic
Pod vodárenskou věží 2, 182 07 Prague 8
e-mail: kramosil@uivt.cas.cz, fax: (420) (02) 85 85 789

Abstract. The most often used combinatorial definition of belief function over a finite basic space S can be obtained through a binary compatibility relation ρ between the states s (elements of S) and some empirical data (observations) x from an observational space E, when x is taken as the value of a random variable X. We shall investigate a generalized version of this model supposing that the values $\rho(s,x)$ defined by the compatibility relation in question are observed through a random binary communication channel so that the values $\rho(s,x)$ are subjected to random changes (deformations) before reaching the subject and being accepted. The resulting randomized basic probability assignments and belief functions will be analyzed in more detail, namely, we shall prove under which conditions and in which sense and degree they can approximate the corresponding original numerical characteristics of uncertainty.

This work has been sponsored by the grant no. A1030803 of the GA AS CR.

1 Introduction – from Compatibility Relations to Belief Functions

The most simple combinatorial definition of non-normalized belief function over a finite nonempty space S reads as follows. *Basic probability assignment* (b.p.a.) over S is a mapping m which takes the power-set $\mathcal{P}(S)$ of all subsets of S into the unit interval $[0,1]$ of real numbers in such a way that $\sum_{A \subset S} m(A) = 1$. Hence, m is nothing else than a probability distribution over the power-set $\mathcal{P}(S)$. The (*non-normalized*) *degree of belief* $bel_m(A)$ generated by the b.p.a. m and ascribed to a subset A of S is defined by

(1) $$bel_m(A) = \sum_{\emptyset \neq B \subset A} m(B),$$

setting $bel_m(\emptyset) = 0$ for the empty subset $\emptyset$ of S.

An alternative way how to arrive at (1) reads as follows. Let S be taken as the set of all possible internal states of a system (answers to a question, solutions to a problem, medical or technical diagnoses, etc.), let E be the space of empirical values (observations, symptoms, hints) concerning the system in question, and let $\rho : S \times E \to \{0,1\}$ (or $\rho \subset S \times E$) be a *compatibility relation* which defines the subject's knowledge as far as the system is concerned. Namely, if $\rho(s,x) = 0$ for some $s \in S$ and $x \in E$, then s cannot be the actual internal state of the system supposing that x was observed, hence, s and x are *incompatible.* If $\rho(s,x) = 1$, then the state s and the empirical value x are *compatible.* So, for each $x \in E$, the set $U(x) = \{s \in S : \rho(s,x) = 1\}$ of states compatible with x is defined.

Let x be the value taken by a random variable X defined on a fixed probability space $\langle \Omega, \mathcal{A}, P \rangle$ with the values in a measurable space $\langle E, \mathcal{E} \rangle$ over E. Under some reasonable measurability conditions, e. g., when E is finite and $\mathcal{E} = \mathcal{P}(E)$, the composed mapping $U(X(\cdot)) = \Omega \to \mathcal{P}(S)$ is a set-valued (generalized) random variable. Setting $m(A) = P(\{\omega \in \Omega : U(X(\omega)) = A\})$ for each $A \subset S$, (1) transforms into

$$bel_m(A) = P\left(\{\omega \in \Omega : \emptyset \neq U(X(\omega)) \subset A\}\right). \tag{2}$$

2 Belief Functions Generated by Randomized Compatibility Relations

Here we shall investigate the case when the compatibility relation ρ is charged by the uncertainty possessing the nature of *randomness.* Hence, given $s \in S$ and $x \in E$, the value $\rho(s,x)$ is either 0 or 1 (ρ is a subset of $S \times E$, s and x are either compatible or incompatible), but the value $\rho(s,x)$ reaches the subject through a communication channel and during this way it may be subjected to a deformation. Let us limit ourselves to the case when the deformation can be only of one kind, namely, the value 0 changes to 1 and, vice versa, 1 changes to 0. Moreover, we shall suppose that the chance with which these deformations can occur can be defined, quantified and processed using the apparatus of the Kolmogorov axiomatic probability theory. In more specific terms, the values $\rho(s,x)$ are processed by *binary information channel* (in particular, by binary symmetric channel, if the probabilities of both the changes, $0 \to 1$ and $1 \to 0$, are the same).

Let S, E, $\langle \Omega, \mathcal{A}, P \rangle$, $X : \langle \Omega, \mathcal{A}, P \rangle \to \langle E, \mathcal{E} \rangle$, $\rho : S \times E \to \{0,1\}$ and $U_\rho(X(\omega)) = \{s \in S : \rho(s, X(\omega)) = 1\}$ keep their standard meanings as introduced in Chapter 1. Let $Y(i,\cdot)$, $i = 0,1$, be random variables defined on the probability space $\langle \Omega, \mathcal{A}, P \rangle$ and taking their values in $\{0,1\}$. Let us denote

$$\begin{aligned} \Omega_1 &= \{\omega \in \Omega : Y(0,\omega) = 0,\ Y(1,\omega) = 1\} \\ \Omega_2 &= \{\omega \in \Omega : Y(0,\omega) = 1,\ Y(1,\omega) = 0\} \\ \Omega_3 &= \{\omega \in \Omega : Y(0,\omega) = 0,\ Y(1,\omega) = 0\} \\ \Omega_4 &= \{\omega \in \Omega : Y(0,\omega) = 1,\ Y(1,\omega) = 1\}. \end{aligned} \tag{3}$$

Let $\rho^* : S \times E \times \Omega = \{0,1\}$ be defined by

$$\rho^*(s,x,\omega) = Y(\rho(s,x),\, \omega), \tag{4}$$

so that ρ^* is the *randomized compatibility relation* defined by the compatibility relation ρ and by the *communication channel* $\langle Y(i,\cdot)\rangle_{i=0,1}$. The are just the values $\rho^*(s,x,\omega)$ (instead of the correct values $\rho(s,x)$) which are at the subject's disposal when computing the belief function bel_ρ. Hence, as a matter of fact, she/he computes the belief function bel_{ρ^*} defined in this way:

$$(5) \qquad U_{\rho^*}(X(\omega)) = \{s \in S : Y(\rho(s, X(\omega)), \omega) = 1\}$$

and, given $A \subset S$,

$$(6) \quad bel_{\rho^*}(A) = P(\{\omega \in \Omega : \emptyset \neq U_{\rho^*}(X(\omega)) \subset A\}) = \\ = P(\{\omega \in \Omega : \emptyset \neq \{s \in S : Y(\rho(s, X(\omega)), \omega) = 1\} \subset A\}).$$

The definiton of bel_ρ is correct supposing that for every $A \subset S$ the subset $\{\omega \in \Omega : U_{\rho^*}(X(\omega)) \subset A\}$ is measurable, i.e., belongs to the σ-field $\mathcal{A}$. If S is finite, bel_{ρ^*} is uniquely defined by the *basic probability assignment* $m^* : \mathcal{P}(S) \to [0,1]$ such that

$$(7) \qquad m^*(A) = P(\{\omega \in \Omega : U_{\rho^*}(X(\omega)) = A\})$$

for every $A \subset S$.

Theorem 2.1. Let $m : \mathcal{P}(S) \to [0,1]$ be defined by $m(A) = P(\{\omega \in \Omega : U_\rho(X(\omega)) = A\})$ for each $A \subset S$, let $m^* : \mathcal{P}(S) \to [0,1]$ be defined by (7) for all $A \subset S$, let $p_i = P(\Omega_i)$ for each $i = 1, \ldots, 4$ and for Ω_i defined by (3). Let the vector random variable $\langle Y(0), Y(1)\rangle$ and the random variable X be statistically independent. Then

$$(8) \qquad \begin{aligned} m^*(\emptyset) &= p_1 m(\emptyset) + p_2 m(S) + p_3, \\ m^*(S) &= p_1 m(S) + p_2 m(\emptyset) + p_4, \\ m^*(A) &= p_1 m(A) + p_2 m(S - A) \end{aligned}$$

for every $\emptyset \neq A \neq S,\ A \subset S$. If S if finite, then both m and m^* are basic probability assignments on $\mathcal{P}(S)$. □

Proof. All the sets Ω_i, $i = 1, \ldots, 4$, are obviously disjoint, measurable (as both $Y(i)$, $i = 0, 1$ are random variables), and $\bigcup_{i=1}^4 \Omega_i = \Omega$, so that $p_1 + p_2 + p_3 + p_4 = 1$. Hence, for each $A \subset S$, (7) yields that

$$(9) \quad m^*(A) = \sum_{i=1}^4 P(\{\omega \in \Omega_i : \{s \in S : Y(\rho(s, X(\omega)), \omega) = 1\} = A\}).$$

Let us analyse the four cases in question.

If $\omega \in \Omega_1$, then no change of the value $\rho(s, X(\omega))$ occurs, no matter whether this value is 0 or 1, so that $\omega \in \Omega_1$ implies that, for all $s \in S$, $Y(\rho(s, X(\omega)), \omega) = \rho(s, X(\omega))$. If $\omega \in \Omega_2$, then the value $\rho(s, X(\omega))$ is changed into $1 - \rho(s, X(\omega))$, no matter which this value and $s \in S$ may be.

Hence, if $\omega \in \Omega_2$, then $Y(\rho(s, X(\omega)), \omega) = 1 - \rho(s, X(\omega))$ for all $s \in S$. If $\omega \in \Omega_3$, then $Y(\rho(s, X(\omega)), \omega) = 0$ for all $s \in S$ and for both the possible values $\rho(s, X(\omega))$, similarly, if $\omega \in \Omega_4$, then $Y(\rho(s, X(\omega)), \omega) = 1$ for all $s \in S$ and for both the values $\rho(s, X(\omega))$. Consequently, given $A \subset S$ we obtain that

$$
\begin{aligned}
(10) \qquad & P(\{\omega \in \Omega_1 : \{s \in S : Y(\rho(s, X(\omega)), \omega) = 1\} = A\}) = \\
&= P(\{\omega \in \Omega_1 : \{s \in S : \rho(s, X(\omega)) = 1\} = A\}) = \\
&= P(\Omega_1 \cap \{\omega \in \Omega : U_\rho(X(\omega)) = A\}) = \\
&= P(\Omega_1)\, P(\{\omega \in \Omega : U_\rho(X(\omega)) = A\}) = p_1 m(A)
\end{aligned}
$$

due to the supposed statistical independence of $\langle Y(0), Y(1)\rangle$ and X. For Ω_2 we obtain that

$$
\begin{aligned}
(11) \qquad & P(\{\omega \in \Omega_2 : \{s \in S : Y(\rho(s, X(\omega)), \omega) = 1\} = A\}) = \\
&= P(\{\omega \in \Omega_2 : \{s \in S : 1 - \rho(s, X(\omega)) = 1\} = A\}) = \\
&= P(\Omega_2 \cap \{\omega \in \Omega : \{s \in S : \rho(X(\omega)) = 0\} = A\}) = \\
&= P(\Omega_2 \cap \{\omega \in \Omega : S - U_\rho(X(\omega)) = A\}) = \\
&= P(\Omega_2 \cap \{\omega \in \Omega : U_\rho(X(\omega)) = S - A\}) = \\
&= P(\Omega_2)\, P(\{\omega \in \Omega : U_\rho(X(\omega)) = S - A\}) = p_2 m(S - A).
\end{aligned}
$$

Consider the subset Ω_3. For $\omega \in \Omega_3$, $Y(\rho(s, X(\omega)), \omega) = 0$ for all $s \in S$, so that, for all such ω,

$$
(12) \qquad \{s \in S : Y(\rho(s, X(\omega)), \omega) = 1\} = \emptyset,
$$

consequently,

$$
(13) \qquad P(\{\omega \in \Omega_3 : \{s \in S : Y(\rho(s, X(\omega)), \omega) = 1\} = A\}) = 0,
$$

if $A \neq \emptyset$. This probability equals to $P(\Omega_3) = p_3$, if $A = \emptyset$. Similarly, for Ω_4, $Y(\rho(s, X(\omega)), \omega) = 1$ for all $s \in S$ and $\omega \in \Omega_4$, so that, for all such ω,

$$
(14) \qquad \{s \in S : Y(\rho(s, X(\omega)), \omega) = 1\} = S.
$$

So,

$$
(15) \qquad P(\{\omega \in \Omega_4 : \{s \in S : Y(\rho(s, X(\omega)), \omega) = 1\} = A\}) = 0,
$$

if $A \neq S$, this probability being $P(\Omega_4) = p_4$, if $A = S$. Combining all the particular cases together, (9) immediately implies (8), so that the theorem is proved. □

Using the results of Theorem 2.1, the rules how to transform belief function bel_m into bel_{m^*} follow then easily, as the following statement proves.

Corollary 2.1. Let the notations and conditions of Theorem 2.1 hold, let $q_m : \mathcal{P}(S) \to [0,1]$ be the so called *commonality function* defined, for each $A \subset S$, by

$$q_m(A) = \sum\nolimits_{B \supset A} m(B). \tag{16}$$

Then

$$bel_{m^*}(A) = p_1\, bel_m(A) + p_2(q_m(S-A) - m(S)) \tag{17}$$

for each $A \subset S,\ A \neq S$, and

$$bel_{m^*}(S) = (p_1 + p_2)\, bel_m(S) + p_4. \tag{18}$$

□

Proof. Let $A \subset S,\ A \neq S$. By definition,

$$bel_{m^*}(A) = \sum\nolimits_{\emptyset \neq B \subset A} m^*(B). \tag{19}$$

As $A \neq S$, all the sets B on the right-hand side of (19) are *proper* subsets of S, so that (8) yields that

$$\begin{aligned} bel_{m^*}(A) &= \sum\nolimits_{\emptyset \neq B \subset A} [p_1\, m(B) + p_2\, m(S-B)] = \\ &= p_1 \sum\nolimits_{\emptyset \neq B \subset A} m(B) + p_2 \sum\nolimits_{\emptyset \neq B \subset A} m(S-B) = \\ &= p_1\, bel_m(A) + p_2 \sum\nolimits_{S \neq B \supset S-A} m(B). \end{aligned} \tag{20}$$

If $A = \emptyset$, there is no B such that $S \neq B \supset S - A$. so that the sum in the right-hand side of the last line is zero by convention and

$$\begin{aligned} bel_{m^*}(\emptyset) &= p_1\, bel_m(\emptyset) = 0 = p_1\, bel_m(\emptyset) + p_2(q_m(S) - m(S)) = \\ &= p_1\, bel_m(\emptyset) + p_2(m(S) - m(S)), \end{aligned} \tag{21}$$

as $q_m(S) = m(S)$. If $\emptyset \neq A \subset S,\ A \neq S$, (20) and (16) yield that

$$bel_{m^*}(A) = p_1\, bel_m(A) + p_2(q_m(S-A) - m(S)) \tag{22}$$

and (17) is proved.

If $A = S$, (8) yields that

$$\begin{aligned} bel_{m^*}(S) &= \sum\nolimits_{\emptyset \neq B \subset S} m^*(B) = \sum\nolimits_{\emptyset \neq B \subset S,\, B \neq S} m^*(B) + m^*(S) = \\ &= p_1 \sum\nolimits_{\emptyset \neq B \subset S,\, B \neq S} m(B) + p_2 \sum\nolimits_{\emptyset \neq B \subset S,\, B \neq S} m(S-B) + \\ &\quad + p_1\, m(S) + p_2\, m(\emptyset) + p_4 = \\ &= p_1 \sum\nolimits_{\emptyset \neq B \subset S} m(B) + p_2 \sum\nolimits_{\emptyset \neq B \subset S} m(B) + p_4 = \\ &= (p_1 + p_2)\, bel_m(S) + p_4. \end{aligned} \tag{23}$$

The assertion is proved. □

The following simple lemma will be useful in the sequel.

Lemma 2.1. For all real numbers $p,\ q \in [1/2,\ 1]$ the inequality

$$1/2 \leq pq + (1-p)\,(1-q) \leq \min(p,q) \tag{24}$$

holds. □

Proof. As $p \geq 1/2$, $p \geq 1-p$ holds, so that

$$pq + (1-p)\,(1-q) \leq pq + p(1-q) = p \tag{25}$$

and analogously for q, so that

$$pq + (1-p)\,(1-q) \leq \min(p,q) \tag{26}$$

is proved. Without any loss of generality we may suppose that $p \leq q$ hold, hence, $q = p + \varepsilon$ for an $\varepsilon \geq 0$. Under this notation

$$\begin{aligned} &pq + (1-p)\,(1-q) = \\ &= p(p+\varepsilon) + (1-p)\,(1-p-\varepsilon) = \\ &= 2p^2 + 2p(1-\varepsilon) + 1 - \varepsilon, \end{aligned} \tag{27}$$

so that $pq + (1-p)\,(1-q) \geq 1/2$ holds iff

$$p^2 - p(1-\varepsilon) + (1/4 - \varepsilon/2) \geq 0 \tag{28}$$

holds. However,

$$0 \leq (p - 1/2)^2 = p^2 - p + 1/4 \tag{29}$$

is trivially valid and $p \geq 1/2$ implies that $(p - 1/2)\,\varepsilon \geq 0$ holds, hence,

$$\begin{aligned} 0 &\leq p^2 - p + 1/4 + (p - 1/2)\,\varepsilon = \\ &= p^2 - p + p\varepsilon + (1/4 - \varepsilon/2) = \\ &= p^2 - p(1-\varepsilon) + (1/4 - \varepsilon/2). \end{aligned} \tag{30}$$

So, (28) is valid and the assertion is proved. □

Remark. An easy inspection of the proof of Lemma 2.1 yields, that if $p,\ q \in (1/2,\ 1)$ holds, then

$$1/2 < pq + (1-p)\,(1-q) < \min(p,q) \tag{31}$$

holds.

3 Combining More Communication Channels

Given a real $p \in [0,1]$, define $\boldsymbol{p}$ as the pair $\langle p,\ 1-p\rangle$ from $[0,1]\times[0,1]$. Given $p,\ q \in [0,1]$ define $\boldsymbol{p} * \boldsymbol{q}$ by $\langle(\boldsymbol{p} * \boldsymbol{q}),\ (\boldsymbol{p} * \boldsymbol{q})_2\rangle$, where

$$(32)\qquad (\boldsymbol{p} * \boldsymbol{q})_1 = p\,q + (1-p)\,(1-q)$$

$$(33)\qquad (\boldsymbol{p} * \boldsymbol{q})_2 = 1 - (p\,q + (1-p)\,(1-q)).$$

Given $p_1, p_2, \ldots, p_n \in [0,1]$ set, by induction,

$$(34)\qquad \boldsymbol{p}_1 * \boldsymbol{p}_2 * \cdots * \boldsymbol{p}_n = (\boldsymbol{p}_1 * \cdots * \boldsymbol{p}_{n-1}) * \boldsymbol{p}_n.$$

If the inequality $1/2 \le p_i \le 1$ holds for each $i \le n$, then the inequality

$$(35)\qquad 1/2 \le (\boldsymbol{p}_1 * \cdots * \boldsymbol{p}_n)_1 \le \min\{p_i : 1 \le i \le n\}$$

holds as well. The proof is almost obvious. Indeed,

$$(36)\qquad 1/2 \le (\boldsymbol{p}_1 * \boldsymbol{p}_2)_1 = p_1\,p_2 + (1-p_1)\,(1-p_2) \le \min\{p_1, p_2\}$$

is valid due to Lemma 5.1 so that

$$(37)\qquad 1/2 \le (\boldsymbol{p}_1 * \cdots * \boldsymbol{p}_n)_1 = \min\left\{\min\{p_i : 1 \le i \le n-1\},\ p_n\right\} = \\ = \min\{p_1 : 1 \le i \le n\}$$

immediately follows.

In order to investigate the role of the communication channel in more detail let us denote by $\hat{\boldsymbol{p}}$ the quadruple (probability distribution) $\langle p_1, p_2, p_3, p_4\rangle$ defined in Theorem 2.1 and by $m^{\hat{\boldsymbol{p}}}$ the modification of the b.p.a. m on $\mathcal{P}(S)$ generated when observing the values of the compatibility relation in question through the communication channel $\langle Y(i,\cdot)\rangle_{i=0}^{1}$, so that $m^{\hat{\boldsymbol{p}}}$ replaces the symbol m^* used above. Consequently, if $p_3 = p_4 = 0$, then $p_2 = 1 - p_1$ and in this case $\hat{\boldsymbol{p}}$ can be identified with the pair $\langle p_1,\ 1-p_1\rangle$, hence, with $\boldsymbol{p}_1$ according to the notation introduced above. The quadruple $\langle p_1,\ 1-p_2,\ 0,\ 0\rangle$ is called *symmetric* as it corresponds to the binary symmetric communication channel in the sense that for the conditional probabilities $p(i/j)$, defined by

$$(38)\ p(i/j) = P\left(\{\omega \in \Omega : Y(\rho(s, X(\omega)), \omega) = i\} / \{\omega \in \Omega : \rho(s, X(\omega)) = j\}\right)$$

for each $i,\ j = 0, 1$, the equalities

$$(39)\qquad p(0/1) = p(1/0) = p_2, \quad p(0/0) = p(1/1) = p_1,$$

hold supposing that the random variable X is stochastically independent with both $Y(0,\cdot)$ and $Y(1,\cdot)$. Indeed, an easy calculation yields that

$$(40)\ p(i/j) = \frac{P(\{\omega \in \Omega : Y(\rho(s, X(\omega)), \omega) = i, \rho(s, X(\omega)) = j\})}{P(\{\omega \in \Omega : \rho(s, X(\omega)) = j\})} =$$

$$= \frac{P(\{\omega \in \Omega : Y(j,\omega) = i,\ \rho(s, X(\omega)) = j\})}{P(\{\omega \in \Omega : \rho(s, X(\omega)) = j\})} =$$
$$= \frac{P(\{\omega \in \Omega : Y(j,\omega) = i\})\, P(\{\omega \in \Omega : \rho(s, X(\omega)) = j\})}{P(\{\omega \in \Omega : \rho(s, X(\omega)) = j\})} =$$
$$= P\left(\{\omega \in \Omega : Y(j,\omega) = i\}\right).$$

Hence, in particular,

$$\begin{aligned}(41)\, p(0/0) &= P\left(\{\omega \in \Omega : Y(0,\omega) = 0\}\right) = \\ &= P\left(\{\omega \in \Omega : Y(0,\omega) = 0,\ Y(1,\omega) = 0\}\right) + \\ &\quad + P\left(\{\omega \in \Omega : Y(0,\omega) = 0,\ Y(1,\omega) = 1\}\right) \ = \ p_3 + p_1 \ = \ p_1,\end{aligned}$$

$$\begin{aligned}p(1/1) &= P\left(\{\omega \in \Omega : Y(1,\omega) = 1\}\right) = \\ &= P\left(\{\omega \in \Omega : Y(0,\omega) = 0,\ Y(1,\omega) = 1\}\right) + \\ &\quad + P\left(\{\omega \in \Omega : Y(0,\omega) = 1,\ Y(1,\omega) = 1\}\right) \ = \ p_1 + p_4 \ = \ p_1,\end{aligned}$$

$$\begin{aligned}p(0/1) &= P\left(\{\omega \in \Omega : Y(0,\omega) = 0\}\right) = \\ &= P\left(\{\omega \in \Omega : Y(0,\omega) = 0,\ Y(1,\omega) = 0\}\right) + \\ &\quad + P\left(\{\omega \in \Omega : Y(0,\omega) = 1,\ Y(1,\omega) = 0\}\right) \ = \ p_3 + p_2 \ = \ p_2,\end{aligned}$$

$$\begin{aligned}p(1/0) &= P\left(\{\omega \in \Omega : Y(0,\omega) = 1\}\right) = \\ &= P\left(\{\omega \in \Omega : Y(0,\omega) = 1,\ Y(1,\omega) = 0\}\right) + \\ &\quad + P\left(\{\omega \in \Omega : Y(0,\omega) = 1,\ Y(1,\omega) = 1\}\right) \ = \ p_2 + p_4 \ = \ p_2,\end{aligned}$$

so that (39) is proved. □

Informally expressed, a binary symmetric channel is defined by the single random event "change the processed value" and its complement "do not change the value", their corresponding probabilities being p_2 and $p_1 = 1 - p_2$ under the notation above. This random event is stochastically independent of the value sent by the channel in case when this value is of random nature.

The following statement describes the situation when a given compatibility relation is modified by sequential processing by two binary symmetric channels.

Theorem 3.1. Let m be a basic probability assignment on the power-set $\mathcal{P}(S)$ of a finite set S, let $\langle p, 1-p, 0, 0\rangle$ and $\langle q, 1-q, 0, 0\rangle$ be symmetric quadruples defining two binary symmetric channels. Then

$$(42) \qquad (m^{\mathbf{p}})^{\mathbf{q}} = m^{\mathbf{p}*\mathbf{q}}. \qquad □$$

Proof. By (8),

(43) $$m^{\mathbf{p}}(A) = p\,m(A) + (1-p)\,m(S-A)$$

for all $A \subset S$. Consequently,

(44) $$(m^{\mathbf{p}})^{\mathbf{q}}(A) = q\,m^{\mathbf{p}}(A) + (1-q)\,m^{\mathbf{p}}(S-A) =$$
$$= q[p\,m(A) + (1-p)\,m(S-A)] + (1-q)\,[p\,m(S-A) + (1-p)\,m(A)] =$$
$$= [pq + (1-p)\,(1-q)]\,m(A) + [p(1-q) + q(1-p)]\,m(S-A) =$$
$$= (\mathbf{p} * \mathbf{q})_1\,m(A) + (\mathbf{p} * \mathbf{q})_2\,m(S-A) \;=\; m^{\mathbf{p}*\mathbf{q}}(A).$$ □

The relation (42) can be immediately generalized to

(45) $$(\ldots(m^{\mathbf{p}_1})^{\mathbf{p}_2}\ldots)^{\mathbf{p}_n} = m^{\mathbf{p}_1 * \mathbf{p}_2 * \cdots * \mathbf{p}_n}$$

for each n-tuple $p_1, p_2, \ldots, p_n$ of real numbers from $[0,1]$. Lemma 2.1 yields that a sequentially repeated processing of a compatibility relation by more binary symmetric communication channels deteriorates the quality of the resulting randomized compatibility relation in the sense that the probability with which the actual original value $\rho(s,x)$ differs from the observed one increases.

4 Dempster Combination Rule for Randomized Belief Functions

Let us consider the case when two basic probability assignments m_1, m_2 on the power-set $\mathcal{P}(S)$ of a finite nonempty set S are randomized by (different, in general) binary symmetric channels and then combined together by the Dempster combination rule. So, let $\mathbf{p}$, $\mathbf{q}$ be symmetric quadruples generated by real numbers p, $q \in [0,1]$. Let A be a subset of S. An easy calculation yields that

(46) $$(m_1^{\mathbf{p}} \oplus m_2^{\mathbf{q}})\,(A) = \sum_{B,C\subset S,\, B\cap C=A} m_1^{\mathbf{p}}(B)\,m_2^{\mathbf{q}}(C) =$$
$$= \sum_{B\cap C=A} [p\,m_1(B) + (1-p)\,m_1(S-B)] \cdot$$
$$[q\,m_2(C) + (1-q)\,m_2(S-C)] =$$
$$= \sum_{B\cap C=A} pq\,m_1(B)\,m_2(C) +$$
$$\sum_{B\cap C=A} p(1-q)\,m_1(B)\,m_2(S-C) +$$
$$\sum_{B\cap C=A} (1-p)\,q\,m_1(S-B)\,m_2(C) +$$
$$\sum_{B\cap C=A} (1-p)\,(1-q)\,m_1(S-B)\,m_2(S-C).$$

Investigating separately the four expressions added together at the right-hand side of (46), we obtain immediately for the first item, that

(47) $$\sum\nolimits_{B \cap C = A} p\, q\, m_1(B)\, m_2(C) = p\, q (m_1 \oplus m_2)\, (A).$$

The fourth expression will be processed dually. Let $\otimes$ be the operation defined dually to the Dempster combination rule so that, for finite basic space S and each $A \subset S$,

(48) $$(m_1 \otimes m_2)\, (A) = \sum\nolimits_{B, C \subset S,\, B \cup C = A} m_1(B)\, m_2(C).$$

This operation can be obtained in the same way as the Dempster operation $\oplus$, just supposing that the compatibility relations $\rho_1 : S \times E \rightarrow \{0,1\}$ and $\rho_2 : S \times E \rightarrow \{0,1\}$ are combined by the maximum operation, hence,

(49) $$\hat{\rho}_{12}(s,x) = \max \{\rho_1(s,x)\, \rho_2(s,x)\}$$

for each $s \in S$ and $x \in E$. Intuitively, $\otimes$ corresponds to the case when not the "pieces of surely valid knowledge", but rather "pieces of doubts" are shared by two or more subjects whose b.p.a.'s and/or belief functions are combined together.

If A, B, $C \subset S$ are such that $B \cap C = A$, then

(50) $$(S - B) \cup (S - C) = S - (B \cap C) = S - A,$$

conversely, if $S - (B \cap C) = S - A$, then $B \cap C = A$. Hence,

(51) $$\sum\nolimits_{B \cap C = A} (1-p)\, (1-q)\, m_1(S-B)\, m_2(S-C) =$$
$$= (1-p)\, (1-q) \sum\nolimits_{S-B,\, S-C,\, B \cap C = A} m_1(S-B)\, m_2(S-C) =$$
$$= (1-p)\, (1-q) \sum\nolimits_{S-B,\, S-C,\, (S-B) \cup (S-C) = S-A} m_1(S-B)\, m_2(S-C) =$$
$$= (1-p)\, (1-q)\, (m_1 \otimes m_2)\, (S-A).$$

In order to at least approximate the second and the third expression in (46) let us introduce the notion of conditioned belief function. Let m be a b.p.a. on $\mathcal{P}(S)$, let $B \subset S$, let m_B be the degenerated b.p.a. on $\mathcal{P}(S)$ uniquely defined by $m_B(B) = 1$, so that $m_B(C) = 0$ for all $C \subset S$, $C \neq B$. Let $m(\cdot/B)$ be the b.p.a. on $\mathcal{P}(S)$ defined by the Dempster product $m \oplus m_B$. Consequently, for each $A \subset S$,

(52) $$m(A/B) = (m \oplus m_B)\, (A) = \sum\nolimits_{C, D \subset S,\, C \cap D = A} m(C)\, m_B(D) =$$
$$= \sum\nolimits_{C,\, C \cap B = A} m(C) = \sum\nolimits_{X \subset S - B} m(A \cup X),$$

so that $m(A/B) = 0$ for each $A \subset S$, $A \not\subset B$, by convention, as in this case there is no C such that $C \cap B = A$. So, we obtain that

$$(53)\qquad \sum_{B\cap C=A} p(1-q)\, m_1(B)\, m_2(S-C) = \\ = \sum_{B\subset S} p(1-q)\, m_1(B) \sum_{C\subset S,\, B\cap C=A} m_B(B)\, m_2(S-C).$$

The relation (52) yields that

$$(54)\qquad m_2((B-A)/B) = \sum_{D,\, D\cap B=B-A} m_2(D).$$

Moreover, if $B \cap C = A$, then $B \cap (S-C) = B - (B\cap C) = B - A$ (but not, in general, *vice versa*), so that the inclusion

$$(55)\qquad \{\langle S-C, B\rangle \in \mathcal{P}(S)\times\mathcal{P}(S) : B\cap C = A\} \subset \\ \{\langle S-C, B\rangle \in \mathcal{P}(S)\times\mathcal{P}(S) : B\cap (S-C) = B-A\}$$

is valid. So, (53) implies that

$$(56)\quad \sum_{B\cap C=A} p(1-q)\, m_1(B)\, m_2(S-C) \le \\ \le \sum_{B\subset S} p(1-q)\, m_1(B) \sum_{S-C,\, B\cap(S-C)=B-A} m_B(B)\, m_2(S-C) = \\ = \sum_{B\subset S} p(1-q)\, m_1(B) \sum_{D,\, D\cap B=B-A} m_B(B)\, m_2(D) = \\ = \sum_{B\subset S} p(1-q)\, m_1(B)\, m_2((B-A)/B).$$

The last expression can be rewritten using the operator E_{m_1} of expected value of a random variable defined on the power-set $\mathcal{P}(S)$ with respect to the probability distribution m_1 on $\mathcal{P}(S)$. In symbols: if $\alpha : \mathcal{P}(S) \to (-\infty, \infty)$ is a mapping, then

$$(57)\qquad E_{m_1}\alpha(\cdot) = \sum_{B\subset S} m_1(B)\, \alpha(B)$$

(let us recall that S is finite so that $E_{m_1}\alpha(\cdot)$ is always defined). Under this notation we arrive at the inequality

$$(58)\ \sum_{B\cap C=A} p(1-q)\, m_1(B)\, m_2(S-C) \le p(1-q)\, E_{m_1} m_2((\cdot - A)/\cdot).$$

For the third expression on the right-hand side of (46) we proceed in the same way as above just with the roles of m_1 and m_2 interchanged, so arriving at the inequality

$$(59)\ \sum_{B\cap C=A} (1-p)\, q\, m_1(S-B)\, m_2(C) \le (1-p)\, q\, E_{m_2} m_1((\cdot - A)/\cdot).$$

Combining (47), (51), (58) and (59) together, we arrive immediately at the following assertion.

Theorem 4.1. Let m_1, m_2 be b.p.a.s over the power-set $\mathcal{P}(S)$ of a finite nonempty set S, let $\boldsymbol{p}$, $\boldsymbol{q}$ be symmetric quadruples defined by real numbers p, q from the unit interval. Then, for each $A \subset S$, the inequality

$$
\begin{aligned}
(60)\qquad (m_1^{\boldsymbol{p}} \oplus m_2^{\boldsymbol{q}})\,(A) \leq{} & p\,q(m_1 \oplus m_2)\,(A) + \\
&+ p(1-q)\,E_{m_1}[m_2((\cdot - A)/\cdot)] + \\
&+ (1-p)\,q\,E_{m_2}[m_1((\cdot - A)/\cdot)] + \\
&+ (1-p)\,(1-q)\,(m_1 \otimes m_2)\,(S-A)
\end{aligned}
$$

holds. □

For some simple cases of basic probability assignments more exact values than those offered by (60) can be obtained. So, let A, B be subsets of S and let $\boldsymbol{p}$, $\boldsymbol{q}$ be as in Theorem 4.1. An easy calculation then yields that for the degenerated b.p.a.s m_A and m_B (defined by the equalities $m_A(A) = 1$ and $m_B(B) = 1$) the following relations are valid:

$$
\begin{aligned}
(61)\qquad & (m_A^{\boldsymbol{p}} \oplus m_B^{\boldsymbol{q}})\,(A \cap B) = p\,q, \\
& (m_A^{\boldsymbol{p}} \oplus m_B^{\boldsymbol{q}})\,(A - B) = p(1-q), \\
& (m_A^{\boldsymbol{p}} \oplus m_B^{\boldsymbol{q}})\,(B - A) = (1-p)\,q, \\
& (m_A^{\boldsymbol{p}} \oplus m_B^{\boldsymbol{q}})\,(S - (A \cup B)) = (1-p)\,(1-q), \\
& (m_A^{\boldsymbol{p}} \oplus m_B^{\boldsymbol{q}})\,(C) = 0
\end{aligned}
$$

for all other $C \subset S$. If some among the sets $A \cap B$, $A - B$, $B - A$ and $S - (A \cup B)$ are identical, the corresponding values of $m_A^{\boldsymbol{p}} \oplus m_B^{\boldsymbol{q}}$ are added together. E.g., if $A \cap B = \emptyset$ and $A \cup B = S$, so that $A \cap B = S - (A \cup B) = \emptyset$, $A - B = A$ and $B - A = B$, (61) converts into

$$
\begin{aligned}
(62)\qquad & (m_A^{\boldsymbol{p}} \oplus m_B^{\boldsymbol{q}})\,(\emptyset) = p\,q + (1-p)\,(1-q), \\
& (m_A^{\boldsymbol{p}} \oplus m_B^{\boldsymbol{q}})\,(A) = p(1-q), \\
& (m_A^{\boldsymbol{p}} \oplus m_B^{\boldsymbol{q}})\,(B) = (1-p)\,q, \\
& (m_A^{\boldsymbol{p}} \oplus m_B^{\boldsymbol{q}})\,(C) = 0
\end{aligned}
$$

for all other $C \subset S$, so that the absolute inconsistency of the b.p.a. $m_A \oplus m_B \equiv m_\emptyset$ is weakened.

5 An Example–Elementary Basic Probability Assignments

The equalities from (61) can be generalized to the case of elementary basic probability assignments with two focal elements one of them being whole the space S. In symbols, given $A \subset S$ and a real number $\varepsilon \in [0, 1]$, the b.p.a. $m_{A,\varepsilon}$ is defined by $m_{A,\varepsilon}(A) = 1 - \varepsilon$, $m_{A,\varepsilon}(S) = \varepsilon$, so that $m_{A,\varepsilon}(C) = 0$ for each $C \subset S$, $A \neq C$, $C \neq S$. Obviously, for $\varepsilon = 0$, $m_{A,\varepsilon}$ reduces to m_A and $m_{S,\varepsilon} \equiv m_S$ for all $\varepsilon \in [0,1]$. Consider two such b.p.a.s. $m_{A,\varepsilon}$ and $m_{B,\eta}$, A, $B \subset S$, ε, $\eta \in [0,1]$,. Let $\boldsymbol{p}$, $\boldsymbol{q}$ be as in Theorem 4.1. A calculation more difficult than that one leading to (61), but still not too hard to be executed, yields that

$$\begin{aligned}
(63)\qquad & \left(m^{\boldsymbol{p}}_{A,\varepsilon} \oplus m^{\boldsymbol{q}}_{B,\eta}\right)(A \cap B) = pq(1-\varepsilon)\,(1-\eta),\\
& \left(m^{\boldsymbol{p}}_{A,\varepsilon} \oplus m^{\boldsymbol{q}}_{B,\eta}\right)(B - A) = (1-p)\,q(1-\varepsilon)\,(1-\eta),\\
& \left(m^{\boldsymbol{p}}_{A,\varepsilon} \oplus m^{\boldsymbol{q}}_{B,\eta}\right)(A - B) = p(1-q)\,(1-\varepsilon)\,(1-\eta),\\
& \left(m^{\boldsymbol{p}}_{A,\varepsilon} \oplus m^{\boldsymbol{q}}_{B,\eta}\right)(S - (A \cup B)) = (1-p)\,(1-q)\,(1-\varepsilon)\,(1-\eta),\\
& \left(m^{\boldsymbol{p}}_{A,\varepsilon} \oplus m^{\boldsymbol{q}}_{B,\eta}\right)(A) = p\,q(1-\varepsilon)\,\eta,\\
& \left(m^{\boldsymbol{p}}_{A,\varepsilon} \oplus m^{\boldsymbol{q}}_{B,\eta}\right)(S - A) = (1-q)\,q(1-\varepsilon)\,\eta,\\
& \left(m^{\boldsymbol{p}}_{A,\varepsilon} \oplus m^{\boldsymbol{q}}_{B,\eta}\right)(B) = p\,q\,\varepsilon(1-\eta),\\
& \left(m^{\boldsymbol{p}}_{A,\varepsilon} \oplus m^{\boldsymbol{q}}_{B,\eta}\right)(S - B) = p(1-q)\,\varepsilon(1-\eta),\\
& \left(m^{\boldsymbol{p}}_{A,\varepsilon} \oplus m^{\boldsymbol{q}}_{B,\eta}\right)(S) = p\,q\,\varepsilon\,\eta,\\
& \left(m^{\boldsymbol{p}}_{A,\varepsilon} \oplus m^{\boldsymbol{q}}_{B,\eta}\right)(\emptyset) = (1-p)\,\varepsilon + (1-q)\,\eta - (1-p)\,(1-q)\,\varepsilon\,\eta,\\
& \left(m^{\boldsymbol{p}}_{A,\varepsilon} \oplus m^{\boldsymbol{q}}_{B,\eta}\right)(C) = 0
\end{aligned}$$

for all $C \subset S$ different from all the subsets of S for which the values ascribed to them by the b.p.a. $m^{\boldsymbol{p}}_{A,\varepsilon} \oplus m^{\boldsymbol{q}}_{B,\eta}$ are explicitly listed above. Equalities from (63) are valid only if all the sets $A \cap B$, $B - A$, $A - B$, $S - (A \cup B)$, A, $S - A$, B, $S - B$, S and $\emptyset$ are pairwise different, if some of them are identical, the values ascribed to them by (63) are added together. If $\varepsilon = \eta = 0$, (63) obviously reduces to (61).

This chapter will be closed by a brief note showing that the operation of randomization (leading from a b.p.a. m to the b.p.a. $m^{\boldsymbol{p}}$) *is not commutative* neither with the operation $\oplus$ of Dempster product nor with the conditioning operation leading from m to $m(\cdot/B)$. In symbols, the inequalities

$$(64)\qquad (m_1 \oplus m_2)^{\boldsymbol{p}} \not\equiv m_1^{\boldsymbol{p}} \oplus m_2^{\boldsymbol{p}}$$

and

$$(65)\qquad (m(\cdot/B))^{\boldsymbol{p}} \not\equiv (m^{\boldsymbol{p}})\,(\cdot/B)$$

are valid in general, as the following simple counter-examples show. Let A, B be two different nonempty and proper subsets of the space S such that $A \cap B \neq \emptyset$. Then $m_A \oplus m_B \equiv m_{A\cap B}$, so that, given $0 < p < 1$,

$$(66)\qquad (m_A \oplus m_B)^{\boldsymbol{p}}\,(A \cap B) = p,$$

$$(m_A \oplus m_B)^{\mathbf{p}}\,(S - (A \cap B)) = 1 - p.$$

However, applying (61) to the case when $p = q$ we obtain that

(67) $$m_A^{\mathbf{p}} \oplus m_B^{\mathbf{q}}\,(A \cap B) = p^2 < p,$$

so that $m_A^{\mathbf{p}} \oplus m_B^{\mathbf{p}} \not\equiv (m_A \oplus m_B)^{\mathbf{p}}$. In the same case,

(68) $$m_A(\cdot/B) \equiv m_A \oplus m_B \equiv m_{A\cap B},$$

hence, $(m_A(\cdot/B))^{\mathbf{p}} \equiv (m_{A\cap B})^{\mathbf{p}}$, consequently,

(69) $$\begin{aligned}(m_A(\cdot/B))^{\mathbf{p}}\,(A \cap B) &= p,\\ (m_A(\cdot/B))^{\mathbf{p}}\,(S - (A \cap B)) &= 1 - p.\end{aligned}$$

At the same time, $(m_A^{\mathbf{p}})\,(\cdot/B) \equiv m_A^{\mathbf{p}} \oplus m_B$, so that

(70) $$\begin{aligned}&(m_A^{\mathbf{p}})\,((A \cap B)/B) = p\\ &(m_A^{\mathbf{p}})\,((S - A) \cap B/B) = (m_A^{\mathbf{p}})\,((B - A)/B) = 1 - p.\end{aligned}$$

Choosing S, A and B in such a way that $B - A \neq S - (A \cap B)$ we arrive at the conclusion that $(m_A^{\mathbf{p}})\,(\cdot/B) \not\equiv (m_A(\cdot/B))^{\mathbf{p}}$.

The paper is almost self-explanatory so that we limit ourselves to refer to [1] and [6] as well-known and already almost classical textbooks dealing with the elements of the Dempster–Shafer theory and the theory of belief functions. The basic notions from the fields of measure theory and probability theory presented at the abstract level suitable for our purposes can be found in [2,3] and [4]. Every of these sources may be replaced by a number of more modern ones.

References

1. D. Dubois, H. Prade: Théorie des Possibilités – Applications à la Représentation de Connaissances en Informatique. Mason, Paris, 1985.
2. S. Guiasu: Information Theory with Applications. McGraw–Hill, New York, 1977.
3. P. R. Halmos: Measure Theory. D. van Nostrand, New York – Toronto – London, 1950.
4. M. Loève: Probability Theory. D. van Nonstrand, New York – Toronto – London, 1960.
5. V. Novák: Fuzzy Sets and their Applications. Adam Hilger, Boston and Philadelphia, 1989.
6. G. Shafer: A Mathematical Theory of Evidence. Princeton Univ. Press, Princeton, 1976.

Quantifying the Correlation between Two Internal-Valued Random Sets

Manuel Montenegro, María Ángeles Gil, María Teresa López and María Asunción Lubiano

Departamento de Estadística e I.O. y D.M., Universidad de Oviedo, 33071 Oviedo, Spain

Abstract. The aim of this paper is to develop a study on the correlation of two interval-valued random sets when we consider either a linear relation or an affine function between them.

1 Introduction

When we have two interval-valued random sets, we can consider the least squares fitting problems associated with a "linear relation" between them (in which both, the slope and the intercept are real numbers), and with an "affine function" (in which the slope is real-valued but the intercept is assumed to be interval-valued).

Diamond (1990) has studied both problems and he has discussed the solutions in some special situations. Recently, Gil *et al.* (2001ab) have developed a general discussion and (unique and nonunique) solutions have been supplied. In addition, cases leading to nonunique solutions have been characterized.

In this paper, we combine the conclusions in Gil *et al.* (2001a) and Gil *et al.* (2001b) to get a comparative study on the linear/affine correlation between two interval-valued random sets. Some remarkable facts from the developed comparison as well as some future directions are finally are pointed out.

2 Preliminaries

Let $\mathcal{K}_c(\mathbb{R})$ be the class of nonempty compact intervals, and let $\mathcal{K}_c^*(\mathbb{R})$ be the subclass of $\mathcal{K}_c(\mathbb{R})$ from which we remove singletons (i.e., $\mathcal{K}_c^*(\mathbb{R}) = \mathcal{K}_c(\mathbb{R}) \setminus \Big\{\{x\} \,\big|\, x \in \mathbb{R}\Big\}$).

$\mathcal{K}_c(\mathbb{R})$ can be endowed with a semilinear structure induced by the product by a scalar and the Minkowski addition. On the other hand, on $\mathcal{K}_c(\mathbb{R})$ one can consider the well-known Hausdorff metric

$$d_H(A,B) = \max\left\{ \sup_{a\in A} \inf_{b\in B} |a-b|, \sup_{b\in B} \inf_{a\in A} |a-b| \right\}$$

for any $A, B \in \mathcal{K}_c(\mathbb{R})$. In the case of compact intervals, this metric can be expressed equivalently in the following simple way:

$$d_H(A,B) = \max\{|\sup A - \sup B|, |\inf A - \inf B|\}.$$

On $\mathcal{K}_c(\mathbb{R})$, we can also use another metric which is topologically equivalent to Hausdorff's one and is more appropriate for computational purposes. This metric has been recently introduced (although in a more general space) by Körner and Näther (2001). On the basis of Radström Theorem (see, for instance, Diamond and Kloeden, 1994), any convex set $A \in \mathcal{K}_c(\mathbb{R})$ can be embedded isometrically *via* its support function s_A into a cone of a Hilbert space of functions. As a consequence, an interval-valued random set can be viewed as a random function which takes on values in a Hilbert space, and any L_2-distance between the support functions of two elements $A, B \in \mathcal{K}_c(\mathbb{R})$ could be expressed as follows:

$$D_K(s_A, s_B) = \sqrt{\sum_{(u,v)\in S^0\times S^0} \big(s_A(u) - s_B(u)\big)\big(s_A(v) - s_B(v)\big)\, K(u,v)}$$

for some $K : S^0 \times S^0 \to \mathbb{R}$ (S^0 being the unit sphere in $\mathbb{R}$, i.e., $S^0 = \{-1, 1\}$) where K represents a symmetric and positive definite kernel, that is, $K(1,1) > 0$, $K(1,-1) = K(-1,1)$ and $K(1,1)K(-1,-1) > K(1,-1)$ $K(-1,1)$.

The square of the distance above could be expressed alternatively by

$$\begin{aligned}[D_K(s_A, s_B)]^2 &= (K(1,1) - K(1,-1))[\sup A - \sup B]^2\\ &+(K(-1,-1) - K(1,-1))[\inf A - \inf B]^2\\ &+4\,K(1,-1)[\operatorname{mid} A - \operatorname{mid} B]^2\end{aligned}$$

with $\operatorname{mid} A = [\sup A + \inf A]/2$ denoting the centre of interval A. If we slightly constrains the kernel K to assess the same "weight" to the squared Euclidean distance between the suprema and the squared Euclidean distance between the infima (i.e., $K(1,1) = K(-1,-1)$) and to assess a nonnegative "weight" to the squared Euclidean distance between the mid-points (i.e., $K(1,-1) \geq 0$), then $D_K(s_A, s_B)$ for $A, B \in \mathcal{K}_c(\mathbb{R})$ can be identified (without loss of generality for the targets in this paper) with a W-distance on $\mathcal{K}_c(\mathbb{R})$ which is defined so that

$$d_W(A,B) = \sqrt{\int_{[0,1]} [f_A(\lambda) - f_B(\lambda)]^2 \, dW(\lambda)}$$

with $f_A(\lambda) = \lambda \sup A + (1-\lambda) \inf A$ for all $\lambda \in [0,1]$, where W can be formalized by means of a probability measure on the measurable space $([0,1], \mathcal{B}_{[0,1]})$ ($\mathcal{B}_{[0,1]}$ being the Borel σ-field on $[0,1]$) associated with a nondegenerate symmetric probability distribution on $[0,1]$.

Remark 1. It should be remarked that the metric employed by Diamond corresponds to d_W for $W(0) = W(1) = .5$. It is obvious that, in the conditions assumed for K, the generalized distance d_W is equivalent to the generalized metric $d_{\boldsymbol{\lambda}}$ by Bertoluzza *et al.* (1995) (see also Lubiano and Gil, 1999), with $\boldsymbol{\lambda} = (W(0), W(.5), W(1))$, but frequently choosing W on $[0,1]$ is more intuitive and easier in practice than choosing $\boldsymbol{\lambda}$. On the other hand, although the measure W has no stochastic meaning, we can formally deal with it in a probabilistic context and hence we can work if required with the probability space $(\Omega \times [0,1], \mathcal{A} \otimes \mathcal{B}_{[0,1]}, P \otimes W)$. The mapping $f_{[0,1]} : \Omega \times [0,1] \to \mathbb{R}$ can be treated as a real-valued random variable which is constant w.r.t. P, and $\sigma^2_{f_{[0,1]}} = \text{Var}\left[f_{[0,1]} | P \otimes W\right] = \int_{[0,1]} \lambda^2 dW(\lambda) - .25 > 0$. We can easily prove for the arbitrary $A, B \in \mathcal{K}_c(\mathbb{R})$ that, due to the symmetry assumed for W, $[d_W(A,B)^2 = [\text{mid}\, A - \text{mid}\, B]^2 + 4\,\sigma^2_{f_{[0,1]}}\, [\text{spr}\, A - \text{spr}\, B]^2$ (with the spread being given by $\text{spr}\, A = [\sup A - \inf A]/2$), whence the greater $\sigma^2_{f_{[0,1]}}$ the greater the influence of the Euclidean distance between the spreads of A and B on $d_W(A,B)$, this influence being the greatest possible one for the metric used by Diamond.

As we have just indicated, from now on we will consider the generalized metric d_W, since choosing W and the interpretation of d_W are usually more intuitive than assigning weigths to the extreme and mid-points of interval-valued data (or, alternatively, assigning the value of $\sigma^2_{f_{[0,1]}}$).

Given a probability space $(\Omega, \mathcal{A}, P)$, a mapping $X : \Omega \to \mathcal{K}_c(\mathbb{R})$ is said to be an *interval-valued random set* (more properly, a compact interval-valued random set) associated with $(\Omega, \mathcal{A}, P)$, if, and only if, X is $(\mathcal{A}, \mathcal{B}_{d_H})$-measurable ($\mathcal{B}_{d_H}$ being the Borel σ-field induced by d_H on $\mathcal{K}_c(\mathbb{R})$ (which coincides with that induced by d_W on this class).

The *expected value of an interval-valued random set* X will be intended in Aumann's sense, that is, it will be defined as the Aumann integral (1965) of X (if it exists), which is given by the set

$$E^A[X|P] = \{E(f|P) \,|\, f : \Omega \to \mathbb{R},\ f \in \mathcal{L}^1(\Omega, \mathcal{A}, P),\ f \in X \ a.s.\,[P]\}.$$

In this case of X being $\mathcal{K}_c(\mathbb{R})$-valued, then

$$E^A[X|P] = [E(\inf X|P), (\sup X|P)].$$

If an interval-valued random set $X : \Omega \to \mathcal{K}_c(\mathbb{R})$ is *integrably bounded* (that is, $|X| \in \mathcal{L}^1(\Omega, \mathcal{A}, P)$, where $|X|(\omega) = \sup\{|x| \,|\, x \in X(\omega)\} = \max\{$ for all $\omega \in \Omega$), then $E^A[X|P]$ exists and it is well-defined.

3 Least squares fitting problems

The two problems we are considering in this paper can be formalized as follows:

Let $(\Omega, \mathcal{A}, P)$ be a probability space, and let X and Y be the *predictor* (independent) and the *response* (dependent) nondegenerate interval-valued random sets.

The *First Least Squares Fitting Problem* (FLSFP) is to find $a, b \in \mathbb{R}$ minimizing the average squared "d_W-error" associated with the "linear relation" $Y = aX + b$, that is, minimizing the function $\phi : \mathbb{R}^2 \to \mathbb{R}$ given by

$$\phi(a,b) = E\big([d_W(Y, aX + b)]^2 \mid P \big).$$

The *Second Least Squares Fitting Problem* (SLSFP) is to find $a \in \mathbb{R}$, $B \in \mathcal{K}_c(\mathbb{R})$ minimizing the average squared "d_W-error" associated with the "affine function" $Y = aX + B$, that is, minimizing the function $\phi : \mathbb{R} \times \mathcal{K}_c(\mathbb{R}) \to \mathbb{R}$ given by

$$\psi(a,B) = E\big([d_W(Y, aX + B)]^2 \mid P \big).$$

Figures 1 and 2 show the expected datum $Y(\omega)$ by a "linear relation" $Y = aX + b$ and by an "affine function" $Y = aX + B$, respectively.

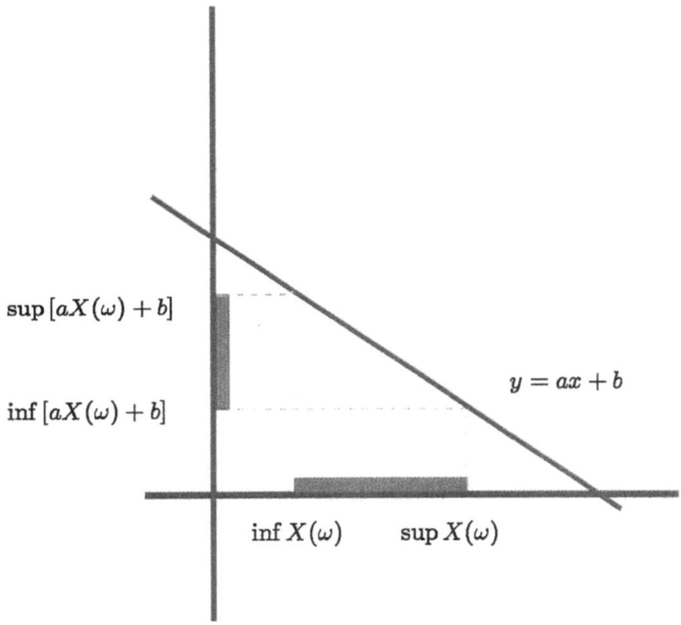

Fig. 1. Graphical representation of $Y(\omega) = aX(\omega) + b$

The case in Figure 1 corresponds to a real-valued intercept, whereas that in Figure 2 corresponds to an interval-valued intercept. In both cases, the least squares fitting problem will deal with the minimization of the average squared W-distance between the expected and the observed interval value of Y.

The analysis of the FLSFP leads to the following conclusion (see Gil *et al.*, 2001a):

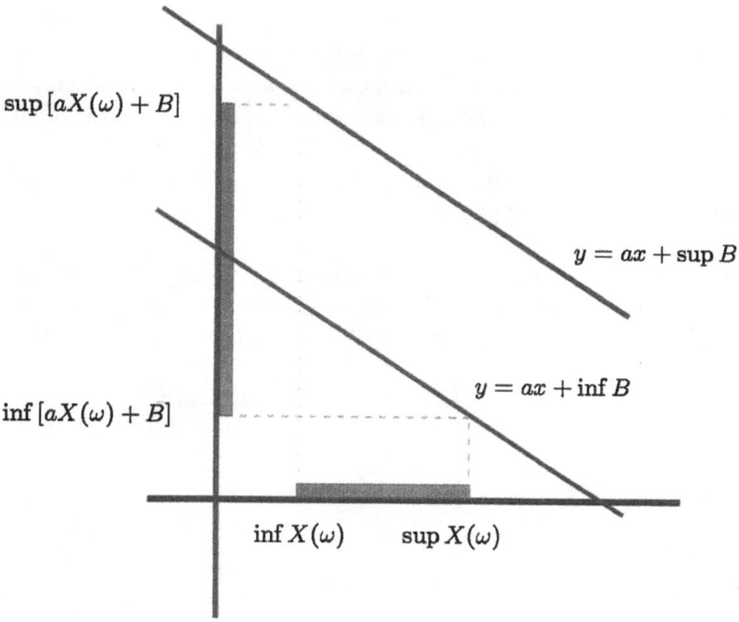

Fig. 2. Graphical representation of $Y(\omega) = aX(\omega) + B$

Theorem 1. *If X and Y are $\mathcal{K}_c^*(\mathbb{R})$-valued almost surely $[P]$ and $E(|X| \mid P) < \infty$ and $E(|Y| \mid P) < \infty$, then the solution of the problem is unique, and ϕ is minimized for $(a^*, b^*) \in (\mathbb{R} \setminus \{0\}) \times \mathbb{R}$ such that*

$$(a^*, b^*) = \begin{cases} (a_1, b_1) & \text{if } a_1^2 > a_2^2, \\ (a_2, b_2) & \text{otherwise,} \end{cases}$$

where a_1, a_2, b_1, b_2 are given in terms of expectations, variances and covariances of the real-valued random variables f_X and f_Y (defined on $(\Omega \times [0,1], \mathcal{A} \otimes \mathcal{B}_{[0,1]}, P \otimes S)$) as follows:

$$a_1 = \frac{\mathrm{Cov}\big(f_X(\cdot), f_Y(\cdot)\big|P \otimes S\big)}{\mathrm{Var}\big(f_X(\cdot)\big|P \otimes S\big)},$$

$$b_1 = E\big(f_Y(\cdot)\big|P \otimes S\big) - a_1 E\big(f_X(\cdot)\big|P \otimes S\big),$$

whenever $a_1 > 0$, and

$$a_2 = \frac{\mathrm{Cov}\big(\overline{f}_X(\cdot), f_Y(\cdot)\big|P \otimes S\big)}{\mathrm{Var}\big(f_X(\cdot)\big|P \otimes S\big)},$$

$$b_2 = E\big(f_Y(\cdot)\big|P \otimes S\big) - a_2 E\big(f_X(\cdot)\big|P \otimes S\big),$$

whenever $a_2 < 0$, with $\overline{f}_A(\lambda) = f_A(1-\lambda)$ for all $\lambda \in [0,1]$ and $A \in \mathcal{K}_c(\mathbb{R})$.

If X and Y are $\mathcal{K}_c^*(\mathbb{R})$-valued almost surely $[P]$, then the slope a^* in the optimal solution of the FLSFP can never vanish. In fact, if X and Y are $\mathcal{K}_c(\mathbb{R})$-valued, then a necessary condition for $a^* = 0$ is that X and Y are not simultaneously $\mathcal{K}_c^*(\mathbb{R})$-valued almost surely $[P]$ (i.e., for almost all $\omega \in \Omega$, either X or Y is real-valued).

On the other hand, the analysis of the SLSFP leads to the following conclusion (see Gil *et al.*, 2001b):

Theorem 2. *If X and Y are $\mathcal{K}_c(\mathbb{R})$-valued and $E(|X| \mid P) < \infty$ and $E(|Y| \mid P) < \infty$, then the solution of the problem is sometimes unique and sometimes nonunique, and ψ is minimized for $(a^*, B^*) \in \mathbb{R} \times \mathcal{K}_c(\mathbb{R})$ such that*

$$(a^*, B^*) = \begin{cases} (a_1, [c_1, c_1 + b_1]) & \text{if SLSFP.1} \\ (a_2, [c_2, c_2 + b_2]) & \text{if SLSFP.2} \\ (a_1', \{c_1'\}) & \text{if SLSFP.3} \\ (a_2', \{c_2'\}) & \text{if SLSFP.4} \\ (0, E^A[X|P]) & \text{if SLSFP.5} \end{cases}$$

where

- SLSFP.1 *iff either* $a_1 > 0, a_2 \geq 0, b_1 > 0$, *or* $a_1^2 \geq a_2^2, a_1 > 0, a_2 < 0, b_1 > 0, b_2 > 0$, *or* $a_1^2\left[1 - \rho^2_{f_X f_{[0,1]}}\right] \geq {a_2'}^2 - \sigma^2_{f_Y}\rho^2_{f_Y f_{[0,1]}}/\sigma^2_{f_X}$, $a_1 > 0, a_2 < 0, b_1 > 0, b_2 \leq 0$,
- SLSFP.2 *iff either* $a_1 \leq 0, a_2 < 0, b_2 > 0$, *or* $a_1^2 \leq a_2^2, a_1 > 0, a_2 < 0, b_1 > 0, b_2 > 0$, *or* $a_2^2\left[1 - \rho^2_{f_X f_{[0,1]}}\right] \geq {a_1'}^2 - \sigma^2_{f_Y}\rho^2_{f_Y f_{[0,1]}}/\sigma^2_{f_X}$, $a_1 > 0, a_2 < 0, b_1 \leq 0, b_2 \leq 0$,
- SLSFP.3 *iff either* $a_1 > 0, a_2 \geq 0, b_1 \leq 0$, *or* ${a_1'}^2 \geq {a_2'}^2, a_1 > 0, a_2 < 0, b_1 \leq 0, b_2 > 0$, *or* $a_2^2\left[1 - \rho^2_{f_X f_{[0,1]}}\right] \leq {a_1'}^2 - \sigma^2_{f_Y}\rho^2_{f_Y f_{[0,1]}}/\sigma^2_{f_X}$, $a_1 > 0, a_2 < 0, b_1 \leq 0, b_2 \leq 0$,
- SLSFP.4 *iff either* $a_1 \leq 0, a_2 < 0, b_2 \leq 0$, *or* ${a_1'}^2 \leq {a_2'}^2, a_1 > 0, a_2 < 0, b_1 \leq 0, b_2 > 0$, *or* $a_1^2\left[1 - \rho^2_{f_X f_{[0,1]}}\right] \leq {a_2'}^2 - \sigma^2_{f_Y}\rho^2_{f_Y f_{[0,1]}}/\sigma^2_{f_X}$, $a_1 > 0, a_2 < 0, b_1 > 0, b_2 \leq 0$,
- SLSFP.5 *iff* $a_1 \leq 0 \leq a_2$.

and with

$$a_1 = \sqrt{\frac{\sigma^2_{f_Y}}{\sigma^2_{f_X}}} \cdot \frac{\rho_{f_X f_Y} - \rho_{f_X f_{[0,1]}}\rho_{f_Y f_{[0,1]}}}{1 - \rho^2_{f_X f_{[0,1]}}},$$

$$a_2 = \sqrt{\frac{\sigma^2_{f_Y}}{\sigma^2_{f_X}}} \cdot \frac{\rho_{\tilde{f}_X f_Y} + \rho_{f_X f_{[0,1]}}\rho_{f_Y f_{[0,1]}}}{1 - \rho^2_{f_X f_{[0,1]}}},$$

$$b_1 = \sqrt{\frac{\sigma^2_{f_Y}}{\sigma^2_{f_{[0,1]}}}} \cdot \frac{\rho_{f_Y f_{[0,1]}} - \rho_{f_X f_{[0,1]}}\rho_{f_X f_Y}}{1-\rho^2_{f_X f_{[0,1]}}},$$

$$b_2 = \sqrt{\frac{\sigma^2_{f_Y}}{\sigma^2_{f_{[0,1]}}}} \cdot \frac{\rho_{f_Y f_{[0,1]}} + \rho_{f_X f_{[0,1]}}\rho_{\widetilde{f}_X f_Y}}{1-\rho^2_{f_X f_{[0,1]}}},$$

$$c_1 = \mu_{f_Y} - a_1\mu_{f_X} - .5\, b_1,\ c_2 = \mu_{f_Y} - a_2\mu_{f_X} - .5\, b_2,$$

$$a_1' = \sqrt{\frac{\sigma^2_{f_Y}}{\sigma^2_{f_X}}} \cdot \rho_{f_X f_Y},\ a_2' = \sqrt{\frac{\sigma^2_{f_Y}}{\sigma^2_{f_X}}} \cdot \rho_{\widetilde{f}_X f_Y},$$

$$c_1' = \mu_{f_Y} - a_1'\,\mu_{f_X},\ c_2' = \mu_{f_Y} - a_2'\,\mu_{f_X},$$

with

$$\mu_{f_{[0,1]}} = E\big[f_{[0,1]}|P \otimes W\big] = .5,$$

$$\mu_{f_X} = E\big[f_X|P \otimes W\big] = E\big[\widetilde{f}_X|P \otimes W\big] = \operatorname{mid} E^A[X|P] = \overline{\operatorname{mid} X},$$

$$\sigma^2_{f_X} = \operatorname{Var}\big[f_X|P \otimes W\big] = \operatorname{Var}\big[\widetilde{f}_X|P \otimes W\big]$$

$$= S^2_{\operatorname{mid} X} + 4\,\sigma^2_{f_{[0,1]}}\left[S^2_{\operatorname{spr} X} + \left(\overline{\operatorname{spr} X}\right)^2\right],$$

$$\rho_{f_X f_Y} = \frac{\sigma_{f_X f_Y}}{\sqrt{\sigma^2_{f_X}\sigma^2_{f_Y}}} = \frac{\operatorname{Cov}\big[f_X, f_Y|P \otimes W\big]}{\sqrt{\sigma^2_{f_X}\sigma^2_{f_Y}}}$$

$$= \frac{S_{\operatorname{mid} X \operatorname{mid} Y} + 4\,\sigma^2_{f_{[0,1]}}\left[S_{\operatorname{spr} X \operatorname{spr} Y} + \overline{\operatorname{spr} X} \cdot \overline{\operatorname{spr} Y}\right]}{\sqrt{\sigma^2_{f_X}\sigma^2_{f_Y}}},$$

$$\rho_{\widetilde{f}_X f_Y} = \frac{S_{\operatorname{mid} X \operatorname{mid} Y} - 4\,\sigma^2_{f_{[0,1]}}\left[S_{\operatorname{spr} X \operatorname{spr} Y} + \overline{\operatorname{spr} X} \cdot \overline{\operatorname{spr} Y}\right]}{\sqrt{\sigma^2_{f_X}\sigma^2_{f_Y}}},$$

$$\rho_{f_X f_{[0,1]}} = -\rho_{\widetilde{f}_X f_{[0,1]}} = 2\sqrt{\frac{\sigma^2_{f_{[0,1]}}}{\sigma^2_{f_X}}}\,\overline{\operatorname{spr} X}.$$

Remark 2. It should be emphasized that all values involved in the computations for the optimal solutions in both probems (but $\sigma^2_{f_{[0,1]}}$) are irrespective of the chosen measure W.

Obviously, in case $a_1 > 0 > a_2$, the solution is not necessarily unique, but for the cases of nonunique solution (in fact, for obtaining two possible solutions, one in the cone corresponding to $a > 0$ and the other one in the cone for $a < 0$) the following conditions are necessary and sufficient:

- if $a_1 > 0, b_1 > 0$ and $a_2 < 0, b_2 > 0$, then the optimal solution is nonunique if, and only if, $a_1 + a_2 = 0,\ b_1 = b_2,\ c_2 = c_1 + 2\,a_1\mu_{f_X}$;

- if $a_1 > 0, b_1 \leq 0$ and $a_2 < 0, b_2 \leq 0$, then the optimal solution is nonunique if, and only if, $a'_1 + a'_2 = 0,\ c'_2 = c'_1 + 2a'_1\mu_{fX}$ (in such a case we have that $b'_1 = b'_2 = 0$);
- if $a_1 > 0, b_1 > 0$ and $a_2 < 0, b_2 \leq 0$, then the optimal solution is nonunique if, and only if, ${a'_2}^2 - a_1^2\left[1 - \rho^2_{fX\,f[0,1]}\right] = \dfrac{\sigma^2_{fY}}{\sigma^2_{fX}}\,\rho^2_{fY\,f[0,1]}$;
- if $a_1 > 0, b_1 \leq 0$ and $a_2 < 0, b_2 > 0$, then the optimal solution is nonunique if, and only if, ${a'_1}^2 - a_2^2\left[1 - \rho^2_{fX\,f[0,1]}\right] = \dfrac{\sigma^2_{fY}}{\sigma^2_{fX}}\,\rho^2_{fY\,f[0,1]}$.

In accordance with the notations we are using, the cases Diamond (1990) has formally examined and for which the uniqueness of the optimal solution has been proven (which are referred to as situations involving *coherent* interval-valued data) correspond to $a_1 \geq a_2 \geq 0$ and $a_1 \leq a_2 \leq 0$.

In the SLSFP, $a^* = 0$ can only happen in cases in which the optimal solution is unique. More precisely, the "affine independence" corresponding to $a^* = 0$ happens if, and only if, $a_1 \leq 0$ and $a_2 \geq 0$. Stochastic independence is a sufficient condition for this affine independence, since when X and Y are *independent interval-valued random sets*, then $a^* = 0$.

4 Correlation analysis of interval-valued random sets

The optimal "slope" a^* equals 0 in a few situations, in which the "unexplained d_W-variation" would equal the highest possible one, σ^2_{fY} for the FLSFP and $\sigma^2_{fY}\left[1 - \rho^2_{fY\,f[0,1]}\right]$ for the SLSFP.

Following the ideas in the real-valued case, in Gil *et al.* (2001a) we have introduced the *extended determination coefficient* of X and Y for the "linear relation", which is defined by

$$r^2_{XY} = \max\left\{\rho^2_{fX\,fY}, \rho^2_{\overline{f}X\,fY}\right\}.$$

Since $0 \leq \phi(a^*, b^*) = \sigma^2_{fY}\left[1 - r^2_{XY}\right]$, then, r^2_{XY} is a symmetric well-defined coefficient varying from 0 to 1, and the smaller r^2_{XY} the greater the unexplained variation. In other words, r^2_{XY} is a measure of the portion of the total variation σ^2_{fY} of an interval-valued random set Y that is explained by the optimal "linear relation" with the interval-valued random set X.

Furthermore,

Proposition 1. *If X and Y are nondegenerate $\mathcal{K}_c(\mathbb{R})$-valued random sets and $E(|X|\,|P) < \infty$ and $E(|Y|\,|P) < \infty$, then*

i) if X and Y are $\mathcal{K}^*_c(\mathbb{R})$-valued almost surely $[P]$, then the extended determination coefficient r^2_{XY} cannot vanish;

ii) a necessary condition for the extended detemination coefficient r^2_{XY} *to vanish is that* X *and* Y *are not simultaneously* $\mathcal{K}^*_c(\mathbb{R})$*-valued almost surely* $[P]$;

iii) if X *and* Y *are independent, then a necessary and sufficient condition for the extended determination coefficient to vanish is that* X *and* Y *are real-valued almost surely* $[P]$.

On the other hand, by following again the ideas in the real-valued case, in Gil *et al.* (2001b) we have introduced the *extended determination coefficient* of X and Y for the "affine function", which is defined by

$$R^2_{XY} = \begin{cases} \dfrac{a_1^2\sigma^2_{f_X}\left[1-\rho^2_{f_X f_{[0,1]}}\right]}{\sigma^2_{f_Y}\left[1-\rho^2_{f_Y f_{[0,1]}}\right]} & \text{if SLSFP.1} \\ \dfrac{a_2^2\sigma^2_{f_X}\left[1-\rho^2_{f_X f_{[0,1]}}\right]}{\sigma^2_{f_Y}\left[1-\rho^2_{f_Y f_{[0,1]}}\right]} & \text{if SLSFP.2} \\ \dfrac{\rho^2_{f_X f_Y}-\rho^2_{f_Y f_{[0,1]}}}{1-\rho^2_{f_Y f_{[0,1]}}} & \text{if SLSFP.3} \\ \dfrac{\rho^2_{\tilde{f}_X f_Y}-\rho^2_{f_Y f_{[0,1]}}}{1-\rho^2_{f_Y f_{[0,1]}}} & \text{if SLSFP.4} \\ 0 & \text{if SLSFP.5.} \end{cases}$$

Since $0 \leq \phi(a^*, B^*) = \sigma^2_{f_Y}\left[1-\rho^2_{f_Y f_{[0,1]}}\right]\left[1-R^2_{XY}\right]$, then R^2_{XY} is a symmetric well-defined coefficient ranging from 0 to 1, and the smaller R^2_{XY} the greater the unexplained variation, so that R^2_{XY} is a measure of the portion of the total variation of Y that is explained by the optimal "affine function" of X.

Furthermore,

Proposition 2. *If* X *and* Y *are nondegenerate* $\mathcal{K}_c(\mathbb{R})$*-valued random sets and* $E(|X| \mid P) < \infty$ *and* $E(|Y| \mid P) < \infty$*, then*

i) $R^2_{XY} = 0$ *if, and only, if, the optimal affine function expressing* Y *as a function of* X *is given by* $Y = E^A[Y|P]$;

ii) if X *and* Y *are independent, then* $R^2_{XY} = 0$.

Remark 3. It should be pointed out that whereas the regression conclusions in the SLSFP generalize those in the FLSFP, the correlation study of the SLSFP is not a generalization of that in the FLSFP, since the supremum of the unexplained d_W-variation is lower for the SLSFP than for the FLSFP.

5 Concluding remarks

Since regression studies are mainly concerned with predicition, it would be very valuable for practical purposes to develop an inferential analysis.

In view of the scheme followed in the communication, a question which arises is why we have introduced extended measures (the W-metric and the objective function ϕ), instead of using a prior real-valued "code" to the interval-valued data, and later handling the coded data by means of the classical techniques. The reason for not having used a "codifier" converting each interval value into a real number, is that the most natural one (like that representing each interval value by its mid-point) would lead to identifying different interval values (those having the same centre but distinct spread). Consequently, the Euclidean distance between the converted values could be equal to 0, whereas the original interval values would have associated really a nonnull error the code would make us ignore.

The studies in this paper, and those suggested at the beginning of this section, could be complemented with a future analysis on the robustness of the conclusions with respect to the choice of the measure W.

Acknowledgements

The research in this paper has been partially supported by DGESIC Grants DGE-99-PB98-1534 and DGE-98-PB97-1282 of the Spanish MEC. Their financial support is gratefully acknowledged.

References

1. Aumann, R.J. (1965), Integrals of set-valued functions, *J. Math. Anal. Appl.*, **12** 1–12.
2. Bertoluzza, C., Corral, N. and Salas, A. (1995), On a new class of distances between fuzzy numbers, *Mathware & Soft Computing*, **2** 71–84.
3. Diamond, P. (1990), Least Squares Fitting of Compact Set-Valued Data, *J. Math. Anal. Appl.*, **147** 531–544.
4. Diamond, P. and Kloeden, P.E. (1994), *Metric Spaces of Fuzzy Sets.* World Sci., New Jersey.
5. Gil, M.A., López,M.T., Lubiano, M.A. and Montenegro, M. (2001a), Regression and correlation analyses of a linear relation between random intervals, *Test*, (accepted, in press).
6. Gil, M.A., Lubiano, M.A., Montenegro, M. and López,M.T. (2001b), Least squares fitting of an affine function and strength of association for interval-valued data, (submitted).
7. Körner, R. and Näther, W. (2001), On the variance of random fuzzy variables, in: C. Bertoluzza, M.A. Gil and D.A. Ralescu (Eds.), *Statistical Modeling, Analysis and Management of Fuzzy Data*, (Physica-Verlag, in press).
8. Lubiano, M.A. and Gil, M.A. (1999), Estimating the expected value of fuzzy random variables in random samplings from finite populations, *Statistical Papers*, **40** 277–295.

How Information Measure Changes Due to Unreliability

Viviana Doldi
Dpt. Matematica
University of Pavia
via Ferrata,1
27100 Pavia ITALY
doldi@dimat.unipv.it

Gloria Naval
Dept. Statistics and O.R.
University of Oviedo
Calle Calvo Sotelo s/n
33007 Oviedo SPAIN
gloria@pinon.ccu.uniovi.es

Carlo Bertoluzza
Dpt. Informatica e Sistemistica
University of Pavia
via Ferrata,1
27100 Pavia ITALY
carlo.bertoluzza@unipv.it

Abstract

It is a common experience that an answer reaches different meaning in account of the reliability of the person to who we had posed the question. That is, the less a person is reliable, the less we are inclined to believe his answer as honest. In order to study this situation, we assign to each person a "membership degree" of his answer (between 0 and 1), that may be view as the degree of belonging of that person to the fuzzy set of "sinceres". Obviously our judgement will introduce changes also in the amount of information we have obtained: the real information that we have after having known the answer, will pay a variation, due to the knowledge of the degrees of belief, with respect to ideal information. In this paper we have found the form that the information's changement assumes, under the hypothesis that the membership function assumes only a finite range of values ($\alpha_0 = 0, \alpha_1, \ldots, \alpha_n = 1$).

1 Definitions

1.1 Questions and Answers

Let Ω be the universe to which we can pose the question and let $\mathcal{F}$ be an algebra of parts of Ω, whose elements represent the population to which, time after time, the questions has to be posed. A question with h answers divides each element of $\mathcal{F}$ in h subsets. Everybody has to reply and nobody can give two or more answers. So we can give the following definitions.

Definition 1. ([1],[2]) A *question* over a structure $(\Omega, \mathcal{F})$, is a map $q_h : \mathcal{F} \to \mathcal{F}^h$ that associates to each element $A \in \mathcal{F}$, an ordered collection $q_h(A) = (A_1, \ldots, A_i, \ldots, A_h)$ of h elements of $\mathcal{F}$ such that:

1. $i \neq j \Rightarrow A_i \cap A_j = \emptyset$;
2. $\cup_{i=1}^{h} A_i = A$.

Definition 2. ([3]) The *answer* i given to the question $(\Omega, \mathcal{F}, q_h)$ is a structure $(\Omega, \mathcal{F}, r_i)$ where $r_i : \mathcal{F} \to \mathcal{F}$ is the map that assigns to each subset $A \in \mathcal{F}$ the subset $r_i(A) = A_i$ of the ordered collection $(A_1, \ldots, A_i, \ldots, A_h)$. A_i is the family of the elements of A, which gave i^{th} answer to the question q_h.

Definition 3. A question is *coherent*([3]) if for all $A, B \in \mathcal{F}$,

$$A \cap B_i \;=\; A_i \cap B \;=\; A_i \cap B_i.$$

Coherent means that the elements of Ω give the same answer whatever the environment of the question is.

Let $\mathcal{F}_r$ be the family of the elements which gave answer r to a suitable question q, and let A be an element of $\mathcal{F}_r$. It is possible that we have some doubts on the correctness or on sincerity of the answer of some elements of A. In this case we associate to this element a *degree of belief* $\widetilde{A}(\omega)$ in $[0, 1]$ which measures till to extent, in our opinion, ω is reliable. $\widetilde{A}(\omega) = 0$ means that ω is completely unreliable. So we constructed a fuzzy set $\widetilde{A}$, and our description of the answer will be the couple $R_A = (\widetilde{A}, A)$. We will denote by $\widetilde{\mathcal{F}}_r = \{(\widetilde{A}, A) | A \in r(\mathcal{F})\}$ the set of all the answers in this last sense.

Definition 4. An answer $(\widetilde{A}, A)$ is *unreliable* if there exists at least an $\omega \in A$ such that $\widetilde{A}(\omega) < 1$.

We will define, on $\widetilde{\mathcal{F}}_r$, an ordering ($\preceq$) (less reliable than) and two operations ($\sqcup, \sqcap$) by means of

$$\begin{aligned} R_A \preceq R_B &\iff A = B,\ \widetilde{A} \subset \widetilde{B}, \\ R_A \sqcup R_B &= (\widetilde{A} \cup \widetilde{B}, A \cup B), \\ R_A \sqcap R_B &= (\widetilde{A} \cap \widetilde{B}, A \cap B). \end{aligned}$$

It is easy to prove that $\preceq$ is compatible with $\sqcup, \sqcap$ and moreover $0_{\sqcup} = (\emptyset, \emptyset)$, $0_{\sqcap} = (\Omega_r, \Omega_r)$ are the neutral elements for $\sqcup$ and $\sqcap$ respectively. Here $\Omega_r = \cup_{A \in \mathcal{F}_r} A$.

1.2 Information Measures

The notion of information we give here has been proposed by J.Kampé de Fèriet and B.Forte ([4]). They remarked that information is naturally associated to propositions, that is, by Stone's theorem, to subsets of a suitable universe, without passing necessarily through a probability.

Let $(\Omega, \mathcal{S})$ be a misurable space, where $\mathcal{S}$ is the family of observable events and let $\mathcal{K}$ be the family of pairs of events in $\mathcal{S}$ which we consider information-independent (J-independent).

Definition 5. An *information measure* (see [4]) over a structure $(\Omega, \mathcal{S}, \mathcal{K})$ is a map $J : \mathcal{S} \to \mathbb{R}^+$ such that:

1. $J(\Omega) = 0$;
2. $J(\emptyset) = +\infty$;
3. $A, B \in \mathcal{S},\ A \subset B, \Longrightarrow J(A) \geq J(B)$;
4. $(\mathcal{A}, \mathcal{B}) \in \mathcal{K},\ A \in \mathcal{A},\ B \in \mathcal{B}, \Longrightarrow J(A \cap B) = J(A) + J(B)$

Definition 6. ([5]) An information measure is *compositive* if it exists a map $F : \mathbb{R}^+ \times \mathbb{R}^+ \to \mathbb{R}^+$ (*composition law*) such that

$$A, B \in \mathcal{S}, A \cap B = \emptyset \quad \Rightarrow \quad J(A \cup B) = F[J(A), J(B)].$$

From now ahead we will indicate function F by an algebraic notation $\top$. The composition law $F(x, y) = x \top y$ furnishes the information of the union of two disjoint subsets. So it must be coherent with the properties of this operation and, consequently, it is defined on the subset

$$\Gamma = \{(x, y) : x = J(A),\ y = J(B), A, B \in \mathcal{S},\ A \cap B = \emptyset\}$$

and it has to satisfy the properties

1. $x \top + \infty = x$;
2. $x \top y = y \top x$;
3. $x \top (y \top z) = (x \top y) \top z$;
4. $x_1 > x_2 \Rightarrow x_1 \top y \geq x_2 \top y$;
5. $(x \top y) + z = (x + z) \top (y + z)$.

The following results also hold:

Theorem 1. ([5])Let Δ be a closed subset and $\overline{\Delta} = \bigcup_{i\in\mathcal{I}}]a_i, b_i[$, $\mathcal{I} \subseteq \mathbb{N}$ its complementary, and for all $i \in \mathcal{I}$ let $f_i\colon [a_i, b_i] \to \mathbb{R}^+$ be a real positive strictly decreasing map with $f_i(b_i) = 0$. Finally let us indicate by $f_i^{(-1)}(r) = f_i^{-1}\{\min(r, f_i(a_i))\}$ the pseudo-inverse of f_i. Every map defined by

$$x \top y = \begin{cases} f_i^{(-1)}[f_i(x) + f_i(y)], & \text{if } (x,y) \in [a_i, b_i]^2 \\ \inf(x,y), & \text{otherwise} \end{cases} \quad (1)$$

is a continue solution of (1)–(4) and, vice versa, every continue solution of (1)–(4) is a map as 1, provided that Δ and f_i have been correctly chosen.

Theorem 2. ([4]) The only continue and universal solutions of (1)–(5) are the two maps

$$x \top y = -k \log(e^{-\frac{x}{k}} + e^{-\frac{y}{k}}), \quad k > 0 \quad (2)$$

$$x \top y = \inf(x,y). \quad (3)$$

where the word *universal* means "compatible with all possible choices of the independent algebras".

Note that 2 is defined if $e^{-x/k}+e^{-y/k} \leq 1$. If $e^{-x/k}+e^{-y/k} > 1$ 2 is not defined as in this case x and y necessarly corrisponds to measure of information of not disjoined events.

This two results are enounced separately because as (1)–(4) must be satisfied in any case, whereas (5) works only if $\mathcal{K}$ is sufficiently large (it has almost the power of continous).

Definition 7. The elements of the subset Δ are called *idempotent* with respect to the composition law $\top$. For them the following relation holds:

$$\xi \in \Delta \Leftrightarrow \xi \top \xi = \xi.$$

2 The Variation $\mathcal{V}$

Let $J(R_A)$ be the ideal information associated to the answer R_A, that is the information we would have if all the elements of A are completely reliable. Moreover let $\widetilde{J}(R_A)$ be the information that we obtain by considering that some elements are not completely reliable, that is the information given by the non reliable only; finally let $J^e(R_A)$ the effective information obtained by composing the previous ones. Then it is obvious that $J^e(R_A)$ should be obtained by adding to $J(R_A)$ a term $\mathcal{V}$ depending both on A and $\widetilde{A}$

$$\widetilde{J}^e(R_A) \;=\; J(R_A) + \mathcal{V}(\widetilde{A}, A) \tag{4}$$

As $\mathcal{V}$ is required to satisfy the relation between effective information and ideal one, it is natural to suppose that $\mathcal{V}$ has to depend in some way from $J(\widetilde{A})$ and $J(A)$, that is:

$$\mathcal{V}(R_A) = \mathcal{V}(\widetilde{A}, A) = G[J(\widetilde{A}), J(A)],$$

and, from the properties of the measure of information, the following relations must hold:

$$\mathcal{V}(0_{\sqcup}) = \mathcal{V}(\widetilde{\emptyset}, \emptyset) = +\infty$$

$$G(+\infty, +\infty) = +\infty;$$

$$\mathcal{V}(0_{\sqcap}) = \mathcal{V}(\widetilde{\Omega_r}, \Omega_r) = 0$$

$$G(0, 0) = 0;$$

$$R_A \preceq R_B \Longrightarrow \mathcal{V}(R_A) = \mathcal{V}(\widetilde{A}, A) \geq \mathcal{V}(R_B) = \mathcal{V}(\widetilde{B}, B)$$

$$J(A) = J(B),\ J(\widetilde{A}) > J(\widetilde{B}) \Longrightarrow G(J(\widetilde{A}), J(A)) \geq G(J(\widetilde{B}), J(B)):$$

If $(\widetilde{A}, A), (\widetilde{B}, B)$ are $\mathcal{V}-$ independent, then
$\mathcal{V}(R_A \sqcap R_B) = \mathcal{V}(\widetilde{A} \cap \widetilde{B}, A \cap B) = \mathcal{V}(\widetilde{A}, A) + \mathcal{V}(\widetilde{B}, B) = \mathcal{V}(R_A) + \mathcal{V}(R_B)$
where $\mathcal{V}-$ independent means that $(\widetilde{\mathrm{A}}, \widetilde{\mathrm{B}})$
and (A, B) are $\mathrm{J}-$ independent,

$$G(J(\widetilde{A} \cap \widetilde{B}), J(A \cap B)) = G(J(\widetilde{A}), J(A)) + G(J(\widetilde{B}), J(B)).$$

So, in order to determine the general form for $\mathcal{V}$, it is enough to find the general form for G which satisfies the above properties.

3 The Finite Case

Now we assume that $\mathrm{Ran}(\widetilde{A}) = (\alpha_0 = 0, \alpha_1, \ldots, \alpha_n = 1)$ for all $A \in \mathcal{F}_r$. So function $\mathcal{V}$ depends only by the α-cuts $A_i = A_{\alpha_i}$ and function G depends only by the values of the informations of the α-cut. We may observe that A and A_i completely determine $A_i^c = A - A_i$, but $J(A)$ and $J(A_i)$ do not determine $J(A_i^c)$. So, in order to take in account the importance of both what we know and what we don't know, the function G in the most general case has to depend on $a_0 = J(A)$, on $a_i = J(A_i)$ for $i = 1, \ldots, n$ and on $a_i^c = J(A_i^c)$ for $i = 1, \ldots, n$

$$G(J(\widetilde{A}), J(A)) = G(a_0, a_1, \ldots, a_n, a_1^c \ldots, a_n^c).$$

The conditions on function G of the previous paragraph take the form

1. $G(+\infty, +\infty, \ldots, +\infty) = +\infty$;
2. $G(0, \ldots, 0) = 0$;
3. $a_0 = b_0,\ a_i > b_i \rightarrow G(a_0, a_1, a_1^c \ldots, a_n, a_n^c) \geq G(b_0, b_1, b_1^c \ldots, b_n, b_n^c)$;
4. $G(a_0{+}b_0, a_1{+}b_1, a_1^c{+}b_1^c, \ldots, a_n{+}b_n, a_n^c{+}b_n^c) = G(a_0, a_1, a_1^c, \ldots, a_n, a_n^c) + G(b_0, b_1, b_1^c, \ldots, b_n, b_n^c)$.

The complete study of this system of functional equations is very hard. So we will treat here only two particular subcases: the universal and the decomposable ones.

4 Universal Variations

In this paragraph we determine the form of function G under the hypothesis that the variation $\mathcal{V}$ is universal, that is compatible with every choice of the family of the couples of $\mathcal{V}-$independent answers. This means that the equations of the previous paragraph, and in particular the last one, have to be satisfied for every choice of the independent variables.
In order to reach this goal, we will consider any α-cutA_α of $\widetilde{A}$. The elements of A_α are reliable to the extent α ($\alpha-$reliable), whereas those of $A_\alpha^c = A - A_\alpha$ are $\alpha-$unreliable. Each α-cut give a contribution to the variation. We suppose that it depends on the subsets A_α and A_α^c through their informations. In a first step we determine the contribution of the α-cuts, and in a seconde step we compose all the contribution to obtain the global variation $\mathcal{V}$.

4.1 One Level: General Results

It is quite evident that the problem of determining the α-cut contribution, is completely equivalent to those of the determination of the variation of the "one-level" unreliable answers, that is of an answer R_A where $\widetilde{A} = \alpha A_\alpha$ (with $A_\alpha \subseteq A$), that is

$$\widetilde{A}(\omega) = \begin{cases} \alpha & \text{if } \omega \in A_\alpha \\ 0 & \text{if } \omega \in A_\alpha^c \end{cases}$$

In this case the conditions of the previous paragraph take the form

1. $G(+\infty, +\infty, 0) = +\infty$;

2. $G(0,0,\infty)=0$;

3. $a=b,\ a^r>b^r\rightarrow G(a,a^r,a^u)\geq G(b,b^r,b^u)$;

$$G(a+b,a^r+b^r,a^u+b^u)=G(a,a^r,a^u)+G(b,b^r,b^u). \tag{5}$$

where $a=J(A),\ a^r=J(A_\alpha),\ a^u=J(A_\alpha^c),\ b=J(B),\ b^r=J(B_\alpha),\ b^u=J(B_\alpha^c)$. The super-indices r,u are to remember that they are the information parts of the $\alpha-$reliable and $\alpha-$unreliable subset.

The following results can be easily obtained from equation 5.

$$\begin{aligned} G(a+b,a+b^r,+\infty+b^u) &= G(a,a,+\infty)+G(b,b^r,b^u). \\ G(a+b,\infty,a+b^u) &= G(a,+\infty,a)+G(b,b^r,b^u), \end{aligned} \tag{6}$$

Combining equations 5 and 6 we can deduce that G depends on a,a^r,a^u only through the difference $x=a^r-a,\ y=a^u-a$

$$G(a,a^r,a^u)\ =\ s(x,y)=s(a^r-a,\ a^u-a)$$

4.2 One Level: Universal Variations

Let us examine now the case where J is compositive. In this case $A=A_\alpha\cup A_\alpha^c$, and therefore $a=J(A)=J(A_\alpha)\top J(A_\alpha^c)=a^r\top a^u$. Let us indicate by g the function of a^r,a^u obtained by function s:

$$g(a^r,\ a^u)\ =\ s(a^r-a^r\top a^u,\ a^u-a^r\top a^u)$$

It can be recognized that the following compatibility conditions on function g hold:

$$\begin{aligned} g(a^r,a^u)+g(b^r,b^u) &= g(a^r+b^r,[a^r+b^u]\top[a^u+b^r]\top[a^u+b^u]), \\ g(+\infty,a)+g(b^r,b^u) &= g(+\infty,a+[b^r\top b^u]), \\ g(a,+\infty)+g(b^r,b^u) &= g(a+b^r,a+b^u). \end{aligned}$$

Now let us remember that we are considering the universal case in the sense specified in paragraph 1.2 for the function J, and in this paragraph for variation $\mathcal{V}$. Then:

1. the above equations have to be satisfied for all a^r,a^u,b^r,b^u,

2. the universal composition laws are

$$\begin{aligned} x\top y &= \sup\{0,-k\log(e^{-\frac{x}{k}}+e^{-\frac{y}{k}})\}, \\ x\top y &= \inf(x,y). \end{aligned} \tag{7}$$

The two cases have been treated in different forms, due to the different aspects of the two laws. Neverteless the formal aspect of the of the final result is the same in both cases. In fact we proved that

$$g(a^r, a^u) \ = \ k(a^r - a^r \top a^u)$$

that is

$$\begin{aligned} \mathcal{V}(A_\alpha, A) \ &= \ k[J(A_\alpha) - J(A)] \\ J^e(R_A) \ = \ J^e(A_\alpha, A) \ &= \ J(A) + k_\alpha[J(A_\alpha) - J(A)] \end{aligned} \tag{8}$$

4.3 Universal Variations: the General Form

Starting from the above result, we can now construct the variation associated to the whole answer $(\widetilde{A}, A)$, by combining (by means of a suitable function Γ) the variations just obtained in the previous sections for each α-cut $A_i = A\alpha_i$.

$$\mathcal{V}(\widetilde{A}, A) \ = \ \Gamma[\mathcal{V}(A_1, A), \ldots, \mathcal{V}(A_n, A)]$$

If $(\widetilde{A}, A)$ and $(\widetilde{B}, B)$ are J-independent, then $\mathcal{V}(\widetilde{A} \cap \widetilde{B}, A \cap B) = \mathcal{V}(\widetilde{A}, A) + \mathcal{V}(\widetilde{B}, B)$. Let us pose $x_i = \mathcal{V}(A_i, A)$, $y_i = \mathcal{V}(B_i, B)$, and let us remember that $\mathcal{V}(A_i \cap B_i, A \cap B) = \mathcal{V}(A_i, A) + \mathcal{V}(B_i, B)$. Then we obtain:

$$\Gamma(x_1 + y_1, \ldots, x_n + y_n) = \Gamma(x_1, \ldots, x_n) + \Gamma(y_1, \ldots, y_n).$$

This is the n-dimensional Cauchy equation ([6]) which has as solution the family of functions

$$\Gamma(x_1, \ldots, x_n) \ = \ \sum_{i=1}^{n} \beta_i x_i, \ \ \beta_i = \text{constant}.$$

Theorem 3. The general form for $\mathcal{V}$ (when the compositional law of J is universal) is

$$\mathcal{V}(\widetilde{A}, A) = \sum_{i=1}^{n} b_i[J(A_i) - J(A)],$$

where $b_i = k_i \cdot \beta_i$ $(k_i = k_{\alpha_i})$ are positive constants. Since higher is the reliability, lower is the variation, constants b_i have to satisfy the condition $\alpha_i > \alpha_j \Rightarrow b_i \leq b_j$.

5 Decomposable Variations

In this paragraph we examine the case where $\mathcal{V}$ is compositive both on the α-cut variations and on the fuzzy variation, that is

$$A \cap B = \emptyset \implies$$
$$\begin{cases} \mathcal{V}(\widetilde{A} \cup \widetilde{B}, A \cup B) &= \mathcal{V}(\widetilde{A}, A) \top^* \mathcal{V}(\widetilde{B}, B), \\ \mathcal{V}(A_i \cup B_i, A \cup B) &= \mathcal{V}(A_i, A) \top \mathcal{V}(B_i, B). \end{cases} \tag{9}$$

Moreover, as in the previous case we suppose that

$$\mathcal{V}(\widetilde{A}, A) = \Gamma_n[\mathcal{V}(A_1, A), \dots, \mathcal{V}(A_n, A)]. \tag{10}$$

If we combine equations 9 and 10, then, by posing $x_i = \mathcal{V}(A_i, A)$, $y_i = \mathcal{V}(B_i, B)$, we obtain the following compatibility equation between function Γ and composition laws $\top$ and $\top^*$.

$$\Gamma_n[x_1 \top y_1, \dots, x_n \top y_n] = \Gamma_n[x_1, \dots, x_n] \top^* \Gamma_n[y_1, \dots, y_n]. \tag{11}$$

5.1 The One Level Case

If $\widetilde{A}$ and $\widetilde{B}$ have the first i levels equal and the others empty, the equation (11) becomes:

$$G_1(x \top y) = G_1(x) \top^* G_1(y),$$

where $G_1(x) = \Gamma_n[x, \dots, x, +\infty, \dots, +\infty]$.
It is easy to verify that G_1 is monotonic. If it is strictly monotonic, then the following results hold:

Theorem 4. If $\Delta_\top$ and $\Delta_{\top^\star}$ are the sets of the idempotents of the norms $\top$ and $\top^\star$ respectively, then $G_1(\Delta_\top) = \Delta_{\top^\star}$.

Theorem 5. Let $x \in]a, b[$ be a non $\top$-idempotent element. By theorem 4 $G_1(]a, b[) =]a^*, b^*[$ is a subset of non $\top^*$-idempotents. Let f and f^* be the generators of $\top, \top^*$ in $]a, b[,]a^*, b^*[$ respectively. Then

$$G_1(x) = f^{*-1}(af(x)),$$

where a is a constant depending on the intervals $]a, b[,]a^*, b^*[$.

Theorem 6. If $x \in \Delta_\top$, then $G_1(x)$ can assume any value provided that the following two conditions are preserved:

Continuity of G_1, Monotonicity of G_1.

5.1.1 The Two Level Case

Now let us consider the family of fuzzy subsets in $\tilde{S}$ assume only the value α_r for some $r < n$ and the value $\alpha_n = 1$. Obviously for them the first r α-cuts are equal and the same holds for the α-cuts A_j with j between $r+1$ and n . That is, they are the sets $\tilde{A}$ such that:

$$\tilde{A}(\omega) = \begin{matrix} \alpha_r, & \text{if } \omega \in B, \\ 1, & \text{if } \omega \in C, \\ 0, & \text{otherwise.} \end{matrix}$$

wher B e C are crisp subsets of Ω. The significant α-cuts are $A_r = B \cup C$ and $A_n = C$. Denoting by x the information of $B \cup C$ and by y the one of C (that is $x = J(B \cup C)$, $y = J(C)$), we want find $\Gamma_n(x, \ldots, x, y, \ldots, y)$ (where the variable x occupies the first r positions), which we will indicate by $G_2(x, y)$ understanding the dependence from r. The equation 11 becomes:

$$G_2(x \top y, z \top w) = G_2(x, z) \top^\star G_2(y, w).$$

G_2 is monotonic in both variables (the proof is immediate). If it is strictly monotonic, then the following results hold:

Theorem 7. If $\Delta_\top$ and $\Delta_{\top^\star}$ are the sets of the idempotents of the norms $\top$ and $\top^\star$ respectively, then $G_2(\Delta_\top, \Delta_\top) = \Delta_{\top^\star}$.

Theorem 8. The general form for G_2 is:

$$G_2(x,y) = \begin{matrix} (a) & inf(x,y) \\ & \text{if } x, y \in \Delta_\top \\ \\ (b) & f_k^{*(-1)}(af_i(x) + bf_i(y)) \\ & \text{if } x, y \in (a_i, b_i) \\ \\ (c) & f_k^{*(-1)}(cf_i(x) + df_j(y)) \\ & \text{if } x \in (a_i, b_i), y \in (a_j, b_j) \text{with} i \neq j \\ \\ (d) & f_k^{*(-1)}(n(x) f_i(y)) \\ & \text{if} x \in \Delta_\top, y \in (a_i, b_i) \end{matrix}$$

where $a = a_i, b = b_i, c = c_i$ are constants depending on subindex i, $d = d_j$ is a constant depending on j and finally $n(x)$ is an arbitrary monotonic function of x which have to preserve

the continuity of G_2 and the monotonicity of G_2.

5.2 The n Level Case

The form of function Γ_n can, under some restrictive hypotheses, be obtained by means of a recurrence procedure which starts from G_2. The philosophy is the following: suppose that we have to compute the variation of a fuzzy set with three meaningful levels. We start by computing the variation associated to the first two by means of function G_2. Then we substitute to these levels an equivalent one, that is an unique level which has the same variation of the first two. What we obtain is a two level subset which is, in a certain sense, equivalent to the original one. Basically this procedure works as the level's variations contribute to the global one without interacting to each other. The form of the procedure is

$$G_i(x_1, \ldots, x_i) = G_2[G_{i-1}(x_1, \ldots, x_{i-1}), x_i] \quad (12)$$

$G_n(x_1, \ldots, x_n)$ is the function $\Gamma(x_1, \ldots, x_n)$ that we need.
If $\Delta_\top$ contains only the elements $0, +\infty$ then we know, by theorem 1, that

$$x \top y = f^{(-1)}[f(x) + f(y)],$$
$$x \top^* y = f^{*-1}[f^*(x) + f^*(y)].$$

Moreover it can be proved that, in this case, $f = f^*$. Then we can give an explicit form of Γ

Theorem 9. The general form for G_n if x_i are not idempotents is:

$$\Gamma(x_1, \ldots, x_n) = f^{(-1)}(\sum_{i=1}^{n} a_i f(x_i)),$$

where a_i are constants.

So the global variation is given by

$$\mathcal{V}(\widetilde{A}, A) = f^{(-1)}(\sum_{i=1}^{n} a_i f(\mathcal{V}(A_i, A))$$

Theorem 10. Another case where we can give an explicit form of the global variation corresponds to $\Delta_\top = \Delta_{\top^*} = \mathbb{R}^+$. In this case the global variation is

$$\mathcal{V}(\widetilde{A}, A) = \max_i \{\mathcal{V}(A_i, A)\}$$

In the other cases we must use the recurrent formula. According to the structure of the idempotent, we can, in certain cases, obtain a complete representation, but we think that it is not important to describe in detail all the cases.

6 Comments and Conclusions

In order to discuss our result, let us consider, as paradigm, the case of subparagraph 4.3, where we proved that, at the α-cut level,

$$J^e(R_A) \;=\; J^e(A_\alpha, A) \;=\; J(A) + k_\alpha[J(A_\alpha) - J(A)]$$

Since $k_\alpha \geq 0$ and $J(A_\alpha) \geq J(A)$, the real information is always greater tha the ideal one. This fact may seem strange: in fact it says that the unreliability, instead of diminsh, increases the information.
But if we think a bit, we can realize that it is really what happens: at theoretical level, as a new amount of information has been added by the people which gives the judgement; at practical level, as the elimination of some elements can help the judge in taking the correct decision.

A second remark refers to the constant k_α. It is reasonable to bound it to the interval $[0,1]$. This means that $J^e(R_A)$ always lies between $J(A)$ and $J(A_\alpha) = J(A^r)$. The lower bound corresponds to discard the unreliability , the upper one corresponds to take in account only the reliable elements. In general in may be viewed as a kind of confidence on the reliability's judgment.

Finally we will indicate some open problems:

1. The independence axiom and the universality notion have been generalized ([7]) so that other information measures would be consistent with the J-independence, beyond the Shannon and the type-inf ones. It would be interesting to analyze the universal variations in this latter case.

2. The last two theorems give an explicit form of the decomposable variations in the limit situations $\Delta = \{0, +\infty\}$, $\Delta = \mathbb{R}^+$. Is it possible find explicit form in other cases? Although not at theoretical level, this problem is important at the practical one.

3. What happens when the range of the membership function is numerable (not difficult) or continuous (more difficult)?

References

[1] Carlo Bertoluzza, Antonia Salas (1999). Pseudoquestionnaires in a deterministic environment. *ESIT'99*, Crete, Greece, june,3-4 (1999)

[2] Viviana Doldi (2000). Pseudoquestionari dal punto di viata deterministico. *Tesi di laurea.* University of Pavia, a/a 1998-99.

[3] Claudia Ronco (1975). Questioni e risposte non attendibili. *in Questionari e Informazione*, tesi di Laurea, University of Pavia, a/a 1974-75.

[4] Joseph Kampé de Fèriet and Bruno Forte (1967). Information et probabilité. *CRAS, Paris, 265 Sèrie A*, 110-114, 143-146, (1967).

[5] Joseph Kampé de Fèriet, Bruno Forte and Piero Benvenuti (1969). Forme Gènèrale de loperation de composition continue d'une information. *CRAS, Paris, 269 Sèrie A*, 529-533, (1969).

[6] Janos Aczel (1966). Lectures on functional equations and their applications. *Academic Press.* (1996)

[7] Carlo Bertoluzza and Angela Boscaini (1977). Su un sistema di equazioni funzionali connesso con la nozione di indipendenza in teoria dell'informazione. *Rend. Istituto Lombardo* (A) vol.111, 69-78 (1977).

Aggregation Methods

On the Aggregation of Some Classes of Fuzzy Relations

Ana Pradera*[1], Enric Trillas[2], and Elena Castiñeira[3]

[1] Department of Experimental Sciences and Engineering. Rey Juan Carlos University. 28933 Móstoles. Madrid. Spain. a.pradera@escet.urjc.es
[2] Department of Artificial Intelligence. Technical University of Madrid. 28660 Boadilla del Monte. Madrid. Spain. etrillas@fi.upm.es
[3] Department of Applied Mathematics. Technical University of Madrid. 28660 Boadilla del Monte. Madrid. Spain. ecastineira@fi.upm.es

Abstract. This paper deals with the aggregation of fuzzy relations under a closure constraint, that is, it studies how to combine a collection of fuzzy relations that present some common properties in order to obtain a single one with the same properties. This aggregation problem is addressed for two important classes of closely related fuzzy relations: generalized distances and indistinguishability operators.

Keywords: Aggregation. Generalized distances. Indistinguishability operators. Triangular norms and conorms. Archimedean operators.

1 Introduction

Information aggregation -that is, combining several incoming data into a single output- is a crucial issue in the construction of many intelligent systems. Very often, the input data presents some kind of imprecision, and therefore a framework with capabilities for both representing and combining such type of knowledge is strongly needed.

Fuzzy Set Theory is a mathematical framework that fulfills such requirements and where investigation on aggregation-related topics has experimented a great development in the last years. It provides several formalisms for representing vagueness (fuzzy sets, fuzzy relations and fuzzy measures), two main aggregation mechanisms (pointwise aggregation and aggregation based on the extension principle) and a very large variety of numerical operators for performing the aggregation.

In any aggregation process, and once the representation formalism and the aggregation method have been chosen, there is still an important remaining decision to make: which aggregation operator should be used? Different criteria may be considered in order to solve this last problem, such as performing empirical tests or analyzing which behavior or mathematical properties the chosen operator should met. Another possibility, which is very often extremely useful, is to impose a closure constraint, that is, only operators that

* Corresponding author

provide an output with the same properties than the inputs may be considered (for example, if the inputs are fuzzy implications, then the output should also be a fuzzy implication).

This work addresses pointwise aggregation procedures where the incoming data is represented by means of fuzzy relations, all of them belonging to a same class, and where the closure constraint is imposed in order to select the aggregation operator. Formally, this problem may be defined as follows:

Definition 1. Let X be a non-empty set and let $R_1, \ldots, R_n : X \times X \to \mathbb{R}$ be n fuzzy relations belonging to a same class C. Let $R : X \times X \to \mathbb{R}$, $R = F(R_1, \ldots, R_n)$, be the fuzzy relation obtained by pointwise-aggregating the input relations by means of some numerical operator $F : \mathbb{R}^n \to \mathbb{R}$, that is, $R(x,y) = F(R_1(x,y), \ldots, R_n(x,y))$ for each $x, y \in X$. We will say that F *is an operator that aggregates relations of class* C when the output relation R belongs to the same class.

This paper studies the former problem for two well-known classes of fuzzy relations: *generalized distances* (section 2) and *indistinguishability operators* (section 3). Section 2 studies the aggregation of two particular types of generalized distances: classical pseudo-distances and generalized distances defined with respect to continuous triangular conorms. Section 3 deals with the aggregation of indistinguishability operators defined with respect to continuous triangular norms.

2 Aggregation of Generalized Distances

Generalized distances were introduced in 1967 (see [8] and [7]) as a generalization of ordinary, boolean and probabilistic metrics. They are functions that assign to each pair from a given universal set a value in an ordered and commutative semigroup. Formally:

Definition 2. Let $\mathcal{C} = (C, *, \leq, e)$ be an ordered and commutative semigroup with neutral element e and X a non-empty set. A function $d : X \times X \to C$ is said to be a *$\mathcal{C}$-generalized distance on X* if it verifies the following properties for any x, y, z in X:

$$\begin{aligned}&(\mathrm{GD1})\ d(x,x) = e\\&(\mathrm{GD2})\ d(x,y) = d(y,x)\\&(\mathrm{GD3})\ d(x,z) \leq d(x,y) * d(y,z)\end{aligned}$$

Next subsections study how to aggregate two important particular cases of generalized distances: ordinary *pseudo-distances* and generalized distances defined with respect to triangular conorms, called *S-generalized distances.*

2.1 Aggregation of Pseudo-distances

Ordinary pseudo-distances are generalized distances defined in $I\!R^+$ by means of the operation $+$, the linear order $\leq$ and neutral element $e = 0$. If the general aggregation problem stated in the introduction is restricted to this kind of relations, the resulting problem may be expressed in the following way:

Definition 3. A function $F : (I\!R^+)^n \to I\!R^+$ is an *operator that aggregates pseudo-distances* when, for any non-empty set X and any arbitrary collection of pseudo-distances $d_i : X \times X \to I\!R^+$, $i = 1 \dots n$, the function $d = F(d_1, .., d_n)$ is a pseudo-distance on X.

According to the definition of pseudo-distance, we are looking for operators $F : (I\!R^+)^n \to I\!R^+$ fulfilling the two following properties:

(1) $F(0, \dots, 0) = 0$
(2) For any family of pseudo-distances $d_1, \dots, d_n : X \times X \to I\!R^+$ and any $x, y, z \in X$,
$F(d_1(x,z), .., d_n(x,z)) \leq F(d_1(x,y), .., d_n(x,y)) + F(d_1(y,z), .., d_n(y,z))$

Next proposition provides a sufficient condition to find such kind of operators:

Proposition 1. *If a function $F : (I\!R^+)^n \to I\!R^+$ is non-decreasing, subadditive and verifies $F(0, \dots, 0) = 0$, then it aggregates pseudo-distances.*

Proof. Function F is subadditive when for any $a_i, b_i \in I\!R^+$ it is
$F(a_1 + b_1, \dots, a_n + b_n) \leq F(a_1, \dots, a_n) + F(b_1, \dots, b_n)$.
Then, as F is non-decreasing and functions d_i are pseudo-distances, the following chain of inequalities holds:
$F(d_1(x,z), .., d_n(x,z)) \leq F(d_1(x,y) + d_1(y,z), \dots, d_n(x,y) + d_n(y,z))$
$\leq F(d_1(x,y), .., d_n(x,y)) + F(d_1(y,z), .., d_n(y,z))$. ■

Some trivial solutions to the former proposition are functions $F = \max$ and $F(x_1, \dots, x_n) = \sum_{i=1}^{n} \alpha_i x_i$, with $\alpha_i \geq 0$. This last operator is a *weighted mean*, which, in fact, is an additive function (see [1]).

In the former, only pseudo-distances giving values in the whole $I\!R^+$ are dealt with. It is many times useful -as it will be shown later- to work with bounded pseudo-distances, that is, pseudo-distances whose range is a closed real interval $[0, c]$, $c \in I\!R^+$. In order to aggregate this kind of functions, operators of the form $F : [0, c]^n \to [0, c]$ are needed, and the concept of subadditivity has to be replaced by subadditivity inside the interval $[0, c]$. Nevertheless, a very similar result to the one given in last proposition may be easily proved:

Proposition 2. *If a function* $F : [0,c]^n \to [0,c]$ *is non-decreasing, subadditive in* $[0,c]$ *and verifies* $F(0,\ldots,0) = 0$*, then it aggregates bounded pseudo-distances with values in* $[0,c]$.

Proof. Function F is subadditive in $[0,c]$ when for any $a_i, b_i \in [0,c]$ such that $a_i + b_i \in [0,c]$ it is

$$F(a_1 + b_1, \ldots, a_n + b_n) \leq F(a_1, \ldots, a_n) + F(b_1, \ldots, b_n).$$

We have to prove that for any family of bounded pseudo-distances $d_1, \ldots, d_n : X \times X \to [0,c]$ and any $x, y, z \in X$,

$$F(d_1(x,z), .., d_n(x,z)) \leq F(d_1(x,y), .., d_n(x,y)) + F(d_1(y,z), .., d_n(y,z)).$$

If pseudo-distances d_i and values $x, y, z \in X$ are taken such as $d_i(x,y) + d_i(y,z) \in [0,c]$ for each i, the proof given in last proposition is still valid. If not, let us suppose that there exists a distance d_j and values x, y, z such that $d_j(x,y) + d_j(y,z) > c$. Then it suffices to find values a and b in $[0,c]$ such that $d_j(x,z) \leq a + b \leq c$ and $a \leq d_j(x,y), b \leq d_j(y,z)$, for example $a = d_j(x,y) - m$ and $b = d_j(y,z) - m$, $m = (d_j(x,y) + d_j(y,z) - c)/2$. Then:

$$\begin{aligned}
&F(d_1(x,z), .., d_j(x,z), .., d_n(x,z)) \\
&\leq F(d_1(x,y) + d_1(y,z), .., a + b, .., d_n(x,y) + d_n(y,z)) \\
&\leq F(d_1(x,y), .., a, .., d_n(x,y)) + F(d_1(y,z), .., b, .., d_n(y,z)) \\
&\leq F(d_1(x,y), .., d_n(x,y)) + F(d_1(y,z), .., d_n(y,z))
\end{aligned}$$ ■

If we restrict ourselves to the $[0,1]$ interval (working with other intervals is just an scaling problem), last proposition gives some examples of operators that allow to aggregate pseudo-distances defined in $[0,1]$. The weighted mean (now with weights in $[0,1]$) is one of them. Among *triangular conorms* (functions $S : [0,1]^2 \to [0,1]$ that are commutative, associative, non-decreasing and with neutral element zero), it is a matter of calculation to see that the three most common ones, $Max(x,y)$, *Prod*$^*(x,y) = x + y - xy$ and $W^*(x,y) = Min(x+y, 1)$ are subadditive in $[0,1]$. Another example is given by Sugeno's t-conorms, defined as $S(x,y) = \min(1, x+y+\lambda xy)$, with $\lambda > -1$, which are subadditive functions if and only if $\lambda \leq 0$.

2.2 Aggregation of S-generalized distances

When working with semigroups $([0,1], S, \leq, 0)$, where the operation S is a triangular conorm, generalized distances are called S-generalized distances. In this case the first and third properties in the definition of generalized distance become $d(x,x) = 0$ and $d(x,z) \leq S\,(d(x,y), d(y,z))$.

The problem of aggregating n S_i-generalized distances in such a way that the output obtained is in turn a generalized distance for some t-conorm S may be reduced to the problem of finding functions $F : [0,1]^n \to [0,1]$ that verify:

(1) $F(0,\ldots,0)=0$
(2) For any family of S_i-generalized distances $d_1,\ldots,d_n : X\times X\to[0,1]$ and any $x,y,z\in X$,

$$F(d_1(x,z),..,d_n(x,z))\leq S\,(F(d_1(x,y),..,d_n(x,y)),F(d_1(y,z),..,d_n(y,z)))$$

Next subsections study the aggregation of S-generalized distances individually in the two following cases: when all the t-conorms involved are the maximum operator and when they are all continuous Archimedean t-conorms.

The maximum operator case

When all the t-conorms involved are taken as the maximum operator, that is, when dealing with *pseudo-ultrametrics*, next result gives a family of solutions to the problem.

Proposition 3. *The operator $F:[0,1]^n\to[0,1]$ defined as*

$$F(x_1,\ldots,x_n)=\max_{i=1}^{n} f_i(x_i),$$

where $f_i:[0,1]\to[0,1]$ are non-decreasing functions satisfying $f_i(0)=0$ for all $i\in\{1,\ldots,n\}$ and $f_i(1)=1$ for at least one i, is an operator that aggregates max*-generalized distances.*

Proof. It is clear that $F(0,\ldots,0)=0$. On the other hand, F is non-decreasing and Dubois and Prade proved in [4] that this operator allows to aggregate n possibility measures into a possibility measure, that is, it verifies the equality $F(\max(a_1,b_1),\ldots,\max(a_n,b_n))=\max(F(a_1,\ldots,a_n),F(b_1,\ldots,b_n))$. ∎

Some examples of concrete aggregation operators obtained from previous result, which may therefore be used to aggregate pseudo-ultrametrics, are the following:

- the t-conorm max;
- the weighted maximum, or *Sugeno Integral*, defined as

$$w\text{-}\max(x_1,\ldots,x_n)=\max_{i=1}^{n}(\min(x_i,w_i)),$$

  where $w^t=(w_1,\ldots,w_n)$, $w_i\in[0,1]$, is a normalized weighting vector such that $\max_{i=1}^{n}(w_i)=1$;
- the operator $F_w(x_1,\ldots,x_n)=\max_{i=1}^{n} x_i^{w_i}$, with $w^t=(w_1,\ldots,w_n)$, $w_i\in\mathbb{R}^+-\{0\}$.

The continuous Archimedean case

Continuous Archimedean operators constitute an important family of triangular conorms. A continuous t-conorm S is said to be *Archimedean* if it satisfies $S(x,x) > x$ for all x in $]0,1[$. This class of operators was characterized by Ling ([6]) by means of the following representation theorem:

Theorem 1. *A continuous t-conorm S is an Archimedean t-conorm if and only if there exists an increasing and continuous function $s : [0,1] \to [0,\infty]$ with $s(0) = 0$ such that for all $a,b \in [0,1]$ it is*

$$S(a,b) = s^{-1}\left(\min(s(1), s(a) + s(b))\right)$$

Function s is called an additive generator *of S, and is uniquely determined up to a positive multiplicative constant.*

The class of continuous Archimedean t-conorms may be further divided into two different subclasses:

- the subclass of those Archimedean t-conorms that are strictly increasing in $[0,1)^2$, which are called *strict t-conorms.* Their additive generators verify $s(1) = \infty$, thus allowing to write S in terms of s and its ordinary inverse, that is, $S(a,b) = s^{-1}\left(s(a) + s(b)\right)$. A typical example of strict t-conorm is $Prod^*(x,y) = x + y - xy$.
- the subclass of Archimedean t-conorms that are not strictly increasing, which are called *non-strict or nilpotent t-conorms.* In this cases $s(1)$ is a finite value, and the function $\widehat{s} = s/s(1) : [0,1] \to [0,1]$, called the *normed additive generator* of S, is uniquely determined. This allows to express S in terms of $\widehat{s}$ by means of $S(a,b) = \widehat{s}^{-1}\left(\min(1, \widehat{s}(a) + \widehat{s}(b))\right)$. The Łukasiewicz t-conorm, $W^*(x,y) = \min(1, x+y)$, is a widely used nilpotent t-conorm.

The problem of aggregating S-generalized distances when the t-conorms considered are all of them continuous Archimedean operators may be reduced to the aggregation of ordinary pseudo-distances. To prove it, we first notice that any S-generalized distance defined with respect to a continuous Archimedean t-conorm S is equivalent to an ordinary pseudo-distance:

Proposition 4. *Let S be a continuous Archimedean t-conorm, s an additive generator of S and X a non-empty set. A function $d : X \times X \to [0,1]$ is a S-generalized distance if and only if the function $s \circ d : X \times X \to [0,\infty]$ is a pseudo-distance.*

Proof. The proof is obtained taking into account the representation of continuous Archimedean t-conorms by means of their additive generators. Let us denote $ord = s \circ d$.

$\Longrightarrow$ We have to prove that *ord* is a pseudo-distance. Both the first and second properties are trivially true. The third one is $ord(x,z) \leq ord(x,y) + ord(y,z)$ for any x,y,z in X.

$$\begin{aligned}
ord(x,z) &= s(d(x,z)) \leq s\left(S(d(x,y),d(y,z))\right) \\
&= s\left[s^{-1}\left(\min(s(1), s(d(x,y)) + s(d(y,z)))\right)\right] \\
&= \min(s(1), s(d(x,y)) + s(d(y,z))) \leq s(d(x,y)) + s(d(y,z)) \\
&= ord(x,y) + ord(y,z).
\end{aligned}$$

$\Longleftarrow$ To prove that $d = s^{-1} \circ ord$ is a S-generalized distance, the two first properties are trivial, so only the inequality $d(x,z) \leq S\left(d(x,y), d(y,z)\right)$ for all x,y,z in X has to be dealt with. Since s is increasing, and due to the representation of S, it is equivalent to

$$ord(x,z) \leq \min(s(1), ord(x,y) + ord(y,z)),$$

which is true since by hypothesis *ord* is a pseudo-distance whose range is included in $[0, s(1)]$. ∎

This equivalence between S-generalized distances defined with respect to continuous Archimedean t-conorms and pseudo-distances allows to solve the aggregation of the former operators in terms of pseudo-distances aggregation. First of all, next theorem deals with the case when all the involved t-conorms are nilpotent:

Theorem 2. *An operator $F : [0,1]^n \to [0,1]$ aggregates n S_i-generalized distances $d_1, \ldots, d_n$ into a S-generalized distance d, with both S and S_i, $i = 1, \ldots, n$, nilpotent continuous Archimedean t-conorms, if and only if*

$$F = \widehat{s}^{-1} \circ G \circ (\widehat{s}_1 \times \ldots \times \widehat{s}_n)$$

where $\widehat{s}$ and $\widehat{s}_i$ are the normed additive generators of S and S_i, respectively, and $G : [0,1]^n \to [0,1]$ is an operator that aggregates pseudo-distances.

Proof. $\Longrightarrow$ Let us define operator $G : [0,1]^n \to [0,1]$ as $G = \widehat{s} \circ F \circ \left(\widehat{s_1}^{-1} \times \ldots \times \widehat{s_n}^{-1}\right)$. It is clear that then operator F can be expressed as stated in the theorem, so we only have to prove that this operator aggregates pseudo-distances, that is, for any bounded pseudo-distances $ord_i : X \times X \to [0,1]$, $i \in \{1, \ldots, n\}$, the operator $ord = G(ord_1, \ldots, ord_n) = \widehat{s} \circ F \circ \left(\widehat{s_1}^{-1} \times \ldots \times \widehat{s_n}^{-1}\right)(ord_1, \ldots, ord_n)$ is a pseudo-distance. According to proposition 4, $\widehat{s_i}^{-1} \circ ord_i$ are S_i-generalized distances and, since by hypothesis $f$aggregate them, *ord* will be, using again proposition 4, a pseudo-distance.

$\Longleftarrow$ We have to prove that $d = \widehat{s}^{-1} \circ G \circ (\widehat{s}_1 \times \ldots \times \widehat{s}_n)(d_1, \ldots, d_n)$ is a generalized distance defined with respect to the nilpotent t-conorm S

when $d_1, \ldots, d_n$ are generalized distances defined with respect to nilpotent t-conorms $S_1, \ldots, S_n$. According to proposition 4, this is equivalent to prove that $\widehat{s} \circ d$ is a pseudo-distance. But this is true since $\widehat{s} \circ d = G \circ (\widehat{s}_1 \times \ldots \times \widehat{s}_n)(d_1, \ldots, d_n)$, G is an operator that aggregates pseudo-distances and $\widehat{s}_i \circ d_i$ are, by proposition 4, pseudo-distances. ■

In a similar way, the following result, related to the aggregation of generalized distances defined with respect to strict continuous Archimedean t-conorms, is obtained:

Theorem 3. *An operator $F : [0,1]^n \rightarrow [0,1]$ aggregates n S_i-generalized distances $d_1, \ldots, d_n$ into a S-generalized distance d, with both S and S_i, $i = 1, \ldots, n$, strict continuous Archimedean t-conorms, if and only if*

$$F = s^{-1} \circ G \circ (s_1 \times \ldots \times s_n)$$

where s and s_i are additive generators of S and S_i, respectively, and $G : (\mathbb{R}^+)^n \rightarrow \mathbb{R}^+$ is an operator that aggregates pseudo-distances.

Proof. The proof is similar to the one given for the non-strict case. ■

Some examples are given below:

Example 1. Aggregation of two generalized distances defined with respect to the strict t-conorm *Prod** into a generalized distance of the same class ($S_1 = S_2 = S =$*Prod**).
The additive generator of *Prod** is $s(x) = -\ln(1-x)$, its inverse is $s^{-1}(x) = 1 - e^{-x}$, and G will be any operator $G : (\mathbb{R}^+)^2 \rightarrow \mathbb{R}^+$ that aggregates pseudo-distances. Some possible choices (see section 2.1):

- $F(x,y) = Max(x,y)$ when taking $G = Max$.
- $F(x,y) = 1 - (1-x)^{w_1}(1-y)^{w_2}$ when taking $G(x,y) = w_1 x + w_2 y$, $w_1, w_2 \geq 0$.

Example 2. Aggregation of two generalized distances defined with respect to the nilpotent t-conorm W^* into a generalized distance of the same class ($S_1 = S_2 = S = W^*$).
The additive generator of W^* is $s(x) = x$, so any operator $G : [0,1]^2 \rightarrow [0,1]$ that aggregates bounded pseudo-distances with values in $[0,1]$ will solve the problem (e.g. the weighted mean or one of the three common t-conorms).

3 Aggregation of T-indistinguishabilities

Triangular norms (t-norms for short) are obtained from t-conorms by means of strong negation functions: a function $T : [0,1] \times [0,1] \rightarrow [0,1]$ is called a *t-norm* if $T^*(x,y) = 1 - T(1-x, 1-y)$ is a t-conorm. T and T^* are said to be *dual*, and this duality allows to translate all the representation properties given for t-conorms to the case of t-norms.

Indistinguishability operators defined with respect to triangular norms were introduced as a generalization of the classical concept of equivalence relation (see [9] and [10]):

Definition 4. Let X a non-empty universal set and T a t-norm. A function $I : X \times X \to [0,1]$ is called a *T-indistinguishability* if, for any $x, y, z \in X$, it verifies the following properties:

$$\begin{aligned}&(\mathrm{I1})\ I(x,x) = 1\\&(\mathrm{I2})\ I(x,y) = I(y,x)\\&(\mathrm{I3})\ T\left(I(x,y), I(y,z)\right) \leq I(x,z)\end{aligned}$$

T-indistinguishabilities aggregation was studied in [2] restricted to the case of T-preorders (relations that are reflexive and T-transitive) and considering quasi-arithmetic means. In the following we show how this aggregation problem can also be studied in the light of the results obtained on S-generalized distances aggregation. This approach is possible thanks to the following simple characterization of T-indistinguishabilities, given in [9]:

Theorem 4. *Let T be a triangular norm and T^* its dual t-conorm. A function $I : X \times X \to [0,1]$ is a T-indistinguishability if and only if $d = 1 - I$ is a T^*-generalized distance.*

The aggregation of T-indistinguishabilities may then be obtained on the basis of T^*-generalized distances aggregation:

Theorem 5. *Let $I_1, \ldots, I_n : X \times X \to [0,1]$ be n T_i-indistinguishability operators defined with respect to some t-norms $T_1, \ldots, T_n$. Let $I : X \times X \to [0,1]$ be defined as $I = F(I_1, \ldots, I_n)$, $F : [0,1]^n \to [0,1]$. Then I is a T-indistinguishability for some t-norm T if and only if*

$$F(x_1, \ldots, x_n) = 1 - G(1 - x_1, \ldots, 1 - x_n)$$

where $G : [0,1]^n \to [0,1]$ is an operator that aggregates n T_i^*-generalized distances into a T^*-generalized distance.

Proof. The proof is easily obtained due to the equivalence between indistinguishabilities and generalized distances stated in previous theorem. ■

Therefore, the aggregation operators that may be used to aggregate T-indistinguishabilities are exactly the dual operators of those that aggregate S-generalized distances.

This means, for example, that in order to aggregate min-indistinguishability operators, the dual operators of the ones given in proposition 3 may be used. When working with continuous Archimedean operators, theorems 2 and 3 have shown that the aggregation of S-generalized distances reduces to the aggregation of pseudo-distances. Combining those results with the last one, the following characterizations are obtained for the nilpotent and the strict case, respectively:

Theorem 6. *An operator $F : [0,1]^n \to [0,1]$ aggregates n T_i-indistinguishability operators into a T-indistinguishability, with both T and T_i, $i = 1 \ldots n$, nilpotent continuous Archimedean t-norms if and only if*

$$F = \widehat{t}^{-1} \circ H \circ (\widehat{t_1} \times \ldots \times \widehat{t_n})$$

where $H : [0,1]^n \to [0,1]$ is an operator that aggregates pseudo-distances and $\widehat{t_i}, \widehat{t}$ are the normed additive generators of t-norms T_i and T, respectively.

Proof. From theorems 2 and 5 it follows that F is expressed as

$$1 - \widehat{s}^{-1} \circ H \circ (\widehat{s}_1 \times \ldots \times \widehat{s}_n) \circ (1 - Id \times \ldots \times 1 - Id)$$

where $\widehat{s}$ and $\widehat{s}_i$ are the normed additive generators of the dual t-conorms of T and T_i, respectively, and Id is the identity. On the other hand, it is well known that if a t-norm T and a t-conorm S are dual, then their additive generators verify $s \circ (1 - Id) = t$. ■

Theorem 7. *An operator $F : [0,1]^n \to [0,1]$ aggregates n T_i-indistinguishability operators into a T-indistinguishability, with both T and T_i, $i = 1 \ldots n$, strict continuous Archimedean t-norms if and only if*

$$F = t^{-1} \circ H \circ (t_1 \times \ldots \times t_n)$$

where $H : (\mathbb{R}^+)^n \to \mathbb{R}^+$ is an operator that aggregates pseudo-distances and t_i, t are additive generators of t-norms T_i and T, respectively.

Proof. The proof is similar to the former one, but now using theorems 3 and 5. ■

Remark Note that this last result could also have been obtained directly from the equivalence that holds between ordinary pseudo-distances and T-indistinguishabilities when considering continuous Archimedean t-norms (see [3]): *given a continuous Archimedean t-norm T with additive generator t, $I : X \times X \to [0,1]$ is a T-indistinguishability if and only if $t \circ I$ is a pseudo-distance.*

Some examples, which according to the results obtained are parallel to the ones given for the case of S-generalized distances, are the following:

Example 3. Aggregation of two indistinguishability operators defined with respect to the strict t-norm $Prod(x,y) = x.y$ into an operator of the same class ($T_1 = T_2 = T = Prod$).

- $F(x, y) = Min(x, y)$ when taking $H = Max$.
- $F(x, y) = x^{w_1} y^{w_2}$ when taking H as a weighted mean (a particular case, when choosing $w_1 = w_2 = 1/2$, is the geometric mean).

Example 4. Aggregation of two indistinguishability operators defined with respect to the nilpotent t-norm $W(x, y) = Max(x + y - 1, 0)$ into an operator of the same class ($T_1 = T_2 = T = W$).
Some possible choices are the weighted mean or the t-norms Min, *Prod,* and W.

4 Conclusions

This paper has studied the pointwise aggregation of both generalized distances and indistinguishability operators under a closure constraint. It gives some sufficient conditions to find operators that are able to aggregate pseudo-distances, and proves that, in the case of continuous Archimedean operators, the two mentioned general problems may be reduced to the aggregation of pseudo-distances.

Acknowledgments

This work has been partially supported by the Spanish CICYT under projects PB98-1379-C02-02 (MEC) and TIC00-1420. The authors also wish to thank Prof. Radko Mesiar (Slovak Technical University) for his valuable comments and suggestions.

References

1. J. Aczél. *Lectures on Functional Equations and their Applications.* Academic Press. New York. (1966).
2. C. Alsina and E. Trillas. "Synthesizing Implications". *International Journal of Intelligent Systems* 7 (1992) 705-713.
3. B. De Baets and R. Mesiar, "Pseudo-metrics and T-equivalences". *J. Fuzzy Math*, Vol. 5, No. 2 (1997) 471-481.
4. D. Dubois and H. Prade. "Aggregation of possibility measures", in *Multiperson Decision Making Using Fuzzy Sets and Possibility Theory,* J. Kacprzyk, M. Fedrizzi (eds), Kluwer Academic Publishers. (1990).
5. E. Klement, R. Mesiar and E. Pap. *Triangular Norms.* Kluwer Academic Publisher. (2000).
6. C.H. Ling. "Representation of Associative Functions". *Publ. Math. Debrecen* 12 (1965) 189-212.
7. B. Schweizer and A. Sklar. *Probabilistic Metric Spaces.* North-Holland (1983).
8. E. Trillas and C. Alsina. *Introducción a los espacios métricos generalizados.* Serie Universitaria 49, Fund. Juan March. (in Spanish). (1979).
9. E. Trillas. "Assaig sobre les relacions d'indistingibilitat". *Actes Congrés Català de Lògica,* (1981) 51-59 (in Catalan).

10. E. Trillas and L. Valverde. "An Inquiry into Indistinguishability Operators", in *Aspects of Vagueness (Eds. H. Skala, S. Termini and E. Trillas), Kluwer*, (1984) 231-256.

Ordinal Sums of Aggregation Operators *

Bernard De Baets[1] and Radko Mesiar[2,3]

[1] Department of Applied Mathematics, Biometrics and Process Control
Faculty of Agricultural and Applied Biological Sciences, Ghent University
Coupure links 653, B-9000 Gent, Belgium
Bernard.DeBaets@rug.ac.be

[2] Department of Mathematics
Faculty of Applied Sciences, Slovak Technical University
Radlinského 11, SK-81368 Bratislava, Slovakia
mesiar@vox.svf.stuba.sk

[3] Systems Research Institute
Polish Academy of Sciences
ul. Newelska 6, 01-447 Warsaw, Poland

Abstract. In this work, aggregation operators are to be understood in their most general sense, i.e. as families of operators, one for each arity. We characterize the smallest and greatest aggregation operators with a predefined behaviour in case all arguments are taken from the same interval (belonging to a system of pairwise disjoint open intervals). Similarly, we characterize the smallest and greatest idempotent aggregation operators with a predefined idempotent behaviour. Relationships with classical ordinal sum constructions are investigated.

1 Introduction

Ordinal sums of semigroups were introduced by Clifford [2] based on an idea of Climescu [3] as a method for constructing a new semigroup from a given system of semigroups indexed by a linearly ordered index set. In the study of t-norms and t-conorms, ordinal sums appeared in Ling's paper [9] for the representation of continuous t-norms (t-conorms) as ordinal sums with Archimedean summands. Jenei [6] recently demonstrated that this ordinal sum construction can be generalized using as summands so-called t-subnorms, still leading to a t-norm. A t-subnorm T only has to satisfy the condition $T \leq \min$, but does not necessarily have 1 as neutral element. In all of the above cases, an associative binary operation is constructed from a given system of associative binary operations.

In recent years, several methods for constructing new associative binary operations on the unit interval from given associative binary operations were proposed, all resembling, yet differing from the ordinal sum of t-norms. We

* This work has been supported in part by grants VEGA 1/7146/20 and 1/8331/01.

mention for instance the uninorms of Yager and Rybalov [4,12] and the nullnorms of Calvo *et al.* [1]. Again, the associativity of the resulting operations allows to consider two arguments only.

T-norms, t-conorms, uninorms, nullnorms and many other operations all belong to the general class of aggregation operators [8].

Definition 1. $A : \bigcup_{n\in\mathbb{N}} [0,1]^n \to [0,1]$ is called an aggregation operator if it satisfies:

(i) boundary conditions: $A(0,\ldots,0) = 0$ and $A(1,\ldots,1) = 1$;

(ii) monotonicity:

$$(x_1,\ldots,x_n) \leq (y_1,\ldots,y_n) \Longrightarrow A(x_1,\ldots,x_n) \leq A(y_1,\ldots,y_n).$$

(iii) identity: $(\forall x \in [0,1])(A(x) = x)$.

Note that the restriction of arguments and values to $[0,1]$ is a matter of scaling only!

All of the methods mentioned above construct a binary operation O on $[0,1]$ starting from some given binary operations O_j on subdomains D_j of $[0,1]$ such that the restriction of O to D_j^2 coincides with O_j. In other words, in the given subdomains the operation O has the prescribed behaviour. Inspired by the ordinal sum construction, it is our aim to develop some methods for constructing new aggregation operators from given ones. Because of the possible lack of associativity of the aggregation operators involved, we have to formulate these methods for general arguments $\mathbf{x} = (x_1,\ldots,x_n)$, $n \in \mathbb{N}$.

This chapter is organized as follows. In the next section, we briefly recall the classical ordinal sum construction and some recent related ones. In Section 3, we introduce lower (smallest) and upper (greatest) ordinal sum constructions for aggregation operators, illustrated by means of several examples. Idempotency preserving ordinal sum constructions are presented in Section 4 and are related to the classical ordinal sum construction. Finally, some conclusions are given.

2 Ordinal sums of associative operations

In this section, we recall the classical ordinal sum construction and relate it to some recently introduced constructions. For the sake of simplicity, we restrict ourselves to the case of one or two given operations. Of course, by induction we can easily generalize these constructions to any finite number of given operations, and following Clifford's approach, even more starting operations could be considered.

Definition 2. [11] An aggregation operator T is called a triangular norm (t-norm) if it is commutative, associative and has 1 as neutral element.

Recall that t-norms were originally defined as binary operations on the unit interval. However, due to their associativity, they can be uniquely extended to any arity n, i.e. to aggregation operators. In the case of associative aggregation operators, we will therefore make no distinction between the binary version and the whole operator.

Proposition 1. *Let T be a t-norm and $]a,b[$ be a subinterval of $[0,1]$ with $a < b$. Then the binary operation $T^* \equiv \langle a,b,T\rangle : [0,1]^2 \to [0,1]$ defined by*

$$T^*(x,y) = \begin{cases} a + (b-a)\,T\left(\dfrac{x-a}{b-a}, \dfrac{y-a}{b-a}\right) & , \text{ if } (x,y) \in [a,b]^2 \\ \min(x,y) & , \text{ elsewhere} \end{cases}$$

is also a t-norm.

The t-norm T^* is called an ordinal sum with summand T on the interval $[a,b]$. The proof of the above proposition is elementary and can be found (in a more general form) in any textbook devoted to t-norms, e.g. [7,10]. Similarly, we can define an ordinal sum $T^* \equiv (\langle a_k, b_k, T_k\rangle; k \in K)$ where the open intervals $]a_k, b_k[$ are pairwise disjoint subintervals of $[0,1]$. For instance, let $K = \{1,2\}$, then $T^*(x,y)$ equals

$$a_i + (b_i - a_i)\,T_i\left(\frac{x-a_i}{b_i-a_i}, \frac{y-a_i}{b_i-a_i}\right)$$

if $(x,y) \in [a_i,b_i]^2$ ($i \in \{1,2\}$), and

$$T^*(x,y) = \min(x,y)$$

elsewhere. Although the domains $[a_1,b_1]$ and $[a_2,b_2]$ may overlap (in case $b_1 = a_2$, for instance), the above definition is correct. Moreover, the n-ary extension of T^* can be written in terms of the n-ary extension of T in the following way. For any $\mathbf{x} = (x_1, \ldots, x_n)$, let

$$\mathbf{x}_i = \min(\mathbf{1}, \max(\mathbf{0}, \frac{\mathbf{x}-a_i}{b_i-a_i})) \ ,$$

then

$$T^*(\mathbf{x}) = a_i + (b_i - a_i)\,T(\mathbf{x}_i)$$

if $\min(x_1,\ldots,x_n) \in]a_i, b_i[$ ($i \in \{1,2\}$), and

$$T^*(\mathbf{x}) = \min(x_1,\ldots,x_n)$$

elsewhere.

Definition 3. [11] An aggregation operator S is called a triangular conorm (t-conorm) if it is commutative, associative and has 0 as neutral element.

Note that if S is a t-conorm, then its dual operator S^d defined by

$$S^d(x,y) = 1 - S(1-x, 1-y)$$

is a t-norm, and vice versa. Therefore, all results for t-conorms can be derived from the corresponding results for t-norms, and vice versa.

Proposition 2. *Let S be a t-conorm and $]a,b[$ be a subinterval of $[0,1]$, with $a < b$. Then the binary operation $S^* \equiv \langle a,b,S\rangle : [0,1]^2 \to [0,1]$ defined by*

$$S^*(x,y) = \begin{cases} a + (b-a)\, S\left(\dfrac{x-a}{b-a}, \dfrac{y-a}{b-a}\right) & , \textit{ if } (x,y) \in [a,b]^2 \\ \max(x,y) & , \textit{ elsewhere} \end{cases}$$

is also a t-conorm.

Triangular norms and conorms are special cases of the more general class of uninorms.

Definition 4. [12] An aggregation operator U is called a uninorm if it is commutative, associative and has a neutral element $e \in [0,1]$.

Obviously, the case $e = 0$ corresponds to the class of t-conorms, while the case $e = 1$ corresponds to the class of t-norms.

Proposition 3. [4] *Let T be a t-norm, S be a t-conorm and $e \in]0,1[$. Then the binary operations $U_* \equiv \langle T,S,e\rangle_* : [0,1]^2 \to [0,1]$ and $U^* \equiv \langle T,S,e\rangle^* : [0,1]^2 \to [0,1]$ defined by*

$$U_*(x,y) = \begin{cases} e\,T\left(\dfrac{x}{e}, \dfrac{y}{e}\right) & , \textit{ if } (x,y) \in [0,e]^2 \\ e + (1-e)\, S\left(\dfrac{x-e}{1-e}, \dfrac{y-e}{1-e}\right) & , \textit{ if } (x,y) \in [e,1]^2 \\ \min(x,y) & , \textit{ elsewhere} \end{cases},$$

and

$$U^*(x,y) = \begin{cases} e\,T\left(\dfrac{x}{e}, \dfrac{y}{e}\right) & , \textit{ if } (x,y) \in [0,e]^2 \\ e + (1-e)\, S\left(\dfrac{x-e}{1-e}, \dfrac{y-e}{1-e}\right) & , \textit{ if } (x,y) \in [e,1]^2 \\ \max(x,y) & , \textit{ elsewhere} \end{cases}$$

are uninorms with neutral element e.

Note that both U_* is the smallest uninorm that coincides on $[0,e]^2$ and $[e,1]^2$ with the ordinal sums $\langle 0,e,T\rangle$ and $\langle e,1,S\rangle$, respectively, while U^* is the greatest such uninorm.

Definition 5. [1] An aggregation operator V is called a nullnorm if it is commutative, associative, has an absorbing element $a \in [0,1]$ and satisfies the boundary conditions:

$$(\forall x \in [0,a])(V(x,0) = x) \quad \text{and} \quad (\forall x \in [a,1])(V(x,1) = x) \ .$$

Proposition 4. [1] *Let T be a t-norm, S be a t-conorm and $a \in]0,1[$. Then the binary operation $V \equiv \langle T,S,a\rangle : [0,1]^2 \to [0,1]$ defined by*

$$V(x,y) = \begin{cases} a\,S\left(\frac{x}{a},\frac{y}{a}\right) & , \ \text{if } (x,y) \in [0,a]^2 \\ a + (1-a)\,T\left(\frac{x-a}{1-a},\frac{y-a}{1-a}\right) & , \ \text{if } (x,y) \in [a,1]^2 \\ a & , \ \text{elsewhere} \end{cases}$$

is a nullnorm with absorbing element a.

The above proposition is not only a construction. It can also be turned into a characterization: any nullnorm with absorbing element $a \in]0,1[$ is of the above type. Similarly as in the case of uninorms expressed in Proposition 3, the nullnorm V in Proposition 4 coincides on $[0,a]^2$ and $[a,1]^2$ with the ordinal sums $(\langle 0,a,S\rangle)$ and $(\langle a,1,T\rangle)$, respectively. Moreover, it is clearly the only nullnorm that does so.

Note that all of the constructions presented in Propositions 1–4 are special cases of the ordinal sum construction introduced by Fuchs [5].

3 Upper and lower ordinal sums of aggregation operators

All of the constructions described in Section 2 start from the binary version of an associative aggregation operator A (resp. family of associative aggregation operators A_i) and a subinterval $]a,b[$ (resp. family of pairwise disjoint subintervals $]a_i,b_i[$) of the unit interval $[0,1]$. The aggregation operator A is first linearly transformed into some other associative binary operator B defined on $[a,b]$ by means of the transformation $B = \phi^{-1} \circ A \circ (\phi,\phi)$, with $\phi : [a,b] \to [0,1]$ defined by $\phi(x) = \frac{x-a}{b-a}$. We will conveniently denote B by $A_{[a,b]}$. Then the newly constructed aggregation operators coincide on the square $[a,b]^2$ (resp. squares $[a_i,b_i]^2$) with the operator $A_{[a,b]}$ (resp. the operators $A_{[a_i,b_i]}$).

In order to generalize these construction methods, we therefore have to figure out how the aggregation operator can be defined outside the square $[a,b]^2$ (resp. the squares $[a_i,b_i]^2$), and more generally, in case of absence of associativity, outside the hypercube $[a,b]^n$ (resp. hypercubes $[a_i,b_i]^n$). Next, we will use $\wedge$ as shorthand for min and $\vee$ as shorthand for max. The notation

$A_{[a,b]}$ denotes again the transformed aggregation operator, i.e.

$$A_{[a,b]}(\mathbf{x}) = a + (b-a)\, A\left(\frac{\mathbf{x}-a}{b-a}\right) ,$$

for any $\mathbf{x} = (x_1, \dots, x_n) \in [a,b]^n$, $n \in \mathbb{N}$.

Proposition 5. *Let A be an aggregation operator and $]a,b[$ be a subinterval of $[0,1]$. Then $A_* \equiv \langle a,b,A\rangle_*$ defined by*

$$A_*(x_1,\dots,x_n) = \begin{cases} 1 & , \text{ if } \min_{i=1}^{n} x_i = 1 \\ b & , \text{ if } b \le \min_{i=1}^{n} x_i \le 1 \\ A_{[a,b]}(b \wedge x_i, \dots, b \wedge x_n) & , \text{ if } a \le \min_{i=1}^{n} x_i < b \\ 0 & , \text{ elsewhere} \end{cases}$$

is the smallest aggregation operator that coincides with $A_{[a,b]}$ on $\bigcup_{n\in\mathbb{N}} [a,b]^n$, while $A^* \equiv \langle a,b,A\rangle^*$ defined by

$$A^*(x_1,\dots,x_n) = \begin{cases} 0 & , \text{ if } \max_{i=1}^{n} x_i = 0 \\ a & , \text{ if } 0 < \max_{i=1}^{n} x_i \le a \\ A_{[a,b]}(a \vee x_i, \dots, a \vee x_n) & , \text{ if } a < \max_{i=1}^{n} x_i \le b \\ 1 & , \text{ elsewhere} \end{cases}$$

is the greatest aggregation operator that coincides with $A_{[a,b]}$ on $\bigcup_{n\in\mathbb{N}} [a,b]^n$.

The aggregation operator A_* will be called a **lower ordinal sum** and the aggregation operator A^* will be called an **upper ordinal sum** with summand A on $[a,b]$. The proof of the above proposition is a simple consequence of the boundary conditions and the monotonicity of aggregation operators. We can easily extend this type of construction to an arbitrary (countable) family of aggregation operators and corresponding family of pairwise disjoint open subintervals of the $[0,1]$. For the sake of simplicity, we will deal with two summands only.

Proposition 6. *Let A_1 and A_2 be two aggregation operators and $0 \le a_1 < b_1 \le a_2 < b_2 \le 1$. Then the lower ordinal sum*

$$A_* \equiv (\langle a_1, b_1, A_1\rangle, \langle a_2, b_2, A_2\rangle)_*$$

defined by

$$A_*(\mathbf{x}) = \begin{cases} (A_i)_{[a_i,b_i]}(\min(b_i,\mathbf{x})) \ , & \textit{if } c(\mathbf{x}) = a_i \\ c(\mathbf{x}) & , \textit{elsewhere} \end{cases}$$

where

$$c(\mathbf{x}) = \max\{u \mid u \in \{0, a_1, b_1, a_2, b_2, 1\} \textit{ and } u \leq \min_{i=1}^{n} x_i\}$$

is the smallest aggregation operator that coincides with $(A_i)_{[a_i,b_i]}$ *on* $\bigcup_{n\in\mathbb{N}} [a_i, b_i]^n$ $(i \in \{1,2\})$, *and the upper ordinal sum*

$$A^* \equiv (\langle a_1, b_1, A_1\rangle, \langle a_2, b_2, A_2\rangle)^*$$

defined by

$$A^*(\mathbf{x}) = \begin{cases} (A_i)_{[a_i,b_i]}(\max(a_i,\mathbf{x})) \ , & \textit{if } d(\mathbf{x}) = b_i \\ d(\mathbf{x}) & , \textit{elsewhere} \end{cases}$$

where

$$d(\mathbf{x}) = \min\{u \mid u \in \{0, a_1, b_1, a_2, b_2, 1\} \textit{ and } u \geq \max_{i=1}^{n} x_i\}$$

is the greatest aggregation operator that coincides with $(A_i)_{[a_i,b_i]}$ *on* $\bigcup_{n\in\mathbb{N}} [a_i, b_i]^n$ $(i \in \{1,2\})$.

From the above proposition we can immediately derive the following result.

Corollary 1. *The lower ordinal sum* A_* *and upper ordinal sum* A^* *of two aggregation operators* A_1 *and* A_2 *coincide if and only if 1 is an absorbing element of* A_1, *0 is an absorbing element of* A_2 *and*

$$0 = a_1 < b_1 = a_2 < b_2 = 1.$$

Hence, under the conditions of Corollary 1 there exists a unique aggregation operator $A = A_* = A^*$ that coincides with $(A_i)_{[a_i,b_i]}$ on $[a_i, b_i]^n$, for any $n \in \mathbb{N}$ and $i \in \{1,2\}$.

The following observations are immediate:

(i) Let T be a t-norm, S be a t-conorm and $a \in]0,1[$. Then the lower ordinal sum

$$(\langle 0, a, S\rangle, \langle a, 1, T\rangle)_*$$

and upper ordinal sum

$$(\langle 0, a, S\rangle, \langle a, 1, T\rangle)^*$$

coincide with the *nullnorm* $\langle T, S, a\rangle$.

(ii) Let T_1 and T_2 be two t-norms and $a \in]0,1[$. Then the lower ordinal sum
$$(\langle 0, a, T_1\rangle, \langle a, 1, T_2\rangle)_*$$
coincides with the classical *ordinal sum of t-norms* $(\langle 0, a, T_1\rangle, \langle a, 1, T_2\rangle)$.

(iii) Let S_1 and S_2 be two t-conorms and $a \in]0,1[$. Then the upper ordinal sum
$$(\langle 0, a, S_1\rangle, \langle a, 1, S_2\rangle)^*$$
is just the classical *ordinal sum of t-conorms* $(\langle 0, a, S_1\rangle, \langle a, 1, S_2\rangle)$.

(iv) Let T be a t-norm, S be a t-conorm and $e \in]0,1[$. Then the lower ordinal sum
$$(\langle 0, e, T\rangle, \langle e, 1, S\rangle)_*$$
is just the *lower uninorm* $\langle T, S, e\rangle_*$ and the upper ordinal sum
$$(\langle 0, e, T\rangle, \langle e, 1, S\rangle)^*$$
is just the *upper uninorm* $\langle T, S, e\rangle^*$.

Note that for any idempotent increasing binary operator $C : [0,1]^2 \to [0,1]$, the aggregation operator $A = C(A_*, A^*)$ also coincides with $(A_i)_{[a_i,b_i]}$ on $\bigcup_{n\in\mathbb{N}} [a_i, b_i]^n$ $(i \in \{1,2\})$. In fact, this is true for any aggregation operator B that satisfies $A_* \leq B \leq A^*$.

4 Preserving idempotency

In general, lower and upper ordinal sums of idempotent aggregation operators are not necessarily idempotent. However, in many applications the idempotency of aggregation operators is regarded as a fundamental property. Moreover, in general, lower (resp. upper) ordinal sums of t-norms (resp. t-conorms) do not coincide with the classical ordinal sum definition.

For these reasons, we will propose yet another method for constructing new aggregation operators from given ones. As these methods are designed to preserve idempotency, we will use the terminology idempotent lower (id-lower for short) ordinal sum and idempotent upper (id-upper for short) ordinal sum.

Proposition 7. *Let A_1 and A_2 be two aggregation operators and $0 \leq a_1 < b_1 \leq a_2 < b_2 \leq 1$. Then the* **id-lower ordinal sum**
$$A_{**} \equiv (\langle a_1, b_1, A_1\rangle, \langle a_2, b_2, A_2\rangle)_{**}$$
defined by
$$A_{**}(\mathbf{x}) = \begin{cases} (A_i)_{[a_i,b_i]}(\min(b_i, \mathbf{x})) \ , & \textit{if } c(\mathbf{x}) = a_i \\ \min\limits_{i=1}^{n} x_i & , \textit{elsewhere} \end{cases}$$

where

$$c(\mathbf{x}) = \max\{u \mid u \in \{0, a_1, b_1, a_2, b_2, 1\} \text{ and } u \leq \min_{i=1}^{n} x_i\}$$

and the **id-upper ordinal sum**

$$A^{**} \equiv (\langle a_1, b_1, A_1 \rangle, \langle a_2, b_2, A_2 \rangle^{**}$$

defined by

$$A^{**}(\mathbf{x}) = \begin{cases} (A_i)_{[a_i,b_i]}(\max(a_i, \mathbf{x})) & , \text{ if } d(\mathbf{x}) = b_i \\ \max_{i=1}^{n} x_i & , \text{ elsewhere} \end{cases}$$

where

$$d(\mathbf{x}) = \min\{u \mid u \in \{0, a_1, b_1, a_2, b_2, 1\} \text{ and } u \geq \max_{i=1}^{n} x_i\}$$

are aggregation operators that coincide with $(A_i)_{[a_i,b_i]}$ *on* $\bigcup_{n \in \mathbb{N}} [a_i, b_i]^n$ $(i \in \{1, 2\})$*, and satisfy*

$$A_* \leq A_{**} \leq A^{**} \leq A^* \ .$$

Moreover, if A_1 *and* A_2 *are idempotent, then* A_{**} *and* A^{**} *are the smallest and greatest idempotent aggregation operators in between* A_* *and* A^**.*

The proof again follows directly from the monotonicity of aggregation operators. It is straightforward that $A_* = A_{**}$ and $A^* = A^{**}$ if and only if $0 = a_1 < b_1 = a_2 < b_2 = 1$. Also the following observations are immediate:

(i) Let T_1 and T_2 be two t-norms and $0 \leq a_1 < b_1 \leq a_2 < b_2 \leq 1$. Then the id-lower ordinal sum

$$(\langle a_1, b_1, T_1 \rangle, \langle a_2, b_2, T_2 \rangle)_{**}$$

coincides with the classical *ordinal sum of t-norms* $(\langle a_1, b_1, T_1 \rangle, \langle a_2, b_2, T_2 \rangle)$.

(ii) Let S_1 and S_2 be two t-conorms and $0 \leq a_1 < b_1 \leq a_2 < b_2 \leq 1$. Then the id-upper ordinal sum

$$(\langle a_1, b_1, S_1 \rangle, \langle a_2, b_2, S_2 \rangle)^{**}$$

is just the classical *ordinal sum of t-conorms* $(\langle a_1, b_1, S_1 \rangle, \langle a_2, b_2, S_2 \rangle)$.

Note that for any idempotent increasing binary operator $C : [0,1]^2 \to [0,1]$, the aggregation operator $A = C(A_{**}, A^{**})$ defined from two idempotent aggregation operators A_1 and A_2 is idempotent and coincides with $(A_i)_{[a_i,b_i]}$ on $\bigcup_{n \in \mathbb{N}} [a_i, b_i]^n$ $(i \in \{1, 2\})$. In fact, this is true for any aggregation operator B that satisfies $A_{**} \leq B \leq A^{**}$.

Example 1. Let $(U_1)^*$ and $(U_2)_*$ be an upper and lower uninorm and $a \in]0, 1[$. Then Corollary 1 can be applied and the unique ordinal sum

$$A^* = A^{**} = A_* = A_{**} \equiv (\langle 0, a, (U_1)^* \rangle, \langle a, 1, (U_2)_* \rangle)$$

is an associative aggregation operator with absorbing element a.

Example 2.

(i) Let T_1 and T_2 be two t-norms and $a \in]0,1[$. Then the upper ordinal sum

$$A^* = A^{**} \equiv (\langle 0, a, T_1 \rangle, \langle a, 1, T_2 \rangle)^*$$

is a non-associative aggregation operator such that $A^*(\mathbf{x}) = a$ whenever

$$\min_{i=1}^{n} x_i \leq a < \max_{i=1}^{n} x_i \quad \text{or} \quad x = \mathbf{a}.$$

(ii) Let S_1 and S_2 be two t-conorms and $a \in]0,1[$. Then the lower ordinal sum

$$B_* = B_{**} \equiv (\langle 0, a, S_1 \rangle, \langle a, 1, S_2 \rangle)_*$$

is a non-associative aggregation operator such that $B_*(\mathbf{x}) = a$ whenever

$$\min_{i=1}^{n} x_i < a \leq \max_{i=1}^{n} x_i \quad \text{or} \quad x = \mathbf{a}.$$

5 Conclusion

We have introduced ordinal-sum like methods for constructing the smallest and greatest aggregation operator having a predefined behaviour in some given subhypercubes of the unit hypercube. In case the predefined behaviour is idempotent, these constructions can be adjusted to obtain the smallest and greatest idempotent aggregation operator having that behaviour.

References

1. T. Calvo, B. De Baets and J. Fodor, *The functional equations of Frank and Alsina for uninorms and nullnorms*, Fuzzy Sets and Systems **120** (2001), 385–394.
2. A. Clifford, *Naturally totally ordered commutative semigroups*, Amer. J. Math. **76** (1954), 631–646.
3. A. Climescu, *Sur l'équation fonctionelle de l'associativité*, Bull. École Polytech. Jassy **1** (1946), 211–224.
4. J. Fodor, R. Yager and A. Rybalov, *Structure of uninorms*, Internat. J. Uncertain. Fuzziness Knowledge-Based Systems **5** (1997), 411–427.
5. L. Fuchs, *Partially Ordered Algebraic Systems*, Pergamon Press, Oxford, 1963.
6. S. Jenei, *Generalized ordinal sum theorem and its consequence to the construction of triangular norms*, BUSEFAL **80**, pp. 52–56.
7. E.-P. Klement, R. Mesiar and E. Pap, *Triangular Norms*, Kluwer Academic Publishers, 2000.
8. A. Kolesárová and M. Komorníkova, *Triangular norm-based iterative compensatory operators*, Fuzzy Sets and Systems **104** (1999), 109–120,
9. C. Ling, *Representation of associative functions*, Publ. Math. Debrecen **12** (1965), 189–212.

10. H.T. Nguyen and E. Walker, *A First Course in Fuzzy Logic*, CRC Press, Boca Raton, 1997.
11. B. Schweizer and A. Sklar, *Statistical metric spaces*, Pacific J. Math **10** (1960), 313–334.
12. R. Yager and A. Rybalov, *Uninorm aggregation operators*, Fuzzy Sets and Systems **80** (1996), 111–120.

Aggregation Principle in the Theory of Nonlinear PDE

Endre Pap[1] and Doretta Vivona[2]

[1] Institute of Mathematics, University of Novi Sad, 21000 Novi Sad, Yugoslavia, e-mail: pap@unsim.ns.ac.yu , pape@eunet.yu
[2] Dipartimento di Metodi e Modelli Matematici per le Scienze Applicate, Universita' "La Sapienza", Via A. Scarpa 10, 00161 Roma, Italy, e-mail: vivona@dmmm.uniroma1.it

Abstract. It is considered a pair of generalized aggregation operators connected by distributive law. It is given a complete characterization of such pairs of operations. The obtained results are applied on nonlinear PDE.

Keywords: pseudo-analysis, nonlinear superposition principle, aggregation operator, PDE.

1 Introduction

Aggregation operators occur in many different fields and their theory and further applications are very actual. We shall consider a pair of generalized aggregation operators called generalized pseudo-addition and generalized pseudo-multiplication connected by distributive law. We apply the obtained results on nonlinear PDE.

It is well-known that the structure of the vector space on the field of real numbers has the origin from the linear superposition principle which is the basic tool for solving linear equations (ODE, PDE - [20], difference equations, etc.). Namely, if u_1 and u_2 are solutions of the considered equation, also $a_1u_1 + a_2u_2$ is a solution for any constants a_1 and a_2. Then the vector space structure allows to develop different methods for solving problems with considered linear equations.

Instead of the field of real numbers in [3,4,13,14,16] it is taken a semiring on the real interval $[a, b] \subset [-\infty, +\infty]$, denoting the corresponding operations as $\oplus$ (pseudo-addition) and $\odot$ (pseudo-multiplication). This structure is applied for solving nonlinear equations (ODE, PDE, difference equations, etc.) using now the pseudo-linear principle ([13–16]), which means that if u_1 and u_2 are solutions of the considered nonlinear equation, then also $(a_1 \odot u_1) \oplus (a_2 \odot u_2)$ is a solution for any constants a_1 and a_2 from $[a, b]$. Based on semiring structure it is developed in [13,14,17–19] the so called pseudo-analysis in an analogous way as classical analysis, introducing $\oplus$-measure, pseudo-integral, pseudo-convolution, pseudo-Laplace transform, etc. Pseudo-analysis was applied for finding weak solutions of Hamilton-Jacobi equation with non-smooth Hamiltonian, [13,17,18].

Jones and Ames [11] have considered a nonlinear superposition principle (NLSP) as a powerful ad hoc technique for finding new solutions of ordinary and partial differential equations, see [2,8]. Namely, they considered an operation $\star$ such that if u_1 and u_2 are solutions of the considered nonlinear equation, then also $u_1 \star u_2$ is a solution of this equation. It was proven by Inselberg [10], Levin [12] and Goard and Broadbridge [8] that the operation $\star$ maybe also noncommutative. This motivated us to develop a further generalization of the real semiring structure to the case when the operations $\oplus$ and $\odot$ are noncommutative and non-associative, and the (left) right distributivity of $\odot$ over $\oplus$ plays a crucial rule.

We give in section 2 a representation theorem- Theorem 1 for such operations and in Theorem 3 and 2 we give a complete characterization for generalized pseudo-addition and pseudo-multiplication. The approach is based on the functional equation technique, given in [1]. More details can be found in [21].

The main problem in the application on nonlinear PDE is the identification of operations $\oplus$ and $\odot$. Goard and Broadbridge [8] have obtained a close connection of NLSP and Lie symmetry algebras [5]. Namely, there are a number of computer added algorithms for finding Lie symmetry algebra [22] and therefore this relation can be used for finding $\oplus$ and $\odot$. With the help of this approach we apply in section 3 the generalized pseudo-analysis on some important nonlinear PDE.

2 A pair of aggregation operators

Definition 1. We call real operations $\oplus$ and $\odot$ generalized pseudo-addition and generalized pseudo-multiplication (from the right), respectively, if they satisfy the following conditions:

(i) $\oplus$ and $\odot$ are functions from $C^2(\mathbb{R}^2)$,
(ii) the equation $t \oplus t = z$ for given z is uniquely solvable,
(iii) $\odot$ is right distributive over $\oplus$:

$$(D_r) \quad (x \oplus y) \odot z = (x \odot z) \oplus (y \odot z).$$

Changing in the previous definition in (iii) that $\odot$ is left distributive over $\oplus$:

$$(D_l) \quad z \odot (x \oplus y) = (z \odot x) \oplus (z \odot y),$$

we obtain generalized pseudo-addition and generalized pseudo-multiplication (from the left), respectively. Since all considerations are analogous we shall take in the future considerations only on the right case.

We shall give a representation theorem for generalized pseudo-addition and generalized pseudo-multiplication. For that purpose first we shall prove several lemmas. First of all for a function of two real variables $u = u(x,y)$ we shall use the following notations

$$(u)_1 = \frac{\partial u}{\partial x} = u_x, \quad (u)_2 = \frac{\partial u}{\partial y} = u_y, \quad (u)_{12} = \frac{\partial^2 u}{\partial x \partial y} = u_{xy}.$$

By [21] we have the following representation theorem.

Theorem 1. *Two real operations $\oplus$ and $\odot$ from $C^2(\mathbb{R}^2)$ with $(x \odot y)_1 \neq 0$ for all x, y, are generalized pseudo-addition and pseudo-multiplication (from the right), respectively, if and only if they are representable by*

$$u \odot z = h^{-1}(f(z)h(u) + \alpha(z)), \tag{1}$$

and

$$x \oplus y = h^{-1}((h(x) \boxplus h(y)), \tag{2}$$

where f and α are arbitrary functions from $C^2(\mathbb{R})$, the function h is given by

$$h(u) = \int_\gamma^u \left(e^{-\frac{1}{a}\int_\beta^s (t \oplus' t)_{12}\, dt}\right) ds,$$

the operation $\oplus'$ is given by $x \oplus' y = \varphi^{-1}(x \oplus y)$, where φ is defined by $\varphi(x) = x \oplus x$ and $\boxplus$ satisfies the functional equation

$$(u \boxplus v)f(z) + \alpha(z) = (uf(z) + \alpha(z)) \boxplus (vf(z) + \alpha(z)).$$

Theorem 2. *If $\oplus$ and $\odot$ are generalized pseudo-addition and pseudo-multiplication (from the right), respectively, and additionally that*

(a) $x \odot 0 = a$ (constant) for every x;
(b) there exists y_0 such that $(x \odot y_0)_1 \neq 0$;

then we have

$$x \oplus y = h^{-1}(h(x) + h(y)), \quad x \odot y = h^{-1}(f(y)h(x)), \tag{3}$$

where (for γ, β arbitrary non-zero constants)

$$h(x) = (\gamma \oplus \beta)_2 \int \frac{(x \oplus \beta)_1}{(x \oplus \beta)_2}\, dx, \tag{4}$$

and f is an arbitrary function from $C^2(\mathbb{R})$ and $f(0) = 0$.

Remark 1. (i) Theorem 2 holds also for $\oplus, \odot \in C^1$, then also $f \in C^1$.
(ii) As a consequence of Theorem 2 we obtain that $\oplus$ is also commutative and associative. Specially, for $f = h$ we obtain the g-calculus, see [14,15].

Definition 2. For given generalized pseudo-addition $\oplus$ and generalized pseudo-multiplication $\odot$ (from the right) we shall call any function h from Theorem 1 in (1) and (2) and Theorem 2 in (3) and (4) a generator of operations $\oplus$ and $\odot$.

Now we can give a complete characterization of generalized pseudo-addition and pseudo-multiplication

Theorem 3. *Let $\oplus$ and $\odot$ be generalized pseudo-addition and pseudo-multiplication, respectively, with $(x \odot y)_1 \neq 0$ for all x, y.*

Then they can be represented in one of the following forms

$$\text{(i)} \qquad x \oplus y = h^{-1}(h(y) + \psi(h(x) - h(y))), \quad x \odot y = h^{-1}(h(x) + \alpha(y));$$

$$\text{(ii)} \qquad x \oplus y = h^{-1}(h(y) + \psi(h(x) - h(y))), \quad x \odot y = h^{-1}(\alpha(y) - h(x)),$$

with ψ odd function;

$$\text{(iii)} \qquad x \oplus y = h^{-1}(h(y) + a(h(x) - h(y))), \quad x \odot y = h^{-1}(h(x)f(y) + \alpha(y)),$$

where $\psi(t) = t \boxplus 0, a$ is a constant and $\boxplus, \alpha, f, h$ are functions from Theorem 1.

3 Applications on nonlinear PDE

3.1 First order equations

We shall consider the following nonlinear PDE of the first order, see [8],

$$c_1(x,y)u_x + c_2(x,y)u_y = g(u), \tag{5}$$

where c_1, c_2 and g are given functions. Taking

$$h(u) = \int \frac{dt}{g(t)}$$

we introduce using (i) from Theorem 3 generalized pseudo-addition $\oplus$ and pseudo-multiplication $\odot$ (from the left) for arbitrary ε

$$u \oplus v = h^{-1}(h(v) + \psi_\varepsilon(h(u) - h(v))), \quad u \odot v = h^{-1}(h(v) + \alpha(u)),$$

respectively, for an arbitrary function α, and $\psi_\varepsilon(x) = G^{-1}(\varepsilon + G(x))$ for arbitrary function G from C^1. Then by [8] we have that if u_1 and u_2 are solutions of equation (5) then also for every ε

$$u_1 \oplus u_2 = h^{-1}(h(u_2) + \psi_\varepsilon(h(u_1) - h(u_2)))$$

is a solution of the equation (5).

For arbitrary but fixed real number a and a solution u of the equation (5) we have that also for every function α

$$a \odot u = h^{-1}(h(u) + \alpha(a))$$

is a solution of the equation (5). Namely, putting $u \odot a$ in (5) we obtain

$$c_1(x,y)(h^{-1}(h(u)+\alpha(a)))_x + c_2(x,y)(h^{-1}(h(u)+\alpha(a)))_y = \frac{1}{(h^{-1}(h(u)+\alpha(a)))},$$

where we have used that $g(u \odot a) = 1/h'(u \odot a)$, and h' is the derivative of h. Hence

$$\frac{c_1(x,y)h'(u)u_x}{h'((h^{-1}(h(u)+\alpha(a))} + \frac{c_2(x,y)h'(u)u_y}{h'((h^{-1}(h(u)+\alpha(a))}$$
$$= \frac{1}{h'(h^{-1}(h(u)+\alpha(a)))}.$$

Since $h'(u) \neq 0$ canceling $h'((h^{-1}(h(u)+\alpha(a))$ and by $h'(u) = 1/g(u)$ we obtain

$$\frac{c_1(x,y)}{g(u)}u_x + \frac{c_2(x,y)}{g(u)}u_y = 1.$$

Summarizing, we have that if u_1 and u_2 are solutions of equation (5) and a_1 and a_2 arbitrary but fixed real numbers, then also for every ε and every α

$$(a_1 \odot u_1) \oplus (a_2 \odot u_2)$$

is a solution of the equation (5).

Taking specially $c_1(x,y) = c_2(x,y) = 1$ and $g(u) = u^2$ we obtain the equation

$$u_x + u_y = u^2.$$

Then we have $h(u) = -1/u$. In this case we have for the operations $\oplus$ and $\odot$

$$u \oplus v = \frac{1}{\frac{1}{v} - \psi\left(\frac{1}{v} - \frac{1}{u}\right)}, \qquad u \odot v = \frac{1}{\frac{1}{v} - \alpha(u)},$$

where $\psi(t) = -\ln(e^t + 1)$, by [8], the same statement as for the general case.

3.2 Multi-dimensional aggregation of solutions

We can consider the extension to n-dimensional case of the equation (5) for $g \neq 0$

$$\sum_{i=1}^{n} c_i(x_1,\ldots,x_n)\frac{\partial u}{\partial x_i} = g(u) \tag{6}$$

considering the m-dimensional pseudo-superposition principle. We have that if $u_1, \ldots, u_m$ are solutions of the equation (6) then also the generalized geometric mean of solutions

$$G(u_1, \ldots, u_m) = f^{-1}(f(u_1)^{a_1} \cdots f(u_m)^{a_m})$$

and the generalized arithmetic mean of solutions

$$A(u_1, \ldots, u_n) = \left(f^{-1}(a_1 f(u_1)^p + \cdots + a_m f(u_m)^p)\right)^{1/p},$$

where $f(x) = \exp\left(\int_\beta^x dt/g(t)\right)$, $a_i \geq 0$ $(i = 1, \ldots, m)$ and $a_1 + \cdots + a_m = 1$, and $p \geq 0$, are solutions of the equation (6).

3.3 Second order equations

We shall need the following special class of operations $\oplus$ and $\odot$.

Theorem 4. *Let ε be an arbitrary but fixed positive real number. If k is a strictly monotone positive function and belongs to C^2, then operations defined by*

$$x \oplus y = k^{-1}(\varepsilon k(x) + k(y)), \quad x \odot y = k^{-1}(k(x)^\varepsilon k(y))$$

are generalized pseudo-addition and pseudo-multiplication (from the left), respectively, which belong to the class (i) in Theorem 3 (introducing an operation $\odot'$ by $x \odot' y = y \odot x$).

Proof. By supposition on k and definition of $\oplus$ and $\odot$ it follows that $\oplus$ and $\odot$ belong to C^2.

We shall show that the equation $t \oplus t = z$ for given z is solvable. Namely, we have

$$t \oplus t = k^{-1}(\varepsilon k(t) + k(t)) = z.$$

Hence

$$\varepsilon k(t) + k(t) = k(z).$$

Therefore we have

$$k(t) = \frac{k(z)}{\varepsilon + 1},$$

which gives us the solution

$$t = k^{-1}\left(\frac{k(z)}{\varepsilon + 1}\right).$$

We shall prove that $\odot$ is left distributive over $\oplus$. Namely, we have

$$\begin{aligned} x \odot (y \oplus z) &= k^{-1}(k(x)^\varepsilon k(y \oplus z)) \\ &= k^{-1}(k(x)^\varepsilon k(k^{-1}(\varepsilon k(y) + k(z)))) \end{aligned}$$

$$
\begin{aligned}
&= k^{-1}(\varepsilon k(x)^{\varepsilon} k(y) + k(x)^{\varepsilon} k(z)) \\
&= k^{-1}((\varepsilon k(k^{-1}(k(x)^{\varepsilon} k(y))) \\
&+ k(k^{-1}(k(x)^{\varepsilon} k(z)))) \\
&= k^{-1}(\varepsilon k(x \odot y) + k(x \odot z)) \\
&= (x \odot y) \oplus (x \odot z).
\end{aligned}
$$

We shall prove now that $\oplus$ and $\odot$ belong to the class (i) in Theorem 3. We take $h(x) = \ln k(x)$, which implies $h^{-1}(x) = k^{-1}(e^{k(x)})$ and $\alpha(x) = \varepsilon \ln k(x)$. So we have

$$
\begin{aligned}
x \oplus y &= k^{-1}(\varepsilon k(x) + k(y)) \\
&= h^{-1} \ln(\varepsilon e^{h(x)} + e^{h(y)}) \\
&= h^{-1} \ln(\varepsilon e^{h(x)} e^{h(y)} e^{-h(y)} + e^{h(y)}) \\
&= h^{-1} \ln(e^{h(y)}(\varepsilon e^{h(x)-h(y)} + 1) \\
&= h^{-1}(h(y) + \ln(\varepsilon e^{h(x)-h(y)} + 1)) \\
&= h^{-1}(h(y) + \psi(h(y) - h(x))),
\end{aligned}
$$

where $\psi(t) = \ln(\varepsilon e^{-t} + 1)$.

For $\odot$ we have

$$
\begin{aligned}
x \odot y &= k^{-1}(k(x)^{\varepsilon} k(y)) \\
&= k^{-1}(e^{\varepsilon \ln k(x) + \ln k(y)}) \\
&= h^{-1}(h(y) + \alpha(x)),
\end{aligned}
$$

where $\alpha(x) = \varepsilon \ln k(x)$. □

Remark 2. Specially for $\varepsilon = 1$ we obtain a semiring which is based on a generator (g-calculus [14,15]).

Example 1. Burgers [6], Hopf [9] and Cole [7] (see also [2]) investigated as a model of turbulence the following equation

$$
v_y + v v_x = \lambda v_{xx}, \tag{7}
$$

where λ is a parameter. Putting $v = u_x$ in (7) and integrating with respect to x we obtain the equation

$$
u_y + \frac{1}{2} u_x^2 = \lambda u_{xx}, \tag{8}
$$

which models the burning of a gas in a rocket, see [2]. We introduce generalized pseudo-addition and generalized pseudo-multiplication (from the left) from Theorem 4 given by

$$
u \oplus v = k^{-1}(\varepsilon k(u) + k(v)), \quad u \odot v = k^{-1}(k(u)^{\varepsilon} k(v)),
$$

respectively, for special $k(u) = e^{-\frac{u}{2\lambda}}$. Then by [8] we have that if u_1 and u_2 are solutions of the equation (8) then also for every $\varepsilon > 0$

$$u_1 \oplus u_2 = -2\lambda \ln\left(\varepsilon e^{-\frac{u_1}{2\lambda}} + e^{-\frac{u_2}{2\lambda}}\right)$$

is a solution of the equation (8).

For arbitrary but fixed real number a and a solution u of the equation (8) we have that also for every ε

$$\begin{aligned} a \odot u &= -2\lambda \ln\left(e^{-\frac{\varepsilon a}{2\lambda}} e^{-\frac{u}{2\lambda}}\right) \\ &= \varepsilon a + u \end{aligned}$$

is a solution of the equation (8). Summarizing we have that if u_1 and u_2 are solutions of equation (8) and a_1 and a_2 arbitrary but fixed real numbers, then also for every $\varepsilon > 0$

$$(a_1 \odot u_1) \oplus (a_2 \odot u_2)$$

is a solution of the equation (8).

We note that if u is a solution and a is an arbitrary real number then $u \odot a$ is a solution of the equation (8) if and only if $\varepsilon = 1$, which gives us the g-calculus.

Example 2. We consider the following PDE of the second order

$$\sum_{i=1}^{n}\sum_{j=1}^{n} a_{ij}(x_1, \ldots, x_n) u_{x_i x_j} + \sum_{i=1}^{n} b_k(x_1, \ldots, x_n) u_{x_k} + c(x_1, \ldots, x_n) u$$

$$= \frac{\lambda}{u} \sum_{i=1}^{n}\sum_{j=1}^{n} a_{ij}(x_1, \ldots, x_n) u_{x_i} u_{x_j}, \tag{9}$$

where a_{ij}, b_k, c are given functions and λ is a constant different from 1. Taking $k(x) = x^{1-\lambda}$ for $x > 0$ and $\lambda \neq 1$ we consider generalized pseudo-addition and pseudo-multiplication (from the left) from Theorem 4

$$u \oplus v = (\varepsilon u^{1-\lambda} + v^{1-\lambda})^{1/(1-\lambda)}, \quad u \odot v = u^{\varepsilon} v,$$

respectively.

If u_1 and u_2 are positive solutions of equation (9) then also for every $\varepsilon > 0$

$$u_1 \oplus u_2 = k^{-1}(\varepsilon k(u_1) + k(u_2)))$$

is a positive solution of the equation (9).

For arbitrary but fixed positive real number a and a solution u of the equation (9) we have that

$$a \odot u = a^{\varepsilon} u$$

is a positive solution of the equation (9). Taking $a \odot (u_1 \oplus u_2)$ with $a = |\beta_0\beta_2|^{1/\varepsilon}$ and $\varepsilon = \frac{|\beta_1|}{|\beta_2|}$ we obtain Levin's result [12].

We note that if u is a solution and a is an arbitrary positive real number then $u \odot a$ is a solution of the equation (9) if and only if $\varepsilon = 1$, which gives us the g-calculus.

Acknowledgment. This paper was written during the visit of the first author at the University "La Sapienza", Rome, and it was supported by University "La Sapienza".

Research of the second author is partially supported by GNFM and MURST.

References

1. J. Aczél, Lectures on Functional Equations and their Applications, Academic Press, New York, 1966.
2. W. F. Ames, Ad hoc Exact techniques for Nonlinear Partial Differential Equations, "Nonlinear Partial Differential Equations in Engineering", Academic Press, New York, 1965.
3. F. Baccelli, G. Cohen, G.J. Olsder and Quadrat, Synchronization and Linearity: an Algebra for Discrete Event Systems, John-Wiley and Sons, New York, 1992.
4. P. Benvenuti and R. Mesiar, Pseudo-arithmetical operations as a basic for the general measure and integration theory, Information Sci. (to appear).
5. G. W. Blumen and S. Kumei, Symmetries and differential equations, Springer-Verlag, New York, 1989.
6. J. M. Burgers, A mathematical model illustring the theory of tubulence, Advan. Appl. Mech. **1** (1948), 171.
7. J. D. Cole, On a qusi-linear parabolic equation occuring in aerodynamics, Quaterly of Applied Mathematics **9** (1951), 225-236.
8. J. M. Goard and P. Broadbridge, Nonlinear Superposition Principles Obtained Lie Symmetry Methods, J. Math. Anal. Appl. **214** (1997), 633-657.
9. E. Hopf, The Partial Differential Equation $u_t + uu_x = \mu u_{xx}$, Commun. Pure Appl. Math. bf 9 (1950), 201-230.
10. A. Inselberg, Noncommutative Superpositions for Nonlinear Operators. J. Math. Anal. Appl. **29** (1970), 294-298.
11. S. E. Jones and W. F. Ames, Nonlinear Superposition, J. Math. Anal. Appl. **17** (1967), 484-487.
12. S.A. Levin, Principles of nonlinear superposition, J. Math. Anal. Appl. **30** (1970), 197-205.
13. V.P. Maslov and S.N. Samborskij, Idempotent Analysis, AMS, Providence, 1992.
14. E.Pap, Null-Additive Set Functions, Kluwer Academic Publishers, Dordrecht-Boston-London, 1995.
15. E. Pap, Decomposable measures and nonlinear equations, Fuzzy Sets and Systems **92** (1997) 205-222.
16. E. Pap, Solving nonlinear equations by non-additive measures, Nonlinear Analysis **30** (1997), 31-40.

17. E. Pap, Applications of decomposable measures, in Handbook Mathematics of Fuzzy Sets-Logic, Topology and Measure Theory (Eds. U. Höhle, S.R. Rodabaugh), Kluwer Academic Publishers, 675-700, 1999.
18. E. Pap and N. Ralević, Pseudo-Laplace Transform, Nonlinear Analysis **33** (1998), 533-550.
19. E. Pap and I. Štajner, Generalized pseudo-convolution in the theory of probabilistic metric spaces, information, fuzzy numbers, optimization, system theory, Fuzzy Sets and Systems **102** (1999), 393-415.
20. E. Pap, Dj. Takači and A. Takači, Partial Differential Equations through Examples and Exercises, Kluwer Academic Publishers, Dordrecht, 1997.
21. E. Pap, D. Vivona, Non-commutative and non-associative pseudo-analysis and its applications on nonlinear partial differential equations, J. Math. Anal. Appl. **246** (2000), 390-408.
22. F. Schwarz, Symmetries of differential equations: from Sophus Lie to computer algebra, SIAM Rev. **30** (1988), 450-481.

Approximation of Membership Functions and Aggregation Operators Using Splines

Gleb Beliakov
School of Computing and Mathematics, Deakin University,
Rusden campus, 662 Blackburn Rd., Clayton 3168, Australia
gleb@deakin.edu.au

Abstract

A good choice of membership functions and aggregation operators is crucial to the behavior fuzzy systems. In many cases there are no theoretical criteria that would justify the use of one or another function, and they are selected based on their goodness of fit to empirical data. This paper discusses a general non-parametric approach to construction of membership functions and aggregation operators based on empirical data. This method is computer oriented: it does not produce operators in closed algebraic form, but the quality of fit and flexibility are superior to other methods. The method is also general, since it can produce membership functions and operators from any class. Restrictions to a particular class can be easily introduced. Examples based on published empirical data are provided.

1 Introduction

In the development of fuzzy systems, one frequently faces the problem of the adequate choice of membership functions and aggregation operators. It is customary (e.g. in fuzzy control) to use triangular or trapezoidal membership functions, and *min*, *max* or product operators for operations on fuzzy sets. These choices are based mostly on the algebraic simplicity of these functions. Fine tuning allows one to adjust some parameters and to obtain the system whose behaviour is close to that of human experts.

Fine tuning is generally *ad hoc* process which relies on the developer's guess and past experience. It does not compromise the overall comprehensibility of the system (it does not change the rule base) but adjusts the form of membership functions and methods of aggregation, so that the system provides the desired output.

Several attempts have been made to develop methods of selecting membership functions and aggregation operators in an objective way. A range of methods for construction of membership functions relies on approximation of experimental data [2,8,20,24,30,31]. Similarly, aggregation operators can also be approximated based on experimental data - experts' estimates of the membership values in the composed set and in the sets-components. This is usually done using linear [30], but mostly non-linear [14,17] regression. The algebraic form of aggregation operator is fixed, and several parameters are fitted to the data. This process depends very much on the operators being used (compensatory operators, generalised means, ordered weighted aggregation, triangular norms), and unfortunately none of the existing methods is general.

The major problem in fixing the algebraic form of membership functions and aggregation operators is that there are no strong theoretical criteria for choosing this form. The semantics of the problem does not translate into any particular algebraic formula, but determines a rather general class of functions (continuous, unimodal; commutative, associative, etc.). On the other hand, notorious difficulties in non-linear regression force one to select the simplest functions of a given class, which may not actually be the best.

This paper develops an alternative, purely data driven way of representing membership functions and aggregation operators based on non-parametric techniques[1]. This method is general: it works independently of the algebraic form of functions, and it is versatile in approximating functions of any shape, while preserving their semantics. On the other hand, it is based on standard well-studied techniques of spline approximation, which makes the algorithms and program code readily available. Furthermore, because our method is numerically efficient, it can be used as a generic mechanism of representing membership functions and aggregation operators in fuzzy systems.

2 Estimation of membership functions

Membership functions of fuzzy sets take many shapes. S-shape, bell-shape, triangular and trapezoidal are the most common examples. Algebraically, these functions are expressed as piecewise polynomials, rational, exponential functions, etc. [11]. If empirical data is available, one can fix the desired algebraic form and fit the parameters to the data using regression techniques. Alternatively, it is possible to use non-parametric methods (for instance, joining the data points with straight lines [24]), and thus to handle a more general class of functions. In this approach, we fix not the algebraic form but the class of functions (such as continuous, square integrable, smooth, etc.) and let the data determine the shape of the estimator.

In order to preserve the semantics of membership functions, we need to examine some of their properties [8,11], and then to ensure that the estimator $f(x)$ complies with them. First, note that membership functions are continuous. Second, their range is at most the unit interval [0,1]. Finally, they are either monotone or unimodal (we consider only simple fuzzy sets, not set combinations, such as "Tall OR Short person", (cf. convex fuzzy sets [8])). While the first two conditions are rather technical, monotonicity (unimodality is monotonicity on two neighbouring intervals) is semantically important for order preservation. That is, if we choose some attribute as the measure of membership in the set, the higher its value, the bigger should be the membership.

[1] The adjective “non-parametric” is misleading. Non-parametric methods (also called distribution-free in statistical literature) actually do involve parameters, either fixed a priori or estimated from the data. Unlike in parametric approach, these parameters are not meaningful in relation to the original problem. A comprehensive discussion of the method of splines in non-parametric regression is given in [9,16].

Therefore, we arrived to the problem of monotone (or isotone) approximation, which translates into the restrictions on the class the membership function estimator can be drawn from. In the subsequent sections we develop a method of monotone approximation using least squares splines.

3 Estimation of aggregation operators

Extensions of classical *max* and *min* operations on fuzzy sets have been extensively studied for some time, both from set-theoretical and empirical perspectives [10,13,21,23,27-31]. Many families of aggregation operators have been constructed, among which triangular norms and conorms play a prominent role [13,23]. Averaging operators have also attracted substantial attention, specifically in applications to decision-making [23,28]. More recently ordered weighted aggregation (OWA) operators and weighted OWA operators have emerged [17,27-29]. Compensatory operators are a useful tool to model connectives based on empirical data [30,31].

The abundance of aggregation operators creates problems with their choice. Except *max* and *min*, and perhaps Lukasiewicz operators, all other operators possess the same essential set-theoretical properties [21]. The equivalence of all aggregation operators to a class of metrics, and therefore equivalence among themselves, has been established in [4,5]. Consequently, the choice is usually based on their ability to fit empirical data and mathematical simplicity [30].

The attempts to build aggregation operators from empirical data have been made since late 1970s. Zimmeramann and Zysno [31] provided empirical data that illustrates poor performance of *max* and *min* operators applied to particular situations, and introduced compensatory operators parameterised with a real parameter p. They used empirical data to find the value of p that provided the best fit. In a similar manner one can use any parameterised family of operators (triangular norms, generalised means [14], OWA [17,29]) and find the best value of the parameter(s) using standard nonlinear regression techniques. Algorithms for learning several parameters (weights of importance) of OWA operators at a time are presented in [17].

A different method to build aggregation operators advocated in this paper is to represent the operator in non-parametric form. The gain is in the quality of fit to empirical data, and in versatility to take great variety of forms, useful to approximate all sorts of connectives.

The most general class of aggregation operators is called generalised aggregation operators [21]. It consists of all monotone non-decreasing functions f: $[0,1]^n \rightarrow [0,1]$, with the property $f(\mathbf{0})=0$ and $f(\mathbf{1})=1$, where the number in bold denotes a vector of length n. Semantically, the monotonicity of the operator is very important (for order preservation), and the boundary conditions allow one to obtain classical logic in the limiting case.

One of the biggest families of operators is that of triangular norms T and conorms C. It is defined by the following properties:

1. $T(a,b)=T(b,a)$; $C(a,b)=C(b,a)$ (commutativity);
2. $T(a,T(b,c))=T(T(a,b),c)$; $C(a,C(b,c))=C(C(a,b),c)$ (associativity);
3. $T(a,b)\leq T(c,d)$; $C(a,b)\leq C(c,d)$, if $a\leq c$ and $b\leq d$ (monotonicity);
4. $T(a,1)=a$; $C(a,0)=a$ (boundary conditions).

Although these are two-argument functions, the associativity property 2 allows one to extend T and C for n-dimensional case.

Archimedian norms and conorms (continuous and $T(a,a)<a$ and $C(a,a)>a$, $a\in(0,1)$) possess additive generators - continuous and monotone (decreasing for norms, increasing for conorms) functions g: $[0,1]\rightarrow[0,\infty)$, $g(1)=0$ ($g(0)=0$ for conorms). The operators can be obtained from

$$T(a,b)=g^{[-1]}(g(a)+g(b)) \text{ or } C(a,b)=g^{[-1]}(g(a)+g(b)),$$

where $g^{[-1]}$ is the pseudoinverse function [23].

Averaging operators are commutative operators with the property [23]

$$min(a,b) \leq M(a,b) \leq max(a,b).$$

Dombi's "aggregative operator" [6] is defined with generator function $g(x)$ (continuous and monotone): $A(a,b)=g^{-1}(g(a)+g(b))$. When $g(x)=x^p$, it gives the class of generalised means [14].

The properties of various classes of aggregation operators are well studied, and the reader is referred to [13,14,21,23,30]. We explicitly listed some of these properties in order to illustrate how they can be used to crystallise a particular family of operators within the general framework of approximating aggregation operators discussed in the subsequent sections.

The approach we take in this paper is to represent general aggregation operators as a linear combination of some functions $b_j(\mathbf{x})$

$$f(\mathbf{x}) = \sum_{j=1}^{J} a_j b_j(\mathbf{x}) .$$

The coefficients a_j are found from the empirical data using linear regression.

The advantage of such a representation is its generality. With a good choice of basis functions, it is possible to approximate all general aggregation operators, regardless of their algebraic form. Thus, using the same algorithm, one can obtain triangular norms, averaging operators, OWA and many more families, based on empirical data.

As in the case of membership functions, we have the problem of monotone approximation because of monotonicity requirement, common to all general aggregation operators. However, we have a multivariate approximation problem now, and hence we need to develop both univariate and multivariate monotone approximation methods.

4 Least squares monotone splines

We will use a standard technique of non-parametric regression – method of least squares splines [7,9,16]. Splines arise as solutions to certain extremal problems in approximation theory (they are the most *smooth* functions approximating the data [7,9]). They can be represented as linear combinations of some basis functions $b_j(x)$

$$f(x) = \sum_j a_j b_j(x) .$$

The coefficients a_j are adjusted to fit the data in the least squares sense.

As the basis functions, we choose to use polynomial B-splines [7,9]. These functions have been extensively studied, they are easy to compute, quite versatile to approximate different forms, and they possess good smootheness. Tensor product of univariate B-splines will be used to approximate aggregation operators in the multivariate case.

Suppose, there is a given set of data points $\{(x_i, y_i)\}_{i=1}^{I}$ on the interval $[a,b]$, and a prescribed set of knots $\{t_j\}_{j=-k}^{N+k+1}$, $t_0=a$, $t_{N+1}=b$, that split $[a,b]$ into N+1 subintervals. The least squares spline $S(x)$ is a piecewise polynomial of order k+1 which minimises the least squares criterion

$$\sum_{i=1}^{I} \left(S(x_i) - y_i\right)^2 .$$

The knots of the spline are the points where the polynomial segments are joined together. The spline $S(x)$ is expressed as

$$S(x) = \sum_{j=-k}^{N} a_j N_j^{k+1}(x), \text{ or } S(x) = \mathbf{Na} \qquad (1)$$

where $N_j^{k+1}(x)$ are normalised B-splines of order k+1, **N** is the row-vector $N_j = N_j(x)$ and **a** is the column-vector of coefficients. The indices run from $-k$ to N, according to notation in [9]. The linear space of functions of the form (1) is the space of polynomial splines of order k+1 on the partition $\{t_j\}$. Its dimension is M=N+k+1.

Functions (1) do not preserve monotonicity of the data. In order to obtain monotone approximation one has to use constrained splines [3,7,15,25]. Restrictions on spline coefficients have to be imposed.

Despite that functions $N_j^{k+1}(x)$ possess many useful properties, such as positivity, local support, recursive definition, numerical stability, etc., they are not well suited to express monotonicity restriction. We look for a different representation of splines in which this condition is expressed better. Let us define the functions

$$T_j^{k+1}(x) = \sum_{m=j}^{N} N_m^{k+1}(x), j = -k,...,N . \qquad (2)$$

These M functions (trapezoidal, or T-splines) also form a basis, and any spline (1) can be represented as

$$S(x) = \sum_{j=-k}^{N} b_j T_j^{k+1}(x) \text{, or } S(x) = \mathbf{Tb} \qquad (3)$$

The advantage of using T-splines is in the form of constraints on the coefficients [6,25]. For any function of the form (3) to be non-decreasing, it is sufficient (also necessary for linear and quadratic splines) that all the relevant coefficients be non-negative: $b_j \geq 0$, j=-k+1,...,N. This way, the condition of monotonicity of the function is translated into the condition of non-negativity of spline coefficients. Unimodal functions are obtained by making part of **b** non-negative and the rest non-positive.

To find the coefficients of the spline (3) we need to minimize the least squares criterion subject to non-negativity condition. It is the classical non-negative least-squares problem NNLS [22]. Efficient methods of its solution exist, and the algorithms are available in [12,19,22]. One such method, LSEI, takes the form

$$\text{Solve } \mathbf{Eb} = \mathbf{e}\text{, } \mathbf{Ab} \approx \mathbf{y}\text{, } \mathbf{Gb} \geq \mathbf{g}\text{,} \qquad (4)$$

where **A** is the matrix of observation equations, $A_{ij} = T_j(x_i)$, $\approx$ stands for "approximately equal" (in the least squares sense), **E** is the matrix of additional observation equations that need to be satisfied exactly (it could be empty), and **G** is the matrix of linear restrictions, in our case **G=I** and **g=0**.

The proposed method of monotone least squares splines consists in filling the matrix **A** with the values of **T** at data points x_i, and solving the NNLS problem using (4). Since T-splines are related to B-splines in (2), standard algorithms for B-splines can be used, with a subsequent linear transformation. On the other hand, once the vector **b** is found from (4), one can obtain the coefficients of the traditional (and more efficient) B-splines representation (1), **a**, using the same transformation.

Figure 1 presents a monotone linear least squares spline, built using LSEI algorithm. For comparison, the usual (unrestricted) linear spline is presented in figure 2. Note its failure to preserve monotonicity of the data.

For multidimensional approximation, we split the V-dimensional domain into $(N+1)^V$ regions ((N+1) with respect to each dimension) using the approximation knots $\{t_j\}_{j=-k}^{N+k+1}$, with t_0 and t_{N+1} coinciding with the ends of the interval [0,1]. Tensor product B-splines are the functions

$$N_{j_1 j_2 \dots j_V}(x_1,\dots,x_V) = \prod_{v=1}^{V} N_{j_v}(x_v),$$

and the V-dimensional spline is the linear combination

$$S(x_1,\dots,x_V) = \sum_{j_1=-k}^{N_1} \dots \sum_{j_K=-k}^{N_V} a_{j_1 \dots j_V} N_{j_1 \dots j_V}(x_1,\dots,x_V) \qquad (5)$$

When the empirical data $\{(\mathbf{x}_i, y_i)\}_{i=1}^{I}$ are given, the coefficients a_j are found by minimising the least-squares criterion.

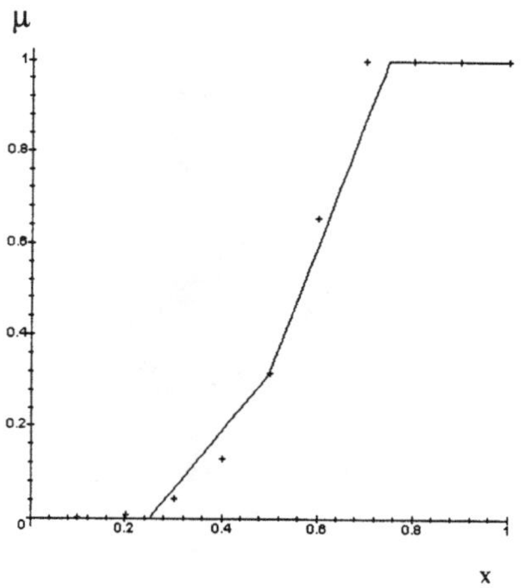

Figure 1. Monotone least squares linear spline.

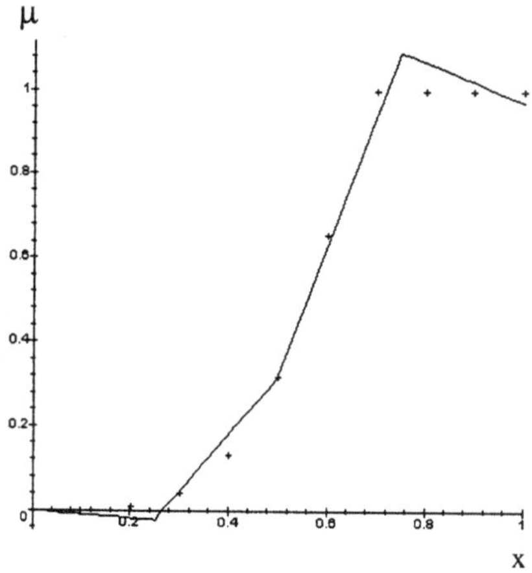

Figure 2. Linear unconstrained least squares spline

For multivariate monotone approximation, tensor products of T-splines are used. They are defined like tensor products of B-splines (5). The monotonicity constraints take a more complicated form compared with the univariate case

$$\sum_{j_1=-k}^{J_1} \dots \sum_{j_V=-k}^{J_V} b_{j_1 \dots j_v \dots j_V} \geq 0,\ j_v = -k-1,\dots N_v,\ J_l = -k,\dots,N_l,\ l \neq v;\ v = 1,2,\dots,V.$$

The LSEI algorithm can be used again, but the matrix **G** is no longer diagonal. The matrices **A** and **E** are also modified as $\mathbf{A}=\mathbf{A}_1\otimes\mathbf{A}_2\otimes\dots\otimes\mathbf{A}_V$, $\mathbf{E}=\mathbf{E}_1\otimes\dots\otimes\mathbf{E}_V$, where ⊗ stands for tensor product of matrices [18]. Further details on monotone spline approximation are presented in [6].

5 Approximation of membership functions: results

Once we have an effective monotone approximation algorithm, we can use it to build membership functions from empirical data. At this point we would also like to impose some additional restrictions on function values, specifically its range. This can be easily done by forcing the spline to interpolate certain points, namely $(a,0)$ and $(b,1)$, using the system **Eb=e** in (4). Because the spline is monotone, its range will be exactly [0,1].

To illustrate the method, we use the data from [24], the fuzzy set "tall people". Quadratic monotone spline with 5 approximation knots on $[a,b]$ is used. The results are presented in figure 3.

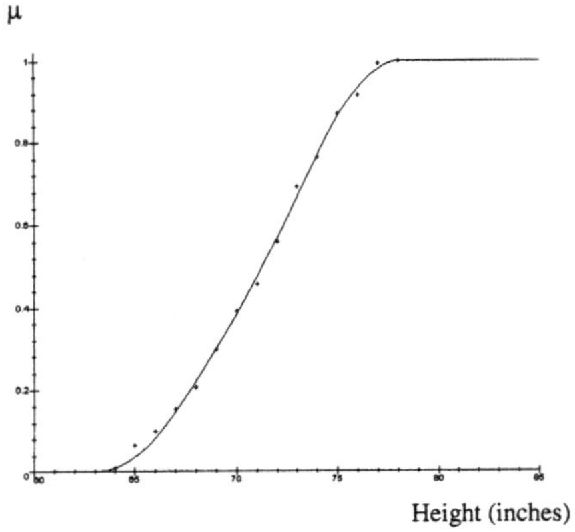

Figure 3. Approximation of membership function of the fuzzy set "tall people" using monotone quadratic spline.

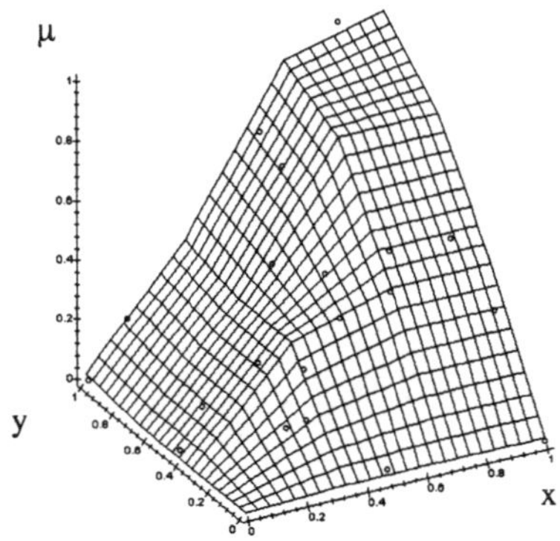

Figure 4. Empirical data used to approximate fuzzy set intersection in the "metallic container" example [30]. Monotone spline aggregation operator.

6 Approximation of aggregation operators: results

In this section we illustrate the use of monotone multivariate splines for approximation of aggregation operators on several examples. First, we consider approximation of empirical data with a generalised aggregation operator. Then, we will require that the operator possess some additional properties of triangular norms and conorms. Finally, we will force the operator to be an Archimedian triangular norm or conorm by approximating its additive generator.

When there are no restrictions on the form of the operator, meaning that it could be any monotone non-decreasing function satisfying boundary conditions $f(\mathbf{0})=0$ and $f(\mathbf{1})=1$, we can use tensor product monotone least squares splines directly. We solve the nonnegative least squares problem with the restrictions described in the previous section. To satisfy the boundary conditions, we force the spline to interpolate the origin and the Ideal [4] point (**1**,1) by specifying the relevant entries of the matrix **E**. As the empirical data, we used the example from [30], the case of fuzzy set "metallic container". The data represent subjects' estimates of the membership values of various objects in the fuzzy sets "metallic object", "container" and "metallic container", taken on three different occasions.

Figure 4 illustrates the resulting aggregation operator, and figure 5 illustrates the quality of approximation (observed vs. predicted values, cf. [30]). For comparison the same plot for *min* operator is provided in figure 6. The straight line corresponds to perfect fit.

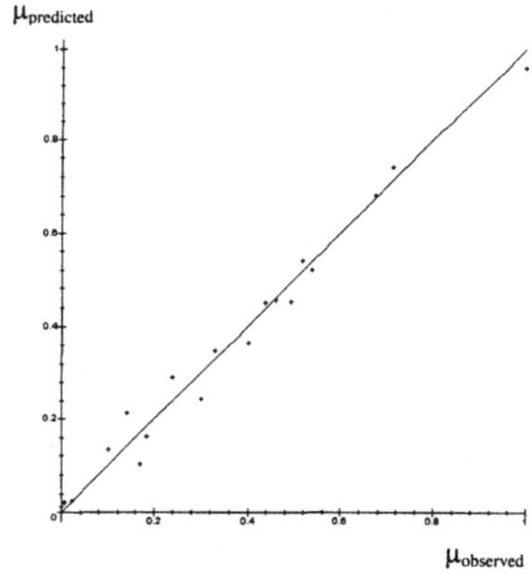

Figure 5. Observed vs. predicted membership values.

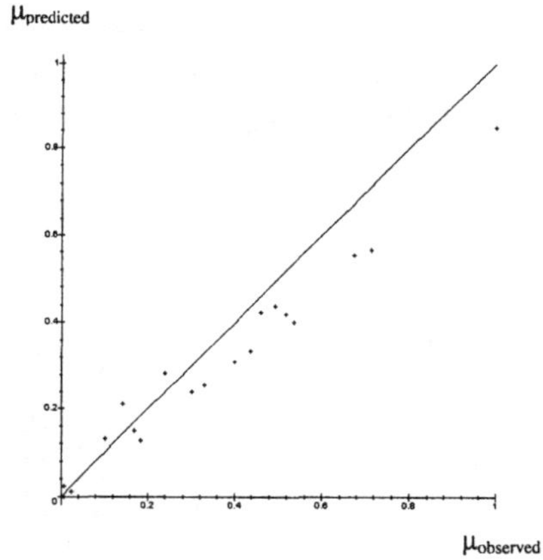

Figure 6. Observed vs. predicted membership values for *min* operator (data from [30]).

In some situations, besides the data, additional information about the aggregation operator is available. It may be required to construct a triangular norm or conorm, for instance, to take advantage of its commutativity and associativity properties. In other cases simpler restrictions, like $T(a,1)=a$ or $C(a,0)=a$, are sufficient.

In the latter case, the restrictions can be introduced as additional interpolation conditions. For bi-linear spline, it is sufficient to interpolate the values

$$S(t_l,1)=t_l,\ S(t_l,0)=0 \text{ or } S(t_l,0)=t_l,\ S(t_l,1)=1,$$

(t_j denote the interpolation knots). These interpolation conditions are translated into the relevant entries of the matrix **E**. Figure 7 illustrates the approximation of a triangular conorm, which takes into account the above conditions.

Another possible restriction of this type is $S(x,x)=x$ (idempotency), which is important for averaging operators. It is also easily translated into the interpolation conditions $S(t_l, t_l) = t_l$, and thus into the entries of the matrix **E**.

Commutativity of the aggregation operator readily translates into the symmetry of the matrix of coefficients **b**. It can be enforced in two ways. The first method (explicit) is to use only half of the matrix **b** and linear combinations of tensor product T-splines

$$T_j(x_1)T_k(x_2) + T_k(x_1)T_j(x_2)$$

as the basis functions. The second method (implicit) is to double up the empirical data and to use $\{(x_{1i}, x_{2i}, y_i)\}_{i=1}^{l}$ and $\{(x_{2i}, x_{1i}, y_i)\}_{i=1}^{l}$ in the general method of tensor product approximation. It will generate nearly symmetric matrix **b**. At the final stage, proper symmeterisation of **b** may be necessary, since in the process of numerical computations the symmetry may not hold.

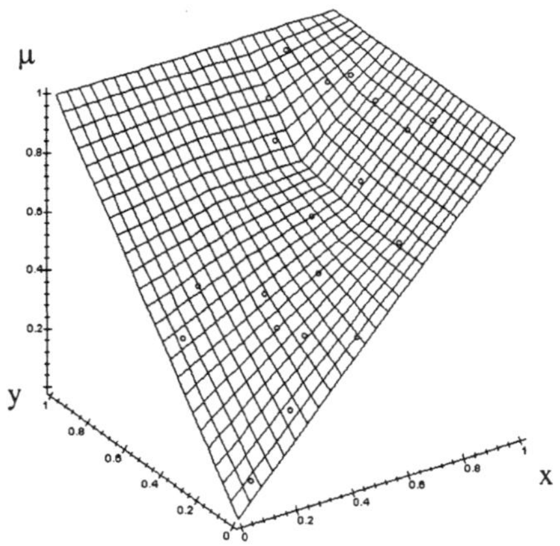

Figure 7. Hamacher sum operator $f(x, y) = \dfrac{x + y - 2xy}{1 - xy}$ approximated with monotone least squares spline. The 20 data points are randomly generated and are marked with circles. The data also contains random noise uniformly distributed in [-0.1,0.1]. Restrictions $f(x,0)=f(0,x)=x$ are added.

7 Approximation of additive generators

Unlike commutativity and boundary conditions, associativity property of aggregation operators does not have direct geometrical interpretation [26]. So it cannot be introduced into the process of multivariate spline approximation by means of any restrictions. Still associativity could be semantically important, and together with commutativity and boundary conditions, it defines the important class of triangular norms (co-norms).

Fortunately, a large proportion of triangular norms (co-norms), called Archimedian norms possess additive generators [23], the monotone functions g: $[0,1]\rightarrow[0,\infty)$, $g(1)=0$ ($g(0)=0$ for co-norms). The generator is unique up to a multiplier, and is due primarily to the associativity [26]. The operators are obtained using

$$T(a,b)=g^{[-1]}(g(a)+g(b)) \text{ or } C(a,b)=g^{[-1]}(g(a)+g(b)). \qquad (6)$$

Instead of approximating the operator itself, we will approximate its additive generator, and then obtain the operator from (6). We write (e.g., for conorms)

$$g(C(a,b)) = g(a) + g(b), \text{ or}$$
$$g(a) + g(b) - g(C(a,b)) = 0.$$

As the empirical data we have the values of a,b and $C(a,b)$, call them x,y and z. Since g is represented by the spline (3), we can write

$$\sum_j b_j\left(T_j(x)+T_j(y)-T_j(z)\right)\approx 0, \text{ or } \sum_j b_j\overline{T}(x,y,z)\approx 0.$$

Next we solve the non-negative linear least squares problem, in which the basis functions are given as $\overline{T}(x,y,z)$. Once the coefficients b_j are found, the additive generator is defined, and the value of the operator C can be numerically determined from g.

Another class of aggregation operators that possesses generator functions is the class of quasi-arithmetic means. They are defined from [1]

$$M(a,b) = g^{-1}\left(\frac{g(a)+g(b)}{2}\right), \qquad (7)$$

where g is continuous and strictly monotone. A particular case is quasi-linear averaging operators ($g(x)=x^p$) [14], see also [10].

Similarly to triangular norms and conorms, generators of quasi-arithmetic means can be found from data. One solves

$$\sum_j b_j\left(\tfrac{1}{2}T_j(x_1)+\tfrac{1}{2}T_j(x_2)-T_j(y)\right)\approx 0.$$

subject to non-negativity of coefficients. Once the generator is found, the operator is obtained from (7). This method is easily generalised for n-dimensional case (averaging operators generally are not associative)

$$M(x_1,\dots,x_n)=g^{-1}\left(\frac{g(x_1)+\dots+g(x_n)}{n}\right),$$

by using

$$\sum_j b_j\left(\tfrac{1}{n}\{T_j(x_1)+\dots+T_j(x_n)\}-T_j(y)\right)\approx 0.$$

In a similar way, other operators that possess additive generators, like Dombi's operator [10], can be found from data.

8 Conclusion

We have presented a general framework for deriving membership functions and aggregation operators from empirical data using non-parametric approach of least squares splines. In traditional (parametric) approaches, the algebraic form of these functions is fixed, and a small number of parameters are varied to fit the data in the least squares sense. These methods are subject to two major difficulties: technical - the selected parameters enter the expression non-linearly, and non-linear approximation is notoriously difficult, and semantical - the selected algebraic form can rarely be translated into a meaningful semantical interpretation. On the other hand, high level concepts with clear semantical meaning, such as continuity, commutativity, idempotency or associativity of operators are not translated into an algebraic formula.

In contrast, the non-parametric approach is purely data driven. The quality of fit is the most important criterion, and any function adequately describing the data is acceptable, unless it contradicts basic semantically important properties. Among the most important semantical properties is order preservation, which translates into monotonicity. Thus, to be useful, any method of non-parametric estimation of membership functions and aggregation operators has to provide adequate tools to ensure monotonicity of the functions.

Polynomial splines are a powerful method of approximation and non-parametric regression. Splines are versatile in approximating functions of any shape, but their well known drawback is not preserving the shape of the derivatives. Special methods to ensure monotonicity or convexity have to be employed. This paper develops one such method, applicable to univariate and multivariate least squares splines. It translates monotonicity into a simple requirement of non-negativity of the coefficients of the spline, and the problem is reduced to standard linear restricted least squares problem.

Because our method is non-parametric, it does not produce operators in a closed algebraic form. From computational viewpoint, however, our method produces results far superior to parametric approaches. The quality of fit is excellent, and can be controlled by specifying adequate number of knots. Furthermore, the presented method is general, which means that it does not require specifying a priori any particular family of operators, be it triangular norms, OWA or averaging operators. On the other hand, this still can be done if necessary, and particular families of operators can be selected in a few different ways. Thus, the advantage of using monotone splines is their generality on the one hand, and a range of tools they provide to select a particular class or property on the other. Linearity of the approximation problem is also a bonus.

Besides being a method for building membership functions and aggregation operators from empirical data, monotone splines are also an effective tool for representation and coding of given operators. Indeed, rather than representing an operator/membership function in algebraic form, one can specify its values at certain points, and then build a spline that accurately approximates it. The numerical evaluation of such approximation is practically as effective as using the original algebraic formula. This way, instead of a formula, one can provide a generic code (e.g., for fuzzy controllers, or for decision, expert systems), suitable for any aggregation, while the actual operators and membership functions used by the concrete system will be determined by the supplied array of spline coefficients.

References

[1] Aczel, J. (1969) *On applications and theory of functioonal equations*, Academic Press, New York.

[2] Amaya Cruz, G.P. and Beliakov, G. (1995), Approximate reasoning and interpretation of laboratory tests in medical diagnostics, *Cybernetics and Systems*, **26**, 713-729.

[3] Beatson, R.K. and Ziegler, Z. (1985). Monotonicity preserving surface interpolation, *SIAM J. Numer. Anal.* **22,** 401-411.

[4] Beliakov, G. (2000). Definition of general aggregation operators through similarity relations, *Fuzzy Sets and Systems* **114**, 437-453.

[5] Beliakov, G. (1999). Aggregation operators as similarity relations, in *Information, Uncertainty, Fusion.*, R. Yager, B. Bouchon-Meunier and L. Zadeh, eds, Kluwer, Boston, 331-342.

[6] Beliakov, G. (2001) Shape preserving approximation using least squares splines, *Approximation theory and applications*, in press.

[7] de Boor C. (1978). *A practical guide to splines*, Springer, Berlin – New York.

[8] Chen, J. and Otto, K. (1995). Constructing membership functions using interpolation and measurement theory, *Fuzzy Sets and Systems* **73**, 313-327.

[9] Dierckx P. (1995). *Curve and surface fitting with splines*, Clarendon press, Oxford.

[10] Dombi, J. (1982). Basic concepts for a theory of evaluation: The aggregative operator, *Europ. J. Oper. Res.* **10**, 282-293.

[11] Dombi, J. (1990). Membership function as evaluation, *Fuzzy Sets and Systems*, **35**, 1-21.

[12] Dongarra, J.J. and Grosse, E. (1987). Distribution of mathematical software via electronic mail, *Comm. ACM* **30**, 403-440.

[13] Dubois, D. and Prade, H. (1985) A review of fuzzy set aggregation connectives, *Information Sciences* **36,** 85-121.

[14] Dyckhoff, H. and Pedrycz, W. (1984). Generalized means as model of compensative connectives, *Fuzzy Sets and Systems* **14**, 143-154.

[15] Elfving, T. and Andersson, L.-E. (1989). An algorithm for computing constrained smoothing spline functions, *Numer.Math.* **52**, 583-595 .

[16] Eubank, R. L. (1999) *Nonparametric regression and spline smoothing*, Marcel Dekker, New York.

[17] Filev, D. and Yager, R. (1998). On the issue of obtaining OWA operator weights, *Fuzzy Sets and Systems* **94**, 157-169.

[18] Halmos, P. (1958). *Finite-dimensional vector spaces*, D.van Nostrand Company, Princeton.

[19] Hanson, R.J. and Haskell, K.H. (1982). Algorithm 587. Two algorithms for the linearly constrained least squares problem, *ACM Trans. Math. Software* **8,** 323-333.

[20] Hisdal, E. (1998) *Logical structures for representation of knowledge and uncertainty*, Physica-Verlag, New York.

[21] Klir, G. and Folger, T. (1992). *Fuzzy sets, uncertainty, and information*, Prentice Hall, Singapore.

[22] Lawson, C. and Hanson, R. (1995). *Solving least squares problems*, SIAM, Philadelphia.

[23] Mizumoto, M. (1989). Pictorial representations of fuzzy connectives, Part I: Cases of t-norms, t-conorms and averaging operators, *Fuzzy Sets and Systems* **31**, 217-242.

[24] Norwich, A.M. and Turksen, I.B. (1984). A model for the measurement of membership and the consequences of its empirical implementation, *Fuzzy Sets and Systems*, **12**, 1-25.

[25] Ramsay, J.O. (1988). Monotone regression splines in action (with comments), *Stat. Science* **3,** 425-461.

[26] Schweizer, B. and Sklar, A. (1961) Associative functions and statistical triangle inequalities, *Publ. Mathematicae Debrecen*, **8**, 169-186.

[27] Yager, R. (1978). Fuzzy decision making including unequal objectives, *Fuzzy Sets and Systems* **1** 87-95.

[28] Yager, R. (1988). On ordered weighted averaging aggregation operators in multicriteria decision making, *IEEE Trans. Syst.,Man, Cybern.* **18**, 183-190.

[29] Yager, R. (1998). Including importances in OWA aggregations using fuzzy systems modeling, *IEEE Trans. Fuzzy Syst* **6**, 286-294.

[30] Zimmermann, H.-J. (1996). *Fuzzy set theory - and its applications*, Kluwer, Boston.

[31] Zimmermann, H.-J. and Zysno, P. (1980). Latent connectives in human decision making, *Fuzzy Sets and Systems,* **4**, 37-51.

The Ordered Weighted Geometric Operator: Properties and Application in MCDM Problems

Francisco Chiclana, Francisco Herrera, and Enrique Herrera-Viedma

Dept. of Computer Science and Artificial Intelligence,
E.T.S. de Ingeniería Informática
University of Granada, 18071- Granada, Spain.
herrera,viedma@decsai.ugr.es

Abstract. The aim of this paper is to present the Ordered Weighted Geometric (OWG) operator. The OWG operator is based on the geometric mean and the OWA operator. It is a fuzzy majority guided aggregation operator proposed to aggregate information given on a ratio scale. Therefore, it allows us to incorporate the concept of fuzzy majority in problems where the information is provided using a ratio scale. Its properties are studied and an application for multicriteria decision making problems with multiplicative preference relations is presented [1].

Keywords: Aggregation, fuzzy majority, decision making, multiplicative preference relations.

1 Introduction

The measurement process for modeling problems consists in the construction of scales by mapping or transforming empirical results into numerical ones in such a way that the information is preserved. We can use different scales to represent that information. Scales which are available, in increasing order of strenght, are as follows [6]:

1. The *nominal scale,* unique up to any 1-1 transformation, which consists essentially of assigning labels to objects.
2. The *ordinal scale* which gives a rank order of objects and is invariant under monotone increasing transformations.
3. The *interval scale,* unique up to positive linear transformation of the form $y = ax + b,\ a > 0$.
4. The *difference scale,* invariant under a transformation of the form y=x+b.
5. The *ratio scale,* invariant under positive linear transformations of the form $y = ax,\ a > 0$.

[1] This research is supported by CICYT and by project PB-981305.

Particularly, in this contribution we are interested in problems where the ratio scale is used to model the information. This is the case, for example, in muticriteria decision making problems modelled by the *Analytic Hierarchy Process* (AHP) designed by Saaty [6,7], in which the performances on the alternatives are ratio-scale measurements provided on the pairwise comparisons of alternatives.

Multicriteria decision making problems are usually solved in a two-phase process [5]:

1. *Aggregation phase:* Using an aggregation operator the performance degrees of alternatives are aggregated for all criteria.
2. *Exploitation phase:* Applying a choice mechanism on the aggregated performance degrees a global ranking of alternatives is achieved.

In any multicriteria decision process the final solution must be obtained from the synthesis of performance degrees of the *majority* of criteria. The majority is traditionally defined as a threshold number of elements. This concept is not always included in the multicriteria decision process. The *fuzzy logic* provides one way to model it.

Fuzzy majority is a soft majority concept expressed by a *fuzzy quantifier* [9], which is manipulated via a fuzzy logic based calculus of linguistically quantified propositions. Therefore, using fuzzy majority guided aggregation operators we can incorporate the concept of majority in the computation of the solution. These operators reflect the fuzzy majority calculating their weights by means of the fuzzy quantifiers, as for example, the *Ordered Weighted Averaging (OWA)* [8].

As shown in [1,2], the proper aggregation operator of ratio-scale measurements is the *geometric mean* and is not the *arithmetic mean.* However, this operator does not allow to incorporate the concept of fuzzy majority in the decision processes. We could use the OWA operator, but this is not possible because it presents a similar behavior to the arithmetic mean.

In this contribution, we present a fuzzy majority guided aggregation operator for synthesizing ratio-scale judgements. We define the *Ordered Weighted Geometric (OWG)* operator. It is based on the geometric mean and the OWA operator. It allows to incorporate the concept of fuzzy majority in the decision process when the information is provided using a ratio scale. We study its properties and present an application for multicriteria decision making processes with multiplicative preference relations.

In order to do this, the paper is set out as follows. The concept of fuzzy majority and the OWA and geometric mean operators are introduced in section 2. Section 3 is devoted to present the OWG operator and its properties. An example of its use in multicriteria decision making is given in section 4. Finally, some concluding remarks are pointed out in section 5.

2 Preliminaries

In this section we present the fuzzy quantifiers, used to representing the fuzzy majority, the OWA operator and the geometric mean.

2.1 Fuzzy Majority

Quantifiers can be used to represent the amount of items satisfying a given predicate. Classic logic is restricted to the use of only two quantifiers, *there exists* and *for all*, that are closely related respectively to the *or* and *and* connectives. However, human discourse is much richer and more diverse in its quantifiers, e.g. *about 5, almost all, a few, many, most, as many as possible, nearly half, at least half.* In an attempt to bridge the gap between formal systems and natural discourse and, in turn, to provide a more flexible knowledge representation tool, Zadeh introduced the concept of fuzzy quantifiers [9].

Zadeh suggested that the semantic of a fuzzy quantifier can be captured by using fuzzy subsets for its representation. He distinguished between two types of fuzzy quantifiers, *absolute* and *relative.* Absolute quantifiers are used to represent amounts that are absolute in nature such as *about 2* or *more than 5.* These absolute linguistic quantifiers are closely related to the concept of count or number of elements. He defined these quantifiers as fuzzy subsets of the non negative real numbers, $\mathcal{R}^+$. In this approach, an absolute quantifier can be represented by a fuzzy subset Q, such that for any $r \in \mathcal{R}^+$ the membership degree of r in Q, Q(r), indicates the degree to which the amount r is compatible with the quantifier represented by Q. Relative quantifiers, such as *most, at least half,* can be represented by fuzzy subsets of the unit interval, [0,1]. For any $r \in [0,1]$, Q(r) indicates the degree to which the proportion r is compatible with the meaning of the quantifier it represents. Any quantifier of natural language can be represented as a relative quantifier or given the cardinality of the elements considered, as an absolute quantifier. Functionally, fuzzy quantifiers are usually of one of three types, *increasing, decreasing,* and *unimodal.* An increasing type quantifier is characterized by the relationship $Q(r_1) \geq Q(r_2)$ if $r_1 > r_2$. These quantifiers are characterized by values such as *most, at least half.* A decreasing type quantifier is characterized by the relationship $Q(r_1) \leq Q(r_2)$ if $r_1 > r_2$.

An absolute quantifier $Q : \mathcal{R}^+ \rightarrow [0,1]$ satisfies:

$$Q(0) = 0, \text{and } \exists k \text{ such that } Q(k) = 1.$$

A relative quantifier, $Q : [0,1] \rightarrow [0,1]$, satisfies:

$$Q(0) = 0, \text{ and } \exists r \in [0,1] \text{ such that } Q(r) = 1.$$

The membership function of a non decreasing relative quantifier can be represented as

$$Q(r) = \begin{cases} 0 & \text{if } r < a \\ \frac{r-a}{b-a} & \text{if } a \leq r \leq b \\ 1 & \text{if } r > b \end{cases}$$

with $a, b, r \in [0, 1]$.

Some examples of relative quantifiers are shown in Figure 1, where the parameters, (a, b) are $(0.3, 0.8)$, $(0, 0.5)$ and $(0.5, 1)$, respectively.

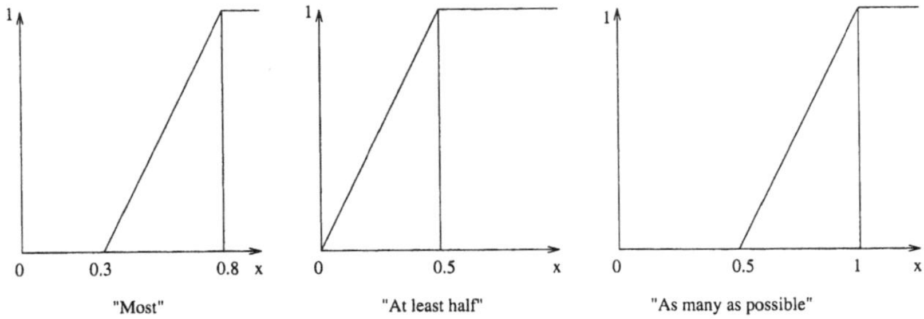

Fig. 1. Relative Fuzzy Quantifiers

2.2 The OWA Operator

The OWA operator was proposed by Yager in [8]. It provides a family of aggregation operators which have the "and" operator at one extreme and the "or" operator at the other extreme.

Definition 1. *An OWA operator of dimension m is a function ϕ,*

$$\phi : \mathcal{R}^m \rightarrow \mathcal{R},$$

that has associated a set of weights or weighting vector $W = [w_1, \ldots, w_m]$ such that,

1. $w_i \in [0, 1]$, *and*
2. $\Sigma_i w_i = 1$;

and is defined for aggregating a list of values $\{a_1, \ldots, a_m\}$ according to the following expression,

$$\phi(a_1, \ldots, a_m) = W \cdot B^T = \Sigma_{i=1}^{m} w_i \cdot b_i$$

where B is the associated ordered value vector, and each element $b_i \in B$ is the i-th largest value in the collection $a_1, \ldots, a_m$.

Proposition 1. The OWA operator satisfies the following properties:

1. *It is an or-and operator, i.e., it remains between the minimum and the maximum of the arguments:*

$$min(a_1, \ldots, a_m) \leq \phi(a_1, \ldots, a_m) \leq max(a_1, \ldots, a_m).$$

2. *It is commutative:*

$$\phi(a_1, \ldots, a_m) = \phi(a_{\pi(1)}, \ldots, a_{\pi(m)}) \ \forall \pi.$$

3. *It is idempotent:*

$$\phi(a_1, \ldots, a_m) = a, \ \textit{if } a_i = a \ \forall i.$$

4. *It is increasing monotonous:*

$$\phi(a_1, \ldots, a_m) \geq \phi(d_1, \ldots, d_m), \ \textit{if } a_i \geq d_i \forall i.$$

5. *It leads to the arithmetic mean when* $w_i = \frac{1}{m} \ \forall i$*:*

$$\phi(a_1, \ldots, a_m) = \Sigma_{i=1}^{m} (\frac{1}{m}) \cdot b_i = (\frac{1}{m}) \Sigma_{i=1}^{m} b_i.$$

6. *It leads to maximum when* $W = [1, 0, \ldots, 0]$.
7. *It leads to minimum when* $W = [0, \ldots, 0, 1]$.

A natural question in the definition of the *OWA* operator is how to obtain the associated weighting vector. In [8], Yager proposed two ways to obtain it. The first approach is to use some kind of learning mechanism using some sample data; and the second approach is to try to give some semantics or meaning to the weights. The final possibility has allowed multiple applications on areas of fuzzy and multi-valued logics, evidence theory, design of fuzzy controllers, and the quantifier guided aggregations.

We are interested in the area of quantifier guided aggregations. The idea consists in calculating weights for the aggregation operations using fuzzy quantifiers representing the concept of *fuzzy majority*. In [8], Yager suggested an interesting way to compute the weights of the *OWA* aggregation operator using fuzzy quantifiers, which, in the case of a non decreasing relative quantifier Q, it is given by the following expression:

$$w_i = Q(i/m) - Q((i-1)/m), i = 1, \ldots, m.$$

When a fuzzy quantifier Q is used to compute the weights of the *OWA* operator ϕ, it is symbolized by ϕ_Q.

2.3 Geometric Mean

As was aforementioned, the geometric mean operator is the traditional aggregation operator to combine ratio-scale judgements in the Saaty's multicriteria decision models. Its main characteristic is that in such decision context it guarantizes the reciprocity property of the multiplicative preference relations used to provide the ratio preferences. The geometric mean is defined as follows:

Definition 2. *A geometric mean operator of dimension* m *is a function* $g : \mathcal{R}^m \to \mathcal{R}$, *defined as*

$$g(a_1, \ldots, a_m) = \Pi_{i=1}^{m} (a_i)^{\frac{1}{m}}.$$

Proposition 2. The geometric mean satisfies the following properties:

1. *It is an or-and operator, i.e., it remains between the minimum and the maximum of the arguments.*
2. *It is commutative.*
3. *It is idempotent.*
4. *It is increasing monotonous.*

3 The OWG Operator

In this section, we present the OWG operator to aggregate ratio-scale judgements. It is based on the OWA operator [8] and on the geometric mean, and therefore, incorporates the advantage of the OWA operator to represent the concept of fuzzy majority and the advantage of geometric mean to deal with ratio-scale judgements. It is defined as follows.

Definition 3. *An OWG operator of dimension* m *is a function,* $\phi^G : \mathcal{R}^m \to \mathcal{R}$, *that has associated a set of weights or exponential weighting vector* $W = [w_1, \ldots, w_m]$ *such that,*

1. $w_i \in [0, 1]$, *and*
2. $\Sigma_i w_i = 1$;

and is defined for aggregating a list of values $\{a_1, \ldots, a_m\}$ *according to the following expression,*

$$\phi^G(a_1, \ldots, a_m) = \Pi_{i=1}^{m} c_i^{w_i}$$

where C *is the associated ordered value vector, and each element* $c_i \in C$ *is the i-th largest value in the collection* $a_1, \ldots, a_m$.

Proposition 3. The OWG operator satisfies the following properties:

1. *It is an or-and operator, i.e., it remains between the minimum and the maximum of the arguments:*

$$min(a_1, \ldots, a_m) \leq \phi^G(a_1, \ldots, a_m) \leq max(a_1, \ldots, a_m).$$

2. *It is commutative:*

$$\phi^G(a_1, \ldots, a_m) = \phi^G(a_{\pi(1)}, \ldots, a_{\pi(m)}), \ \forall \pi.$$

3. It is idempotent:

$$\phi^G(a_1, \ldots, a_m) = a, \ \text{if } a_i = a \ \forall i.$$

4. It is increasing monotonous:

$$\phi^G(a_1, \ldots, a_m) \geq \phi^G(d_1, \ldots, d_m), \ \text{if } a_i \geq d_i \forall i.$$

5. It leads to the geometric mean when $w_i = \frac{1}{m} \ \forall i$*:*

$$\phi^G(a_1, a_2, \ldots, a_m) = \Pi_{k=1}^{m}(c_k)^{\frac{1}{m}} = g(a_1, a_2, \ldots, a_m).$$

6. It leads to maximum when $W = [1, 0, \ldots, 0]$*:*

$$\phi^G(a_1, a_2, \ldots, a_m) = max_{i=1}^{m}(a_i).$$

7. It leads to minimum when $W = [0, \ldots, 0, 1]$*:*

$$\phi^G(a_1, a_2, \ldots, a_m) = min_{i=1}^{m}(a_i).$$

We can obtain W using the same method that in the OWA operator case, i.e., the weighting vector may be obtained using a fuzzy quantifier, Q, representing the concept of fuzzy majority. When a fuzzy quantifier Q is used to compute the weights of the OWG operator ϕ^G, then, it is symbolized by ϕ^G_Q.

In the following section, we present an example of the use of the OWG operator in a multicriteria decision making problem under multiplicative preference relations.

4 Solving a Multicriteria Decision Making Problem Using the OWG Operator

Let $X = \{x_1, x_2, \ldots, x_n, \ (n \geq 2)\}$ be a finite set of alternatives. The alternatives must be classified from best to worst (ordinal ranking), using the information known according to a finite set of general criteria or experts $E = \{e_1, e_2, \ldots, e_m, \ (m \geq 2)\}$. We assume that the experts' preferences over the set of alternatives, X, are represented by means of the multiplicative preference relations on X, i.e.,

$$A^k \subset X\text{x}X, \ A^k = [a_{ij}^k]$$

where a_{ij}^k indicates a ratio of preference intensity for alternative x_i to that of x_j, i.e., it is interpreted as x_i is a_{ij}^k times as good as x_j. Each a_{ij}^k is assessed using the ratio scale proposed by Saaty, that is, precisely the 1 to 9 scale [6]: $a_{ij}^k = 1$ indicates indifference between x_i and x_j, $a_{ij}^k = 9$ indicates that x_i is absolutely preferred to x_j, and $a_{ij}^k \in 2, 3, \ldots, 8$ indicates intermediate evaluations. In order to guarantee that A^k is "self-consistent", only some pairwise comparison statements are collected to construct it. The rest of the values are what satisfy the following conditions [6]:

1. Multiplicative Reciprocity Property: $a_{ij}^k \cdot a_{ji}^k = 1 \; \forall i, j$.
2. Saaty's Consistency Property: $a_{ij}^k = a_{it}^k \cdot a_{tj}^k \; \forall i, j, t$.

Then, we consider multiplicative preference relations assessed in Saaty's discrete scale, which has only the following set of values:

$$\{\frac{1}{9}, \frac{1}{8}, \frac{1}{7}, \ldots, \frac{1}{2}, 1, 2, \ldots, 7, 8, 9\}.$$

The multicriteria decision making problem when the experts express their preferences using multiplicative preference relations have been solved by Saaty using the decision AHP, which obtains the set of solution alternatives by means of the eigenvector method [6]. However, this decision process is not guided by the concept of majority.

Here, we present an alternative decision process to the AHP proposed by Saaty in order to show the application of the OWG operator. Following the choice scheme proposed in [5], i.e.,

$$\textbf{Aggregation} + \textbf{Exploitation},$$

we design a selection process based on fuzzy majority to choose the best alternatives from multiplicative preference relations. This process is defined using the quantifier guided OWG operator to aggregate the preferences and to define a choice function of alternatives, called *multiplicative quantifier guided dominance degree*, which obtains the best alternatives from the aggregated information. This degree is defined as a multiplicative version of quantifier guided dominance degree proposed for fuzzy preference relations in [3,4].

Definition 4. Quantifier guided dominance degree for an alternative x_i, symbolized $MQGDD_i^k$, from a multiplicative preference relation, A^k, is defined according to the following expression:

$$MQGDD_i^k = \phi_Q^G(a_{i1}^k, \ldots, a_{in}^k).$$

In what follows, we present the phases of selection process based on fuzzy majority and designed to deal with multicriteria decision making problems under multiplicative preference relations.

1. Aggregation phase

This phase defines a collective multiplicative preference relation, $A^c = [a_{ij}^c]$, which indicates the global preference according to the fuzzy majority of experts' opinions. A^c is obtained from $\{A^1, \ldots, A^m\}$ by means of the following expression:

$$a_{ij}^c = \phi_Q^G(a_{ij}^1, \ldots, a_{ij}^m),$$

where ϕ_Q^G is the OWG operator guided by the concept of fuzzy majority represented by the fuzzy quantifier Q.

2. Exploitation phase

Using the quantifier guided choice degree defined for multiplicative preference relations, this phase transforms the aggregated or global information about the alternatives into a global ranking of them, supplying the set of solution alternatives.

Firstly, using the OWG operator ϕ_Q^G we obtain the choice degrees of alternatives from A^c:

$$[MQGDD_1, \ldots, MQGDD_n],$$

with

$$MQGDD_i = \phi_Q^G(a_{i1}^c, \ldots, a_{in}^c).$$

And secondly, the application of choice degree of alternatives over X allows us to obtain the following solution set of alternatives:

$$X^{sol} = \{x_i \,|\, x_i \in X, MQGDD_i = sup_{x_j \in X} MQGDD_j\}$$

whose elements are called maximum dominance ones.

4.1 Example

Consider the following illustrative example of the classification method of alternatives studied in this contribution. Assume that we have a set of four experts, $E = \{e_1, e_2, e_3, e_4\}$, and a set of four alternatives, $X = \{x_1, x_2, x_3, x_4\}$. Suppose that experts supply their opinions by means of the following multiplicative preference relations:

$$A^1 = \begin{bmatrix} 1 & 3 & 5 \\ \frac{1}{3} & 1 & 2 \\ \frac{1}{5} & \frac{1}{2} & 1 \end{bmatrix}, A^2 = \begin{bmatrix} 1 & 2 & 7 \\ \frac{1}{2} & 1 & 5 \\ \frac{1}{7} & \frac{1}{5} & 1 \end{bmatrix}, A^3 = \begin{bmatrix} 1 & 2 & 3 \\ \frac{1}{2} & 1 & 2 \\ \frac{1}{3} & \frac{1}{2} & 1 \end{bmatrix}, A^4 = \begin{bmatrix} 1 & 5 & 3 \\ \frac{1}{5} & 1 & 9 \\ \frac{1}{3} & \frac{1}{9} & 1 \end{bmatrix}.$$

In the decision process we use the fuzzy majority criterion with the fuzzy quantifier *"at least half "*, with the pair $(0, 0.5)$, and the corresponding OWG operator with the weighting vector, $W = [\frac{1}{2}, \frac{1}{2}, 0, 0]$.

Selection Process Based on Fuzzy Majority

1. Aggregation phase

The collective multiplicative preference relation obtained in this phase is the following:

$$A^c = \begin{bmatrix} 1 & 15^{\frac{1}{2}} & 23^{\frac{1}{2}} \\ \frac{1}{2} & 1 & 45^{\frac{1}{2}} \\ \frac{1}{3} & \frac{1}{2} & 1 \end{bmatrix}.$$

For example a_{21}^c is obtained as

$$a_{21}^c = \phi_Q^G(\frac{1}{3}, \frac{1}{2}, \frac{1}{2}, \frac{1}{3}) = (\frac{1}{3})^{\frac{1}{2}} \cdot (\frac{1}{3})^{\frac{1}{2}} \cdot (\frac{1}{2})^0 \cdot (\frac{1}{2})^0 = \frac{1}{3}.$$

2. Exploitation phase

The quantifier guided choice degree of alternatives acting over the collective multiplicative preference relation and with the weighting vector $W = [\frac{2}{3}, \frac{1}{3}, 0]$ supplies the following values:

$$MQGDD_1 = 8.52, \;\; MQGDD_2 = 3.55, \;\; MQGDD_3 = 0.79.$$

These values represent the dominance that one alternative has over "at least half"of the alternatives according to "at least half" of the experts. For example the value $MQGDD_1$ is obtained as

$$MQGDD_1 = \phi_Q^G(1, 15^{\frac{1}{2}}, 23^{\frac{1}{2}}) = 23^{\frac{1}{2}^{\frac{2}{3}}} \cdot 15^{\frac{1}{2}^{\frac{1}{3}}} \cdot 1^0 = 8.52.$$

Clearly the solution set is:

$$X^{sol} = \{x_1\}.$$

5 Concluding Remarks

In this contribution, we have presented a new aggregation operator for the synthesis of ratio judgements, called OWG operator. It has been designed incorporating the advantages of the geometric mean to deal with ratio judgements and the advantages of the OWA operator to represent the concept of fuzzy majority in the aggregation processes.

We have studied its properties and also have illustrated its use in a multicriteria decision making problem with multiplicative preference relations. Particularly, we have developed a selection process of alternatives based on a quantifier guided dominance degree.

In the future, we will research the use of the OWG operator for designing consensus processes in multicriteria decision making problems with multiplicative preference relations.

References

1. Azcel, J., Alsina, C. (1983) Procedures for synthesizing ratio judgements. Journal of Mathematical Psychology. **27**, 93-102.
2. Azcel, J., Alsina, C. (1987) Synthesizing judgements: A functional equations approach, Mathematical Modelling. **9**, 311-320.
3. Chiclana, F., Herrera, F., Herrera-Viedma, E., Poyatos, M.C. (1996) A clasification method of alternatives for multiple preference ordering criteria based on fuzzy majority. Journal of Fuzzy Mathematics. **4**, 801-813.

4. Chiclana, F., Herrera, F., Herrera-Viedma, E. (1998) Integrating three representation models in fuzzy multipurpose decision making based on fuzzy preference relations. Fuzzy Sets and Systems. **97**, 33-48.
5. Roubens, M. (1997) Fuzzy sets and decision analysis. Fuzzy Sets and Systems. **90**, 199-206.
6. Saaty, Th.L. (1980) The Analytic Hierarchy Process. McGraw-Hill, New York.
7. Vargas, L.G. (1990) An overview of the analytic hierarchy process and its applications. European Journal of Operational Research. **48**, 2-8.
8. Yager, R.R. (1988) On ordered weighted averaging aggregation operators in multicriteria decision making. IEEE Transactions on Systems, Man, and Cybernetics. **18**, 183-190.
9. Zadeh, L.A. (1983) A computational approach to fuzzy quantifiers in natural languages. Computers and Mathematics with Applications. **9**, 149-184.

On Dominance and Dispersion of a Class of Weighting Lists

Tomasa Calvo, Javier Martín, Gaspar Mayor, and Jaume Suñer

University of the Balearic Islands, Dept. of Mathematics and Computer Science, 07071-Palma de Mallorca, Spain

Abstract. The class of weighting lists with a prefixed minimum and maximum values is studied. It is introduced the concept of degree of Dominance of a weighting list as a generalization of the degree of Orness. It is proved that, with good conditions, there always exist two unique lists with minimum and maximum dominance respectively. From the concepts of dominance and dispersion, it is solved the problem of obtaining the weighting list in the class considered here of maximum dispersion with a given degree of dominance.

1 Introduction

The process of information aggregation appears in many applications related to the development of intelligent systems. One can see aggregation in neural networks, fuzzy logic controllers, vision systems, expert systems, etc. We are interested in operators that can provide for aggregations lying between the logical *or* and *and*. In this framework two important types of operators are available: the weighted averaging (WA) operators and the ordered weighted averaging (OWA) operators ([1]). Besides obvious differences between them, they have in common that both need a list of weights to be defined. In this work we introduce the concept of Dominance of a weighting list as a measure of the "importance" of the weights on the left-hand side of the list. In the case of the weighting list associated to an OWA operator, it coincides with the degree of Orness of the operator. On the other hand, as usual, the Dispersion of a weighting list is defined as the entropy of the list. In this paper we investigate these measures independently of the use of the weighting lists to construct WA operators, OWA operators or any other aggregation operator. In some cases it could be interesting to work with prefixed maximum and minimum weights, thus in this paper we deal with the class $W_{r,s}^{a,b}$ of n-dimensional lists $(w_1, ..., w_n)$ with minimum $w_r = a$ and maximum $w_s = b$. In [2], a method of obtaining weighting lists associated to OWA operators is given. It consists of solving the mathematical programming problem of finding the weighting list with a given degree of orness which has maximum entropy. The same problem for the case of multi-dimensional OWA operators is considered in [3]. We apply this method to the case of weighting lists with prefixed maximum and minimum weights, that is, we solve the problem of obtaining the weighting list of maximum dispersion (maximum entropy) with a fixed degree of dominance for lists of the class $W_{r,s}^{a,b}$.

2 The class $W_{r,s}^{a,b}$

Let $n \geq 3$. Let us consider the set W of n-dimensional weighting lists, that is,

$$W = \{(w_1, \dots, w_n) : \sum_{i=1}^{n} w_i = 1, w_i \geq 0 \ \forall i = 1, \dots, n\}$$

Given $r, s \in \{1, \dots, n\}, r \neq s$ and $a, b \in [0, 1]$ with $a \leq b$, let us consider the following subset of W, formed by the lists $(w_1, ..., w_n) \in W$ with minimum $w_r = a$ and maximum $w_s = b$:

$$W_{r,s}^{a,b} = \{w \in W : w_r = a = \bigwedge_{i=1}^{n} w_i \ , \quad w_s = b = \bigvee_{i=1}^{n} w_i\}$$

Example 1. If $a = b$, then it must be $a = \frac{1}{n}$ and $W_{r,s}^{\frac{1}{n},\frac{1}{n}} = \{(\frac{1}{n}, \dots, \frac{1}{n})\}$. On the other hand, $W_{r,s}^{0,1} = \{(0, \dots, w_s = 1, \dots, 0)\}$, whereas $W_{r,s}^{0,\frac{1}{n}} = \emptyset$.

Remark 1. Observe that $W = \bigcup_{a,b;r,s} W_{r,s}^{a,b}$, but this union is not formed by disjoint sets: $(\frac{1}{n}, \dots, \frac{1}{n}) \in W_{r,s}^{\frac{1}{n},\frac{1}{n}} \ \forall r, s$. However, when $a \neq a'$ or $b \neq b'$, $W_{r,s}^{a,b} \cap W_{r',s'}^{a',b'} = \emptyset$.

In the third example above, we have seen that $W_{r,s}^{a,b}$ can be the empty set. The following proposition gives the conditions that a and b must satisfy in order to $W_{r,s}^{a,b} \neq \emptyset$. Of course, theses conditions do not depend on the particular value of r and s.

Proposition 1. *$W_{r,s}^{a,b}$ is not the empty set if, and only if, $(n-1)a + b \leq 1$ and $a + (n-1)b \geq 1$.*

Proof. Let us suppose first that $W_{r,s}^{a,b} \neq \emptyset$. Given $w \in W_{r,s}^{a,b}$, we have

$$1 = \sum_{i=1}^{n} w_i = \sum_{i \neq s} w_i + b \geq (n-1)a + b$$

and

$$1 = \sum_{i=1}^{n} w_i = \sum_{i \neq r} w_i + a \leq (n-1)b + a$$

Conversely, if both inequalities are satisfied, then we can construct the following weighting list w:

$$w_r = a, \qquad w_s = b, \qquad w_i = \frac{1 - (a+b)}{n-2} \quad \forall i \neq r, s$$

Obviously,

$$a \leq \frac{1-(a+b)}{n-2} \leq b \quad \text{and} \quad a+b+(n-2)w_i = 1;$$

in other words, $w \in W_{r,s}^{a,b}$. □

Example 2. Let us consider the case $n = 6$ with $a = w_4 = 0.05$, $b = w_2 = 0.30$. Then

$$5 \cdot 0.05 + 0.30 = 0.55 < 1 \quad \text{and} \quad 0.05 + 5 \cdot 0.30 = 1.55 > 1$$

For example, the following lists belong to $W_{4,2}^{0.05,0.30}$:

$$(0.10, 0.30, 0.20, 0.05, 0.15, 0.20), \ (0.15, 0.30, 0.30, 0.05, 0.10, 0.10).$$

The inequalities in the proposition above define the region shown in the following figure:

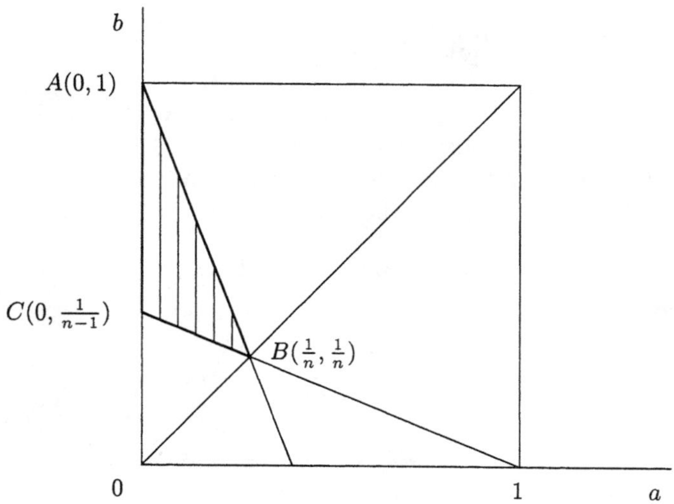

Fig. 1. Region of $[0,1]^2$ where $W_{r,s}^{a,b}$ is not empty.

In the case $n = 3$, when the class $W_{r,s}^{a,b}$ is not empty, it contains a unique list. Next proposition characterizes this kind of classes for $n \geq 4$.

Proposition 2. *Let $n \geq 4$. $W_{r,s}^{a,b}$ contains a unique list if, and only if, $(n-1)a + b = 1$ or $a + (n-1)b = 1$.*

Proof. Let us suppose first that $(n-1)a + b < 1$ and $a + (n-1)b > 1$, that is, $a < \dfrac{1-(a+b)}{n-2} < b$. We know that the list w with $w_r = a, w_s = b$ and $w_i = \dfrac{1-(a+b)}{n-2}$ $\forall i \neq r, s$ belongs to $W_{r,s}^{a,b}$.

By taking two components, both different from r and s, and adding to one of them and subtracting to the other one a convenient quantity, we obtain a new list of the same class different from w.

Conversely, let us suppose that $(n-1)a+b=1$. We will prove that the unique list of $W_{r,s}^{a,b}$ is $(a,\ldots,a,w_s=b,a,\ldots,a)$. If $w \in W_{r,s}^{a,b}$, then

$$\sum_{i\neq r,s} w_i = 1-(a+b) = (n-2)a, \quad \text{i.e.,} \quad \sum_{i\neq r,s}(w_i-a)=0,$$

but $w_i \geq a \ \forall i$, hence $w_i = a \ \forall i \neq r,s$.

Analogously, when $a+(n-1)b=1$, it can be proved that the unique list in $W_{r,s}^{a,b}$ is $(b,\ldots,b,w_r=a,b,\ldots,b)$. □

Observe that $W_{r,s}^{a,b}$ contains a unique list if, and only if, the pair (a,b) belongs to AB or BC in Fig. 1.

3 Dominance of lists in $W_{r,s}^{a,b}$

Next we define a concept which, in the case of the weighting list associated to an OWA operator, it coincides with the degree of Orness introduced in [1]. We call it the degree of Dominance and it measures the "importance" of the weights on the left-hand side of the list.

Definition 1. Assuming w is a weighting list $(w_1,\ldots,w_n)$, then the *degree of dominance* of w is defined as

$$\alpha(w) = \frac{1}{n-1}\sum_{i=1}^{n}(n-i)w_i \ .$$

Remark 2. As we know, $\forall w \in W, \ 0 \leq \alpha(w) \leq 1$. We have

$$\alpha(w)=0 \Longleftrightarrow w=(0,0,\ldots,1)$$

and

$$\alpha(w)=1 \Longleftrightarrow w=(1,0,\ldots,0)$$

On the other hand, $\alpha(1/n,\ldots,1/n)=0.5$.

Let us consider now the case when $(n-1)a+b<1$ and $a+(n-1)b>1$, that is, the class $W_{r,s}^{a,b}$ consisting of infinite lists. We are going to construct two lists $\underline{w}$ and $\overline{w}$ with minimum and maximum dominance, respectively.

Let us take $k=\frac{1-(n-1)a-b}{b-a}$, $t=[k]$ (the greatest integer less than or equal to k) and $R=a+(k-t)(b-a)$.

We define $\underline{w}$ to be the list with $\underline{w}_r = a, \underline{w}_s = b$ and the other $n-2$ components are

$$(\overbrace{a,\ldots,a}^{n-t-3}, R, \overbrace{b,\ldots,b}^{t})$$

Analogously, $\overline{w}$ will be the list with $\overline{w}_r = a, \overline{w}_s = b$ and the other $n-2$ components are

$$(\overbrace{b,\ldots,b}^{t}, R, \overbrace{a,\ldots,a}^{n-t-3})$$

It is easy to prove that both lists are in $W_{r,s}^{a,b}$.

Proposition 3. *The unique lists in* $W_{r,s}^{a,b}$ *with minimum and maximum dominance are, respectively,* $\underline{w}$ *and* $\overline{w}$.

Proof. We must prove that $\alpha(\underline{w}) \leq \alpha(w) \leq \alpha(\overline{w})\ \forall w \in W_{r,s}^{a,b}$.

Let $d = w - \underline{w}$. We have $d_r = d_s = 0$ and there exists $l \in \{1,\ldots,n\}$ such that $d_i \geq 0\ \forall i = 1,\ldots,l$ and $d_i \leq 0\ \forall i = l+1,\ldots,n$.

Moreover,

$$\sum_i d_i = \sum_{i \leq l} d_i + \sum_{i > l} d_i = 0,$$

that is,

$$\sum_{i \leq l} d_i = -\sum_{i > l} d_i.$$

Let us observe now that $\alpha(\underline{w}) \leq \alpha(w)$ is equivalent to

$$\sum_i (n-i)\underline{w}_i \leq \sum_i (n-i) w_i,$$

that is, $\sum_i i\underline{w}_i \geq \sum_i i w_i$, or $\sum_i i d_i \leq 0$.

But

$$\begin{aligned}
\sum_i i d_i &= \sum_{i \leq l} i d_i + \sum_{i > l} i d_i \\
&\leq \sum_{i \leq l} l d_i + \sum_{i > l} (l+1) d_i \\
&= l \sum_{i \leq l} d_i - (l+1) \sum_{i \leq l} d_i \\
&= -\sum_{i \leq l} d_i \leq 0.
\end{aligned}$$

It can be easily seen that if $w \neq \underline{w}$, then we have a strict inequality, which proves that $\underline{w}$ is the unique list in $W_{r,s}^{a,b}$ with minimum dominance.

The proof that $\overline{w}$ is the list with maximum dominance is completely analogous. □

We will denote by α_{min} and α_{max} the dominance of $\underline{w}$ and $\overline{w}$, respectively. Let us see now an example of the calculation of these lists with minimum and maximum dominance.

Example 3. Let us consider the class $W_{4,2}^{0.05,0.30}$ with $n = 6$. We are going to obtain α_{min} and α_{max}.

In this case, we have $k = 1.8, t = 1, R = 0.25$ and, thus,

$$\underline{w} = (0.05, 0.30, 0.05, 0.05, 0.25, 0.30) \quad \text{with} \quad \alpha_{min} = 0.39,$$

and

$$\overline{w} = (0.30, 0.30, 0.25, 0.05, 0.05, 0.05) \quad \text{with} \quad \alpha_{max} = 0.72.$$

As we have proved, any list $w \in W_{4,2}^{0.05,0.30}$ satisfies $0.39 \leq \alpha(w) \leq 0.72$.

4 Maximum dispersion problem

In this section we propose the problem of obtaining the weighting list of maximum dispersion (maximum entropy) with a fixed degree of dominance for lists of the class $W_{r,s}^{a,b}$; that is, we want to solve the mathematical programming problem

$$max: -\sum_{i=1}^{n} w_i \ln w_i$$

$$subject\ to: \frac{1}{n-1} \sum_{i=1}^{n} (n-i) w_i = \alpha,$$

$$\sum_{i=1}^{n} w_i = 1, \qquad w_i \geq 0, \quad i = 1, \ldots, n,$$

$$w_r = a \leq w_i \leq b = w_s, \quad i = 1, \ldots, n,$$

where, as shown in the previous section, $\alpha \in [\alpha_{min}, \alpha_{max}]$.

Let us observe that this problem has only interest for $n \geq 5$ because for $n = 4$, there is only one list satisfying all the restrictions.

A similar problem was studied in [2] and, more recently, it was considered in the multi-dimensional case ([3]).

First of all we solve the mathematical programming problem without considering the restriction $w_r = a \leq w_i \leq b = w_s$, $i = 1, \ldots, n$, but assuming $w_r = a$ and $w_s = b$. In this case we can establish the following result:

Proposition 4. *Given* $\alpha \in [\alpha_{min}, \alpha_{max}]$, *and assuming* $n \geq 4$, *the mathematical programming problem*

$$max : -\sum_{i=1}^{n} w_i \ln w_i$$

$$subject\ to : \frac{1}{n-1}\sum_{i=1}^{n}(n-i)w_i = \alpha,$$

$$\sum_{i=1}^{n} w_i = 1, \qquad w_i \geq 0, \quad i = 1,\ldots,n,$$

$$w_r = a, \ w_s = b$$

has a unique solution given by $(w_1, \ldots, w_n)$ *with*

$$w_j = (1-a-b)\frac{x^j}{\sum_{i\neq r,s} x^i}, \quad j \neq r,s, \quad and \quad w_r = a, \quad w_s = b,$$

where x *is the only real positive zero of the equation*

$$\sum_{i\neq r,s}\left(\frac{n+c}{1-a-b} - i\right)x^{i-1} = 0$$

with $c = -\alpha(n-1) - ra - sb$.

Proof. Some elementary calculations show that the restriction

$$\frac{1}{n-1}\sum_{i=1}^{n}(n-i)w_i = \alpha$$

is equivalent to

$$\sum_{i\neq r,s} i\, w_i = n + c \quad \text{where} \quad c = -\alpha(n-1) - ra - sb\ .$$

The Lagrange Multiplier Theorem gives us a method to solve our problem. Hence, we look for the maximum of the following function

$$F(w_1, \ldots, w_n, \lambda, \mu) = -\sum_{i=1}^{n} w_i \ln w_i + \lambda(\sum_{i\neq r,s} i\, w_i - n - c) + \mu(\sum_{i=1}^{n} w_i - 1)\ .$$

Calculating the partial derivatives of F we obtain the following equations:

$$\frac{\partial F}{\partial w_i} = -(\ln w_i + 1) + \lambda\, i + \mu = 0, \qquad i \neq r, s$$

with solutions given by $w_i = e^{\lambda\, i} e^{-1+\mu}$. It is easy to prove that the solution of this system corresponds to a maximum. If we say $x = e^{\lambda}$, $y = e^{1-\mu}$, then we have that $w_i = x^i/y$. Substituting these values in the restrictions we obtain

$$\sum_{i=1}^{n} w_i = 1 \implies \sum_{i\neq r,s} x^i = (1-a-b)y \implies y = \frac{\sum_{i\neq r,s} x^i}{(1-a-b)},$$

$$\sum_{i\neq r,s} i\, w_i = n + c \implies \frac{\sum_{i\neq r,s} i\, x^i}{y} = n + c$$

and from this

$$\sum_{i\neq r,s} \left(\frac{n+c}{1-a-b} - i \right) x^i = 0.$$

Since $x > 0$, this equation is equivalent to

$$p(x) = \sum_{i\neq r,s} \left(\frac{n+c}{1-a-b} - i \right) x^{i-1} = 0.$$

Let us prove now that the coefficients of the polynomial $p(x)$ have a single change of sign.

Let us suppose first that $r, s \notin \{1, n\}$. Then we will show that the first coefficient $\frac{n+c}{1-a-b} - 1$ is positive. This is equivalent to say that

$$\frac{n - \alpha(n-1) - ra - sb}{1-a-b} > 1,$$

that is,

$$n - \alpha(n-1) - ra - sb > 1 - a - b,$$

and this is equivalent to say that

$$(n-r)a + (n-s)b + \sum_{i\neq r,s} (n-i)w_i = \alpha(n-1) < n - ra - sb - 1 + a + b$$

which is equivalent to the inequality

$$\sum_{i\neq r,s} (n-i)w_i < n - 1 + a + b - na - nb.$$

But

$$n - 1 + a + b - na - nb = (n-1)(1-a-b) = \sum_{i \neq r,s} (n-1)w_i$$

and we obtain the desired result since $n - i \leq n - 1$ and $w_i > 0$ for all i.

On the other hand, the coefficient of x^{n-1} is negative:

$$\begin{aligned} n - \alpha(n-1) - ra - sb - n + na + nb &= a(n-r) + b(n-s) - \alpha(n-1) \\ &= -\sum_{i \neq r,s} (n-i)w_i < 0. \end{aligned}$$

Therefore, there is at least a change of sign. Now, as the coefficients of $p(x)$ form a strictly decreasing sequence, we conclude that there is a single change of sign.

By applying the Descartes signs Rule we know that $p(x)$ has at most a positive real root. On the other hand, $p(0) > 0$ and $\lim_{x \to +\infty} p(x) = -\infty$. Therefore, we can affirm that $p(x)$ has a unique real positive zero.

The other cases, when r and s can be 1 or n are dealt with in a similar way.

To summarize, we have proved that the problem stated above has a unique solution given by

$$w_j = (1-a-b)\frac{x^j}{\sum_{i \neq r,s} x^i}, \quad j \neq r, s, \quad \text{and} \quad w_r = a, \quad w_s = b,$$

where x is the only real positive zero of the equation

$$p(x) = \sum_{i \neq r,s} \left(\frac{n+c}{1-a-b} - i \right) x^{i-1} = 0$$

with $c = -\alpha(n-1) - ra - sb$. □

Let us consider again the mathematical programming problem but now with the restrictions $w_r = a \leq w_i \leq b = w_s, \quad i = 1, \ldots, n$. In this case, we would proceed as follows:

First of all, we solve the problem stated in proposition 4. If the solution is in the hypercube $[a, b]^n$, then this is the list we are looking for. If not, some other calculations will be necessary.

In case the list is not in this hypercube, this means that the solution to our problem must lie somewhere in its border. Thus, we look for it by consecutively substituting each one of the free components of the list (the components w_i for i different from r and s) by a and b and solving the corresponding $(n-3)$-dimensional problem stated in proposition 4. We must first, of course, make sure that the corresponding substitution is possible (all the restrictions in proposition 4 are still satisfied). Thus we obtain at most $2(n-2)$ lists. If all of them are in the hypercube, then the solution will be the list with greater dispersion. If one or more lists are not in it, then we must repeat the same construction. Observe that this procedure will end with the solution to our problem.

We are going to illustrate this process with two examples. In the first one, we obtain as a solution of the mathematical programming problem a weighting list in the hypercube and thus, this is the required list. The second example needs extra calculation as the list we obtain is not in the hypercube.

Example 4. Let us consider $n = 6$ and the class $W_{4,2}^{0.05,0.30}$ of lists of the form $(w_1, 0.30, w_3, 0.05, w_5, w_6)$. We fix a dominance $\alpha = 0.65$ (recall that the interval of possible values for α is $[0.39, 0.72]$) and we are looking for the list of maximum dispersion.

According to the proposition above, we have to find the unique real positive root of the polynomial $p(x) = 2 - 2x^4 - 3x^5$. This root is $x = 0.8185$; hence $w_1 = 0.2615, w_3 = 0.1752, w_5 = 0.1173, w_6 = 0.0960$.

Observe that $a = 0.05 < w_i < b = 0.30\ \ \forall i = 1,3,5,6$ and thus this is the solution to our problem. Then

$$w = (0.2615, 0.30, 0.1752, 0.05, 0.1173, 0.0960)$$

is the weighting list with dominance 0.65 and maximum dispersion.

Example 5. Let us consider the same problem, that is, $n = 6$ and the class $W_{4,2}^{0.05,0.30}$ of lists of the form $(w_1, 0.30, w_3, 0.05, w_5, w_6)$. We fix now a dominance $\alpha = 0.41$ and we are looking for the list of maximum dispersion.

According to the proposition above, we have to find the unique real positive solution to the equation $3.846 + 1.846x^2 - 0.154x^4 - 1.154x^5 = 0$. This root is $x = 1.43367$; hence $w_1 = 0.049, w_3 = 0.1, w_5 = 0.206, w_6 = 0.295$.

Observe that $w_1 < a = 0.05$ and thus this is not a solution to our problem. We must then look for it at the border of the intersection of the hypercube $[0.05, 0.30]^6$ with the hyperplanes $w_2 = 0.30$ and $w_4 = 0.05$. We have to assign consecutively the values $a = 0.05$ and $b = 0.30$ to w_i for $i = 1,3,5,6$ and solve the corresponding problems. The components w_1 and w_3 cannot take the value 0.30 because of the restriction $\alpha = 0.41$. We have thus 6 substitutions to make:

a) $w_1 = 0.05$. In this case we obtain the list $(0.05, 0.30, 0.10, 0.05, 0.20, 0.30)$, with a dispersion of $D_1 = 1.5741$.

b) $w_3 = 0.05$. We obtain the list $(0.075, 0.30, 0.05, 0.05, 0.225, 0.30)$, with a dispersion of $D_2 = 1.55185 < D_1$.
c) $w_5 = 0.05$. We obtain the list $(0.061, 0.30, 0.131, 0.05, 0.05, 0.408)$. In this case, the list is not in the hypercube, but, even so, its dispersion takes the value $D_3 = 1.4634 < D_1 = 1.5741$. This means that, in the border, D will take even a lower value.
d) $w_5 = 0.30$. It happens like in (c). We obtain a list not in the hypercube, $(0.041, 0.30, 0.082, 0.05, 0.30, 0.227)$, but with a dispersion of $D_4 = 1.5448 < D_1 = 1.5741$.
e) $w_6 = 0.05$. We obtain the list $(0.007, 0.30, 0.061, 0.05, 0.532, 0.05)$. Like in (c) and (d), it is not in the hypercube, but it has a dispersion of $D_5 = 1.20186 < D_1 = 1.5741$.
f) $w_6 = 0.30$. We obtain the same list as in (a).

Then

$$w = (0.05, 0.30, 0.10, 0.05, 0.20, 0.30)$$

is the weighting list with dominance 0.41 and maximum dispersion.

5 Conclusions

In this paper we have dealt with some measures associated to weighting lists independently of their use to construct weighted averaging operators, OWA operators or any other aggregation operator. First of all we have introduced the concept of Dominance of a weighting list as a measure of the "importance" of the weights on the left-hand side of the list. When the weighting list is associated to an OWA operator, this concept coincides with the degree of Orness of the operator. Then we have restricted the set of weighting lists to the class $W_{r,s}^{a,b}$ of lists with given minimum and maximum values: $w_r = a \leq w_i \leq b = w_s \ , \quad i = 1, \ldots, n$. This situation could be interesting in some cases concerning aggregation of information. Finally, we have solved the mathematical programming problem of obtaining the weighting list of maximum dispersion (maximum entropy) with a fixed degree of dominance for lists of the class $W_{r,s}^{a,b}$.

References

1. Yager, R. R. (1988) On ordered weighted averaging aggregation operators in multi-criteria decision making. IEEE Trans. Systems Man Cybernetics **18**, 183–190
2. O'Hagan, M. (1990) Using maximum entropy-ordered averaging operator to construct a fuzzy neuron. Proceedings 24th Annual IEEE Asilomar Conf. on Signals, Systems and Computers. Pacific Grove. CA, 618–623
3. Carbonell M., Mas M., Mayor G. (1997) On a class of Monotonic Extended OWA Operators. Proceedings Sixth International Conference on Fuzzy Systems **3**, 1695–1700

Fuzzy Sets

On the Definition of Coherence Measure for Fuzzy Sets[1]

A. Sancho-Royo
Depto. de Matemáticas
Escuela de Arte de Granada
18001 Granada
alejandrosancho_royo@hotmail.com

J.L. Verdegay
Depto. de Ciencias de la Computación e I.A.
Universidad de Granada
18071 Granada
verdegay@ugr.es

Abstract

Studying comparison methods for fuzzy sets is an essential task for the good understanding of the underlying theory in this field. Most of these tools deal with fuzzy sets from the view of similarity, order relationships and so forth. In this paper however, based on a former comparison measures introduced by the authors, the so called Coherence Measures, the extension and analysis of these tools to a measurable Lebesgue set X is carried out, with which coherence measures are linked to the Fishburn-Yager's ambiguity measures. Besides, two methods for constructing coherence measures, one from ambiguity measures and another from metrics on $P^f(X)$, the set of fuzzy sets on X, are shown and exemplified by a variety of measures and metrics. Finally some illustrative examples testing the coherence measures introduced are provided.

Keywords: Coherence measures, ambiguity measures, fuzzy sets.

---

[1] Research supported by the Spanish "Dirección General de Enseñanza Superior e Investigación Científica" under project PB98-1305

1 Introduction

Coherence measures have been recently proposed as comparison tools for finite fuzzy sets [5]. These measures provide information on both the similarity and the ambiguity at once. The aim of this paper, based upon [6], is to extend the concept of coherence measures from finite sets to measurable Lebesgue fuzzy sets, and then to study the properties and characteristics of the corresponding measures. From this point of view, Section 2 introduces Coherence Measures and shows some properties being valid for both finite and non finite fuzzy sets. In Section 3 the relationship between coherence measures and ambiguity ones is analysed. Coherence measures construction methods for the non finite case are studied, and conditions for the extension of an ambiguity measure to a coherence one are provided by the so called Theorem of Extension. As an illustration of these results, last section shows four applications of this Theorem of Extension by presenting some theoretic and practical examples. Among them, the analysis carried out on the ambiguity measures of Yager [8] and of De Luca and Termini [11] is to be remarked. Finally, last example, shows the meaning of coherence measures by means of a practical example. Along the paper in order to facilitate the reading and to adhere the limitations in length, only relevant results and the main properties of the measures are presented, and hence the proofs are omitted[2].

2 Coherence Measures

Definition 1. Let X be a measurable set and $P^f(X)$ the set of fuzzy sets on X. One says that cohe: $P^f(X)\times P^f(X) \rightarrow [0,1]$ is a *coherence measure* on $P^f(X)$ if and only if the three following axioms hold:

C1) cohe(A,B) = cohe(B,A)
C2) cohe(A,B^c) = 1 - cohe(A,B)
C3) cohe(∅,X) = 0

It is clear that C1 shows the map cohe as a symmetric measure. C2 presents the basic idea on the concept of coherence measure: if the term coherence is meant as the possibility of coexistence of two evaluations, then is clear that (in the [0,1] interval) such possibility between A and B^c is the opposite to such another between A and B. Finally C3 shows that the minimum coherence is to be attained when the sets ∅ and X are compared. In the following the main results that can be obtained from these axioms are shown (an asterisk will be used to distinguish those results valid for both the finite and non finite case).

Remark. Let X be a measurable Lebesgue set with a finite positive measure m. If $\chi(X)$ denotes the characteristic function of X,

$$m = \lambda (X) = \cap_X \chi(x)dx$$

[2] Proofs can be obtained from the authors on request

Then, as it is well known, there is an interval $I \subset X$ such that

$$0 < \lambda (I) = \cap_I dx < \lambda (X) = \cap_X dx$$

Lemma 2 (*). Let cohe:$P^f(X) \times P^f(X) \rightarrow [0,1]$ be a coherence measure then:

a) $cohe(A^c, B^c) = cohe(A, B)$
b) $cohe(\varnothing, \varnothing) = cohe(X, X) = 1$
c) If $A^*(x) = 0.5\ \forall x$, then $\forall A \in P^f(X)\ \ cohe(A, A^*) = 0.5$

The following lemma is a negative result on the monotony of these measures.

Lemma 3 (*). Let cohe:$P^f(X) \times P^f(X) \rightarrow [0,1]$ be a coherence measure. Then $\forall A,B,C,D \in P^f(X)$, neither is true that

(1) If $A \subseteq B$ and $C \subseteq D$ then $cohe(A,C) \leq cohe(B,D)$

nor

(2) If $A \subseteq B$ and $C \subseteq D$ then $cohe(A,C) \geq cohe(B,D)$

where, as usual, if $A,B \in P^f(X)$, $A \subseteq B$ if and only if $A(x) \leq B(x)$, $\forall x \in X$.

3 Coherence and Ambiguity

As it is well known, in Fuzzy Sets and Systems Theory ambiguity measures have been typically used as measures of fuzziness, but formerly they come from the classical Sets Theory. In order to relate coherence measures and ambiguity ones, recall first the definition of ambiguity for classical sets.

Definition 4. (Fishburn, 1993). Let X be any set, and denote P(X) the set of subsets on X. Then

$$\alpha: P(X) \rightarrow [0,1]$$

is an *ambiguity measure* if and only if the following axioms hold:

A1) $\alpha(\varnothing) = 0$
A2) $\alpha(A) = \alpha(A^c)$
A3) $\alpha(A \cup B) + \alpha(A \cap B) \leq \alpha(A) + \alpha(B)$

The extension of this definition to the fuzzy case, i.e., to fuzzy sets, can be straightforward by using the usual operations of union, intersection and complementation (Yager, 1995). Hence,

Definition 5. (Yager, 1995). Let X be any referential set. Then

$$\alpha: P^f(X) \rightarrow [0,1]$$

is an *ambiguity measure* if and only if the following axioms hold

A1. $\alpha(\varnothing) = 0$

A2. $\alpha(A) = \alpha(A^c)$
A3. $\alpha(A \cup B) + \alpha(A \cap B) \leq \alpha(A) + \alpha(B)$

where

$$A \cup B(x) = \max(A(x), B(x))$$
$$A \cap B(x) = \min(A(x), B(x))$$
$$A^c(x) = 1 - A(x)$$

In order to avoid misunderstandings, in the following such a measure α will be referred as an ambiguity measure in Fishburn-Yager sense. The following lemma shows a first link between both coherence and ambiguity measures.

Lemma 6. Let cohe:$P^f(X) \times P^f(X) \rightarrow [0,1]$ be a coherence measure. Then α:$P^f(X) \rightarrow [0,1]$ defined as $\alpha(A) = 1-$ cohe(A, A) is an ambiguity measure in Fishburn-Yager sense if and only if:

$$\text{cohe}(A, A) + \text{cohe}(B, B) \leq \text{cohe}(A \cup B, A \cup B) + \text{cohe}(A \cap B, A \cap B)$$

Let α now an ambiguity measure in Fishburn-Yager sense. Do it makes sense to extend α to a coherence measure ß such that $ß(A,A) = 1 - \alpha(A)$?. The following counterexamples give negative answers to this question

Counterexample 1: Consider $\alpha(A) = 0$, $\forall A \in P^f(X)$. It is obvious that α is an ambiguity[3] measure. If $ß(A,A) = 1 - \alpha(A)$ is a coherence, by axiom C2:

$$ß(A,A^c) = 1 - ß(A,A) = \alpha(A)$$

hence $ß(A,A^c) = 0$, $\forall A \in P^f(X)$. However, by lemma 2, part c), for A^* holds $ß(A^*,A^*) = 0.5$, what is contradictory with $A^* = A^{*c}$.

Counterexample 2: Consider α defined by $\alpha(\varnothing) = \alpha(X) = 0$, and $\alpha(A) = 1$, $\forall A \in P^f(X)$, $A \neq \varnothing, X$. By a parallel reasoning to the previous one, a contradiction can be obtained.

Consequently one can conclude that not always is possible to find such an extension. In the following however necessary conditions for the existence of such an extension are shown.

Lemma 7. Let α: $P^f(X) \rightarrow [0,1]$ be an ambiguity measure. To extend α to a coherence measure ß: $P^f(X) \times P^f(X) \rightarrow [0,1]$ such that $ß(A,A) = 1 - \alpha(A)$, it is necessary that $\alpha(A^*) = 0.5$, where $A^*(x) = 0.5$, $\forall x$.

Lemma 8. Let X be a Lebesgue measurable set, with a finite measure $m \neq 0$, $A,B \in P^f(X)$ and ß:$P^f(X) \times P^f(X) \rightarrow [0,1]$ a measure defined by:

$$\beta(A,B) = \cap_X f(A(x), B(x))dx$$

[3] For the sake of brevity, in the remaining we will use "ambiguity" instead of "ambiguity measure in the Fisburn-Yager sense" and "coherence" instead of "coherence measure".

Then ß is a coherence measure if and only if the function $f:[0,1]^2 \rightarrow [0,1]$ verifies:

a) $f(x,y) = f(y,x)$
b) $f(x, 1-y) = (1/m) - f(x,y)$
c) $f(1-x,y) = (1/m) - f(x,y)$
d) $f(0,1) = 0$

The following lemma will give conditions for a desirable and intuitive property of the coherence measures: The nearest from $\varnothing$ or X respectively are two elements A and B, the greater coherence measure is.

Lemma 9. Let X be a measurable set, $m = l(X) \neq 0$, and $A,B \in P^f(X)$. Consider $A^*(x) = 0.5$, $\forall x \in X$, and $ß:P^f(X) \times P^f(X) \rightarrow [0,1]$ a coherence measure defined by:

$$\beta(A,B) = \cap_X f(A(x), B(x))dx$$

If f is monotonous in the interval $[0, 0.5]^2$ then:

1) $A \subseteq B \subseteq A^*, A' \subseteq B' \subseteq A^* \Rightarrow \beta(A,A') \geq \beta(B,B')$
2) $A^* \subseteq B \subseteq A, A^* \subseteq B' \subseteq A' \Rightarrow \beta(A,A') \geq \beta(B,B')$

It is patent therefore that is more meaningful a proximity between two very clear evaluations than between two ambiguous evaluations.

Next lemma shows a) the way in which coherence measures can be constructed from metrics on $P^f(X)$, and b) the existence of such measures.

Lemma 10. Let X be a measurable set with a measure $m \neq 0$. Let

$$d:P^f(X) \times P^f(X) \rightarrow [0,1]$$

be a bounded metric defined by:

$$d(A,B) = (\cap_X h(A(x), B(x))dx)^{1/r},\ r \geq 1$$

Then a coherence measure defined as

$$\beta(A,B) = [1 + d(A,B^c) - d(A,B)]/2$$

can be constructed if and only if:

a) $h(0,1) = (1/m)$
b) $h(a, 1-b) = h(1-a,b)\ \forall a,b \in [0,1]$

Therefore the application of this lemma to different metrics will permit to obtain a number of coherence measures which, eventually, shall can be compared. This is the aim of the following examples

Example 1. Case of r-metrics ($r \geq 1$) on $P^f(X)$. As it is known,

$$d(A,B) = [(1/m) \cap_X | A(x) - B(x) |^r dx]^{1/r}$$

It is evident that a) and b) above are verified. Hence from this metric several coherence measures, all of them depending on a parameter r, can be defined.

Example 2. Consider the metrics that can be constructed from $h:[0,1] \to [0,1]$

$$h(a,a) = 0 \qquad \forall a \in [0,1],$$
$$h(a,b) = 1/m \qquad \forall a,b \in [0,1],\ a \neq b$$

If $G = \{x \in X / A(x) \neq B(x)\}$, and g is the measure of G , then in this case:

$$d(A,B) = (g/m)^{1/r},\ \forall r \geq 1$$

Parallel to the above lemma, but now concerning the construction of ambiguity measures, next result shows a production tool for these measures.

Lemma 11: Let X be a measurable set with $m = l(X) \neq 0$, and $\alpha:P^f(X) \to [0,1]$ defined by

$$\alpha(A) = \cap_X g(A(x))\, dx$$

Then α is an ambiguity measure (in Fishburn-Yager sense) if and only if $g:[0,1] \to [0,1]$ verifies:

a) $g(0) = 0$
b) $g(a) = g(1-a)$

This lemma suggest to think on a direct way for extending an ambiguity measure to a coherence one. The following result however shows how that direct extension may be not trivial in general.

Lemma 12. Let X be a measurable set with $m = l(X) \neq 0$ and $\alpha:P^f(X) \to [0,1]$, defined by

$$\alpha(A) = \cap_X g(A(x))\, dx$$

Then, there is not any function $k:[0,1]^2 \to [0,1]$ such that:

$$\beta\,(A,B) = \cap_X k \cdot g(A(x), B(x))\, dx$$

is a coherence measure extending α, that is to say such that: $\alpha(A) = 1 - \beta(A,A)$.

General conditions under which an ambiguity measure can be extended to a coherence measure are shown in the following theorem, which because of this reason is called of extension. This theorem concretely enables two (similar and parallel) ways to perform that extension according to the use of either the max or min operator, and therefore it shows as from each ambiguity measure two coherence measures can be obtained.

Theorem of Extension 13. Let X be a measurable set with $m = l(X) \neq 0$ and $\alpha:P^f(X) \to [0,1]$, defined by

$$\alpha(A) = \cap_X g(A(x))\, dx$$

with $\alpha(A^*) = 0.5$. Then it can be defined coherence measures

$$\beta:P^f(X) \times P^f(X) \to [0,1]$$

in such a way that $ß(A,A) = 1 - \alpha(A)$.

The proof is based upon the consideration of the functions:

$$ß(A,B) = 1 - \alpha(AUB) \text{ and } ß'(A,B) = 1 - \alpha(A \cap B)$$

both defined on the set

$$J_{11} = \{x \in X / A(x) \in [0, 0.5) \text{ and } B(x) \in [0, 0.5)\}$$

It is shown that in J_{11} both ß and ß' are coherence measures, and then the proof is successively straightforward to the sets:

$$J_{12} = \{x \in X / A(x) \in [0, 0.5) \text{ and } B(x) \in [0.5, 1]\}$$
$$J_{21} = \{x \in X / A(x) \in [0.5, 1] \text{ and } B(x) \in [0, 0.5)\}$$
$$J_{22} = \{x \in X / A(x) \in [0.5, 1] \text{ and } B(x) \in [0.5, 1]\}$$

where in all the cases it is also shown as ß and ß' are coherence measures. Consequently the following general form of ß(A,B) is obtained

$$\beta(A,B) = \cap_{J33} [(1/m) - g(\max(A(x),B(x))]dx + \cap_{J3\spadesuit} g(\max(A(x), 1-B(x))dx +$$
$$+ \cap_{J\spadesuit 3} g(\max(1- A(x), B(x))dx + \cap_{J\spadesuit\spadesuit} [(1/m) - g(\max(1- A(x),1- B(x)))dx$$

4 Theorem of Extension Applications

Ways in which the Theorem of Extension can be applied are focused in this section by means of four different examples.

1. Let consider first the ambiguity measure defined in Yager (1995), and suppose it is normalised so that it can be extended to a coherence measure,

$$Fuzz(A) = k \cdot \sum_{i=1..m} D(a_i); \quad D(a_i) = \min(a_i, 1- a_i)$$

From Lemma 7, if A^* is such that $A^*(x) = 0.5\ \forall x$, in order to Fuzz(·) can be extended, it is necessary that $Fuzz(A^*) = 0.5$. Hence $k = 1/m$, and by applying the Theorem of Extension, the following coherence measure is obtained

$$\beta_{Ymax} (A,B) = \cap_{J33} [(1/m)-(1/m) \cdot (\max(A(x),B(x))]dx +$$
$$+\cap_{J3\spadesuit} (1/m) \cdot \max(A(x),1-B(x))dx + \cap_{J\spadesuit 3} (1/m) \cdot \max(1- A(x), B(x))$$
$$dx +$$
$$+\cap_{J\spadesuit\spadesuit} [(1/m)-(1/m) \cdot (\max(1- A(x), 1- B(x))) dx$$

As now will be clear another coherence measure, $ß_{Ymin}$, could be obtained whether min were used instead of max.

2. Let consider now the application of the theorem to the De Luca and Termini's ambiguity measure, De Luca and Termini (1972),

$$Fuzz(A) = -(\sum_{i=1..m} a_i \cdot \ln(a_i) + \sum_{i=1..m} (1-a_i) \cdot \ln(1- a_i))$$

If it is normalised, so that can be extended to a coherence measure,

$$\mathrm{Fuzz}(A^*) = -2 \cdot m \cdot 0.5 \cdot \ln(0.5) = m \cdot \ln 2$$

Therefore the normalised ambiguity measure is defined by:

$$\mathrm{Fuzz}^*(A) = (2 \cdot m \cdot \ln 2)^{-1} \mathrm{Fuzz}(A)$$

The application of the theorem to this measure provides two other coherence measures, which in the following will be referred as $ß_{Dmax}$ and $ß_{Dmin}$.

3. Consider any function $g:[0,1] \rightarrow [0,1]$ verifying a) $g(0) = 0$, b) $g(a) = g(1-a)$, and c) $g(0.5) = 1/(2 \cdot m)$. From lemmas 7 and 11 above, one can construct an ambiguity measure

$$\alpha(A) = \cap_X g(A(x))\, dx, \text{ with } \alpha(A^*) = 0.5$$

to which one can associate two other coherence measures. Concretely the quadratic function $g(\cdot)$ defined as

$$g(a) = (2/m)a(1-a)$$

verifies the above three conditions. Therefore, the application of the theorem will provide again two new coherence measures, β_{2max} and β_{2min}. In particular, if the operator max is used,

$$\begin{aligned}\beta_{2max} = &\cap_{J33} (1/m)\cdot(1 - 2\max(A(x), B(x)) \cdot (1 - \max(A(x), B(x)))\, dx + \\ &+\cap_{J3\spadesuit} (2/m) \cdot\max(A(x), 1- B(x)) \cdot (1- \max(A(x), 1- B(x)))dx + \\ &+\cap_{J\spadesuit 3} (2/m) \cdot\max(1- A(x), B(x)) \cdot (1- \max(1- A(x), B(x)))\, dx + \\ &+\cap_{J\spadesuit\spadesuit} (1/m) \cdot (1- 2\max(1 - A(x), 1- B(x)) \cdot (1- \max(1- A(x), 1- B(x)))\, dx\end{aligned}$$

The following result is of a remarkable importance because it shows as the above measures are monotonous ones in the interval $[0,0.5]^2$.

Lemma 14. The coherence measures obtained from the ambiguity measures of Yager, De Luca and Términi, and the above quadratic function g, respectively denoted $ß_{Ymax}$, $ß_{Ymin}$, $ß_{Dmax}$, $ß_{Dmin}$, $ß_{2max}$ and $ß_{2min}$, verify the hypotheses of the lemma 10. Concretely, these measures can be generically defined as:

$$\beta(A,B) = \cap_X f(A(x), B(x))\, dx$$

being f a monotonous function on its arguments in $[0,0.5]^2$

According to this result, one can conclude, as announced, that the nearest are two elements A, B from ∅ or X, the greater coherence measure is.

4. This last example shows two important properties of the measures of coherence here considered: First, they are context-dependent, that is, these measures depend on X, and second its sensitivity to the vagueness of components. Let $A= (a,b,\alpha,\beta)$ be a fuzzy number with a trapezoid membership function. The parameters a,b, α and β have the meaning that the next figure illustrate,

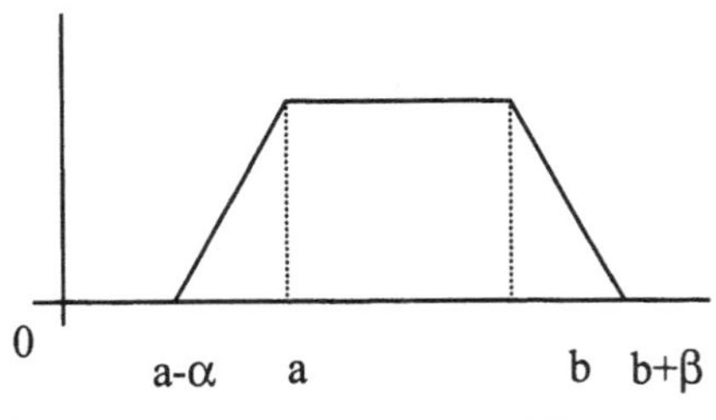

Consider the linguistic variable "age" defined on [0,100] with labels:

child (0, 10, 0, 5); young (15, 25, 5, 5); adult (25, 60, 5, 10); old (65, 100, 5, 0)

A possible representation of the labels could be the following:

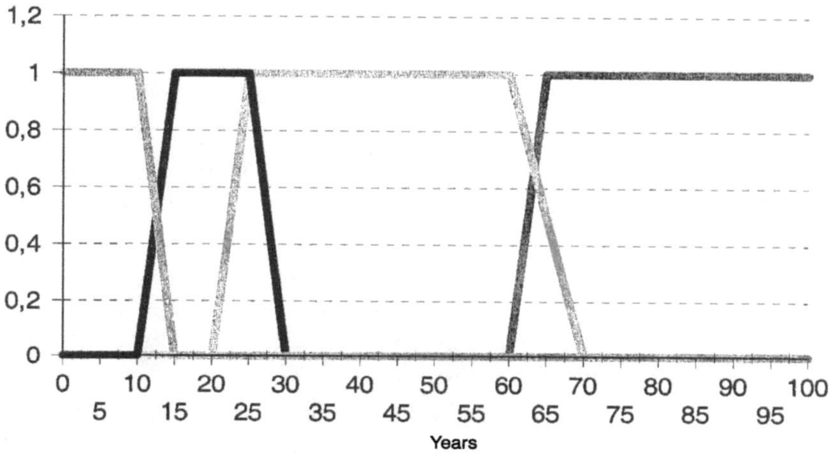

Then coherence measures for β_{Ymax} (Yager's ambiguity) and β_1 (coherence based on the r-metric for r = 1) are shown in the following table

	X=[0,100] β_{Ymax}	X=[0,100] β_1	X=[0,50] β_{Ymax}	X=[0,50] β_1	X=[15,25] β_{Ymax}	X=[15,25] β_1
Child-Young	.74	.75	.48	.50	0	0
Adult-Young	.63	.55	.38	.33	.31	.25
Adult-Old	.25	.55	.45	.45	.75	.75
Child-Old	.50	.63	.74	.75	1	1

Then, on the one hand, as it can be seen the coherences between the labels Child and Old are greater on X = [0,50] than on X = [0,100]. This is because on the interval [15,60] both labels coincide. It is also because of this reason that the coherences between Child and Old equals 1 at third column. On the other hand, the coherence on Child and Young has a high value on X = [0,100], but it is lower when only the first part of the life is considered. It is clear, finally, that in the interval X = [15,25], where Child and Young may be understood as having opposite meanings, the coherences are equal to 0.

References

[1] Bortolan, G. and R. Degani, A Review of Some Methods for Ranking Fuzzy Subsets *Fuzzy sets ans Systems* (1985), 15, (1-19)

[2] DeLuca, A. and S. Términi, A Definition of a Non-probabilistic Entropy in the Setting of Fuzzy Sets *Inf. Control* (1972) 20, (301-312)

[3] Dubois, D. and H. Prade, Fuzzy Sets and Systems. Theory and applications. Orlando :Academic Press (1980)

[4] Fishburn P.C., On the Theory of Ambiguity. *Int. J. Inform. Management Sci.* (1991) 2, 1-16

[5] Fishburn P.C., The Axioms and Algebra of Ambiguity. *Theory and Decision* (1993) 34, 119-137

[6] Sancho-Royo, A. and J.L. Verdegay, Coherence Measures on Finite Fuzzy Sets. *International Journal of Uncertainty, Fuzziness and Knowledge-Based Systems* 8, 6, 641-663 (2000).

[7] Sancho-Royo, A. and J.L. Verdegay, Coherence Measures for Fuzzy Sets. *Proceedings of the Eigth International Conference Information Processing and Management of Uncertainty in Knowledge-Based Systems* (IPMU'2000). Vol III. Madrid, 2000, 1443-1448.

[8] Wong S.K.M., Z.W. Wang and P. Bollmann-Sdorra, On Qualitative Measures of Ignorance *Int. Journ. Intell. Systems* (1996) 11, 27-47

[9] Yager, R.R., On a Measure of Ambiguity. *Int. Jour. of Intelligent Systems* 1995, vol.10, 1001-1019

[10] Yager, R.R., On the Measure of Fuzziness and Negation. Part I :Membership in the Unit Interval . *Int.Journ. Intell. Systems* (1979) 5, (221-229)

[11] Yager, R.R., On the Measure of Fuzziness and Negation. Part II:Lattices *Inf. Control* (1980) 44, (236-280).

Caracterizing k-Additive Fuzzy Measures

Pedro Miranda
Departamento de Estadística, I.O. y D.M.
Calvo Sotelo s/n, 33007 Oviedo, Spain
pmm@pinon.ccu.uniovi.es

Michel Grabisch
Université Pierre et Marie Curie- LIP6
8, rue du Capitaine Scott, 75015 Paris, France
Michel.Grabisch@lip6.fr

1 Introduction

Recently, Grabisch has proposed the concept of k-additive measures to cope with the complexity problem involved by the use of fuzzy measures [8]. The concept has proven to be useful in multicriteria decision making, since it brings a model which is both flexible and simple to use.

However, as far as we are concerned with decision making, a better understanding of k-additive measures in terms of behavioural properties, i.e. related to the preferences of the decision maker, is desirable. In other terms, we are looking for a representation theorem in the spirit of what was done by Schmeidler [16] or Chateauneuf [2] to cite a few, for the Choquet integral with respect to a fuzzy measure.

Based on preliminary results [9] borrowing ideas from social welfare theory, the aim of this paper is to go further on in the characterization of k-additive measures. An emphasis will be done on 2-additive measures, which are the most useful in practice.

2 Basic concepts

Let us start with some basic concepts that will be needed in the following. Till the end, we will use the following notations: We will consider a set of criteria X which is a finite set with cardinality n; elements of X will be denoted by x_i, x_j and so on and also by i, j; subsets of X are denoted by $A, B, ...$; subsets $\{x_i\}, \{x_i, x_j\}$ are sometimes denoted by i, ij in order to simplify notation. Actions are mappings $f : X \mapsto \mathbb{R}$; we denote them by $f, g, ...$; the set of actions is denoted by F; the evaluation of action f

over the criterium i is denoted by $f(x_i)$ or f_i. We will write $f = g$ when $f_i = g_i$, $\forall i \in X$. If $f_i = k$, $\forall i \in X$, for some $k \in \mathbb{R}$ we will denote f by k; we will often identify an action f with the vector of its evaluations over X, i.e. $f \equiv (f_1, ..., f_n)$. We consider a preference relation $\succeq$ on $F \times F$. Our goal in next sections will be to characterize, i.e. to find a set of axioms on $\succeq$, such that

$$f \succeq g \Leftrightarrow \mathcal{C}_\mu(f) \geq \mathcal{C}_\mu(g),$$

where μ is a fuzzy measure and $\mathcal{C}_\mu$ its Choquet integral.

In order to be self-contained, we write down some definitions:

Definition 1 *[17] A (discrete)* fuzzy measure *on X is a set function $\mu : \mathcal{P}(X) \longrightarrow [0,1]$ satisfying*

(i) $\mu(\emptyset) = 0, \quad \mu(X) = 1.$

(ii) $A \subset B$ implies $\mu(A) \leq \mu(B)$ (monotonicity).

Definition 2 *[4] The* Choquet integral *of a function $f : X \rightarrow \mathbb{R}^+$ is defined by*

$$\mathcal{C}_\mu(f) := \int_0^\infty \mu(\{x | f(x) > \alpha\}) d\alpha,$$

which in our case reduces to:

$$\mathcal{C}_\mu(f) := \sum_{i=1}^{n} (f(x_{(i)}) - f(x_{(i-1)})\mu(A_i),$$

where parenthesis mean a permutation such that $0 \leq f(x_{(1)}) \leq ... \leq f(x_{(n)})$ and $A_i = \{x_{(i)}, ..., x_{(n)}\}$. Another equivalent expression is

$$\mathcal{C}_\mu(f) := \sum_{i=1}^{n} f(x_{(i)})(\mu(A_i) - \mu(A_{i+1}))$$

with $A_{n+1} = \emptyset$.

Definition 3 *[19] An* ordered weighted averaging operator (OWA) *is an operator defined by*

$$OWA_w(f) = \sum_{i=1}^{n} w_i f_{(i)},$$

where w is the weight vector, $w = (w_1, ..., w_n) \in [0,1]^n$ and such that $\sum_{i=1}^{n} w_i =$ 1.

Definition 4 *A fuzzy measure is said to be* symmetric *if it satisfies*

$$|A| = |B| \Rightarrow \mu(A) = \mu(B).$$

An equivalent definition for a symmetric fuzzy measure is given by next lemma:

Lemma 1 *Let μ be a fuzzy measure. Then, μ is a symmetric fuzzy measure if and only if for every action $f = (f_1, ..., f_n) \in F$ and for every permutation on the indices π, we have*

$$\mathcal{C}_\mu(f) = \mathcal{C}_\mu(\pi f),$$

where πf is defined by $\pi f_i = f_{\pi(i)}$.

For a symmetric fuzzy measure, the following can be proved:

Proposition 1 *[7, 6, 13] Let μ be a fuzzy measure on X. Then, the following are equivalent:*

1. *there exists $w \in [0,1]^n$ such that $\mathcal{C}_\mu = OWA_w$.*
2. *μ is a symmetric fuzzy measure.*

As a consequence of this result, the following can be proved:

Lemma 2 *Let us suppose that we are given an operator defined by*

$$\mathcal{H}(f) = \sum_{j=1}^{n} w_j f_{(j)}.$$

Then, this operator is a Choquet integral of a symmetric fuzzy measure if and only if the following conditions hold:

- **C1** $w_i \geq 0$.
- **C2** $\sum_{i=1}^{n} w_i = 1$,

We will come back to these conditions in next sections.

Definition 5 *[15] Let μ be a fuzzy measure on X. The* Möbius transform *of μ is defined by*

$$m_\mu(T) := \sum_{K \subset T} (-1)^{|T \setminus K|} \mu(K), \forall T \subset X.$$

We will denote the Möbius transformation of μ by m when there is no confusion. It can be proved [3] that

Proposition 2 *Any Choquet integral $\mathcal{C}_\mu : [0,1]^n \rightarrow \mathbb{R}$ can be written as*

$$\mathcal{C}_\mu(f) = \sum_{T \subset X} m(T) \bigwedge_{i \in T} f_i, \quad f \in [0,1]^n,$$

where $\bigwedge$ denotes the minimum.

Clearly, we have the following lemma:

Lemma 3 *Consider μ a fuzzy measure. Then, μ is a symmetric fuzzy measure if and only if its Möbius transform m is such that $m(A)$ only depends on the cardinality of A, i.e.*

$$|A| = |B| \Rightarrow m(A) = m(B).$$

Definition 6 *[8] A fuzzy measure μ is said to be $k-$*additive *if its Möbius transform satisfies $m(A) = 0$ if $|A| > k$ and there exists at least a subset B such that $|B| = k$ and $m(B) \neq 0$.*

We present now the concept of comonotone actions that will be needed in the following sections. This concept appears in Hardy *et al.* [11]. It is defined as follows:

Definition 7 *[11] A pair of actions f, g is said to be* comonotone *if and only if*

$$(f_i - f_j)(g_i - g_j) \geq 0, \quad \forall i, j.$$

An equivalent definition for comonotonicity is given by next lemma:

Lemma 4 *Let f, g be two actions. Then, f and g are comonotone if and only if they are ranked in the same way, i.e. if there is a permutation π such that*

$$f_{\pi(1)} \leq f_{\pi(2)} \leq \dots \leq f_{\pi(n)},$$

$$g_{\pi(1)} \leq g_{\pi(2)} \leq \dots \leq g_{\pi(n)}.$$

We approach the problem of characterizing k-additive measures in several steps: In next section, we deal with symmetric measures; then the symmetric 2-additive case is considered; finally, we deal with the general symmetric k-additive. We then study the characterization for general fuzzy measures, and from the results obtained we characterize 2-additive measures and finally k-additive measures.

3 Characterization of OWA

In this section we deal with the problem of characterizing the preference relation given by an OWA operator. Then, suppose an OWA operator $(w_1, ..., w_n)$ and the preference relation given by

$$f \succeq g \Leftrightarrow \sum_{i=1}^{n} w_i f_{(i)} \geq \sum_{i=1}^{n} w_i g_{(i)}.$$

In order to characterize this relation we use the following result due to Weymark [18]. We first introduce some axioms:

- **A1** (weak order). $\succeq$ is complete and transitive.
- **A2** (continuity). For every $f \in F$, if $\succ$ denotes the strict preference, the sets $\{g \in F | g \succ f\}$ and $\{g \in F | g \prec f\}$ are open sets (in the topology of F induced by the natural topology on $\mathbb{R}^n$).
- **A3** (symmetry). For every $f, g \in F$, if there is a permutation π on X such that $f = \pi g$, then $f \sim g$, where $\sim$ denotes the equivalence between both actions.
- **A4** (weak independence of income source). For all comonotone actions f, g, h, $f \succeq g \Leftrightarrow f + h \succeq g + h$.

With these axioms Weymark proved the following:

Theorem 1 *[18] Let $\succeq$ be a preference relation over $F \times F$. Then, $\succeq$ satisfies* **A1**, **A2**, **A3** *and* **A4** *if and only if*

$$\exists \mathcal{H} : [0,1]^n \to \mathbb{R} \text{ such that } \forall f, g \in F,\ f \succeq g \Leftrightarrow \mathcal{H}(f) \geq \mathcal{H}(g)$$

and

$$\mathcal{H}(f) = \sum_{i=1}^{n} w_i f_{(i)},$$

where $f_{(1)} \leq f_{(2)} \leq \dots \leq f_{(n)}$, and $w_i \in \mathbb{R}$.

Note that in this result we have no condition over the weights of the functional. We use this result to characterize all symmetric fuzzy measures. For the sake of simplicity, we will establish our result in several propositions.

Let us consider the following axiom.

- **A5** (monotonicity). $f_i \geq g_i, \forall i \Rightarrow f \succeq g$.

It is easy to see that the Choquet integral verifies **A5**. Now, we have the following proposition.

Proposition 3 *If* **A1**, **A2**, **A3** *and* **A4** *hold, then* **A5** *is equivalent to* **C1**.

Let us now consider the following axiom:

- **A6** (non-triviality). There exist $f, g \in F$ such that $f \succ g$.

Then, the following proposition holds:

Proposition 4 *If* **A1**, **A2**, **A3**, **A4** *and* **A5** *hold, then* **A6** *is equivalent to* $\sum_{i=1}^n w_i > 0$.

Now, we can normalize and thus we can suppose that $\sum_{i=1}^n w_i = 1$. Then, applying Lemma 2 and Proposition 1 we obtain the following:

Theorem 2 *Let $\succeq$ be a binary relation on $F \times F$. The following are equivalent:*

1. *$\succeq$ satisfies* **A1**, **A2**, **A3**, **A4**, **A5** *and* **A6**.
2. *there is a unique symmetric fuzzy measure μ such that $\succeq$ is represented by C_μ.*

4 Characterization of 2-additive OWA

In this section we deal with the problem of characterizing 2-additive symmetric fuzzy measures. In order to do this, we are going to use a result proved by Ben Porath and Gilboa in [14]. They denote by F_M the set of increasing actions and use next definition.

Definition 8 *Let f be an action. We say that i f-*precedes *j if $f_i \leq f_j$ and there is no k such that $f_i < f_k < f_j$.*

Ben Porath and Gilboa use the set of axioms of Weymark except **A4** which is changed into a weaker version **A4'**. Besides **A5** is changed into a stronger version **A5'**, and finally they also add some other axioms. Namely:

- **A4'** (order-preserving gift). For every f, f', g, g' in F_M, for every $i \in X$, if $f_j = f'_j$ and $g_j = g'_j$ for every $j \neq i$ and $f'_i = f_i + t, g'_i = g_i + t$ for some $t \in \mathbb{R}$, then $f \succeq g$ if and only if $f' \succeq g'$.
- **A5'** (strong monotonicity). If $f_i \geq g_i$ for all $i \in X$, and there exists a j such that $f_j > g_j$, then $f \succ g$.
- **A7** (order-preserving transfer). For every f, f', g, g' in F, and for all $i, j \in X$, if i $f-, g-, f'-$ and $g'-$precedes j, if $f'_i = f_i + t, g'_i = g_i + t, f'_j = f_j - t, g'_j = g_j - t$ for some $t > 0$, if $f'_k = f_k, g'_k = g_k$ for all $k \neq i, j$, then $f \succeq g$ iff $f' \succeq g'$.
- **A8** (inequality aversion). For every f, f' in F_M, for all $i \in X$, if $f'_i = f_i + t, f'_{i+1} = f_{i+1} - t$ for some $t > 0$, if $f'_j = f_j$ for all $j \neq i, i+1$, then $f' \succ f$.

Then, they prove the following:

Theorem 3 *Let $\succeq$ be a binary relation on $F \times F$. The following are equivalent:*

1. *$\succeq$ satisfies* **A1**, **A2**, **A3**, **A4'**, **A5'**, **A7** *and* **A8**.
2. *there is a unique number $\delta, 0 < \delta < 1/(n-1)$, such that $\succeq$ is represented by the following functional:*

$$\mathcal{H}(f) = \sum_{i \in X} f_i - \delta[\sum_{1 \leq i \leq j \leq n} |f_i - f_j|]. \tag{1}$$

Grabisch [10] has shown that (1) is the Choquet integral of a 2-additive symmetric fuzzy measure. However, this does not cover all of them. The problem is that for his results, the coefficient multiplying $f_{(i)}$ is $1 + (n - 2i)\delta$, and thus the weights are non-increasing. It can be proved [14] that **A8** is equivalent to have a strictly decreasing order in the weights of the OWA operator. As this is not always the case for fuzzy measures, we have to remove it.

It can be seen that the axiom giving 2-additivity is **A7** as we will prove below (Proposition 7).

We will use this set of axioms in order to characterize 2-additive symmetric fuzzy measures. As in the previous section we do it in several propositions.

Proposition 5 *If we have a 2-additive symmetric fuzzy measure (at most), then its weights in the OWA expression verify*

$$w_i - w_{i+1} = w_1 - w_2, \quad \forall i.$$

Remark that 1-additive symmetric fuzzy measures also verify this property. In this case all coefficients are equal and thus $w_1 - w_2 = 0$. This can be seen just from the symmetry or even from the expression of the OWA operator.

Let us now prove the reciprocal of this result.

Proposition 6 *If we have an OWA such that the weights are equidistant, then the corresponding symmetric fuzzy measure is 2-additive or 1-additive.*

Joining both results we obtain:

Corollary 1 *Let μ be symmetric fuzzy measure and $C_\mu(f) = \sum_{i=1}^{n} f_{(i)} w_i$. Then, μ is 2-additive if and only if there exist two constants k_1, k_2 satisfying $w_i = k_1 + (n - i)k_2$, $\forall i$.*

Now, it suffices to find an axiom that gives equidistance in the weights for characterizing 2-additive symmetric fuzzy measures. This is solved in next proposition.

Proposition 7 *If* **A1**, **A2**, **A3**, **A4**, **A5** *and* **A6** *hold, then* **A7** *is equivalent to $w_1 - w_2 = w_i - w_{i+1}$.*

Then, we have proved the following:

Theorem 4 *Let $\succeq$ be a binary relation on $F \times F$. The following are equivalent:*

1. *$\succeq$ satisfies* **A1**, **A2**, **A3**, **A4**, **A5**, **A6** *and* **A7**.
2. *there is a unique 2-additive (or 1-additive) symmetric fuzzy measure μ such that $\succeq$ is represented by C_μ.*

Remark that we have not used **A8**. Remark also that **A7** gives equidistant weights and thus the 2-additivity in the symmetric case. We will use this fact in next section.

5 Characterization of k-additive OWA

Let us now turn to the general case. From the preceding analysis, we just have to remove **A7** and put another axiom for the k-additive case, which we call **A7(k)**. We follow the same sequence as in the previous section:

Proposition 8 *Let μ be a symmetric fuzzy measure and let us denote $C_\mu(f) = \sum_{i=1}^n w_i f_{(i)}$. Then, μ is a k-additive fuzzy measure if and only if*

$$\sum_{j=0}^{k-1}(-1)^j \binom{k-1}{j} w_{i+j} = m_k, \forall i = 1, ..., n-k+1,$$

where $m_k = m(C)$, $|C| = k$.

Let us now consider the following axiom:

- **A7(k)** (k-dimensional order preserving transfer). $\forall f, g, f', g' \in F$ and $i \in X$, if
  1. $f'_i = f_i + t, f'_{i+1} = f_i - \binom{k-1}{1}t, ..., f'_{i+j} = f_{i+j} + (-1)^j \binom{k-1}{j}t, f'_k = f_k, k \neq i, i+1, ..., i+k-1$
     $g'_i = g_i + t, g'_{i+1} = g_i - \binom{k-1}{1}t, ..., g'_{i+j} = g_{i+j} + (-1)^j \binom{k-1}{j}t, g'_k = g_k, k \neq i, i+1, ..., i+k-1$
  2. f, f' and g, g' are comonotone.

  then $f \succeq g \Leftrightarrow f' \succeq g'$.

The following proposition holds:

Proposition 9 *If* **A1, A2, A3, A4, A5** *and* **A6** *hold, then* **A7(k)** *is equivalent to $\sum_{j=0}^{k-1}(-1)^j \binom{k-1}{j} w_{i+j}$ constant, i.e. $\sum_{j=0}^{k-1}(-1)^j \binom{k-1}{j} w_{i+j}$ does not depend on i.*

In summary, we have proved the following.

Theorem 5 *Let $\succeq$ be a binary relation on $F \times F$. The following are equivalent:*

1. *$\succeq$ satisfies* **A1, A2, A3, A4, A5, A6** *and* **A7(k)**.
2. *there is a unique (at most) k-additive symmetric fuzzy measure μ such that $\succeq$ is represented by C_μ.*

Remark that **A7(k)** is much more difficult to interpret than **A7**. This is a weakness in this characterization. A possible way of interpretation has been given by T. Gadjos in [5]. He considers **A7(k)** as a taxation scheme. Then, **A7** means that the decision maker cares about inequality. **A7(3)** represents the fact that the application of **A7** depends on the location in which the policy is applied; **A7(4)** is considered as the fact that the application of **A7(3)** depends on the location in which it is applied and so on. When the application of **A7(k)** does not depend on the location where this policy is applied, then the decision maker respects **A7(k)**. This dependency is interpreted as an inequality aversion for the decision maker. Then, **A7(k)** for different choices of k can also be seen as a scale to measure the sensitiveness to inequalities of the decision maker.

Another possibility of characterization for symmetric k-additive measures can be derived from the results of Calvo and De Baets ([1]) and Kao-Van and De Baets ([12]), in which they introduce the concept of binomial OWA operators.

Definition 9 *Let* $k \in \{1, ..., n\}$. *The* binomial OWA operator C_k^n *is the OWA operator with weight vector* $W_k = (w_{k1}, ..., w_{kn})$ *defined by*

$$w_{ki} = \frac{\binom{n-i}{k-1}}{\binom{n}{k}}.$$

Then, they prove the following:

Theorem 6 *Let* $k \in \{1, ..., n\}$. *Consider an* n*-ary aggregation operator* $\mathcal{H}$*, then the following equivalence holds:*

1. $\mathcal{H}$ *is the Choquet integral w.r.t. a symmetric* k*-additive fuzzy measure* μ *on* X.

2. $\mathcal{H}$ *is a weighted sum of the first* k *binomial OWA operators.*

We feel that this result can help to characterize symmetric k-additive measures. However, a wide study of the binomial OWA operators must be done.

We have to remark as a conclusion that the properties that characterize the k-additive symmetric case are rather special. For the general k-additive case, it can be seen that these properties do not hold. In fact, the most important tool that was used in the proofs of the results was the fact that $m(A) = m(B)$ whenever $|A| = |B|$, and this property is due to the symmetry. This implies that even if these results can give us some idea about the general case, this one is much more difficult.

This will not be the case for general measures. We will prove in the next section that removing the symmetry we can obtain a characterization of Choquet integral.

6 Characterization of Choquet integral for the general case

Now, let us turn to the general case. Then, it is obvious that the symmetry axiom **A3** must be removed. Indeed, it can be proved that we have just to remove **A3** in order to characterize the general case. To prove this, we need the following result due to Schmeidler [16]:

Theorem 7 *Let $I : F \mapsto \mathbb{R}$ satisfying $I(1_X) = 1$ be given. Suppose also that the functional I satisfies*

1. *Comonotonic additivity. f and g comonotonic (Definition 7) imply $I(f+g) = I(f) + I(g)$.*
2. *Monotonicity. $f_i \geq g_i$, $\forall i$ implies $I(f) \geq I(g)$.*

Then, defining $\mu(A) = I(1_A)$, $\forall A$, we have

$$I(f) = \int_0^\infty \mu(f \geq \alpha) d\alpha + \int_{-\infty}^0 (\mu(f \geq \alpha) - 1) d\alpha.$$

This expression is the Choquet integral for real functions.

Now, the following can be proved:

Theorem 8 *Let $\succeq$ be a binary relation on $F \times F$. The following are equivalent:*

1. *$\succeq$ satisfies* **A1**, **A2**, **A4**, **A5** *and* **A6**.
2. *there is a unique fuzzy measure μ such that $\succeq$ is represented by C_μ.*

Proof: It is clear that Choquet integral satisfies all these axioms. Let us see that this is the only functional verifying them.

Let $\mathcal{H}$ be a functional verifying the set of axioms. We will denote by $\mathcal{H}_\pi$ the restriction of $\mathcal{H}$ to a simplex H_π; H_π is defined as follows: for a permutation π of the indices, $H_\pi = \{(x_1, ..., x_n) | x_{\pi(1)} \leq x_{\pi(2)} \leq ... \leq x_{\pi(n)}\}$. Now, we extend $\mathcal{H}_\pi$ to $[0,1]^n$ by symmetry, i.e. given $(x_1, ..., x_n)$ we take a permutation α such that $(x_{\alpha(1)}, x_{\alpha(2)}, x_{\alpha(n)}) \in H_\pi$ and we define $\bar{\mathcal{H}}(x_1, ..., x_n) = \mathcal{H}_\pi(x_{\alpha(1)}, x_{\alpha(2)}, x_{\alpha(n)})$. Thus, $\bar{\mathcal{H}}$ is symmetric. Symmetry axiom, together with **A1**, **A2** and **A4** is the set of axioms used by Weymark in [18]. Then, we know that this is equivalent to

$$\bar{\mathcal{H}} = \sum_{i=1}^n p_i f_{(i)},$$

for some $p_i \in \mathbb{R}$, $i = 1, ..., n$, and $\mathcal{H}$ is comonotone additive.

Then, $\bar{\mathcal{H}}$ is linear in each simplex. In particular $(\bar{\mathcal{H}})_\pi$ is linear but we have $(\bar{\mathcal{H}})_\pi = \mathcal{H}_\pi$.

Thus, $\mathcal{H}$ itself is linear in each simplex. Now, we define $\mu(A) = \mathcal{H}(1_A)$.

By **A5** and **A6** we know that μ is a fuzzy measure. Then, we have the conditions of the result of Schmeidler characterizing Choquet integral. So that $\succeq$ is represented by a Choquet integral. □

Remark that this result is just a version of the conditions of Schmeidler while having an order over the set of actions. In fact, **A4** is a version for actions of the linearity property for each simplex.

This result is very similar to the one proved by Chateauneuf in [2]. He uses the following set of axioms:

- **B1** $\succeq$ is a non-trivial weak order.
- **B2** (Continuity with respect to monotone uniform convergence)
  1. $f_n, f, g \in F, f_n \succeq g, f_n \downarrow^u f \Rightarrow f \succeq g$.
  2. $f_n, f, g \in F, g \succeq f_n, f_n \uparrow^u f \Rightarrow g \succeq f$.
- **B3** (Monotonicity) $f_i \geq g_i + \epsilon$ (where $\epsilon > 0$ is a constant) $\Rightarrow f \succ g$.
- **B4** (Comonotonic independence) $f, g, h \in F, f$ and h comonotonic, g and h comonotonic, then $f \sim g \Rightarrow f + h \sim g + h$.

and then he proves the following:

Theorem 9 *Let $\succeq$ be a binary relation on $F \times F$. The following are equivalent:*

1. *$\succeq$ satisfies* **B1**, **B2**, **B3** *and* **B4**.
2. *there is a unique fuzzy measure μ such that $\succeq$ is represented by C_μ.*

It is easy to see that **B1** is equivalent to **A1** and **A6**, **B2** is equivalent to **A2**, **B3** implies **A5** and finally **B4** is implied by **A4**.

7 Characterization of 2-additive fuzzy measures

Now, we are going to deal with the problem of characterizing 2-additive fuzzy measures. Of course, we only need to add an axiom to the set of axioms found in last section. First, we have to note that we can not use **A7** because this axiom is supposed in a symmetric case. Thus, our axiom must be a generalization of **A7**. It is easy to see that equidistance is not true for the general 2-additive case. Indeed, it can be proved that the only 2-additive fuzzy measures that are equidistant for all orders are the symmetric ones.

Proposition 10 *A fuzzy measure is 2-additive (or 1-additive) if and only if $\forall A \subset X, \forall i, j \in A$,*

$$\mu(A) - \mu(A\backslash\{i\}) - \mu(A\backslash\{j\}) + \mu(A\backslash\{ij\}) = \mu(\{ij\}) - \mu(\{i\}) - \mu(\{j\}).$$

Let us now consider the following axiom:

- **A9** Let f, g be actions s.t. i f, g-precedes j. Let f_1, g_1 be actions s.t. $f_1 \sim f, g_1 \sim g$ and s.t the order between i and j has changed. Let us now consider f', g', f_1', g_1' coming resp. from f, g, f_1, g_1 by adding $t > 0$ to the i-th coordinate; t s.t. the order of all actions does not change. Then, defining the difference of two actions h_1, h_2 as the action h s.t $\mathcal{C}(h_1) - \mathcal{C}(h_2) = \mathcal{C}(h)$, then we have
$$f' - f_1' \sim g' - g_1'.$$

Now, the following can be proved:

Proposition 11 *If $\succeq$ satisfies* **A1, A2, A4, A5** *and* **A6**, *then* **A9** *is equivalent to*
$$\mu(A) - \mu(A \backslash i) - \mu(A \backslash j) + \mu(A \backslash ij) = f(i, j), \quad \forall A.$$

Remark that this axiom is much more difficult to interpret than the other ones. Here, we have two income profiles f, g. It could be interpreted as saying that the amount of income in both systems is the same, or equivalently, that the amount of income depends only on i, j and not on the income of the other ones.

Then, we have proved:

Theorem 10 *Let $\succeq$ be a binary relation on $F \times F$. The following are equivalent:*

1. *$\succeq$ satisfies* **A1, A2, A4, A5, A6** *and* **A9**.
2. *there is a unique 2-additive fuzzy measure μ such that $\succeq$ is represented by $\mathcal{C}_\mu$.*

8 Characterization of k-additive fuzzy measures

In this section we are going to deal with the general k-additive case. We will use the results obtained in last section and then change the 2-additive case for the general k-additive one. For the k-additive case, we have the following result:

Proposition 12 *A fuzzy measure is (at most) k-additive if an only if*
$$\sum_{\substack{B \subset \{i_1, \ldots, i_k\} \\ i_1, \ldots, i_k \in A}} \mu(A \backslash B)(-1)^{|A|-|B|} = f(i_1, \ldots, i_k), \forall A \, s.t. i_1, \ldots, i_k \in A.$$

We consider the axiom:

- **A9(k)** Let f, g be actions such that $f_{i_1} = ... = f_{i_k}, g_{i_1} = ... = g_{i_k}$. We define for all $A \subset \{i_1, ..., i_k\}$ $f_{A,j} = f_j - t$ if $j \in A, f_{A,j} = f_j$ otherwise $g_{A,j} = g_j - t$ if $j \in A, g_{A,j} = g_j$ otherwise. $t > 0$ s.t. the order does not change. Then, for $f' = \sum_{A\subset\{i_1,...,i_k\}} f_A(-1)^{k-|A|}, g' = \sum_{A\subset\{i_1,...,i_k\}} g_A(-1)^{k-|A|}$, we have $f' \sim g'$.

Now, the following can be proved

Proposition 13 *If* $\succeq$ *verifies* **A1, A2, A4, A5** *and* **A6** *then* **A9(k)** *is equivalent to*

$$\sum_{\substack{B\subset\{i_1,...,i_k\}\\ i_1,...,i_k\in A}} \mu(A\backslash B)(-1)^{|A|-|B|} = f(i_1, ..., i_k), \forall A \textit{ such that } i_1, ..., i_k \in A.$$

Then, we have proved:

Theorem 11 *Let* $\succeq$ *be a binary relation on* $F \times F$. *The following are equivalent:*

1. $\succeq$ *satisfies* **A1, A2, A4, A5, A6** *and* **A9(k)**.
2. *there is a unique* k*-additive fuzzy measure* μ *such that* $\succeq$ *is represented by* C_μ.

9 Conclusions and future research

We have found some results characterizing different types of fuzzy measures, from the symmetric case to the general k-additive one. The goal of the paper was to provide some interpretable axioms characterizing these measures. Axioms for 2-additive measures (in the symmetric and in the general case) can be interpreted from an economical point of view. However, it must be noted that axioms for the k-additive general case, are rather difficult to interpret, even for the symmetric case; they are just a generalization of those from the 2-additive case. Maybe it could be possible to find better axioms considering the Shapley interaction ([8]) instead of the Möbius transform; however, the Choquet integral in terms of Shapley interaction is rather complicated and thus a deep study must be done.

References

[1] T. Calvo and B. De Baets. Aggregation operators defined by k-order additive/maxitive fuzzy measures. *Int. J. of uncertainty, Fuzziness and Knowledge-Based Systems*, (6):533–550, 1998.

[2] A. Chateauneuf. Modeling attitudes towards uncertainty and risk through the use of Choquet integral. *Annals of Operations Research*, (52):3–20, 1994.

[3] A. Chateauneuf and J. Y. Jaffray. Characterizations of lower probabilities and other monotone capacities through the use of Möbius inversion. *Mathematical Social Sciences*, 1989.

[4] G. Choquet. Theory of capacities. *Annales de l'Institut Fourier*, (5):131–295, 1953.

[5] T. Gajdos. Measuring inequalities without linearity in envy: Choquet integral for symmetric capacities. (Working paper).

[6] M. Grabisch. Pattern classification and feature extraction by fuzzy integral. In *3d European Congr. on Intelligent Techniques and Soft Computing (EUFIT)*, pages 1465–1469, Aachen (Germany), August 1995.

[7] M. Grabisch. The application of fuzzy integrals in multicriteria decision making. *European J. of Operational Research*, (89):445–456, 1996.

[8] M. Grabisch. k-order additive discrete fuzzy measures and their representation. *Fuzzy Sets and Systems*, (92):167–189, 1996.

[9] M. Grabisch. k-additive measures: Recent issues and challenges. In *5th Int. Conf. on Soft Computing and Information/Intelligent Systems*, pages 394–397, Izuka (Japan), October 1998.

[10] M. Grabisch. On lower and upper approximation of fuzzy measures by k-order additive measures. In *7th Int. Conf. on Information Processing and Management of Uncertainty in Knowledge-Based Systems (IPMU'98)*, pages 1577–1584, Paris (France), July 1998.

[11] G.H. Hardy, J.E. Littlewood, and G. Pólya. *Inequalities.* Cambridge Univ. Press, Cambridge (UK), 1952.

[12] K. Kao-Van and B. De Baets. A decomposition of k-additive Choquet and k-maxitive Sugeno integrals. *Int. J. of Uncertainty, Fuzziness and Knowledge-Based Systems*, to appear.

[13] T. Murofushi and M. Sugeno. Some quantities represented by the Choquet integral. *Fuzzy Sets and Systems*, (56):229–235, 1993.

[14] E. Ben Porath and I. Gilboa. Linear measures, the Gini index, and the income-equality trade-off. *Journal of Economic Theory*, (64):443–467, 1994.

[15] G. C. Rota. On the foundations of combinatorial theory I. Theory of Möbius functions. *Zeitschrift für Wahrscheinlichkeitstheorie und Verwandte Gebiete*, (2):340–368, 1964.

[16] D. Schmeidler. Integral representation without additivity. *Proc. of the Amer. Math. Soc.*, (97(2)):255–261, 1986.

[17] M. Sugeno. *Theory of fuzzy integrals and its applications.* PhD thesis, Tokyo Institute of Technology, 1974.

[18] J. A. Weymark. Generalized Gini inequality indices. *Mathematical Social Sciences*, (1):409–430, 1981.

[19] R. R. Yager. On ordered weighted averaging aggregation operators in multicriteria decision making. *IEEE Trans. Systems, Man & Cybern.*, (18):183–190, 1988.

Design of Takagi-Sugeno Controllers Using Piecewise Constant Functions and a Normalized Fuzzification Transform

Felipe Fernández[1] and Julio Gutiérrez[2]
Dep. Tecnología Fotónica, Facultad de Informática
Universidad Politécnica de Madrid, 28660 Madrid, Spain
[1]felipe.fernandez @es.bosch.com [2]jgr@dtf.fi.upm.es

Abstract

Takagi-Sugeno fuzzy controllers are today one of the most promising technique to describe input-output relations of nonlinear systems using fuzzy rules. This chapter presents an extension of this modelling technique mainly based on the use of global fuzzy parameters and convolution operators to specify different uncertainties of a system: imprecision of inputs, vagueness of antecedent linguistic labels and smoothness requirements of outputs. The presented approach provides an efficient method to specify and implement an extended zero order product-sum Takagi-Sugeno controller with fuzzy inputs, antecedent terms fuzzy partition with an additional uniform vagueness, and singletons outputs with an additional output filter. It introduces a similarity transformation that greatly simplifies the involved computation. The most relevant feature of this approach is a global transformation of imprecision of inputs, uniform vagueness of antecedent terms and smoothness requirements of outputs into a single convolution transform applied to the corresponding antecedent terms partition. The kernels of the fuzzification transforms used are even B-spline functions. Some practical considerations and examples are also given.

1 Introduction

Fuzzy set theory, introduced by Zadeh in 1965, was motivated by the necessity of having a mathematical tool to cope with the wide gap between the precision and sharply defined concepts of classical mathematics and the imprecision and vague concepts usually related to the real world.

Fuzzy control is mainly based on the unsharp boundaries of fuzzy sets, and it allows to describe transfer functions of nonlinear systems using a set of rules and a complementary specification of the corresponding linguistic terms.

Fuzzy tools provide a formal treatment of imperfect knowledge and allow modelling vagueness of linguistic terms and imprecision attached to the inputs of different systems. Moreover, the efficient computations of the involved fuzzy algorithms have become important with the emergence of advanced information systems with critical real time behaviour.

This paper describes an extension of an MISO zero-order Takagi-Sugeno-Kang controller [10] considering fuzzy inputs variables and incorporating into the model an additional smoothing output filter.

The antecedent linguistic terms mainly considered are fuzzy partitions with uniform fuzziness. These partitions of unity are initially decomposed into crisp partitions and additional fuzzification functions, in order to simplify the corresponding specification process.

A unified approach is used to model three types of uncertainty associated with the description of a fuzzy controller: imprecision of each input, uniform vagueness of each antecedent terms partition and output smoothness required

The corresponding uncertainties are modelled by the convolution operations: input fuzzification, antecedent term fuzzification and output filtering

The main idea of the paper is the use of convolution operators as bridges between crisp and fuzzy models. This way a fuzzy set specification is divided into two parts: crisp and uncertainty specification (Figure 1).

This crisp-fuzzy breaking down is in a sense analogous to the standard splitting used in classical engineering to cope with imprecision, errors and noise.

For practical purposes, we have only considered linguistic terms that form convex fuzzy partitions [8] and we have reduced the kernel of convolutions used to even B-spline functions [5]. This choice does not limit too much the expressive power of the model, simplifies very much the corresponding specification and analysis process, and provides a rich set of interesting properties to the fuzzy controllers considered.

The rest of the paper is organised as follows: section 2 reviews some general definitions and terminology on fuzzy sets and fuzzy partitions; the fuzzification transform is introduced in section 3; section 4 describes an extended model of Takagi-Sugeno controller and presents a similarity transformation used for the efficient computation of the corresponding system; in section 5 an application example is shown; and section 6 concludes the work.

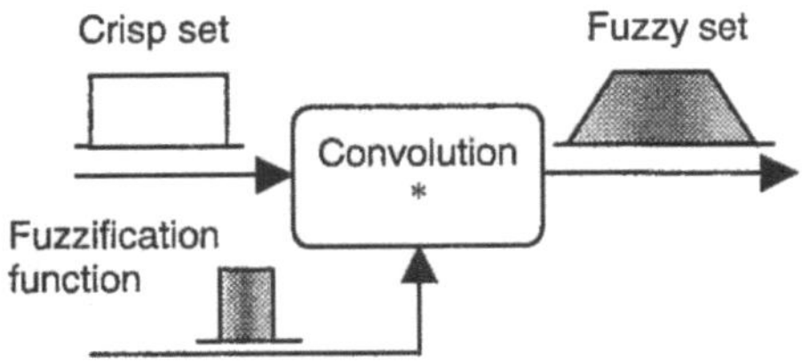

Figure 1. Transformation of a crisp set into a fuzzy set by convolution.

2 Basic Fuzzy Concepts

In this section we gather some general terminology and definitions used in this paper. We also review the main standard concepts required [1][8] and introduce new ones on fuzzy sets, fuzzy numbers and fuzzy partitions.

A multidimensional fuzzy set A can be defined as a mapping A: $R^n \rightarrow [0,1]$. For convenience of ulterior development, we introduce the non-standard concept of S-fuzzy set (signal fuzzy set) defined as function: $R^n \rightarrow [0,\infty)$.

A fuzzy set A is normal when Height(A)=1. A normal convex fuzzy set is usually called in the literature fuzzy number, L-R fuzzy number or fuzzy interval [8].

In this paper, for a more general consideration of fuzzy numbers we relax the normality condition and only maintain the convexity constraint.

To accomplish general functional transformations, we introduce the nonnormal class (into the S-fuzzy sets and S-fuzzy numbers) to designate those ones with Height(A)≠1 (subnormal when 0≤Height(A)<1 and supernormal when Height(A)>1).

For interest of ulterior development, we recall the following standard concepts [8]:

- Cardinality of fuzzy set A, on a discrete domain U, is defined by

$$|A| = \sum_{u \in U} A(u)$$

- Area of fuzzy set A, on a continuous domain U, is defined by

$$|A| = \int_U A(u)\, du$$

In this paper we name a S-fuzzy set C-normal when its area or cardinality is $|A|=1$.

Generally a set of linguistic terms is used in the antecedent description of a fuzzy controller. These linguistic terms can be seen as qualitative values used to describe fuzzy rules.

A set of M linguistic terms $\{A_1, A_2, \dots A_M\}$ is defined in the domain U of a given scalar variable u. It is generally required that the linguistic terms satisfy the property of coverage, i.e. for each domain element is assigned at least one fuzzy set A_j with nonzero membership degree.

For practical reasons, the linguistic terms are usually constrained to be normal or subnormal fuzzy numbers. Also the model here considered, and presently in many other fuzzy control models [1][13][14], imposes stronger conditions on the linguistic terms used:

- Ruspini-partition of unity $\{Aj\}$ of a domain U is defined by the following constraints

$$0 \le Aj(u) \le 1 \qquad \forall u\in U \quad 1\le j\le M$$

$$\sum_{j=1}^{M} A_j(u) = 1 \qquad \forall u\in U$$

$$\sum_{u \in U} A_j(u) \; > 0 \quad 1\le j\le M$$

First equation is the standard membership constraint. Second equation means that for each u, the sum of all membership degrees $A_j(u)$ equals one. Third equation implies that none of the fuzzy sets $A_j(u)$ is empty. This fuzzy segmentation of domain U is also called *fuzzy partition* [1][8]. A hard or *crisp partition* $\{B_j\}$ can be considered as a particular case: $B_j(u)\in\{0,1\}$.

- A sequence $T=\{(t_0,t_1,...,t_M) \mid (a=t_0< t_1< ...< t_M=b)\}$ with $[a,b]\in$ U, defines a basic crisp partition, determined by a set of M crisp intervals $\{A_0, A_1,..., A_{M-1}\} =\{[t_0,t_1),[t_1,t_2),\ldots,[t_{M-1},t_M],\}$

In this paper, a particular extension of a fuzzy partition [7] is considered in order to avoid bound problems in window-convolution operations applied on fuzzy partitions, which are used to model fuzzification transforms:

- A constant extension of a fuzzy partition $\{A_j\}^+$ ($1\le j\le M$) defined on a domain $U=[\alpha,\beta]$ onto a bigger domain $U^+= [\alpha-w, \beta+w] \mid (w>0)$ is characterised by

$$\{A_j(u)\}^+ = \{ \begin{array}{lcl} u\in[\alpha,\beta] & \rightarrow & \{A_j(u)\}; \\ u\in(\alpha-w,\alpha) & \rightarrow & \{A_j(\alpha)\}; \\ u\in(\beta,\beta+w) & \rightarrow & \{A_j(\beta)\}\ \} \end{array}$$

- An important parameter of a fuzzy partition is the *overlapping factor ov*, which is the maximum number of membership functions with non-null membership degrees among all the elements of domain U.

$$\mathrm{ov}(\{A_j\}) = \max_{u\in U} \Big(\sum_{1\le j\le M} \lceil A_j(u) \rceil \Big)$$

where $\lceil\alpha\rceil$ denotes the ceiling function (smallest integer $\ge \alpha$).

Finally in this section we review one type of uncertainty measurement of special interest for fuzzy partition characterisation: degree of fuzziness.

- Any set that is not crisp has some degree of fuzziness that results from the imprecision of its boundaries [8][6]. For measuring fuzziness of a fuzzy set, we can use the function f to express the lack of distinction between the membership $A(u)$ and its complement $1\text{-}A(u)$:

$$f(A) = \int_{Supp(A)} (1-2\,|\,A(u)-0.5\,|)\, du$$

Analogously, it is possible to define the right and left fuzziness of a fuzzy number, respectively delimited on the left and right bounds. For example, the corresponding fuzziness of a normal trapezoidal fuzzy number B are [6]:

$$f(B)=(\alpha+\beta)/2;\ f_l(B)=\alpha/2;\ f_r(B)=\beta/2$$

where α and β are the bases length of the corresponding left and right rectangular triangles.

3 Fuzzification Transform

This section introduces the concept of *fuzzification transform*, which is a generalisation of the concept of fuzzification function [4][8]. This transform allows a unified consideration of the fuzziness associated to the input variables and to the antecedent terms of a fuzzy system, and models the smoothing output filter of a fuzzy controller.

• The fuzzification transform $\mathcal{F}$ applies an even fuzzification function Φ (even C-normal S-fuzzy number) onto a fuzzy number f (normal or subnormal), defined on a continuous extended domain U, and gives a new fuzzy number f' defined by means of the following cross-correlation/convolution operation

$$\mathcal{F}_\Phi(f)\ (v)=\Phi * f\ (v)=\int_U f(u)\cdot\Phi(u-v)\,du=f'(v)$$

A Particular interesting case of fuzzification transform is the Dirac impulse fuzzification transform $\mathcal{F}_\delta$, normally called in the literature singleton fuzzification transform:

$$\mathcal{F}_\delta(f)=\delta * f=f$$

It is convenient to notice that the fuzzification convolution modifies, in general, the support, core and kernel of the corresponding fuzzy number, but it preserves the area and partition of unity condition as it is shown bellow.

On the contrary, if a max-min operation [3] [11][6] is used to define an analogous fuzzification transform (instead of sum-product), the corresponding operation modifies the support but not the core of the corresponding fuzzy number, and therefore it does not preserve the corresponding fuzzy partition.

Some important properties of this fuzzification transform are:

- **Partition of unity conservation.** The fuzzification transform of a fuzzy partition ($\{Aj\}$ j=1..M) is another fuzzy partition, i. e. partitions of unity are closed under fuzzification transform:

$$\mathcal{F}_\Phi(\{A_j\})=\Phi *\{A_j\}=\{\Phi * A_j\}=\{A'_j\}$$

Proof. It is a consequence of the distributive property of convolution operation

$$\sum_{j=1}^{M}\Phi *\{A_j\}=\Phi * 1=1 \qquad \forall u\in U$$

□

- **Area preservation.** The fuzzification transform preserves the area of a fuzzy number A

$$|A*\Phi|=|A|$$

Proof. It is a consequence of the commutative and distributive property of integral operator

$$\int_U F_\Phi(A)dv = \int_U \int_U \Phi(u-v)A(u)\, du\, dv = \int_U \int_U \Phi(u-v)\, dv\, A(u)\, du = 1\cdot |A| \qquad \forall u \in U$$

□

- **Closed in S-Fuzzy numbers set**. The set of S-fuzzy numbers is closed under the fuzzification transform.

Proof. Since the fuzzification transform preserves the convexity property of a fuzzy number.

□

- **Smoothness.** Fuzzification transform is a smoothing transform: If f and Φ have smoothness of order m and n respectively ($f \in C^{m-2}$ and $\Phi \in C^{n-2}$), then $f*\Phi$ has smoothness of order m+n ($f*\Phi \in C^{m+n-2}$). Smoothness of order k means [2] that the derivative of order k of the function becomes impulsive, and the differentiability class C^k is the space of functions that are k times continuously differentiable.

Proof. Since the order of Fourier transforms F of f: Φ and $f * \Phi$ are respectively

$$F(f_j) = o(|s|^{-m});\ F(\Phi) = o(|s|^{-n});\ F(f * \Phi) = o(|s|^{-(m+n)})$$

hence the smoothness order of $f * \Phi$ is $m+n$ (its $(m+n)$-th derivative is impulsive) and consequently $f * \Phi$ belongs to the class C^{m+n-2}.

□

We close this section with three interpretations of fuzzification transform:

1. As a cross-correlation between a linguistic term $A(.)$ and a fuzzy input variable $X(.)$ at position v. This provides a measure of matching or closeness between the fuzzy term A and the fuzzy variable X.

$$F_X(A)\,(v) = X * A\ (v) = \langle X(u-v), A\,(u)\rangle$$

This transform makes easier the real time computation a fuzzy proposition (X is A) when the fuzzification transform is carried out during the compilation time of the corresponding fuzzy algorithm.

2. As a mapping operator (spatially or shift invariant linear operator) with respect to a fuzzification function $\Phi(.)$ of a fuzzy number $A(.)$.

$$F_\Phi(A)\,(v) = \Phi * A\ (v) = \langle \Phi\,(u-v), A\,(u)\rangle$$

This operator uses Φ as a subscript to remind the fact that the transform depends not only on the fuzzy number A but also on the fuzzification function Φ. This way, it is possible to control the fuzziness degree of a fuzzy partition by means of the corresponding fuzzification operator.

3. As a convolution filtering (multivariate lowpass filter) of a signal z with the smoothing function Φ.

$$F_\Phi(z)\,(v) = \Phi * z\ (v) = \langle \Phi(v-u), z\,(u)\rangle$$

so that the lowpass window function Φ can be used for filtering the output z of fuzzy controller. This local averaging has the effect of suppressing the high-frequency variations while preserving the basic shape of z.

4 Extended T-S Model

Zero-order Takagi-Sugeno controllers specify a fuzzy system by means of a set of r rules of the form:

R_r: If x_1 is A_{r1} and ... and x_N is A_{rN} then z is c_r

where R_r is rth rule, $x_1,\ldots,x_N$ are scalar input variables, $A_{r1}, \ldots, A_{rN}$ are fuzzy sets of antecedent linguistic terms, z is the output variable and c_r is a constant function. In this additive model, the output z is a convex combination of the corresponding consequents c_r. The output value of a T-S controller is

$$z = \frac{\sum_{r \in R\,\text{active}} (u_r \cdot c_r)}{\sum_{r \in R\,\text{active}} (u_r)}$$

where $u_r = u_{r1} \times u_{r2} \times \ldots \times u_{rN}$ is the firing degree of the rth rule, and $u_{ri} = A_{ri}(x_i)$ is matching degree between the scalar variable x_i and linguistic term A_{ri}., and R_{active} is the set of active rules.

T-S model has also an equivalent multidimensional form, which is of interest for our purpose:

R_r: If $\boldsymbol{x}$ is $\boldsymbol{A}_r$ then z is c_r

where $\boldsymbol{x}=(x_1,\ldots,x_N)$ is the multivariate input variable and $A_r=A_{r1}(x_1)\times \ldots \times A_{rN}(x_N)$ is the multivariate fuzzy number of the rth rule defined by means of the corresponding tensor product.

The MISO fuzzy controller considered in this paper is an extension of T-S model. Its rules are expressed in conjunctive canonical form:

R_r: If X_1 is A'_{r1} and ... and X_N is A'_{rN} then z is c_r

where $X_1,\ldots,X_N$ are fuzzified input variables that are symmetrical C-normal S-fuzzy numbers, and $A'_{r1},\ldots, A'_{rN}$ are fuzzified terms that are normal or subnormal S-fuzzy numbers. Moreover, each fuzzy term A'_{ri} belongs to the corresponding partition of unity $\{A'_{ij}\}$. These fuzzy partitions are considered as a fuzzified version of an original crisp or fuzzy one $\{A_{ij}\}$.

In order to simplify and improve the specification and implementation of this T-S controller the following additional processes are introduced, applying the fuzzification transform previously defined (Figure 2):

1. The fuzzy inputs are considered the result of a Fuzzification transform applied on the corresponding scalar inputs, in order to contemplate the inputs imprecision:

$$F_{\Phi xi}(\delta_{xi})(v) = \Phi Xi * \delta_{xi}(v) = Xi\,(v)$$

where ΦXi is the fuzzification function applied to input x_i, $\delta_{xi}(v)=\delta(v-xi)$ and $Xi\,(v)= \Phi Xi\,(v-xi)$.

2. The fuzzy partitions mainly consider are the result of a Fuzzification transform applied on the original crisp partitions, in order to contemplate the uniform vagueness (fuzziness) of the antecedent terms:

$$F_{\Phi Ai}(\{A_{ij}\})\,(v) = \Phi Ai^{*}\{A_{ij}\}(v) = \{A_{ij}'\}(v)$$

where ΦA_i is the fuzzification function applied to the original crisp partition $\{A_{ij}\}$ of variable x_i, and $\{A'_{ij}\}$ is the corresponding fuzzy partition obtained.

3. The output of the controller is the result of applying an additional output fuzzification transform, in order to consider the corresponding smoothing constraint (multivariate lowpass filter) in the direction of each variable x_i:

$$F_{\Phi Zi}(z)\,(v) = \Phi zi^{*}z\ (v)$$

where Φzi is the filter convolution function applied on the direction of axis x_i.

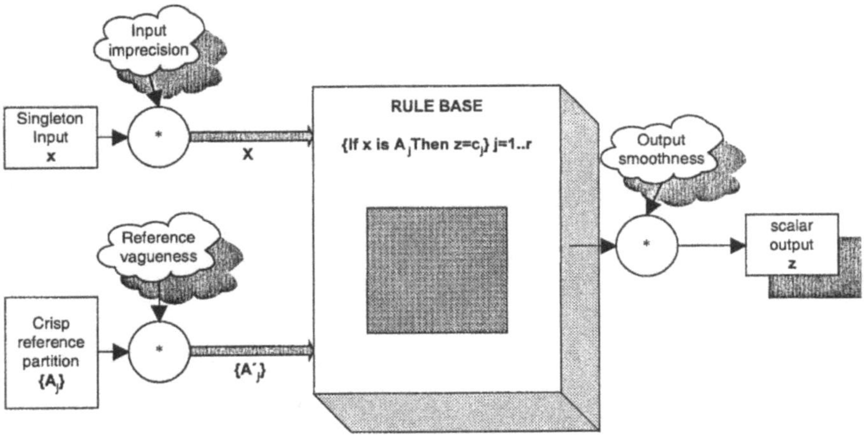

Figure 2. Extended Takagi-Sugeno model considered

Therefore, we can express a rule R_r by the following equivalent multidimensional form

$$R_r\text{: If } (\mathbf{\Phi X}^{*}\delta_x \text{ is } \mathbf{\Phi A}^{*}A_r)^{*}\ \mathbf{\Phi z} \text{ then } z \text{ is } c_r$$

where $\delta x=(\delta x_1, \ldots ,\delta x_N)$ is a multivariate Dirac impulse, $\mathbf{\Phi X} = \Phi X_1(x_1)\times \ldots \times \Phi X_N(x_N)$, $\mathbf{\Phi A} = \Phi A_1(x_1) \times\ldots\times \Phi A_N(x_N)$ and $\mathbf{\Phi Z} = \Phi Z_1(x_1) \times\ldots\times \Phi Z_N(x_N)$ are multivariate fuzzification functions defined by means of the indicated tensor products, and $A_r=A_{r1}(x_1)\times\ldots\times A_{rN}(x_N)$ is the multivariate fuzzy number of the rth rule also defined by means of the indicated tensor product.

All these fuzzification transforms can be combined (Figure 3), taking into account the additive nature of T-S controller, the commutative and distributive properties of convolution operator, and the tensor product structure of the antecedent terms of rules. It results

$$^{o}R_r\text{: If } (\delta_x \text{ is } \mathbf{\Phi X}^* \mathbf{\Phi A}^* \mathbf{\Phi z}\ ^*A_r) \text{ then } z \text{ is } c_r$$

or the following equivalent expression

$$R_r\text{: If } (\delta_x \text{ is } \Phi^* A_r) \text{ then } z \text{ is } c_r$$

where $\Phi = \Phi A * \Phi X * \Phi z$.

This way, it is possible to apply a global fuzzification Φ_i to the corresponding crisp partition $\{A_{ij}\}$ of each variable x_i, obtaining a new fuzzy partition $\{A'''_{ij}\}$

$$\{A'''_{ij}\} = F_{\Phi i}(\{A_{ij}\})\,(v) = \Phi_i^* \{A_{ij}\}\,(v)$$

where $\Phi_i = \Phi A_i * \Phi X_i * \Phi z_i$. This multiple convolution can be executed during the compilation time of the corresponding algorithm, in order to reduce dramatically the corresponding execution time.

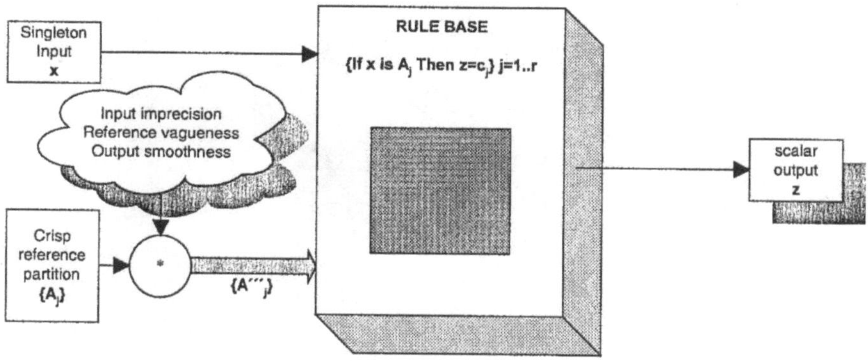

Figure 3. Canonical reduced form of the extended Takagy-Sugeno model.

Using previous transformations, the output z of the controller can be computed in a similar form to a standard T-S fuzzy controller with singleton input variables:

$$z = \frac{\sum_{r \in R\,\text{active}} (u_r \cdot c_r)}{\sum_{r \in R\,\text{active}} (u_r)} = \sum_{r \in R\,\text{active}} (u_r \cdot c_r)$$

where $u_r = u_{r1} \times u_{r2} \times \ldots \times u_{rN}$ is also the firing degree of the rth rule and

$$u_{ri} = \Phi A_i * \Phi X_i * \Phi z_i * A_{ri}(x_i) = A'''_{ri}\,(x_i)$$

is matching degree between the scalar variable x_i and the transformed linguistic term A'''_{ri}

The computation of output z does not use any division since in the new partition of unity obtained, the denominator of previous fraction equals one for every point of domain U^N [5][1].

If a nonuniform partition with a nonuniform fuzziness is required, it is possible to specify first a nonuniform triangular fuzzy partition and then apply an additional fuzzification transform. Another possibility is to introduce an additional input equalisation transform, with a suitable smoothness order, to convert the initial nonuniform crisp partition into a uniform crisp one (Figure 4)

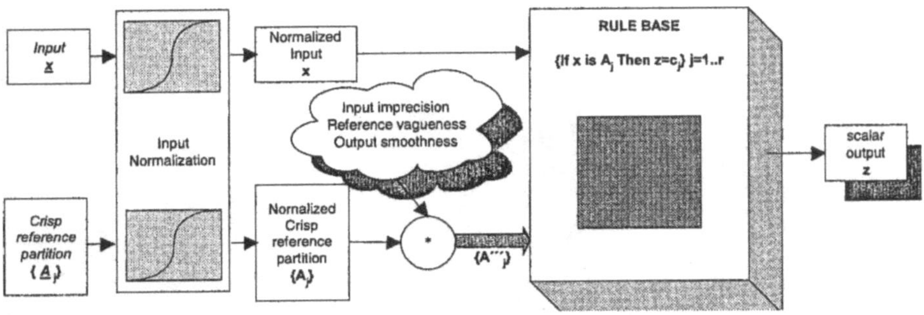

Figure 4. Extended Takagy-Sugeno model with nonuniform fuzziness.

The main advantages of the extended T-S controller presented are:

- It simplifies the specification of a uniform fuzziness system by means of the a crisp-fuzzy decomposition:

  Fuzzy controller = Crisp controller + Fuzzification transform

- The model has more expressive power because it incorporates in the model the imprecision of inputs and output smoothing requirements.

- It is simpler to compute because it does not use any division for output evaluation or any convolution type operation during the execution time.

Next section presents a simple case study on fuzzy control in order to show practically the capability of the model considered.

5 Application Example

A classical experiment of nonlinear feedback control system is the control of verticality of an inverted pendulum, also called cart-pole system. If we call θ the angle between the vertical and the pendulum, the inputs to the fuzzy controller will be θ and the angular speed $\dot{\theta}$

The mathematical model of the pendulum used for simulation has been the same applied by Yamakawa [12] and Driankov et al. [4]

The set of fuzzy rules implemented in our experiment has been indicated in Table 1, which is similar to the one used by other authors [9].

$\dot{\theta}$ / θ	NB	NS	ZR	PS	PB
NB	PB	PB	PB	ZR	ZR
NS	PB	PS	PS	ZR	ZR
ZR	PB	PS	ZR	NS	NB
PS	ZR	ZR	NS	NS	NB
PB	ZR	ZR	NB	NB	NB

Table 1. Fuzzy rules of inverted pendulum

We have selected a well-known fuzzy model in order to have a practical reference for analysing and evaluating the techniques we have developed.

What we have studied is the influence on the smoothness of control surface produced by the global fuzzification transform applied and the corresponding performance effects in the control.

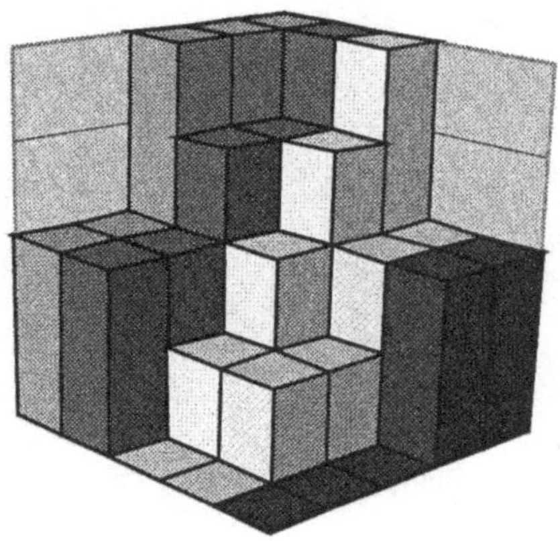

Figure 5. Initial crisp control surface for an inverted pendulum

Uniform Crisp partitions (see Figure 5) are initially considered for the set of linguistic labels, with constant extension in the extremes to determine the ulterior convolution operation. Both inputs: angle and angular speed have the same crisp linguistic terms and the same crisp partition. The universe of discourse is symmetrical respect to 0 and it is in the range [-5,+5]. A new fuzzified set of labels is obtained by the application of a convolution filter on the original crisp linguistic terms. All the membership functions have been convolved tree times with an even C-normal rectangular pulse of 2.0 units of width or, what is the same, convolved one time with an even C^2 cubic B-spline of 6.0 units of support.

Notice that only the table of rules, the antecedent crisp partitions, and the global fuzzy parameters: support size and B-spline order, have been used to specify the reduced form of corresponding fuzzy controller

The initial control surface of the crisp controller before applying the fuzzification transforms is shown in Figure 5 (a piecewise constant surface).

The final C^3 control surface obtained after applying the corresponding fuzzification transform is shown in Figure 6. It is noticeable the improvement in surface smoothness in relation with other classical methods [4]. From the analysis

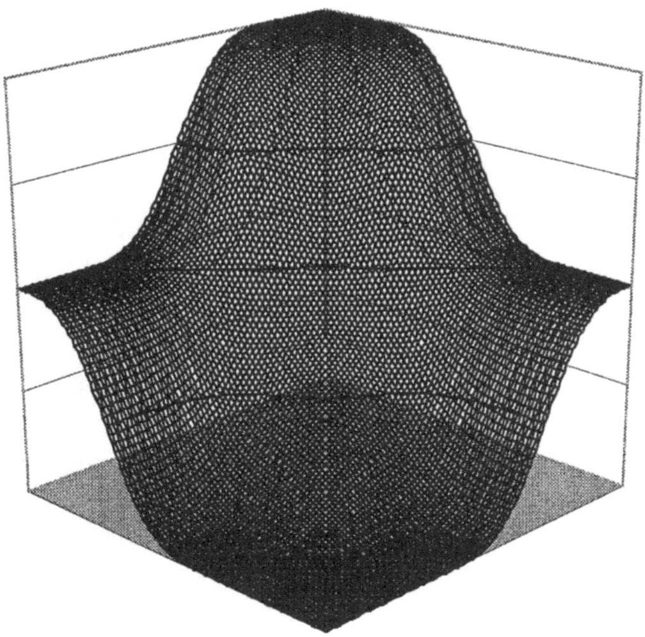

Figure 6. Fuzzified control surface for an inverted pendulum

of responses supplied by the simulator, we have observed a significant improvement in the movement continuity.

6 Conclusions

The main practical contribution of this paper is a direct derivation of a fuzzy system using a set of crisp rules plus global fuzzification parameters, which is of interest in many circumstances of control applications. The fuzzy model developed is mainly based on the additional application of standard fuzzification transform to specify the fuzziness (imprecision) of input variables, common fuzziness (vagueness) of antecedent linguistic terms and the smoothness requirements of output function.

We have used crisp partitions for the antecedent linguistic terms, and even B-spline fuzzification functions. The utilisation of fuzzified input variables, fuzzified antecedent terms and output filtering, in an integrated form, gives more expressive power to the fuzzy source language, allows direct specification of control-surface smoothness and does not involve an additional computation in execution time, using the referred transforms.

This way, the description of fuzzy system with uniform fuzziness can be decomposed into a crisp one and a suitable fuzzification function.

References

1. R. Babuska, Fuzzy Modelling for Control, Kluwer Academic Publisher, 1998.
2. R. N. Bracewell, The Fourier Transform and Its Applications, McGraw-Hill, 1986.
3. T. Chiueh, "Optimisation of Fuzzy Logic Inference Architecture", Computer, IEEE, vol. 25, No. 5, May 1992, pp. 67-71.
4. D. Driankov, H. Hellendoorn, M. Reinfrank, An Introduction to Fuzzy Control, Springer-Verlag, 1993.
5. G. Farin, Curves and Surfaces for Computer-Aided Geometric Design, 4th Ed., Academic Press, 1997.
6. F. Fernández and J. Gutiérrez, "A Transformational Approach to Fuzzy Matching", Proc. of 7th International Conference IPMU, 1998, Vol. II, pp. 1317-1324.
7. F. Fernández and J. Gutiérrez, "Transformation and Optimization of Fuzzy Controllers Using Signal Processing Techniques". Proc. of Int. Conf. 6th Fuzzy Days, Dortmund, May 1999, Lecture Notes in Computer Science 1625, Springer-Verlag, pp. 75-87.
8. G. Klir, B. Yuan, Fuzzy Sets and Fuzzy Logic, Prentice Hall, 1995.
9. B. Kosko, Fuzzy Engineering, Prentice Hall, 1997.
10. M. Sugeno, Fuzzy Modeling and Control. Selected Works of M. Sugeno, Computing Engineering, CRC, 1999.
11. H. Watanabe, W. Dettloff and K. Yount, "A VLSI Fuzzy Logic Controller with Reconfigurable, Cascadable architecture" IEEE Journal of Solid-state Circuits, Vol. 25, No. 2, April 1990, pp. 376-381.
12. T. Yamakawa, "Stabilization of an inverted pendulum by a high speed fuzzy logic controller hardware system.", Fuzzy Sets and Systems, vol. 32, 1989.
13. J. Zhang and A. Knoll, Constructing Fuzzy Controllers with B-spline Models, IEEE International Conference on Fuzzy Systems, 1996.
14. J. Zhang and A. Knoll, Unsupervised Learning of Control Surfaces Based on B-spline Models, IEEE International Conference on Fuzzy Systems, 1997, pp. 1725-1730.

Fuzzy Temporal Rules: A Rule-based Approach for Fuzzy Temporal Knowledge Representation and Reasoning

Purificación Cariñena, Alberto Bugarín, Manuel Mucientes, Félix Díaz-Hermida, and Senén Barro

Grupo de Sistemas Intelixentes, Dept. Electrónica e Computación
Univ. Santiago de Compostela, 15782 Santiago de Compostela. Spain.
{puri,alberto,manuel}@dec.usc.es, felixdh@usc.es, senen@dec.usc.es

Abstract. In this paper a model for the representation and execution of a type of fuzzy control rules that explicitly handle time variable (Fuzzy Temporal Rules) is presented. The model here described permits using temporal references for the occurrence of events. These references are allowed to be described either in an absolute manner or related to occurrence of other events. A complete grammar that formally describes the representation language of the model is presented, together with its semantic counterpart. This knowledge and reasoning representation model is illustrated by means of a number of examples that show the substantial increase in the expresiveness that FTRs exhibit when compared to usual fuzzy control rules.

Keywords: fuzzy temporal rules, temporal reasoning, knowledge representation and reasoning

1 Introduction

The control environment, in which the fuzzy set theory has been applied with undoubted success, is essentially an application field in which variables are dynamic and changeable. In spite of this, it is curious to note that there has been a tendency, it would seem, to opt for simple and basic fuzzy reasoning models, without paying hardly any attention to the possibility of representations of knowledge that explicitly manipulate time and reason on it. In our opinion, this noticeably limits the possibilities for the expansion of fuzzy reasoning to applications which demand more expressive forms of dealing with expert knowledge. The greater complexity required at an operational level by fuzzy temporal rules (FTRs) - fuzzy temporal rule being understood as one which represents information of a temporal type in an explicit manner - as opposed to simple fuzzy rules may be, without doubt, one of the causes of this. On the other hand, the fact that there are still no well-defined models nor computer aid tools for the design of FTR-based systems, means that the use of this form of knowledge representation is very limited, which, in turn, limits the interest of the research and technical communities in FTRs.

In this work, our objective is to present a formal FTR model, which may be used for representation of and reasoning on fuzzy temporal knowledge, and which is endowed with substantial expressive capabilities. We introduce the formal definition of a grammar that describes Fuzzy Temporal Propositions (FTPs), as those making up the FTRs. The aim is to implement a language, close to the natural one, which allows experts to describe their knowledge (including the temporal component) in a legible and flexible way. We then analyze the FTR execution process, describing the semantic expressions associated to the syntactic rules in the proposed grammar, including some examples by way of illustration.

Some of the aspects related to the model of FTPs, mainly concerning the semantics associated with part of the propositions here formalised, can be found in [2,4,5], although outside the formal and integrational setting proposed in this paper.

1.1 Some Approaches to the Concept of Fuzzy Temporal Rule

The first attempt to formalize the representation of fuzzy time by means of intervals associated to fuzzy sets was described in [17]. However, arguably the first formal work with regard to the formalization of the concept of fuzzy time is that of [9], where the foundations for the representation of imprecision and uncertainty in temporal knowledge with the theory of possibility were laid. With some variants, the concepts there introduced and the manner of representing them appear in the majority of works relating to fuzzy time.

With regard to models of fuzzy temporal reasoning (fuzzy reasoning that explicitly takes into account the presence of temporal references), these fundamentally deal with constraint network models [3,12] and fuzzy rules which, in one way or another, explicitly introduce time as another decision variable. In [14], a model for fuzzy proposition and temporal reasoning, that deals with three forms of temporal relationship is presented. The model is not capable of handling persistence over time of conditions of the value of the variables that are handled, although all basic temporal relations [1] amongst temporal entities (time instants or intervals) are dealt with.

In [16], the concept of "time dependent fuzzy set" is introduced, whilst in [11] a reasoning method that incorporates a vague time delay into fuzzy *if-then* rules is proposed. Except for the specific mathematical support with which rules are evaluated, this is a similar proposal to [7], which deals with establishing a validity time for the result inferred by a rule, an idea which is also present in the faded temporal fuzzy controller described in [10]. [15] puts forward a model for the representation and manipulation of vague time, based on the theory of possibility and following the temporal entity representational scheme of [9].

2 Model of Fuzzy Temporal Propositions

In the following, we present the main features of our model of FTRs, and also a formal grammar which encompasses the degree of expressiveness of the model. A first approach to this problem was presented in [6].

2.1 Time Entities

For representing temporal entities, and following [9], we assume a discrete time axis τ, that is discretized in time points t_n, $n \in \mathbb{N}$. Time point $t_0 \in \tau$ represents the time origin, and $\forall n \in \mathbb{N}$ $\delta = t_n - t_{n-1}$ is assumed to be a constant. The following temporal entities [3] are also considered:
- **Instant** i. Represented as a normalized and unimodal possibility distribution $\mu_i(t)$ that represents the possibility of i being precisely time point $t \in \tau$.
- **Temporal extent (duration)** D. It represents quantities of time. A fuzzy temporal extent or duration is represented by a possibility distribution μ_D over the set of integer numbers $\mathbb{Z}$ (assuming they represent units of time δ).
- **Interval** $I(i_b, i_e, D)$. It is described by means of a possibility distribution μ_I that is calculated as in [9], according to the possibility theory. For example, if the beginning i_b and ending i_e instants are known, μ_I comprises the time points that are possibly after i_b and before i_e. In a similar way it is calculated when either i_b or i_e and duration D are known.

Furthermore, we consider the basic temporal relationships (qualitative and quantitative) [3] between these entities, at the level of instants and intervals ($i - i$, $i - I$, $I - I$), and between temporal extents ($D - D$). We assume that all these relationships between temporal entities can be reduced to relationships between time points and temporal extents. Some examples of this kind of relationships are: *before, at the end of...* We do not consider in any case expressions that make reference to the future.

In this manner, we may have absolute and relative temporal entities. We should strictly consider that the specification of time associated to a fact in absolute terms is any one relative to a fixed entity of time, whilst a specification of time associated to a fact in relative terms will be the one that depends on a temporal entity that is linked to the occurrence of other facts.

For instance, we may have an instant i which is given by a reference to a fact occurring at time i_{ref}, bearing in mind that it always has to be prior (or equal) to t_{now}, the current time point. In this case, we have: $i = D \oplus i_{ref}$, and using fuzzy addition operator $\oplus$, this is defined as:

$$\forall t \in \tau, \mu_{D \oplus i_{ref}}(t) = Sup_{t=t'+k\delta} min \left(\mu_D(k), \mu_{i_{ref}}(t')\right), t' \in \tau, k \in \mathbb{Z} \quad (1)$$

2.2 Model of Fuzzy Temporal Rules and Propositions

We assume that we are operating with discrete signals S, described by means of a function $S(t)$, which represents the history of crisp values associated to a variable, together with the occurrence time points of each one of the aforementioned values. This is what most real-time applications [13] demand.

Two types of signals are defined: **observed** signals, whose values are supplied from outside the system, by means of sensors, file readings, ... and **inferred** signals, whose values are supplied by the system itself, by means of inference processes based on prior observations and/or inferences.

FTRs take the form:

IF PC_1 and PC_2 and ... and PC_M THEN C_1 and C_2 and ... and C_N

where PC_m, $m = 1,...,M$, are propositions of the antecedent part of the rule, and C_n, $n = 1,...,N$, of the consequent part of the rule (conclusions), which take the form C_n: S_n is V_n in T_n, S_n being an inferible signal, V_n the value (represented by a non-temporal fuzzy set) inferred for this signal and T_n the time (fuzzy instant or interval) associated to the inferred value. For the antecedent part, a **fuzzy temporal proposition** consists of a signal and a set of different constraints on it:

- **Value Constraints** (VC). Spatial (non temporal) value constraints on the signal, which may be given in an absolute manner ($VC(u) = \mu_{VC}(u)$), or related to another spatial reference value V_{ref} ($VC(u) = (\Delta \oplus \mu_{V_{ref}})(u)$). For example, as in "*high*" or "*much greater than pressure in heater 2*"

- **Temporal Constraints** (TC). Absolute or relative temporal constraints over the set of temporal points where the signal will be evaluated. They may be instants (TCi) or intervals (TCI). Examples of this type of constraints are "*throughout the last half an hour*", "*before the maximum value of pressure*".

- **Temporal Context**. In some cases a temporal constraint may act as a temporal context for signal evaluation, establishing a temporal window (interval) within which the proposition will be evaluated, as in "*a few minutes ago*" or "*the last half an hour*"

We may also have **operators** belonging to one of the following types:

- **Quantifiers** (O_Q): *all, the majority, between 3 and 5, approximately half,...* In some cases it may be of interest to quantify the fuzzy temporal propositions, as in "*the temperature has been high during the majority of the last half an hour*".

- **Specification operators** (O_S): *first, last, maximum, minimum,...* These select one candidate from amongst various, according to a specific criterion (spatial and/or temporal).

- **Reduction operators** (O_R): *mean value, accumulated value,...* In this case the constraint operates on the spatial values that are observed or inferred for the proposition, in order to return a new one, calculated on the basis of the former ones.

In order to formalize the description of which combinations of these elements are allowed, a grammar is presented in the next section. The description of the grammar comprises all rules that permit the construction of a temporal specification language.

3 A Grammar for Fuzzy Temporal Rules

3.1 Rewriting Rules of the Grammar

We introduce a grammar describing the structure of FTPs, which contemplates all the elements mentioned above. The complete set of syntactic rules, combining temporal and spatial values and constraints, is shown in Table 1, using the BNF (Backus-Naur Form) metalanguage.

It can be seen in the table how the first three rules establish the general structure of a propositional clause PC. Rules R5-R6 deal with the different types of value constraints which may act on the signal: absolute and/or relative constraints. In rules R7 to R21 the structure of the temporal constraints and temporal relations between temporal entitites (instants, intervals, time extents) is described, enabling a great flexibility in the use of temporal references in the propositions. Finally, rules R22 to R25 correspond to the description of the different kinds of operators: reduction, spatial or temporal specification, quantification.

3.2 Semantic Expressions Associated to the Syntactic Rules

The next step after defining the rewriting rules for a grammar for FTPs is to describe their semantic counterpart: how the propositions are evaluated during the process of execution of the FTRs, in order to obtain a degree of fulfillment(DOF) for a FTP. In principle, for each one of the constraints present in a proposition an associated DOF can be obtained. This DOF indicates the degree in which this constraint is verified according to the *evaluation instance*, understood as the set of data considered (spatial and temporal values and, where appropriate, associated DOFs). The evaluation time for a rule will be the current time point t_{now}, which is used as the reference time point for the consequent part of the rule. Furthermore, it should be borne in mind that during the evaluation of propositions in real time, the evaluation scenario will alter as time advances. In the case of there being a temporal context defined explicitly for the proposition, different evaluation instances may be obtained from it, so that the remaining constraints will be evaluated on each one of them. In the absence of other explicit criteria, it will be considered that the result of the evaluation of a proposition in a given temporal context is the one that is obtained on the basis of the best of the possible evaluation instances.

Table 2 shows the semantic rules corresponding to the grammar in Table 1.

Table 1. Rewriting rules of the grammar (using BNF metalanguage).

(R1) <Propositional Clause>::= (<Proposition> |
| <Proposition><Spatial Relation><Proposition>)[<Temporal Constraint>]
(R2) <Proposition>::= <Generalised Signal> <Temporal Instant> |
| (<Operator> | <Quantifier>) <Generalised Signal> [<Value Constraint>]
<Temporal Interval>
(R3) <Generalised Signal>::= <Signal> [<Value Constraint>]
(R4) <Signal>::= TEMPERATURE | PRESSURE | ...
(R5) <Value Constraint>::= HIGH | LOW | TALL | MORE THAN 30 | ...
(R6) <Spatial Relation>::= GREATER THAN | LOWER THAN | SIMILAR TO |...
(R7) <Temporal Constraint>::= <Temporal Instant> | <Temporal Interval>
(R8) <Temporal Instant>::= [<Instant-Instant Relation>] <Instant> |
| <Instant-Interval Relation> <Interval>
(R9) <Temporal Interval>::= [<Interval-Interval Relation>] <Interval> |
| <Interval-Instant Relation> <Instant>
(R10) <Instant-Instant Relation>::= [<Instant-Instant Relation>]
(<Time Distance> | [APPROXIMATELY] EQUAL)
(R11) <Instant-Interval Relation>::= [<Instant-Interval Relation>]
(<Time Distance> | [<Instant-Instant Relation>]
(BEGINNING | END) | BELONGS)
(R12) <Time Distance>::= [<Time Extent>] (AFTER | BEFORE)
(R13) <Time Extent>::= <Temporal Quantity> [<Temporal Unit>]
(R14) <Temporal Quantity>::= $k \in \mathbb{Z}$| LITTLE | MUCH | AT LEAST SOME |...
(R15) <Temporal Unit>::= ...| SEC | MIN | HOUR |...
(R16) <Instant>::= <Direct Instant> | <Propositional Clause>
(R17) <Direct Instant>::= $t \in \tau$| NOW | TODAY | AT NOON |...
(R18) <Interval-Instant Relation>::= [<Interval-Instant Relation>]
(<Time Distance> | [APPROXIMATELY] (UNTIL | FOLLOWS) |
| INCLUDES)
(R19) <Interval-Interval Relation>::= [<Interval-Interval Relation>]
(<Time Distance> | ([APPROXIMATELY] (STARTS WITH |
| STARTED BY | AT | FINISHES WITH | FINISHED BY | UNTIL |
| FOLLOWS)) | INCLUDES | DURING |
| OVERLAPS (SINCE) | OVERLAPPED BY (UP TO))
(R20) <Interval>::= <Direct Interval> | <Propositional Clause>
(R21) <Direct Interval>::= (<Instant>, <Instant>, <Time Extent>) |
| BETWEEN<Instant>AND<Instant> | YESTERDAY | TODAY |...
(R22) <Operator>::= <Reduction Operator> | <Specification Operator>
(R23) <Reduction Operator>::= MEAN_VALUE | ACCUMULATED_VALUE | ...
(R24) <Specification Operator>::= MAXIMUM | MINIMUM | LAST | ...
(R25) <Quantifier>::= [APPROXIMATELY] (ALL | THE_MAJORITY |
| BETWEEN_3_AND_5 | A_HALF | ...)

The first rule establishes that from a propositional clause PC a set of three elements is obtained when the rule is executed: history of signal values ($S(t)$), and degrees of fulfillment of spatial and temporal constraints in the proposition. In these semantic rules, SF stands for "spatial fulfillment" and TF for

Table 2. Semantic expressions associated to rules in Table 1. In expressions, U stands for the non-temporal universe of discourse

(R1) <Propositional Clause>: $PC(t) = (S(t), SF_{PC}(t), TF_{PC}(t))$
<Prop. Clause>::= <Proposition> [<Temp. Constr.>]
$SF_{PC}(t) = SF_P(t),\ TF_{PC}(t) = TC(t) \wedge TF_P(t)$
<Prop. Clause>::= <Prop.><Spatial Rel.><Prop.> [<Temp. Constr.>]
$SF_{PC}(t) = SF_P(t) \wedge \left[\bigvee_{t' \in TF'_P} SR(S(t), S'(t')) \wedge SF_{P'}(t') \wedge TF_{P'}(t')\right]$
$TF_{PC}(t) = TC(t) \wedge TF_P(t)$
(R2) <Proposition>: $P(t) = (S(t), SF_P(t), TF_P(t))$
<Prop.>::=<Gen. Signal> <Temp. Instant>
$SF_P(t) = SF_{GS}(t), TF_P(t) = TCi(t)$
<Prop.>::=<Operator> <Gen. Signal> [<Val. Constr.>] <Temp. Interval>
with <Operator>::=<Specification Operator>
$SF_P(t) = SF_{GS}(t) \wedge SF_{O_S}(t) \wedge \mu_{VC}(t), TF_P(t) = TCI(t)$
with <Operator>::=<Reduction Operator>
$P(t_{now}) = S_{O_R}(t_{now}) \Rightarrow PC(t_{now}) = (S_{O_R}(t_{now}), SF_{PC}(t_{now}))$
<Prop.>::=<Quantifier> <Gen. Signal> [<Val. Constr.>] <Temp. Interval>
$SF_P(t) = SF_{GS}(t) \wedge \mu_{VC}(t), TF_P(t) = TCI(t)$
(R3) <Gen. Signal>: $GS(t) = (S(t), SF_{GS}(t))$
$SF_{GS}(t) = \mu_{VC}(S(t))$
(R4) <Signal>: $S(t),\ t \in \tau$
(R5) <Value Constraint>: $\mu_{VC}(u), u \in U$
(R6) <Spatial Relation>: $\mu_{SR}(u, u'), u, u' \in U$
(R7) <Temporal Contraint>: $TR(t)$
(R8) <Temporal Instant>: $TCi(t) = \mu_{i-i}(k) \oplus i(t)$
$TCi(t) = \mu_{i-I}(k) \oplus I(t)$
(R9) <Temporal Interval>: $TCI(t) = \mu_{I-i}(k) \oplus i(t)$
$TCI(t) = \mu_{I-I}(k) \oplus I(t)$
(R10) <Instant-Instant Relation>: $\mu_{i-i}(k), k \in \mathbb{Z}$
(R11) <Instant-Interval Relation>: $\mu_{i-I}(k), k \in \mathbb{Z}$
(R12) <Time Distance>: $\mu_D(k) \oplus \mu_{AFTER/BEFORE}(k)$
(R13) <Time Extent>: $\mu_D(k)$
(R14) <Temporal Quantity>: $k \in \mathbb{Z} \mid \mu_{LITTLE} \mid \ldots$
(R16) <Instant>::=<Direct Instant>: $i(t) = \mu_i(t)$
<Instant>::=<Propositional Clause>: $i(t) = TF_{PC}(t)$
(R17) <Direct Instant>: $t \in \tau \mid \mu_{NOW}(t) \mid \mu_{TODAY}(t) \mid \ldots$
(R18) <Interval-Instant Relation>: $\mu_{I-i}(k), k \in \mathbb{Z}$
(R19) <Interval-Interval Relation>: $\mu_{I-I}(k), k \in \mathbb{Z}$
(R20) <Interval>::=<Direct Interval>: $I(t) = \mu_I(t)$
<Interval>::=<Propositional Clause>: $I(t) = TF_{PC}(t)$
(R21) <Direct Interval>::= $\mu_I(t)$ defined as mentioned in section 2.1
(R23) <Reduction Operator>: $S_{O_R}(t_{now}) = O_R(S(t)), t \in SUPP_{t_{now}}(TCI)$
(R24) <Specification Operator>: $SF_{O_S}(t)$ degree of fulfillment of the specification
(R25) <Quantifier>: any valid quantifier operator O_Q may be used as stated in section 4.1

"temporal fulfillment", whilst the subscripts indicate the entity being referred to.

All time dependent expressions are defined over the time points $t \in \tau$, according to the assumed discretization, except for the case of reduction operators in R2, where a single value of the signal is obtained at t_{now} (R23) when the rule is executed, with its corresponding spatial degree of fulfillment if there exists a value constraint in the proposition acting on this "reduced" spatial value. In the next section an explanation on the meaning of these semantic rules is presented, together with some examples.

4 Execution of Fuzzy Temporal Rules

The execution of a rule involves the evaluation of each one of the propositions PC_m, $m = 1,...,M$, which make up its antecedent part, and for which an individual DOF will have to be obtained. The calculation of a global DOF for the entire antecedent part, is made by means of the usual conjunction process in fuzzy control: $DOF_{ant\_part} = DOF_1 \wedge DOF_2 \wedge \ldots \wedge DOF_M$. This global value will be the one that is transmitted to the consequent part when the rule is executed.

4.1 Execution of Independent Propositions

A proposition PC_m is defined as **independent** if all its associated constraints are absolute, i.e. can be evaluated independently from any other temporal fact or proposition. It corresponds to an instantiation of rule R1 as

<Propositional Clause>::=<Proposition>

and no other recursive instantiation of this rule.

The calculation expression for DOF_m depends on the kind of proposition we are dealing with. If the temporal reference for the proposition is an instant (first case in rule R2, Table 2), we have [4,5]:

$$DOF_m(t_{now}) = \bigvee_{t \in SUPP_{t_{now}}(TF_{PC_m})} SF_{PC_m}(t) \wedge TF_{PC_m}(t) \qquad (2)$$

In the case of the temporal reference being an interval (the remaining options in rule R2), we must distinguish the three situations in Table 2: specification operator, reduction operator and quantifier [1].

For the first case (**specification**), the expression for $DOF_m(t_{now})$ will be the same as in (2). In the case of **reduction** operators, the spatial value obtained is not a function of t, as we previously mentioned, so the calculation of $DOF_m(t_{now})$ will be as follows (applying also rule R23):

$$DOF_m(t_{now}) = SF_{PC_m}(t_{now}) \qquad (3)$$
$$SF_{PC_m}(t_{now}) = \mu_{VC_m}(S_{O_R}(t_{now}))$$

[1] For implementing these operators, respectively denoted as O_R, O_S and O_Q, any of the valid models in the literature may be used (e.g., [8])

Finally, the structure of the expression for this calculation in the third case (**quantification**) is a function of the particular quantifier in the proposition (R25). In general:

$$DOF_m(t_{now}) = O_{Q_{t \in SUPP_{t_{now}}(TF_{PC_m})}} [SF_{PC_m}(t), TF_{PC_m}(t)] \qquad (4)$$

where O_Q may be modelled using any valid quantifier model [8]. For instance, when $Q = \forall$:

$$DOF_m(t_{now}) = \bigwedge_{t \in SUPP_{t_{now}}(TF_{PC_m})} [SF_{PC_m}(t) \vee [1 - TF_{PC_m}(t)]] \qquad (5)$$

and when $Q = \exists$ (this is assumed to be the default case):

$$DOF_m(t_{now}) = \bigvee_{t \in SUPP_{t_{now}}(TF_{PC_m})} [SF_{PC_m}(t) \wedge TF_{PC_m}(t)] \qquad (6)$$

Fulfillment of the value constraints. Different cases may come about, depending on the type of constraints present in the proposition:
(i) The value constraint VC in rule R3 is an absolute value (e.g. VC ="high"). Then, $\mu_{VC}(u) = \mu_{high}(u)$ (R5). This case includes those constraints that are "relative" to an absolute reference value: $\mu_{VC}(u) = (\Delta \oplus V_{ref})(u)$, where Δ represents the spatial relationship with respect to a reference value V_{ref} ($SR(u, u') = \Delta(u - u')$, e.g., "*The temperature is much greater than 30° C* ").
(ii) If a reduction or a specification operator exists, a second value constraint (rule R2) will be added (with t-norm *minimum*) to the result of applying the first one (in the case this exists).
Example 1: "*At some point in the last few minutes, the minimum value among high temperatures has been very high*".
PC : (GS = (S =temperature, VC_1 = high), TCI=the last few minutes, O_S=minimum, VC_2=very high).

The value constraint VC_2 "*very high*" is applied on the value instance obtained after applying specification operator O_S in the temporal reference $TCI(t)$ "*the last few minutes*" and the value instance of observed temperature values, previously filtered through value constraint VC_1 "*high*".

Fulfillment of the temporal constraints. The evaluation of the degree of fulfillment or membership to the temporal part of the proposition implies obtaining a distribution $TF_{PC}(t)$, associated to the set of time points on which the rest of the constraints have to be evaluated.
(i) Only temporal constraints TCI or TCi and context TC, both absolute temporal references, are present: $TF_{PC}(t)$ will be determined by the possibility distributions associated to these references (either temporal instants or intervals, fuzzy or not), $TF_{PC}(t) = TCI(t) \wedge TC(t)$ (and analogously for the case of instants TCi).

(ii) If a temporal constraint TC is relative to another absolute temporal reference T^* (instant or interval) we have (eq. (1)) $TC = D \oplus T^*$, D representing the relationship between temporal entities, and thus, $TF_{PC}(t) = (D \oplus T^*)(t)$.
Example 2: "*Temperature was high at some point during the last 30 minutes*".

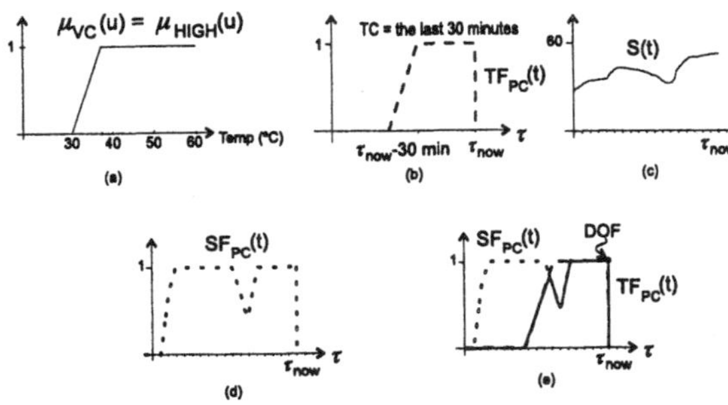

Fig. 1. Calculation of DOF for proposition "*Temperature was high at some point during the last 30 minutes*"

We assume that the membership function in Fig. 1(a) represents the value constraint "*high*", time membership function in (b), the time interval "*the last 30 minutes*" (temporal constraint), and the recent history of temperature observed values ($S(t)$) is the one described in (c). The fulfillment of the spatial part $SF_{PC}(t)$ (in (d)) must be combined with the temporal constraint $TF_{PC}(t)$, as shown in (e), in order to calculate the DOF. In this example, we must use the expression for existential quantification (6).

4.2 Execution of Dependent Propositions

When in a proposition PC_m constraints that are a function of relative values appear, PC_m can be decomposed into a set of several related propositions (**dependent** propositions), making all possible value or temporal dependences explicit: $PC_m = (P^1, P^2, ..., P^K)$. Thus, in order to obtain DOF_m each one of the constraints in P^k, $k = 1,...,K$, has to be evaluated. Dependencies in the propositions can be either spatial (of value) or temporal. Depending on the type of constraint which produces the dependency, this evaluation provides the corresponding value and time instances, and associated DOFs.

Value Constraints. In dependent propositions, the reference value makes reference to the value instance obtained after another proposition has been evaluated. This corresponds to an instantiation of rule R1 in Table 1 as: <Propositional Clause>::= <Proposition><Spatial Relation><Proposition>. Here, in order to evaluate PC_m two propositions (denoted as P^k and $P^{k'}$) should be evaluated.

(i) In the case of relative value constraints,

$$SF_{P^k}(t) = \bigwedge_{t^{k'} \in TC^{k'}} \mu_{SR}(S^k(t), S^{k'}(t')) \wedge SF_{P^{k'}}(t')$$

$SF_{P^{k'}}$ being the value instance obtained after evaluating the proposition $P^{k'}$ being referred to ($SF_{P^{k'}}$ can be provided by the evaluation of a value constraint $VC^{k'}$, of a specification operator...)
(ii) Whenever a reduction or specification operator exists, the degree of spatial fulfillment SF_{P^k} corresponds to the compatibility between the resultant of applying operator O^k to the corresponding value instance of proposition P^k over the temporal reference, and the value constraint given by SR applied on the value instance of the dependent proposition $P^{k'}$.
Example 3: "*Throughout a minute the mean value of temperature in heater 1 is greater than the mean value of temperature in heater 2*". According to the proposed model of propositions, $PC = (P^1, SR, P^2, TC)$:
P^1 : (S^1=temperature in heater 1, O_R^1=mean value), SR=greater than
P^2 : (S^2=temperature in heater 2, O_R^2=mean value)
TC=TCI=(ib, ie, D=1 minute).

The evaluation of both propositions is linked through the references in the specification of P^1 with respect to P^2, by means of a spatial relation SR. Therefore, P^2 must initially be evaluated: over the temporal context (in the case of it existing) or over all the history of values, temporal instances will be taken (intervals in this case, 1 minute long). In each one of these instances, the operator O_R^2 will be evaluated, providing the mean value, in that minute, of all the temperature values of heater 2. In order to evaluate proposition P^1, we will obtain from P^2 the set of temporal instances (intervals of 1 minute) and the associated value instances (for each interval 1 minute long, the mean value of temperature in heater 2). This set will be the reference set for the possible evaluation instances for P^1. From each element, the temporal part will be used to select values of temperature 1, in order to subsequently obtain the mean value (constraint O_R^1), and then the constraint given by the spatial relation SR (mean value of temp. 1 "greater than" mean value of temp. 2) will be evaluated. In this way, we obtain a set of values SF_{PC} for each evaluation instance of P^1. The spatial fulfillment for $PC(SF_{PC})$ will be obtained from the best of the possible instances: the one that verifies all the constraints to the highest degree.

Temporal Constraints. We say that a dependent proposition through temporal constraints exists when in a proposition P^k a reference is made to the temporal instance that has been calculated for another proposition $P^{k'}$.
(i) The reference value is given by the time of occurrence of a fact. This corresponds to instantiation of rules (R8) or (R9) giving a temporal relation to an <Instant> or an <Interval>, and then:
(R16) <Instant>::= <Propositional Clause>

(R20) <Interval>::= <Propositional Clause>
In this case, the temporal reference (instant or interval) in a proposition P^k is given by a reference to a proposition $P^{k'}$ describing the occurrence of the considered fact, so this second proposition must initially be solved. Evaluating $P^{k'}$ we obtain the spatial values verifying the fact, $SF_{P^{k'}}$ (degree of fulfillment of this fact), and the set of time points verifying the constraint with a non-null value ($TF_{P^{k'}}$). Therefore, we have that $TF_{P^k}(t) = (D \oplus TF_{P^{k'}})(t)$.
Example 4: *"Pressure was high a little before temperature was low at some point during the last half an hour"*. $PC = (P^1, TC)$
$P^1 : (GS^1 = (S^1\text{=pressure}, VC^1\text{=high}), TCI^1\text{=a little before}(P^2), Q^1{=}\exists)$
$P^2 : (GS^2 = (S^2\text{=temperature}, VC^2\text{=low}), TCi^2{=}t)$
TC=the last half an hour.

The DOF of proposition P^1 depends on the evaluation instance of proposition P^2. Figure 2(a) shows the history of recent temperature values $S^2(t)$, assuming $\delta = 5min$. These values are matched with the value constraint "*low*" in order to obtain SF_{P^2}, shown as *Temp. low* in Fig. 2(b), where the representation of the temporal context TC "*the last half an hour*" is also given. TF_{P^2} represents the temporal instance obtained after the evaluation of P^2. It is the result of considering both the membership to the temporal context "*the last half an hour*" and the value constraint "*low*". Furthermore, it provides the temporal reference for the evaluation of P^1. Within the temporal context TC we have different temporal instances in which the value constraint has to be evaluated, thus we obtain a SF_{P^2} for each one: how low the temperature is.

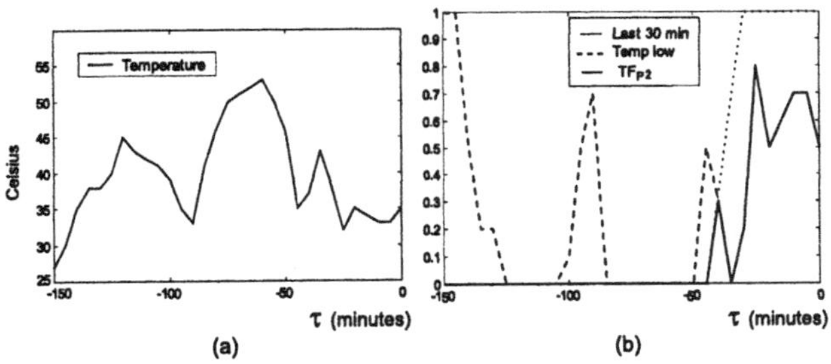

Fig. 2. Calculation of the temporal instance for proposition P^2 in example 4. In the time axis, we are assuming t_{now} as the time origin ($t = 0$), in order to make the representation more simple

The process of calculating the fulfillment of the temporal constraint TCI^1 is shown graphically in Fig. 3. The temporal relationship "*a little before*" is assumed to be defined as the possibility distribution shown in Fig. 3 (a). The temporal reference TCI^1 is obtained as the fuzzy addition between this possibility distribution and the temporal instance TF_{P^2}, as shown in Fig. 3 (b).

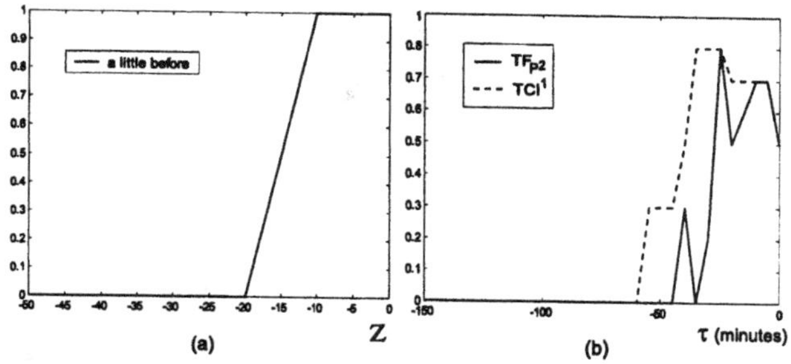

Fig. 3. Calculation of the temporal reference for proposition P^1 in example 4: "*a little before* (TF_{P^2})"

(ii) Finally, we can also have temporal constraints on any operator. In the following example we can see both cases (specification operator and temporal constraint on the selected value):

Example 5: *"Between 6 and 8, pressure was high a little after the last time temperature was high"*. $PC = (P^1)$

P^1:(GS^1=(S^1=pressure, VC^1=high), TCI^1=a little after P^2)

P^2:(GS^2=(S^2=temperature, VC^2=high), O_S^2=last, TC^2=between 6 and 8).

P^2 will be the first to be evaluated, providing $P^2(t)$ ($SF_{P^2}(t)$ and $TF_{P^2}(t)$), with $t \in SUPP_{TF_{P^2}}$ being the time points in TC^2 verifying $SF_{VC^2}(t) \neq 0$. Thus, TCI^1 will be obtained as: $TCI^1(t) = (D \oplus TF_{P^2})(t)$.

5 Discussion

The generalization of fuzzy rules to FTRs, which allows an explicit representation and handling of time, can, no doubt, contribute to extending the application domain of fuzzy logic, or at least, to making the design of solutions for problems associated to dynamic systems and processes easier. In this sense, the control environment is a paradigmatic one, although, paradoxically, FTRs are not yet being used in it as we think they should.

In this work we introduce a model of FTRs that attempts to represent the semantic expressiveness of expert knowledge. The expressive capacity of the model and how it directly deals with imprecision and uncertainty linked to information and knowledge, make it, in our opinion, very promising for application in environments such as process control [13] or monitoring.

Regarding our current and future work, our aim is to extend the language, in such a way that definitions for other temporal facts are included and also other cases of interest in fuzzy temporal reasoning systems are considered.

Acknowledgements

Authors wish to acknowledge support from the Secretaría Xeral de I+D (Xunta de Galicia) through grant PGIDT99PXI20603A, the Spanish Ministry of Education and Culture (CICYT) and the European Commission through grant 1FD97-0183, and the Spanish Ministry of Science and Technology and the European Commission through grant TIC2000-0873.

References

1. Allen, J.F. (1984). Towards a general theory of action and time. Artificial Intelligence, **23**, 123–154
2. Barro, S., Bugarín, A. et al. (1997) Petri nets for fuzzy reasoning on dynamic systems. Proceedings of the 7th IFSA World Congress, 279–284
3. Barro, S., Marín R. et al. (1994) A model and a language for the fuzzy representation and handling of time. Fuzzy Sets and Systems, **61**, 153–175
4. Bugarín, A., Cariñena, P. et al. (1999) Fuzziness in Petri Nets, vol. 22 of *Studies in Fuzziness*, chapter Reasoning with Fuzzy Temporal Rules on Petri Nets, 174–202. Physica-Verlag
5. Cariñena, P., Bugarín, A. et al. (1999) Enhanced fuzzy temporal rules and their projection onto fuzzy Petri nets. International Journal of Intelligent Systems **14**, 8, 775–804
6. Cariñena, P., Bugarín, A. et al. (1999) A language for expressing expert knowledge using fuzzy temporal rules. Proceedings 1999 EUSFLAT-ESTYLF Joint Conference, 171–174
7. Carse, B., Fogarty, T.C., Munro, A. (1998) Artificial evolution of fuzzy rule bases which represent time: a temporal fuzzy classifier system. International Journal of Intelligent Systems **13**, 905–927
8. Delgado, M., Sánchez, D., Vila, M.A. (2000) Fuzzy cardinality based evaluation of quantified sentences. International Journal of Approximate Reasoning **23**, 1, 23–66
9. Dubois, D., Prade, H. (1989) Processing fuzzy temporal knowledge. IEEE Transactions on Systems, Man and Cybernetics **19**, 4, 729–744
10. Gadeo, M.A., Velasco, J.R. (2000) Faded temporal fuzzy logic controller and temporal fuzzy logic controller. comparative study. Proceedings Eighth International Conference on Information Processing and Management of Uncertainty in Knowledge-based Systems - IPMU 2000, vol. 2, 732–737
11. Maeda, H., Asaoka, S., Murakami, S. (1996) Dynamical fuzzy reasoning and its application to system modeling. Fuzzy Sets and Systems **80**, 101–109
12. Marín, R., Cárdenas, M.A. et al. (1997) Obtaining solutions in fuzzy constraint networks. International Journal of Approximate Reasoning **16**, 261–288
13. Mucientes, M., Iglesias, R. et al. (1999) Use of fuzzy temporal rules for avoidance of moving obstacles in mobile robotics. Proceedings 1999 EUSFLAT-ESTYLF Joint Conference, 167–170
14. Qian, D.Q. (1992) Representation and use of imprecise temporal knowledge in dynamic systems. Fuzzy Sets and Systems, **50**, 59–77
15. Raha, S., Ray, K.S. (1999) Approximate reasoning with time. Fuzzy Sets and Systems **107**, 59–79
16. Virant, J., Zimic, N. (1996) Attention to time in fuzzy logic. Fuzzy Sets and Systems **82**, 39–49
17. Vitek, M. (1983) Fuzzy information and fuzzy time. Proc. IFAC Symp. Fuzzy Information, Knowledge Representation and Decision Analysis, 159–162

On a New Method to T-transitive Fuzzy Relations

Luis Garmendia
DB/DC; IBM Learning Services
E-mail: luisgarmendia@es.ibm.com

Adela Salvador
Dep. Matemática Aplicada
E.T.S.I. Caminos. Univ. Politécnica de Madrid
E-mail: ma09@dumbo.caminos.upm.es

Abstract

This paper provides a new method to construct a T-transitive fuzzy relation that is contained in the initial fuzzy relation.

Keywords: fuzzy relation, T-transitive.

1. Introduction

It is well known the importance of the T-transitive property on fuzzy relations, especially because it is a necessary property for a fuzzy relation to be a T-preorder or a T-indistinguishability.

It is proposed a new original method to modify the membership degrees of any fuzzy relation in order to transform it into a T-transitive relation that is contained in the initial one and conserves the μ-T-conditionality and α-reflexivity properties. The T-transitive closure of a fuzzy relation also conserves those properties and it also is T-transitive, but the difference is that it contains the initial relation.

The transformed relation of a reflexive relation is a T-preorder. The symmetry property is not kept, but it is possible to find the greatest symmetric and T-transitive relation contained in a symmetric relation.

It is proved that the given algorithm is computable when the universe of the fuzzy relation is finite.

2. Preliminaries

Let T be a triangular t-norm and let $E=\{a_1, ..., a_n\}$ be a finite set. A fuzzy relation $R:E\times E\rightarrow[0,1]$ is T-transitive when $T(R(a,b), R(b,c))\leq R(a,c)$ for all a, b, $c\in E$.
Given a fuzzy relation R, it is going to be called element $a_{i,j}$ to the relation between a_i and a_j, and it might also represent its relational degree $R(a_i, a_j)$. A relational element $a_{i,j}$ of a fuzzy relation is called T-transitive when $T(a_{i,k}, a_{k,j})\leq a_{ij}$ for all k=1..n.
The initial fuzzy relation R that is wanted to be transformed into a T-transitive relation is called R^0, and the relation obtained by modifying the first m membership degrees (of the first m modified relational elements) is called R^m. Let $a_{i,j}{}^m$ be the relational element of R^m, whose relational degree is $R^m(a_i, a_j)$.
It is proposed a method to obtain a T-transitive relation contained in R^0, so if n is greater or equal than m, then the relational degree of $a_{i,j}{}^n$ is less or equal than the relational degree of $a_{i,j}{}^m$, so $R= R^0\supseteq R^1\supseteq...\supseteq R^m\supseteq...\supseteq R^n$.

3. Concepts to understand the new proposed T-transitivization method

The proposed method consists on transforming a fuzzy relation R^0 into a T-transitive relation R_T contained in R^0 through n^2-1 steps and verifying $R= R^0\supseteq R^1\supseteq...\supseteq R^m\supseteq...\supseteq R^{n^2-1}=R_T$.
The most original aspect of this method is that every step will assure one more element of the previous step to be T-transitive in all of the fuzzy relations constructed in further steps (this element could be called T-transitivized element), it is, if it is chosen to T-transitivize the element $a_{i,j}{}^m$ of R^m (on the m+1th step), then $a_{i,j}{}^r$ would be a T-transitive element of R^r for all $r\geq m$.
To make this possible, every step must choose a non T-transitivized element from the relation of the previous step with minimum relational degree to be made T-transitive by reducing the relational degree of other non transitivized elements (with a greater relational degree). So, when it is chosen the element $a_{i,j}{}^m$ of R^m to be T-transitivized (on the m+1th step), then $a_{i,j}{}^m = a_{i,j}{}^r$ for all $r\geq m$.
When using this strategy the algorithm terminates in n^2-1 steps (by T-transitivizing n^2-1 elements) reaching a T-transitive relation.

Definition 1

Let τ be a set of pairs (i,j) where i,j =1..n. Lets denote that $a_{i,j}{}^m\in\tau^m$ when $(i, j)\in\tau^m$. τ^m is a subset of τ is inductively defined as follows:
1) $\tau^0=\varnothing$
2) $\tau^{m+1}=\tau^m \cup (i, j)$ when $a_{i,j}{}^m\in(\tau^m)'$ is the chosen element of R^m to be T-transitivized in the m+1th step.

Using the notation suggested previously, it is defined τ^m as the set of the m T-transitivized elements of R^m and $(\tau^m)'$ as the set of the n^2-m non T-transitivized elements that will be candidates to be T-transitivized in the m+1th step.

Definition of R^{m+1} from R^m.

Let $a_{i,j}^m$ be the chosen element of $(\tau^m)'$ to be T-transitivized in the m+1th step. $(a_{i,j}^m = \mathrm{Min}\{a_{v,w}$ such that $a_{v,w} \in (\tau^m)'\}$.
Then it is defined $a_{r,s}^{m+1}$ as

$$\begin{cases} J^T(a_{s,j}^m, a_{i,j}^m) & \text{if } r=i,\ T(a_{r,s}^m, a_{s,j}^m) > a_{i,j}^m \text{ and } a_{i,s}^m \le a_{s,j}^m \\ J^T(a_{i,r}^m, a_{i,j}^m) & \text{if } s=j,\ T(a_{i,r}^m, a_{r,s}^m) > a_{i,j}^m \text{ and } a_{i,r}^m \ge a_{r,s}^m \\ a_{r,s}^m & \text{on other cases} \end{cases}$$

Transition from R^m to R^{m+1}.

Once it is chosen the element $a_{i,j}^m$ to T-Transitivize ($a_{i,j}^m$ is the element with minimum relational degree in $(\tau^m)'$, it is, $a_{i,j}^m = \mathrm{Min}\{a_{v,w}$ such that $a_{v,w} \in (\tau^m)'\}$), some elements $a_{i,k}^m$ or $a_{k,j}^m$, k=1..n, are candidates to be reduced in R^{m+1}. When $T(a_{i,k}^m, a_{k,j}^m) > a_{ij}^m$, it is chosen to be reduced the element with minimum relational degree between $a_{i,k}^m$ and $a_{k,j}^m$.
If $a_{i,k}^m \le a_{k,j}^m$ then it is defined $a_{i,k}^{m+1} = J^T(a_{k,j}^m, a_{ij}^m)$ and if $a_{i,k}^m > a_{k,j}^m$ then it is defined $a_{k,j}^{m+1} = J^T(a_{i,k}^m, a_{ij}^m)$. Other elements keep its relational degrees ($a_{r,s}^{m+1} = a_{r,s}^m$).

4. The algorithm is computable

Lemma 1

If $a_{i,j}^m \in (\tau^m)'$ is the mth element to T-transitivize then $a_{i,j}^m = a_{i,j}^{m+1} = \dots = a_{i,j}^{n^2-1}$

Proof

The mth element to T-transitivize $a_{i,j}^m$ is not modified in further steps because $a_{i,j}^m = \mathrm{Min}\{a_{v,w}$ such that $a_{v,w} \in (\tau^m)'$. It never causes intransitivity of other elements because its relational degree is less or equal than the relational degree of the elements to T-transitivize, so when T-transitivizing $a_{r,s}^{m+q} \in (\tau^{m+q})'$ in further steps, it holds for all $0 \leq q \leq n^2\text{-}m\text{-}1$ that $T(a_{i,j}^m, x) \leq Min(a_{i,j}^m, x) \leq a_{i,j}^m \leq a_{r,s}^{m+q}$, so $a_{i,j}^{m+q}$ is never reduced and $a_{i,j}^m = a_{i,j}^{m+1} = ... = a_{i,j}^{n^2-1}$.

Lemma 2

If $a_{i,j}^m \in (\tau^m)'$ is the mth element to T-transitivize then $a_{i,j}^{m+1}$ is a T-transitive element in R^{m+1}.

Proof

By the definition of R^{m+1}, $a_{r,s}^{m+1} = a_{r,s}^m$ except for some elements $a_{i,k}^{m+1}$ or $a_{k,j}^{m+1}$ if for some k=1..n, $T(a_{i,k}^m, a_{k,j}^m) > a_{ij}^m$. In this case, if $a_{i,k}^m \leq a_{k,j}^m$ then $a_{k,j}^{m+1} = J^T(a_{i,k}^m, a_{i,j}^m)$ and $a_{i,j}^{m+1} = a_{i,j}^m = T(a_{i,k}^m, J^T(a_{i,k}^m, a_{i,j}^m) = T(a_{i,k}^{m+1}, a_{k,j}^{m+1})$. If $a_{i,k}^m > a_{k,j}^m$ then $a_{i,k}^{m+1} = J^T(a_{k,j}^m, a_{i,j}^m)$ and $a_{i,j}^{m+1} = a_{i,j}^m = T(J^T(a_{k,j}^m, a_{i,j}^m), a_{k,j}^m) = T(a_{i,k}^{m+1}, a_{k,j}^{m+1})$. On both cases the element $a_{i,j}^{m+1}$ is a T-transitive element in R^{m+1}.
If for some k=1..n, $T(a_{i,k}^m, a_{k,j}^m) \leq a_{ij}^m$ then $a_{i,j}^{m+1} = a_{i,j}^m \geq T(a_{i,k}^m, a_{k,j}^m) = T(a_{i,k}^{m+1}, a_{k,j}^{m+1})$ so $a_{i,j}^{m+1}$ is a T-transitive element in R^{m+1}.

Lemma 3

If $a_{i,j}^m \in (\tau^m)'$ is the mth element to T-transitivize then $a_{i,j}^r$ is a T-transitive element of R^r for all $r \geq m+1$.

Proof

By lemma 2, $a_{i,j}^{m+1}$ is a T-transitive element in R^{m+1} so for all k=1..n, $a_{i,j}^{m+1} \geq T(a_{i,k}^{m+1}, a_{k,j}^{m+1})$. For any $0 \leq q$, $1 \leq r,s \leq n$, $a_{r,s}^{m+1} \geq a_{r,s}^{m+1+q}$ so $a_{i,j}^{m+1+q} = a_{i,j}^{m+1} \geq T(a_{i,k}^{m+1}, a_{k,j}^{m+1}) \geq T(a_{i,k}^{m+1+q}, a_{k,j}^{m+1+q})$.

Theorem 1

R^T is a T-transitive relation

Proof

$R^T = R^{n^2-1}$ is a T-transitive relation because by lemma 3 its n^2-1 T-transitivized elements of (τ^{n^2-1}) are T-transitive elements in R^{n^2-1}. The only non T-transitivized element $a_{f,g}^{n^2-1} \in (\tau^{n^2-1})'$ is also T-transitive in R^{n^2-1} because $a_{f,g}^{n^2-1} \geq a_{r,s}^{n^2-1}$ for all $1 \leq r,s \leq n$ so $a_{f,g}^{n^2-1} \geq T(a_{f,g}^{n^2-1}, a_{f,g}^{n^2-1}) \geq T(a_{f,k}^{n^2-1}, a_{k,g}^{n^2-1})$ for all k=1..n. So $R^T = R^{n^2-1}$ is a T-transitive relation.

Example 1

Let E be the set $\{a_1, a_2, a_3\}$ and let $R: E \times E \rightarrow [0, 1]$ be a fuzzy relation defined by the matrix

$$R^0 = \begin{pmatrix} 0.7 & 0.9 & 0.2 \\ 0.5 & 0.6 & 0.1 \\ 0.4 & 1 & 0.8 \end{pmatrix}.$$

For example, $R(a_1, a_2) = a_{1,2} = 0.9$.
The element to Min-transitivize in the first step is $a_{2,3}^0 = 0.1$ because it is the element with lowest relational degree. $a_{2,3}^0$ is not a Min–transitive element in R^0 because $\mathrm{Min}(a_{2,1}^0, a_{1,3}^0) = \mathrm{Min}(0.5, 0.2) \geq 0.1 = a_{2,3}^0$. To make $a_{2,3}^0$ a Min–transitive element in R^0 it must be reduced ether $a_{2,1}^0$ or $a_{1,3}^0$.
In this case $a_{1,3}^0 \leq a_{2,1}^0$ so $a_{1,3}^1 := J^{Min}(a_{2,1}^0, a_{2,3}^0) = a_{2,3}^0 = 0.1$, and the first step relation is represented by:

$$R^1 = \begin{pmatrix} 0.7 & 0.9 & 0.1 \\ 0.5 & 0.6 & 0.1 \\ 0.4 & 1 & 0.8 \end{pmatrix}.$$

So $\tau^1 = \{(2, 3)\}$and using the suggested notation $\tau^1 = \{a_{2,3}^1\}$. In this point it is know that $a_{2,3}^{1+q} \in \tau^{1+q}$ for all integer $q \geq 0$.
By lemma 1, $a_{1,3}^0 = a_{1,3}^1 = a_{1,3}^2 = a_{1,3}^q$ for all integer $q \geq 0$. As $a_{1,3}^0$ is the element with lowest relational degree, then $\mathrm{Min}(a_{1,3}^q, x) \leq a_{r,s}^q$ for any $1 \leq r,s \leq 3$, so $a_{1,3}^q$ is never modified in further steps because it never causes other elements not to be Min-transitive.
By lemma 2, $a_{1,3}^1$ is a Min-transitive element in R^1, and by lemma 3, $a_{1,3}^{1+q}$ is a Min-transitive element in R^{1+q} for all integer $q \geq 0$. This is because in further steps all elements have a smaller or equal relational degree.
The second step must Min-transitivize an element with minimum relational degree in $(\tau^1)'$ which is the element $a_{1,3}^1$, but this element is already Min-transitive so $R^2 = R^1$ and $\tau^2 = \{a_{2,3}^2, a_{1,3}^2\}$.
The third step must Min-transitivize the element $a_{3,1}^2 = 0.4$. As $\mathrm{Min}(a_{3,2}^2, a_{2,1}^2) = \mathrm{Min}(1, 0.5) \geq 0.5 = a_{3,1}^2$, then $a_{2,1}^2$ must be reduced defining $a_{2,1}^3 := 0.4$.
All elements in R^3 are Min-transitive, so

$$R^3 = R^4 = \ldots\ldots = R^8 = R^{Min} = \begin{pmatrix} 0.7 & 0.9 & 0.1 \\ 0.4 & 0.6 & 0.1 \\ 0.4 & 1 & 0.8 \end{pmatrix}.$$

When T is the product or Lucasiewicz t-norm,

$$R^{Prod} = R^{W} = \begin{pmatrix} 0.7 & 0.9 & 0.2 \\ 0.4 & 0.6 & 0.1 \\ 0.4 & 1 & 0.8 \end{pmatrix}.$$

5. Some properties of the algorithm

Property 1

If $R(a_i, a_i)=\alpha$, then $R^m(a_i, a_i)=\alpha$ for all $m \geq 0$.

Proof.

An element $a_{i,i}$ could be only modified when T-transitivizing some other element $a_{r,s}$ with i=r or i=s. In this case $T(a_{i,i}, a_{i,s}) \leq Min(a_{i,i}, a_{i,s}) \leq a_{i,s}$ and $T(a_{r,i}\ a_{i,i}) \leq Min(a_{r,i}, a_{i,i}) \leq a_{r,i,}$ so the diagonal elements never cause other element not to be T-transitive so they are never modified.

Corollary 1

When R is reflexive (α-reflexive) then R^T is reflexive (α- reflexive).

Proof

It is trivial from property 1 that the algorithm conserves the reflexive property of fuzzy relations.

Example 2

If $R_1 \subseteq R_2$, not always $R_1^T \subseteq R_2^T$

A counter example is given.
Let be the following fuzzy relations:

$$R_1 = \begin{pmatrix} 0.5 & 0.6 & 0.5 \\ 0.5 & 1 & 0.5 \\ 0.9 & 1 & 1 \end{pmatrix} \subseteq \begin{pmatrix} 0.5 & 0.6 & 1 \\ 1 & 1 & 1 \\ 0.9 & 1 & 1 \end{pmatrix} = R_2.$$

R_1 is Min-transitive, so $R_1^{Min} = R_1$, and R_1^{Min} is not contained in

$$R_{2Min} = \begin{pmatrix} 0.5 & 0.5 & 1 \\ 1 & 1 & 1 \\ 0.5 & 0.5 & 1 \end{pmatrix}.$$

Property 2

If R_1 and R_2 are T-transitive fuzzy relations then $R_1 \cap_{Min} R_2$ is also a T-transitive fuzzy relation.

Proof

If R_1 is a T-transitive fuzzy relation then $T(a_{i,k}^1, a_{k,j}^1) \le a_{ij}^1$.
If R_2 is a T-transitive fuzzy relation then $T(a_{i,k}^2, a_{k,j}^2) \le a_{ij}^2$.
T-norms are monotonous, so

$$T(Min(a_{i,k}^1, a_{i,k}^2), Min(a_{k,j}^1, a_{k,j}^2)) \le T(a_{i,k}^1, a_{k,j}^1) \le a_{ij}^1,$$
$$T(Min(a_{i,k}^1, a_{i,k}^2), Min(a_{k,j}^1, a_{k,j}^2)) \le T(a_{i,k}^2, a_{k,j}^2) \le a_{ij}^2,$$

and $T(Min(a_{i,k}^1, a_{i,k}^2), Min(a_{k,j}^1, a_{k,j}^2)) \le Min(a_{i,j}^1, a_{i,j}^2)$, so $R_1 \cap_{Min} R_2$ is also a T-transitive fuzzy relation.

Definition 2

It is denoted R_T^{Min} to the Min-intersection of all possible output of the T-transitization algorithm.
The algorithm might construct different T-transitive fuzzy relations depending on which is the chosen element in τ' with minimum relational degree in τ' to be T-transitivize in each step (it might be several elements in τ' with the same relational degree).
R_T^{Min} is the greatest fuzzy relation that is contained in all possible T-transitivized fuzzy relations of a fuzzy relation R.

Corollary 2

$R_T^{Min} \subseteq R^{Ti} \subseteq R$ for all possible T-transitivized relation R^{Ti} of a fuzzy relation R.

Corollary 3

R_T^{Min} is a T-transitive fuzzy relation

Proof

Trivial from property 2.

Example 3

The T-transitivization of fuzzy relations algorithm does not conserve the symmetry property of fuzzy relations.

A counter example is given.
Let R be a symmetric fuzzy relation defined by the matrix

$$R = \begin{pmatrix} 0.1 & 0.7 & 0.4 \\ 0.7 & 0.5 & 0.2 \\ 0.4 & 0.2 & 0.9 \end{pmatrix}.$$

A possible Min-transitivized fuzzy relation of R might be

$$R^{Min} = \begin{pmatrix} 0.1 & 0.1 & 0.1 \\ 0.7 & 0.5 & 0.2 \\ 0.4 & 0.2 & 0.9 \end{pmatrix}$$

Which is not symmetric.

Example 4

The following example shows that a fuzzy relation R_T^{Min} of a symmetric fuzzy relation R might be symmetric.
Let R be a symmetric fuzzy relation defined by the matrix

$$R= \begin{pmatrix} 0.1 & 0.7 & 0.4 \\ 0.7 & 0.5 & 0.2 \\ 0.4 & 0.2 & 0.9 \end{pmatrix}.$$

All the possible Min-transitivized fuzzy relation of R are:

$$R^{Min}{}_1 = \begin{pmatrix} 0.1 & 0.1 & 0.1 \\ 0.7 & 0.5 & 0.2 \\ 0.4 & 0.2 & 0.9 \end{pmatrix},$$

$$R^{Min}{}_2 = \begin{pmatrix} 0.1 & 0.7 & 0.4 \\ 0.1 & 0.5 & 0.2 \\ 0.1 & 0.2 & 0.9 \end{pmatrix},$$

$$R^{Min}{}_3 = \begin{pmatrix} 0.1 & 0.1 & 0.4 \\ 0.7 & 0.5 & 0.2 \\ 0.1 & 0.2 & 0.9 \end{pmatrix},$$

$$R^{Min}{}_4 = \begin{pmatrix} 0.1 & 0.7 & 0.1 \\ 0.1 & 0.5 & 0.2 \\ 0.4 & 0.2 & 0.9 \end{pmatrix}$$

and the Min-intersection of all the possible Min-transitivized fuzzy relations is

$$R_{Min}{}^{Min} = \begin{pmatrix} 0.1 & 0.1 & 0.1 \\ 0.1 & 0.5 & 0.2 \\ 0.1 & 0.2 & 0.9 \end{pmatrix}$$

which is Min-transitive, conserves the α-reflexivity and is symmetric.

Theorem 2

If E is a finite set then the algorithm is computable.

Proof

If E is a finite set of n elements, the algorithm must take n^2-1 steps to make T-transitive all the n^2 elements of a fuzzy relation R. In each step it is necessary to check at least n-1 possible values of k to assure the T-transitivity of an element. So the algorithm is of polynomial complexity of O(Dim^3 R) order.
However it is possible to implement faster algorithms when using the fact that is not necessary to check whether an T-transitiviced element $a_{r,s} \in \tau^m$ should be reduced in further steps to make T-transitive an element $a_{f,g} \in (\tau^m)'$ (for r=f or s=g) because $a_{r,s} \le a_{f,g}$ and always $T(a_{r,s}, x) \le a_{f,g}$.
It could also be used the fact that the diagonal elements are never modified, as property 1 shows.

6. Conclusions

It is given a new original algorithm to give a T-transitive fuzzy relation from a fuzzy relation. The new fuzzy relation is contained in the initial one. It could be found several T-transitive relations contained in a fuzzy relation, but not the closest T-transitive relation contained in a given fuzzy relation. This is the difference between this algorithm and others to find the closest T-transitive relation that contains a fuzzy relation, which is the T-transitive closure. A lower T-transitive relation might be much closer to the original fuzzy relation than its T-transitive closure.
This algorithm also conserves the α-reflexive property of fuzzy relations, so it could be very useful to construct several T-preorders from a reflexive fuzzy relation in order to make fuzzy inference.

Acknowledgements

The authors would like to thank the support of Enric Trillas and all his investigation team.

References

[1] L. Garmendia, C. Del Campo, S. Cubillo, A. Salvador. *A method to make some fuzzy relations T-transitive*. International Journal of Intelligent Systems, vol. 14, pp. 873-882. 1999.

[2] H. Hashimoto. *Fuzzy Sets and Systems* 29, pp 229-234. 1989.

[3] M. A. Mishrel. *Fuzzy Sets and Systems* 52, pp 337-343. 1992.

[4] E. Trillas. *In Advanced Methods in Artificial Intelligence*; Bouchon-Meunier, B et al (eds); Springer-Verlag; Berlin pp 85-100. 1993.

[5] B. Schweizer, A. Skalar. *Probabilistic Metric Spaces*. North-Holland, New York, 1983.

Intuitionistic Fuzzy Relations and Measures of Consensus

Janusz Kacprzyk and Eulalia Szmidt
Systems Research Institute, Polish Academy of Sciences
ul. Newelska 6, 01–447 Warsaw, Poland
E-mail: {szmidt, kacprzyk}@ibspan.waw.pl

Abstract

Zadeh's (1983) calculus of linguistically quantified statements is employed to represent and handle a fuzzy majority in the derivation of a measure (degree) of consensus under intuitionistic fuzzy preferences. We follow the concept of a fuzzy majority introduced by Kacprzyk (1984, 1985a, b, 1986, 1987), Fedrizzi (1988), Kacprzyk and Fedrizzi (1986, 1988, 1989). The proposed consensus measure expresses a degree to which, say, "most of the important individuals agree as to almost all of the relevant options". Individual testimonies are assumed to be individual intuitionistic fuzzy preference relations that, as opposed to ordinary fuzzy preference relations, can better reflect the fact that during the consensus reaching proccess individuals can be, first, unsure as to their preferences, and second, can change them. We obtain new interval valued measures of consensus meant as, on the one hand, reflecting a possible hesitation of individuals, and on the other hand, providing a best and worst possible result.

Keywords: consensus, degree of consensus, intuitionistic fuzzy sets, intuitionistic fuzzy preference relation, linguistically quantified statements.

1 Introduction

Fuzzy preference relations have been a topic of intense research for many years, and a most advanced and comprehensive source of information is here presumably Fodor and Roubens' (1994) book. They have found numerous applications notably in group decision and consensus reaching models under imprecise (fuzzy) information. As a further step, a concept of a fuzzy majority was introduced by Kacprzyk (1984, 1985a, b, 1986, 1987), leading to conceptually new models and solution concepts. Both the idea of a fuzzy preference relation and a fuzzy majority have also been employed to derive a soft measure of consensus by Fedrizzi (1988), and Kacprzyk and Fedrizzi

(1986, 1988, 1989), and the proposed consensus measure expresses a degree to which, say, "most of the important individuals agree as to almost all of the relevant options". That new degree of consensus can therefore be equal to 1 which stands for full consensus, when, say, "*most* of the (*important*) individuals agree as to *almost all* (of the *relevant*) alternatives (issues , options, variants, ...)". For a comprehensive review of group decision making and consensus reaching under fuzziness, see Kacprzyk and Nurmi (1998). Morover, some new results in this area are given by Kacprzyk and Zadrożny (1999, 2000).

Basically, in those works, the point of departure is a set of individual fuzzy preference relations which associate with each pair of options a number from $[0,1]$. So, we have a set of n options, $S = \{s_1, \ldots, s_n\}$, and a set of m individuals, $I = \{1, \ldots, m\}$. Each individual k provides his or her individual fuzzy preference relation, R_k, given by $\mu_{R_k} : S \times S \to [0,1]$. It is convenient to represent (individual) fuzzy preference relation by a matrix $[r^k_{ij}]$ such that $r^k_{ij} = \mu_{R_k}(s_i, s_j)$; $i,j = 1, \ldots, n$; $k = 1, \ldots, m$; $[r^k_{ij}] + [r^k_{ji}] = 1$.

The degree of consensus is now derived in three steps:

1. for each pair of individuals we derive a degree of agreement as to their preferences between *all* the pairs of alternatives,

2. we aggregate these degrees to obtain a degree of agreement of each pair of individuals as to their preferences between Q_1 (a fuzzy linguistic quantifier as, e.g., "most", "almost all", "much more than 50%", ...) pairs of *relevant* alternatives, and

3. we aggregate these degrees to obtain a degree of agreement of Q_2 (a fuzzy linguistic quantifier similar to Q_1) pairs of *important* individuals as to their preferences between Q_1 pairs of *relevant* alternatives. This is meant to be the *degree of consensus* sought.

Notice that we assume here that both the individuals and alternatives are assigned different degrees of importance and relevance, respectively. This may be useful in the context of consensus reaching because a higher impact of opinions of more important (e.g., competent) individuals, and that of the individuals' opinions concerning more relevant options may speed up the consensus reaching process.

It is easy to notice that in the above process of the derivation of a degree of consensus a crucial role is played by a fuzzy majority that was introduced by Kacprzyk (1984, 1985a, b, 1986, 1987) [and later extended by Fedrizzi (1988), Kacprzyk and Fedrizzi (1986, 1988, 1989)] as being equated with a fuzzy linguistic quantifier in Zadeh's (1983) sense; this is clearly a natural and simple formal representation of a fuzzy majority.

The proposed consensus measure expresses a degree to which, say, "most of the important individuals agree as to almost all of relevant options". The fuzzy majorities, "most" and "almost all" are equated with fuzzy linguistic quantifiers, Q_1 and Q_2. For instance, a fuzzy linguistic quantifier Q = "most" may be given as [cf. Kacprzyk (1984, 1985a, b, 1986, 1987)]:

$$Q_{\text{"}most\text{"}}(x) = \begin{cases} 1 & \text{for} \quad x > 0.8 \\ 2x - 0.6 & \text{for} \quad 0.3 \leq x \leq 0.8 \\ 0 & \text{for} \quad x < 0.3 \end{cases} \tag{1}$$

and this form of "most" will be used throughout this paper.

To handle the fuzzy majority we will employ Zadeh's (1983) calculus of linguistically quantified statements.

The relevance of options is assumed to be given as a fuzzy set defined in the set of alternatives S such that $\mu_B(s_i) \in [0,1]$ is a *degree of relevance* of option s_i, from 0 for fully irrelevant to 1 for fully relevant, through all intermediate values, and the more relevant the option the higher this degree.

The relevance of a pair of options, $(s_i, s_j) \in S \times S$, may be defined, say, as

$$b_{ij}^k = \frac{1}{2}[\mu_B(s_i) + \mu_B(s_j)] \tag{2}$$

which is clearly the most straightforward solution; evidently, $b_{ij}^k = b_{ji}^k$, and b_{ii}^k do not matter; for each i, j, k.

And analogously, the *importance of individuals*, I, is defined as a fuzzy set in the set of individuals such that $\mu_I(k) \in [0,1]$ is a *degree of importance* of individual k, from 0 for fully unimportant to 1 for fully important, through all intermediate values.

Then, the importance of a pair of individuals, (k_1, k_2), b_{k_1,k_2}^I, may be defined in various ways, e.g., analogously as (2), i.e.

$$b_{k_1,k_2}^I = \frac{1}{2}[\mu_I(k_1) + \mu_I(k_2)] \tag{3}$$

We start with a strict agreement (cf. Section 3), and as it may be viewed too rigid, then we use the degree of a *sufficient agreement* (at least to degree $\alpha \in [0,1]$).

The three step procedure of finding consensus is a starting point for employing the intuitionistic fuzzy sets (cf. Section 2) instead of fuzzy sets for modeling *individual preference relations.* In effect, each individual k provides his or her *(individual) intuitionistic fuzzy preference relation*, giving not only R_k, (described, as previously by its membership function μ_{R_k}), but giving also Π_k - so called hesitation margins, $\pi_k : S \times S \to [0,1]$. It is convenient to represent (individual) hesitation margins by a matrix $[\pi_{ij}^k(s_i, s_j)]; i, j = 1, \ldots, n; k = 1, \ldots, m$. Such a representation of individual preferences (taking into account another degree of freedom, i.e. a hesitation margins) makes it possible to express a hesitation of individuals (concerning their degrees of preferences), and leads to finding out a best and worst possible degree of soft consensus.

Notice that we concentrate here, initially, on how to derive a soft degree of consensus assuming a standard form of a fuzzy preference relation. We do not consider here advanced concepts and properties related to fuzzy preference structures that have been dealt with by many authors, notably De Baets, Fodor, Roubens, etc. For more information on those relevant issues, we refer the reader to, e.g., De Baets and Fodor (2000) or Fodor and Roubens (1994).

First, intuitionistic fuzzy sets (Atanassov, 1999) are presented in a very brief way. Next, a degree of consensus under fuzzy preferences and fuzzy majority is considered. Finally, a new degree of consensus under intuitionistic fuzzy preferences and fuzzy majority is introduced.

2 Brief Introduction to Intuitionistic Fuzzy Sets

As opposed to a fuzzy set (Zadeh, 1965) in $X = x$, given by:

$$A^{'} = \{< x, \mu_{A'}(x) > | x \in X\} \tag{4}$$

where $\mu_{A'} : X \rightarrow [0, 1]$ is the membership function of the fuzzy set $A^{'}$: $\mu_{A'(x)} \in [0, 1]$; an intuitionistic fuzzy set (Atanassov, 1986, 1999) $A \in X$ is given by

$$A = \{< x, \mu_A(x), \nu_A(x) > | x \in X\} \tag{5}$$

where: $\mu_A : X \rightarrow [0, 1]$ and $\nu_A : X \rightarrow [0, 1]$ such that

$$0 \leq \mu_A(x) + \nu_A(x) \leq 1 \tag{6}$$

and $\mu_A(x)$, $\nu_A(x) \in [0, 1]$ denote the degree of membership and non-membership of x in A, respectively.

Obviously, each fuzzy set corresponds to the following intuitionistic fuzzy set:

$$A = \{< x, \mu_{A'}(x), 1 - \mu_{A'}(x) > | x \in X\} \tag{7}$$

For each intuitionistic fuzzy set in X, we will call

$$\pi_A(x) = 1 - \mu_A(x) - \nu_A(x) \tag{8}$$

an *intuitionistic fuzzy index* (the hesitation margin) of x in A and it is a hesitancy degree of whether x belongs to A or not [cf. Atanassov (1986, 1999)]. It is obvious, that $0 \leq \pi_A(x) \leq 1$ *for each* $x \in X$.

On the other hand, for each fuzzy set $A^{'}$ in X, evidently,

$$\pi_{A'}(x) = 1 - \mu_{A'}(x) - [1 - \mu_{A'}(x)] = 0, \text{ for each } x \in X \tag{9}$$

Therefore, to summarize, if we want to fully describe an intuitionistic fuzzy set, we must use any two functions from the triplet:

{membership function,
non-membership function.
intuitionistic index}

In other words, the application of intuitionistic fuzzy sets instead of fuzzy sets means the introduction of another degree of freedom into a set description (i.e. in addition to μ_A we also have ν_A or π_A).

Example 1 (Atanassov, 1999) Let E be the set of all countries with elective governments. Assume that we know for every country $x \in E$ the percentage of the electorate who have voted for the corresponding government. Let it be denoted by $M(x)$ and let $\mu(x) = \frac{M(x)}{100}$. Let $\nu(x) = 1 - \mu(x)$. This number corresponds to that part of electorate who have not voted for the government. By means of the fuzzy set theory we cannot consider this value in more detail. However, if we define $\nu(x)$ as the number of votes given to parties or persons outside the government, then we can show the part of electorate who have not voted at all and the corresponding number will be $1 - \mu(x) - \nu(x)$. Thus we can construct the set $\{\langle x, \mu(x), \nu(x)\rangle | x \in E\}$ and obviously, $0 \leq \mu(x) + \nu(x) \leq 1$.

□

Below we will briefly mention basic results on intuitionistic fuzzy sets (Atanassov, 1999), namely on basic operations and relations over intuitionistic fuzzy sets taking as a point of departure respective definitions of relations and operations over fuzzy sets and extending them. Conversely, relations and operations on fuzzy sets will turn out to be particular cases of these new definitions.

Here is the definition of basic relations and operations on intuitionistic fuzzy sets:

Definition 1 (Atanassov, 1999)
For every two intuitionistic fuzzy sets A and B the following relations and operations can be defined ("iff" means "if and only if"):

$$A \subset B \quad \textit{iff} \quad (\forall x \in E)(\mu_A(x) \leq \mu_B(x) \& \nu_A(x) \geq \nu_B(x)), \tag{10}$$

$$A \supset B \quad \textit{iff} \quad B \subset A, \tag{11}$$

$$A = B \quad \textit{iff} \quad (\forall x \in E)(\mu_A(x) = \mu_B(x) \& \nu_A(x) = \nu_B(x)), \tag{12}$$

$$\overline{A} = \{\langle x, \nu_A(x), \mu_A(x)\rangle | x \in E\}, \tag{13}$$

$$A \cap B = \{\langle x, \min(\mu_A(x), \mu_B(x)), \max(\nu_A(x), \nu_B(x))\rangle | x \in E\}, \tag{14}$$

$$A \cup B = \{\langle x, \max(\mu_A(x), \mu_B(x)), \min(\nu_A(x), \nu_B(x))\rangle | x \in E\}, \tag{15}$$

$$A + B = \{\langle x, \mu_A(x) + \mu_B(x) - \mu_A(x).\mu_B(x), \nu_A(x).\nu_B(x)\rangle, | \, x \in E\} \tag{16}$$

$$A.B = \{\langle x, \mu_A(x).\mu_B(x), \nu_A(x) + \nu_B(x) - \nu_A(x).\nu_B(x)\rangle \mid x \in E\}, \tag{17}$$

$$A@B = \{\langle x, (\frac{\mu_A(x) + \mu_B(x))}{2}, \frac{(\nu_A(x) + \nu_B(x))}{2}\rangle | x \in E\}, \tag{18}$$

$$A\$B = \{\langle x, \sqrt{\mu_A(x).\mu_B(x)}, \sqrt{\nu_A(x).\nu_B(x)}\rangle | x \in E\}, \tag{19}$$

$$A * B = \{\langle x, \frac{\mu_A(x)+\mu_B(x)}{2.(\mu_A(x).\mu_B(x)+1)}, \frac{\nu_A(x)+\nu_B(x)}{2.(\nu_A(x).\nu_B(x)+1)}\rangle | x \in E\}, \tag{20}$$

$$A \bowtie B = \{\langle x, 2.\frac{\mu_A(x).\mu_B(x)}{\mu_A(x)+\mu_B(x)}, 2.\frac{\nu_A(x).\nu_B(x)}{(\nu_A(x)+\nu_B(x)}\rangle | x \in E\}, \tag{21}$$

for which we will accept that if

$$\mu_A(x) = \mu_B(x) = 0, , \textit{ then } \frac{\mu_A(x).\mu_B(x)}{\mu_A(x)+\mu_B(x)} = 0$$

$$\textit{and if } \nu_A(x) = \nu_B(x) = 0, \textit{then } \frac{\nu_A(x).\nu_B(x)}{\nu_A(x)+\nu_B(x)} = 0.$$

The relations (10), (11) and (12) defined above are analogous to the relations of inclusion and equality in the ordinary fuzzy set theory. Here it is also true that, for every two intuitionistic fuzzy sets A and B,

$$A \subset B \text{ and } B \subset A \text{ iff } A = B. \tag{22}$$

Each of the above operations (13)–(21) has also its counterpart in the fuzzy set theory. The first four of them were defined in the present form by Atanassov in 1983 and this was his first step towards the investigation of properties of intuitionistic fuzzy sets.

Intuitionistic fuzzy sets can be useful in modeling many real situations, and, examples in negotiation processes are given in Szmidt and Kacprzyk (1996a, 1996b, 1996c, 1997a, 1998b, 1998c]).

3 Degrees of Consensus under Fuzzy Preferences and a Fuzzy Majority

By following the reasoning in Kacprzyk (1987), and Kacprzyk and Fedrizzi (1986, 1988, 1989), we will now consecutively show how "soft" degrees of consensus are derived using Zadeh's (1983) fuzzy-logic-based calculus of linguistically quantified statements.

In the most basic case, we start with the degree of strict agreement between individuals k_1 and k_2 as to their preferences between alternatives s_i and s_j given by

$$v_{ij}(k_1,k_2) = \begin{cases} 1 & \text{if } r_{ij}^{k_1} = r_{ij}^{k_2} \\ 0 & \text{otherwise} \end{cases} \tag{23}$$

Next, the degree of agreement between individuals k_1 and k_2 as to their preferences between *all* the pairs of *relevant* alternatives is

$$v_B(k_1,k_2)=\frac{\sum_{i=1}^{n-1}\sum_{j=i+1}^{n}[v_{ij}(k_1,k_2)\wedge b_{ij}^B]}{\sum_{i=1}^{n-1}\sum_{j=i+1}^{n} b_{ij}^B} \tag{24}$$

The degree of agreement between individuals k_1 and k_2 as to their preferences between Q_1 *relevant* pairs of alternatives is

$$v_{Q_1}^B(k_1,k_2)=\mu_{Q_1}[v_B(k_1,k_2)] \tag{25}$$

In turn, the degree of agreement of *all* the pairs of *important* individuals as to their preferences between Q_1 pairs of *relevant* alternatives is

$$v_{Q_1}^{I,B}=\frac{\sum_{k_1=1}^{m-1}\sum_{k_2=k_1+1}^{m}[v_{Q_1}^B(k_1,k_2)\wedge b_{k_1,k_2}^I]}{\sum_{k_1=1}^{m-1}\sum_{k_2=k_1+1}^{m} b_{k_1,k_2}^I} \tag{26}$$

Finally, the degree of agreement of Q_2 pairs of *important* individuals as to their preferences between Q_1 pairs of *relevant* alternatives, called the *degree of $Q1/Q2/I/B$-consensus*, is

$$con(Q_1,Q_2,I,B)=\mu_{Q_2}(v_{Q_1}^{I,B}) \tag{27}$$

Since the strict agreement (23) may be viewed too rigid, we can use the degree of sufficient agreement (at least to degree $\alpha\in[0,1]$) of individuals k_1 and k_2 as to their preferences between options s_i and s_j, defined by , i.e.

$$v_{ij}^{\alpha}(k_1,k_2)=\begin{cases}1 & \text{if } \mid r_{ij}^{k_1}-r_{ij}^{k_2}\mid\leq 1-\alpha\leq 1\\ 0 & \text{otherwise}\end{cases} \tag{28}$$

and by following (24)–(27) define the degree of *sufficient* (at least to degree α) agreement of Q_2 pairs of *important* individuals as to their preferences between Q_1 pairs of *relevant* alternatives, called the *degree of $\alpha/Q1/Q2/I/B$-consensus*.

We can also explicitly introduce the strength of agreement into (23), and use the degree of strong agreement of individuals k_1 and k_2 as to their preferences between options s_i and s_j defined by

$$v_{ij}^{s}(k1,k2)=s(\mid r_{ij}^{k_1}-r_{ij}^{k_2}\mid) \tag{29}$$

where s: $[0,1]\longrightarrow[0,1]$ is some function representing the degree of strong agreements exemplified by

$$s(x)=\begin{cases}1 & \text{for } x\leq 0.05\\ -10x+1.5 & \text{for } 0.05<x<0.15\\ 0 & \text{for } x\geq 0.15\end{cases} \tag{30}$$

Then, by following (24)–(27), we can analogously define a degree of strong agreement of Q_2 pairs of *important* individuals as to their preferences between Q_1 pairs of *relevant* alternatives, called a *degree of $s/Q1/Q2/I/B$-consensus.*

4 Degrees of Consensus under Intuitionistic Fuzzy Preferences and a Fuzzy Majority

A basic reason for employing intuitionistic fuzzy sets when looking for a measure of consensus is to obtain a possibility of having an additional degree of freedom, i.e. to make it possible to formally reflect a possible hesitation of individuals as to their preferences, and in consequence, as to the degree of consensus obtained. On the other hand, the derivation of measures of consensus follows the line of reasoning as in the case of fuzzy preference realtions.

First, the degree of strict agreement between individuals $k1$ and $k2$ as to their preferences between options s_i and s_j is

$$v_{ij}(k_1, k_2) = \begin{cases} 1 & \text{if } r_{ij}^{k_1} = r_{ij}^{k_2} \text{ and } \pi_{ij}^{k_1} = \pi_{ij}^{k_2} \\ 0 & \text{otherwise} \end{cases} \tag{31}$$

so now, when useing intuitionistic fuzzy sets in the process of looking for the "basic" degree of consensus we demand that both values of r_{ij}^k and π_{ij}^k (for different k) are equal.

Next, following (24) - (26) we obtain the degree of agreement of Q_2 pairs of *important* individuals as to their preferences between Q_1 pairs of *relevant* alternatives, called the *degree of* $Q1/Q2/I/B$*-consensus*

$$con(Q_1, Q_2, I, B) = \mu_{Q_2}(v_{Q_1}^{I,B}) \tag{32}$$

As we will see when considering examples, the strict agreement is far too rigid, but as it was in a case of fuzzy sets, we can use the degree of sufficient agreement (at least to degree $\alpha \in [0, 1]$) of individuals k_1 and k_2 as to their preferences between options s_i and s_j, defined by

$$v_{ij,min}^{\alpha}(k_1, k_2) = \begin{cases} 1 & \text{if} \quad a_1 \leq 1 - \alpha \leq 1 \\ 0 & \text{otherwise} \end{cases} \tag{33}$$

where

$$a_1 = max\{| r_{ij}^{k_1} - r_{ij}^{k_2} |, \quad | (r_{ij}^{k_1} + \pi_{ij}^{k_1}) - (r_{ij}^{k_2} + \pi_{ij}^{k_2}) |\} \tag{34}$$

$$v_{ij,max}^{\alpha}(k_1, k_2) = \begin{cases} 1 & \text{if} \quad a_2 \leq 1 - \alpha \leq 1 \\ 0 & \text{otherwise} \end{cases} \tag{35}$$

where

$$a_2 = min\{| r_{ij}^{k_1} - r_{ij}^{k_2} |, \quad | (r_{ij}^{k_1} + \pi_{ij}^{k_1}) - (r_{ij}^{k_2} + \pi_{ij}^{k_2}) |\} \tag{36}$$

It is worth noticing that a sufficient agreement is given by a number from the interval $[v_{ij,min}^{\alpha}(k_1, k_2), v_{ij,max}^{\alpha}(k_1, k_2)]$. It is a result of the fact that when considering intuitionistic fuzzy preferences of every individual k, we must take into account not only values r_{ij}^k (as in a case of fuzzy preferences) but also hesitancy margins π_{ij}^k concerning every pair of (s_i, s_j) options. In this way we try to reflect a real human behaviour, i.e. situations when individuals are not able to tell definitively that they are for an option i-th to extent $a \in [0,1]$, and against an option j-th to extent $1-a$. Individuals often express some margin of hesitancy π_{ij}^k which can disappear (eg. after some discussion) supporting r_{ij}^k or r_{ji}^k. Then our discussion (under the absence of hesitancy) reduces to looking for consensus under fuzzy preference relations. If π_{ij}^k exist, the next step of our procedure is to find out the degree of agreement between individuals k_1 and k_2 as to their preferences between *all* the pairs of *relevant* alternatives is [cf. (24) and (33)]

$$v_{B,min}^{\alpha}(k_1,k_2) = \frac{\sum_{i=1}^{n-1}\sum_{j=i+1}^{n}[v_{ij,min}^{\alpha}(k_1,k_2) \wedge b_{ij}^{B}]}{\sum_{i=1}^{n-1}\sum_{j=i+1}^{n} b_{ij}^{B}} \tag{37}$$

and [cf. (24) and (35)]

$$v_{B,max}^{\alpha}(k_1,k_2) = \frac{\sum_{i=1}^{n-1}\sum_{j=i+1}^{n}[v_{ij,max}^{\alpha}(k_1,k_2) \wedge b_{ij}^{B}]}{\sum_{i=1}^{n-1}\sum_{j=i+1}^{n} b_{ij}^{B}} \tag{38}$$

The degree of agreement between individuals k_1 and k_2 as to their preferences between Q_1 *relevant* pairs of alternatives is

$$v_{Q_1,min}^{\alpha,B}(k_1,k_2) = \mu_{Q_1}[v_{B,min}^{\alpha}(k_1,k_2)] \tag{39}$$

$$v_{Q_1,max}^{\alpha,B}(k_1,k_2) = \mu_{Q_1}[v_{B,max}^{\alpha}(k_1,k_2)] \tag{40}$$

In turn, the degree of agreement of *all* the pairs of *important* individuals as to their preferences between Q_1 pairs of *relevant* alternatives is

$$v_{Q_1,min}^{\alpha,I,B} = \frac{\sum_{k_1=1}^{m-1}\sum_{k_2=k_1+1}^{m}[v_{Q_1,min}^{\alpha,B}(k_1,k_2) \wedge b_{k_1,k_2}^{I}]}{\sum_{k_1=1}^{m-1}\sum_{k_2=k_1+1}^{m} b_{k_1,k_2}^{I}} \tag{41}$$

$$v_{Q_1,max}^{\alpha,I,B} = \frac{\sum_{k_1=1}^{m-1}\sum_{k_2=k_1+1}^{m}[v_{Q_1,max}^{\alpha,B}(k_1,k_2) \wedge b_{k_1,k_2}^{I}]}{\sum_{k_1=1}^{m-1}\sum_{k_2=k_1+1}^{m} b_{k_1,k_2}^{I}} \tag{42}$$

Finally, the degree of agreement of Q_2 pairs of *important* individuals as to their preferences between Q_1 pairs of *relevant* alternatives, called the *degree of Q1/Q2/I/B-consensus*, is given as a number from the interval

$$con^{\alpha}(Q_1,Q_2,I,B) \in [\mu_{Q_2}(v_{Q_1,min}^{\alpha,I,B}), \quad \mu_{Q_2}(v_{Q_1,max}^{\alpha,I,B})] \tag{43}$$

We can also explicitly introduce the strength of agreement into (31), and use the degree of strong agreement of individuals k_1 and k_2 as to their preferences between options s_i and s_j defined by

$$v^s_{ij,min}(k1,k2) = s(max\{\mid r^{k_1}_{ij} - r^{k_2}_{ij} \mid, \quad \mid (r^{k_1}_{ij} + \pi^{k_1}_{ij}) - (r^{k_2}_{ij} + \pi^{k_2}_{ij}) \mid\}) \quad (44)$$

$$v^s_{ij,max}(k1,k2) = s(min\{\mid r^{k_1}_{ij} - r^{k_2}_{ij} \mid, \quad \mid (r^{k_1}_{ij} + \pi^{k_1}_{ij}) - (r^{k_2}_{ij} + \pi^{k_2}_{ij}) \mid\}) \quad (45)$$

where $s : [0,1] \longrightarrow [0,1]$ is some function representing the degree of strong agreements exemplified by

$$s(x) = \begin{cases} 1 & \text{for } x \leq 0.05 \\ -10x + 1.5 & \text{for } 0.05 < x < 0.15 \\ 0 & \text{for } x \geq 0.15 \end{cases} \quad (46)$$

Then, by following (37)–(42), we consecutively obtain:

$$v^s_{B,min}(k_1,k_2) = \frac{\sum_{i=1}^{n-1}\sum_{j=i+1}^{n}[v^s_{ij,min}(k_1,k_2) \wedge b^B_{ij}]}{\sum_{i=1}^{n-1}\sum_{j=i+1}^{n} b^B_{ij}} \quad (47)$$

$$v^s_{B,max}(k_1,k_2) = \frac{\sum_{i=1}^{n-1}\sum_{j=i+1}^{n}[v^s_{ij,max}(k_1,k_2) \wedge b^B_{ij}]}{\sum_{i=1}^{n-1}\sum_{j=i+1}^{n} b^B_{ij}} \quad (48)$$

$$v^{s,B}_{Q_1,min}(k_1,k_2) = \mu_{Q_1}[v^s_{B,min}(k_1,k_2)] \quad (49)$$

$$v^{s,B}_{Q_1,max}(k_1,k_2) = \mu_{Q_1}[v^s_{B,max}(k_1,k_2)] \quad (50)$$

$$v^{s,I,B}_{Q_1,min} = \frac{\sum_{k_1=1}^{m-1}\sum_{k_2=k_1+1}^{m}[v^{s,B}_{Q_1,min}(k_1,k_2) \wedge b^I_{k_1,k_2}]}{\sum_{k_1=1}^{m-1}\sum_{k_2=k_1+1}^{m} b^I_{k_1,k_2}} \quad (51)$$

$$v^{s,I,B}_{Q_1,max} = \frac{\sum_{k_1=1}^{m-1}\sum_{k_2=k_1+1}^{m}[v^{s,B}_{Q_1,max}(k_1,k_2) \wedge b^I_{k_1,k_2}]}{\sum_{k_1=1}^{m-1}\sum_{k_2=k_1+1}^{m} b^I_{k_1,k_2}} \quad (52)$$

and, finally, the degree of strong agreement of Q_2 pairs of *important* individuals as to their preferences between Q_1 pairs of *relevant* alternatives, called the *degree of $s/Q1/Q2/I/B$-consensus* is given as a number from the following interval

$$con^s(Q_1,Q_2,I,B) \in [\mu_{Q_2}(v^{s,I,B}_{Q_1,min}), \quad \mu_{Q_2}(v^{s,I,B}_{Q_1,max})] \quad (53)$$

Example 2 Suppose that $n = m = 3$, $Q_1 = Q_2 =$ "most" are given by (1), $\alpha = 0.9$, $s(x)$ is defined by (30), and the individual preference relations are:

$$R_1 = \begin{bmatrix} - & 0.1 & 0.5 \\ 0.9 & - & 0.5 \\ 0.4 & 0.3 & - \end{bmatrix} \quad \Pi_1 = \begin{bmatrix} - & 0 & 0.1 \\ 0 & - & 0.2 \\ 0.1 & 0.2 & - \end{bmatrix}$$

$$R_2 = \begin{bmatrix} - & 0.1 & 0.5 \\ 0.9 & - & 0.5 \\ 0.2 & 0.2 & - \end{bmatrix} \quad \Pi_2 = \begin{bmatrix} - & 0 & 0.3 \\ 0 & - & 0.3 \\ 0.3 & 0.3 & - \end{bmatrix}$$

$$R_3 = \begin{bmatrix} - & 0.2 & 0.1 \\ 0.8 & - & 0.6 \\ 0.2 & 0.3 & - \end{bmatrix} \quad \Pi_3 = \begin{bmatrix} - & 0 & 0.7 \\ 0 & - & 0.1 \\ 0.7 & 0.1 & - \end{bmatrix}$$

If we assume the relevance of the alternatives to be $b_i^B = 1/s_1 + 0.6/s_2 + 0.2/s_3$, the importance of the individuals to be $b_k^I = 0.8/1 + 1/2 + 0.4/3$, $\alpha = 0.9$ and $Q =$ "most" given by (1), then we obtain the following degrees of consensus:

$$con(\text{“most”}, \text{“most”}, I, B) = 0$$

$$con^{0.9}(\text{“most”}, \text{“most”}, I, B) \in [1.0, 1.0]$$

which can be expressed as 1.0, and

$$con^{s}(\text{“most”}, \text{“most”}, I, B) \in [0.8, 1]$$

The results obtained are intuitively appealing. First, the "basic" degree of consensus is just equal to zero because, naturally, the underlying requirements as to what consensus should be are very rigid. The degree of consensus increases both in the case of allowing for a sufficient ($\alpha = 0.9$) agreement, and a strong agreement because both the presence of α and a "mild" function $s(x)$ assumed indicate that our requirement as to the meaning of consensus is much less rigid.

□

5 Concluding Remarks

We extended earlier ideas of Kacprzyk (1984, 1985a, b, 1986, 1987), Kacprzyk and Fedrizzi (1986, 1988, 1989), and Fedrizzi and Kacprzyk (1988), and extended soft measures of consensus employing intuitionistic fuzzy sets when modeling preference relations to better reflect human behavior – by taking into account a hesitancy of individuals. Next, by obtaining as a result an interval of possible values we can evaluate the smallest (worst) and the largest (best) values of degrees of consensus. When individuals are sure as to their preferences, our considerations boils down to solutions obtained by using fuzzy preference relations.

References

[1] Atanassov K. (1986), Intuitionistic fuzzy sets, Fuzzy Sets and Systems, 20, pp. 87–96.

[2] Atanassov K. (1999), Intuitionistic Fuzzy Sets: Theory and Applications. Springer-Verlag.

[3] De Baets, B. and J. Fodor (2000) twenty years of fuzzy preference structures (1978 – 1997). Belgian Journal of Operational Research, Statistics and Computational Science.

[4] Fedrizzi, M. and Kacprzyk, J. (1988). On measuring consensus in the setting of fuzzy preference relations. In J. Kacprzyk and M. Roubens (Eds.): Non-Conventional Preference Relations in Decision-Making, Springer-Verlag, Heidelberg, pp. 129–141.

[5] Fodor, J. and M. Roubens (1994) Fuzzy Preference Modelling and Multicriteria Decision Support. Kluwer, Dordrecht.

[6] Kacprzyk, J. (1984) Collective decision making with a fuzzy majority rule. In: Proceedings of Sixth WOGSC (World Organization of General Systems and Cybernetics) International Congress (Paris, 1984), AFCET, Paris, pp. 153-160.

[7] Kacprzyk, J. (1985a) Group decision making with a fuzzy majority via linguistic quantifiers. Part I: a consensory - like pooling, Cybernetics and Systems: An International Journal, 16, pp. 119–129.

[8] Kacprzyk, J. (1985b) Group decision making with a fuzzy majority via linguistic quantifiers. Part II: a competitive-like pooling, Cybernetics and Systems: An International Journal, 16, pp. 131–144.

[9] Kacprzyk, J. (1986) Group decision making with a fuzzy majority, Fuzzy Sets and Systems, 18, pp. 105–118,

[10] Kacprzyk, J. (1987) On some fuzzy cores and 'soft' consensus measures in group decision making. In J.C. Bezdek (Ed.): The Analysis of Fuzzy Information, Vol. II, CRC Press, Boca Raton, USA, pp. 119–130.

[11] Kacprzyk, J. and Fedrizzi, M. (1986). 'Soft' consensus measures for monitoring real consensus reaching processes under fuzzy preferences, Control and Cybernetics, 15, pp. 309–323.

[12] Kacprzyk, J. and Fedrizzi, M. (1988). A 'soft' measure of consensus in the setting of partial (fuzzy) preferences, European Journal of Operational Research, 34, pp. 315–325.

[13] Kacprzyk, J. and Fedrizzi, M. (1989). A 'human-consistent' degree of consensus based on fuzzy logic with linguistic quantifiers, Mathematical Social Sciences, 18, pp. 275–290.

[14] Kacprzyk, J., Fedrizzi, M. and Nurmi, H. (1992a). Fuzzy logic with linguistic quantifiers in group decision making and consensus formation. In R.R. Yager and L.A. Zadeh (Eds.): An Introduction to Fuzzy Logic Applications in Intelligent Systems, Kluwer, Dordrecht, pp. 263–280.

[15] Kacprzyk, J., Fedrizzi, M. and Nurmi, H. (1992b). Group decision making and consensus under fuzzy preferences and fuzzy majority, Fuzzy Sets and Systems, 49, pp. 21–31.

[16] Kacprzyk J. and H. Nurmi (1998) Group decision making under fuzziness. In R. Sowiski (Ed.): Fuzzy Sets in Decision Analysis, Operations Research and Statistics, Kluwer, Boston, pp. 103–136.

[17] Kacprzyk, J., Nurmi, H. and Fedrizzi, M., Eds. (1996). Consensus under Fuzziness, Kluwer, Boston.

[18] Kacprzyk J. and Zadrożny S. (2000) Collective choice rules under linguistic preferences: an example of the computing with words/perceptions paradigm. IEEE'2000 Conf. on Fuzzy Systems, San Antonio, USA, 7-10 May, pp. 786-791.

[19] Szmidt E. and Kacprzyk J. (1996a). Intuitionistic fuzzy sets in group decision making, Notes on IFS, 2, pp. 15-32.

[20] Szmidt E. and Kacprzyk J. (1996b). Group decision making via intuitionistic fuzzy sets, Proceeding of FUBEST'96 (Sofia, Bulgaria, 1996), pp. 107-112.

[21] Szmidt E. and Kacprzyk J. (1996c). Remarks on some applications of intuitionistic fuzzy sets in decision making, Notes on IFS, 2, (1996), pp. 22-31.

[22] Szmidt E. and Kacprzyk J. (1997a). Intuitionistic fuzzy sets for more realistic group decision making, Proceedings of TRANSITIONS'97 (Warsaw, Poland, 1997a), pp. 430-433.

[23] Szmidt E. and Kacprzyk J. (1998a) Intuitionistic Fuzzy Linguistic Quantifiers. Notes on IFS, Vol.3, No.5. pp. 111-122.

[24] Szmidt E. and Kacprzyk J. (1998b) Group Decision Making under Intuitionistic Fuzzy Preference Relations. Proceedings of the 7th Int. Conference IPMU'98 (Paris, La Sorbonne, July 6-10), pp. 172-178.

[25] Szmidt E. and Kacprzyk J. (1998c) Applications of Intuitionistic Fuzzy Sets in Decision Making. Proceedings of the 8th Congreso EUSFLAT'99 (Pamplona, Univ. De Navarra, September 8-10), pp. 150-158.

[26] L.A. Zadeh (1965) Fuzzy sets. Information and Control, 8, pp. 338-353.

[27] Zadeh, L.A. (1983). A computational approach to fuzzy quantifiers in natural languages. Computers and Mathematics with Applications, 9, No. 1, pp. 149–184.

[28] Zadrożny S. and Kacprzyk J. (1999) Collective choice rules: a classification using the OWA operators. EUSFLAT-ESTYLF'99, Palma de Mallorca, September 22-25, pp. 21-24.

A Soft Design of Acceptance Sampling Plans by Variables

Przemysław Grzegorzewski[1,2]

[1] Systems Research Institute, Polish Academy of Sciences,
Newelska 6, 01-447 Warsaw, Poland
[2] Faculty of Math. and Inf. Sci., Warsaw University of Technology,
Plac Politechniki 1, 00-661 Warsaw, Poland

Abstract. A soft method for designing single sampling plans by variables with relaxed quality levels is suggested. Since small deviations of the parameter from its target value are very often of no importance our soft method for designing sampling plans is more flexible than the conventional one.
Key Words: acceptance sampling, sampling plan by variables, fuzzy sets, hypotheses testing, testing fuzzy hypotheses.

1 Introduction

The goal of statistical quality control (SQC) is to draw conclusions about the quality of a population of products by means of statistical methods applied to sampling results. According to the time of inspection we can distinguish between statistical process control and acceptance sampling. The purpose of acceptance sampling is to investigate whether a particular lot of final or semifinished products (goods or services) satisfy the quality requirements. If during the inspection the produced units are only classified into one of the two disjoint categories: "good" or "bad" then we deal with acceptance sampling by attributes. However, quality specifications are frequently written in terms of measurements like weight, length, diameter, life time, etc. If such continuous quality characteristic is used in acceptance sampling procedure we deal with acceptance sampling by variables.

The statistical tools of acceptance sampling are called sampling plans. Classical acceptance sampling plans have been studied by many researchers. They are thoroughly elaborated e.g. in Schilling (1982).

Before designing a sampling plan a producer and consumer specify statistical requirements of the plan concerning their risks and quality levels. Various economic and technological factors must be taken into account while defining these parameters which makes it difficult for producers and consumers to uniquely specify these factors. Determination involves careful and complex negotiations between producers and consumers. Nevertheless it happens sometimes that a desired plan requires needlessly large samples if the producer and consumer's standpoints are too rigid.

To relax this rigidity of the conventional design plans with relaxed risks and quality levels are considered. Single sampling plans by attributes with relaxed requirements were first discussed by Ohta and Ichihashi (1988), Kanagawa and Ohta (1990), Tamaki, Kanagawa and Ohta (1991) and Grzegorzewski (1998, 2001).

In the present paper we propose a soft method of designing acceptance sampling plans by variables. This method is based on the generalized concept of probabilities of type I and type II errors for fuzzy hypothesis testing problem, suggested by Arnold (1996). We consider situations with relaxed acceptable and rejectable quality levels. This method is more flexible than conventional methods, since small deviations of the requirement from its target value are very often of no importance.

2 Sampling plans by variables

Let X denote a quality characteristic under study of a product unit. An item is called nonconforming if the measurement x of X lies above an upper specification limit USL or below a certain lower specification limit LSL or if it lies outside of a specified closed interval $[LSL, USL]$. Which of these cases is appropriate depends on the specific situation.

In a single sampling plan by variables one draws a random sample of n items $X_1, \ldots, X_n$ from the lot of size N, takes measurements, i.e. determines the realizations $X_1 = x_1, \ldots, X_n = x_n$ of the sample vector and compute the realization $T(x_1, \ldots, x_n)$ of the test statistic $T(X_1, \ldots, X_n)$. If $T(x_1, \ldots, x_n)$ falls in a specific acceptance region then the whole lot is accepted, otherwise, it is rejected.

Sampling plans by variables are in fact statistical tests for a location parameter (in general, tests for the mean). Suppose $X_1, \ldots, X_n$ are normally distributed, i.e. $X_i \sim N(m, \sigma^2)$. Under our assumptions the most natural test statistic T is the sample mean

$$T(X_1, \ldots, X_n) = \overline{X}_n = \frac{1}{n} \sum_{i=1}^{n} X_i. \tag{1}$$

The sample mean is an unbiased estimator of the unknown process mean, i.e. $E\overline{X}_n = m$. It is also normally distributed. In real quality control we have a sampling without replacement and the variance of $\overline{X}_n$ is equal to

$$Var(\overline{X}_n) = \frac{\sigma^2}{n} \frac{N-n}{N-1}. \tag{2}$$

However, in practice, the sample size is small compared to the lot size (say, $\frac{n}{N} \leq 0.1$) and we can assume that the approximate distribution of the sample mean is

$$\overline{X}_n \sim N\left(m, \frac{\sigma^2}{n}\right). \tag{3}$$

Now, without loss of generality, let assume that only one – the upper specification limit USL is given. If the realization of $\overline{X}_n$ is not too large it may be interpreted as evidence that the process mean m is small enough and as evidence of a small fraction nonconforming in the lot (the fraction nonconforming in the lot is a ratio $\frac{M}{N}$, where M denotes an unknown number of nonconforming items in the lot). Therefore, consequently, we will accept this lot. The actual requirement for the acceptance is

$$\overline{X}_n \leq USL - k\sigma, \tag{4}$$

where $k \in R$ is called an acceptance factor, while if

$$\overline{X}_n > USL - k\sigma \tag{5}$$

the lot is rejected.

Similarly, for the lower specification limit LSL the decision criteria are as follows

$$\begin{array}{lll} \text{if} & \overline{X}_n \geq LSL + k\sigma & \text{then accept the lot} \\ \text{if} & \overline{X}_n < LSL + k\sigma & \text{then reject the lot,} \end{array} \tag{6}$$

while for the double (two-sided) specification limits we have

$$\begin{array}{lll} \text{if} & LSL + k'\sigma \leq \overline{X}_n \leq USL - k'\sigma & \text{then accept the lot} \\ \text{if} & \overline{X}_n < LSL + k'\sigma \quad \text{or} \quad \overline{X}_n > USL - k'\sigma & \text{then reject the lot.} \end{array} \tag{7}$$

If the true population variance σ^2 is unknown one has to use sample data to estimate it. The counterparts of the decision criteria given above are now:

$$\begin{array}{lll} \text{if} & \overline{X}_n \leq USL - kS_n & \text{then accept the lot} \\ \text{if} & \overline{X}_n > USL - kS_n & \text{then reject the lot.} \end{array} \tag{8}$$

for the upper specification limit,

$$\begin{array}{lll} \text{if} & \overline{X}_n \geq LSL + kS_n & \text{then accept the lot} \\ \text{if} & \overline{X}_n < LSL + kS_n & \text{then reject the lot} \end{array} \tag{9}$$

for the lower specification limit and

$$\begin{array}{lll} \text{if} & LSL + k'S_n \leq \overline{X}_n \leq USL - k'S_n & \text{then accept the lot} \\ \text{if} & \overline{X}_n < LSL + k'S_n \quad \text{or} \quad \overline{X}_n > USL - k'S_n & \text{then reject the lot} \end{array} \tag{10}$$

for the double specification limits, where $S_n = \sqrt{S_n^2}$ and S_n^2 is a sample variance given by

$$S_n^2 = \frac{1}{n-1}\sum_{i=1}^{n}(X_i - \overline{X}_n)^2. \tag{11}$$

Therefore given specification limit and mathematical model (whether variance σ^2 is known or unknown) any single sampling plan by variables may be described by an ordered pair (n, k), i.e. by the number of items one has draw from the lot and the acceptance factor.

Acceptance sampling doesn't reduce to single-sampling only. There are also double-sampling plans, sequential-sampling plans, variables sampling schemes and other techniques. For more details we refer the reader to Montgomery (1991), Mittag and Rinne (1993), Schilling (1982), etc. However, further on by a sampling plan (or a plan, for short) we will understand a single acceptance sampling plan by variables.

It is seen that the procedure of a single-sampling plan by variables is equivalent to a hypothesis testing for the mean. Namely, the sampling plan for the upper specification limit is equivalent to the hypotheses testing problem

$$H : m \leq m_0 \quad \text{against} \quad K : m > m_0, \tag{12}$$

the sampling plan for the lower specification limit is equivalent to the hypotheses testing problem

$$H : m \geq m_0 \quad \text{against} \quad K : m < m_0, \tag{13}$$

while the sampling plan for the double specification limits is equivalent to the hypotheses testing problem

$$H : m = m_0 \quad \text{against} \quad K : m \neq m_0. \tag{14}$$

However, in the case of sampling plans the parameter m_0 is not explicitly specified.

Further on, without loss of generality, we restrict our considerations to single specification limit problem since the construction of plans for given double specification limits is approached in the same way as for plans single specification limits.

An important measure of the discriminatory power of an acceptance sampling plan is the operating-characteristic (OC) curve. This curve plots the probability of accepting the lot versus the fraction nonconforming in the lot θ. That is, it shows the probability that a lot submitted with a certain fraction nonconforming will be either accepted or rejected.

In the case of the upper specification limit USL the OC curve is a graph of a following, so called, OC function

$$L_{n,k}(\theta) = P(\overline{X}_n \leq USL - k\sigma \mid \theta). \tag{15}$$

The common way to determine a sampling plan is to specify four numbers: the quality levels – the acceptable quality level (AQL) and rejectable quality level (RQL), where $AQL < RQL$, with corresponding risks – the producer's risk (α) and consumer's risk (β), where $\beta < 1 - \alpha$. Then we are looking for such a plan that its OC curve would pass through the two points $(AQL, 1 -$

α) and (RQL, β). Thus the plan parameters – the sample size n and the acceptance factor k – are the solutions of

$$\begin{cases} P(\text{ acceptance } \mid AQL) = 1 - \alpha \\ P(\text{ acceptance } \mid RQL) = \beta. \end{cases} \tag{16}$$

Usually (16) cannot be realized since the sample size n must be integer valued and a desired plan does not exist. Therefore instead of (16) we are looking for a plan for which given requirements are only approximately satisfied, i.e.

$$\begin{cases} P(\text{ acceptance } \mid AQL) \approx 1 - \alpha \\ P(\text{ acceptance } \mid RQL) \approx \beta, \end{cases} \tag{17}$$

or we express the requirements in the following way

$$\begin{cases} P(\text{ acceptance } \mid AQL) \geq 1 - \alpha \\ P(\text{ acceptance } \mid RQL) \leq \beta, \end{cases} \tag{18}$$

which ensures that we are on the safe side. This holds regardless of upper or lower specification limits (because the OC curve turned out to be the same for both cases).

Therefore conditions (16) for the plan under study might be expressed in the following way

$$\begin{cases} L_{n,k}(AQL) = 1 - \alpha \\ L_{n,k}(RQL) = \beta. \end{cases} \tag{19}$$

Direct formulas for n and k for plans with known or unknown process variance can be found in Montgomery (1991), Mittag and Rinne (1993), Schilling (1982), etc.

But now let us additionally briefly discuss the definitions and interpretation of these specific points on the OC curve used in the plan determination. Suppose the quality level is measured by the fraction nonconforming in the lot. Then the *acceptable quality level* (AQL) represents the poorest level of quality for the producer's process that the consumer would consider to be acceptable as a process average (compare ISO 2859). The consumer often tries to design the sampling plan so that the OC curve gives a high probability $1 - \alpha$ of acceptance at the AQL. Thus the probability of rejecting the lot having good quality is equal to α and is called the *producer's risk.* It is worth noting that the AQL is a property of the producer's process and is not a property of the sampling plan. It is also not a target value for the producer's process but it is just a simple standard against which to judge the lots.

However the consumer often is also interested in the other end of the OC curve. He needs the protection against individual lots of poor quality. Thus he establishes the poorest level of quality that he is willing to accept in an individual lot, called the *rejectable quality level* (RQL). The probability of accepting the lot having such poor quality is called the *consumer's risk* β. Note that RQL is also not a property of the plan but a level of quality specified by the consumer to protect himself.

3 Sampling plans with relaxed quality levels

Various economic and technological factors must be taken into account while defining AQL, RQL, α and β, which makes it difficult for producers and consumers to uniquely specify these four main factors. Hence their determination involves careful and complex negotiations between producers and consumers. However, in practice it is not essential that quality levels are exact – it suffices that they are close, in some sense, to the desired values. As it was stated above, a plan satisfying very rigid requirements (16) may not exist at all, and then we have to adopt some approximations. Moreover, the definitions of the AQL and RQL are also not precise but rather descriptive (actual definitions of these parameters may even differ in different sampling schemes). Therefore, concluding, it seems reasonable to substitute crisp parameters AQL and RQL by their relaxed counterparts.

Suppose we have specified the relaxed acceptable quality level and relaxed rejectable quality level $\widetilde{AQL}$ and $\widetilde{RQL}$, respectively. Then, according to (16), the desired sampling plan (n, k) should satisfy following equations

$$\begin{cases} P(\text{ acceptance } \mid \widetilde{AQL}) = 1 - \alpha \\ P(\text{ acceptance } \mid \widetilde{RQL}) = \beta. \end{cases} \tag{20}$$

Now we have two tasks: to propose a natural and effective method for modelling relaxed quality levels $\widetilde{AQL}$ and $\widetilde{RQL}$ and then to interpret (20) .

Let $\widetilde{AQL}$ denote a fuzzy set representing relaxed acceptable quality level with the following membership function $\mu_{AQL} : [0,1] \to [0,1]$,

$$\mu_{AQL}(\theta) = \begin{cases} 1 & \text{if} \quad \theta \leq \theta_1 \\ f(\theta) & \text{if} \quad \theta_1 < \theta \leq \theta_2 \\ 0 & \text{if} \quad \theta > \theta_2, \end{cases} \tag{21}$$

where $f : [0,1] \to [0,1]$ is a nonincreasing function. This membership function corresponds to the acceptable quality level described as "rather smaller than θ_1 but surely not greater than θ_2". Such a model of relaxed quality level seems to be natural, since usually the producer and consumer can easily specify values they surely accept, values they do not accept completely, and intermediate values for possible negotiations.

Similarly, let $\widetilde{RQL}$ denote a fuzzy set representing relaxed rejectable quality level with the following membership function $\mu_{RQL} : [0,1] \to [0,1]$,

$$\mu_{RQL}(\theta) = \begin{cases} 0 & \text{if} \quad \theta < \theta_3 \\ g(\theta) & \text{if} \quad \theta_3 \leq \theta < \theta_4 \\ 1 & \text{if} \quad \theta \geq \theta_4, \end{cases} \tag{22}$$

where $g : [0,1] \to [0,1]$ is a nondecreasing function. This membership function shows a grade of conviction that the individual lot with given quality level should be rejected.

Without loss of generality we consider a plan with the upper specification limit USL. Since $X \sim N(m, \sigma^2)$ then the probability that a random item is conforming is

$$P(X < USL \mid m, \sigma) = \Phi\left(\frac{USL - m}{\sigma}\right), \tag{23}$$

where Φ denotes the cumulative distribution function of the standard normal distribution $N(0,1)$. For the fraction nonconforming θ we have

$$\Phi\left(\frac{USL - m}{\sigma}\right) = 1 - \theta. \tag{24}$$

Hence

$$\frac{USL - m}{\sigma} = u_{1-\theta}, \tag{25}$$

where $u_\theta = \Phi^{-1}(\theta)$ is the quantile of order θ from the standard normal distribution. Therefore we get a following relationship

$$m = m(\theta) = USL - u_{1-\theta}\,\sigma. \tag{26}$$

In particular, if θ is equal to AQL or RQL then

$$\begin{cases} m_{AQL} = USL - u_{1-AQL}\,\sigma, \\ m_{RQL} = USL - u_{1-RQL}\,\sigma. \end{cases} \tag{27}$$

However, if the acceptable quality level is fuzzy then, by the extension principle, m_{AQL} is no longer a crisp number but a fuzzy set $\widetilde{m_{AQL}}$ with the following membership function $\mu_H : R \to [0,1]$

$$\mu_H(m) = \begin{cases} 1 & \text{if} \quad m \leq m_1 \\ h(m) & \text{if} \quad m_1 < m \leq m_2 \\ 0 & \text{if} \quad m > m_2, \end{cases} \tag{28}$$

where $m_1 = USL - u_{1-\theta_1}\sigma$, $m_2 = USL - u_{1-\theta_2}\sigma$ and

$$h(m) = \sup_{\{\theta : m = USL - u_{1-\theta}\,\sigma\}} \mu_{AQL}(\theta). \tag{29}$$

Similarly, for the fuzzy rejectable quality level we get the corresponding fuzzy set $\widetilde{m_{RQL}}$ with the following membership function $\mu_K : R \to [0,1]$

$$\mu_K(m) = \begin{cases} 0 & \text{if} \quad m < m_3 \\ k(m) & \text{if} \quad m_3 \leq m < m_4 \\ 1 & \text{if} \quad m \geq m_4, \end{cases} \tag{30}$$

where $m_3 = USL - u_{1-\theta_3}\sigma$, $m_4 = USL - u_{1-\theta_4}\sigma$ and

$$k(m) = \sup_{\{\theta : m = USL - u_{1-\theta}\,\sigma\}} \mu_{RQL}(\theta). \tag{31}$$

Now suppose that we consider fuzzy null hypothesis H against fuzzy alternative K described by their membership functions $\mu_H : \Theta \to [0,1]$ and $\mu_K : \Theta \to [0,1]$, respectively. These membership functions give the degree to which parameter θ belongs to each hypothesis. To verify such fuzzily formulated hypotheses Arnold (1996) generalized the definition of probabilities of type I and type II errors. If $M_\psi : \Theta \to [0,1]$ denotes a power function of a given test ψ then the quantities

$$\alpha(\psi) = \sup_{\theta \in \Theta_H} \{(\mu_H(\theta) - \mu_K(\theta)) M_\psi(\theta)\} \tag{32}$$

and

$$\beta(\psi) = \sup_{\theta \in \Theta_K} \{(\mu_K(\theta) - \mu_H(\theta))(1 - M_\psi(\theta))\} \tag{33}$$

where

$$\begin{aligned} \Theta_H &= \{\theta \in \Theta : \mu_H(\theta) > \mu_K(\theta)\} \\ \Theta_K &= \{\theta \in \Theta : \mu_H(\theta) < \mu_K(\theta)\} \end{aligned} \tag{34}$$

are generalized probabilities of type I and type II errors, respectively. A test ψ is said to be a test on significance level α ($\alpha \in (0,1)$) if the inequality $\alpha(\psi) \le \alpha$ holds.

It is easily seen that in the traditional situation (where $\Theta_H \cap \Theta_K = \emptyset$) Arnold's formulas reduce to

$$\begin{aligned} \alpha(\psi) &= \sup_{\theta \in \Theta_H} M_\psi(\theta) \\ \beta(\psi) &= \sup_{\theta \in \Theta_K} (1 - M_\psi(\theta)), \end{aligned} \tag{35}$$

which are classical probabilities of type I and type II errors, respectively.

Now let us go back to designing sampling plans. In our problem $\alpha(\psi) = \alpha(n,k)$, $\beta(\psi) = \beta(n,k)$ and $M_\psi(\theta) = M_{n,k}(m) = 1 - L_{n,k}(m)$. Thus, according to (19), (32), (33) and (34) we get the following counterpart of (20), i.e. the system of requirements for the plan with fuzzy quality levels:

$$\begin{cases} \sup_{m \in \Theta_1} \{(\mu_H(m) - \mu_K(m))(1 - L_{n,k}(m))\} = \alpha \\ \sup_{m \in \Theta_2} \{(\mu_K(m) - \mu_H(m)) L_{n,k}(m)\} = \beta, \end{cases} \tag{36}$$

where

$$\begin{aligned} \Theta_1 &= \{m \in R : \mu_H(m) > \mu_K(m)\} \\ \Theta_2 &= \{m \in R : \mu_H(m) < \mu_K(m)\}. \end{aligned} \tag{37}$$

Then solving (36) for n and k we get the desired plan (n,k). Of course, the result for the sample size n is always rounded to the next bigger integer.

4 Example

Suppose that we want to design a sampling plan by variables with the single upper specification limit USL for given fuzzy acceptable and rejectable quality levels $\widetilde{AQL}$ and $\widetilde{RQL}$ and given producer's and consumer's risks α and β. Suppose the membership function μ_{AQL} is piecewise linear, i.e.

$$\mu_{AQL}(\theta) = \begin{cases} 1 & \text{if} \quad \theta \leq \theta_1 \\ \frac{\theta_2-\theta}{\theta_2-\theta_1} & \text{if} \quad \theta_1 < \theta \leq \theta_2 \\ 0 & \text{if} \quad \theta > \theta_2. \end{cases} \tag{38}$$

Moreover, we assume that $\widetilde{RQL}$ is the fuzzy complement of $\widetilde{AQL}$, i.e.

$$\mu_{RQL}(\theta) = 1 - \mu_{AQL}(\theta) \quad \text{for each} \quad \theta \in [0,1]. \tag{39}$$

Membership functions of such fuzzy acceptable and rejectable quality levels are shown in Fig. 1.

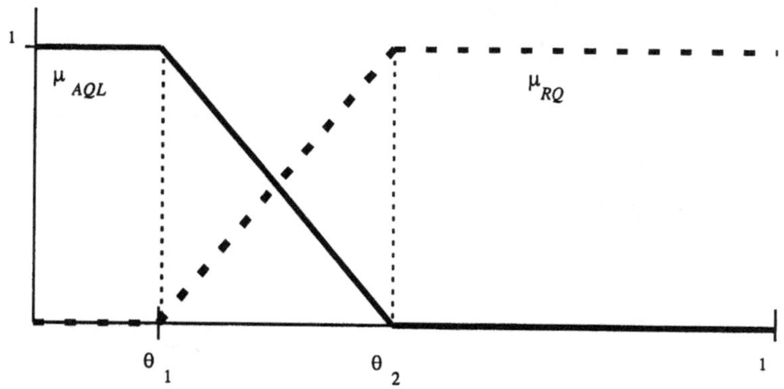

Fig. 1. Membership functions of fuzzy acceptable and rejectable quality levels

This assumption leads to natural fuzzy hypotheses testing problem which is a generalization of the test for crisp hypotheses $H : m \leq m_1$ against $K : m > m_1$.

Although the membership function of the process mean μ_H corresponding to $\widetilde{AQL}$ is not piecewise linear, it can be often well approximated by such a function (e.g. if $0.2 \leq \theta \leq 0.95$). Therefore we have

$$\mu_H(m) \approx \begin{cases} 0 & \text{if} \quad m \leq m_1 \\ \frac{m-m_1}{m_2-m_1} & \text{if} \ m_1 < m \leq m_2 \\ 1 & \text{if} \quad m > m_2, \end{cases} \tag{40}$$

where $m_1 = USL - u_{1-\theta_1}\sigma$ and $m_2 = USL - u_{1-\theta_2}\sigma$.

Since $\widetilde{RQL}$ is the fuzzy complement of $\widetilde{AQL}$ then the process mean corresponding to $\widetilde{RQL}$ is

$$\mu_K(m) = 1 - \mu_H(m) \quad \forall m \in R. \tag{41}$$

Let us additionally assume that the process is normally distributed and known variance σ^2. In the case of crisp quality levels our plan would be equivalent to testing hypothesis H against K described with the OC function

$$L(m) = P\left(\frac{\overline{X} - m_1}{\sigma}\sqrt{n} \leq k \mid m\right), \qquad \forall m \in R. \tag{42}$$

Since $X_1, \ldots, X_n$ are independent identically distributed random variables from $N(m, \sigma^2)$ hence

$$\begin{aligned} L(m) &= P\left(\frac{\overline{X} - m}{\sigma}\sqrt{n} \leq \frac{m_1 - m}{\sigma}\sqrt{n} + k \mid m\right) \\ &= \Phi\left(\frac{m - m_1}{\sigma}\sqrt{n} - k\right). \end{aligned} \tag{43}$$

Substituting this OC function (43) and suitable membership functions μ_H (40) and μ_K (41) into (36) we get

$$\begin{cases} \sup\limits_{m_1 \leq m \leq m_0} \left\{\left[2\frac{m_2-m}{m_2-m_1} - 1\right] \cdot \right. \\ \qquad \left. \cdot \left(1 - \Phi\left(\frac{m-m_1}{\sigma}\sqrt{n} - k\right)\right)\right\} = \alpha \\ \sup\limits_{m_0 \leq m \leq m_2} \left\{\left[1 - 2\frac{m_2-m}{m_2-m_1}\right] \cdot \right. \\ \qquad \left. \cdot \Phi\left(\frac{m-m_1}{\sigma}\sqrt{n} - k\right)\right\} = \beta, \end{cases} \tag{44}$$

where $m_0 = \frac{m_1+m_2}{2}$. After some calculations we get

$$\begin{cases} \sup\limits_{0 \leq t \leq 1} t\Phi\left((1-t)\frac{u_{1-\theta_2} - u_{1-\theta_1}}{2}\sqrt{n} - k\right) = \alpha \\ \sup\limits_{0 \leq t \leq 1} t\Phi\left(k - (1+t)\frac{u_{1-\theta_2} - u_{1-\theta_1}}{2}\sqrt{n}\right) = \beta. \end{cases} \tag{45}$$

In order to find n and k satisfying the system of equations given above we have to find the maximum of a function

$$\lambda(t) = t\Phi(\eta - \xi t), \tag{46}$$

where η and ξ are real numbers (depending on $u_{1-\theta_1}$, $u_{1-\theta_2}$, n and k). It can be shown (compare Arnold, 1998) that $\lambda(t)$ has exactly one relative maximum which is the absolute maximum on $[0, 1]$. However, we advise to apply an effective solution of the system given above which is an approximate one.

Let t_0 denote a point where λ reaches its maximum. Thus $\frac{d}{dt}\lambda(t)\big|_{t=t_0} = 0$. It means that t_0 is a solution of the equation

$$\Phi(\eta - \xi t) - \xi \phi(\eta - \xi t) = 0, \tag{47}$$

where ϕ is the density function of the standard normal distribution. In computing t_0 the following approximation given by Hastings (1955) will be useful:

$$\Phi(x) = 1 - \left(a_1 z + a_2 z^2 + a_3 z^3\right) \phi(x), \tag{48}$$

where $z = (1 + 0.33267x)^{-1}$, $a_1 = 0.4361836$, $a_2 = -0.1201676$, $a_3 = 0.9372980$ (the error in $\Phi(x)$, for $x \geq 0$, is less than 1×10^{-5}).

5 Conclusions

In the present paper we have proposed a method for designing single acceptance sampling plans by variables with relaxed acceptable and rejectable quality levels . Since small deviations of the parameter (quality level) from its target value are very often of no importance our soft method for designing sampling plans is more flexible than the conventional one. By relaxing quality levels one can reduce sample size. Our soft method for designing sampling plans is also general: it may be applied for determining more complicated acceptance sampling plans by variables.

References

1. Arnold B. F. (1996) An Approach to Fuzzy Hypothesis Testing. *Metrika* **44**, 119–126.
2. Arnold B. F. (1998). Testing Fuzzy Hypotheses with Crisp Data. *Fuzzy Sets and Systems* **94**, 323–333.
3. Grzegorzewski P. (1998). A Soft Design of Acceptance Sampling Plans by Attribute. In: *Proceedings of the VIth International Workshop on Intelligent Statistical Quality Control*, Würzburg, September 14–16, pp. 29–38.
4. Grzegorzewski P. (2001). Acceptance Sampling Plans by Attributes with Fuzzy Risks and Quality Levels. In: *Frontiers in Frontiers in Statistical Quality Control*, vol. 6 (Wilrich P.Th., Lenz H.J., Eds.). Springer, Heidelberg, pp. 36–46.
5. Hastings C. (1955). *Approximations for Digital Computers*, Princeton University Press.
6. ISO 2859, International Standard *Sampling Procedures for Inspection by Attributes.*
7. Kanagawa A., Ohta H. (1990). A Design for Single Sampling Attribute Plan Based on Fuzzy Sets Theory. *Fuzzy Sets and Systems* **37**, 173–181.
8. Mittag H.J., Rinne H. (1993), *Statistical Methods of Quality Assurance*, Chapman and Hall.
9. Montgomery D.C. (1991). *Introduction to Statistical Quality Control*, Wiley, New York.

10. Ohta H., Ichihashi H. (1988). Determination of Single-Sampling Attribute Plans Based on Membership Functions. *Int. J. Prod. Res.* **26**, 1477–1485.
11. Schilling E.G. (1982). *Acceptance Sampling in Quality Control*, Dekker, New York.
12. Tamaki F., Kanagawa A., Ohta H. (1991). A Fuzzy Design of Sampling Inspection Plans by Attributes. *Japanese Journal of Fuzzy Theory and Systems* **3**, 315–327.

Network Based Technologies

On the Problem of Performing Exact Partial Abductive Inference in Bayesian Belief Networks using Junction Trees

Luis M. de Campos[1], José A. Gámez[2], and Serafín Moral[1]

[1] Dpto. de Ciencias de la Computación e I.A. Universidad de Granada.
18071 - Granada - SPAIN
{lci,smc}@decsai.ugr.es

[2] Dpto. de Informática. Universidad de Castilla-La Mancha.
02071 - Albacete - SPAIN
jgamez@info-ab.uclm.es

Abstract. Partial abductive inference in Bayesian belief networks has been usually expressed as an extension of *total* abductive inference (abduction over all the variables in the network). In this paper we study the transformation of the partial problem in a total one, analyzing and trying to improve the method previously appeared in the literature. We also outline an alternative approach, and compare both methods by means of experimentation. The experimental results reveal that the problem of partial abductive inference is difficult to solve by exact computation.

1 Introduction

Bayesian belief networks (BBNs) are frequently used as the kernel of *Probabilistic Expert Systems*, because they provide an efficient representation of the joint probability distribution, and allow to calculate probabilities by means of *local* computation.

A *Bayesian belief network* (Pearl [12], Jensen [5]) is a directed acyclic graph (DAG) where each node represents a random variable, and the topology of the graph shows the (in)dependence relations among the variables. If $X_{\mathcal{U}} = \{X_1, \ldots, X_n\}$ is the set of variables in the network, then the joint probability for them can be calculated as:

$$p(X_{\mathcal{U}}) = \prod_{X_i \in X_{\mathcal{U}}} p(X_i | pa(X_i)), \qquad (1)$$

where $pa(X_i)$ contains the parents of X_i.

Probabilistic reasoning in a Bayesian network is carried out by means of propagation algorithms. These algorithms proceed by sending flows of messages through the nodes of a graphical structure called *junction tree*. A *junction tree* (Jensen, [5]) is a higher level graphical structure, obtained from the original BBN by means of a process called *compilation*, and its use avoids to introduce restrictions about the topology of the BBN.

In the context of probabilistic reasoning, abductive or diagnostic inference corresponds to finding the maximum 'a posteriori' probability state of the system variables given some observed evidence. If X_O is the set of observed variables, $X_O = x_O$ is the observed evidence and X_U is the set of unobserved variables, then the goal is to obtain the configuration x^*_U of X_U such that:

$$x^*_U = \arg\max_{x_U} P(x_U|x_O). \tag{2}$$

Usually, x^*_U is known as the *most probable explanation* (MPE) [11,14].

Dawid [2] developed an efficient algorithm to calculate the most probable explanation (MPE) in a junction tree. The algorithm is based on the probabilities propagation algorithm described in [1], but replacing summation by maximum in the calculation of the messages. However, in general we are interested not only in the MPE, but in the K MPEs, and Nilsson [9] has proved that using Dawid's algorithm only the three most probable explanations can directly be identified, but the fourth and subsequent explanations cannot be found directly. Seroussi and Goldmard [13] developed a method able to find the K MPEs for every K. In this method a message is equivalent to a matrix of K messages in the probabilities propagation algorithm, so the algorithm has a considerable computational cost. Later, Nilsson [10] has developed a more efficient method for finding the K MPEs for every K. This method is based in the combination of Dawid's algorithm with a divide and conquer technique.

Sometimes we are interested in obtaining the K MPEs only for a subset of the network's variables called *explanation set* [8]. This problem is known as *Partial Abductive Inference* and we think that in practical applications is more interesting than the classical abductive inference problem, because we can select as the explanation set the variables representing diseases in a medical diagnosis problem, the variables representing critical components (starter, battery, alternator, ...) in a car diagnosis problem, ...

Now, if we denote by $X_E \subset X_U$ the explanation set, then the goal is to obtain the configuration x^*_E of X_E such that:

$$x^*_E = \arg\max_{x_E} P(x_E|x_O) = \arg\max_{x_E} \sum_{x_R} P(x_E, x_R|x_O), \tag{3}$$

where $X_R = X_U \backslash X_E$. In general, x^*_E is not equal to project the configuration x^*_U over the variables of X_E. So, we need to obtain x^*_E directly (eq. 3).

Therefore, the problem of partial abductive inference can be solved in two steps:

1. Marginalize out (by summation) over the variables not in the explanation set. This process will yield a junction tree containing only the variables in the explanation set (X_E).
2. Apply an algorithm of *total* abductive inference [10,13].

However, this process is more complex than it looks, because summation and maximum have to be used simultaneously and these operations do not have a commutative behaviour. This fact motivates that not all junction tree obtained from the original BBN will be valid. Thus, this method can be only directly applied when X_E is included in a node of the junction tree, or when the variables of X_E constitute a subtree of the complete junction tree. Therefore, the problem is what to do when the variables of the explanation set are associated with several disconnected subtrees of the junction tree?. Xu [15] gives a method for transforming the initial junction tree into another one containing a node in which the variables of X_E are included. The problem is that if X_E contains many variables, then the size of the probability table associated with the node containing X_E will be to large. Nilsson [10] outlines how to slightly modify Xu's algorithm in order to allow (when possible) that the variables of X_E constitute a sub-tree and not a single node.

In this paper we study this algorithm and try to contribute to its improvement. We also outline an alternative approach and compare both methods by experimentation. The paper is organized as follows: second section introduces the junction tree representation. In the third section we revise the algorithm of Xu-Nilsson, trying to improve it by adding an intermediate step and introducing heuristics. In the fourth section we outline an alternative approach for building a valid junction tree. The fifth section describes the experiments, and their results are discussed in the sixth section. Finally, in the seventh section we consider the conclusions.

2 Junction Tree Representation

If $\mathcal{G}$ is the directed acyclic graph representing the BBN, a junction tree representation for $\mathcal{G}$ is obtained by a process known as compilation. Thus, a junction tree is a tree whose nodes are subsets of variables (clusters) which satisfies the two following properties:

1. For each variable X_i in the Bayesian network, there is at least a cluster C_j in the tree containing the set of variables $\{X_i\} \cup pa(X_i)$.
2. *Running intersection property:* If C_i and C_j are two clusters in the junction tree, then the variables in $C_i \cap C_j$ are contained in every cluster along the path between C_i and C_j.

Every conditional probability distribution in the BBN $P(X_i|pa(X_i))$ is assigned to one (and only one) clique C_j such that $\{\{X_i\} \cup pa(X_i)\} \subseteq C_j$. The potential function $\psi(C_j)$ associated to each clique is built by combining the probability distributions assigned to it. If a clique does not have any probability distribution assigned, then a unitary potential is built. After this initialization of the cliques, if $\mathcal{T}$ denote the set of clusters in the junction tree, then the following expression represents a factorization of the joint probability distribution:

$$P(X_{\mathcal{U}}) = \prod_{C_j \in \mathcal{T}} \psi(C_j). \tag{4}$$

Running intersection property is necessary in order to ensure that computations can be carried out in a local manner, i.e., to ensure consistence in the message passing scheme (see [5] for details). Both properties are guaranteed from the compilation process.

Associated with each edge (C_i, C_j) of the junction tree there is a *separator*, $S_{ij} = C_i \cap C_j$. These separators are used to store the messages during the propagation, and initially they contain a unitary potential.

Figure 1.(a) shows the *Asia* Bayesian network [7], and figure 1.(b) shows a junction tree for it. The separators are indicated in the links.

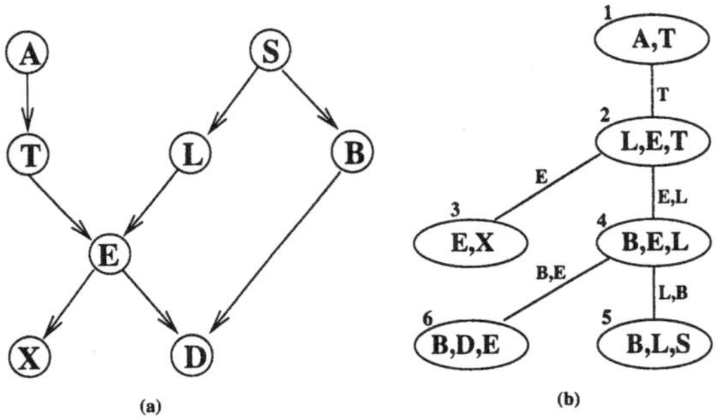

Fig. 1. (a) The Asia Bayesian network. (b) A junction tree for Asia.

3 Transforming the Junction Tree

The modification of the junction tree $\mathcal{T}$ to include a sub-tree containing a given subset of variables (namely X_E) is performed by the Xu-Nilsson's algorithm as follows:

1. Identify the smallest subtree $\mathcal{T}'$ of $\mathcal{T}$ that contains the variables of X_E.
2. Pass sum-flows from the rest of the cliques to $\mathcal{T}'$. In this way $\mathcal{T}'$ factorizes over the variables contained in its cliques.
3. The rest of the process consists in the selection of two neighbours C_i and C_j in $\mathcal{T}'$, and in their fusion into a new node C_{ij} obtained from $C^*_{ij} = C_i \cup C_j$ by deleting the variables that are not necessary to maintain the running intersection property and do not belong to X_E. C^*_{ij} is important because though we produce a clique C_{ij} in the process we have to compute with potentials defined on the whole set C^*_{ij}. Figure 2 shows an example for the Bayesian network Asia taking $X_E = \{A, T, B\}$.

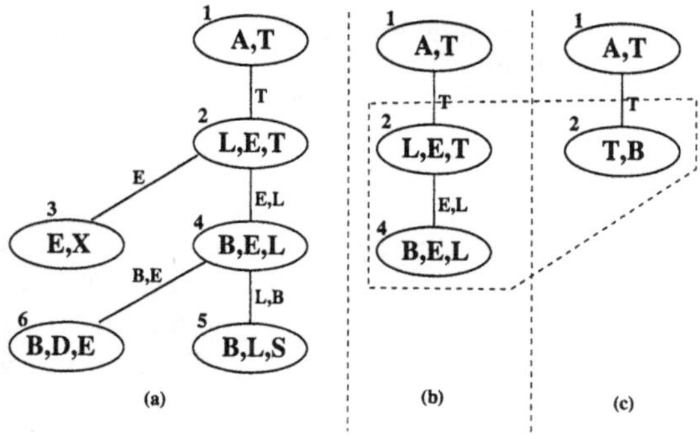

Fig. 2. (a) The initial join tree. (b) $\mathcal{T}'$ for $X_E = \{A, T, B\}$. (c) The junction tree obtained by the fusion process.

The potential assigned to C_{ij} is obtained as:

$$\psi(C_{ij}) = \sum_{C^*_{ij} \setminus C_{ij}} \frac{\psi(C_i) \cdot \psi(C_j)}{\psi(S_{i,j})} \tag{5}$$

Step 3 is applied while $\mathcal{T}'$ contains variables not in X_E. The process is equivalent to pass sum-flows from the initial $\mathcal{T}'$ to X_E (the only variables finally contained in $\mathcal{T}'$), so $\mathcal{T}'$ factorizes over X_E (or over $X_E \cap (X_O = x_O)$ if the evidence $X_O = x_O$ has been entered previously) and then an algorithm to obtain the K MPEs can be applied.

If we know that the separator contains a unitary potential, the division performed in eq. 5 is not necessary. This will be our case if we assume that the junction tree has not been used for another propagation, because in abductive inference it is enough to send the messages from the leaves to the root [10], and so we are sure that the separators in $\mathcal{T}'$ contain (the initials) unitary potentials. So, in the rest of the paper we omit the division.

In the rest of this section we study some aspects of the algorithm and propose some improvements.

3.1 Introducing an Intermediate Step

After identifying the subtree $\mathcal{T}'$ and before beginning the process of fusion, an intermediate step can be introduced, which could be viewed as an optimization of the previous method.

The idea is to look for the variables not in X_E that are only included in one clique of $\mathcal{T}'$, then it is clear that these variables can be marginalized out directly[1]. This idea, although very simple, has two advantages:

[1] Notice that as a consequence of the deletion of these variables, the resulting clique may not be a clique, i.e., can be a subset of one of its neighbours. This is not

i) The fusion process is more efficient because the potentials induced during the combination are smaller, due to the absence of the previously removed variables.
ii) It could improve the quality of the final junction tree. For example, if we suppose that the junction tree in figure 3.(a) is $\mathcal{T}'$ for $X_E = \{A, B, C, D\}$, then figure 3.(b) shows the junction tree obtained when the fusion process is applied directly. However, the variable E can be marginalized out in clique 2, obtaining the junction tree shown in figure 3.(c). In this case there is no need to apply the fusion process and so the junction tree shown in (c) is the final junction tree.

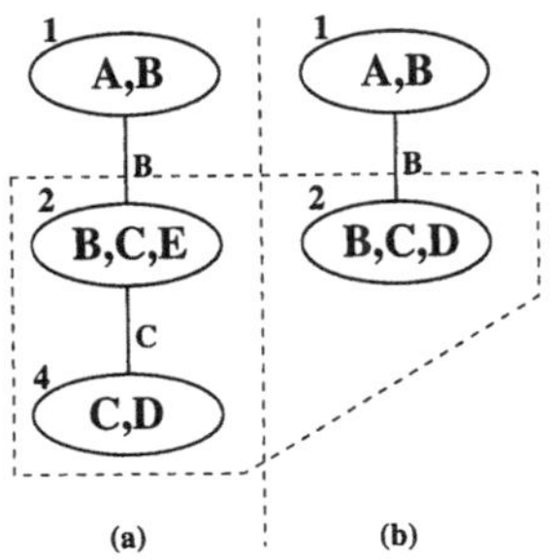

Fig. 3.

It is clear that the obtained junction tree is better to perform propagation because the smaller size of its potentials.

3.2 Introducing Heuristics

It is clear that the way the neighbours to fuse are selected has influence in the process efficiency. For example, if we consider the junction tree in figure 1.(b) and the explanation set $X_E = \{A, B\}$, then we identify the subtree $C_1 - C_2 - C_4$ as $\mathcal{T}'$. So, we have two possibilities to perform the fusion:

1. $((C_1, C_2)C_4)$. Although the fusion (C_1, C_2) produces the node $C_{12} = \{A, L, E\}$, the combination of C_1 and C_2 induces a potential over the set $C^*_{12} = \{A, T, L, E\}$. The fusion (C_{12}, C_4) induces a potential over the set $C^*_{(12)4} = \{A, B, L, E\}$ and produces the node $C_{124} = \{A, B\}$. So, if all the variables have two possible states, this process of fusion involves two potentials of size 16.
2. $(C_1(C_2, C_4))$. In this case, the fusion (C_2, C_4) induces a potential over the set $C^*_{24} = \{L, E, T, B\}$ and produces the node $C_{24} = \{T, B\}$, and the

a problem because the subset will be absorbed by its superset neighbour during the fusion process.

fusion (C_1, C_{24}) induces a potential over the set $C^*_{1(24)} = \{A, T, B\}$ and produces the node $C_{124} = \{A, B\}$. So, following this sequence, the fusion process only involves a potential of size 16 and other of size 8.

Therefore, if we select the neighbours to fuse in an appropriate way, the size of the induced potentials will be smaller, and so the fusion process will be more efficient. To implement these ideas, we propose to set out the problem as a deletion problem (like triangulation but deleting links instead of nodes or variables), because in this way we can use similar heuristics to the ones proposed for this kind of problems (see Kjærulff [6]). More precisely, if $s(C_i)$ represents the size of the potential associated to C_i, we propose the following heuristics:

H1 Select the link (C_i, C_j) with smaller $s(C^*_{ij})$. With this heuristic we prefer the creation of smaller potentials.
H2 Select the link (C_i, C_j) with smaller $s(C_{ij})$. With this heuristic we prefer the creation of smaller nodes. Using this heuristic we expect an earlier deletion of the variables not in X_E.

Before we continue, it is important to emphasize that on the contrary to the case of triangulation, in the fusion process not all the links have to be removed, so we need to identify which are the links candidates for deletion.

Definition 1. Given a junction tree $\mathcal{T}'$ and an explanation set X_E, a link (C_i, C_j) with separator $S_{i,j}$ has to be removed if:

i) $S_{i,j} \not\subseteq X_E$, or
ii) $S_{i,j} \subseteq X_E$, but $S_{i,j} = C_i$ or $S_{i,j} = C_j$.

The second condition of the previous definition is necessary to deal with non-maximal nodes, which can be introduced by the intermediate step presented in the previous subsection.

Therefore, the fusion process for the junction tree $\mathcal{T}'$ and the explanation set X_E could be expressed by the following pseudocode:

1. Select an heuristic H_k from $\{H_1, H_2\}$.
2. Let $\mathcal{L}$ be the set containing all the links in $\mathcal{T}'$ identified by definition 1.
3. While $\mathcal{L} \neq \emptyset$ do
   (a) Choose the link (C_i, C_j) using H_k, and remove it from $\mathcal{L}$.
   (b) Obtain C_{ij} from (C_i, C_j).
   (c) For all links in $\mathcal{L}$ containing C_i or C_j, replace C_i or C_j by C_{ij}.
4. At this point $\mathcal{L}$ contains the (links of the) junction tree defined over X_E.

In section 5 we present some preliminary results about the application of the heuristics to some real Bayesian networks.

4 An Alternative Approach

One possible problem of the previous method is that the quality of the final junction tree (on which the abductive inference algorithm will be applied), depends on the initial junction tree, which was obtained for general purposes and not thinking in abductive inference. Figure 4 shows an example of this: In (a) we can see the Bayesian network; (b) and (c) show two different junction trees, both of the same quality (size); (d) and (e) show the final junction trees obtained from (b) and (c) respectively.

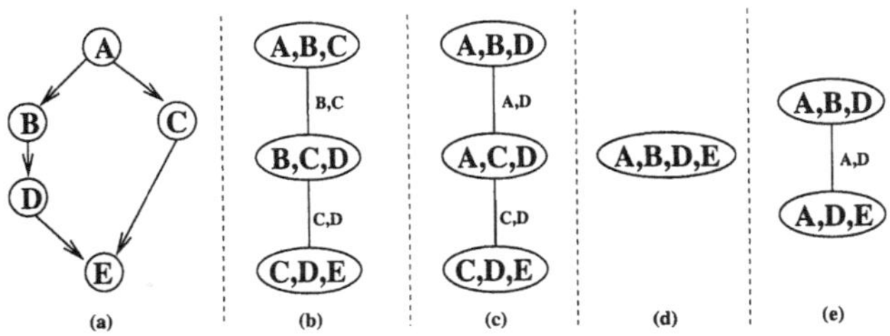

Fig. 4. Different initial junction trees can yield different final junction trees

The junction tree in figure 4.(d) is worse than the one in figure 4.(e), because the greater size of its potentials.

An alternative approach could be to obtain a specific junction tree for a given set X_E [4]. This task can be achieved by taking advantage of the available degrees of freedom in the compilation process. Concretely, during the triangulation we can use constrained deletion sequences, in such a way that we start to delete the variables of X_E only when all the variables not in X_E have been deleted.

Using this kind of deletion sequences, and adding all the clusters (and not only those which are maximal) to the tree, we can build a junction tree in which a subtree for X_E can be identified. If only cliques are added to the tree, it is necessary to apply *maximum cardinality search* (see [7]) beginning with a variable of X_E and breaking ties in favor of the variables in X_E during the numbering of the graph's nodes. Figure 5 shows the junction tree for the Asia BBN and the explanation set $X_E = \{A, B, T\}$ considered in the previous examples.

After building a junction tree in this way, we only have to identify $\mathcal{T}'$ for X_E, to marginalize out the variables not in $\mathcal{T}'$ (steps 1 and 2 of the procedure in Section 3) and then to apply the intermediate step explained in subsection 3.1, but the fusion process (step 3 of the procedure in section 3) is avoided. In section 6 we compare both methods.

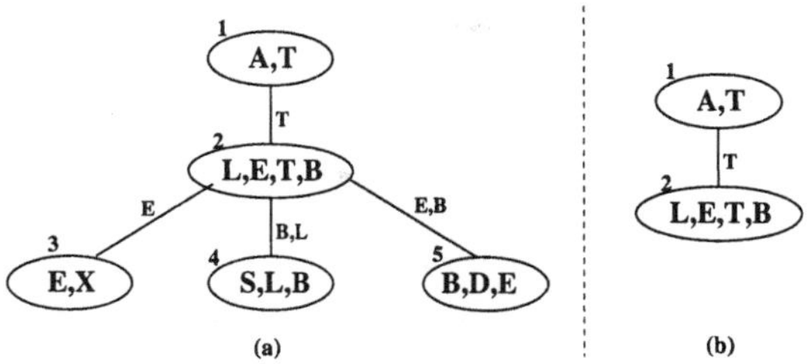

Fig. 5. (a) Specific junction tree for Asia and $X_E = \{A, B, T\}$.(b) Identified $\mathcal{T}'$

5 Experimental Evaluation

In order to gather more information about the complete abductive process, i.e., (obtaining a valid junction tree for a given explanation set) + (the propagation process), we have performed a battery of experiments over a set of Bayesian networks. Concretely, we have used two real-world Bayesian networks and a randomly generated one. Table 1 describes some information about the used Bayesian networks.

For each network we have generated 10 different orderings of their variables, so all the results are the average over 10 runs. The last three variables of the ordering have been selected as evidence. The abductive inference process has been carried out for each network taking as explanation set the first 1, 2, 3, ... variables of the corresponding network (for the Diabetes network we have taken 5, 10, 15, ... variables), and obtaining the junction tree in which abductive inference is applied by using the heuristics H1 and H2, and the method described in section 4.

Figures 6 to 8 show the obtained results with respect to the size of the junction tree (size is shown in the y axis). The picture on the left shows the size of the junction tree which is built during the fusion process using heuristic H1 and H2. The size of the junction tree is obtained as:

$$s(\text{initial junction tree}) + \sum_{\text{all } C^*_{ij} \text{ generated}} s(C^*_{ij}).$$

We have considered $s(C^*_{ij})$ and not $s(C_{ij})$ because the potential over the first one is always built.

The picture in the center shows the sizes of the expanded junction trees obtained by H2 and the method described in section 4 (where a specific junction tree is searched). The size of the initial junction tree is also shown.

The picture on the right shows the sizes of the final junction trees including only explanation variables (over which abductive inference is performed) using heuristic H2 [2] and the method described in section 4.

[2] The final junction tree obtained by H1 and H2 is the same.

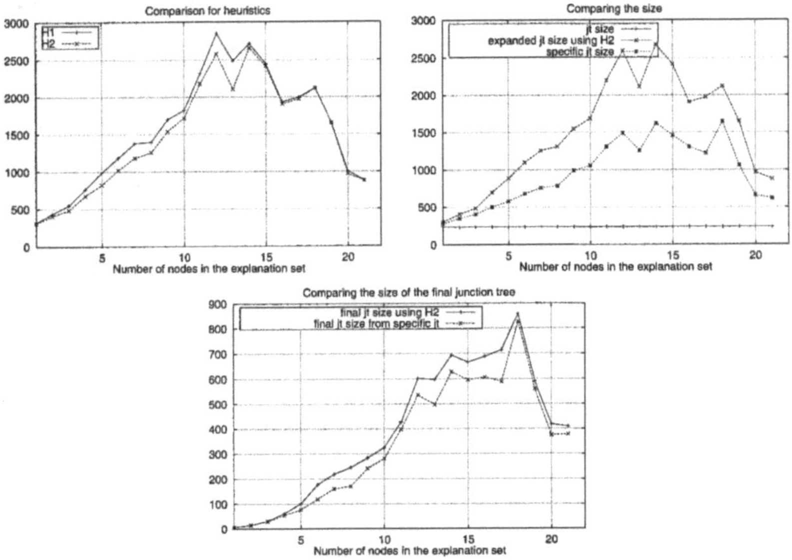

Fig. 6. Experimental results for the random Bayesian network

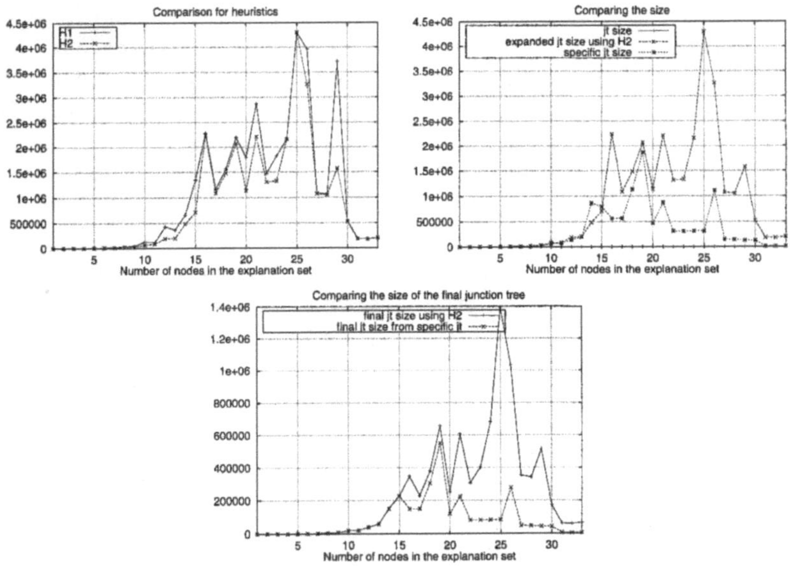

Fig. 7. Experimental results for the Alarm Bayesian network

Table 1. Some data about the networks used in the experiments

			node potential size		
Network	nodes	links	min	max	mean
random	25	30	2	24	8.36
Alarm	37	46	2	108	20.3
Diabetes	413	602	3	280000	15633.1

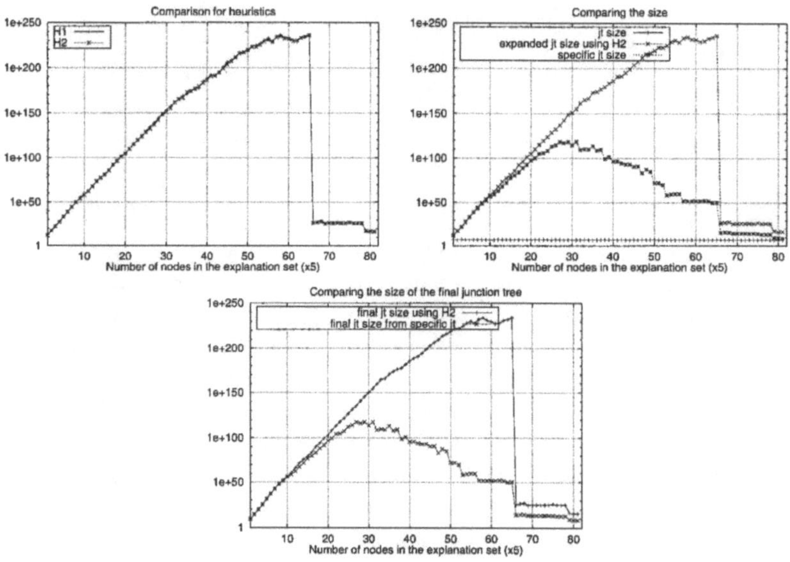

Fig. 8. Experimental results for the Diabetes Bayesian network

Finally, figure 9 shows the average time cost of the whole process (obtaining junction tree + propagation) for the *random* Bayesian network. The experiments have been carried out over a Pentium II 300Mhz computer, running under Linux operating system. The programs have been developed in Java.

6 Discussion

From the experiments we can obtain the following conclusions:

- The junction tree (JT) created during the fusion process has a size much greater than the size of the initial junction tree. Heuristic H2 improves the results provided by H1 and, in general, we can expect that if an arbitrary selection is implemented in the fusion process, the size of the obtained junction tree will be even greater.

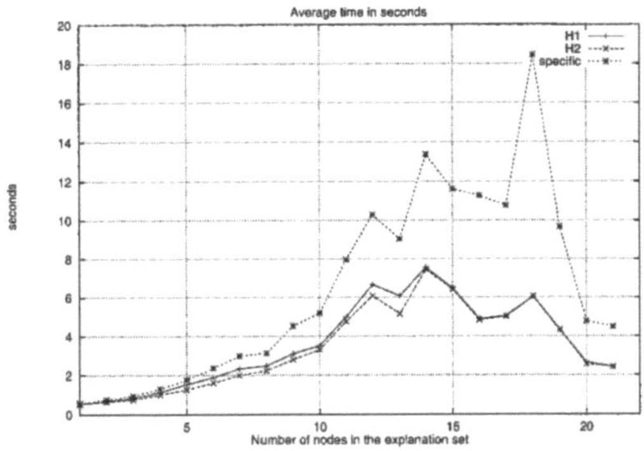

Fig. 9. A plot of the average time in the *Random* network

- Respect to the size of the final junction tree, which includes only the variables of the explanation set, we can observe that the specific method obtains junction trees of higher quality. This is a logical consequence of the application of a specific process. Therefore, the propagation process carried out to search the K MPEs will be more efficient (in general) over this junction tree than over the junction tree obtained by the fusion process.
- If we compare the size of the whole junction tree obtained by the specific process with the size of the whole junction tree obtained by the fusion process (using H2), we can see that the first one has a smaller size. However, the computation time employed when the specific method is used is greater than the computation time employed when the fusion process is used. We think that the following observations could explain this fact:
  - The size of a junction tree obtained by a constrained triangulation is much greater than the size of a junction tree obtained without constrains. This fact motivates that the process of initializing the greater junction tree is a high time consuming process (setting to 1 all configurations of a big potential).
  - The process of finding the subtree $\mathcal{T}'$ by means of marginalization of the variables not in $\mathcal{T}'$ takes much more time for the greater junction tree, because the great size of the potentials.
  - Finally, the specific method avoids the fusion process, but this advantage does not compensate for the time employed in the previous steps.

7 Concluding Remarks

The main conclusion that can be extracted from this paper is that though partial abductive inference has always been expressed as an extension of *total* abductive inference, the transformation of the initial problem (initial junction tree) in the final problem (a junction tree defined over the explanation set) is a complex problem that should receive more attention. In fact, given the great size of the junction tree created by the transformation process, the amount of necessary computer memory can be so high, that the problem becomes unsolvable by exact computation, even for medium-size networks.

In this paper we have contributed to improve an existing method (the only one known by the authors), and we also have introduced an alternative approach. The second approach has the advantage that it produces smaller final junction trees, although the first steps of the process take more time due to the great size of the whole junction tree. As future research we plan to investigate how to obtain smaller junction trees, and in the use of alternative ways to represent the potentials, as probability trees or multiple tables (like in lazy propagation), in order to reduce the time for potential initialization.

Finally, we think that, due to the size of the junction tree, in many cases approximate methods will have to be used, so we also plan to investigate in the development of this kind of methods [3].

Acknowledgements

This work has been supported by the Spanish Comisión Interministerial de Ciencia y Tecnología (CICYT) under Project TIC97-1135-CO4-01.

References

1. S.K. Andersen, K.G. Olesen, F.V. Jensen, and F. Jensen. Hugin: a shell for buiding belief universes for expert systems. In *Proceedings of the 11th International Joint Conference on Artificial Intelligence*, Detroit, 1989.
2. A.P. Dawid. Applications of a general propagation algorithm for probabilistic expert systems. *Statistics and Computing*, 2:25–36, 1992.
3. L.M. de Campos, J.A. Gámez, and S. Moral. Partial Abductive Inference in Bayesian Belief Networks using a Genetic Algorithm. *Pattern Recognition Letters*, 20(11-13):1211–1217, 1999.
4. J.A. Gámez. *Inferencia abductiva en redes causales.* PhD thesis, Departamento de Ciencias de la Computación e I.A. Escuela Técnica Superior de Ingeniería Informática. Universidad de Granada, 1998.
5. F.V. Jensen. *An introduction to Bayesian Networks.* UCL Press, 1996.
6. U. Kjærulff. Triangulation of graphs - algorithms giving small total space. Technical Report R 90-09, Department of Mathematics and Computer Science. Institute of Electronic Systems. Aalborg University, March 1990.
7. S.L. Lauritzen and D.J. Spiegelhalter. Local computations with probabilities on graphical structures and their application to expert systems. *J.R. Statistics Society. Serie B*, 50(2):157–224, 1988.
8. R. E. Neapolitan. *Probabilistic Reasoning in Expert Systems. Theory and Algorithms.* Wiley Interscience, New York, 1990.

9. D. Nilsson. An algorithm for finding the M most probable configurations of discrete variables that are specified in probabilistic expert systems. *MSc. Thesis*, University of Copenhagen, 1994.
10. D. Nilsson. An efficient algorithm for finding the M most probable configurations in Bayesian networks. *Statistics and Computing*, 2:159–173, 1998.
11. J. Pearl. Distributed revision of composite beliefs. *Artificial Intelligence*, 33:173–215, 1987.
12. J. Pearl. *Probabilistic Reasoning in Intelligent Systems.* Morgan Kaufmann, San Mateo, 1988.
13. B. Seroussi and J.L. Goldmard. An algorithm directly finding the K most probable configurations in Bayesian networks. *International Journal of Approximate Reasoning*, 11:205–233, 1994.
14. B.K. Sy. Reasoning MPE to multiply connected belief networks using message passing. In *Proceedings of the 11th National Conference on AI*, pages 570–576. AAAI, 1993.
15. H. Xu. Computing marginals for arbitrary subsets from marginal representation in markov trees. *Artificial Intelligence*, 74:177–189, 1995.

Computing Probabilities of Events in Bayesian Networks

Rolf Haenni[1], Jürg Kohlas[2], and Norbert Lehmann[2]

[1] Computer Science Department, University of California, Los Angeles, CA, 90095, USA
[2] Department of Informatics, University of Fribourg, Switzerland

Abstract. This paper proposes a new approach for computing probabilities of events in Bayesian networks. The idea is to replace the outward phase of the propagation algorithm by a second (partial) inward propagation phase. The benefit of this idea is that the attention can be focussed on optimizing the inward phase.[1]

1 Introduction

Several architectures have been developed for computing marginal distributions of variables in Bayesian networks. The following three architectures are the most popular ones:

- the HUGIN architecture [2],
- the Lauritzen-Spiegelhalter architecture (LS-architecture for short) [3],
- the Shenoy-Shafer architecture (SS-architecture for short) [7].

All these techniques are based on a message-passing scheme related to certain graphical structures (join or junction trees), where the two main operations of *multiplication* and *marginalization* (summation) of potentials are always performed locally on relatively small families of variables. A common feature of the three architectures is that they use a two-phase computation, consisting of a so-called *inward propagation*, in which information is collected, and an *outward propagation* phase, in which information is distributed. At the end of the outward phase, the marginal distributions of certain families of variables are available. This permits (by summation) to compute the probabilities of events related to such a family of variables.

The main difference between these architectures is the way in which the outward phase is performed. The HUGIN and the LS-architecture need a further operation of *division* to prepare or to perform the outward phase. These are relatively costly operations, which are avoided in the SS-architecture. It has been shown that the SS-architecture is at least as efficient as the HUGIN architecture considered so far to be the most efficient one (see [5]).

[1] Research supported by grant No. 21-53500.98 of the Swiss National Foundation for Research.

This paper proposes an alternative approach for computing probabilities of events. The new feature is that outward propagation is replaced by a second *partial inward propagation*. In this new approach, the question of selecting an appropriate architecture is therefore only of minor importance. Furthermore, eliminating the outward phase allows an optimization of the inward phase, not possible otherwise.

The underlying idea of the method presented in this paper has first been developed for the framework of *probabilistic argumentation systems* [1]. The same technique has then been applied to the closely related domain of belief function networks [4]. Clearly, since Bayesian networks can be considered as special cases of belief function networks, it is not surprising, that the method can also be adapted to Bayesian networks. Possibly, it is an approach which can be formulated in the general theory of valuation networks [7], although this has still to be verified.

The basic theorem on which the method is based is formulated in Section 2. In Section 3, the theoretical result is used to design a two-phase inward procedure. Finally, the optimization of the inward propagation is discussed in Section 4.

2 Probability of Events and Normalization Constants

Consider a set of *variables* $V = \{X_1, \ldots, X_n\}$ where every variable X_i has a corresponding finite *frame* Θ_i. Furthermore, if I is a subset of indices in $N = \{1, \ldots, n\}$, then $\mathbf{X}_I$ denotes a vector of variables X_i with $i \in I$. The cartesian product $\Theta_I = \prod_{i \in I} \Theta_i$ represents the set of all such vectors relative to I. A *potential* on Θ_I (or a potential on I for short) is a mapping $\psi : \Theta_I \rightarrow \mathbb{R}^+$. It corresponds to an $|I|$-dimensional table which is written as $\psi(\mathbf{X}_I)$. I is called the *domain* of $\psi(\mathbf{X}_I)$. In the following, a potential on I is either a probability distribution over Θ_I, a conditional probability distribution over Θ_J given Θ_K (where $J \cup K = I$ and $J \cap K = \emptyset$), or an evidence $\mathbf{X}_I \in E_I$, where E_I is a subset of Θ_I. In this latter case, the potential is a table with $\psi(\mathbf{X}_I) = 1$ if $\mathbf{X}_I \in E_I$ and $\psi(\mathbf{X}_I) = 0$ otherwise.

Let $p(\mathbf{X}_N)$ be a probability distribution over all n variables and suppose that there exists a corresponding factorization

$$p(\mathbf{X}_N) = \prod_{I \in \mathcal{H}} \psi(\mathbf{X}_I), \tag{1}$$

where $\mathcal{H}$ is a family of domains $I \subseteq N$ (a hypergraph). Furthermore, suppose that a number of evidences, represented by potentials $\psi_E(\mathbf{X}_I)$ with $I \in \mathcal{H}^* \subseteq \mathcal{H}$, are added. These potentials describe the observations that $\mathbf{X}_I \in E_I$. The conditional distribution of the n variables given these evidences (abbreviated by E) is then given by

$$p(\mathbf{X}_N | E) = \frac{1}{c} \cdot \prod_{I \in \mathcal{H}} \psi(\mathbf{X}_I) \cdot \prod_{I \in \mathcal{H}^*} \psi_E(\mathbf{X}_I), \tag{2}$$

where

$$c = \sum_{\mathbf{X}_N \in \Theta_N} [\prod_{I \in \mathcal{H}} \psi(\mathbf{X}_I) \cdot \prod_{I \in \mathcal{H}^*} \psi_E(\mathbf{X}_I)] \tag{3}$$

is the *normalization constant* of the factorization. Finally, suppose that $H \subseteq \Theta_N$ represents an *event* (also called a hypothesis), then

$$p(\mathbf{X}_N \in H|E) = \sum_{\mathbf{X}_N \in H} p(\mathbf{X}_N|E) \tag{4}$$

is the conditional probability of the event H given the evidence E. Note that H is often given as a set $H_I \subseteq \Theta_I$. In such a case, H can simply be considered as the cylindrical extension of H_I to Θ_N.

The expression in (4) represents the classical way of computing conditional probabilities of events. However, the following theorem shows, that there is an interesting alternative.

Theorem 1. *Suppose that $\psi_H(\mathbf{X}_N)$ represents the potential obtained by considering the event H as an additional evidence. If*

$$c' = \sum_{\mathbf{X}_N \in \Theta_N} [\psi_H(\mathbf{X}_N) \cdot \prod_{I \in \mathcal{H}} \psi(\mathbf{X}_I) \cdot \prod_{I \in \mathcal{H}^*} \psi_E(\mathbf{X}_I)] \tag{5}$$

denotes the new factorization constant, then

$$p(\mathbf{X}_N \in H|E) = \frac{c'}{c}. \tag{6}$$

Proof. The proof of this theorem is based on the fact that $\psi_H(\mathbf{X}_N)$ can be seen as a filter for the sum in (5). It selects all the values of $\mathbf{X}_N$ which are in H. The second normalization factor can therefore be written as

$$c' = \sum_{\mathbf{X}_N \in H} [\prod_{I \in \mathcal{H}} \psi(\mathbf{X}_I) \cdot \prod_{I \in \mathcal{H}^*} \psi_E(\mathbf{X}_I)].$$

Finally, the equivalence between (4) and (6) can be demonstrated as follows:

$$\begin{aligned} \frac{c'}{c} &= \frac{1}{c} \cdot \sum_{\mathbf{X}_N \in H} [\prod_{I \in \mathcal{H}} \psi(\mathbf{X}_I) \cdot \prod_{I \in \mathcal{H}^*} \psi_E(\mathbf{X}_I)] \\ &= \sum_{\mathbf{X}_N \in H} [\frac{1}{c} \cdot \prod_{I \in \mathcal{H}} \psi(\mathbf{X}_I) \cdot \prod_{I \in \mathcal{H}^*} \psi_E(\mathbf{X}_I)] \\ &= \sum_{\mathbf{X}_N \in H} p(\mathbf{X}_N|E) = p(\mathbf{X}_N \in H|E). \end{aligned}$$

This theorem shows that the probability of an event is determined by the normalization constants of two slightly different factorizations. This will be exploited in the next section for an efficient computation of this probability.

3 Computing Normalization Constants

As shown in the previous section, the problem of computing probabilities of events can be reduced to the problem of computing two related normalization constants c and c'. The first normalization constant c remains the same for all possible events. In contrast, the second normalization constant c' depends on H and must therefore be recomputed for every event of interest.

This section shows how normalization constants can be computed efficiently. The general idea is the same as in the architectures mentioned at the beginning. The point is that a factorization on a hypergraph (as required in (2), for example) can be transformed into an equivalent factorization on a join tree [7]. The computation can then be arranged as a message-passing scheme between the nodes of the join tree. A message between two nodes I and J is a potential on $I \cap J$ that contains the information required by the receiving node. In this way, the information is propagated through the entire join tree. The benefit of this is that the potentials are always multiplied locally on relatively small domains.

The propagation algorithm of all three architectures includes two phases. The first phase (called the inward phase) is shown in Fig. 1. Messages are sent from the leaves of the join tree towards an arbitrarily chosen root. If R denotes the domain of the root, then, after the inward phase, it is possible to derive probabilities of events $H_R \subseteq \Theta_R$. During the second phase (called the outward phase), messages are sent from the root to the leaves of the join tree. At the end, it is possible to compute probabilities of events relative to all the domains appearing in the join tree. Figure 2 illustrates the outward phase of the propagation algorithm in a join tree.

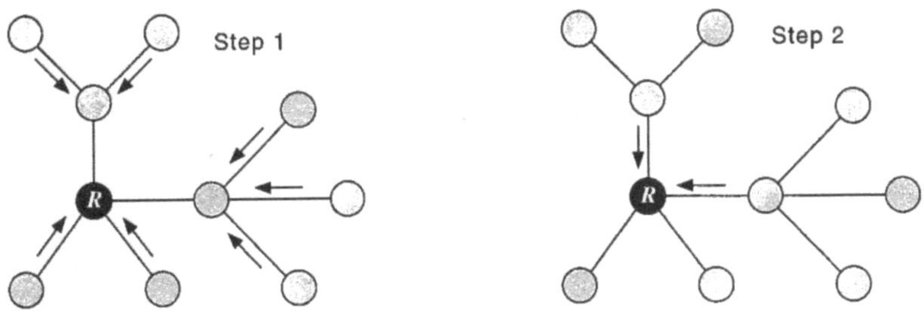

Fig. 1. The inward propagation phase

At the beginning of the propagation process, a corresponding potential $\psi(\mathbf{X}_I)$ is stored for every node I of the network. As soon as all incoming messages $M_1(\mathbf{X}_{I\cap I_1})$ to $M_k(\mathbf{X}_{I\cap I_k})$ are received at the node I, a new potential

$$\tilde{\psi}(\mathbf{X}_I) \;=\; \psi(\mathbf{X}_I) \cdot \prod_{i=1,\ldots,k} M_i(\mathbf{X}_{I\cap I_i}) \tag{7}$$

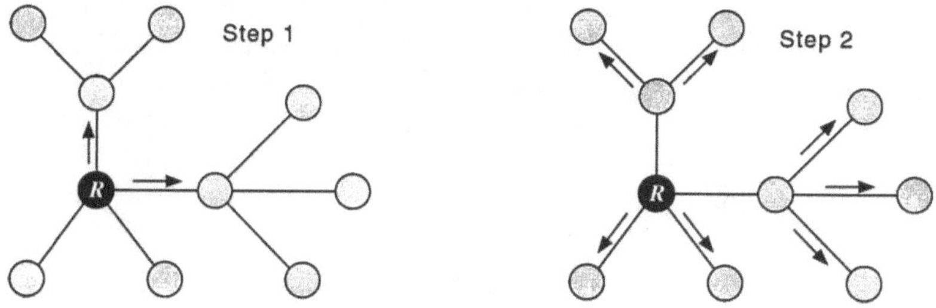

Fig. 2. The outward propagation phase

can be computed and stored. In Fig. 3, this situation is depicted for a node with $k+1$ neighbors.

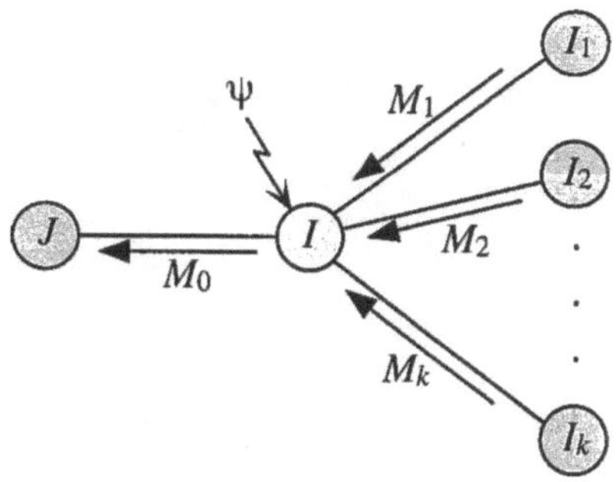

Fig. 3. Receiving and sending messages

If $L = I - J$ denotes the set of variables contained in I but not in its neighbor J, then the message $M_0(\mathbf{X}_{I \cap J})$ to be sent from I to J is determined by

$$M_0(\mathbf{X}_{I \cap J}) = \sum_{\mathbf{X}_L \in \Theta_L} \tilde{\psi}(\mathbf{X}_I). \tag{8}$$

Note that at the beginning, only the leaves of the join tree are able to send their messages. In a second step, all the neighbors of the leaves can send their messages, and so on. Finally, the potential $\tilde{\psi}(\mathbf{X}_R)$ is obtained at the root. It determines the first normalization constant by

$$c = \sum_{\mathbf{X}_R \in \Theta_R} \tilde{\psi}(\mathbf{X}_R). \tag{9}$$

Thus, the first normalization constant c is already known at the end of the inward phase. This value remains the same for all further computations.

For the computation of the normalization constant c', suppose that H_I is an event relative to a node I appearing in the join tree. In addition, let

$\psi_H(\mathbf{X}_I)$ be the corresponding potential on I representing the event H_I. This new potential can then be introduced at the corresponding node I. The product $\psi_H(\mathbf{X}_I) \cdot \tilde{\psi}(\mathbf{X}_I)$ determines a new potential $\tilde{\psi}'(\mathbf{X}_I)$ for the node I. By recomputing the messages along the unique path from I towards the root R, a new potential $\tilde{\psi}'(\mathbf{X}_R)$ is obtained at the root, from which the second normalization constant can be derived:

$$c' = \sum_{\mathbf{X}_R \in \Theta_R} \tilde{\psi}'(\mathbf{X}_R). \tag{10}$$

Finally, the probability of the event H_I is obtained by (6). Therefore, it is possible to compute probabilities of events in join trees without the outward phase. However, recomputing the messages along the unique path towards the root is necessary for every event of interest. Such a partial inward phase is shown in Fig. 4 for an event H_I.

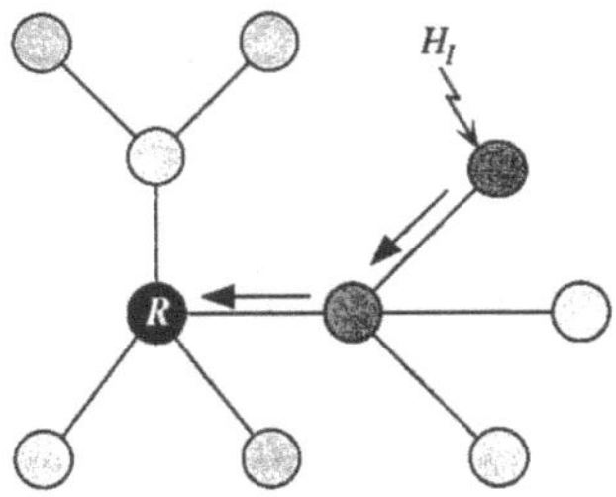

Fig. 4. Partial inward phase for an event H_I

If the event of interest concerns a domain I which is a subset of several nodes of the join tree, then the corresponding potential $\psi_H(\mathbf{X}_I)$ can be implanted on any of these nodes. Clearly, it is important to select the node with the smallest distance to the root (if possible, the root itself). This guarantees that the number of messages to be recomputed is minimal.

Sometimes, the event of interest H_I can be factorized into several events $H_{I_1}, \ldots, H_{I_n}$ so that each of the sets $I_1, \ldots, I_n$ is a strict subset of I. In this case, the potential $\psi_H(\mathbf{X}_I)$ representing the event H_I can be written as

$$\psi_H(\mathbf{X}_I) = \prod_{i=1}^{n} \psi_{H_i}(\mathbf{X}_{I_i}), \tag{11}$$

where $\psi_{H_1}(\mathbf{X}_{I_1}), \ldots, \psi_{H_n}(\mathbf{X}_{I_n})$ are corresponding potentials for the events $H_{I_1}, \ldots, H_{I_n}$. The second normalization constant c' can then be obtained by introducing these potentials on corresponding nodes of the join tree and by performing a partial inward phase towards the root as shown in Fig. 5. Consequently, even though there is no node for an event H_I in the join tree which contains I as subset, it may nevertheless be possible to compute the

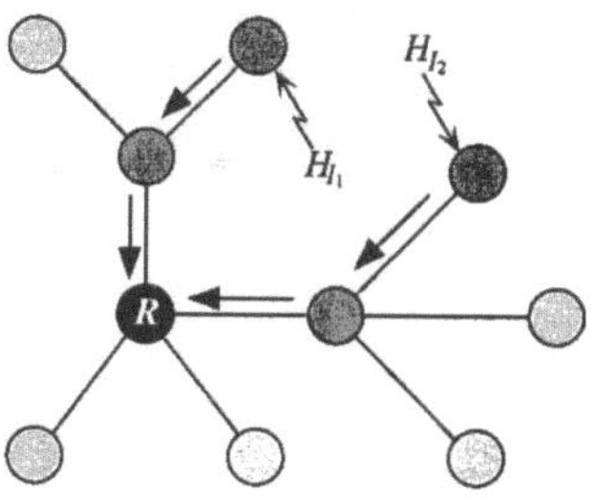

Fig. 5. Another partial inward phase

second normalization constant c'. Therefore, if there is no corresponding node for the set I, it is not always necessary to reconstruct the join tree. This is clearly an advantage of this alternative approach for computing probabilities of events over the three architectures presented in Section 1.

4 Optimizations

As the method proposed in this paper uses only inward but not outward propagation, it is important to organize the inward phase as efficient as possible. Several aspects of the procedure sketched in the previous section can be further optimized. First of all, consider the combination of the incoming messages during the first inward phase (see Fig. 3). The result is a product of potentials as described by (7). Clearly, because multiplication of potentials is commutative and associative, there are many different ways to compute this product.

A strategy for finding a good sequence of multiplications is based on the fact that multiplying potentials is less expensive for small domains. Observe that the k messages received at node I are potentials on different domains $I \cap I_1$ to $I \cap I_k$. Therefore, it is advantageous to start with a pair of messages M_i and M_j, such that the union of their domains $I \cap (I_i \cup I_j)$ is as small as possible. The same strategy is then applied for selecting a pair of messages in the second step, and so on. Note that each step of the procedure, resulting potentials from previous steps may be selected.

For example, consider a node I with four incoming messages M_1 to M_4. The product of the four messages can then be computed in 18 different ways. Two of them are depicted in Fig. 6. If $L_1 = \{1,2\}$, $L_2 = \{1\}$, $L_3 = \{2,3,4\}$, and $L_4 = \{3,4\}$ are the domains of the incoming messages, then

$$[M_1(\mathbf{X}_{L_1}) \cdot M_2(\mathbf{X}_{L_2})] \cdot [M_3(\mathbf{X}_{L_3}) \cdot M_4(\mathbf{X}_{L_4})]$$

represents the optimal way of computing the corresponding product (it includes three multiplications on the domains $\{1,2\}$, $\{2,3,4\}$, and $\{1,2,3,4\}$, respectively). It can easily be verified that the optimal solution is obtained from the strategy described above. It corresponds to the right side of Fig. 6.

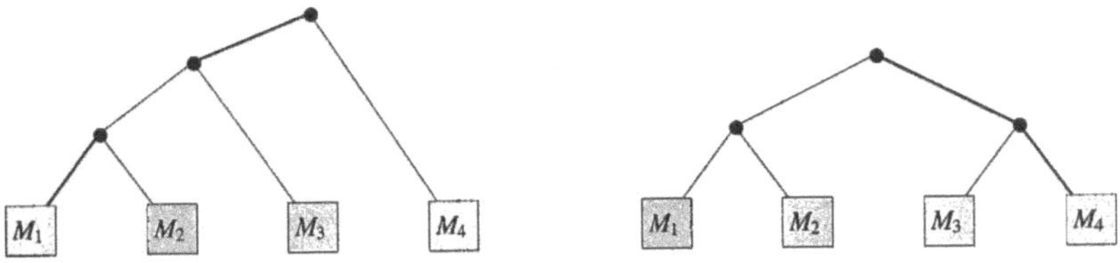

Fig. 6. (a) One way for computing the product of incoming messages. **(b)** Another way for computing the product of incoming messages

A second important problem is the optimization of the second (partial) inward phase. As described in Section 3, the partial inward phase consists in recomputing the messages along the unique path between a particular node and the root of the join tree.

A trivial solution for this is to recompute entirely the product of the incoming messages at each node on the path. Clearly, this presupposes that all incoming messages have been stored during the first inward phase. More formally, let $M_1(\mathbf{X}_{I\cap I_1})$ to $M_k(\mathbf{X}_{I\cap I_k})$ be the messages received and stored at node I during the first inward phase. If $M'_j(\mathbf{X}_{I\cap I_j})$, $1 \leq j \leq k$, is the new message received during the partial inward phase, replacing the old message $M_j(\mathbf{X}_{I\cap I_j})$, then the new potential obtained for I can be computed as follows:

$$\tilde{\psi}'(\mathbf{X}_I) \quad = \quad M'_j(\mathbf{X}_{I\cap I_j}) \cdot \psi(\mathbf{X}_I) \cdot \prod_{\substack{i=1,\ldots,k \\ i \neq j}} M_i(\mathbf{X}_{I\cap I_i}). \tag{12}$$

The problem with this approach is that the number k of multiplications required at node I remains the same for the first and the second inward phase. Depending on the sequence of multiplications selected during the first inward phase, certain computations are repeated unnecessarily during the second inward phase.

A better solution is possible, if not only the incoming messages are stored during the first inward phase, but also the potential $\tilde{\psi}(\mathbf{X}_I)$. The new potential $\tilde{\psi}'(\mathbf{X}_I)$ can then be computed with constantly two operations: one division on $I \cap I_j$ and one multiplication on I:

$$\tilde{\psi}'(\mathbf{X}_I) \quad = \quad M'_j(\mathbf{X}_{I\cap I_j}) \cdot \frac{\tilde{\psi}(\mathbf{X}_I)}{M_j(\mathbf{X}_{I\cap I_j})} \tag{13}$$

$$= \quad \frac{M'_j(\mathbf{X}_{I\cap I_j})}{M_j(\mathbf{X}_{I\cap I_j})} \cdot \tilde{\psi}(\mathbf{X}_I). \tag{14}$$

Note that the division-by-zero problem is automatically handled, since every 0-value in $M_j(\mathbf{X}_{I\cap I_j})$ is also a 0-value in $M'_j(\mathbf{X}_{I\cap I_j})$ and in $\tilde{\psi}(\mathbf{X}_I)$. This solution performs better than the trivial approach as soon as $k \geq 3$. In contrast, the trivial approach is preferred for $k = 2$, because multiplication is computationally less expensive than division, and also for $k = 1$, because only one multiplication is required.

Another approach uses the concept of binary join trees [6]. A binary join tree is a join tree such that no node has more than three neighbors. Therefore, if I is an arbitrary node in a binary join tree, then $k = 2$ is the maximal number of messages received at node I. A binary join tree can be constructed during the first inward phase by inserting initially empty nodes. For example, consider the case where I receives four incoming messages M_1 to M_4, and suppose that their product is computed as depicted on the right side of Fig. 6. A corresponding binary join tree can then be constructed according to Fig. 7.

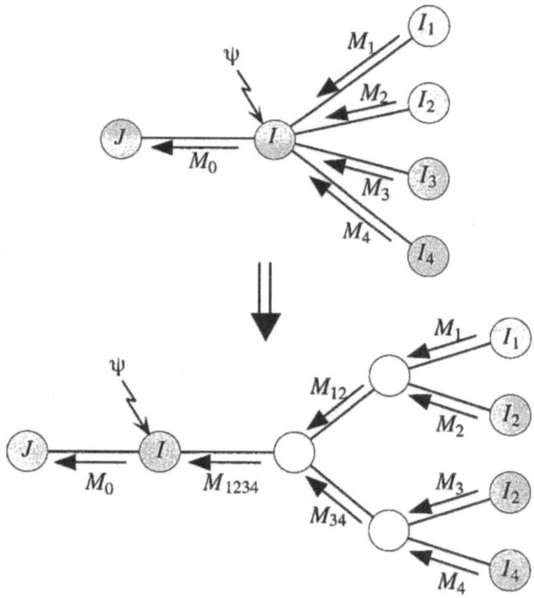

Fig. 7. Constructing a binary join tree

Let $L_{12} = L_1 \cup L_2$ be the domain of a newly inserted empty node. If $M_1(\mathbf{X}_{L_1})$ and $M_2(\mathbf{X}_{L_2})$ are the corresponding incoming messages, then $\tilde{\psi}(\mathbf{X}_{L_{12}}) = M_1(\mathbf{X}_{L_1}) \cdot M_2(\mathbf{X}_{L_2})$ is the potential to be computed during the first inward phase. Note that no initial potential $\psi(\mathbf{X}_{L_{12}})$ is needed. During the second inward phase, the new potential to be computed is either $\tilde{\psi}'(\mathbf{X}_{L_{12}}) = M_1'(\mathbf{X}_{L_1}) \cdot M_2(\mathbf{X}_{L_2})$ or $\tilde{\psi}'(\mathbf{X}_{L_{12}}) = M_1(\mathbf{X}_{L_1}) \cdot M_2'(\mathbf{X}_{L_2})$, depending on whether M_1 or M_2 has changed.

The strength of this approach is that during the first and the second inward phase only one multiplication is required at each node of the join tree. However, because new nodes are inserted during the first inward phase, the size of the join tree has increased. Therefore, the average length of the path to be recomputed during the second inward phase has increased as well.

5 Conclusion

The approach to compute the probability of certain events on a Bayesian network replaces the usual method, which consists of computing the marginal of all variables in an outward phase, by a second inward phase. In the first method, the outward propagation, depending on the architecture used, contains a lot of multiplications and even divisions of potentials. But once the outward propagation is terminated, the computation of the probability of an event reduces to summing up. In contrast, in the method presented here, the second inward phase, contains multiplications of potentials along the path to the root.

In both cases the first inward phase constitutes a necessary preparation. In the method proposed here, only this necessary phase is executed. The other computations needed to process queries are executed only on demand. In the classical method, by the outward propagation one precomputes a lot data, in expectation of query demands. It all depends on how many queries are finally to be processed to decide which one of the two methods are more efficient.

References

1. R. Haenni, J. Kohlas, and N. Lehmann. Probabilistic argumentation systems. Technical Report 99-9, Institute of Informatics, University of Fribourg, 1999.
2. F. Jensen, S. Lauritzen, and K. Olesen. Bayesian updating in causal probabilistic networks by local computations. *SIAM Journal on Computing*, 4:269–282, 1990.
3. S. Lauritzen and D. Spiegelhalter. Local computations with probabilities on graphical structures and their application to expert systems. *Journal of Royal Statistical Society*, 50(2):157–224, 1988.
4. N. Lehmann and R. Haenni. An alternative to outward propagation for Dempster-Shafer belief functions. In A. Hunter and S. Parsons, editors, *ECSQARU'99, Qualitative and Quantitative Approaches to Reasoning with Uncertainty*. Springer, 1999.
5. V. Lepar and P. Shenoy. A comparison of Lauritzen-Spiegelhalter, Hugin and Shenoy-Shafer architectures for computing marginals of probability distributions. In G. Cooper and S. Moral, editors, *Proceedings of the 14th Conference on Uncertainty in Artificial Intelligence (UAI-98)*, pages 328–337. Morgan Kaufmann, 1998.
6. P. Shenoy. Binary join trees. In *Proceedings of the 12th Conference on Uncertainty in Artificial Intelligence (UAI-96)*, pages 492–499. Morgan Kaufmann, 1996.
7. P. Shenoy and G. Shafer. Axioms for probability and belief functions propagation. In R. Shachter and al., editors, *Uncertainty in Artificial Intelligence 4*. North Holland, 1990.

Approximate Bayesian Networks

Dominik Ślęzak[1,2]

[1] Polish-Japanese Institute of Information Technology
Koszykowa 86, 02–008 Warsaw, Poland
[2] Institute of Mathematics, Warsaw University
Banacha 2, 02–097 Warsaw, Poland

Abstract. We introduce the notion of an approximate Bayesian network, which almost keeps the information entropy of data and encodes knowledge about approximate dependencies between features. Presented theoretical results, as well as relationships to fundamental concepts of the rough set theory, provide a novel methodology of applying the Bayesian net models to the real life data analysis.

1 Introduction

Bayesian network (BN) is a directed acyclic graph (DAG) designed to encode knowledge about conditional independence statements between considered variables, within a given probabilistic space ([1,2,10]). Roughly speaking, the power of such an encoding increases while removing DAG's edges, unless it causes a loss of control of exactness of derivable statements. BN-structures can be also used to model data and the flow of information while reasoning about new cases by analogy to records gathered in data tables (cf. [18,19]).

Classical BN corresponds to the notion of exact probabilistic independence, which is too accurate while mining real life data, because of the risk of possible noises or fluctuations. Thus, one needs a methodology of generalization of fundamental concepts and results concerning Bayesian networks, to let them deal with appropriately defined approximate independence statements.

The idea of basing such a generalization onto the rough set framework ([7]) originates in the fact that it provides a wide range of tools for expressing data inconsistency, in particular, those related to frequency-based rough membership functions ([8,9]). The notion of a rough membership decision reduct (cf. [13,14,16,17]) corresponds to the probabilistic notion of a Markov boundary, crucial for effective construction of BN-models ([10]). Various criteria of the reduction of noises and redundant information by the approximate preserving of rough membership information ([12–14,16,17,20]) can be thus used to approximate the concepts related to Markov boundaries and Bayesian networks.

We focus on approximations dedicated to the information measure of entropy ([3,4,6,15]), by letting a reasonably small increase of its quantity while reducing conditions (cf. [14,16,18,19]). After recalling the basics of data analysis in Section 2, we thus introduce the notion of an entropy-based approximate decision reduct in Section 3. In Section 4 we consider possibilities of using the approximate decision reduct framework for searching for Bayesian data models (cf. [3,8,10,15,19]). In Section 5 we introduce the entropy-based notion of an approximate conditional independence, which generalizes the classical probabilistic model and its properties providing a kind of graphical representation of probabilistic information ([10,11]). In Section 6 we recall the notions related to Bayesian networks and show how to generalize them onto the case of the analysis of approximate dependencies between features. Section 7 contains the proof of the main result concerning approximate Bayesian networks and Section 8 concludes the paper with final remarks.

2 Frequencies in Data

Data can be represented as an information system $\mathbf{A} = (U, A)$, where each attribute $a \in A$ is identified with function $a : U \rightarrow V_a$, for V_a denoting the set of all possible values on a ([7]). Let us write $A = \langle a_1, \ldots, a_n \rangle$ according to some ordering over the set of attributes. For any $B \subseteq A$, one can consider information function $B : U \rightarrow V_B^U$, which labels objects $u \in U$ with vectors $B(u) = \langle a_{i_1}(u), \ldots, a_{i_m}(u) \rangle$, where values of successive $a_{i_j} \in B$, $j = 1, \ldots, m$, occur due to the ordering assumed on A. The set $V_B^U = \{B(u) : u \in U\}$ gathers all vectors of values on B supported in $\mathbf{A}$.

Reasoning about data can be stated, e.g., as the classification problem concerning a distinguished decision to be predicted under information provided over the rest of attributes. For this purpose, one represents data as a decision table $\mathbf{A} = (U, A \cup \{d\})$, $d \notin A$. To express conditions→decision dependencies, one can use frequencies of occurrence of $v_d \in V_d$ conditioned by $w_B \in V_B^U$, provided by

$$P_{\mathbf{A}}(v_d / w_B) = \frac{|\{u \in U : B(u) = w_B \wedge d(u) = v_d\}|}{|\{u \in U : B(u) = w_B\}|} \tag{1}$$

Then, for a given $\alpha \in [0,1]$, α-inexact decision rule $(B = w_B) \Rightarrow_\alpha (d = v_d)$ is satisfied iff $P_{\mathbf{A}}(v_d / w_B) \geq \alpha$, i.e., iff for at least $\alpha \cdot 100\%$ of objects $u \in U$ such that $B(u) = w_B$ we have also $d(u) = v_d$. The strength of the rule is provided by quantity $P_{\mathbf{A}}(w_B) = |\{u \in U : B(u) = w_B\}| \,/\, |U|$. It corresponds to the chance that an object $u \in U$ will satisfy the rule's left side.

In the rough set literature, frequencies are best known as rough membership functions, introduced in [9] to measure degrees of inclusion of indiscernibility classes into concepts being approximated.

Definition 1. Let $\mathbf{A} = (U, A)$, $B \subseteq A$ and $X \subseteq U$ be given. The rough membership function $\mu_B^X : U \rightarrow [0,1]$ is defined by

$$\mu_B^X(u) = |[u]_B \cap X| \,/\, |[u]_B| \tag{2}$$

where $[u]_B = \{u' \in U : B(u) = B(u')\}$ is the B-indiscernibility class of u.

The general rough set principle of reduction of possibly large amount of redundant conditional information takes here the following form:

Definition 2. Let $\mathbf{A} = (U, A \cup \{d\})$ be given. Let $V_d = \{v_1, \ldots, v_r\}$, where, for each $k = 1, \ldots, r$, $X_k = \{u \in U : d(u) = v_k\}$ is called the k-th decision class. We say that $B \subseteq A$ preserves rough membership information iff

$$\forall_{u \in U} \forall_{k=1,\ldots,r} \left[\mu_B^{X_k}(u) = \mu_A^{X_k}(u)\right] \tag{3}$$

We say that B is a rough membership decision reduct (μ-decision reduct, in short) iff it satisfies (3) and none of its proper subsets does it.

One can easily show the following equivalent forms of (3):

Proposition 1. *Let $\mathbf{A} = (U, A \cup \{d\})$ and $B \subseteq A$ be given. The following conditions are equivalent:*

- *B preserves rough membership information.*
- *B makes d conditionally independent on $A \setminus B$, in terms of $P_{\mathbf{A}}$.*
- *B satisfies, for each $u \in U$, equality $\mu_{d/B}(u) = \mu_{d/A}(u)$, for*

$$\mu_{d/B}(u) = P_{\mathbf{A}}(d(u)/B(u)) = \mu_B^{X_{d(u)}}(u) \tag{4}$$

Several alternative definitions of a frequency-based decision reduct were proposed within the rough set framework (see e.g. [13,14,17]). We focus on the above one because it clearly emphasizes the analogies between frequency based and rough set based methodologies of data analysis. The following correspondence is of the greatest importance:

*If we treat $P_{\mathbf{A}}$ as the empirical probability distribution spanned over $A \cup \{d\}$, then each μ-decision reduct is actually a **Markov boundary** of d within A, i.e., irreducible subset $B \subseteq A$, which makes d independent on the rest of A.*

3 Approximate Decision Reducts

The notion of a μ-decision reduct enables us to handle inconsistencies but its conditions turn out to be too rigorous with respect to possible noises or fluctuations in real life data. A solution is to set up a numeric measure labeling subsets of conditional attributes with their capability of defining decision in terms of rough membership information. Then we would be likely to focus on subsets, which approximately preserve it under the attribute reduction.

Each $B \subseteq A$ induces in $\mathbf{A} = (U, A \cup \{d\})$ the bunch of $\mu_{d/B}(u)$-inexact decision rules $(B = B(u)) \Rightarrow_{\mu_{d/B}(u)} (d = d(u))$, for successive objects $u \in U$. One can thus measure the quality of B by arithmetic or geometric average of accuracy of those rules, i.e., respectively, by

$$E_{\mathbf{A}}(d/B) = \frac{1}{|U|} \sum_{u \in U} \mu_{d/B}(u) \qquad G_{\mathbf{A}}(d/B) = \sqrt[|U|]{\Pi_{u \in U} \mu_{d/B}(u)} \tag{5}$$

For instance, in [17,20] we consider various generalizations of the following:

Definition 3. Let $\varepsilon \in [0,1)$, $\mathbf{A} = (U, A \cup \{d\})$ and $B \subseteq A$ be given. We say that B preserves (E,ε)-approximately rough membership information iff

$$E_{\mathbf{A}}(d/B) \geq (1-\varepsilon)E_{\mathbf{A}}(d/A) \tag{6}$$

We say that B is an (E,ε)-approximate μ-decision reduct iff it satisfies (6) and none of its proper subsets does it.

Analogous notion can be formulated by replacing (6) with condition

$$G_{\mathbf{A}}(d/B) \geq (1-\varepsilon)G_{\mathbf{A}}(d/A) \tag{7}$$

One can see that $E_{\mathbf{A}}(d/A) = G_{\mathbf{A}}(d/A) = 1$ iff $\mathbf{A}$ is consistent, i.e., iff each $[u]_A$ belongs to some decision class. Then, we can consider subsets $B \subseteq A$, which almost define d, by means of $E_{\mathbf{A}}(d/B) \geq 1-\varepsilon$ or $G_{\mathbf{A}}(d/B) \geq 1-\varepsilon$.

$G_{\mathbf{A}}$ corresponds to the measure of conditional entropy, known from the information theory ([4,6]), occurring in the rough set, statistical and machine learning applications in various forms (cf. [3,5,15,16]). Let $\mathbf{A} = (U, A \cup \{d\})$, where $V_d = \{v_1, \ldots, v_r\}$, and $B \subseteq A$ be given. Let us put

$$H_{\mathbf{A}}(d/B) = \sum_{w_B \in V_B^U} P_{\mathbf{A}}(w_B)h(\langle P_{\mathbf{A}}(v_1/w_B), \ldots, P_{\mathbf{A}}(v_r/w_B)\rangle) \tag{8}$$

where $h : \triangle_{r-1} \to [0,1]$ is defined over the (r-1)-dimensional simplex

$$\triangle_{r-1} = \{s = \langle s[1], \ldots, s[r]\rangle \in [0,+\infty)^r : s[1] + \ldots + s[r] = 1\} \tag{9}$$

by attaching to each probabilistic distribution $s \in \triangle_{r-1}$ its entropy

$$h(s) = -\sum_{k:\, s[k]>0} s[k]\log_2(s[k]) \tag{10}$$

Proposition 2. *For any* $\mathbf{A} = (U, A \cup \{d\})$ *and* $B \subseteq A$, *we have*

$$H_{\mathbf{A}}(d/B) = -\log_2(G_{\mathbf{A}}(d/B)) \tag{11}$$

Proof. $-|U| \cdot H_{\mathbf{A}}(d/B) =$
$= -\sum_{w_B \in V_B^U} |\{u \in U : B(u) = w_B\}| h(\langle P_{\mathbf{A}}(v_1/w_B), \ldots, P_{\mathbf{A}}(v_r/w_B)\rangle)$
$= \sum_{w_B, v_d : P_{\mathbf{A}}(v_d/w_B)>0} |\{u \in U : (B,d)(u) = (w_B, v_d)\}| \log_2(P_{\mathbf{A}}(v_d/w_B))$
$= \sum_{w_B, v_d : P_{\mathbf{A}}(v_d/w_B)>0} |\{u \in U : (B,d)(u) = (w_B, v_d)\}| \log_2(P_{\mathbf{A}}(d(u)/B(u)))$
$= \sum_{u \in U} \log_2(P_{\mathbf{A}}(d(u)/B(u))) = \log_2(\Pi_{u \in U} P_{\mathbf{A}}(d(u)/B(u)))$

By taking the logarithm of both sides of inequality (7), we get the following condition (12), expressing the information approximation in terms of entropy:

Definition 4. Let $\varepsilon \in [0,1)$, $\mathbf{A} = (U, A \cup \{d\})$ and $B \subseteq A$ be given. We say that B preserves (H,ε)-approximately rough membership information iff

$$H_{\mathbf{A}}(d/B) + \log_2(1-\varepsilon) \leq H_{\mathbf{A}}(d/A) \tag{12}$$

We say that B is an (H,ε)-approximate μ-decision reduct iff it satisfies (12) and none of its proper subsets does it.

Let us conclude this part with two important properties of the above notion:

Proposition 3. *The notions of a μ-decision reduct and an $(H, 0)$-approximate μ-decision reduct are equivalent.*

Proof. For $\varepsilon = 0$, (12) takes the form of $H_{\mathbf{A}}(d/B) \leq H_{\mathbf{A}}(d/A)$. According to [4], we know that $H_{\mathbf{A}}(d/B) \geq H_{\mathbf{A}}(d/A)$, where equality holds iff B makes d conditionally independent on $A \setminus B$. Thus, one has (12) iff $H_{\mathbf{A}}(d/B) = H_{\mathbf{A}}(d/A)$ iff B preserves rough membership information.

Theorem 1. *The problem of finding minimal (H, ε)-approximate μ-decision reduct is NP-hard, for any constant $\varepsilon \in [0, 1)$.*

Proof. In [17] we prove the NP-hardness of the Minimal Graph α-Covering Problem for any $\alpha \in (0, 1]$ – a generalization of the classical complexity result for $\alpha = 1$. Then, we show how to construct, for any $\varepsilon \in [0, 1)$, the polynomial reduction of the Minimal Graph $\alpha(\varepsilon)$-Covering Problem (for appropriately chosen $\alpha(\varepsilon) \in (0, 1]$) to the problem of finding a minimal (E, ε)-approximate μ-decision reduct. Actually, analogous reduction can be constructed also for H instead of E, i.e., the polynomial reduction of the Minimal Graph $\alpha(\varepsilon)$-Covering Problem (for $\alpha(\varepsilon)$ chosen slightly differently than in case of E) to the problem being considered here.

4 Approximate Bayesian Models

Rough set applications to the data analysis are usually based on the search for minimal (inexact) decision rules of various kinds ([12–14,16,17,20]). Recently, some interest on possibilities of combining the rough set framework with the Bayesian techniques arises (see e.g. [8,19]). Bayesian models contain the rules with decision situated at their left side. In general, they are related to the analysis of distribution $P_{\mathbf{A}}(A/d)$, letting an object $u \in U$ be classified as, e.g., having decision value

$$v = \arg\max_{v_d \in V_d} [prior(v_d) P_{\mathbf{A}}(A(u)/v_d)] \tag{13}$$

for $prior : V_d \to [0, 1]$ expressing prior probabilities of decision values, their frequencies in observed data, subjective preferences of an expert, etc..

Let us set up an arbitrary ordering $A = \langle a_1, \ldots, a_n \rangle$ and denote by V_i the set of all values of a_i. We can decompose $P_{\mathbf{A}}(A/d)$ by noting that for any supported combination of values $v_d \in V_d$, $v_i \in V_i$, $i = 1, \ldots, n$, one has

$$P_{\mathbf{A}}(v_1, \ldots, v_n/v_d) = \prod_{i=1}^{n} P_{\mathbf{A}}(v_i/v_d, v_1, \ldots, v_{i-1}) \tag{14}$$

The attribute reduction can be now related to sub-component distributions:

Proposition 4. *Let $\mathbf{A} = (U, A \cup \{d\})$, $A = \langle a_1, \ldots, a_n \rangle$, be given. Let us assume that for each table $\mathbf{A}_i = (U, \{d, a_1, \ldots, a_{i-1}\} \cup \{a_i\})$, $i = 1, \ldots, n$, a μ-decision reduct B_i has been found. Then, for any given $u \in U$, the decision value calculated by (13) is equal to*

$$v = \arg\max_{v_d \in V_d} \left[prior(v_d) \prod_{i:\, d \in B_i} P_{\mathbf{A}}(a_i(u)/v_d, (B_i \setminus \{d\})(u)) \right] \tag{15}$$

Proof. First, let us consider the case of $v_d \in V_d$ such that $P_{\mathbf{A}}(A(u)/v_d) = 0$. Then there is such $i = 1, \ldots, n$ that $P_{\mathbf{A}}(a_i(u)/v_d, a_1(u), \ldots, a_{i-1}(u)) = 0$ and $P_{\mathbf{A}}(v_d, a_1(u), \ldots, a_{i-1}(u)) > 0$. Subset B_i must contain d because otherwise $P_{\mathbf{A}}(a_i(u)/B_i(u)) > 0$. Thus, $P_{\mathbf{A}}(a_i(u)/v_d, (B_i \setminus \{d\}(u))$ occurs in the product in (15) and makes it equal to 0 for the considered v_d.

Now, let us consider $v_d \in V_d$ such that $P_{\mathbf{A}}(A(u)/v_d) > 0$. In this case, the value of the product in (15) is positive. We obtain

$$\frac{\prod_{i=1}^{n} P_{\mathbf{A}}(a_i(u)/v_d, a_1(u), \ldots, a_{i-1}(u))}{\prod_{i:\, d \in B_i} P_{\mathbf{A}}(a_i(u)/v_d, (B_i \setminus \{d\})(u))} = \prod_{i:\, d \notin B_i} P_{\mathbf{A}}(a_i(u)/B_i(u)) \tag{16}$$

what is a positive quantity independent on the choice of v_d. Thus, one can see that for any $v_k, v_l \in V_d$ inequality $P_{\mathbf{A}}(A(u)/v_k) \leq P_{\mathbf{A}}(A(u)/v_l)$ holds iff substitution of v_k to the product in (15) gives not more than in case of v_l.

Obviously, the above equivalence can be considered only over the input vectors occurring in data. In case of combinations not included in V_A^U, it remains to trust into the generalization ability of the classification model related to formula (15). According to the general rough set principle of reduction, one can regard that that ability as dependent on solving the following:

Optimization problem: *For any $\mathbf{A} = (U, A \cup \{d\})$, find such ordering $A = \langle a_1, \ldots, a_n \rangle$ that μ-decision reducts B_i for $\mathbf{A}_i$ provide minimal $\sum_{i=1}^{n} |B_i|$.*

In [19] we consider also the approximate Bayesian models:

Definition 5. Let $\varepsilon \in [0, 1)$ and $\mathbf{A} = (U, A \cup \{d\})$, $A = \langle a_1, \ldots, a_n \rangle$, be given. We say that collection $\mathcal{B} = \langle B_1, \ldots, B_n \rangle$ of subsets $B_i \subsetneq \{d, a_1, \ldots, a_{i-1}\}$, $i = 1, \ldots, n$, is (H, ε)-approximately consistent with $\mathbf{A}$ iff

$$\sum_{i=1}^{n} H_{\mathbf{A}}(a_i/B_i) + \log_2(1 - \varepsilon) \leq H_{\mathbf{A}}(A/d) \tag{17}$$

Condition (17) means that the aggregate entropy of $\mathcal{B}$ approximates the information entropy of distribution $P_{\mathbf{A}}(A/d)$. One can obtain such $\mathcal{B}$ by decomposing $\varepsilon \in [0, 1)$ onto $\varepsilon_1, \ldots, \varepsilon_n \in [0, 1)$, satisfying $(1-\varepsilon_1) \cdot \ldots \cdot (1-\varepsilon_n) \geq 1-\varepsilon$, and setting up components $B_i \in \mathcal{B}$ as (H, ε_i)-approximate μ-decision reducts for particular decision tables $\mathbf{A}_i$. Indeed, then we have $H_{\mathbf{A}}(A/d) =$

$$\begin{aligned} &= \textstyle\sum_{i=1}^{n} H_{\mathbf{A}}(a_i/d, a_1, \ldots, a_{i-1}) \\ &\geq \textstyle\sum_{i=1}^{n} [H_{\mathbf{A}}(a_i/B_i) + \log_2(1 - \varepsilon_i)] \\ &= \textstyle\sum_{i=1}^{n} H_{\mathbf{A}}(a_i/B_i) + \log_2 [\prod_{i=1}^{n}(1 - \varepsilon_i)] \\ &\geq \textstyle\sum_{i=1}^{n} H_{\mathbf{A}}(a_i/B_i) + \log_2(1 - \varepsilon) \end{aligned} \tag{18}$$

The choice of $\varepsilon_i \in [0,1)$, $i = 1, \ldots, n$, influences the degree of keeping classification calculations, like e.g. those in (15), close to observed data. On the other hand, by appropriate tuning of approximation coefficients, one can get simplified and more efficient model, which is still reliable enough.

Optimization problem (ε): *For any $\mathbf{A} = (U, A \cup \{d\})$, find such ε-decomposition $\varepsilon_1, \ldots, \varepsilon_n \in [0,1)$ and ordering $A = \langle a_1, \ldots, a_n \rangle$ that (H, ε_i)-approximate μ-decision reducts B_i for $\mathbf{A}_i$ provide minimal $\sum_{i=1}^{n} |B_i|$.*

Obviously the above problem is substantially more complex than, e.g., that of finding minimal (H, ε)-approximate μ-decision reducts – the effective search for reducts is worth almost nothing unless an "appropriate" strategy of choosing the attribute ordering is provided.

5 Approximate Independence

The property of preserving rough membership information by a given subset of conditional attributes is a special case of the following:

Definition 6. Let $\mathbf{A} = (U, A \cup \{d\})$ and mutually disjoint $X, Y, Z \subseteq A \cup \{d\}$ be given. We say that Y makes X conditionally independent on Z iff for all possible configurations of w_X, w_Y and w_Z – being vectors of values over X, Y and Z, respectively – we have implication

$$(P_{\mathbf{A}}(w_Y, w_Z) > 0) \Rightarrow (P_{\mathbf{A}}(w_X / w_Y, w_Z) = P_{\mathbf{A}}(w_X / w_Y)) \tag{19}$$

Proposition 5. *Let $\mathbf{A} = (U, A \cup \{d\})$ and mutually disjoint $X, Y, Z \subseteq A \cup \{d\}$ be given. Then Y makes X conditionally independent on Z iff*

$$\forall_{u \in U} \left[P_{\mathbf{A}}(X(u)/Y(u)) = P_{\mathbf{A}}(X(u)/Y(u), Z(u))\right] \tag{20}$$

Just like in the special case of decision tables, a kind of approximate version of independence seems to be necessary. We restrict ourselves to the one based on entropy, although there are also other possibilities (see e.g. [16,18]).

Definition 7. Let $\varepsilon \in [0,1)$, $\mathbf{A} = (U, A \cup \{d\})$ and mutually disjoint $X, Y, Z \subseteq A \cup \{d\}$ be given. We say that Y makes X conditionally (H, ε)-approximately independent on Z iff

$$H_{\mathbf{A}}(X/Y) + \log_2(1 - \varepsilon) \leq H_{\mathbf{A}}(X/Y \cup Z) \tag{21}$$

Proposition 6. *Let $\varepsilon \in [0,1)$ and $\mathbf{A} = (U, A \cup \{d\})$ be given. For mutually disjoint $X, Y, Z \subseteq A \cup \{d\}$, let us denote by $I_{\mathbf{A}}^{H,\varepsilon}(X/Y/Z)$ the statement that Y makes X conditionally (H, ε)-approximately independent on Z. Let mutually disjoint $X, Y, Z, W \subseteq A \cup \{d\}$ be given. The following rules of reasoning about conditional independence statements are satisfied:*
Symmetry:

$$I_{\mathbf{A}}^{H,\varepsilon}(X/Y/Z) \Rightarrow I_{\mathbf{A}}^{H,\varepsilon}(Z/Y/X) \tag{22}$$

Decomposition:

$$I_{\mathbf{A}}^{H,\varepsilon}(X/Y/Z \cup W) \Rightarrow I_{\mathbf{A}}^{H,\varepsilon}(X/Y/Z) \tag{23}$$

Weak union:

$$I_{\mathbf{A}}^{H,\varepsilon}(X/Y/Z \cup W) \Rightarrow I_{\mathbf{A}}^{H,\varepsilon}(X/Y \cup Z/W) \tag{24}$$

Dynamic contraction:

$$I_{\mathbf{A}}^{H,\varepsilon}(X/Y \cup Z/W) \wedge I_{\mathbf{A}}^{H,\varepsilon}(X/Y/Z) \Rightarrow I_{\mathbf{A}}^{H,\varepsilon(2-\varepsilon)}(X/Y/Z \cup W) \tag{25}$$

Proof. We have $H_{\mathbf{A}}(X/Y) = H_{\mathbf{A}}(X \cup Y) - H_{\mathbf{A}}(Y)$, where

$$H_{\mathbf{A}}(B) = -\frac{1}{|U|}\sum_{u \in U} \log_2 P_{\mathbf{A}}(B(u)) \tag{26}$$

for any $B \subseteq A \cup \{d\}$. Thus, (21) can be rewritten as inequality

$$H_{\mathbf{A}}(X \cup Y \cup Z) \geq H_{\mathbf{A}}(X \cup Y) + H_{\mathbf{A}}(Y \cup Z) - H_{\mathbf{A}}(Y) + \log_2(1-\varepsilon) \tag{27}$$

It is equivalent to both $I_{\mathbf{A}}^{H,\varepsilon}(X/Y/Z)$ and $I_{\mathbf{A}}^{H,\varepsilon}(Z/Y/X)$ – it implies (22). To show (23), let us assume its left side. Then we have

$$H_{\mathbf{A}}(X/Y) + \log_2(1-\varepsilon) \leq H_{\mathbf{A}}(X/Y \cup Z \cup W) \leq H_{\mathbf{A}}(X/Y \cup Z) \tag{28}$$

where the second inequality is provided by [4]. The left side of (24) provides

$$H_{\mathbf{A}}(X/Y \cup Z \cup W) - \log_2(1-\varepsilon) \geq H_{\mathbf{A}}(X/Y) \geq H_{\mathbf{A}}(X/Y \cup Z) \tag{29}$$

Finally, the left side of (25) implies that $H_{\mathbf{A}}(X/Y \cup Z \cup W) \geq$

$$\geq H_{\mathbf{A}}(X/Y \cup Z) + \log_2(1-\varepsilon) \geq H_{\mathbf{A}}(X/Y) + \log_2(1-\varepsilon) + \log_2(1-\varepsilon) \tag{30}$$

what gives the right side, for $2\log_2(1-\varepsilon) = \log_2(2(1-\varepsilon))$.

It can be shown, by generalizing Proposition 3, that the notions of conditional independence and conditional (H,ε)-approximate independence are equivalent for $\varepsilon = 0$. As a consequence, the above result implies that probabilistic independence satisfies the axioms of so called *semi-graphoids* – the theory being developed in purpose of the graph-based reasoning about dependencies among variables (cf. [10,11]). Moreover, stability of the degrees of approximation in (22–24), as well as the polynomial bound for their aggregation in (25), enable to regard Definition 7 as providing a dynamically stable model of the semi-graphoid-based inference.

6 Approximate Bayesian Networks

Bayesian networks (BN) have the structure of a directed acyclic graph (DAG) $\mathcal{D} = (V, \vec{E})$, where $\vec{E} \subseteq V \times V$. The objective of the BN-based methodology is to encode conditional independence statements involving groups of probabilistic variables corresponding to elements of V, in terms of the following graph-theoretic notion ([10]):

Definition 8. Let DAG $\mathcal{D} = (V, \vec{E})$ and mutually disjoint $X, Y, Z \subseteq V$ be given. We say that Y d-separates X from Z iff any path between any node in X and any node in Z comes through:

- a serial or diverging connection covered by some element of Y, or
- a converging connection not covered by Y, having no descendant in Y;

where:

- descriptions '*serial*', '*diverging*' and '*converging*' correspond to directions of arrows meeting within a given path, in a given node;
- b is a descendant of a iff there is a directed path from a towards b in $\mathcal{D}$.

Let us formulate the notion of a Bayesian network in terms of data analysis:

Definition 9. Let $\mathbf{A} = (U, A \cup \{d\})$ and DAG $\mathcal{D} = (A \cup \{d\}, \vec{E})$ be given. We say that $\mathcal{D}$ is a Bayesian net for $\mathbf{A}$ iff for any mutually disjoint $X, Y, Z \subseteq A \cup \{d\}$ such that Y d-separates X from Z this is also true that Y makes X conditionally independent on Z, in terms of distribution induced by $\mathbf{A}$.

Theorem 2. *([10]) Let $\mathbf{A} = (U, A \cup \{d\})$, $A = \langle a_1, \ldots, a_n \rangle$, be given. Let us assume that for each table $\mathbf{A}_i = (U, \{d, a_1, \ldots, a_{i-1}\} \cup \{a_i\})$ a μ-decision reduct B_i is provided. Then DAG $\mathcal{D} = (A \cup \{d\}, \vec{E})$, where*

$$\vec{E} = \bigcup_{i=1}^{n} \{\langle b, a_i \rangle : b \in B_i\} \tag{31}$$

is a Bayesian network for $\mathbf{A}$.

The above construction corresponds to the model of the Bayesian classification considered in Proposition 4. Actually, one can treat DAG defined by (31) as the visualization of the flow and synthesis of information while searching for the frequency-based weights of decision classes. The Optimization Problem considered in Section 4 can be now regarded as corresponding to the extraction of optimal Bayesian networks from data. The quantity of $\sum_{i=1}^{n} |B_i|$ relates to the number of edges in (31). It should be minimized to achieve possible large number of conditional independence statements derivable from the graphical structure of $\mathcal{D}$.

Still, only by basing the process of DAG's creation on an approximate μ-decision reducts, we can expect a structure with the number of edges substantially lower than $n(n+1)/2$. Let us thus recall the notion of an (H, ε)-approximately consistent Bayesian model introduced in Section 4 and adapt it to the current framework as follows:

Definition 10. Let $\varepsilon \in [0,1)$, $\mathbf{A} = (U, A \cup \{d\})$ and DAG $\mathcal{D} = (A \cup \{d\}, \vec{E})$ be given. We say that $\mathcal{D}$ is (H,ε)-approximately consistent with $\mathbf{A}$ iff

$$\sum_{a \in A \cup \{d\}} H_{\mathbf{A}}(a/\pi_{\mathcal{D}}(a)) + \log(1-\varepsilon) \leq H_{\mathbf{A}}(A \cup \{d\}) \tag{32}$$

where $\pi_{\mathcal{D}}(a) = \{b \in A \cup \{d\} : \langle b, a\rangle \in \vec{E}\}$ is the set of parents of a in $\mathcal{D}$.

Condition (32) seems to keep the aggregate information induced by $\mathcal{D}$-based local conditional distributions somehow close to that encoded within the whole of $P_{\mathbf{A}}(A \cup \{d\})$. This idea can be compared to that of studying the Bayesian likelihood of a DAG under data observed, proposed in [2]. There, likelihood means the probability $\mathbf{P}(\mathbf{A}/\mathcal{D})$ of obtaining a table with frequency distribution equal to $P_{\mathbf{A}}$ by random sampling based on probabilities $P_{\mathbf{A}}(a/\pi_{\mathcal{D}}(a))$, $a \in A \cup \{d\}$. An application of the Stirling's approximation to the formula for $\mathbf{P}(\mathbf{A}/\mathcal{D})$ derived in [2] leads to the following (cf. [1,6]):

$$-\frac{\log_2(\mathbf{P}(\mathbf{A}/\mathcal{D}))}{|U|} \approx \sum_{a \in A} H_{\mathbf{A}}(a/\pi_{\mathcal{D}}(a)) - H_{\mathbf{A}}(A \cup \{d\}) \tag{33}$$

It encourages to tune $\varepsilon \in [0,1)$ in purpose of searching for the balance between likelihood and generalization abilities of DAG-models determined by condition (32). Still, the fundamental question is whether the closeness (likelihood) understood in terms of (H,ε)-approximate consistency implies somehow the closeness understood in terms the quality of information about dependencies between features.

Definition 11. Let $\varepsilon \in [0,1)$, $\mathbf{A} = (U, A \cup \{d\})$ and DAG $\mathcal{D} = (A \cup \{d\}, \vec{E})$ be given. We say that $\mathcal{D}$ is an (H,ε)-approximate Bayesian network for $\mathbf{A}$ iff for any mutually disjoint $X, Y, Z \subseteq A \cup \{d\}$ such that Y d-separates X from Z this is also true that Y makes X conditionally (H,ε)-approximately independent on Z.

The following result seems to answer to the question stated above positively. In particular, it generalizes Theorem 2, since any DAG $\mathcal{D}$ built on the basis of μ-decision reducts is $(H,0)$-approximately consistent with a given $\mathbf{A}$, as well as any $(H,0)$-approximate Bayesian network is a Bayesian network.

Theorem 3. *Let $\varepsilon \in [0,1)$ and $\mathbf{A} = (U, A \cup \{d\})$ be given. Each DAG which is (H,ε)-approximately consistent with $\mathbf{A}$ is an (H,ε)-approximate Bayesian network for $\mathbf{A}$.*

7 Proof of Theorem 3

Proof. Let DAG $\mathcal{D} = (A \cup \{d\}, \vec{E})$ be given. Assume that for some mutually disjoint $X, Y, Z \subseteq A \cup \{d\}$ subset Y d-separates X from Z in $\mathcal{D}$. Let us denote such a d-separation statement by $\langle X/Y/Z\rangle_{\mathcal{D}}$. Consider subsets

$$\begin{aligned} X' &= \{a \in A \cup \{d\} \setminus Y : \langle \{a\}/Y/Z\rangle_{\mathcal{D}}\} \\ Z' &= \{a \in A \cup \{d\} \setminus Y : \langle \{a\}/Y/X\rangle_{\mathcal{D}} \wedge \neg\langle \{a\}/Y/Z\rangle_{\mathcal{D}}\} \end{aligned} \tag{34}$$

One can see that $X \subseteq X'$ and $Z \subseteq Z'$, subsets X', Y, Z' are mutually disjoint and d-separation statement $\langle X'/Y/Z'\rangle_{\mathcal{D}}$ holds. In particular:

1. For any $a \in X'$, we have $\pi_{\mathcal{D}}(a) \subseteq X' \cup Y$, because of implication

$$\langle \{a\}/Y/Z\rangle_{\mathcal{D}} \Rightarrow \forall_{b \in \pi_{\mathcal{D}}(a)\setminus Y} \langle \{b\}/Y/Z\rangle_{\mathcal{D}} \tag{35}$$

2. For any $a \in Z'$, we have $\pi_{\mathcal{D}}(a) \subseteq Z' \cup Y$, because of implications

$$\begin{array}{l} \langle \{a\}/Y/X\rangle_{\mathcal{D}} \Rightarrow \forall_{b \in \pi_{\mathcal{D}}(a)\setminus Y} \langle \{b\}/Y/X\rangle_{\mathcal{D}} \\ \neg\langle \{a\}/Y/Z\rangle_{\mathcal{D}} \Rightarrow \forall_{b \in \pi_{\mathcal{D}}(a)\setminus Y} \neg\langle \{b\}/Y/Z\rangle_{\mathcal{D}} \end{array} \tag{36}$$

3. For any $a \in Y$, we have $\pi_{\mathcal{D}}(a) \subseteq X' \cup Y$ or $\pi_{\mathcal{D}}(a) \subseteq Y \cup Z'$, because if not $\pi_{\mathcal{D}}(a) \subseteq X' \cup Y$, then there exists $b \in \pi_{\mathcal{D}}(a) \setminus Y$ which is not in X', what means $\neg\langle \{b\}/Y/Z\rangle_{\mathcal{D}}$. Due to implications

$$\begin{array}{l} \exists_{b \in \pi_{\mathcal{D}}(a)\setminus Y} \neg\langle \{b\}/Y/Z\rangle_{\mathcal{D}} \Rightarrow \forall_{b \in \pi_{\mathcal{D}}(a)\setminus Y} \neg\langle \{b\}/Y/Z\rangle_{\mathcal{D}} \\ \exists_{b \in \pi_{\mathcal{D}}(a)\setminus Y} \neg\langle \{b\}/Y/Z\rangle_{\mathcal{D}} \Rightarrow \forall_{b \in \pi_{\mathcal{D}}(a)\setminus Y} \langle \{b\}/Y/X\rangle_{\mathcal{D}} \end{array} \tag{37}$$

   we thus know that $\pi_{\mathcal{D}}(a) \setminus Y \subseteq Z'$.

Let $\mathcal{D}$ be (H,ε)-approximately consistent with $\mathbf{A} = (U, A \cup \{d\})$, $\varepsilon \in [0,1)$. We will prove that $I^{H,\varepsilon}_{\mathbf{A}}(X'/Y/Z')$, i.e., that the following inequality holds:

$$H_{\mathbf{A}}(X' \cup Y \cup Z') \geq H_{\mathbf{A}}(X' \cup Y) + H_{\mathbf{A}}(Y \cup Z') - H_{\mathbf{A}}(Y) + \log_2(1-\varepsilon) \tag{38}$$

Let us set up such an ordering $A \cup \{d\} = \langle a_0, \ldots, a_n\rangle$ that if $(a_i, a_j) \in \vec{E}$, then $i < j$. For $i = 1, \ldots, n$, let us consider $\varepsilon_i \in [0,1)$ which satisfies equality

$$H_{\mathbf{A}}(a_i/\pi_{\mathcal{D}}(a_i)) + \log_2(1-\varepsilon_i) = H_{\mathbf{A}}(a_i/A_{i-1}) \tag{39}$$

where $A_{i-1} = \{a_0, \ldots, a_{i-1}\}$. Then inequality $\sum_{i=1}^{n} \log_2(1-\varepsilon_i) \geq \log_2(1-\varepsilon)$ holds, because otherwise $\mathcal{D}$ would not be able to satisfy (32). Let us note that for any $B \subseteq A$ the following is true:

$$H_{\mathbf{A}}(B) = \sum_{i:a_i \in B} H_{\mathbf{A}}(a_i/B \cap A_{i-1}) \tag{40}$$

Thus, $H_{\mathbf{A}}(X' \cup Y \cup Z') =$

$$\begin{array}{l} = \sum_{i:a_i \in X' \cup Y \cup Z'} H_{\mathbf{A}}(a_i/(X' \cup Y \cup Z') \cap A_{i-1}) \\ \geq \sum_{i:a_i \in X' \cup Y \cup Z'} H_{\mathbf{A}}(a_i/A_{i-1}) \\ = \sum_{i:a_i \in X' \cup Y \cup Z'} [H_{\mathbf{A}}(a_i/\pi_{\mathcal{D}}(a_i)) + \log_2(1-\varepsilon_i)] \\ \geq \sum_{i:a_i \in X' \cup Y \cup Z'} H_{\mathbf{A}}(a_i/\pi_{\mathcal{D}}(a_i)) + \sum_{i=1}^{n} \log_2(1-\varepsilon_i) \\ \geq \sum_{i:a_i \in X' \cup Y \cup Z'} H_{\mathbf{A}}(a_i/\pi_{\mathcal{D}}(a_i)) + \log_2(1-\varepsilon) \end{array} \tag{41}$$

By comparing (38) and (41), one can see that it is enough to show that

$$\sum_{i:a_i \in X' \cup Y \cup Z'} H_{\mathbf{A}}(a_i/\pi_{\mathcal{D}}(a_i)) \geq H_{\mathbf{A}}(X' \cup Y) + H_{\mathbf{A}}(Y \cup Z') - H_{\mathbf{A}}(Y) \tag{42}$$

For any $i = 0, \ldots, n$, inclusions proved in points 1.,2.,3. can take the form of

$$\begin{array}{l} a_i \in X' \Rightarrow (\pi_{\mathcal{D}}(a) \subseteq (X' \cup Y) \cap A_{i-1}) \\ a_i \in Z' \Rightarrow (\pi_{\mathcal{D}}(a) \subseteq (Y \cup Z') \cap A_{i-1}) \\ a_i \in Y \Rightarrow [(\pi_{\mathcal{D}}(a) \subseteq (X' \cup Y) \cap A_{i-1}) \vee (\pi_{\mathcal{D}}(a) \subseteq (Y \cup Z') \cap A_{i-1})] \end{array} \tag{43}$$

Thus, they imply

$$\begin{array}{l} a_i \in X' \Rightarrow H_{\mathbf{A}}(a_i/\pi_{\mathcal{D}}(a_i)) \geq H_{\mathbf{A}}(a_i/(X' \cup Y) \cap A_{i-1}) \\ a_i \in Z' \Rightarrow H_{\mathbf{A}}(a_i/\pi_{\mathcal{D}}(a_i)) \geq H_{\mathbf{A}}(a_i/(Y \cup Z') \cap A_{i-1}) \\ a_i \in Y \Rightarrow H_{\mathbf{A}}(a_i/\pi_{\mathcal{D}}(a_i)) \geq H_{\mathbf{A}}(a_i/(X' \cup Y) \cap A_{i-1}) \\ \qquad +H_{\mathbf{A}}(a_i/(Y \cup Z') \cap A_{i-1}) - H_{\mathbf{A}}(a_i/Y \cap A_{i-1}) \end{array} \tag{44}$$

where third inequality holds because, on the one hand, $H_{\mathbf{A}}(a_i/Y \cap A_{i-1})$ is not less than both $H_{\mathbf{A}}(a_i/(X' \cup Y) \cap A_{i-1})$ and $H_{\mathbf{A}}(a_i/(Y \cup Z') \cap A_{i-1})$, and, on the other hand, we know from (43) that $H_{\mathbf{A}}(a_i/\pi_{\mathcal{D}}(a_i))$ is not smaller than at least one of them. We obtain that the left side of (42) is not less than

$$\begin{array}{l} \sum_{i:a_i \in X'} H_{\mathbf{A}}(a_i/(X' \cup Y) \cap A_{i-1}) + \\ \sum_{i:a_i \in Z'} H_{\mathbf{A}}(a_i/(Y \cup Z') \cap A_{i-1}) + \\ \sum_{i:a_i \in Y} [H_{\mathbf{A}}(a_i/(X' \cup Y) \cap A_{i-1}) + \\ \qquad H_{\mathbf{A}}(a_i/(Y \cup Z') \cap A_{i-1}) - H_{\mathbf{A}}(a_i/Y \cap A_{i-1})] \end{array} \tag{45}$$

which – after re-grouping its components – appears to be equal to

$$\begin{array}{l} \sum_{i:a_i \in X' \cup Y} H_{\mathbf{A}}(a_i/(X' \cup Y) \cap A_{i-1}) + \\ \sum_{i:a_i \in Y \cup Z'} H_{\mathbf{A}}(a_i/(Y \cup Z') \cap A_{i-1}) - \\ \sum_{i:a_i \in Y} H_{\mathbf{A}}(a_i/Y \cap A_{i-1}) = \\ = H_{\mathbf{A}}(X' \cup Y) + H_{\mathbf{A}}(Y \cup Z') - H_{\mathbf{A}}(Y) \end{array} \tag{46}$$

Thus, finally we get (42), what implies that Y makes X' conditionally (H, ε)-approximately independent on Z'. Now, it is enough to recall that $X \subseteq X'$, $Z \subseteq Z'$ and apply the inference rules described in Proposition 6 to obtain the wanted statement $I_{\mathbf{A}}^{H,\varepsilon}(X/Y/Z)$.

8 Conclusions

Introduced notion of an entropy-based approximate Bayesian network reflects the need of dealing with approximate independence statements in case of the real life data analysis. Presented results provide the framework for the efficient extraction and application of approximate BN-models to the data classification and description tasks.

Acknowledgements: Supported by the grants of Polish National Committee for Scientific Research, No. 8T11C02319, 8T11C02417, 8T11C02519.

References

1. Bouckaert, R.R.: Properties of Bayesian Belief Network Learning Algorithms. In: Proc. of UAI'94, University of Washington, Seattle, Morgan Kaufmann, San Francisco, CA (1994) pp. 102–109.
2. Cooper, F.G., Herskovits, E.: A Bayesian Method for the Induction of Probabilistic Networks from Data. In: Machine Learning, **9**, Kluwer Academic Publishers, Boston (1992) pp. 309–347.
3. Duentsch, I., Gediga, G.: Uncertainty measures of rough set prediction. Artificial Intelligence **106** (1998) pp. 77–107.
4. Gallager, R.G.: Information Theory and Reliable Communication. John Wiley & Sons, New York (1968).
5. Kapur, J.N., Kesavan, H.K.: Entropy Optimization Principles with Applications. Academic Press (1992).
6. Li, M., Vitanyi, P.: An Introduction to Kolmogorov Complexity and Its Applications. Springer Verlag (1997).
7. Pawlak, Z.: Rough sets – Theoretical aspects of reasoning about data. Kluwer Academic Publishers, Dordrecht (1991).
8. Pawlak, Z.: Decision rules, Bayes' rule and rough sets. In: Proc. of RSFD-GrC'99, Yamaguchi, Japan, LNAI **1711** (1999) pp. 1–9.
9. Pawlak, Z., Skowron, A.: Rough membership functions. In: Advances in the Dempster Shafer Theory of Evidence, John Wiley & Sons Inc., New York, (1994) pp. 251–271.
10. Pearl, J.: Probabilistic Reasoning in Intelligent Systems: Networks of Plausible Inference. Morgan Kaufmann (1988).
11. Pearl, J., Paz, A.: Graphoids: A graph-based logic for reasoning about relevance relations. In: Advanves in Artificial Intelligence II, B. Du Boulay, D. Hogg and L. Steels (eds.), North-Holland, Amsterdam (1987) pp. 357–363.
12. Polkowski, L., Skowron, A. (eds.): Proc. of RSCTC'98, June 22–26, Warsaw, Poland, Springer Verlag, Berlin (1998).
13. Polkowski, L., Skowron, A. (eds.): Rough Sets in Knowledge Discovery. Physica Verlag, Heidelberg (1998), parts **1**, **2**.
14. Polkowski, L., Tsumoto, S., Lin, T.Y. (eds.): Rough Set Methods and Applications: New Developments in Knowledge Discovery in Information Systems. Physica Verlag / Springer Verlag (2000).
15. Rissanen, J.: Modeling by the shortest data description. Authomatica **14** (1978) pp. 465–471.
16. Ślęzak, D.: Approximate reducts in decision tables. In: Proc. of IPMU'96, July 1–5, Granada, Spain (1996) **3**, pp. 1159–1164.
17. Ślęzak, D.: Normalized decision functions and measures for inconsistent decision tables analysis. Fundamenta Informaticae **44/3**, IOS Press (2000) pp. 291–319.
18. Ślęzak, D.: Foundations of Entropy-Based Bayesian Networks: Theoretical Results & Rough Set Based Extraction from Data. In: Proc. of IPMU'00, July 3–7, Madrid, Spain (2000) **1**, pp. 248–255.
19. Ślęzak, D.: Data Models based on Approximate Bayesian Networks. In: Proc. of JSAI RSTGC'2001, May 20–22, Shimane, Japan (2001).
20. Ślęzak, D., Wróblewski, J.: Application of Normalized Decision Measures to the New Case Classification. In: Proc. of RSCTC'00, October 16–19, Banff, Canada (2000).

Stochastic Algorithms for Searching Causal Orderings in Bayesian Networks

Luis M. de Campos
Depto. de Ciencias de la Computación e I.A.
E.T.S.I.I, Universidad de Granada
18071 - Granada, SPAIN
lci@decsai.ugr.es

Juan F. Huete
Depto. de Ciencias de la Computación e I.A.
E.T.S.I.I, Universidad de Granada
18071 - Granada, SPAIN
jhg@decsai.ugr.es

Abstract

The structure of a Bayesian network depends heavily on the ordering of its variables: given any ordering it is always possible to build a Bayesian network whose arcs are consistent with the initial ordering; however, the topology of the network, and therefore the number of conditional independence relationships that may be explicitly represented can vary greatly from one ordering to another. As a sparse representation is always preferable to a denser representation of the same model, the task of determining the ordering giving rise to the network with minimum number of arcs is important. In this work we propose methods to obtain a good approximation to the optimal ordering, using only partial information. More precisely, we only use conditional independence relationships of order zero and one, and search for the ordering which best preserves this information. The search process will be guided by genetic algorithms and simulated annealing.

1 Introduction

One of the most interesting problems when dealing with Bayesian networks [13] is that of developing automatic methods capable of learning the network directly from raw data, as an alternative or a complement [10] to the (difficult and time-consuming) method of eliciting opinions from experts. In general, learning Bayesian networks is NP-hard [8]. Therefore, in order to facilitate the learning process, any kind of previous information about the model to be recovered may be quite useful (to reduce the search space). This information may be an ordering of the variables in the network [1, 7, 9, 15], knowledge about the (possible) presence of some causal or (in)dependence relationships [10, 14], or some restrictions relative to the type of network to be recovered [5, 6]. Usually, an expert provides this kind of information; nevertheless, if there is no expert available, it may be interesting to develop tools capable of obtaining this information as a previous step to the learning process.

In this work we focus on the problem of obtaining an ordering on the set of variables in the network. In general, if we require an optimal ordering then obtaining it may require as much information as the learning of the complete structure itself, and the calculus may be quite complex as well [3, 12]. So, we propose the following general criterion: *To use only partial information about the problem in order to get a 'good' approximation of the ordering.*

The type of partial information we use will be a subset of the set of dependence/independence relationships that could be represented in the network (more precisely, marginal and conditional (in)dependence relationships of order one), and the methods to perform the search of the ordering will be genetic algorithms and simulated annealing.

The rest of the paper is organized as follows: in the next section we briefly recall some general ideas about Bayesian networks, which will be used in the further development. In Sections 3 and 4 we describe our methods. Section 5 shows some preliminary experiments with the proposed methods. Finally, Section 6 contains the concluding remarks.

2 Bayesian Networks

A Bayesian network [13] is a directed acyclic graph (dag), where the nodes represent the variables in the domain, and the arrows represent dependence or causality relationships among the variables. The strength of these connections is modelized by means of probability distributions: for each variable x_i we store a set of conditional probabilities of the form $P(\mathtt{x_i} \mid \Pi(\mathtt{x_i}))$, where $\mathtt{x_i}$ and $\Pi(\mathtt{x_i})$ represent a possible assignment of values to x_i and to the set $\Pi(x_i)$ of parents of x_i in the dag. The absence of a direct connection between two variables is interpreted as the existence of an independence relationship between them. The set of all the independence relationships represented in a Bayesian network may be determined using the d-separation criterion [13].

Given a Bayesian network, we can extract an ordering θ for its variables in the following way: if there is an arrow $x_i \rightarrow x_j$ in the graph then x_i precedes x_j in the ordering θ, i.e., $\theta(x_i) \prec \theta(x_j)$. Such an ordering θ is a *causal ordering* [3]. It is interesting to note that, given a dag, the causal ordering is not unique; for example $\theta_1 = \{x_1, x_2, x_3, x_4, x_5, x_6\}$ and $\theta_3 = \{x_1, x_4, x_2, x_3, x_5, x_6\}$ are two valid causal orderings for the network on the left side of figure 1.

It can be shown (using d-separation) that for a dag G, given a causal ordering θ, the following independence relationship (known as the Markov condition) is true: the variable x_i is conditionally independent of all the variables that precede it in the ordering, given its parent set $\Pi(x_i)$, i.e., $\langle x_i, Prec_\theta(x_i) \setminus \Pi(x_i) \mid \Pi(x_i) \rangle$, where $Prec_\theta(x_i) = \{x_j \mid \theta(x_j) \prec \theta(x_i)\}$ and $\langle ., . | . \rangle$ denotes d-separation.

Given an ordering θ, the Markov condition provides a systematic method to build Bayesian networks: for each node x_i, to assign, as the parents of x_i in the dag, the minimal subset of predecessors of x_i in the ordering θ, $\Pi_\theta(x_i)$, which makes x_i conditionally independent of the rest of its predecessors.

However, different orderings may give rise to different networks. For example, let us start from the network on the left side of figure 1. Let $\theta_1 = \{x_1, x_2, x_3, x_4, x_5, x_6\}$ and $\theta_2 = \{x_6, x_3, x_2, x_4, x_1, x_5\}$ be two different orderings. If we apply the previous process, for θ_1 we recover the original graph and for the ordering θ_2 we get the much more dense graph on the right side of figure 1.

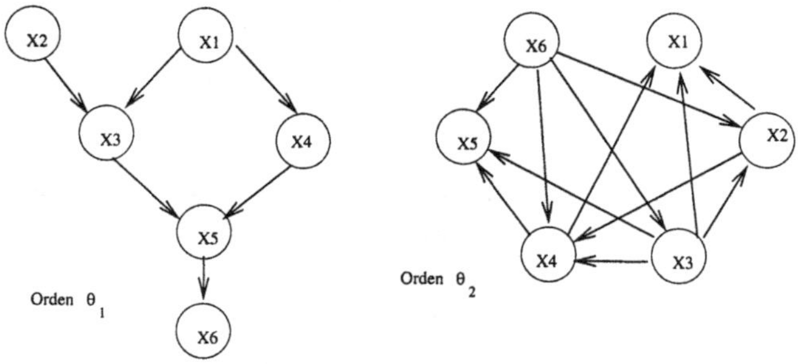

Figure 1: Dags obtained using orderings θ_1 and θ_2

After assigning the corresponding conditional probabilities to the nodes, the two models represent the same joint probability distribution. However, the set of independence relationships represented in these dags is not the same. In the graph associated to θ_2 only a few independences are preserved, whereas using θ_1 we get the same set of dependence/independence relationships as in the original model.

3 Approximating a Causal Ordering

We seek to find a good causal ordering for the variables in a (unknown) Bayesian network from a database. Given any ordering, it is possible to build a Bayesian network representing the joint probability distribution, this network being an Independence map [13] of the underlying probabilistic model. However, the density of the resultant dag may change drastically depending on the selected ordering. Our goal is to find an ordering able to represent as much true independence relationships as possible. Given this ordering, the search space to find an optimal Bayesian network reduces considerably [1, 9]. Several approaches to deal with this problem can be found in the literature [3, 12, 15]. Our approach is situated between the works of Singh and Valtorta [15] and those of Larrañaga et al. [12]. The basic idea is to use only a subset of the (in)dependence relationships of the model to learn a draft of the network and next apply a combinatorial optimization tool to search for the ordering which preserves as much of these dependences and independences as possible.

When dealing with conditional independence relationships whose true values have to be estimated from a database by means of conditional independence tests, two problems appear: the number of tests and their order (i.e., the number of variables involved in the conditioning set). On one hand, the number of conditional independence tests that may be necessary to perform can increase exponentially with the number of variables; on the other hand, computing the truth value of a conditional independence test requires a number of calculations which grows exponentially with the order of the test. Moreover, another problem is not related with efficiency but reliability: conditional independence tests of high order are not reliable except if the size of the database is enormous. So, we propose using only conditional independence tests of order zero and one (i.e. $I(x_i, x_j|\emptyset)$ and $I(x_i, x_j|x_k)$, respectively) for several reasons: i) this kind of tests are quite reliable even for moderate datasets, ii) the number of tests is polynomial $O(n^3)$, and iii) this set of independences is quite expressive for sparse structures, as those that we usually find in real applications. These independences are sufficient even for characterizing and learning some specific kinds of Bayesian networks [5, 6]. We shall call *0-1 Independences* to the set of conditional independence relationships of order zero and one which are true for a given model.

Our algorithm will take the set I_{0-1}^M of 0-1 Independences obtained from the data set as the input. In an initialization step, we build an undirected graph (denoted G_{0-1}) as a basic skeleton of the network: starting from the complete undirected graph, we remove those links $x_i - x_j$ such that there is a 0-1 independence between x_i and x_j in I_{0-1}^M (either $I(x_i, x_j|\emptyset)$ or $I(x_i, x_j|x_k)$ for some x_k). For example, let us suposse that the underlying model is isomorphic to the graph I) in figure 2. In this case the set of 0-1 Independences is $I_{0-1}^M = \{I(x_2, x_3|x_1)\}$. The initialization step produces the undirected graph II) in figure 2.

In a second step we shall execute the search process, which tries to find an optimal ordering. For both the genetic and the simulated annealing algorithms, each cromosome and each configuration represents an ordering of the variables. For any ordering θ being considered, we direct the skeleton G_{0-1} as follows: if $x_i - x_j \in G_{0-1}$, and $\theta(x_i) \prec \theta(x_j)$ then we direct the link as $x_i \rightarrow x_j$. For the example in figure 2, let us consider the following orderings: $\theta_1 = \{x_1, x_2, x_3, x_4\}$; $\theta_2 = \{x_2, x_3, x_4, x_1\}$; $\theta_3 = \{x_1, x_2, x_4, x_3\}$ and $\theta_4 = \{x_3, x_1, x_2, x_4\}$. Using these

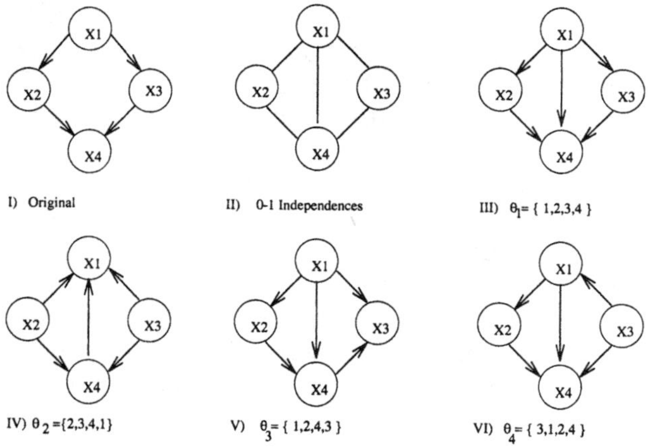

Figure 2: Different orderings of G_{0-1}

orderings we obtain the dags III), IV), V) and VI) respectively in figure 2.

Now, let us describe the different components of the two search processes. We assume a basic knowledge of genetic algorithms [11] and simulated annealing [2].

3.1 The Genetic Approach

• *Fitness function:* For each individual θ of the population we try to measure the degree $g(\theta)$ in which, after directing G_{0-1} according to the ordering θ (thus obtaining a dag G^{θ}_{0-1}), the dependence and independence relationships in I^{M}_{0-1} are preserved in the dag. Let us denote $I^{G^{\theta}}_{0-1}$ to the set of independence relationships of order zero and one that are valid in G^{θ}_{0-1} (using d-separation). So, we count the number of dependence and independence relationships that are true in the model but are not in $I^{G^{\theta}}_{0-1}$. Therefore, our fitness function is:

$$g(\theta) = \sum_{\substack{x_i, x_j \\ x_i \neq x_j}} \left(I(x_i, x_j | \emptyset) \otimes \langle x_i, x_j | \emptyset \rangle \right) + \sum_{\substack{x_i, x_j, x_k \\ x_i \neq x_j \neq x_k}} \left(I(x_i, x_j | x_k) \otimes \langle x_i, x_j | x_k \rangle \right)$$

where we assume that an independence relationship takes on a binary value (0 for dependence, 1 for independence) and $\otimes$ corresponds to the exclusive-or operator. A value $g(\theta) = 0$ represents that I^{M}_{0-1} and $I^{G^{\theta}}_{0-1}$ are equivalent, and the greater the value of $g(\theta)$ is, the greater number of dependence and independence relationships are not preserved. Obviously, we shall prefer those orderings giving a value of g as low as possible. For the example in figure 2, we have $g(\theta_1) = 0$, $g(\theta_2) = 2$, $g(\theta_3) = 1$ and $g(\theta_4) = 0$, thus θ_1 and θ_4 are the preferred orderings.

• *Crossover operator:* Each cromosome representing an ordering θ is a chain of variables, where if x_i appears before x_j then x_i precedes x_j in θ. The crossover operator takes two orderings θ_{p1} and θ_{p2} as the input and produces two children θ_{h1} and θ_{h2} as the output. The idea is to randomly select a subchain from a parent and preserve the relative ordering of the elements for the other parent. For example, let us consider the orderings $\theta_{p1} = \{1,2,3,4,5,6,7\}$ and $\theta_{p2} = \{2,3,6,5,4,1,7\}$. We randomly select two cut points (suposse these points are 1 and 4) which represent the segment of the cromosome that will be interchanged. So, the first child inherits the subchain of the second parent, $\theta_{h1} = \{*,3,6,5,*,*,*\}$ and the second child inherits the subchain of the first parent, $\theta_{h2} = \{*,2,3,4,*,*,*\}$. The rest of elements in each child is obtained preserving the relative ordering of the variables of the other parent, i.e., $\theta_{h1} = \{1,3,6,5,2,4,7\}$ and $\theta_{h2} = \{6,2,3,4,5,1,7\}$.

• *Mutation operator:* We randomly select two elements of the cromosome to be interchanged, and we actually interchange them with probability p_m. For example, for the ordering $\theta = \{1,2,3,4,5,6,7\}$, if the selected elements are in positions 3 and 6, then the mutation produces (with probability p_m) the cromosome $\theta_m = \{1,2,6,4,5,3,7\}$.

3.2 The Simulated Annealing Approach

• *Energy function*: It is the same fitness function that has been used in the genetic approach. Our objective is also to minimize its value.

• *Perturbation mechanism:* The new configuration (ordering) is obtained by modifying a randomly selected segment s in the current configuration. Two mechanisms (randomly selected with 0.5 probability) have been implemented. In the first one we use a transportation function that moves the segment toward a new random position p (interchanging the elements); the second one is the inverse function that inverts the ordering of the variables within the segment. For example, consider the configuration $\theta = \{1,\mathbf{2},\mathbf{3},\mathbf{4},5,6,7,8,9\}$, the segment $s = [2,3,4]$ and the position $p = 6$. After using the transportation function we obtain the configuration $\theta_T = \{1,6,7,8,5,\mathbf{2},\mathbf{3},\mathbf{4},9\}$ and the inverse function gives $\theta_I = \{1,\mathbf{4},\mathbf{3},\mathbf{2},5,6,7,8,9\}$.

• *Temperature function:* A proportional decreasing function has been implemented, i.e., $T_k = \alpha T_{k-1}$, where $\alpha \in (0,1)$ and T_0 is a fixed initial temperature.

• *Stopping criterion:* The algorithm stops when: i) all the 0-1 independences have been captured by the current configuration θ, ii) the energy is not modified after two consecutive iterations or iii) 100 changes in the value of the temperature have been performed.

4 Evaluating the Solution

In the previous two techniques the fitness or energy function intends to preserve the set of dependences and independences of order zero and one. This criterion is used to guide the search for the best ordering. However, some important remarks have to be done:

R1: It can not be guaranteed that all the 0-1 independences will be preserved after directing the graph G_{0-1} even using the optimal ordering. For instance, consider figure 3, where the graph I) represents the original model and the graph II) is the skeleton G_{0-1}, obtained by removing all 0-1 independences from a complete graph. In this case, and in order to preserve the 0 independences, we have that variables $x_1, \ldots, x_4$ must precede x_5 and x_6 in the ordering. Now, consider the link $x_5 - x_6$: directing it as $x_5 \rightarrow x_6$ we find that $\langle x_1, x_6 | \emptyset \rangle$ does not hold and directing the link as $x_5 \leftarrow x_6$ we have that $\langle x_4, x_5 | \emptyset \rangle$ is not preserved.

The reason for this behavior is that, since we are using only partial information, the learned skeleton G_{0-1} includes some unnecessary links inducing false dependence relationships. Therefore, we cannot expect to always preserve all the independence relationships.

R2: For non-sparse graphs, the set of 0-1 independences is not very significant and therefore, the output ordering may be far from the optimum. For example, consider the graph III) in figure 3, where the set I^M_{0-1} is empty. At the initialization step we obtain the complete graph IV) and any ordering used to direct it preserves (trivially) all the 0-1 independences.

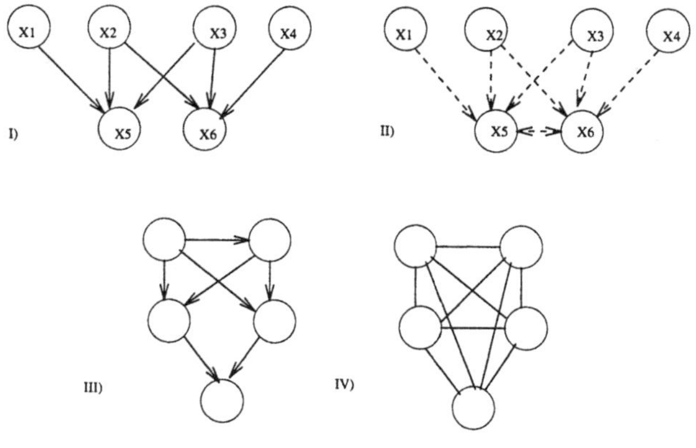

Figure 3: Evaluating the solution

Considering these facts, we conclude that the search processes may not reach the minimum of the fitness function (remark R1) and, even if the minimum value is obtained, we can not always guarantee the correctness of the output ordering (remark R2).

Therefore, our purpose now is to study the goodness of the output ordering

θ obtained after applying the proposed methodology. In other words, we are looking for a value measuring the quality of an ordering θ, i.e., how much θ fits an optimal causal ordering for the original model. Remember that, for a given dag, the optimal ordering is not unique. Different orderings give rise to different, but equivalent [16], graph structures (in all these graphs the links and the non-adjacent head to head connections are preserved).

Therefore, our proposal intends to capture the degree of equivalence between models: Starting from the skeleton of the original network model (i.e., without considering the true directionality of arrows), we can direct this undirected graph using the ordering θ. Then, we compare the resultant network with the original one. For this purpose, we define a quantitative version of the concept of equivalence between dags [16], i.e., we measure how much of the non-adjacent head to head connections two dags have in common:

Definition: *Let G_1 and G_2 be two dags with the same skeleton. We define the equivalence degree between G_1 and G_2, denoted by Equiv(G_1,G_2), as the number of links that are in at least one non-adjacent head to head connection in G_1 but do not belong to any non-adjacent head to head connection in G_2 and vice-versa.*

Obviously, when Equiv(G_1, G_2)=0 then the two dags G_1 and G_2 are equivalent. For example, let G be the graph I) in figure 3 and let $\theta_1 = \{x_2, x_3, x_4, x_5, x_6, x_1\}$ and $\theta_2 = \{x_1, x_2, x_5, x_6, x_3, x_4\}$ be two orderings. If we direct the skeleton of the graph G using θ_1 and θ_2, we obtain the graphs I) and II) in figure 4, respectively. In this case, Equiv$(G, G^{\theta_1}) = 1$ since the arrow $x_1 \to x_5$ is in the connection $x_1 \to x_5 \leftarrow x_2$ (it also belongs to $x_1 \to x_5 \leftarrow x_3$) in G, but this connection is not in G^{θ_1}. Analogously, Equiv$(G, G^{\theta_2}) = (3{+}2) = 5$: (3) after inverting the arrows $x_3 \to x_5$, $x_3 \to x_6$ and $x_4 \to x_6$ we have lost the connections $x_1 \to x_5 \leftarrow x_3$, $x_2 \to x_6 \leftarrow x_3$ and $x_2 \to x_6 \leftarrow x_4$ respectively, and (2) because in G^{θ_2} a new non-adjacent head to head connection $x_5 \to x_3 \leftarrow x_6$ which does not belong to G appears.

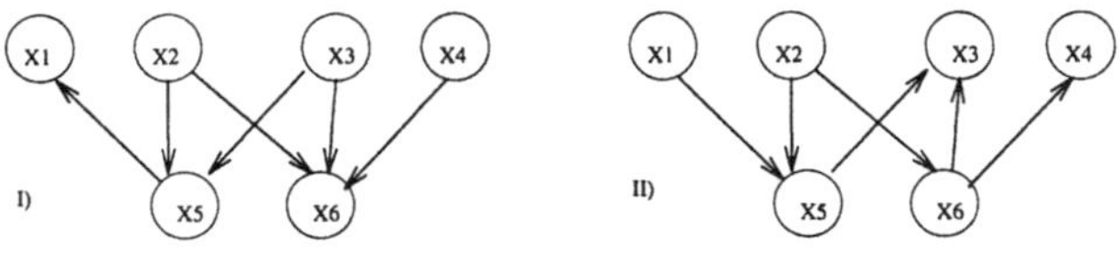

Figure 4: Directing the graph using θ_1 and θ_2

5 Experimental Results

In order to empirically test the behavior of our techniques, we have carried out the following experiments. We start from a dag G as our underlying dependence model M. We obtain the set I_{0-1}^M of 0-1 independences from this graph (using d-separation), and using this set we build the skeleton G_{0-1}. Then, either the genetic or the simulated annealing algorithms will be executed, giving an ordering θ of variables as the output. To measure the quality of this ordering θ, we re-direct the original model G using θ (obtaining a new dag G^{θ}) and calculate the equivalence degree between these two dags (G and G^{θ}).

Given a number of nodes $n = 10, 15, 20, 25$ and the density of the graph $p = 3, 4, 5$, represented by the maximum number of parents allowed for any node, we have carried out 12 basic experiments, $(n = 10, p = 3)$, $(n = 10, p = 4)$, ... For each experiment a set of ten different initial dags has been randomly generated.

The parameters used in the genetic algorithm are: Population size 61; mutation probability 0.05; number of generations 1000.

The average results (for ten dags) obtained using this technique are shown in table 1. The first column represents the number of nodes in the dag; the second one indicates the density p; the third and fourth columns represent the number of links in the original dag G and the number of links in G_{0-1}, respectively; fifth and sixth columns indicate the ratio of zero and first order independences that exist in the model; the seventh column represents the percentage of 0-1 independences that, being true in the model, are still preserved after directing G_{0-1}; finally, the last column represents the equivalence degree obtained using the output ordering given by the genetic algorithm.

Table 1: Results using genetic algorithms

n	p	Org.	Lrn.	I0	I1	Ftn.	Eqv.
10	3	7.4	9.3	0.66	0.66	100	0.1
10	4	12.3	18.6	0.33	0.34	100	1.1
10	5	17.9	27.5	0.15	0.17	100	2.0
15	3	12.8	15.8	0.64	0.64	100	0.1
15	4	21.7	43.6	0.20	0.22	99.3	1.8
15	5	26.6	53.2	0.21	0.22	99.9	2.0
20	3	19.4	28.8	0.55	0.56	99.5	0.8
20	4	26.5	50.8	0.40	0.40	99.0	3.6
20	5	36.4	89.6	0.31	0.27	98.2	4.1
25	3	22.3	28.4	0.66	0.67	99.2	1.5
25	4	38.3	91.0	0.43	0.43	98.3	4.8
25	5	43.5	127.0	0.35	0.34	97.2	8.3

We also have carried out the same set of experiments using simulated annealing as search algorithm. The parameters used are: Initial temperature $T_0 = 1$; decreasing factor $\alpha = 0.9$; the number L_k of iterations maintaining the temperature is $L_k = 50 * n$, where n is the number of nodes. The results are displayed in table 2.

Table 2: Results using simulated annealing

n	p	Org.	Lrn.	I0	I1	Ftn.	Eqv.
10	3	9.1	12.4	0.48	0.49	99.95	0.5
10	4	12.7	21.0	0.36	0.35	99.98	1.3
10	5	13.4	18.8	0.35	0.35	98.43	2.5
15	3	13.5	19.0	0.59	0.59	99.72	0.8
15	4	18.1	29.1	0.49	0.48	99.65	1.2
15	5	26.4	56.4	0.22	0.20	99.98	2.7
20	3	18.0	22.1	0.62	0.63	99.82	0.3
20	4	27.0	53.2	0.40	0.38	99.19	2.2
20	5	35.7	96.6	0.31	0.28	99.45	5.1
25	3	25.7	47.4	0.56	0.56	99.78	1.9
25	4	35.3	90.7	0.47	0.45	99.24	5.2
25	5	43.8	120.9	0.36	0.32	99.49	4.5

Since we are showing average data, and in order to do not mislead some results, we also present the individual data obtained in one of the above experiments. Table 3 shows the results for the ten dags with 20 nodes and a maximum of 4 parents.

Table 3: Simulated annealing, 20 nodes, 4 parents

Org.	Lrn.	I0	I1	Ftn.	Eqv.
33	71	0.41	0.37	99.59	0
30	56	0.03	0.08	98.87	9
29	55	0.42	0.37	96.76	0
30	64	0.29	0.26	100	5
26	56	0.35	0.35	99.24	1
28	61	0.43	0.41	99.82	3
26	55	0.40	0.36	100	1
22	35	0.53	0.53	99.32	2
21	30	0.52	0.49	99.72	0
25	49	0.58	0.56	98.59	1

To conclude the experimental work, we will consider the performance of the proposed methodology in more realistic circumstances, where our objective is now to learn a whole Bayesian network from a database of cases. Figure 5 shows a hand-constructed belief network named ALARM [4] (37 nodes and 46 arcs). In the experiment we use four databases *DB1*,*DB2*,*DB3* and *DB4* obtained by selecting, respectively, the first 5000, 6000, 7000 and 10000 cases of the original ALARM dataset.

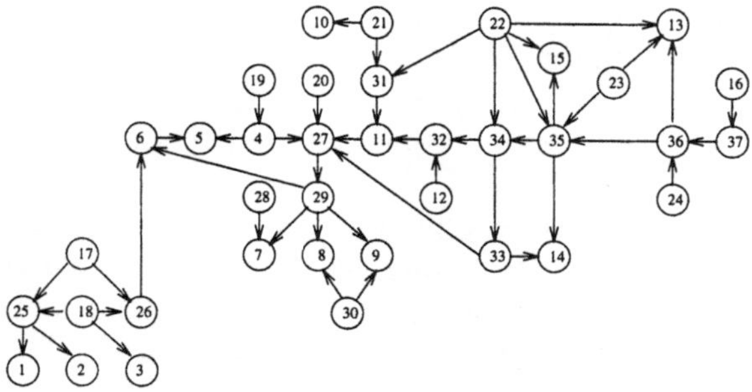

Figure 5: ALARM Network

In the learning process we consider two main steps: first, learning an ordering of the variables θ, and second using an algorithm for learning the network structure which takes the ordering θ as the input. In this way, we can judge the quality of the ordering by evaluating the quality if the network eventually generated. Particularly, in the experimentation we use an independence-based approach for learning Belief Network structures [5] (which also makes an intensive use of zero and first order independence statements, evaluated in the previous step).

In order to measure the quality of the ordering, we will compare the learned network with the one obtained by the aforementioned learning algorithm using the Alarm 'correct' ordering as the input. In that case, the algorithm recovers the original network, except the arrows $21 \rightarrow 31$ and $12 \rightarrow 32$.

Using both Genetic Algorithms and Simulated Annealing approach, the fitness values (percentage of 0-1 independences preserved) for the best orderings obtained for all the databases belong to the interval $[96.6, 97.7]$, although there are many different orderings having the same fitness value. Two general comments about the results obtained in our experiments must be done:

i) If there are not 0-1 independence relationships among the variables in a set W, then we could change the relative ordering among the variables in W (without modifying the fitness value). Analyzing these orderings will be relevant to get a better (having less arrows) network. This is the case for the set $W = \{35, 15, 34\}$ (see Table 4.

ii) As it could be expected, the degree in which the database reflects the set of 0-1 Independences is important for getting a good ordering. In our experimentation we found that, for variables 29 and 9, the 0-1 dependences with many of the variables which are ancestors of 27 in the original Alarm network are not reflected. The consequence of this fact is that 29 and 9 should precede variable 27 in the ordering (although variable 27 precedes both variables 29 and 9 in the Alarm's original ordering): if it is not the case, then the fitness value decreases to aprox. 81%.

Depending on the specific ordering being used, some other arrows can be inverted with respect to the original Alarm network; however, they are not incorrectly inverted because give rise to isomorphical structures (for example, we could get the arrow $4 \rightarrow 19$; note that the direction of this arrow does not matter).

In Table 4 we present the result obtained by using one of the orderings obtained for $DB4$ (for the other databases the results are similar) when we are considering the previous comments. In each row, the results obtained by using the different relative orderings between $35, 15$ and 34 can be found. On the average, we add 2.16 edges, miss 0.66 edges and invert 1.83 edges.

Table 4: Results for DB4

Ordering	Added	Missing	Inverted
$35 \prec 34 \prec 15$	none	none	$27-29$
$35 \prec 15 \prec 34$	none	none	$27-29$
$34 \prec 35 \prec 15$	$23-4$; $36-34$	none	$34-35$; $27-29$
$15 \prec 35 \prec 34$	$23-15$; $36-15$	none	$15-35$; $27-29$
$34 \prec 15 \prec 35$	$34-15$; $36-1$ $36-34$; $23-34$	$36-35$	$34-35$; $15-35$ $27-29$
$15 \prec 34 \prec 35$	$15-34$; $23-15$ $23-34$; $36-15$ $36-34$	$36-35$ $34-35$ $23-35$	$15-35$; $27-29$

Looking into the tables we can conclude that there exist three main factors that are relevant to the quality of the solution:

- *The number of variables*: the time needed to obtain the solution increases and the quality of the solution decreases with this parameter.
- *The number of 0-1 independence relationships in the original model*: For a given set of nodes, the quality of the ordering increases with the relative cardinality of the set I^M_{0-1}.
- *The number of links in G_{0-1}*: We obtain better results when this graph has a small number of links.

Although a more rigorous and exhaustive experimental work have to be carried out, we provisionally propose the following heuristic rules to be confident on the quality of the ordering determined by our methods:

I.- The ratio for the set of 0-1 independences should be greater than 0.30
II.- The number of links in G_{0-1} should be less than 30% of the total number or links in the complete graph.

If these rules do not hold, perhaps we could use some conditional independence tests of order greater than one, in order to get an initial model G_{0-1} as sparse as possible. Next, we would also use genetic algorithms or simulated annealing.

6 Concluding Remarks

The problem of obtaining a good causal ordering for the set of variables in a Bayesian network has been studied. This ordering would be given as the input to an algorithm that learns Bayesian networks. In general, to obtain an optimal solution to this problem will be necessary to learn the network (i.e., to have information about the complete set of valid conditional independence statements). Our approach is based on using partial information to obtain a good approximation of the ordering. The initial knowledge is limited to the set of zero and first order conditional independence relationships. The main reasons for using only this information are: reliability, expressiveness and efficiency. We use simulated annealing and genetic algorithms as searching mechanisms. The obtained results shown the validity of our approach. In future works we will study methods that refine a given ordering (e.g., the output ordering provided by our algorithms) to obtain an optimal solution. These methods could be based on the idea of the reliability about the particular position of any given variable x_i in the ordering, which in turns is directly related to the number of 0-1 independences where this variable x_i is involved.

This work has been supported by the CICYT under Project n. TIC96-0781.

References

[1] S. Acid and L.M. de Campos. Benedict: An algorithm for learning probabilistic belief netwoks. In *Proc. of the IPMU-96 Conference*, 979-984, 1996.

[2] N. Ansari and E. Hou. *Computational Intelligence for Optimization.* Kluwer Academic Publishers, 1997.

[3] R. Bouckaert. Optimizing causal orderings for generating dag's from data. In *Proc. of the Eighth Conference on Uncertainty in Artificial Intelligence*, 9-16, 1992.

[4] I. Beinlich, H. Seurmondt, R. Chavez, and G. Cooper. The alarm monitoring system: a case study with two probabilistic inference techniques for belief networks. In *Proc. of the Second European Conference on Artificial Intelligence in Medicine*, 247-256, 1989.

[5] L.M. de Campos. Independency relationships and learning algorithms for singly connected networks. *Journal of Experimental and Theoretical Artificial Intelligence* 10:511-549, 1998.

[6] L.M. de Campos and J.F. Huete. On the use of independence relationships for learning simplified belief networks. *International Journal of Intelligent Systems*, 12:495-522, 1997.

[7] L.M.de Campos and J.F. Huete. A new approach for learning belief networks using independence criteria. *International Journal of Approximate Reasoning* 24:11-37, 2000.

[8] D. Chickering, D. Geiger, and D. Heckerman. Learning bayesian networks is NP-hard. Technical Report MSR-TR-94-17, Microsoft Research, 1994.

[9] G.F. Cooper and E. Herskovits. A bayesian method for the induction of probabilistic networks from data. *Machine Learning*, 9:309-347, 1992.

[10] D. Heckerman, D. Geiger, and D.M. Chickering. Learning Bayesian networks: The combination of knowledge and statistical data. *Machine Learning*, 20:197-243, 1995.

[11] J.H. Holland. *Adaptation in Natural and Artificial Systems*. Ann Arbor, MI: The University of Michigan Press, 1975.

[12] P. Larrañaga, C.M. Kuijpers, R.H. Murga, and Y. Yurramendi. Learning bayesian network structure by searching for the best ordering with genetic algorithms. *IEEE Transactions on Systems, Man and Cybernetics- Part A: Systems and Humans*, 26(4):487-493, 1996.

[13] J. Pearl. *Probabilistic Reasoning in Intelligent Systems: Networks of Plausible Inference*. Morgan and Kaufmann, San Mateo, 1988.

[14] P. Spirtes, C. Glymour, and R. Scheines. *Causation, Prediction and Search*. Lecture Notes in Statistics 81. Springer Verlag, New York, 1993.

[15] M. Singh and M. Valtorta. Construction of bayesian networks structures from data: A survey and an efficient algorithm. *International Journal of Approximate Reasoning*, 12:111-131, 1995.

[16] T. Verma and J. Pearl. Equivalence and synthesis of causal models. In *Proc. of the Sixth Conference on Uncertainty in Artificial Intelligence*, 220-227, Mass, 1990.

SYMBIONT: A Cooperative Evolutionary Model for Evolving Artificial Neural Networks for Classification

Nicolás García-Pedrajas[1], César Hervás-Martínez[1], and José Muñoz-Pérez[2]

[1] Dept. of Computing and Numerical Analysis
Escuela Politécnica Superior
University of Córdoba

[2] Dept. of Languages and Computer Science
Escuela Superior de Ingeniería Informática
University of Málaga

Abstract. A new cooperative evolutionary model, called *Symbiont*, for evolving artificial neural networks is presented in this paper. This model is based on the idea of developing subnetworks, called *nodules*, that must cooperate to form a solution, instead of evolving a complete network. The performance of the model in solving two real-world problems of classification is compared with a multilayer perceptron trained using back-propagation. Symbiont has proved to show better generalization than the multilayer perceptron and to evolve smaller networks.

Keywords: Neural networks, cooperative evolution, genetic algorithms, evolutionary programming.

1 Introduction

In the area of neural network design one of the main problems is finding suitable architectures for solving specific problems. The election of such architecture is very important, as a network smaller than needed would be unable to learn and a network larger than needed would end in over-training.

The problem of finding a suitable architecture and the corresponding weights of the network is a very complex task (for a very interesting review of the matter the reader can consult [13]). Modular systems are often used in machine learning as an approach for solving such complex problems. Some efforts have been made in designing modular neural networks (e.g. [14]), but in all of them the design of the networks is helped by methods outside evolutionary computation. In our model the whole network, both structure and weights, is evolved.

The underlying idea is based on evolving two populations, one of subnetworks, in our model called *nodules*, and another of networks. The networks are combinations of the individuals of the nodule populations. So the nodules must learn to cooperate in forming good networks. The idea of evolving two populations is taken from D. E. Moriarty[6], who proposes a population of networks and another population of neurons. We have taken a step forward developing networks with two hidden layers and with no restriction in the structure.

This paper is organized as follows: Section 2 explains the proposed model. Section 3 makes a comparison between our model and a standard algorithm for training neural networks in the task of solving two classification problems. Section 4 presents the conclusions of our work and states some future work that would be interesting to do in order to improve the model.

2 Cooperative evolutionary model

Symbiont is a cooperative evolutionary model, that is, each member of the population is a partial solution of the problem; the combination of several individuals makes up the solution itself. A nodule is made up of a variable number of units with free interconnection among them (see Figure 1).

Some parameters of the nodule are given by the problem:

n	Number of inputs
m	Number of outputs
f^{output}	Transfer function of the output layer
$\mathbf{x} = (x_1, \ldots, x_{n_i})$	Input vector
$\mathbf{o} = (o_1, \ldots, o_{n_o})$	Output vector of the network

the rest of the parameters depend on each nodule:

h	Number of units of the nodule
f^i	Transfer function of unit i
p_i	Partial output of the i-th unit
y_i	Output of the i-th unit
$\mathbf{w}_i$	Weight vector of unit i

For simplicity the connections that are not present in the nodule are considered as having 0 weight, so we can use a weight vector of fixed length for all nodes. A node could have connections from input nodes, from other nodes and to output nodes. The weight vector is ordered as follows:

$$\mathbf{w}_i = (\overbrace{w_{i,0}}^{bias}, \overbrace{w_{i,1}, \ldots, w_{i,n}}^{input}, \overbrace{w_{i,n+1}, \ldots, w_{i,n+h}}^{hidden}, \overbrace{w_{i,n+h+1}, \ldots, w_{i,n+h+m}}^{output}) \quad (1)$$

As there is no restriction in the connectivity of the nodule the transmission of the impulse along the connections must be defined in a way that avoids recurrence. The transmission has been defined in three steps:

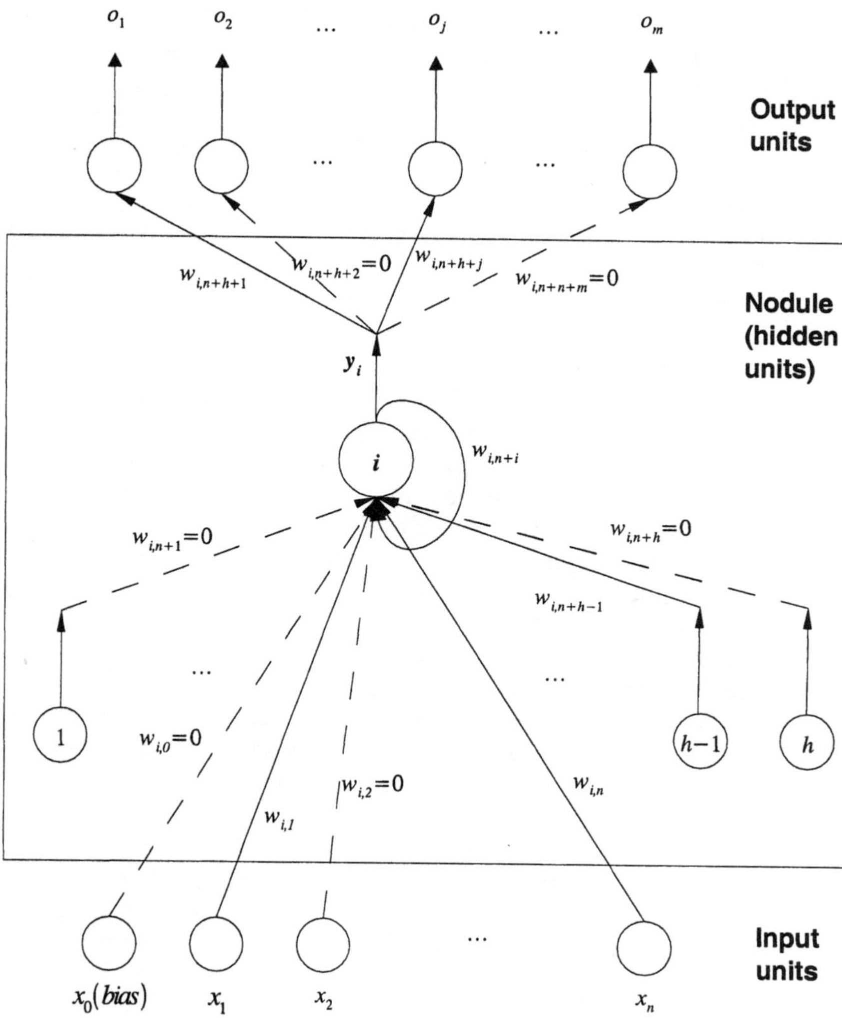

Fig. 1. Model of a nodule

Step 1. Each unit generates its output as a function of only the inputs of the nodule (that is, the inputs of the whole network), its *partial output*:

$$p_i = f^i\left(\sum_{j=0}^{n} w_{i,j}x_j\right), \tag{2}$$

Step 2. These partial outputs are propagated along the connections. Then, each unit generates its output as a function of all its inputs:

$$y_i = f^i\left(\sum_{j=0}^{n} w_{i,j}x_j + \sum_{j=1}^{h} w_{i,n+j}p_j\right). \tag{3}$$

Step 3. Finally, the output layer of the network generates its output from the nodule:

$$o_j = f^{output}\left(\sum_{i=1}^{h} w_{i,n+h+j}y_i\right). \tag{4}$$

These three steps are repeated over all the nodules. The actual output of the network is the sum of the output generated by each nodule.

Defined in this way a nodule is equivalent to a subnetwork of two hidden layers with the same number of units in both layers. This equivalent model is shown in Figure 2. So, the nodule of Figure 1 could be seen as the genotype of a nodule whose phenotype is the subnetwork shown on Figure 2. These difference is important, as the model of Figure 1 considered as a phenotype would be a recurrent network.

The basic idea is the evolution of subnetworks (nodules) that can be combined among them, instead of evolving whole networks. The nodules are combined to make up a network that is a solution to the problem. The evolution enforces the nodules to develop responses to different features of the available data.

Symbiont consists of two different populations that evolve concurrently: the population of networks and the population of *nodules*. Each individual of the population of networks is formed by the combination of a fixed number of nodules. The population of nodules is divided into N subpopulations that evolve independently. The whole evolutionary process is shown on Figure 3.

2.1 Nodule populations

Each nodule population consists of a fixed number of nodules codified directly as subnetworks (see Figure 1). The population is subject to the operation of replication and mutation. With these features the algorithm falls in the class of evolutionary programming[2].

There is no limitation in the structure of the nodule nor in the connection among the units. There are only three restrictions to avoid unnecessary complexity in the resulting nodules. These restrictions, that could be removed without affecting the model, are the following: two units cannot have two connections in the same direction, there can be no connections to an input node, and there can be no connections from an output node.

The algorithm for the generation of a new nodule population is based on a modification of the GNARL[1] algorithm. The description is the following:

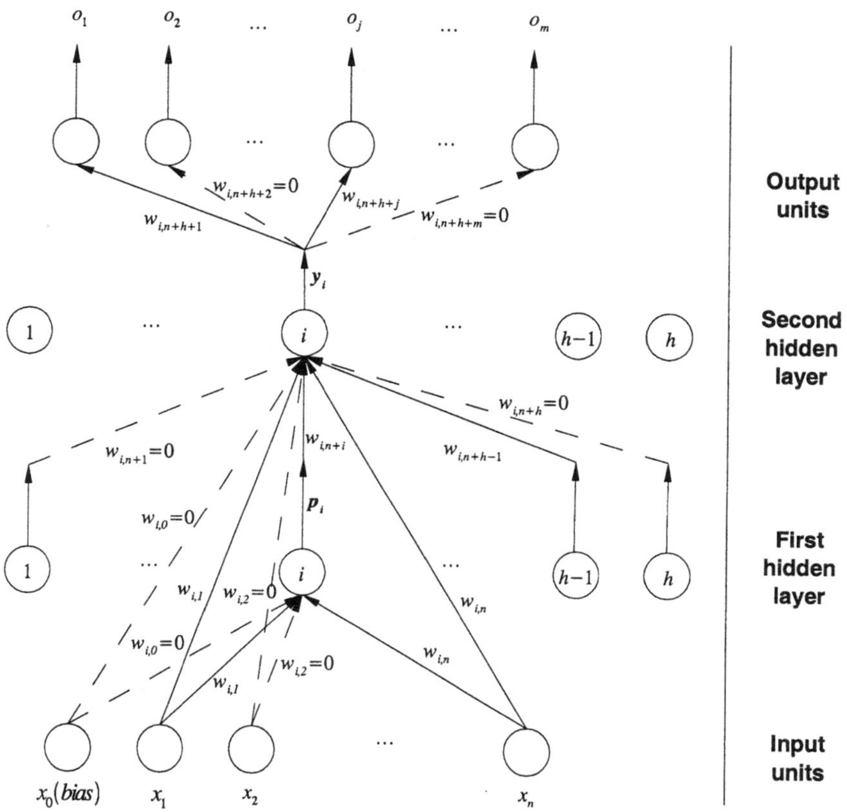

Fig. 2. Equivalent two hidden layer model. Every connection from an input node represents two connections, as the input value is used in two steps (see Equations 2 and 3). Every connection from another node of the nodule represents a connection between the first and second hidden layer (see Equation 3)

- The nodules of the first population are created randomly. The number of units of the nodule, n_h, is obtained from a uniform distribution: $n_h \in U[0, n^h_{max}]$. Each node is created with a number of connections, n_c, taken from a uniform distribution: $n_c \in U[0, n^c_{max}]$. The initial value of the weights is uniformly distributed in the interval $[w_{min}, w_{max}]$.
- The new population is generated replicating the best 50% of the former population. The rest 50% is removed and substituted by mutated copies of the best 50%.
- There are two types of mutation: parametric and structural. The severity of the mutation is determined by the relative fitness, F_r, of the nodule.

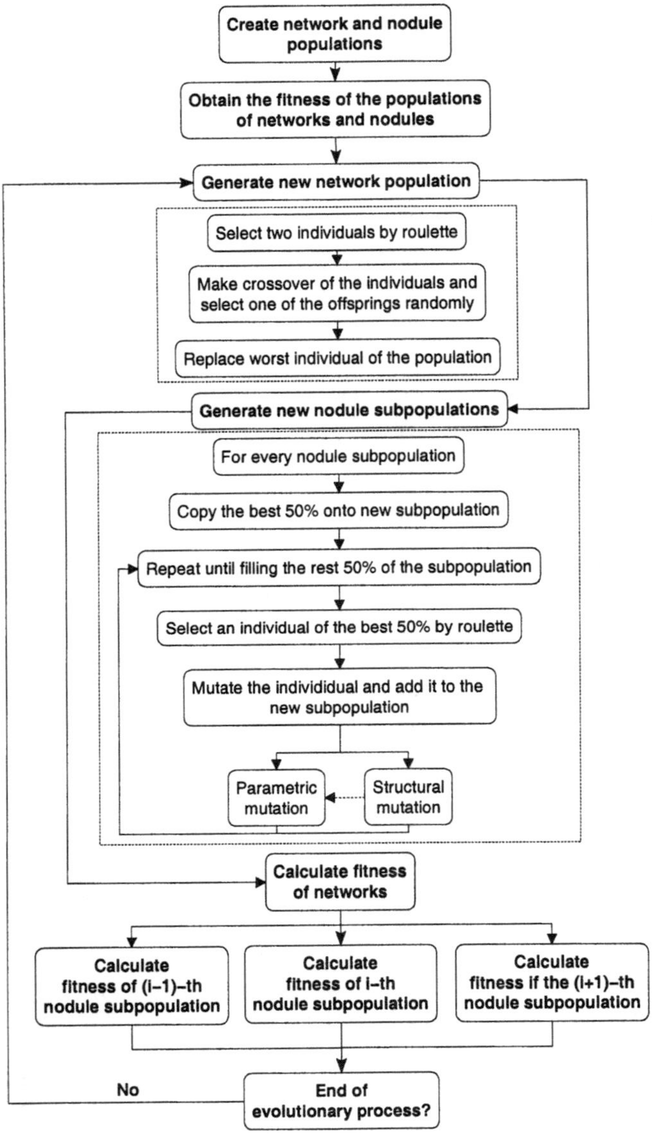

Fig. 3. Evolutionary process

Given a nodule ν its relative fitness is defined as:

$$F_r(\nu) = 1 - \frac{f_\nu}{f_{max}}, \tag{5}$$

where f_{max} must be set by the user. In order to avoid dramatic modifications of the nodule an *instantaneous relative fitness* is defined:

$$\hat{F}_r(\nu) = U(0,1]F_r(\nu). \tag{6}$$

Parametric mutation affects all the weights of the nodule. For each weight, w_{ij}, of the nodule the following operation is carried out:

$$w_{ij} = w_{ij} + \Delta w_{ij}, \quad \forall w_{ij} \in \nu, \tag{7}$$

where

$$\Delta w_{ij} \in N(0, \alpha \hat{F}_r(\nu)). \tag{8}$$

The value of α used in all our experiments has been $\alpha = 1.0$.

Structural mutation is more complex because it implies a modification of the structure of the nodule. The behavioral link between parents and their offspring must be enforced to avoid generational gaps that produce inconsistency in the evolution. There are seven possible mutations, for each one there is a minimum value, Δ_m, and a maximum value, Δ_M. The number of elements involved in the mutations is calculated as follows:

$$\Delta = \Delta_m + \lfloor U(0,1)\hat{F}_r(\nu)(\Delta_M - \Delta_m) \rfloor. \tag{9}$$

The mutations that the nodules suffer are the following:

Addition of a unit. The unit is added with no connections to enforce the behavioral link with its parent.

Deletion of a unit. A unit is selected randomly and deleted together with its connections.

Addition of a connection. A connection is added, with weight 0, to a randomly selected unit. There are three types of connection: from an input unit, from another hidden unit and to an output unit. The selection of the type is made according to the relative number of each type of units: input, output and hidden. Otherwise, when there is a significant difference among these three types, the connections may end highly biased.

Deletion of a connection. A connection is selected following the same criterion of the addition of connections.

Modification of a connection. A connection is selected randomly. Its origin, if it is an input connection, or its destination, if an output connection, is modified.

Modification of the type of a connection. A connection is selected randomly and its type is modified. It usually implies the modification of its origin or destination.

Modification of a transfer function. The transfer function of a randomly selected unit is modified. The unit can have two different sigmoidal transfer functions: hyperbolic tangent, $y = \frac{e^x - e^{-x}}{e^x + e^{-x}}$, or logistic, $y = \frac{1}{1+e^{-ax}}$.

2.2 Network population

The network population is formed by a fixed number of networks. Each network is the combination of a nodule of each population of nodules. So the networks are strings of integer numbers of fixed length. The value of the numbers is not significant as they are just labels of the nodules.

The network population is evolved using the ***steady-state*** genetic algorithm[12][11]. This term may lead to confusion as it has been proved to show higher variance[10] and is a more aggressive and selective selection strategy[3] than the standard genetic algorithm. This algorithm is selected because we need a population of networks that evolves more slowly than the population of nodules, as the changes in the population of networks have a major impact in the fitness of the nodules. This algorithm has three features that are different from the standard genetic algorithm:

- The crossover generates just one individual. Two parents are chosen by means of a Montecarlo algorithm. One of the two offsprings is selected randomly.
- The offspring selected replaces the worst individual of the population instead of replacing one of its parents. In some implementations the worst individual is not the one that has the lowest fitness value and is chosen following a criterion of "less adaptation".
- Fitness is assigned to the members of the population in function of their rank and not as their absolute fitness value. In our model this feature has been ignored, and the absolute value of the fitness has been used.

The algorithm allows to add mutation to the model, always at very low rates. Usually mutation rate is in the interval (1%, 5%).

In our model we have modified this standard algorithm allowing the replacement of the n worst individuals instead of replacing just the worst one. In our experiments n ranges from 1 to 5.

2.3 Fitness assignment

The assignment of fitness to networks is straightforward. Each network is assigned a fitness value in function of its performance in solving a given problem. In this paper the two problems presented are of classification and the fitness of each network is the number of patterns of the training set that are correctly classified. The classification is made following the Bayesian criterion of the maximum: the pattern is assigned to the class whose corresponding output is the highest one. Ties are resolved arbitrarily assigning the pattern to a *default class*.

Assigning fitness to the nodules is a much more complex problem. In fact, the assignment of fitness to the individuals that form a solution in cooperative evolution is one of its key topics. The performance of the model highly depends on that assignment. A discussion of the matter can be found in the Introduction of [7]. The algorithm that we present here is new and can be applied not only to modular neural network but also to any model of cooperative coevolution.

Our credit assignment must fulfill the following requirements to be useful and to reward the best cooperating nodules:

- It must enforce competition among the populations to avoid that two populations might develop similar responses to the same characteristics of the data, that is, the specialization of the nodules is enforced.
- It must enforce cooperation. The nodules must develop complementary features that could solve the problem together.
- It must measure the contribution of the nodule to the fitness of the network. A nodule that is present in a good network must not get a high fitness if its contribution to the performance of the network is not significant. Likewise, a nodule that is in a poor performance network must not be penalized if its contribution to the fitness of the network is high. Otherwise, a good nodule that is temporally assigned to poor rated networks could be lost in the evolution of the populations of nodules.

Some methods for calculating the fitness of the nodules have been tried. The best one consists of the weighted sum of three different criteria. These criteria, for obtaining the fitness of a nodule ν in a population π, are:

1. Substitution (σ). N networks are selected. In these networks the nodule of population π is substituted by the nodule ν. The fitness is measured as the difference of the fitness of the network with the nodule substituted and the original one. If the fitness is negative, it is set to 0. This criterion enforces competition among nodules of the same population.
2. Difference(δ). The nodule is removed from all the networks where it is present. The fitness is measured as the mean of the difference in performance of these networks. If the fitness is negative it is set to 0. This criterion enforces competition among population of nodules.
3. Best n (β_n). The fitness is the mean of the fitness of the best N networks where the nodule ν is present. Only the best N are selected because the importance of the worst networks of the population must not be significant. This criterion rewards the nodules that are in the best networks.

Considered isolated, none of these criteria is able to fulfill the three desired features above mentioned. Nevertheless, when the weighting sum of all of them is used, they have given a very good performance in the problems used as tests, as it will be shown on Section 3. Typical values of the weights of the components of the fitness used in our experiment are ($\sigma = 0.70, \delta = 0.29, \beta_n = 0.01, N = 10$).

3 Performance comparison

The performance of the developed model is tested in two classification problems with different features. In order to get a clear idea of the goodness of the model we have solved these problems with a multilayer perceptron (MLP) trained with standard back-propagation[8] and a momentum term. We used three permutations of the data set and made 10 repetitions over each permutation.

The MLP networks were trained using a validation set, after every 25 epochs the validation error was measured and the learning process stopped when this error started to grow. So, the data set was divided into three parts: 50% for learning, 25% for validation and 25% for testing the generalization error.

The Symbiont model was trained with and without a validation set. The best results were obtained without a validation set. The main reason is the absence of over-training effect, so adding the validation set to the training set gives more information to the network and has not the negative effect of over-training.

3.1 Classification of Iberian pig carcasses

The data set consists of 118 patterns. Each pattern is the near-infrared (NIR) transmission spectra of a fat sample of an Iberian pig carcass. For each one the NIR transmission was measured at intervals of 2 nm ranging from 110 to 2498 nm. A more detailed description of this data set can be found in [4] where this problem is also solved using the Extended Delta-Bar-Delta rule([5]). A principal components analysis was carried out in the original data set. The first 14 principal components were selected as the inputs of the network.

The samples are from three classes of Iberian pigs: pigs fed mainly with acorns, pigs fed with acorns and a feed compound, and pigs fed only with a feed compound. From a quality control point of view the correct classification of each class is very important because of the difference in price among the three classes.

From the whole data set 89 patterns (60 for learning and 29 for validating for the MLP network) were chosen for training and the remaining 29 were used for testing the generalization of the network. Three different permutations of these sets were used, making 10 experiments on each set. The summary of results are shown on Table 2. The error measure used is:

$$E = \frac{1}{P} \sum_{p=1}^{P} e_i, \tag{10}$$

where P is the number of patterns and e_i is 0 if the pattern p_i is correctly classified and 1 otherwise.

The networks were trained with a learning coefficient $\eta = 0.1$ and a momentum coefficient $\mu = 0.1$. The network had 12 hidden units. This number was obtained after some trials with different configurations. The two layers of the network are completely connected. The tolerance used in the classification was 0.45. An output, o, is considered 0 if $o \in [0, 0.45)$, and is considered

Table 1. Symbiont parameters for NIR data set

Parameter	Value
Number of networks	1000
Number of nodule populations	5
Number of nodules on each population	50
f_{max}	45
Max. number of nodes	6
Max. number of connections	10
Nodule fitness components	$\sigma = 3.45, \delta = 1.50,$ $\beta_n = 0.05, n = 10$
Percent. of worst individuals replaced on network population	1.0%
Mutation rate on network pop.	5.0%
Regularization term	Yes

1 if $o \in (0.55, 1]$. If the output falls in the interval $[0.45, 0.55]$ it is considered undefined. This is usually known as the *451045 criterion.*

Table 2. Results using NIR data. Error rates for training and generalization

Method	Training				Generalization				Structure	
	Ave.	Sd.	Best	Worst	Ave.	Sd.	Best	Worst	Units	Conns.
Symbiont	.0200	.0150	.0000	.0674	.1816	.0665	.0690	.2759	12.03	69.33
BP	.1463	.0949	.0000	.3506	.2368	.1180	.0345	.5517	12	204

The population of Symbiont's networks was trained 100 generations. After that number of generations the performance of the system remains almost constant. The parameters of the evolutionary process are shown on Table 1. The parameters that have a major impact in the performance of the model are the weights of the components of the nodule fitness. It is important to note that the number of useful nodules is learned by the system. If a number of nodules higher than needed is set some of these nodules converge to void nodules.

The results show that Symbiont obtains the best generalization values, moreover its variance is significatively lower than the variance of the MLP network. Symbiont performance is also better in learning, showing that Symbiont is almost unaffected by over-training.

3.2 Classification of the Pima Indians data set

This data set is from the UCI machine learning repository. The data set contains data of 768 individuals, all of them females at least 21 years old of

Pima Indian heritage. The patterns are divided into two classes. The class of each pattern shows whether the patient shows signs of diabetes according to the World Health Organization criteria.

There are 8 attributes for each pattern. Former results can be found in [9]. Following this previous work we have divided the data set in 576 patterns for training and 192 patterns for generalization. The results, using the same 3 models of the previous test on NIR data, are shown in Table 4.

Table 3. Symbiont parameters for PIMA data set. Only the parameters that are different from NIR problem are shown

Parameter	Value
Number of networks	250
f_{max}	576
Max. number of nodes	6
Max. number of connections	10
Nodule fitness components	$\sigma = 0.70, \delta = 0.29,$ $\beta_n = 0.01, n = 10$
Percent. of worst individuals replaced on network population	1.2%

The BP networks had 20 units in the hidden layer, this number was obtained after some trials on different values. The learning parameter has a value of $\eta = 0.2$ and the momentum parameter has a value of $\mu = 0.1$. The training was repeated 10 times on each permutation of the data.

Table 4. Results using PIMA data set. Error rates for training and generalization

Method	Training				Generalization				Structure	
	Ave.	Sd.	Best	Worst	Ave.	Sd.	Best	Worst	Units	Conns.
Symbiont	.2194	.0057	.2101	.2361	.2019	.0179	.1771	.2240	5	38.7
BP	.2735	.0130	.2540	.3040	.2481	.0297	.2083	.3229	20	220

The parameters using Symbiont model are shown on Table 3. The populations were evolved 100 generations. As we can see on Table 4 Symbiont outperformed clearly MLP networks and has also lower variance. The best network generalizes better than it learns, that is an effect that also appears in almost all the bibliography consulted[14][15].

4 Conclusions and Future Work

We have developed a new evolutionary model for the design of artificial neural networks. This model is based on a new idea, the concept of nodule. Instead of trying to evolve whole networks, a task that is not feasible in many problems, we evolve subnetworks (*nodules*) that must cooperate in solving the given task. A population of networks keeps track of the best combinations of nodules for solving the problem.

This model has proved to perform better than standard algorithms in two real problems of classification. Moreover, it has showed better results than the most successful method for training neural networks by means of gradient descent.

As work for the future, our main goals focus on two directions. First, the credit assignment to nodules must be modified to achieve a better fulfillment of the objectives stated above. Second, the combination of modules must enforce the cooperation among them. We have observed that sometimes the cooperation of the nodules is not as good as desired. In those cases, each nodule tries to solve the problem by itself. The result is a poor combination of nodules, and networks with low performance.

It would be also very interesting to carry out a fine tuning of the parameters of the model using an evolutionary strategy. Currently, it is not feasible because of the enormous time that such experiment would spend.

Acknowledgments

The authors would like to acknowledge R. Moya-Sánchez for her helping in the final version of this paper and an anonymous referee for her/his very useful comments.

This work was supported in part by the Project ALI98-0676-CO2-02 of the Spanish Comisión Interministerial de Ciencia y Tecnología.

References

1. Angeline, P. J., Saunder, G. M., and Pollack, J. B. (1994) An evolutionary algorithm that constructs recurrent neural networks. IEEE Transactions on Neural Networks **5**(1), 54–65.
2. Fogel, D. B., (1992) Evolving artificial intelligence. PhD thesis, University of California, San Diego
3. Goldberg, D., Deb., K (1991) A comparative analysis of selection schemes used in genetic algorithms. In Rawlins, G., ed., Foundations of Genetic Algorithms, 94–101, Morgan Kaufmann
4. Hervás, C., Garrido, A., Lucena, B., García-Pedrajas, N., and de Pedro, E. (1994) Near infrared spectroscopy for classification of Iberian pig carcasses using an artificial neural network. Journal of Near Infrared Spectroscopy **2**, 177 – 184
5. Minai, A. A., and Williams, R. D. (1990) Acceleration of back-propagation through learning rate and momentum adaptation. In International Joint Conference on Neural Networks **1**, 676–679
6. Moriarty, D. E. and Miikkulainen, R. (1998) Forming neural networks through efficient and adaptive coevolution. Evolutionary Computation, **4**(5)

7. Potterm, M. A. (1997) The Design and Analysis of a Computational Model of Cooperative Coevolution. PhD thesis, Goerge Mason University, Fairfax, Virginia
8. Rumelhart, D., Hinton, G., and Williams, R. J. (1986) Learning internal representations by error propagation. In D. Rumelhart and J. McClelland, eds., Parallel Distributed Processing, 318–362. MIT Press, Cambridge, MA
9. Smith, J. W., Everhart, J. E., Dickson, W. C., Knowler, W. C., and Johannes, R. S. (1988) Using the ADAP learning algorithm to forecast the onset of diabetes mellitus. In Proceedings of the Symposium on Computer Applications and Medical Care, 261–265. IEEE Computer Society Press
10. Syswerda, G. (1989) uniform crossover in genetic algorithms. In Morgan-Kaufmann, editor, Proc 3rd Int. Conf. on Genetic Algorithms, 2–9
11. Whitley, D. (1989) The genitor algorithm and selective pressure. In Morgan-Kaufmann, editor, Proc 3rd Internation Conf. on Genetic Algorithms, 116–121
12. Whitley, D., and Kauth, J. (1988) Genitor: a different genetic algorithm. In Proceedings of the Rocky Mountain Conference on Artificial Intelligence, 118–130, Denver, CO
13. Yao, X. (1999) Evolving artificial neural networks. Proceedings of the IEEE, **9**(87), 1423–1447
14. Yao, X., and Liu, Y. (1997) A new evolutionary system for evolving artificial neural networks. IEEE Transactions on Neural Networks, **8**(3), 694–713
15. Yao, X., and Liu, Y. (1998) Making use of population information in evolutionary artificial neural networks. IEEE Transactions on Systems, Man, and Cybernetics – Part B: Cybernetics, **28**(3), 417–425

Functional Equivalence between S-neural Networks and Fuzzy Models

Claudio Moraga, Karl-Heinz Temme

Department of Computer Science, Computer Engineering and Computing Education.
University of Dortmund; 44221 Dortmund; Germany
{moraga | temme}@LS1.cs.uni-dortmund.de

Abstract. A family of S-functions is introduced and characterized. S-functions may be used as activation functions in neural networks and allow the interpretation of the activity of the artificial neurons as fuzzy *if-then* rules, where the degree of satisfaction of the premises for a given input is calculated by means of the symmetric summation. These rules are appropriate to model compensating systems.

Introduction

Neural networks based fuzzy modeling is a well established area within Computational Intelligence. Special feedforward networks have been proposed, where the first hidden layers realize the fuzzification -(association of physical crisp inputs to linguistic terms)- and compute the corresponding degree of satisfaction. Further layers compute the fuzzy inference and, if needed, additional layers will cope with defuzzification. Probably one of the best known representatives of this class is the ANFIS system (see Jang (1993), Jang and Sun (1995)) since it is presently included in Matlab®, however similar networks have been discussed in the literature (see *e.g.* Glorennec et al. (1992), Horikawa et al. (1992), Keller et al. (1992), Yi and Oh (1992)). Since the neural network is trained with a gradient descent algorithm, ANFIS-like systems use the product as t-norm conjuncting the premises of a rule in order to preserve differentiability. This is not necessarily the best way to relate premises, since this largely depends on the kind of system under modeling and, moreover, the product may result to be "quite negative" (see below).

Consider, for instance the following rule to decide upon buying books:

*"**If** the author of the book is famous **and** the price is convenient **then** it is recommendable to buy the book"*

If both premises are satisfied to a degree 0.7, then the recommendation to buy the book would have a degree 0.49, which in this context would have the possible interpretation: *"it is doubtful that the book should be bought"*. Furthermore if the first premise is satisfied to a degree 0.7 and the other one, to a degree 0.5, then the recommendation to buy that book would only have a degree 0.35. It becomes apparent that this is not the right model for using the rule as humans would do. The given rule is a typical example where the goal of satisfying both premises may be better expressed by means of an aggregation operator (see e.g. Dubois and Prade (1985)) rather than by a t-norm.

Another important neuro-fuzzy modeling architecture is represented by the NARA system (Takagi and Hayashi (1991), Takagi et al. (1992), Han and Moraga (1996)). In this case a (possibly fuzzy) partition of the problem space is done first and every block of the partition is associated to a conclusion. Every block represents a premise at a high level of abstraction thus avoiding the problem of choosing the proper connectives to relate elementary premises; but the resulting rules may possibly have a difficult interpretation for a human user.

The rest of the chapter is organized as follows. In the next section a new class of activation functions will be discussed and the relationship between the neural networks obtained by using the new activation functions and a related fuzzy rule-based system using aggregation operators will be explained. Furthermore it will be shown, that the present method applied to neural networks makes them appropriate for fuzzy modeling, even if no architectural constraints are introduced. A discussion on some activation functions will close the presentation.

S-Activation Functions

Definition 1:

A function $f: R \rightarrow (0,1)$ is said to be an S-Activation (or simply S-function) if it satisfies the following conditions:

- f is continuous, strictly monotonously increasing and invertible
- $\forall x \in R$, $f(-x) = 1 - f(x)$, (from where $f(0) = 1/2$)
- $\lim_{x \to -\infty} f(x) = 0$; $\lim_{x \to \infty} f(x) = 1$

It becomes apparent that the classical logistic function (see *e.g.* Amari (1968)) is a particular S-Activation function. The same applies to $f(x) = 1/(1+k^{-x})$, $k>1$, real, known as the generalized logistic function (Temme et al. (1999)), the asymmetric Elliot function (Georgiu (1992)) given by $f(x) = ½[1+ x/(1+|x|)]$ and trigonometric functions like *e.g.* $f(x) = 1-(1/\pi)\text{arccot}(x)$. Definition 1 comprises thus a family of "soft step" functions.

Observations:

- f(x) is overall differentiable with respect to x *i.e.* an S-Activation function may be used in neural networks trained with the backpropagation algorithm.
- $\forall x \in R$ f(x) may be interpreted as a right-open fuzzy set.
- f(x) is a *squashing* function (Hornik et al. (1989)). It follows that neural networks with one hidden layer using S-activation functions and an output linear node are universal approximators (Hornik et al. (1989), Funuhashi (1989)).

- f(x) is invertible. It follows that feedforward neural networks using *allover* S-activation functions are also universal approximators (Moraga (1997)).

These last two properties are roughly equivalent to saying that for any physical system there exists at least one neural network of this kind, which can identify the system with arbitrary precision if enough representative performance examples are available.

Definition 2:

A neural network using allover S-activation functions, except possibly at the output node(s), which may be linear, will be called S - neural network (SNN).

Definition 3:

Let f be an S-function. Moreover $\forall\ x_1, x_2 \in R$, let $f(x_1) = v_{x1}$ and $f(x_2) = v_{x2}$. Then:

$$f(x_1) \otimes f(x_2) =_{def} f(\, f^{-1}(v_{x1}) + f^{-1}(v_{x2})\,)$$

is an aggregation operator and f is its generating function.

Lemma 1:

The aggregation operator given in definition 3 has the following properties:

- $\otimes$: $(-\infty, \infty) \rightarrow (0,1)$
- $\otimes$ is associative

$$\left(\bigotimes_{j=1}^{n} f(x_j) = f \sum_{j=1}^{n} f^{-1}(v_{x_j}) \right)$$

- $\otimes$ is commutative
- $\otimes$ is continuous, except at the points (0,1) and (1,0)
- $\otimes$ is strict monotone in $(0,1) \times (0,1)$

Proof: See Theorem 4 in Dombi (1982).

Lemma 2:

$((0,1), \otimes)$ is an Abelian group. Its neutral element is (1/2).

Proof: From Lemma 1, $\otimes$ is associative and commutative. Furthermore

$$f(x + (-x)) = f(0) = 1/2 = f(x) \otimes f(-x) \quad = \quad f(x) \otimes (1 - f(x))$$

i.e. $((0,1), \otimes)$ is an Abelian group with 1/2 as neutral element and the inverse of an element f(x) is given by 1-f(x).

Moreover for argument values in [0, ½] the symmetric summation behaves as a t-norm and for values in [½, 1], as its dual t-conorm. Klement et al. (1996) proved that the former t-norm and t-conorm belong to the Hamacher family (see Hamacher (1978)).

The above given definition 3 supports the following interpretation. Consider a node in the hidden layer of an S - neural network with n inputs. The operation of the node may be expressed as:

$$y = f(w_1x_1 + w_2x_2 + ... + w_nx_n),$$

where w_1 , ..., w_n are real-valued input weights to the node. After definition 3 the operation at the node may also be expressed as

$$y = f(w_1x_1) \otimes f(w_2x_2) \otimes \; ... \; \otimes \; f(w_nx_n)$$

$$\forall \; x_i , w_i \in R \text{ let } f_{w_i}(x_i) =_{def} f(w_ix_i)$$

then

$$y = f_{w_1}(x_1) \otimes f_{w_2}(x_2) \otimes ... \otimes f_{w_n}(x_n).$$

i.e. y is given by an aggregation of fuzzy sets evaluated at x_1, ..., x_n. These fuzzy sets are right-open if the corresponding weights are positive; otherwise they are left-open.

Thus each node of the hidden layer of an SNN *learns* a rule of the form:

if x_1 *is at least* T_1 ***and ... and*** x_n *is at least* T_n ***then***

$$y = f_{w_1}(x_1) \otimes f_{w_2}(x_2) \otimes \; ... \; \otimes f_{w_n}(x_n)$$

where T_j is the linguistic term represented by f_{w_j} and all weights are assumed to be positive. It is fairly obvious that the value of y represents the degree of satisfaction of all premises (of a given rule) under aggregation. Since f(x) is asymptotic to 1, *i.e.* the fuzzy sets are normal in the limit, a reference value has to be agreed upon in order to apply the *"at least"* conditional. Following Benítez et al. (1997), the value of x_j leading to $f_{w_j}(x) = 0.9$ will be taken.

It becomes apparent that an SNN with one hidden layer and a linear output node may be interpreted as an additive fuzzy system (Kosko (1994)). An extension to realize a Takagi-Sugeno type of conclusion (Takagi and Sugeno (1985)) would only require one additional processing node (per rule) to learn the required linear combination of the inputs, scaled by the corresponding degree of satisfaction y. An SNN without architecture constraints other than being feedforward may be interpreted as a fuzzy system possibly comprising chained rules.

Lemma 3: Let x, y, z $\in$ R s.t. x + y = z. Then the inverse of f(z) in the group ((0,1), $\otimes$) is given by the $\otimes$-aggregation of the inverses of f(x) and f(y) respectively.

Proof: $f(-z) = 1 - f(z)$
but $f(-z) = f(-x-y) = f((-x) + (-y))$
then $f(-z) = f(-x) \otimes f(-y)$

Observation:

Let *inv* : $(0,1) \rightarrow (0,1)$ denote the inversion in the group $((0,1), \otimes)$. Then *inv* has the following properties:

- *inv* is continuous
- *inv* is strictly monotonously decreasing
- *inv* is involutive: *inv* (*inv* (f(x))) = f(x)
- 1/2 is the only solution to *inv* (f(x)) = f(x)
- $\lim_{x \to -\infty}$ *inv* (f(x)) = 1; $\lim_{x \to \infty}$ *inv* (f(x)) = 0
- an extension to [0,1] leads to *inv* (0) = 1 and *inv* (1) = 0
- *inv* distributes over $\otimes$. (Lemma 3)

It becomes apparent, that *inv* satisfies all the conditions to be a *strong negation* in fuzzy logic (Alsina et al. (1983))

Corollary 3.1 From the point of view of fuzzy logic, *inv* and $\otimes$ induce a DeMorgan-like symmetric law in the group.

For the fine tuning of an S neural network, some bias signals may be required at the nodes of the hidden layer. In what follows it will be shown, that these net-parameters may be given an adequate interpretation as linguistic modifiers of the corresponding fuzzy expression of the premises.

Consider a node in the hidden layer of an S - neural network with n inputs, where the node has its own bias b. The operation of the node may be expressed as:

$$y = f(w_1x_1 + w_2x_2 + ... + w_nx_n + b)$$

and transformed into

$$y = f_{w_1}(x_1) \otimes f_{w_2}(x_2) \otimes ... \otimes f_{w_n}(x_n) \otimes f(b)$$

Let $u = f_{w_1}(x_1) \otimes f_{w_2}(x_2) \otimes ... \otimes f_{w_n}(x_n)$. It may be seen, that u represents the output of the node without bias and $u \in (0,1)$. Then: $y = u \otimes f(b)$

Define $\Lambda^{(b)}$ to be a linguistic modifier induced by b.

$$\Lambda^{(b)}: (0,1) \rightarrow (0,1) \text{ and } \Lambda^{(b)}(u) =_{def} u \otimes f(b)$$

It follows that $y = \Lambda^{(b)}(u)$, *i.e.* the output of the node with bias may be interpreted as the output of the node without bias modified by $\Lambda^{(b)}$. Since b is a constant (once the node is adjusted), then f(b) will also have a constant value and for all values of u between 0 and 1, f(b) will modify these values of u according to the characteristics of the aggregation operator $\otimes$.

Discussion

It has been shown that a node having an S-activation function computes the aggregation of the degrees of satisfaction of premises for a given input vector. This value may be taken directly as a crisp conclusion or may be used to scale more structured conclusions (learnt in subsequent nodes). The aggregation operator has a unique relationship to the S-activation function. A particular S-activation function may be selected to satisfy predefined optimality criteria, like *e.g.* efficient computability or flexibility. For example, the *generalized logistic function* $f(x) = [1 + k^{-x}]^{-1}$, $k > 1$, real, discussed in Temme et al. (1999) (see Fig. 1) has these properties since

$$\frac{\partial f(x)}{\partial x} = (\ln k) f(x)(1 - f(x))$$

and

$$\frac{\partial f(x)}{\partial k} = \frac{x}{k} f(x)(1 - f(x))$$

i.e. both partial derivatives have roughly the same computation complexity and the value of k may *also* be adjusted within a gradient descent algorithm. For a given topology a neural network using *this* S-activation function converges faster to a minimal error or reaches a smaller error than a classical neural network (where $k = e$ and this value remains constant) within the same number of generations. It becomes apparent that adjustment of k corresponds to an adjustment of the edge of the corresponding fuzzy set. This suggests that a better matching between rules and training data may be obtained.

The aggregation operator generated by the generalized logistic function is given by:

$$f(x) \otimes f(y) = \frac{f(x)f(y)}{inv(f(x))\, inv(f(y)) + f(x)f(y)}$$

This operator is known to be a *symmetric summation* (Silvert (1979)).

If on the other hand a good table look–up possibility is available, then the work with a trigonometric S-function like $g(x) = 1-(1/\pi)\cot^{-1}(vx)$ with $v \geq 1$ and $dg(vx)/dx = v[\pi(1+v^2x^2)]^{-1}$, for instance, could also be considered. (See Fig. 2). This function leads to the following aggregation operator:

$$g(x) \otimes g(y) = 1 - (1/\pi)\cot^{-1}[v(\cot(\pi(inv(g(x))) + \cot(\pi(inv(g(y))))]$$

since $\pi(1 - g(x)) = \cot^{-1}(vx)$ and from lemma 3, $(1 - g(x)) = inv(g(x))$.

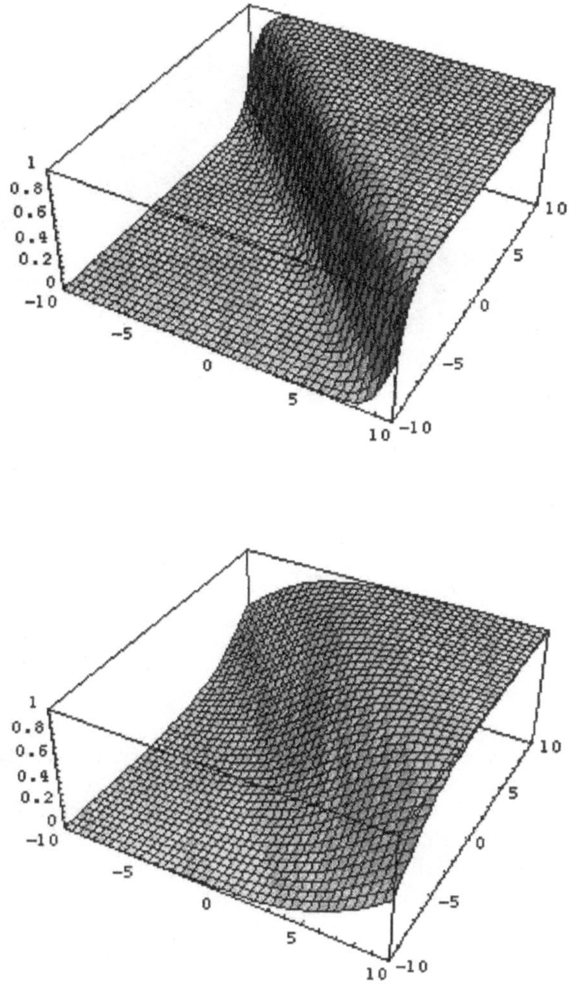

Fig. 1. (top) f(x+y) with k = 5; (bottom) f(x+y) with k = 3/2

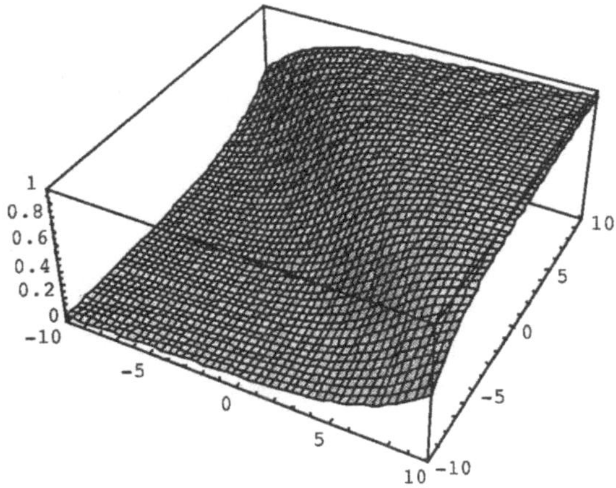

Fig. 2. $g(x+y) = 1 - (1/\pi)\cot^{-1}((1/3)(x+y))$

References

Alsina C., Trillas E., Valverde L. (1983): On some logical connectives for fuzzy sets theory. Jr. of Mathematical Analysis and Applications **93**, 15-26

Amari S. (1968): Geometrical Theory of Information. Kyoritsu-Shuppan, Tokyo

Benítez J.M., Castro J.L., Requena I.(1997): Are neural networks black boxes? IEEE Trans. on Neural Networks **8**, 1156-1163

Dombi J. (1982): Basic concepts for a theory of evaluation: The aggregative operator. European Jr. Operation Research **10**, 282-293

Dubois D., Prade H. (1985): A review of fuzzy set aggregation connectives. Information Sciences **36**, 85-121

Funahashi K.I. (1989): On the approximate realization of continuous mappings by neural networks. Neural Networks **2**, 183–192

Georgiou G.M. (1992): Parallel distributed processing in the complex domain. Ph.D. Thesis, Dept. C. Sc., Tulane University, New Orleans, Lousiana

Glorennec P.Y., Barret C., Brunet M. (1992): Application of Neuro–Fuzzy Networks to identification and control of nonlinear dynamic systems. Proc. Int. Conference on Information Processing and Management of Uncertainty in Knowledge–based Systems (IPMU), 507–510, Palma de Mallorca

Han J., Moraga C. (1996): Parametric Feedforward Network based Adaptive Fuzzy Modeling. Proc. Int. Symp. Intelligent Industrial Automation and Soft Computing, B–159–165, Reading UK, ICSC Academic Press

Horikawa S.I., Furuhashi T., Uchikawa Y. (1992): A new type of Fuzzy Neural Network for Linguistic Fuzzy Modeling. Proc. 2nd. Int. Conference on Fuzzy Logic and Neural Networks. 1053–1056, Iizuka, Japan

Hornik K., Stinchcombe M., White H. (1989): Multilayer Feedforward Networks are universal approximators. Neural Networks **2**, 359–366

Jang J.S.R. (1993): ANFIS: Adaptive Network based Fuzzy Inference System. IEEE Trans. on Systems, Man and Cybernetics **23**, (3), 665–685

Jang J.S.R., Sun C.T. (1995): Neuro–fuzzy Modeling and Control. Proceedings IEEE **83**, (3), 378–406

Klement, P.; Mesiar, R.; Pap, E. (1996): On the relationship of associative compensatory operators to triangular norms and conorms, Int'l Jr. of Uncertainty, Fuzziness and Knowledge-based Systems **4** (2) 129-144

Kosko B. (1994): Fuzzy systems as universal approximators. IEEE Trans. Computers **43**, (11), 1324–1333

Keller J.M., Tager R.R., Tahani H. (1992): Neural Network implementation of fuzzy logic. Fuzzy Sets and Systems **45**, (1), 1–12

Moraga C. (1997): Properties of Parametric Feedforward Networks. Proceedings XXIII Conferencia Latinoamericana de Informática, 861–870, Valparaíso, Chile

Silvert W. (1979): Symmetric summation: A class of operations on fuzzy sets. IEEE Trans. on Systems, Man and Cybernetics **9**, 659-667

Takagi H., Hayashi I. (1991): NN-driven fuzzy reasoning. Int. Journal of Approximate Reasoning **5**, (3), 191–212

Takagi H., Sugeno M. (1985): Fuzzy identification of systems and its application to modeling and control. IEEE Trans. on Systems, Man and Cybernetics **15**, (1), 116-132

Temme K.-H., Heider R., Moraga C. (1999): Generalized neural networks for fuzzy modeling. Proc., Int'l Conference of the European Society of Fuzzy Logic and Technology, EUSFLAT'99, 469-472, Palma de Mallorca, Spain

Takagi H., Susuki N., Koda T., Kojima Y. (1992): Neural Networks designed on approximate reasoning architecture and their applications. IEEE Trans. Neural Networks **3**, (5), 752–760

Yi H.J., Oh K.W. (1992): Neural Network based Fuzzy Production Rule Generation and its application to an Approximate Reasoning Approach. *Proceedings 2nd. Int. Conference on Fuzzy Logic and Neural Networks.* 333–336, Iizuka, Japan

Logic and Logic Based Systems

Towards Mathematical Morpho-Logics

Isabelle Bloch[1] and Jérôme Lang[2]

[1] ENST-TSI, CNRS URA 820, 46 rue Barrault 75013 Paris, France - Isabelle.Bloch@enst.fr

[2] IRIT-UPS, 118 route de Narbonne 31062 Toulouse, France - lang@irit.fr

Abstract. In this paper, we suggest a new way to process information represented in a logical framework based on mathematical morphology. We show how the basic morphological operations can be expressed in a logical setting. We give some properties, show some links with revision and fusion, and ideas illustrate possible use of morpho-logics to approximation, reasoning and decision.

1 Introduction

Mathematical morphology is originally based on set theory. It has been introduced in 1964 by Matheron [16,17], in order to study porous media. But this theory evolved rapidly to a general theory of shape and its transformations, and was applied in particular in image processing and pattern recognition [20]. Additionally to its set theoretical foundations, it also relies on topology on sets, on random sets, on topological algebra, on integral geometry, on lattice theory.

In the knowledge representation community, propositional formulas are used to encode either pieces of knowledge (which may be generic – for instance, integrity constraints – or factual) or "preference items" (such as opinions, desires or goals) and are then used for complex reasoning or decision making tasks. These tasks often make use of operations on propositional formulas which are very similar to those considered in mathematical morphology. We give a (non-exhaustive) list of examples:

- *belief revision* (as shown by Katsuno and Mendelzon [11]) consists of the following operation: let φ and ψ be two propositional formulas. The models of the revision $\varphi \circ \psi$ of φ by ψ are the models of ψ which are closest (with respect to a given distance) to a model of φ. Intuitively, using the language of mathematical morphology, it means that φ has to be dilated enough to intersect with some models of ψ. *Belief update* [11] proceeds to the same kind of dilation but on each individual model of φ and then takes the union of all obtained sets of models.
- *belief merging* [12] consists in finding the best compromise between a finite set of formulas φ_1, ... φ_n, which amounts to selecting the models which minimize the aggregation (using some given operator) of the distances to each of the φ's. This amounts intuitively to dilate simultaneously all the φ's until they intersect. Similar operations are at work for the aggregation of preferences in group decision making as proposed in [14].

- one of the tasks involved in *similarity-based reasoning* [8,7] consists in determining if a formula φ approximatively entails a formula ψ by looking to what extent ψ has to be extended so as to contain all models of φ, which again corresponds to a dilation.
- *reasoning with supermodels* [9] uses models of a formula φ which are robust enough to resist some perturbations. In some cases, obtaining supermodels consists in eroding the formula so as to be far enough from the countermodels of φ. Again this corresponds to a classical operation of mathematical morphology (erosion). Another close notion, evoked in [14], is the search for the most representative worlds of a formula.
- in *abductive reasoning* [18], preferred explanations of a formula are defined based on a set of axioms, several of which being closed to properties of morphological operators.

Our aim is therefore to investigate how and why mathematical morphology can be applied on logical formulas. First we note that the fact that a propositional formula can be equivalently defined by the set of its models enables us to apply easily all (set-theoretic) definitions of mathematical morphology to logical objects (worlds, formulas). This will lead us not only to rewriting well-known logical operations used for reasoning or decision making, but also to designing new kinds of logical objects or notions by transposing basic morphological operations to propositional logic. There are two ways of doing that: first, one may define modal logics from mathematical morphology, by establishing links between accessibility relations and structuring elements, and constructing modal operators $\Box$ and $\Diamond$ from erosion and dilation for instance [4] (based for instance on links between morphological operators and approximation operators in the theory of rough sets [3]). Second, one may view morphological operators as transformations on formulas. Here we choose to explore the latter way for reasoning or decision making, etc.

In Section 2, we introduce some notations and logical concepts that are used throughout the paper. In Section 3 we propose definitions for dilation and erosion of logical formulas, by extending these two fundamental morphological operations to the logical framework. We also list some properties, and give some applications for fusion, revision, and specifying formulas. In Section 4, we define opening and closing on formulas, and give some properties and interpretations for approximating and filtering formulas. In Section 5 we provide a few simple examples showing the effects of these four operations. In Section 6, we suggest a few other operations acting on a formula.

2 Basic logical concepts

Let PS be a finite set of propositional symbols. $PROP_{PS}$ is the propositional language generated by PS and the usual connectives. Well-formed formulas of $PROP_{PS}$ will be denoted by Greek letters φ, ψ... Interpretations will be denoted by ω, ω' and the set of all interpretations for $PROP_{PS}$ by Ω_{PS}. $Mod(\varphi) = \{\omega \in \Omega_{PS} \mid \omega \models \varphi\}$ is the set of all models of φ (i.e. all interpretations for which φ is true).

The underlying idea for constructing morphological operations on logical formulas is to consider set interpretations of formulas and interpretations. Since $PROP_{PS}$ is isomorphic to $2^{\Omega_{PS}}$, i.e., knowing a formula is equivalent to knowing the set of its models, we can identify φ with the set of its models $Mod(\varphi)$, and then apply set-theoretic morphological operations. We recall that $Mod(\varphi \vee \psi) = Mod(\varphi) \cup Mod(\psi)$, $Mod(\varphi \wedge \psi) = Mod(\varphi) \cap Mod(\psi)$, and $Mod(\varphi) \subset Mod(\psi)$ iff $\varphi \models \psi$.

3 Dilation and erosion

3.1 Definitions

Let us first recall the definitions of dilation and erosion of a set X by a structuring element B in $\mathbb{R}^n$, denoted respectively by $D_B(X)$ and $E_B(X)$:

$$D_B(X) = \{x \in \mathbb{R}^n \mid B_x \cap X \neq \emptyset\}, \tag{1}$$

$$E_B(X) = \{x \in \mathbb{R}^n \mid B_x \subset X\}, \tag{2}$$

where B_x denotes the translation of B at x,

In these equations, B defines a neighborhood that is considered at each point. It can also be seen as a relationship between points.

Using the previous equivalences, we propose to define dilation and erosion of a formula as follows:

$$Mod(D_B(\varphi)) = \{\omega \in \Omega_{PS} \mid B_\omega \wedge \varphi \textit{ consistent}\}, \tag{3}$$

$$Mod(E_B(\varphi)) = \{\omega \in \Omega_{PS} \mid B_\omega \models \varphi\}. \tag{4}$$

In these equations, the structuring element B represents a relationship between worlds, i.e. $\omega' \in B_\omega$ iff ω' satisfies some relationship with ω. The condition in Equation 3 expresses that the set of worlds in relation to ω should be consistent with φ. The condition in Equation 4 is stronger and expresses that all worlds in relation to ω should be models of φ.

3.2 Structuring element

There are several possible ways to define structuring elements in a context of formulas. We suggest here a few ones. The relationship defined in the previous section can be any relationship between worlds. It defines a "neighborhood" of worlds. If it is symmetrical, it leads to symmetrical structuring elements. If it is reflexive, it leads to structuring elements such that $\omega \in B_\omega$, which leads to interesting properties, as will be seen later. For instance, this relationship can be an accessibility relation as in normal modal logics [10]. An interesting way to choose the relationship is to base it on distances between worlds. This allows to define sequences of increasing structuring elements defined as the balls of a distance. From any distance δ between worlds, a distance from a world to a formula is derived as a distance from a point to a set: $d(\omega, \varphi) = \min_{\omega' \models \varphi} \delta(\omega, \omega')$.

The most commonly used distance between worlds in knowledge representation (especially in belief revision [6], belief update [11], merging [12] or preference representation [14]) is the Hamming distance d_H where $d_H(\omega, \omega')$ is the number of propositional symbols that are instantiated differently in both worlds. By default, we take δ to be d_H.

Then dilation and erosion of size n are defined from Equations 3 and 4 by using the distance balls of radius n as structuring elements:

$$Mod(D^n(\varphi)) = \{\omega \mid \exists \omega', \omega' \models \varphi \text{ and } d_H(\omega, \omega') \leq n\} = \{\omega \mid d(\omega, \varphi) \leq n\}, \tag{5}$$

$$Mod(E^n(\varphi)) = \{\omega \mid \forall \omega', d_H(\omega, \omega') \leq n \Rightarrow \omega' \models \varphi\} = \{\omega \mid d(\omega, \neg\varphi) > n\}. \tag{6}$$

From operations with the unit ball we define the external (respectively internal) boundary of φ as $D^1(\varphi) \wedge \neg\varphi$ (respectively $\varphi \wedge \neg E^1(\varphi)$), corresponding to the worlds that are exactly at distance 1 of φ (resp. of $\neg\varphi$).

3.3 Properties

The main properties of dilation and erosion, which are satisfied in mathematical morphology on sets, hold also in the logical setting proposed here. They are summarized below. The proofs are not given here, but they are straightforward based on set/logic equivalences.

Monotonicity: Both operators are increasing with respect to φ, i.e. if $\varphi \models \psi$, then $D_B(\varphi) \models D_B(\psi)$ and $E_B(\varphi) \models E_B(\psi)$, for any structuring element B. Dilation is increasing with respect to the structuring element, while erosion is decreasing, i.e. if $\forall \omega \in \Omega_{PS}, B_\omega \subset B'_\omega$, then $D_B(\varphi) \models D_{B'}(\varphi)$ and $E_{B'}(\varphi) \models E_B(\varphi)$.

Extensivity: Dilation is extensive ($\varphi \models D_B(\varphi)$) if B is derived from a reflexive relation (as is the case for distance based dilation, since if $\omega \models \varphi$, then $d(\omega, \varphi) = 0$), and erosion is anti-extensive ($E_B(\varphi) \models \varphi$) under the same conditions.

Iteration: Dilation and erosion satisfy an iteration property. For instance for distance based operations, we have:

$$D^{n+n'}(\varphi) = D^{n'}[D^n(\varphi)] = D^n[D^{n'}(\varphi)],$$

$$E^{n+n'}(\varphi) = E^{n'}[E^n(\varphi)] = E^n[E^{n'}(\varphi)].$$

This means that the effects of these operations increase with the size of the structuring element, and that the computation can be done either by successive applications of "small" structuring elements or directly by the sum of the structuring elements.

Commutativity with union or intersection: Dilation commutes with union or disjunction (this is a fundamental property of dilation[1]): for any family $\varphi_1, ...\varphi_m$ of formulas, we have: $D_B(\vee_{i=1}^m \varphi_i) = \vee_{i=1}^m D_B(\varphi_i)$. Erosion on the other hand commutes with intersection or conjunction.

In general dilation (resp. erosion) does not commute with intersection (resp. union), and only an inclusion relation holds: $D_B(\varphi \wedge \psi) \models D_B(\varphi) \wedge D_B(\psi)$.

Adjunction relation: (E_B, D_B) is an adjunction[2], i.e. $D_B(\psi) \models \varphi$ iff $\psi \models E_B(\varphi)$.

Duality: Dilation and erosion (respectively opening and closing) are dual operators with respect to the negation: $E_B(\varphi) = \neg D_B(\neg\varphi)$ which allows to deduce properties of an operator from those of its dual operator.

Relations to distances: Equation 5 shows how to derive a dilation from a distance. Conversely, we have: $d(\omega, \varphi) = \min\{n \in \mathbb{N} \mid \omega \models D^n(\varphi)\}$, and similarly, we have $d(\omega, \neg\varphi) = \min\{n \in \mathbb{N} \mid \omega \models \neg E^n(\varphi)\}$.

Distances between formulas can also be derived from dilation, as minimum distance and Hausdorff distance. For instance the minimum distance is expressed as: $d_{min}(\varphi, \psi) = \min_{\omega \models \varphi, \omega' \models \psi} d_H(\omega, \omega') = \min\{n \in \mathbb{N} \mid D^n(\varphi) \wedge \psi \neq \emptyset \textit{ and } D^n(\psi) \wedge \varphi \neq \emptyset\}$. This means that the minimum distance is attained for the minimum size of dilation of both formulas such that they become consistent.

Examples of dilations of erosions are shown in Section 5.

3.4 Computational complexity

The commutation of dilation with disjunction, along with the iteration property, allows to recover results of [14]. In particular, when φ is a consistent conjunction of literals, i.e., $\varphi = l_1 \wedge l_2 \wedge ... \wedge l_n$, then

$$D^1(\varphi) = \vee_{j=1}^n (\wedge_{i \neq j} l_i).$$

This property, together with the commutation of dilation with disjunction, gives the following result [14]: if k is a fixed integer, then the dilation of

[1] More generally a dilation in a complete lattice is defined as an operator that commutes with union.

[2] Moreover, if two operators form an adjunction there are an erosion and a dilation respectively.

size k $D^k(\varphi)$ of a DNF formula φ can be computed in time $\mathcal{O}(n^k)$ – thus in polynomial time. In a similar way, erosion commutes with intersection and can be computed in polynomial time from a CNF formula.

When φ is not under DNF, computing $D^k(\varphi)$ directly from φ (without rewriting φ under DNF first) is a difficult problem that we leave for further research. Note that, however, inference from the dilation of a formula is (theoretically) not harder than inference from the formula itself. Namely, given any two formulas φ and ψ and any integer k, determining whether $D^k(\varphi) \models \psi$ is coNP-complete[3]. Obviously, a similar result holds for inference from erosion.

3.5 Fusion and revision from dilation

Interestingly, belief revision and belief fusion operators can be recovered from dilations.

We start with some basics about belief revision. A *faithful assignment* [11] is a mapping which associates to each formula φ a preorder $\leq_\varphi$ on Ω_{PS} such that (1) if $\omega \models \varphi$ and $\omega' \models \varphi$ then $\omega \sim_\varphi \omega'$; (2) if $\omega \models \varphi$ and $\omega' \models \neg\varphi$ then $\omega <_\varphi \omega'$; (3) if $\models \varphi_1 \leftrightarrow \varphi_2$ then $\leq_{\varphi_1} = \leq_{\varphi_2}$. As shown by Katsuno and Mendelzon, a revision operator $\circ$ satisfies the "AGM" postulates [1] iff there exists a faithful assignment that maps each formula φ to a total preorder $\leq_\varphi$ such that for every propositional formula μ we have $Mod(\varphi \circ \mu) = \min(Mod(\mu), \leq_\varphi)$[4]. The preorder $\leq_\varphi$ expresses the distance of a world ω relatively to φ, i.e., $\omega \leq_\varphi \omega'$ means that ω is closer to φ than ω'. Therefore, a faithful assignment can be defined from a distance d from a world to a formula in the following way: $\omega \leq_\varphi \omega'$ iff $d(\omega, \varphi) \leq d(\omega', \varphi)$. In particular, the revision operator induced by the choice of the distance d_H is known as Dalal's revision operator. Now, it can be easily seen that $\varphi \circ \psi = D^n(\varphi) \wedge \psi$, with $n = \min\{k \in \mathbb{N} \mid D^k(\varphi) \wedge \psi \text{ is consistent}\}$.

We now recall some basics about belief fusion as defined by Konieczny and Pino-Pérez [12]. If d is a distance function from an interpretation to a formula, the Δ_{max} quasi-fusion of the m formulas $\varphi_1, \ldots, \varphi_m$ is defined by: $Mod(\Delta_{max}(\{\varphi_1, \ldots, \varphi_m\})) = \min(\Omega_{PS}, \leq_{\{\varphi_1,\ldots,\varphi_m\}})$ where $\omega \leq_{\{\varphi_1,\ldots,\varphi_m\}}$

[3] Here is a sketch of the proof: first, we have that $D^k(\varphi) \not\models \psi$ iff $\exists \omega \models D^k(\varphi)$ s.t. $\omega \models \neg\psi$, and second, $\omega \models D^k(\varphi)$ iff there is a world $\omega' \models \varphi$ such that $d(\omega, \omega') \leq k$. This leads us to the following nondeterministic algorithm: *1. guess two interpretations ω and ω'; 2. check that $d(\omega,\omega') \leq k$; 3. check that $\omega' \models \varphi$; 4. check that $\omega \models \neg\psi$.* This nondeterministic polynomial algorithm shows the membership of the complementary problem of INFERENCE FROM DILATION to NP, hence, INFERENCE FROM DILATION is in coNP. As to hardness, it is proved by the following polynomial reduction from UNSAT to INFERENCE FROM DILATION: a formula φ is in UNSAT iff $D^k(\varphi) \models new$, where *new* is a propositional variable not appearing in φ.

[4] The notation $\min(A, \leq)$ where $\leq$ is a total preorder, stands for $\{\omega \in A \mid \forall \omega' \in A, \omega \leq \omega'\}$.

ω' iff $\max_{i=1..m} d(\omega, \varphi_i) \leq \max_{i=1..m} d(\omega', \varphi_i)$. It can be easily seen that $\Delta_{max}(\varphi_1, ..., \varphi_m) = D^n(\varphi_1) \wedge D^n(\varphi_2) \wedge ... \wedge D^n(\varphi_m)$, where $n = \min\{k \in \mathbb{N} \mid D^k(\varphi_1) \wedge ... \wedge D^k(\varphi_n)$ is consistent$\}$.

3.6 Ultimate erosion

In some problems, it might be interesting to find the most pertinent worlds that are models of a formula. This problem is solved in [14] by taking the absolute maximum of the internal distance function (i.e. the function that associates to each world its distance to $\neg\varphi$). Mathematical morphology offers other tools that could also be interesting. Ultimate erosion is one of them. It consists in eroding iteratively φ and, at each step n, keeping the connected components of $E^n(\varphi)$ that disappear in $E^{n+1}(\varphi)$. It corresponds exactly to the regional maxima of the internal distance. In the first approach (absolute maximum), the result is the most restrictive. It gives the center of the largest component of φ, and if φ is not connected, the other components are not represented. On the contrary the second approach (ultimate erosion) provides several components, which represent all parts of φ, belonging to different connected components, or connected by narrow sets of worlds. It could be interesting to relate this approach to the notions of supermodels [9] and of preferred explanations [18]. For instance, it is easy to prove that $\omega \models E^k(\varphi)$ iff ω is a $(k, 0)$-supermodel of φ.

Another solution to this problem is provided by the morphological skeleton, as shown in Section 6.

4 Opening and closing

4.1 Definitions

Let B be any structuring element, and $\check{B}$ its symmetrical (they are different only in case of non symmetrical relation). Opening and closing of a formula φ by B are defined respectively as:

$$O_B(\varphi) = D_{\check{B}}(E_B(\varphi)), \tag{7}$$

$$C_B(\varphi) = E_{\check{B}}(D_B(\varphi)). \tag{8}$$

4.2 Properties

Monotonicity: Opening and closing are both increasing with respect to φ, for any structuring element. Opening is decreasing with respect to the structuring element, while closing is increasing.

Extensivity and anti-extensivity: Closing is extensive and opening is anti-extensive for any structuring element. This is proved by the fact that opening can be written as[5]:

$$Mod(O_B(\varphi)) = \bigvee\{B_\omega \mid \omega \in \Omega_{PS},\ B_\omega \models \varphi\}.$$

Idempotence: Contrary to dilation and erosion which satisfy iterativity properties, opening and closing are idempotent operators, i.e. $O_B[O_B(\varphi)] = O_B(\varphi)$ and $C_B[C_B(\varphi)] = C_B(\varphi)$[6]. Moreover, for distance based operations we have:

$$O^n[O^{n'}(\varphi)] = O^{n'}[O^n(\varphi)] = O^{\max(n,n')}(\varphi),$$

$$C^n[C^{n'}(\varphi)] = C^{n'}[C^n(\varphi)] = C^{\max(n,n')}(\varphi).$$

Duality: Opening and closing are dual operators with respect to the negation: $O_B(\varphi) = \neg C_B(\neg\varphi)$.

4.3 Approximation from opening and closing

The two basic morphological filters[7] are opening and closing. They can be seen as approximation operators, since they "simplify" formulas by either suppressing some irregularities for opening, or adding some parts of $\neg\varphi$ for closing (see examples in Section 5). Families of filters can be built from these two ones. For instance, granulometry [20] consists in applying successively openings with structuring elements of increasing size, such decomposing a formula in parts of different characteristic sizes. Another example is alternate sequential filters [21], which consist in building sequences of opening/closing (or closing/opening), with structuring elements of increasing size. Such transformations are increasing and idempotent, and allow to filter progressively parts of φ and $\neg\varphi$.

5 Examples

In this Section, we show a few simple examples illustrating the four basic morphological operations. We make use of a graph representation of worlds, where each node represents a world and a link represents an elementary connection between two worlds, i.e. being at distance 1 from each other. We also introduce the notion of connectedness of a formula.

---

5 Indeed, we have $\omega \models O_B(\varphi)$ iff $\check{B}_\omega \wedge E_B(\varphi)$ is consistent. Let $\omega' \models \check{B}_\omega \wedge E_B(\varphi)$. $\omega' \models \check{B}_\omega$ is equivalent to $\omega \models B_{\omega'}$. And $\omega' \models E_B(\varphi)$ is equivalent to $B_{\omega'} \models \varphi$, qed.

6 Anti-extensivity of opening guarantees that $O_B[O_B(\varphi)] \models O_B(\varphi)$. Moreover, we have (ignoring the subscript for simplicity) $O[O(\varphi)] = D[C[E(\varphi)]]$. Since closing is extensive, we have $E(\varphi) \models C[E(\varphi)]$. Since dilation is increasing, we have $D[E(\varphi)] \models D[C[E(\varphi)]]$, i.e. $O(\varphi) \models O[O(\varphi)]$, qed.

7 A morphological filter is an increasing and idempotent operator.

Connectedness: A formula φ is said to be connected iff: $\forall(\omega, \omega') \in \Omega^2_{PS}$ such that $\omega \models \varphi$ and $\omega' \models \varphi$, there exists a sequence of ω_i, $i = 0...m$, such that $\forall i, \omega_i \models \varphi$, $\omega_0 = \omega$, $\omega_m = \omega'$, and $\forall i < m, d_H(\omega_i, \omega_{i+1}) = 1$. This means that there is a path from any model of φ to any other model that is obtained by changing one propositional symbol at each step, while remaining in $Mod(\varphi)$.

Using the graph representation, a connected formula is a connected component of the graph, in the usual graph theoretical sense. A ball of radius 1 centered at ω is constituted by ω and the extremities of the arcs originating in ω. This allows for an easy visualization of the effects of transformations, but is not tractable from a computational point of view if $|\Omega_{PS}|$ is high. Typically, if $|PS| = n$, then the graph has $|\Omega_{PS}| = 2^n$ nodes, and each node has n arcs (if all worlds are considered to be admissible or physically possible).

Let us consider an example with three propositional symbols a, b, c. The possible worlds are represented in Figure 1.

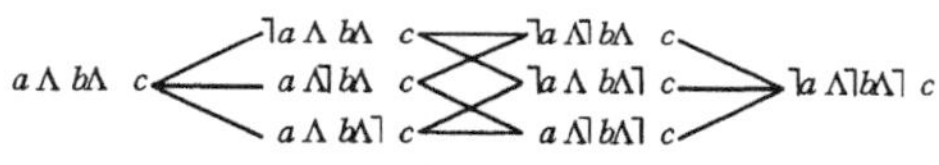

Fig. 1. Graph representation of possible worlds with 3 symbols. An arc between two nodes ω and ω' means that $d_H(\omega, \omega') = 1$.

Let us consider $\varphi = \neg a \wedge b \wedge c$. Then we have:

$$D^1(\varphi) = (\neg a \wedge b) \vee (\neg a \wedge c) \vee (b \wedge c),$$

$$D^2(\varphi) = \neg a \vee b \vee c = \neg(a \wedge \neg b \wedge \neg c).$$

These results are illustrated in Figure 2. They show the extensivity of dilation, and the iteration property ($D^1(D^1(\varphi)) = D^2(\varphi)$). On this example, the external boundary of φ is not connected:

$$D^1(\varphi) \wedge \neg\varphi = (a \wedge b \wedge c) \vee (\neg a \wedge \neg b \wedge c) \vee (\neg a \wedge b \wedge \neg c).$$

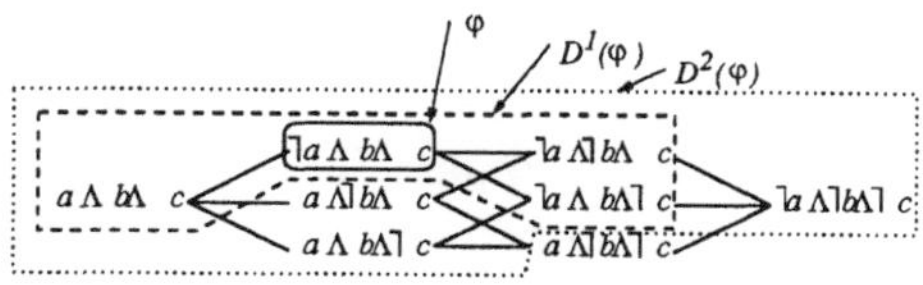

Fig. 2. An example of φ and two successive dilations.

One of the interesting effects of dilation is that it connects formulas if their components are separated by a size less than the size of the structuring element. Let us take for example the following non connected formula:

$$\varphi = (a \wedge b \wedge c) \vee (\neg a \wedge \neg b \wedge c) \vee (\neg a \wedge b \wedge \neg c).$$

Then we have:

$$D^1(\varphi) = \neg a \vee b \vee c = \neg(a \wedge \neg b \wedge \neg c),$$

which is connected. For instance, $\neg a \wedge b \wedge c$ is at distance 1 of both $a \wedge b \wedge c$ and $\neg a \wedge \neg b \wedge c$, and the addition of this world in the dilation connects these two parts of φ. In a similar way, it connects $\neg a \wedge \neg b \wedge c$ and $\neg a \wedge b \wedge \neg c$ (see Figures 1 and 2).

In a similar way, dilation fills holes of φ (connected components of $\neg\varphi$) which are smaller than the structuring element.

By duality, we have the opposite effects for erosion: it reduces the number of worlds that are models of φ, it may disconnect a formula, or even suppress small components (smaller than the structuring element).

Let us now consider opening. Opening is a morphological filter (defined as an increasing and idempotent operator). To show the filtering effect, we consider the example in Figure 3, where:

$$\varphi = (\neg a \wedge b) \vee (\neg a \wedge c) \vee (b \wedge c) \vee (\neg a \wedge \neg b \wedge \neg c),$$

$$E^1(\varphi) = \neg a \wedge b \wedge c,$$

$$O^1(\varphi) = D^1[E^2(\varphi)] = (\neg a \wedge b) \vee (\neg a \wedge c) \vee (b \wedge c).$$

This illustrates the anti-extensivity of opening. The part $\neg a \wedge \neg b \wedge \neg c$ has been filtered out by the opening, and the result is more regular than φ in the sense that it can be covered by distance balls of radius 1 without intersection with its negation (in this example, there is only one such ball, centered at $\neg a \wedge b \wedge c$). Similarly, it may disconnect formulas by suppressing "narrow" parts of it.

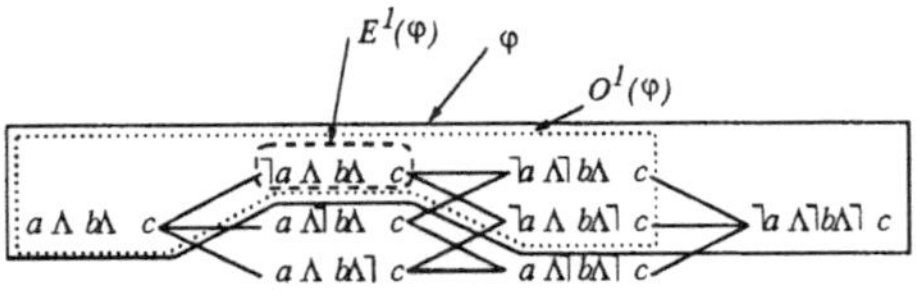

Fig. 3. An example of opening.

If we apply again the opening operation, it does not change anything (idempotence property). This can be interpreted as follows: once parts of φ smaller than the structuring element have been removed, the other remaining unchanged, there are no more such parts, and a second application of the same transformation (with the same structuring element) has no effect.

By duality, closing is extensive, and connects parts of φ if the separation between them is smaller than the structuring element. This is illustrated in Figure 4, where:

$$\varphi = (a \wedge b \wedge c) \vee (\neg a \wedge \neg b \wedge c) \vee (\neg a \wedge b \wedge \neg c),$$

$$D^1(\varphi) = \neg a \vee b \vee c = \neg(a \wedge \neg b \wedge \neg c),$$

$$C^1(\varphi) = E^1[D^1(\varphi)] = (\neg a \wedge b) \vee (\neg a \wedge c) \vee (b \wedge c).$$

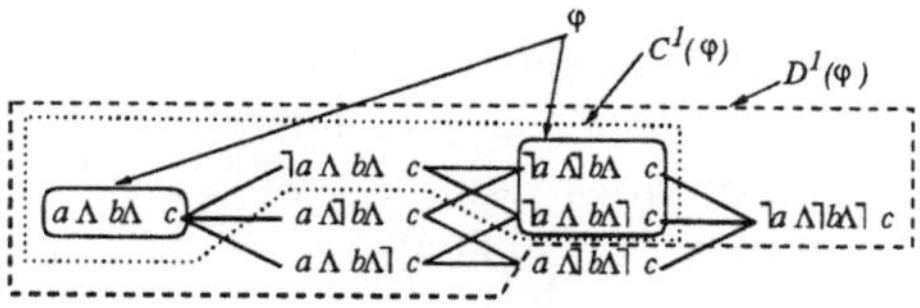

Fig. 4. An example of closing.

It is easy to check on this example the idempotence property of closing.

6 Some derived operators

In this Section, we give some ideas on other operators. These are just a few examples, that need to be completed.

Conditioning and reconstruction: First, we consider problems for which transformations have to be done subject to some constraints (e.g. integrity constraints). Mathematical morphology provides useful tools for this, which are geodesic or conditional operations [20,21,19,15]. Let us take the example of dilation. A geodesic dilation is defined in classical morphology by replacing the distance ball by a geodesic distance ball. In the discrete case, it amounts to taking the intersection of the dilation by the conditioning set. Translating this property to the logical framework, we define a geodesic dilation of φ conditionally to ψ by: $D^n_\psi(\varphi) = [D^1(\varphi) \wedge \psi]^n$, where the supscript n means that the operation of dilation/conjunction is iterated n times. This constraints the result to satisfy ψ. For instance ψ can represent integrity constraints (as in [13]), or a restriction of allowed worlds, etc.

If this conditional operation is iterated until convergence (achieved in a finite number of steps if Ω_{PS} is finite), this defines a morphological reconstruction $D^\infty_\psi(\varphi)$. The result is exactly equal to the connected components of φ that are consistent with ψ. This allows to find all models of φ which are connected to models of ψ. For instance, it allows to restrict preferences expressed by φ in order to make them consistent with ψ, the result being maximum for this property. ψ can represent other preferences, or constraints (but less strict than integrity constraints). While conditional operations lead to complete satisfaction of constraints, reconstruction leads only to consistency with constraints.

Skeleton: Another morphological approach for simplifying a formula and retaining only its most significant parts is the skeleton. In a continuous space, the skeleton of a set is defined as the centers of maximal balls included in the set [20,21]. The centers of maximal balls of radius n can be computed by taking the difference between the erosion of size n and its opening by a ball of radius going towards 0. In the discrete case, this opening is performed with a ball of radius 1, at the cost of lost of homotopy. We define a maximal ball included in φ as follows: a ball $B^n(\omega)$ of radius n centered at ω is maximal iff $B^n(\omega) \models \varphi$, and there do not exist ω', n' with $(\omega, n) \neq (\omega', n')$ such that $B^{n'}(\omega') \models \varphi$ and $B^n(\omega) \models B^{n'}(\omega')$. The skeleton of φ is then defined as:

$$Mod(Skel(\varphi)) = \{\omega \in \Omega_{PS} \mid \exists n \in \mathbb{N},\ B^n(\omega)\ maximal\ in\ \varphi\}. \tag{9}$$

One interesting property of this definition is that it is invertible, and φ can be reconstructed from its skeleton: $\varphi = \vee_n D^n(\psi_n)$ where ψ_n is the set of centers of maximal balls of radius n ($Skel(\varphi) = \vee_n \psi_n$). ψ_n is computed by: $\psi_n = E^n(\varphi) \wedge \neg O^1[E^n(\varphi)]$.

Let us consider again the example of Figure 1, and take:

$$\varphi = (\neg a \wedge b) \vee (\neg a \wedge c) \vee (b \wedge c) \vee (\neg a \wedge \neg b \wedge \neg c).$$

We have:

$$\begin{aligned} E^0(\varphi) &= \varphi, \\ O^1[E^0(\varphi)] &= (\neg a \wedge b) \vee (\neg a \wedge c) \vee (b \wedge c), \\ E^1(\varphi) &= \neg a \wedge b \wedge c, \\ Mod(O^1[E^1(\varphi)]) &= \emptyset. \end{aligned}$$

Therefore, $\psi_0 = \neg a \wedge \neg b \wedge \neg c$, $\psi_1 = \neg a \wedge b \wedge c$, and there is no maximal ball of radius greater than 1 in φ. Finally, we obtain:

$$Skel(\varphi) = (\neg a \wedge \neg b \wedge \neg c) \vee (\neg a \wedge b \wedge c).$$

The first term corresponds to the "irregularity" of φ (which had been filtered by opening in Figure 3), and the second one corresponds to the central part of $(\neg a \wedge b) \vee (\neg a \wedge c) \vee (b \wedge c)$ (see Figure 5). This is an example where the resulting skeleton is not connected, although φ is.

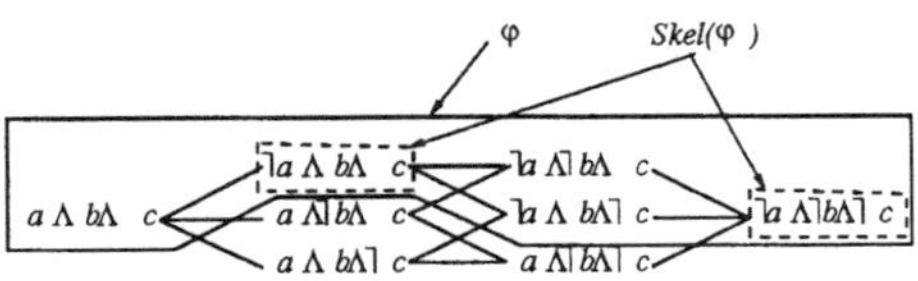

Fig. 5. An example of skeleton.

The skeleton obtained by this approach represents all parts of the formula, and may have branches representing irregularities at the boundary of φ. It can be filtered e.g. by suppressing centers of maximal balls with a small radius (i.e. applying the skeleton on an erosion of φ), or by first opening the formula to filter out non significant parts before computing the skeleton.

Homotopic skeletons can be obtained by other morphological transformations, called thinning. This is left for future work.

Other operators, acting on set of formulas, can be derived from morphological operators. They can be used in various problems in knowledge representation such as fusion, revision, update, etc. They are not detailed here.

7 Conclusion

We have defined in this paper the bases for morpho-logics, at the cross-road between mathematical morphology and formal logic, two domains that to our knowledge were so far completed disconnected. We have shown how to define basic morphological operators on logical formulas, and how these operators can be used in knowledge representation, reasoning and decision making.

Future work is threefold. First, further morphological operators can be investigated in a logical setting. Such operators are connected operators that consider connected components as entities and process them as such, hit-or-miss transformations and derived thinning and thickening (which allow to test a neighborhood of a world not only against φ, but partly against φ and partly against $\neg\varphi$, leading to other types of transformation like homotopic skeleton, convex hull etc.), watershed (for instance to separate the main components of a connected formulas, or finding zones of influence of several connected components), etc. Also the more general lattice framework for mathematical morphology can be exploited on the lattice structure of formulas and interpretations, based on the fundamental adjunction relation.

Second, other ways of logical processing of knowledge and information can be investigated. New operators for merging, fusion, finding compromises, negotiations, etc. can be constructed from morphological operators. Other types of distance can also be used, like geodesic distances or distances based on actions and plans. Another promising extension of our work concerns similarity-based reasoning [8,7]: some approximate entailments have links with morphological operations, either using binary morphology as in this paper, or its extensions to functions [20] or to fuzzy sets [5].

Last, computational aspects of propositional morphological operators deserve some attention. Since the cardinal of Ω_{PS} is exponentially large in the size of the input, it is generally not reasonable to work explicitely on the interpretations but on the formulas, possibly put in a specific normal form (as for DNF for dilation). Bailleux and Marquis [2] have studied the problem DISTANCE-SAT consisting in finding a model of a formula φ close enough to a given partial interpretation. This work is probably a first step towards the practical computation of dilations and erosions induced by distances.

References

1. C. E. Alchourrón, P. Gärdenfors, and D. Makinson. On the Logic of Theory Change: Partial Meet Contraction and Revision Functions. *Journal of Symbolic Logic*, 50:510–530, 1985.
2. O. Bailleux and P. Marquis. DISTANCE-SAT: Complexity and Algorithms. In *National Conference on Artificial Intelligence AAAI'99*, pages 642–647, 1999.
3. I. Bloch. On Links between Mathematical Morphology and Rough Sets. *Pattern Recognition*, 33(9):1487–1496, 2000.
4. I. Bloch. Using Mathematical Morphology Operators as Modal Operators for Spatial Reasoning. In *ECAI 2000, Workshop on Spatio-Temporal Reasoning*, pages 73–79, Berlin, Germany, 2000.
5. I. Bloch and H. Maître. Fuzzy Mathematical Morphologies: A Comparative Study. *Pattern Recognition*, 28(9):1341–1387, 1995.
6. M. Dalal. Investigations into a Theory of Knowledge Base Revision: Preliminary Report. In *AAAI'88*, pages 475–479, 1988.
7. D. Dubois, F. Esteva, P. Garcia, L. Godo, and H. Prade. A Logical Approach to Interpolation based on Similarity Relations. *International Journal of Approximate Reasoning*, 17(1):1–36, 1997.
8. F. Esteva, P. Garcia, and L. Godo. A Modal Account of Similarity-Based Reasoning. *International Journal of Approximate Reasoning*, 16:235–260, 1997.
9. M. L. Ginsberg, A. J. Parkes, and A. Roy. Supermodels and Robustness. In *Fifteenth National Conference on Artificial Intelligence AAAI'98*, pages 334–339, Madison, Wisconsin, July 1998.
10. G. E. Hughes and M. J. Cresswell. *An Introduction to Modal Logic*. Methuen, London, UK, 1968.
11. H. Katsuno and A. O. Mendelzon. Propositional Kowledge Base Revision and Minimal Change. *Artificial Intelligence*, 52:263–294, 1991.
12. S. Konieczny and R. Pino-Pérez. On the Logic of Merging. In *6th International Conference on Principles of Knowledge Representation and Reasoning*, pages 488–498, Trento, Italy, 1998.
13. S. Konieczny and R. Pino-Pérez. Merging with Integrity Constraints. In A. Hunter and S. Parsons, editors, *ECSQARU'99*, volume 1638 of *LNCS*, pages 232–244, London, July 1999. Springer.
14. C. Lafage and J. Lang. Représentation logique de préférences pour la décision de groupe. In *RFIA 2000*, volume III, pages 267–276, Paris, France, February 2000.
15. C. Lantuejoul and F. Maisonneuve. Geodesic Methods in Image Analysis. *Pattern Recognition*, 17(2):177–187, 1984.
16. G. Matheron. *Eléments pour une théorie des milieux poreux*. Masson, Paris, 1967.
17. G. Matheron. *Random Sets and Integral Geometry*. Wiley, New-York, 1975.
18. R. Pino-Pérez and C. Uzcátegui. Jumping to Explanations versus jumping to Conclusions. *Artificial Intelligence*, 111:131–169, 1999.
19. M. Schmitt and J. Mattioli. *Morphologie mathématique*. Masson, Paris, 1994.
20. J. Serra. *Image Analysis and Mathematical Morphology*. Academic Press, London, 1982.
21. J. Serra. *Image Analysis and Mathematical Morphology, Part II: Theoretical Advances*. Academic Press (J. Serra Ed.), London, 1988.

Fuzzy Sets from a Mathematical-Naïve Point of View

E. Trillas[1] and **C. Alsina**[2]

[1] Univ. Politécnica de Madrid, Campus de Montegancedo
28660 Boadilla del Monte. Madrid, Spain. etrillas@fi.upm.es
[2] Univ. Politècnica de Catalunya, Diagonal 649
08028 Barcelona. Spain. alsina@ea.upc.es

Abstract. This paper introduces, in a naïve style, a symbolic and axiomatic generalization of Set Theory, the Loose-Set Theory, as a framework for the Standard Theories of Fuzzy Sets. Those theories are placed inside Set Theory and, among them, the case of Functionally Expressible Loose-Set Theories are distinguished as isomorphic to a very general Fuzzy Set Theory.
Keywords: Loose-Sets, Sets, Fuzzy Sets.

1 Introduction

Around thirty six years after the introduction of Fuzzy Sets by Lotfi A. Zadeh in 1965 [2], it seems that there are enough theoretical results and practical applications to review the grounds of Fuzzy Set Theory. In this line, papers [3] and [4] and [7] constitute an attempt to do it from inside Fuzzy Set Theory.

This paper does not try to introduce a mathematically sophisticated purely axiomatic Loose-Set Theory like, for example, Zermelo-Frankel's Set Theory. What is now presented is only an outline, by looking from outside fuzzy sets, of the concept of Loose-Set in a mathematical naïve way similar to the Naïve Set Theory as P.R. Halmos presented it in his well known book [1].

In building the axiomatics for Loose-Sets not only the classical Set Theory is presupposed but also the basic entities of Mathematical Analysis, as it is usual in all introductions to Fuzzy Set Theory. This paper means, perhaps, no more than either an attempt to a better understanding of the diverseness of structures that can be reached by means of fuzzy sets or a way to see more clearly where Fuzzy Sets can be, mathematically, rooted in.

2 The concept of Loose-Set

Given a set $X = \{x, y, z, ...\}$ of primary symbols and a set $E = \{\underset{r}{\in}; r \in J, \{0,1\} \subset J \subset [0,1]\}$ of secondary symbols, the elements in a set $L = \{\varphi, \psi, \alpha, \beta, ...\}$ will be called *loose-sets* (*l-sets*, for short) whenever the following axioms are satisfied.

A1. $(\forall x \in X)(\forall \varphi \in L)(\exists! a \in J) : x \underset{a}{\in} \varphi$;
A2. $\varphi, \psi \in L$ are *identical*, $\varphi \equiv \psi$, if $(\forall x \in X)(\forall a \in J)$ $x \underset{a}{\in} \varphi$ if and only if $x \underset{a}{\in} \psi$;
A3. There are symbols $\sigma, \omega \in L$ such that $(\forall x \in X) x \underset{0}{\in} \sigma$ and $x \underset{1}{\in} \omega$.
A4. $\varphi \in L$ is *contained* in $\psi \in L$, $\varphi \leq \psi$, if $(\forall x \in X)$, $(\forall a, b \in J) x \underset{a}{\in} \varphi$ and $x \underset{b}{\in} \psi$ imply $a \leq b$.
A5. $(\forall \varphi \in L)(\forall \psi \in L)(\exists \varphi + \psi \in L)$:
$\varphi + \psi \equiv \psi + \varphi$, $\varphi + \sigma \equiv \varphi$, $\varphi + \omega \equiv \omega$, $\varphi \leq \varphi + \psi$, $\psi \leq \varphi + \psi$.
A6. $(\forall \varphi \in L)(\forall \psi \in L)(\exists \varphi \cdot \psi \in L)$:
$\varphi \cdot \psi \equiv \psi \cdot \varphi$, $\varphi \cdot \sigma \equiv \sigma$, $\varphi \cdot w \equiv \varphi$, $\varphi \cdot \psi \leq \varphi$, $\varphi \cdot \psi \leq \psi$.
A7. $(\forall \varphi \in L)(\exists - \varphi \in L) : -(-\varphi) \equiv \varphi$ and $\varphi \leq \psi$ implies $-\psi \leq -\varphi$.

The structure $(X, E, L, \equiv, \leq, +, \cdot, -)$ will be called a *Loose-Set Theory* (LST, for short). Thus in a LST since for any $x \in X$ the number $a \in J$ such that $x \underset{a}{\in} \varphi$ is unique we can write $a = \varphi(x)$ and read the above axioms in a functional language.

Of course, more general definitions for Loose-Set theories can be given, e.gr., either by avoiding commutative laws in A5 and A6, or by weakening the involutive law $\neg(\neg\varphi) \equiv \varphi$ in A7.

Theorem 2.1. In a Loose-Set Theory we have the following facts:

(i) Relation $\equiv$ is an equivalence relation;
(ii) Relation $\leq$ is a partial order;
(iii) The L-sets σ and ω are unique;
(iv) $\varphi \equiv \psi$ if and only if $\varphi \leq \psi$ and $\psi \leq \varphi$;
(v) For any φ in L we have $\sigma \leq \varphi \leq \omega$;
(vi) $-\sigma \equiv \omega$ and $-\omega \equiv \sigma$;
(vii) For any φ, ψ in L:

$$\begin{aligned}(\varphi \cdot \psi)(x) &\leq \mathrm{Min}\,(\varphi(x), \psi(x)) \\ &\leq \mathrm{Max}\,(\varphi(x), \psi(x)) \\ &\leq (\varphi + \psi)(x);\end{aligned}$$

(viii) If $(\varphi + \psi)(x) = 0$ then $\varphi(x) = \psi(x) = 0$;
(ix) If $(\varphi \cdot \psi)(x) = 1$ then $\varphi(x) = \psi(x) = 1$;
(x) $\varphi \cdot \psi \leq \varphi \leq \varphi + \psi$ and $\varphi \cdot \varphi \leq \varphi \leq \varphi + \varphi$.

Proof. The first five properties follow from the fact that the relation $\equiv$ becomes equivalent to the pointwise equality of functions and $\leq$ is the usual ordering of functions induced by the order in their range J. For (vi) note that $-\sigma \leq \omega$ yields $-\omega \leq -(-\sigma) = \sigma \leq -\omega$, so $\sigma \equiv -\omega$ and $-\sigma \equiv -(-\omega) \equiv \omega$. (A5) implies (vii) and from this we obtain (viii), (ix) and (x). ∎

Definition 2.1. A Loose-Set Theory will be called *regular* when the following three properties hold:

(a) $(\varphi + \psi)(x) = 0$ if and only if $\varphi(x) = \psi(x) = 0$;
(b) $(\varphi \cdot \psi)(x) = 1$ if and only if $\varphi(x) = \psi(x) = 1$;
(c) $\varphi(x) = 0$ if and only if $(-\varphi)(x) = 1$.

Note that $\varphi(x) = 1$ means $(-(-\varphi))(x) = 1$ which by (c) becomes equivalent to $(-\varphi)(x) = 0$. Thus (c) can be also presented in the form "$\varphi(x) = 1$ if and only if $(-\varphi)(x) = 0$".

The regularity requirements of Definition 2.1 make sense because one can build LST's where these conditions do not hold (see Example 3.2).

Note 2.1. For each $a \in J$ the symbol $\underline{a}$ with *constant* value a, i.e., "$(\forall x \in X) : \underline{a}(x) = a$" may be included in L or not, but $\sigma \equiv \underline{0}$ and $\omega = \underline{1}$ are always in L. When $L \supset \{\underline{a} | a \in J\}$ then $x \underset{t}{\in} \underline{a} \cdot \underline{b}$ implies $t \leq \text{Min}(a, b)$ and $x \underset{u}{\in} \underline{a} + \underline{b}$ implies $\text{Max}(a, b) \leq u$, hence $x \underset{t}{\in} \underline{a} \cdot \underline{a}$ yields $t \leq a$ and $x \underset{u}{\in} \underline{a} + \underline{a}$ yields $a \leq u$.

Note 2.2. If we denote by L^* the subset of L given by

$$L^* = \{\varphi \in L \mid \varphi(x) \in \{0, 1\}\}$$

then $\sigma, \omega \in L^*$ (so $L^* \neq \emptyset$) and these are the only constant functions in L^*. But if we are in the regular case then L^* must be closed by $+, \cdot$ and $-$.

Definition 2.2. An L-set ψ is *contradictory* with an L-set φ if $\psi \leq -\varphi$.

An L-set ψ is *selfcontradictory* when over $\psi \leq -\psi$.

An L-set ψ is *incompatible* with an L-set φ if $\psi \cdot \varphi \equiv \sigma$. An L-set ψ is *selfincompatible* when $\psi \cdot \psi \equiv \sigma$.

Both relations are symmetric because $\psi \leq -\varphi$ implies $-(-\varphi) \equiv \varphi \leq -\psi$, and $\psi \cdot \varphi \equiv \varphi \cdot \psi$. It is immediate to show the following

Theorem 2.2. σ and ω are contradictory. σ is selfcontradictory and ω is not; If $\psi \leq \varphi$ and φ is selfcontradictory, ψ and φ are contradictory; σ and ω are incompatible; σ is selfincompatible.

3 Functionally expressible L-set theories

In this section we want to deal with the case that the binary operations $+, \cdot$ can be obtained by means of pointwise functional expressions. To this end we introduce the following

Definition 3.1 Let $(X, E, L, \equiv, \leq, +, \cdot, -)$ a Loose-Set Theory. We will say that the LST is *functionally expressible* (FE, for short) if for each couple φ, ψ in L there exists functions $F_{\varphi\psi} : J \times J \to J$, $G_{\varphi\psi} : J \times S \to J$, $N_{\varphi}, N_{\psi} : J \to J$ such that for all x in X:

(i) $(\varphi \cdot \psi)(x) = F_{\varphi\psi}(\varphi(x), \psi(x))$,
(ii) $(\varphi + \psi)(x) = G_{\varphi\psi}(\varphi(x), \psi(x))$,
(iii) $(-\varphi)(x) = N_{\varphi}(\varphi(x)), (-\psi)(x) = N_{\psi}(\psi(x))$.

In the case that for all φ, ψ we have $F_{\varphi\psi} = F$, $G_{\varphi\psi} = G$ and $N_{\varphi} = N$, $n_{\varphi} = n$ then we will say that our LST is universally functionally expressible (UFE, for short).

The properties of $\cdot, +$ and $-$ assumed in an LST force the operations $F_{\varphi\psi}$, $G_{\varphi,\psi}$, N_{ψ}, N_{φ} to have the corresponding properties in J, e.g., for any $r \in$Im φ, $s \in$Imψ we need to have

(a) $F_{\varphi\psi}(r,s) \leq \text{Min}(r,s) \leq \text{Max}(r,s) \leq G_{\varphi\psi}(r,s)$
(b) $F_{\varphi\psi}(r,s) = F_{\varphi\psi}(s,r)$; $G_{\varphi\psi}(r,s) = G_{\varphi\psi}(s,r)$;
(c) $r \leq s$ imply $N_{\varphi}(r) \geq N_{\varphi}(s)$, $N_{\varphi}((N_{\varphi})(r)) = r$.

So when $J = [0,1]$ and $N_{\varphi}(0) = 1$, N_{φ} is a strong negation. If 0,1 $\in$Im $\varphi \cap$ Im ψ then

(d) $F_{\varphi\psi}(r,1) = G_{\varphi\psi}(r,0) = r$, $F_{\varphi\psi}(r,0) = 0$, $G_{\varphi\psi}(r,1) = 1$.

From this it is immediate to stablish criteria for regularity in the sense of Definition 2.1 by checking the suitable properties of $F_{\varphi\psi}$, $G_{\varphi\psi}$ and N_{φ}. Additional requirements on the operations $F_{\varphi\psi}$ and $G_{\varphi\psi}$ yield the corresponding properties for $+$ and $\cdot$, e.g., if the operations on J are non-decreasing in both variables then

$$\text{“}\varphi \leq \psi \text{ and } \eta \leq \theta \text{ imply } \varphi \cdot \eta \leq \psi \cdot \theta, \varphi + \eta \leq \psi + \sigma\text{”},$$

or if some class of duality is assumed, e.g., $N_{\varphi} = N$ for all φ and $F_{\varphi\psi} \geq N \circ G_{\varphi\psi} \circ (N \times N)$ then $(-\varphi) + (-\psi) \leq -(\varphi \cdot \psi)$ so De Morgan's Laws may hold in this framework, and, of course, the lattice structure is not obtained when dealing with operations on J with no idempotent elements.

Example 3.1. Consider $X = \mathbb{R}$, $J = [0,1]$ and a probability space. Let L denote the set of strictly increasing continuous probability distributions functions F_Z such that $F_Z(0) = 0$, $F_Z(1) = 1$ (where Z denotes any random variable in the probability space with values in [0,1]) adding in L the 0, 1 functions. We consider the pointwise ordering in L and $x \underset{a}{\in} F_Z$ whenever $F_Z(x) = a$. For $F_X, F_Y \in L \backslash \{0,1\}$ define

$$\begin{aligned} F_X + F_Y &= F_{\text{Min}(X,Y)} \\ F_X \cdot F_Y &= F_{\text{Max}(X,Y)} \\ -F_X &= F_{1-X} \end{aligned}$$

Then by Sklar's theorem [6] we have an FE-LST because there exist copulas C_{XY} such that

$$F_{\text{Min}(X,Y)}(t) = C_{XY}(F_X(t), F_Y(t))$$

$$F_{\mathrm{Max}(X,Y)}(t) = F_X(t) + F_Y(t) - $$
$$-C_{XY}(F_X(t), F_Y(t))$$
$$F_{1-X}(t) = 1 - F_X(1-t) = N_X(F_X(t))$$

where $N_X(u) = 1 - F_X(1 - F_X^{-1}(u))$. Clearly these operations can not be universally functionally expressible.

Another example of this type may be found in [4].

Example 3.2. Let $X = J = [0,1]$ and consider $L = \{\varphi_\alpha \mid 0 \leq \alpha \leq 1\}$ where for each $0 \leq \alpha < 1$, $\varphi_\alpha : [0,1] \to [0,1]$ is given by $\varphi_\alpha(x) = \alpha x$, and $\varphi_1(x) = 1$, for all x in [0,1]. Then we will write $x \underset{a}{\in} \varphi_\alpha$ whenever $\varphi_\alpha(x) = a$. Take $\sigma = \varphi_0$, $\omega = \varphi_1$ and define:

$$\varphi_\alpha + \varphi_\beta = \varphi_{\mathrm{Max}(\alpha,\beta)},$$
$$\varphi_\alpha \cdot \varphi_\beta = \varphi_{\mathrm{Min}(\alpha,\beta)},$$
$$-\varphi_\alpha = \varphi_{1-\alpha}.$$

It is immediate to see that we have defined a Loose-Set Theory. This structure is not regular because e.g. $\varphi_{1/2}(0) = 0$ but $(-\varphi_{1/2})(0) = \varphi_{\frac{1}{2}}(0) = 0 \neq 1$; it admits contradictory elements (φ_α and φ_β such that $\alpha + \beta \leq 1$) and selfcontradictory members (φ_α with $\alpha \leq 1/2$). Moreover this structure is not UFE. If there would exist a function $N : [0,1] \to [0,1]$ such that

$$(-\varphi_\alpha)(x) := N(\varphi_\alpha(x)),$$

then we would need to have for any $\alpha \neq 1$ and $x \neq \alpha$

$$(1-\alpha)(x) = N(\alpha x)$$

which in turn implies

$$(1-\alpha)(x) = N(\alpha x) = N(x\alpha) = (1-x)\alpha$$

which is a contradiction with the assumption $\alpha \neq x$.

Note also that for $\alpha \neq 0, 1$ we have $\varphi_\alpha \cdot (-\varphi_\alpha) \neq \varphi_0$, $\varphi_\alpha + (-\varphi_\alpha) \neq \varphi_1$.

Example 3.3. Consider $X = [0,1]$, $L = \{f \mid f : [0,1] \to [0,1]\}$ and $x \underset{a}{\in} f$ if and only if $f(x) = a$. Let $\sigma = 0$ be the zero function, $\omega = 1$ be the constant one function and consider the usual pointwise ordering in L. For any f, g in L define

$$(f+g)(x) = \begin{cases} \mathrm{Max}(f(x), g(x)) \text{ if } f \equiv 0 \text{ or } g \equiv 0 \\ \\ \mathrm{Max}(\sup\{f(x)\} \\ \sup\{g(x)\}), \qquad \text{otherwise.} \end{cases}$$

Then A5 is satisfied but $+$ is neither regular nor universally functionally expressible. If there would exist $G : [0,1] \times [0,1] \to [0,1]$ such that $(f+g)(x) =$

$G(f(x), g(x))$ then taking $f \equiv 1/2$ and $g(x) = 0$ whenever $x \leq 1/2$ and $g(x) = 1$ whenever $1/2 < x < 1$ we would obtain:

$$\begin{aligned}\frac{1}{2} &= f\left(\frac{1}{2}\right) = (f+0)\left(\frac{1}{2}\right) = \\ &= G\left(f\left(\frac{1}{2}\right), 0\left(\frac{1}{2}\right)\right) = G\left(\frac{1}{2}, 0\right) \\ &= G\left(f\left(\frac{1}{2}\right), g\left(\frac{1}{2}\right)\right) = (f+g)\left(\frac{1}{2}\right) \\ &= \text{Max}\left\{\frac{1}{2}, 1\right\} = 1\end{aligned}$$

which is impossible.

Note also that taking g as defined above we have $g\left(\frac{1}{2}\right) = 0$ but $(g + g)\left(\frac{1}{2}\right) = \text{Max}(1,1) = 1$, i.e., + can not be regular.

Note. It should be pointed out that in a FELST it is not rare to have constant selfcontradictory l-sets different from $\underline{0} \equiv \sigma$: it is enough the existence of some $r \in J - \{0\}$ such that $r < N(r)$, because then $\underline{r} \leq -\underline{r}$. In fact, in a such a theory any l-set φ such that $\varphi(x) < N(\varphi(x))$ for any $x \in X$, is selfcontradictory. Thus in any LST on which the law: $\varphi \leq \zeta$, $\eta \leq \sigma$ imply $\varphi \cdot \eta \leq \zeta \cdot \theta$, do hold:

a) If $\varphi \leq \zeta$ and ζ is selfincompatible, φ and ζ are incompatible.
b) If $\varphi \leq \zeta$ and φ, ζ are incompatible, φ is selfincompatible.

If a LST is FE, incompatible φ and ζ means $(\varphi \cdot \zeta)(x) = F(\varphi(x), \zeta(x)) = 0$ for all $x \in X$, hence a sufficient condition for having incompatible couples of l-sets, both different of σ, in a FELST is that function F have zero divisors. In any FELST, L-set ω is not selfincompatible because $\omega \cdot \omega \equiv \omega$.

4 Classical Sets

In this section we devote our attention to the classical Sets Theory.

Theorem 4.1. In any regular LST, L^* is a Boolean Algebra of L-sets.

Proof. From axioms A5, A6, A7 and definition 2.1, for any μ, σ in L^* and each x in X, it is:

- $(\mu \cdot \sigma)(x) = \text{Min}(\mu(x), \sigma(x))$
- $(\mu + \sigma)(x) = \text{Max}(\mu(x), \sigma(x))$
- $(-\mu)(x) = 1 - \mu(x)$.

Hence, L^* is closed for $\cdot, +$ and $-$. Then, L^* is itself a FELST on which $J = \{0, 1\}$, $F = \text{Min}$, $G = \text{Max}$ and $N = 1-\text{id}$. Consequently, since $F = NoGo(N \times N)$ it follows $\mu + \sigma = -((-\mu) \cdot (-\sigma))$ for any μ, σ in L^*.

As function $F = \text{Min}$ is associative: $(\mu \cdot (\sigma \cdot \delta))(x) = F(\mu(x), (\sigma \cdot \delta)(x)) = F(\mu(x), F(\sigma(x), \delta(x))) = F(F(\mu(x), \sigma(x)), \delta(x)) = ((\mu \cdot \sigma)(\cdot\delta)(x)$, for any x in X. Then, $\mu \cdot (\sigma \cdot \delta) \equiv (\mu \cdot \sigma) \cdot \delta$, and operation $\cdot$ is associative.

For any r, s in $\{0, 1\}$ is $r = \text{Max}(\text{Min}(r, s), \text{Min}(r, 1 - s))$. Consequently, it follows $\mu \equiv (\mu \cdot \sigma) + \mu \cdot (-\sigma))$, for any μ, σ in L^* and, by applying Huntington's theorem (see [5]), L^* is a Boolean Algebra. ∎

Corollary 4.1. In any regular LST and for any μ, σ, δ in L^* we have:

- $\mu \cdot \mu \equiv \mu$; $\mu + \mu \equiv \mu$
- $\mu \cdot (-\mu) \equiv \sigma$; $\mu + (-\mu) \equiv \omega$
- $\mu \cdot (\sigma + \delta) \equiv \mu \cdot \sigma + \mu \cdot \delta$; $\mu + \sigma \cdot \delta \equiv (\mu + \delta) \cdot (\mu + \delta)$.

Proof. It is immediate since L^* is a Boolean Algebra, or because of the properties of Min, Max and 1–id in $\{0, 1\}$. ∎

Corollary 4.2. In any regular LST the only selfcontradictory element in L^* is σ.

Proof. If $\mu \in L^*$ is such that $\mu \leq -\mu$, it follows $\mu \cdot \mu \leq (-\mu) \cdot \mu \equiv \sigma$. Hence $\mu \equiv \sigma$. ∎

Corollary 4.3. In any regular LST there is coincidence between contradiction and incompatibility in L^*.

Proof. If μ, σ are in L^* and $\mu \leq -\sigma$, it follows $\mu \cdot \sigma \leq (-\sigma) \cdot \sigma \equiv \sigma$ and $\mu \cdot \sigma \equiv \sigma$. Reciprocally, if $\mu \cdot \sigma \equiv \sigma$, from $\mu \equiv \mu \cdot \sigma + \mu \cdot (-\sigma)$ it follows $\mu \equiv \mu \cdot (-\sigma) \leq -\sigma$. ∎

Theorem 4.2. Any regular LST is a generalization of Set Theory.

Proof. In fact, L^* is a part of L and being a Boolean Algebra by Stone's theorem (see [5]) L^* must be isomorphic to a Boolean Algebra of sets. ∎

This Boolean Algebra can be easily identified with a subalgebra of $P(X)$, because $\mu \in L^*$ is defined by means of a function $\mu : X \to \{0, 1\}$ which assigns to each primary symbol x the number $\mu(x)$ such that $x \underset{\mu(x)}{\in} \mu$. Consequently, this function μ is the Characteristic Function of the set $\underset{\sim}{\mu} = \mu^{-1}(1)$.

As it is well known, the Boolean Algebras $(P(X), \cap, U, c)$ and $(\{0, 1\}^X$, Min, Max, 1-id) are isomorphic. Since the Boolean Algebra $(L^*, \cdot, +, -)$ is a subalgebra of $(\{0, 1\}^X$, Min, Max, 1-id), it must be isomorphic to the corresponding subalgebra of $(P(X), \cap, U, c)$. Hence,

Theorem 4.3. Any regular LST contains a Boolean Algebra isomorphic to a subalgebra of $P(X)$.

Because of ω is defined by $\omega(x) = 1$ for any x in X, the corresponding set in $P(X)$ is X itself and, from this point of view, ω *can be identified with* X. Analogously, σ *can be identified with the empty set* $\emptyset$.

Notice that regularity is an essential condition for theorems 4.2 and 4.3. This fact is shown by the non-regular LST of Example 3.2 which does not contain any Boolean Algebra isomorphic to $\{0,1\}^{[0,1]}$. In fact, it only contains the trivial Boolean Algebra $\{\varphi_0, \varphi_1\}$.

5 Fuzzy Sets

Now let's try to locate Fuzzy Sets Theory in the LST context.

Theorem 5.1. Any FELST is isomorphic to a theory of fuzzy sets.

Proof. The operator $\sim: L \to J^X$ defined by $\sim(\varphi) = \underset{\sim}{\varphi}$, with $\underset{\sim}{\varphi} \in J^X$ given as $\underset{\sim}{\varphi}(x) = \varphi(x)$ for each φ in L, is one-to-one and onto:

- If $f \in J^X$, the l-set φ defined by $\varphi(x) = f(x)$ verifies $\sim(\varphi) = f$.
- If $\sim(\varphi) = \sim(\zeta)$, or $\varphi(x) = \zeta(x)$ for any x in X, it is $\varphi \equiv \zeta$.

With the corresponding functions $F : J \times J \to J, G : J \times J \to J$ and $N : J \to J$, let's define in J^X the operations $(f \wedge g)(x) = F(f(x), g(x)), (f \vee g)(x) = G(f(x), g(x))$ and $f'(x) = N(f(x))$, for each x in X and any f, g in J^X. It is, obviously, $\sim(\varphi \cdot \zeta) = \sim(\varphi) \wedge \sim(\zeta), \sim(\varphi + \zeta) = \sim(\varphi) \vee \sim(\zeta)$ and $\sim(-\varphi) = (\sim(\varphi))'$. Hence, the given structure is isomorphic to the fuzzy set theory $(J^X, \wedge, \vee, \cdot)$. ■

Theorem 5.2. In a FELST with $J = [0,1]$ functions F and G are a t-norm and a t-conorm, respectively, if and only if the following laws do hold:

- $\varphi \leq \zeta$, $\eta \leq \theta$ imply $\varphi \cdot \eta \leq \zeta \cdot \theta$ and $\varphi + \eta \leq \zeta + \theta$ (Monotonicity)
- $\varphi \cdot (\zeta \cdot \eta) \equiv (\varphi \cdot \zeta) \cdot \eta$, and $\varphi + (\zeta + \eta) \equiv (\varphi + \zeta) + \eta$ (Associativity).

Thus any FELST with $J = [0,1]$ on which the laws of Monotonicity and Associativity of both operations $\cdot$ and $+$ do hold, is isomorphic to a standard theory of fuzzy sets $([0,1]^X, T, S, N)$ with a t-norm T, a t-conorm S and a strong negation N. In these theories De Morgan's Laws do hold if and only if $T = NoSo(N \times N)$.

Let us remark here that while characteristic functions and fuzzy sets may have a pointwise partial order, this is not the case of probabilities. If two probabilities P_1 and P_2 in Boolean algebra a would be ordered, pointwise, i.e., $P_1 \leq P_2$ then since for all A in a we would have $P_1(A) \leq P_2(A)$ and $P_1(A^c) \leq$

$P_2(A^c)$ we would conclude $P_1 = P_2$. This makes clear why Probability Theory and LST's theory (including any theory of Fuzzy Sets) are different kind of theories.

6 Singletons

For each primary symbol $x \in X$ and any $r \in J$, the symbol x/r is defined by virtue of:

$$(x/r)(z) = \begin{cases} r, \text{ if } z = x \\ 0, \text{ otherwise.} \end{cases}$$

and it is called the *r-singleton* of x which may be in L or not. Note that the symbols x/r belong eventually to L, but x is in X. The only singletons that are in L^* are $x/0 \equiv \sigma$ and $x/1$ which corresponds to the classical singletons $\{x\}$. Results in this section suppose that any x/r is in L.

Theorem 6.1.

a) If $x \underset{a}{\in} \varphi$, then $x/a \leq \varphi$;
b) $x/r \leq y/s$ *iff* $x = y$ and $r \leq s$;
c) $x/r \equiv y/s$ *iff* $x = y$ and $r = s$.

In a LST in which the associative law $\varphi + (\zeta + \eta) \equiv (\varphi + \zeta) + \eta$ holds, it is possible to define $\varphi_1 + \varphi_2 + ... + \varphi_n$ and, it this case, $\varphi_i \leq \varphi_1 + \ldots + \varphi_n$ $(1 \leq i \leq n)$. Hence, in such a case:

$$x_i/a_i \leq x_1/a_1 + \ldots + x_n/a_n \, (1 \leq i \leq n).$$

Definition 6.1. An *l-set* φ is *finite* if $\varphi(x) > 0$ for only a finite subset of primary symbols x in X.

Of course, if $X = \{x_1, ..., x_n\}$ is a finite set, that is, there is only a finite number of primary symbols, any L-set is finite.

Theorem 6.1. In a LST on which the associative law of + holds, for any finite *l-set* φ is: $\varphi \leq x_1/\varphi(x_1) + ... + x_n/\varphi(x_n)$, with $\{x_1, ..., x_n\}$ the finite subset of primary symbols such that $\varphi(x_i) > 0$.

Proof. Let $\varphi^+ \equiv x_1/\varphi(x_1) + ... + x_n/\varphi(x_n)$. Since it is $x_i/\varphi(x_i) \leq \varphi^+$ $(1 \leq i \leq n)$, it follows $\varphi(x_i) \leq \varphi^+(x_i)$ $(1 \leq i \leq n)$ and, of course, for any $x \in X$ such that $x \notin \{x_1, ..., x_n\}$ it is $\varphi(x) = 0 \leq \varphi^+(x)$. Hence, $\varphi \leq \varphi^+$. ■

Theorem 6.2. In a FELST in which G is a t-conorm, for any finite *l-set* φ it is

$$\varphi \equiv x_1/\varphi(x_1) + ... + x_n/\varphi(x_n),$$

with $\{x_1, ..., x_n\}$ the finite subset of primary symbols such that $\varphi(x_i) > 0$.

Proof. Taking φ^+ as in theorem 6.2, it is $\varphi^+(x) = G((x_1/\varphi(x_1)(x), ..., (x_n/\varphi(x_n)(x))$. Then, $\varphi^+(x_1) = G(\varphi(x_1), 0, ..., 0) = \varphi(x_1), ..., \varphi^+(x_n) = G(0, 0, ..., \varphi(x_n)) = \varphi(x_n)$, and if $x \notin \{x_1, ..., x_n\}$ it is $\varphi^+(x) = G(0, 0, ..., 0) = 0$ and $\varphi(x) = 0$. Hence, $\varphi^+ \equiv \varphi$. ■

Corollary 6.1. In a regular LST on which $X = \{x_1, ..., x_n\}$ is a finite set, any $\mu \in L^*$ can be identified with the set $\{x_{ij} \in X; \mu(x_{ij}) > 0\}$.

Proof. For any $\mu \in L^*$ it is $\mu(x_i) \in \{0, 1\}$, $1 \leq i \leq n$. As L^* is a FELST with G =Max, applying theorem 6.2 results $\mu \equiv x_{i1}/1 + ... + x_{ik}/1$, where $\{x_i, ..., x_{ik}\}$ is the subset of X such that $\mu(x_{ij}) > 0$. Finally, function $\underset{\sim}{\mu}$ is $\underset{\sim}{\mu}(x)$ =Max$((x_{i1}/1)(x), ..., (x_{ik}/1)(x))$ and, then, $\underset{\sim}{\mu}$ is the Characteristic Function of set $\{x_{i1}, ..., x_{ik}\}$. ■

Last Remark. To connect *l-set* theory and its applications it should be reflected that any reasonable thing asserted on the elements of a given set specifies an *l-set*. To such end it seems fine to proceed like Halmos does in [1].

Let p be any property linguistically labeled P whose graded use in a universe X is translated by a function t (x verifies p) $= t$("x is P")$\in [0, 1]$. Then let us provisionally establish the following axiom.

A8. (Specificity) For any set X, any predicate P and any function $t(x \text{ is } P) \in [0, 1]$, $x \in X$, there exists an LST whose primary symbols are the elements of X and with an *l-set* $\underset{\sim}{P} \in L$ such that:

$$\text{“}x \underset{r}{\in} \underset{\sim}{P} \text{ if and only if } (\forall x \in X)(r = t(x \text{ is } P))\text{”}.$$

At each particular case, function t may have a concrete meaning, e.g., $t(x$ is $P)$ may be the truth value of "x is P". Obviously, in the case that t takes values in $\{0, 1\}$, A8 is Halmos' specificity axiom.

References

1. P.R. Halmos, 1960, Naïve Set Theory, Van Nostrand (New York).
2. L.A. Zadeh, 1965, Fuzzy Sets, *Information and Control,* 8, 338-353.
3. E. Trillas, C. Alsina and J. Jacas, 1999, On Contradiction in Fuzzy Logic (*Soft Computing*) 3, 197-199.
4. E. Trillas, C. Alsina and J. Jacas, 1999, On Logical Connectives for Fuzzy Set Theory with or without Nonempty Self-contradictions (*Int. Jour. of Intel. Systems*), 15, 155-164.
5. G. Birkhoff, 1973, Lattice Theory, AMS Pubs. (Providence).
6. B. Schweizer and A. Sklar, 1983, Probabilistic metric spaces, Elsevier, North-Holland, New York.
7. E. Trillas and C. Alsina, 1999, A reflection on what is a membership function (*Mathware & Soft-Computing*) VI, 2-3, 201-215.

On the Implementation of Fril++ for Object-Oriented Logic Programming with Uncertainty and Fuzziness

T.H. Cao, J.M. Rossiter, T.P. Martin, J.F. Baldwin

Artificial Intelligence Group
Department of Engineering Mathematics
University of Bristol
United Kingdom BS8 1TR
Tru.Cao@bristol.ac.uk

Abstract. Uncertain and fuzzy object-oriented logic programming is a combination of logic programming, object-oriented programming, and uncertain and fuzzy logic to exploit the advantages of all three disciplines in dealing with real world problems. This paper presents our implementation of Fril++, the Fril-based uncertain and fuzzy object-oriented logic programming language. Fril++ syntax is introduced and related semantic issues, particularly, ones of uncertain multiple inheritance and uncertain membership evaluation, are discussed and solutions to them are proposed. The implemented compiler translating a Fril++ source program into a Fril target program is then presented with examples.

1 Introduction

It is now widely accepted that taxonomic information, and in particular a class hierarchy, is an important part of a knowledge base. This is not only because objects in the real world are naturally associated with classes, but also because taxonomic information helps to organise knowledge through classification and provide efficient computation through inheritance. For development of such a system, object-oriented programming has provided advantageous methodologies and techniques. This is why extension of the classical object-oriented model with uncertainty and fuzziness, which are another essential aspect of knowledge, has been the quest and focus of significant research effort, e.g. [8], [9], [4], [12], [15], [3] and [7].

Meanwhile, logic programming has also been an important tool for knowledge base building, which provides a declarative way for problem specification, well-founded semantics for formal reasoning, and non-deterministic mechanism for solution searching. However, research on combining all together logic programming, object-oriented programming, and uncertain and fuzzy logic appears to be sporadic.

The benefit of such a combination is not only that the advantages of the three disciplines can be exploited, but also that one discipline sheds light on existing problems resulting from combining the other two. In particular, those are ones of multiple inheritance and uncertain inheritance, which have not been adequately solved in previous works, as reviewed in [1], on extending the classical object-oriented model to the uncertain and fuzzy object-oriented model.

The work on Fril++ ([3]), extending Fril ([2]) with object-oriented features, is among a few attempts towards object-oriented logic programming with uncertainty and fuzziness. However, that work still lacked a coherent framework for the implementation of Fril++ to be completed. Thus, in [1], we have proposed a general framework for object-oriented extension of existing uncertain and fuzzy logic programming systems. Two schemes, namely, *probability-based* and *possibility-based*, have been provided in the framework, intended for uncertain and fuzzy logic programming systems with formulas weighted by probability-based degrees or possibility-based degrees, respectively.

This paper applies the proposed probability-based scheme to our implementation of Fril++ by writing a compiler to translate a Fril++ source program into a Fril target program, following the approach of [11]. Section 2 presents an overview of Fril++ class hierarchy and implementation approach. Section 3 introduces Fril++ syntax and Section 4 discusses related semantic issues. Then Section 5 presents our translation strategy and illustrates translated codes. Finally, Section 6 presents concluding remarks of the paper.

2 Overview

2.1 Class Hierarchy

Like any other object-oriented system, a Fril++ system is associated with a class hierarchy. Besides particular classes for the domain of the system, there are two special classes, namely, *Fril* and *Fril++*, which are common to all Fril++ systems. The Fril class is at the top of a class hierarchy, containing all Fril built-in predicates, which can be inherited by all classes in a Fril++ system. The Fril++ class is a subclass of the Fril class, but a super-class of any other class, to define new common predicates for all Fril++ systems and to override some Fril built-in predicates. The predicates in the Fril and Fril++ classes can also be overridden.

As discussed in [1], for a class hierarchy in an uncertain and fuzzy object-oriented system, we assume that a class is totally subsumed by any of its super-classes or, in other words, a class totally subsumes any of its subclasses. The first reason is that a set of classes with a graded inclusion or inheritance relation actually forms a *network* rather than a *hierarchy*. Indeed, if a class A has an inclusion degree to a class B, then usually B also has an inclusion degree to A, due to fuzzy matching of their descriptions. The second reason is that a concept is naturally classified into sub-concepts totally subsumed by it, though the sub-concepts can overlap each other.

2.2 Implementation Approach

As shown in [11], object-oriented logic programs can be translated into normal logic programs, such as Prolog ones, to be executed almost as efficiently as the original programs would be. We follow this approach in the implementation of Fril++ by writing a compiler, using Fril itself, to translate a Fril++ source program into a Fril target program.

Fril is a logic programming language that can handle both uncertainty and fuzziness and, unlike other Prolog-like languages, Fril's syntax is Lisp-like with list as the primary data and program structure. A Fril atom, i.e., a predicate, has the following form:

(*predicate-name arg*1 *arg*2 ... *argN*)

where values of *arg*1, *arg*2, ..., and *argN* can be fuzzy sets. The form of a Fril clause is as follows:

(*head-atom body-atom*1 *body-atom*2 ... *body-atomN*)

which can be associated with a support pair defining a lower bound and an upper bound of the conditional probability of the head given the body of the clause.

A Fril++ program, which contains class definitions and logical clauses, has the same list format as a Fril program as presented below.

3 Fril++ Syntax

3.1 Class Definition

A Fril++ *class* definition contains the following sections: *super-class* declaration, *constant* declaration, *part* declaration, and *property* definition. The super-class section declares the *immediate* super-classes of the class. The constant section declares the constant labels and their values associated with the class, which can be inherited or overridden like class properties. The part section declares the identifiers and classes of the objects to be included as parts of an instance of the class.

The property section defines the *properties*, i.e., attributes and methods, of the class, which in the logic-based object-oriented model are represented by logical clauses. As in the probability-based scheme of the framework proposed in [1], each class property is associated with a support pair defining lower and upper bounds of the probability for the property being applicable to a member of the class.

Constants, parts, and properties can have either one of the visibility modifier **public**, **protected**, or **private** as in C++ ([14]), with **public** as the default. For examples, let us start with a simple one of the class BIRD defined in Fril++ as follows:

```
((class bird extends (winged_animal))
     (properties ((no-of-legs 2))
                 ((fly)) : (0.9 0.95)
     )
)
```

Here words printed in boldface are Fril++ reserved words. For the property *fly*, 0.9 and 0.95 are respectively a lower bound and an upper bound of the conditional probability of an object being able to fly given that it is a bird.

For another example, one can have the following definition of the class PERSON:

```
((class person extends (universal))
     (parts (left_eye human_eye)
            (right_eye human_eye)
     )
     (properties ((age [0:1 120:1]))
                 ((height [0:1 2.4:1]))
     )
)
```

Here [0:1 120:1] is a special fuzzy set, which is equivalent to a crisp one, defining the age of a person to be in between 0 and 120 years of age. Similarly, [0:1 2.4:1] defines the height of a person to be in between 0 and 2.4 metres. In the part section, *left_eye* and *right_eye* are part identifiers representing the eyes of a person, whereas *human_eye* is the class of those parts.

Then the class MAN can extend the class PERSON as follows:

```
((class man extends (person))
     (constants (young [0:1 30:1 40:0 120:0])
                (tall [0:0 1.5:0 1.8:1 2.4:1])
     )
     (properties ((handsome) (age young) (height tall)) )
)
```

The property is a rule saying "A man is handsome if he is *young* and *tall*", where *young* and *tall* are defined in the constant section as linguistic labels of fuzzy sets. Here [0:1 30:1 40:0 120:0] represents a fuzzy set on [0, 120] whose membership function takes value 1 on [0, 30], value 0 on [40, 120], and is linearly decreasing on [30, 40]. Meanwhile, the membership function of [0:0 1.5:0 1.8:1 2.4:1] is linearly increasing on [1.5, 1.8].

3.2 Message Passing

Message passing is concerned with which object a message is sent to and where definitions for the property that the message refers to are. These can be specified by one of the following:

- The Fril++ reserved word **self**
- The Fril++ reserved word **super**
- A class identifier
- An object identifier, possibly followed by a sequence of part identifiers.

The reserved word **self** represents the currently referred object, which is the default receiver of the message. The reserved word **super** means that definitions for the property that the message refers to are to be searched in super-classes of the class where the message is passed. A class containing definitions to be used for the referred property can also be designated as with the third case above. Meanwhile, the fourth case is for specifying an object to which the message is sent, which can be a part of another object. In any case, definitions to be used for the referred property are ones asserted for a receiver object itself or ones that the object inherits from classes, subject to overriding and multiple inheritance as discussed in Section 4.

For example, with the class MAN defined above, suppose that John belongs to that class. Then the following Fril++ queries respectively asks about the colour of John's left eye and the support for John being a handsome man:

    ? ((John.left_eye.colour COLOUR))
    qs ((John.handsome))

where *?* and *qs* are query predicates built into Fril++.

4 Semantic Issues

4.1 Uncertain Inheritance

In the uncertain and fuzzy object-oriented model, the membership of an object to a class is not a matter of "to be or not to be" as in the classical model, but rather a matter of degree. Here, for the probability-based scheme of the framework proposed in [1], uncertain membership is measured by support pairs. Uncertain membership of an object and uncertain applicability of a property to a class naturally make inheritance become uncertain. However, as reviewed in [1], this problem has not been adequately solved in previous works.

It was mainly due to the procedural interpretation of method properties (i.e., ones distinguished from attribute properties in the classical object-oriented model terminology), as implicitly assumed in those works, for which it was not clear what an execution of a method with some uncertainty degree could mean. From the logic programming viewpoint, it simply means that the rule representing the method is weighted and applied with that uncertainty degree, just as in an uncertain and fuzzy logic program. This viewpoint was applied and exemplified in [3], which however did not consider uncertain applicability of properties to a class.

We now derive a support pair for a property p of a class C being applicable to an object O. Let $(l \;\; u)$ be the applicability degree of p to C, and $(\alpha \;\; \beta)$ be the membership degree of O to C. Also, we write $p(x)$ and $p(O)$ to denote "p is applicable to x" and "p is applicable to O", and $C(x)$ and $C(O)$ to denote "x is a member of C" and "O is a member of C", respectively. Then, applying Jeffrey's rule ([10]), the probability of $p(O)$ is defined by:

$$\Pr(p(O)) = \Pr(p(x) \mid C(x)) \times \Pr(C(O)) + \Pr(p(x) \mid \neg C(x)) \times \Pr(\neg C(O)).$$

Here $l \leq \Pr(p(x) \mid C(x)) \leq u$, $\alpha \leq \Pr(C(O)) \leq \beta$, and $\Pr(\neg C(O)) = 1 - \Pr(C(O))$.

Assuming that $\Pr(p(x) \mid \neg C(x))$ is totally unknown, i.e., only $0 \leq \Pr(p(x) \mid \neg C(x)) \leq 1$ is known, one obtains:

$$l \times \alpha \leq \Pr(p(O)) \leq u \times \alpha + (1 - \alpha)$$

whence the support pair for p being applicable to O is:

$$(l \times \alpha \quad u \times \alpha + (1 - \alpha)) \tag{4.1}$$

This result satisfies intuition in the following special cases:

- $(\alpha \;\; \beta) = (1 \;\; 1)$: $l \leq \Pr(p(O)) \leq u$. That is, if O is a full member of C, then O inherits p from C with the same support pair as defined in C.
- $(\alpha \;\; \beta) = (0 \;\; 0)$: $0 \leq \Pr(p(O)) \leq 1$. That is, if O is certainly not a member of C then, from only this source of information, nothing can be said about the applicability of p to O.
- $(l \;\; u) = (1 \;\; 1)$: $\alpha \leq \Pr(p(O)) \leq 1$. Here, as O can inherit p from other classes, the upper bound of $\Pr(p(O))$ is not limited by the upper bound β of $\Pr(C(O))$.
- $(l \;\; u) = (0 \;\; 0)$: $0 \leq \Pr(p(O)) \leq (1 - \alpha)$. Here, if O is not a full member of C, i.e., $\alpha \neq 1$, then the fact p is not applicable to C does not entail that p is not applicable to O.

We note that in general the lower and upper bounds of $\Pr(p(O))$ also depend on β, but not in this case as shown by Formula (4.1) when $\Pr(p(x) \mid \neg C(x))$ is totally unknown.

For example, suppose that the class PENGUIN is defined as follows:

```
((class penguin extends (bird))
    (properties ((fly)) : (0 0) )
    ....
)
```

and Penny is a member of PENGUIN but Billie is not, that is, the support pairs for Penny and Billie being members of PENGUIN are (1 1) and (0 0), respectively. Then, by Formula (4.1), the support pairs for the property *fly* being applicable to Penny and Billie are respectively (0 0) and (0 1). In other words, one can infer that Penny cannot fly but cannot say anything about whether Billie can fly or not, from only this source of information.

4.2 Multiple and Overriding Inheritance

For multiple inheritance, the procedural interpretation of methods also raises the problem of deciding which method among those inherited of the same name is to be selected for execution. Meanwhile, from the logic programming viewpoint, that selection problem disappears, as discussed and exemplified in [11] on logic-based object-oriented programming and in [3] on its extension with uncertainty and fuzziness.

Indeed, in the logic-based object-oriented model, each object is viewed as a knowledge base of clauses representing all the properties that the object can have. Then inherited properties of the same name are included in the object's knowledge base just as clauses whose heads are predicates of the same name, which are usual in logic programming. A message sent to the object is viewed as a query on the object's knowledge base, which is answered by a Prolog style proof procedure. There can be different and, moreover, possibly conflicting answers to the query, and it is a role of uncertain and fuzzy logic to resolve the conflict and combine the answers. The particular solution depends on the uncertain and fuzzy logic theorem prover being applied.

For an example, suppose that there is a shape which resembles both a circle and a square, as illustrated in Figure 1, and one wants to evaluate its area approximately. The problem can be solved by considering the shape as a partial member of both the class CIRCLE and the class SQUARE with support pairs, for instance, (0.7 0.8) and (0.6 0.7) respectively.

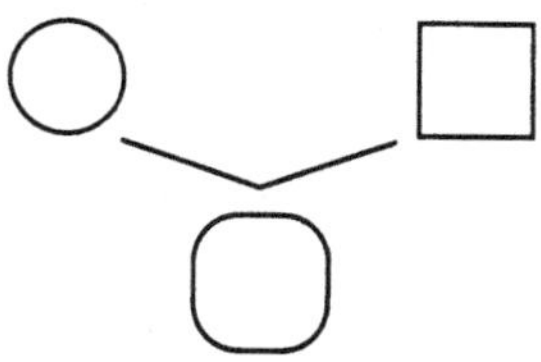

Figure 1: A shape resembling a circle and a square

The classes CIRCLE and SQUARE can be defined as subclasses of the class SHAPE as follows:

```
((class circle extends (shape))
      (properties ((radius _ ))
                  ((area A)
                        (radius R) (times R R R2) (times 3.14 R2 A))
      )
)
((class square extends (shape))
      (properties ((length _ ))
                  ((area A) (length L) (times L L A))
      )
)
```

where A, R, $R2$, and L are variables whose values can be fuzzy numbers, i.e., fuzzy sets on the set of all real numbers, and *times* is a Fril built-in predicate generally for fuzzy multiplication.

Then the knowledge base of the shape virtually contains the above rules for evaluating its area, which are inherited from CIRCLE and SQUARE, respectively with the support pairs (0.7 1) and (0.6 1) as computed by Formula (4.1). As shown in [1] using Fril, given approximate radius and length of the shape, both of the rules are applied and the two resulting support pair-weighted fuzzy sets can be combined into an expected fuzzy set, which can then be defuzzified to give an approximately estimated area of the shape.

Further, with overriding inheritance, it is possible for an object or a class not to inherit some properties from its super-classes, but use their own definitions of those properties, as in the classical object-oriented model. In Fril++, we adopt overriding inheritance as a default, that is, a property (possibly associated with a support pair) in a class is assumed to override properties of the same name in super-classes of the class. Also, a property asserted for an object is assumed to override properties of the same name in classes.

However, in the case with uncertainty, the uncertain membership of an object to a class raises a new issue regarding overriding inheritance. Specifically, if an object is not a full member of a class, then the question is whether a property that the object inherits from the class would override properties of the same name in super-classes of the class. In Fril++, we assume that overriding inheritance is effective only with the full membership, i.e., with the support pair (1 1).

For example, the property ((*fly*)) : (0 0) of Penny in the example above, which is inherited from the class PENGUIN, overrides the property ((*fly*)): (0.9 0.95) in the class BIRD. Now, suppose that Polly is a bird, but is not certainly a penguin, with the support pair (0.6 0.8) for instance. Then, by Formula (4.1), Polly has the following support pairs for its property *fly*:

((fly)): (0.9 0.95)

((fly)): (0 0.4)

which are inherited from BIRD and PENGUIN, respectively.

In this case, as Polly is not a full member of PENGUIN, there is no overriding inheritance, but multiple inheritance instead. As in Fril, normally the intersection rule is applied to combine support pairs, but Dempster's rule ([13]) can be applied instead for those obtained from sources of independent and possibly conflicting viewpoints. Here Dempster's rule gives the combined support pair (0.782609 0.826087) for the property *fly* of Polly. Recently, in [5], we have proposed probabilistic default reasoning as a suitable approach to uncertain multiple inheritance.

4.3 Uncertain Membership Evaluation

Uncertain membership may be asserted as subjective probability degrees or evaluated according to object and class descriptions. It seems that there is no universally applicable method for evaluating the membership degree of an object to a class on the basis of their uncertain and fuzzy descriptions. Therefore, for flexibility, we propose that each class has a user-defined method for computing the membership degree of an object to the class. Nevertheless, as discussed in [1], there are good default definitions for such an uncertain membership evaluation method, which are *hierarchy-based* or *description-based.*

The hierarchy-based evaluation relies on the following assumptions proposed in [6]:

1. If an object is a member of a class with some *positive characteristic* degree, then it is a member of any super-class of that class with the same degree.
2. If an object is a member of a class with some *negative characteristic* degree, then it is a member of any subclass of that class with the same degree.

For fuzzy truth degrees, for instance, the positive and negative characteristics could be defined to be **true** and **false** characteristics, respectively. Here, probability lower bounds are considered as positive characteristic degrees, while probability upper bounds are considered as negative characteristic ones. Consequently, if an object is a member of a class with a support pair $(l\ \ u)$, then it is a member of any super-class of that class with the support pair $(l\ \ 1)$, and a member of any subclass of that class with the support pair $(0\ \ u)$.

Meanwhile, the description-based evaluation may be performed as weighted fuzzy pattern matching of class properties to object properties. Let, for every i from 1 to n, R_i be the value of property A_i of a class C, V_i be the value of A_i of an object O, and $(l_i\ \ u_i)$ be the support pair for the applicability of A_i to C. Then, on the basis of the evidential logic matching method of [2], the support pair for O being a member of C is defined to be $(F(\Sigma_{i=1,n}\{w_i\,\alpha_i\})\ \ F(\Sigma_{i=1,n}\{w_i\,\beta_i\}))$ where:

- $w_i = (l_i + u_i) / \Sigma_{i=1,n}\{(l_i + u_i)\}$, which measures a weight of A_i in evaluation of the membership of O to C.
- $(\alpha_i\ \ \beta_i)$ is the support pair obtained by the semantic unification of R_i to V_i, based on mass assignment theory.
- F: $[0, 1] \rightarrow [0, 1]$ is a function whose choice determines the nature of the combination of $A_1, A_2, \ldots, A_n$.

Another approach studied in [5] to the description-based object recognition is using inverse Jeffrey's rule as follows:

$$\Pr(C(O)) = \frac{\Pr(p(O)) - \Pr(p(x) \mid \neg C(x))}{\Pr(p(x) \mid C(x)) - \Pr(p(x) \mid \neg C(x))}$$

which is derived from the expression of Jeffrey's rule for a property p presented in Section 4.1. Then probabilistic default reasoning is applied to combine such probability degrees obtained for O being members of different classes with respect to their subclass relation.

5 Translation into Fril

5.1 Translation Strategy

Following [11], the execution of an object-oriented logic program is considered as having two phases, namely, the *label phase* and the *body phase*. In the label phase, the system determines the actual classes whose definitions for the currently called property are to be executed. Then, once those classes have been determined, the system enters the body phase to execute the property as defined in the bodies of the classes.

Corresponding to these label phase and body phase are *label clauses* and *body clauses* of a target program, which is a normal logic program, translated from an object-oriented logic program. The label clauses provide entry points to the definitions to be executed for a property call, and to realise overriding inheritance such that if a definition of a property is found in a class, then the definitions of the property in its super-classes are excluded. Meanwhile the body clauses are the translation of definitions of class properties.

There are following important differences between the classical object-oriented model and the uncertain and fuzzy one, which is out of the scope of [11], due to uncertain class membership and uncertain property applicability:

- In the classical model, an object as an instance of a class inherits properties only from that class or its super-classes. Whereas, since in the uncertain and fuzzy model an object can be a partial member of a class, it can inherit with uncertainty degrees properties from any class.
- In the classical model, a property of a class is fully applicable to an object as a member of the class. Whereas, in the uncertain and fuzzy model, this applicability can be uncertain and, moreover, an associated uncertainty degree is not determinable at translation-time if the membership degree of an object to a class can change at run-time.

They make a difference between the translation of an uncertain and fuzzy object-oriented logic program and that of a classical one, for both of the label clauses and the body clauses.

Regarding the first difference, for the label clauses of the translation of a classical object-oriented logic program, when a property is applied to an object, its definition is first searched in the local knowledge base of the object. If it is found therein, then it is the definition to be executed. Otherwise, it is searched in the class which the object is an instance of and then, if still not found, in super-classes of that class. Meanwhile, in the uncertain and fuzzy case, every class containing a definition of the property is considered.

Therefore, in Fril++, a definition of a property is first searched in the local knowledge base of the object that the property is applied to. If it is found therein, then it is the definition to be executed. Otherwise, not as in the classical case, all the classes that contain the property are considered. If the object is a full member of one of those classes, then all of its super-classes are excluded due to overriding inheritance. At the end, if there are more than one definition to be executed, one has multiple inheritance.

Regarding the second difference, the body clauses of the translation of an uncertain and fuzzy object-oriented logic program are weighted by support pair variables, whose values are functions of uncertain applicability degrees of properties and uncertain membership degrees of objects as computed by Formula (4.1), which are determined at run-time. This can be realised for Fril++ as Fril allows variables to be support pairs of clauses.

If the membership degree of an object to a class can change at run-time, overriding inheritance, which requires the full membership as discussed in Section 4.2, is not determinable at translation-time. Therefore, in order to gain execution efficiency at run-time, we distinguish *static* objects from *dynamic* objects, where membership degrees of the former to classes cannot be changed after they are created and thus overriding inheritance can be performed at translation-time.

The next sections illustrate specifically how the presented strategy is realised in the translation of Fril++ class definitions and message passing into Fril codes.

5.2 Label Clauses

For illustrating examples, let us use the following simple class hierarchy, excluding the default Fril and Fril++ classes introduced in Section 2.1, where CIRCLE and SQUARE are defined as in Section 4.2:

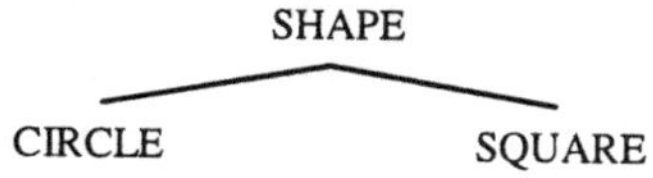

The main label clauses for executing a Fril++ program are defined by the following predicates:

1. For each property, the predicate that defines all the classes containing it. For instance, in the current example, those for the properties *radius*, *length*, and *area* are:

   ((property radius (circle)))
   ((property length (square)))
   ((property area (circle square))).
2. The predicate that identifies the actual classes for executing a property

applied to an object, with respect to overriding inheritance and the visibility of the property at the place where it is called. For overriding inheritance, that depends on the membership of the object to the classes containing the property, whereas the visibility depends on public, protected, or private declarations of the property in the class hierarchy of discourse.

3. The predicate that executes the body clauses of a property from the actual classes as identified in the above overriding inheritance and visibility checking process. The body clauses are the translation of the definitions of the property in those classes as presented below.

5.3 Body Clauses

Each property definition in a class is translated into a body clause. For example, the body clause for the property *area* of SQUARE is as follows:

```
((square (area  A) (X  Y) SELF)
      (eq  SUPP  (X  1))
      (query SELF (length  L) (square))
      (query SELF  (times  L  L  A)  (Fril))
) : SUPP.
```

Here *SELF* is a variable to represent, and pass around, an object currently referred to at run-time. (*X Y*) is the support pair for *SELF* being a member of SQUARE. *SUPP* is the support pair for the applicability of the property *area* of SQUARE to *SELF*; the Fril built-in predicate *eq* equates *SUPP* with (*X* 1) in accordance with Formula (4.1).

The predicate *query* is the basic one that each property call in a Fril++ source program is translated into. The last argument of this predicate for a property call is the list of the classes whose definitions of the property are visible at the place of that property call. For instance, the list (*square*) in one predicate *query* above says that only the definition of the property *length* in the class SQUARE is visible there. Meanwhile, for the other predicate *query*, the list (*Fril*) says that only the definition of the property *times* in the class Fril is visible.

We note that, in the translation, *times* is treated like any other property, though in the given definition of *area* of SQUARE, *times* is intended to be the one built into Fril. To bypass classes in searching for a definition of a property, one can designate a class whose definition for the property is the only one to be executed, as mentioned in Section 3.2 about message passing. For example, the definition of *area* of SQUARE can be modified as follows for that purpose:

```
((area  A) (length  L) (Fril.times  L  L  A))
```

Then its translation becomes:

```
((square (area  A) (X  Y) SELF)
      (eq  SUPP  (X  1))
      (query SELF (length  L) (square))
      (times  L  L  A)
) : SUPP.
```

This gains execution efficiency at run-time as compared to the previous translation.

We recall that, if a property is applied to an object, a definition for the property is first searched in the local knowledge base of the object and, if it is found therein, it is the only definition to be executed. Properties of an object are also stored as Fril clauses in its knowledge base. For example, suppose the following clauses for an object *ufo*:

```
((ufo (isa circle) )) : (0.7 0.8)
((ufo (isa square) )) : (0.6 0.7)
((ufo (radius [1.0: 0 1.2: 1 1.4: 0]) ))
((ufo (length [1.8: 0 2.2: 1 2.6: 0]) ))
```

where [1.0: 0 1.2: 1 1.4: 0] and [1.8: 0 2.2: 1 2.6: 0] are fuzzy sets defining the linguistic terms *about 1.2* and *about 2.2*, respectively. The clauses express that *ufo* is a member of CIRCLE and SQUARE with the support pairs (0.7 0.8) and (0.6 0.7), respectively, and has the radius of *about 1.2* and the length of *about 2.2*.

Fril++ queries are also translated accordingly. For example, the following query asks for the area of *ufo*:

```
? ((ufo.area A))
```

and its translation is:

```
? ((query ufo (area A) (circle square)).
```

Meanwhile, the translation for constants, with or without overriding inheritance, is similar to that for properties. The translation for message passing to **self** or **super** is straightforward from its description in Section 3.2. The translation for message passing to an object identifier followed by a sequence of part identifiers is similar to the translation for message passing to just an object identifier.

6 Conclusion

We have presented Fril++ syntax and discussed related semantic issues in translating an uncertain and fuzzy object-oriented logic program into a normal uncertain and fuzzy logic program. We have pointed out that, not as in the classical object-oriented model, in the uncertain and fuzzy model an object can inherit with uncertainty degrees properties from any class, and overriding inheritance depends on uncertain membership of objects to classes. Our translation strategy has then been presented and translated codes for Fril++ class definitions and message passing have been illustrated. The presented compiler has been implemented with the current version of Fril.

For a completed version of Fril++ to be released, there remain problems to be solved and their solutions to be implemented. Those include handling high-ordered predicates (i.e., ones whose arguments are also predicates) and optimising translated codes. These are among the topics that are currently investigated. As a programming language, Fril++ can then be used for developing uncertain and fuzzy object-oriented systems. Our direct application of Fril++ is for building a machine learning system incorporating a class library of different uncertain and fuzzy learning algorithms.

References

[1] Baldwin, J.F., Cao, T.H., Martin, T.P. and Rossiter, J.M. 2000. Towards soft computing object-oriented logic programming. In Proceedings of the 9th IEEE International Conference on Fuzzy Systems, pp. 768-773.

[2] Baldwin, J.F., Martin, T.P. and Pilsworth, B.W. 1995. *Fril - Fuzzy and Evidential Reasoning in Artificial Intelligence*. Research Studies Press.

[3] Baldwin, J.F., Martin, T.P. and Vargas-Vera, M. 1998. Fril++: object-based extensions to Fril. In Martin, T.P. and Fontana, F.A. (eds), *Logic Programming and Soft Computing*, Research Studies Press, pp. 223-238.

[4] Bordogna, G., Lucarella, D. and Pasi, G. 1994. A fuzzy object oriented data model. In Proceedings of the 3rd IEEE International Conference on Fuzzy Systems, pp. 313-318.

[5] Cao, T.H. 2000. Uncertain inheritance and recognition as probabilistic default reasoning. To appear in *International Journal of Intelligent Systems*.

[6] Cao, T.H. and Creasy, P.N. 2000. Fuzzy types: a framework for handling uncertainty about types of objects. *International Journal of Approximate Reasoning*, 25, 217-253.

[7] Dubitzky, W., Büchner, A.G., Hughes, J.G. and Bell, D.A. 1999. Towards concept-oriented databases. *Data & Knowledge Engineering*, 30, 23-55.

[8] George, R., Buckles, B.P. and Petry, F.E. 1993. Modelling class hierarchies in the fuzzy object-oriented data model. *International Journal for Fuzzy Sets and Systems*, 60, 259-272.

[9] Itzkovich, I. and Hawkes, L.W. 1994. Fuzzy extension of inheritance hierarchies. *International Journal for Fuzzy Sets and Systems*, 62, 143-153.

[10] Jeffrey, R. 1965. *The Logic of Decision*. McGraw-Hill.

[11] McCabe, F.G. 1992. *Logic and Objects*. Prentice Hall.

[12] Rossazza, J-P., Dubois, D. and Prade, H. 1997. A hierarchical model of fuzzy classes. In De Caluwe, R. (ed.), *Fuzzy and Uncertain Object-Oriented Databases: Concepts and Models*, World Scientific, pp. 21-61.

[13] Shafer, G. 1976. *A Mathematical Theory of Evidence*. Princeton University Press.

[14] Stroustrup, B. 1997. *The C++ Programming Language* (3rd edition). Addison-Wesley.

[15] Van Gyseghem, N. and De Caluwe, R. 1997. The UFO database model: dealing with imperfect information. In De Caluwe, R. (ed.), *Fuzzy and Uncertain Object-Oriented Databases: Concepts and Models*, World Scientific, pp. 123-185.

On some Simplifications of the Axiomatization of Monoidal Logic

Siegfried Gottwald *
Institut für Logik und Wissenschaftstheorie
Universität Leipzig, D-04109 LEIPZIG, Germany
e-mail: gottwald@rz.uni-leipzig.de

Abstract. The class of t-norms has gained central importance in considerations on fuzzy sets as well as in fuzzy logic, mainly because they are natural candidates for non-idempotent conjunction and intersection operations.
For an inferential, and therefore syntactical treatment of such t-norm based conjunction connectives one needs an axiomatic basis, either for some particular t-norm, or preferably for whole classes of t-norms. Monoidal logic was a first attempt to find a logical calculus designed to handle the case of left continuous t-norms. Here its axiomatization shall be simplified and transformed in such a way that it becomes easy to compare monoidal logic syntactically with other, more recent systems for the treatment of t-norm based logics.

1 Introduction

By a t-norm based residuated logic we shall mean an infinitely valued logic with truth degree set the real unit interval $\mathcal{I} = [0,1]$, which has as its basic connectives an idempotent conjunction $\wedge$ and an idempotent disjunction $\vee$ determined by the truth degree functions min and max, respectively, together with a non-idempotent conjunction connective & determined by some t-norm $\boldsymbol{t}$ as truth degree function, and together with an implication connective $\rightarrow$ determined by a truth degree function $\rightarrowtail$ which is given via the adjointness condition

$$z \leqslant (x \rightarrowtail y) \quad \Leftrightarrow \quad \boldsymbol{t}(x,z) \leqslant y \,. \tag{1}$$

from the t-norm $\boldsymbol{t}$.

The most natural approach toward an axiomatization of such a t-norm based residuated system, or even of a whole class of such t-norm based residuated systems, is the semantical one which either starts from some standard logical matrix, which specifies (for a given formalized propositional language) the relevant truth degree structure together with the set of designated truth degrees, or which starts from a whole class of suitable truth degree structures

* The author gratefully acknowledges fruitful discussions during the COST action #15 on "Many-Valued Logic for Computer Science Applications".

with specified designated degrees each. Of course, suitablility here means that the propositional language and the algebraic structures have coinciding signatures. In both cases one has the usual notion of logical validity (of a well-formed formula of the language in a structure – or in a whole class of structures) available.

The problem of axiomatization then is the problem to determine a suitable logical calculus $\mathbb{K}$ which has as its set of (formal) theorems just the set of logically valid formulas.

2 Monoidal logic

The adjointness condition (1) which is crucial for the introduction of a suitable implication connective in the t-norm based systems forces the corresponding t-norm to be left continuous. Here left continuity of a t-norm $\boldsymbol{t}$ is understood as left continuity of the binary real function $\boldsymbol{t}$ in both its arguments. This comes from the fact that one has the following result.

Proposition 1 *For a given t-norm* $\mathbf{t}$ *there exists an adjoint operation* $\rightarrowtail$ *in* $[0,1]$ *such that this pair* $\mathbf{t}, \rightarrowtail$ *satisfies the adjointness condition* (1) *iff* $\mathbf{t}$ *is left continuous.*

It is a routine matter to show that the adjointness condition (1) even forces that the adjoint operation $\rightarrowtail$ in $[0,1]$ is determined by the formula

$$u \rightarrowtail v = \sup\{w \mid \boldsymbol{t}(u,w) \leq v\}\,.$$

Thus one gets from (1) that the implication in each t-norm based system is the R-implication connected with the given t-norm conjunction.

Having in mind the basic t-norm properties it is obvious that for each left continuous t-norm $\boldsymbol{t}$ the algebraic structure $\langle [0,1], \boldsymbol{t}\rangle$ is an abelian semigroup. But even more, the richer algebraic structure

$$\langle [0,1], \min, \max, \boldsymbol{t}, \rightarrowtail, 0, 1\rangle$$

is a residuated lattice in the sense of the following definition.

Definition 1 *An algebraic structure* $\langle L, \cap, \cup, *, \rightarrowtail, 0, 1\rangle$ *is a* residuated lattice *iff one has that*

(i) $\langle L, \cap, \cup, 0, 1\rangle$ *is a lattice with zero and unit element (with ordering* $\leqslant$*);*
(ii) $\langle L, *, 1, \leqslant\rangle$ *is a commutative lattice-ordered monoid;*
(iii) the binary operations $*$ *and* $\rightarrowtail$ *form an adjoint pair, i.e. satisfy for all* $x, y, z \in L$ *the adjointness condition*

$$z \leqslant (x \rightarrowtail y) \quad \Leftrightarrow \quad x * z \leqslant y\,. \qquad (2)$$

And this is the basic type of algebraic structure for the approach toward t-norm based systems which is realized by the monoidal logic of Höhle [10]: Monoidal logic is the logic of the class of all residuated lattices, as classical logic is the logic of the class of all Boolean algebras.

3 An adequate axiomatization of monoidal logic

The axiomatization of HÖHLE [10] for the monoidal logic is given in a language which has as its basic vocabulary the set $\mathcal{J} = \{\rightarrow, \&, \wedge, \vee, \neg\}$ of connectives, interpreted in each residuated lattice $\langle L, \sqcap, \sqcup, *, \rightarrowtail, 0, 1\rangle$ as the operations $\rightarrowtail, *, \sqcap, \sqcup$, respectively, and as an additional unary operation – defined by $-x =_{\mathrm{def}} x \rightarrowtail 0$ for each $x \in L$.

This monoidal logic was originally axiomatized by a set of axioms $\mathsf{Ax}_{\mathsf{ML}}$ determined by the following schemata:

(Ax$_{\mathsf{ML}}$1) $(\varphi \rightarrow \psi) \rightarrow ((\psi \rightarrow \chi) \rightarrow (\varphi \rightarrow \chi))$,
(Ax$_{\mathsf{ML}}$2) $\varphi \,\&\, \psi \rightarrow \varphi$,
(Ax$_{\mathsf{ML}}$3) $\varphi \,\&\, \psi \rightarrow \psi \,\&\, \varphi$,
(Ax$_{\mathsf{ML}}$4) $(\varphi \rightarrow (\psi \rightarrow \chi)) \rightarrow (\varphi \,\&\, \psi \rightarrow \chi)$,
(Ax$_{\mathsf{ML}}$5) $(\varphi \,\&\, \psi \rightarrow \chi) \rightarrow (\varphi \rightarrow (\psi \rightarrow \chi))$,
(Ax$_{\mathsf{ML}}$6) $\varphi \wedge \psi \rightarrow \varphi$,
(Ax$_{\mathsf{ML}}$7) $\varphi \rightarrow \varphi \vee \psi$,
(Ax$_{\mathsf{ML}}$8) $\psi \rightarrow \varphi \vee \psi$,
(Ax$_{\mathsf{ML}}$9) $(\varphi \rightarrow \chi) \rightarrow$
$((\psi \rightarrow \chi) \rightarrow (\varphi \vee \psi \rightarrow \chi))$,
(Ax$_{\mathsf{ML}}$10) $\varphi \wedge \psi \rightarrow \psi$,
(Ax$_{\mathsf{ML}}$11) $(\varphi \,\&\, \psi) \,\&\, \chi \rightarrow \varphi \,\&\, (\psi \,\&\, \chi)$,
(Ax$_{\mathsf{ML}}$12) $(\varphi \rightarrow \psi) \rightarrow$
$((\varphi \rightarrow \chi) \rightarrow (\varphi \rightarrow \psi \wedge \chi))$,
(Ax$_{\mathsf{ML}}$13) $\varphi \,\&\, \neg\varphi \rightarrow \psi$,
(Ax$_{\mathsf{ML}}$14) $(\varphi \rightarrow \varphi \,\&\, \neg\varphi) \rightarrow \neg\varphi$,

and has as its (only) inference rule the rule of detachment (w.r.t. the implication connective $\rightarrow$).

The logical calculus which is constituted by this axiom system and its inference rule, and which has the standard notion of derivation, shall be denoted by $\mathbb{K}_{\mathsf{ML}}$.

The main theoretical results from which the adequacy of this axiomatization results are the following ones.

Proposition 2 *The (extended) logical calculus $\mathbb{K}_{\mathsf{ML}}$ is sound, i.e. derives only such formulas which are valid in all residuated lattices.*

Proof. It is (essentially) a routine matter to check that all the axioms of the axiom system $\mathsf{Ax}_{\mathsf{ML}}$ are valid in each residuated lattice. And easily one gets that the rule of detachment (MP) leads from wffs which are valid in some residuated lattice $\mathfrak{L}$ again to a wff which is valid in $\mathfrak{L}$. □

Proposition 3 *The* LINDENBAUM *algebra of the (extended) logical calculus $\mathbb{K}_{\mathsf{ML}}$ is a residuated lattice.*

The proof needs the derivation of a lot of particular theorems of $\mathbb{K}_{\mathsf{ML}}$. This shall not be done here. All the necessary details are given in [10] as well as in [9, 11, 12].

Theorem 4 (Completeness Theorem) *For each wff φ of $\mathcal{L}_t$ the following assertions are equivalent:*

(*i*) *φ is derivable within the logical calculus $\mathbb{K}_{\mathsf{ML}}$;*
(*ii*) *φ is valid in all residuated lattices.*

4 Some modifications of this axiom system

The previously mentioned axiomatization of HÖHLE [10] for the monoidal logic shall now be given in a language which has as its basic vocabulary the sets $\mathcal{J}^* = \{\to, \&, \wedge, \vee\}$ and $\mathcal{K}^* = \{0\}$ of connectives and of truth degree constants, interpreted in each residuated lattice $\langle L, \cap, \cup, *, \rightarrowtail, 0, 1\rangle$ as the operations $\rightarrowtail, *, \cap, \cup$ and the truth degree 0, respectively. This language is usually extended by the definitions

$$\neg\varphi =_{\text{def}} \varphi \to 0\,, \qquad 1 =_{\text{def}} \neg 0\,, \tag{3}$$

and then becomes the full language of t-norm based systems.

Theorem 5 *This monoidal logic $\mathsf{Ax}_{\mathsf{ML}}$ one can also adequately axiomatize by the following axiom system $\mathsf{Ax}^*_{\mathsf{ML}}$:*

($\mathsf{Ax}^*_{\mathsf{ML}}1$) $(\varphi \to \psi) \to ((\psi \to \chi) \to (\varphi \to \chi))$,
($\mathsf{Ax}^*_{\mathsf{ML}}2$) $\varphi \,\&\, \psi \to \varphi$,
($\mathsf{Ax}^*_{\mathsf{ML}}3$) $\varphi \,\&\, \psi \to \psi \,\&\, \varphi$,
($\mathsf{Ax}^*_{\mathsf{ML}}4$) $(\varphi \to (\psi \to \chi)) \to (\varphi \,\&\, \psi \to \chi)$,
($\mathsf{Ax}^*_{\mathsf{ML}}5$) $(\varphi \,\&\, \psi \to \chi) \to (\varphi \to (\psi \to \chi))$,
($\mathsf{Ax}^*_{\mathsf{ML}}6$) $\varphi \wedge \psi \to \varphi$,
($\mathsf{Ax}^*_{\mathsf{ML}}7$) $\varphi \to \varphi \vee \psi$,
($\mathsf{Ax}^*_{\mathsf{ML}}8$) $\psi \to \varphi \vee \psi$,
($\mathsf{Ax}^*_{\mathsf{ML}}9$) $(\varphi \to \chi) \to$
$((\psi \to \chi) \to (\varphi \vee \psi \to \chi))$,
($\mathsf{Ax}^*_{\mathsf{ML}}10$) $\varphi \wedge \psi \to \psi \wedge \varphi$,
($\mathsf{Ax}^*_{\mathsf{ML}}11$) $\varphi \,\&\, (\varphi \to \psi) \to \varphi \wedge \psi$,
($\mathsf{Ax}^*_{\mathsf{ML}}12$) $0 \to \varphi$,

together with the rule of detachment (w.r.t. the implication connective $\to$) as inference rule.

The logical calculus which is constituted by this axiom system and its inference rule, and which has the standard notion of derivation, shall be denoted by $\mathbb{K}^*_{\mathsf{ML}}$.

There are two points which have to be considered: the change in the basic vocabulary, and the change in the axiom schemata.

Obviously, the first nine schemata coincide. So only the remaining one have to be considered.

To get the equivalence of these two axiom systems we first prove that the axiom schemata of $\mathsf{Ax_{ML}}$ which are missing in $\mathsf{Ax^*_{ML}}$, are derivable in $\mathbb{K}^*_{\mathsf{ML}}$.

Proposition 6 (*i*) *The logical calculus* $\mathbb{K}^*_{\mathsf{ML}}$ *allows to derive*

$$(\mathsf{Ax_{ML}}11) \qquad (\varphi \,\&\, \psi) \,\&\, \chi \to \varphi \,\&\, (\psi \,\&\, \chi)\,,$$
$$(\mathsf{Ax_{ML}}14) \qquad (\varphi \to \varphi \,\&\, \neg\varphi) \to \neg\varphi\,.$$

(*ii*) *From* $\mathsf{Ax^*_{ML}}1$ *together with* $\mathsf{Ax^*_{ML}}6, \mathsf{Ax^*_{ML}}7$ *one can derive*

$$(\mathsf{Ax_{ML}}10) \qquad \varphi \wedge \psi \to \psi\,.$$

(*iii*) *From the axiom schemata* $\mathsf{Ax^*_{ML}}1, \ldots, \mathsf{Ax^*_{ML}}7$ *one can derive*

$$(\mathsf{Ax_{ML}}12) \qquad (\varphi \to \psi) \to ((\varphi \to \chi) \to (\varphi \to \psi \wedge \chi))\,.$$

(*iv*) *From the schemata* $\mathsf{Ax^*_{ML}}11, \mathsf{Ax^*_{ML}}12$ *together with* (6) *one can derive*

$$(\mathsf{Ax_{ML}}13) \qquad \varphi \,\&\, \neg\varphi \to \psi\,.$$

Proof. One first has from $\mathsf{Ax^*_{ML}}2$ and $\mathsf{Ax^*_{ML}}5$

$$\vdash_{\mathsf{ML}} \varphi \to (\psi \to \varphi)\,. \tag{4}$$

And one gets

$$\vdash_{\mathsf{ML}} (\varphi \to (\psi \to \chi)) \to (\psi \to (\varphi \to \chi)) \tag{5}$$

from $\mathsf{Ax^*_{ML}}3$ via importation/exportation $\mathsf{Ax^*_{ML}}4, \mathsf{Ax^*_{ML}}5$ and chaining $\mathsf{Ax^*_{ML}}1$. Hence one has wffs similar to axioms schemata of the logical calculi $\mathbb{K}^m_{\mathrm{RT}}$ of the general ROSSER/TURQUETTE calculi of finitely many-valued systems, which means that one gets

$$\vdash_{\mathsf{ML}} \varphi \to \varphi \tag{6}$$

as in $\mathbb{K}^m_{\mathrm{RT}}$, cf. e.g. [5, 13]. And applying this last result with the wff $(\varphi \to \psi)$ instead of φ additionally gives

$$\vdash_{\mathsf{ML}} \varphi \,\&\, (\varphi \to \psi) \to \psi \tag{7}$$

by an application of importation $\mathsf{Ax^*_{ML}}4$ and of chaining $\mathsf{Ax^*_{ML}}1$.

(*i*) One immediately has

$$\vdash_{\mathsf{ML}} (\varphi \,\&\, \psi) \,\&\, \chi \to (\varphi \,\&\, \psi) \,\&\, \chi\,,$$

and therefore

$$\vdash_{\mathsf{ML}} (\varphi \,\&\, \psi) \to (\chi \to (\varphi \,\&\, \psi) \,\&\, \chi)\,,$$

via exportation $\mathsf{Ax}^*_{\mathsf{ML}}9$ and chaining $\mathsf{Ax}^*_{\mathsf{ML}}1$, as well as

$$\vdash_{\mathsf{ML}} \varphi \to (\psi \to (\chi \to (\varphi \,\&\, \psi) \,\&\, \chi)) .$$

So (5) together with chaining $\mathsf{Ax}^*_{\mathsf{ML}}1$ gives

$$\vdash_{\mathsf{ML}} \varphi \to (\chi \to (\psi \to (\varphi \,\&\, \psi) \,\&\, \chi)) .$$

Now two applications of importation $\mathsf{Ax}^*_{\mathsf{ML}}8$, again together with chaining $\mathsf{Ax}^*_{\mathsf{ML}}1$, give

$$\vdash_{\mathsf{ML}} (\varphi \,\&\, \psi) \,\&\, \chi \to \varphi \,\&\, (\psi \,\&\, \chi) .$$

Furthermore one gets via chaining $\mathsf{Ax}^*_{\mathsf{ML}}1$ from the schemata $\mathsf{Ax}^*_{\mathsf{ML}}6, \dots, \mathsf{Ax}^*_{\mathsf{ML}}8$

$$\vdash_{\mathsf{ML}} \varphi \,\&\, (\varphi \to \mathsf{0}) \to \mathsf{0} . \tag{8}$$

Having in mind that according to (5) one can write $\mathsf{Ax}^*_{\mathsf{ML}}1$ as

$$\vdash_{\mathsf{ML}} (\psi \to \chi) \to ((\varphi \to \psi) \to (\varphi \to \chi)) ,$$

this gives

$$\vdash_{\mathsf{ML}} (\varphi \to \psi \,\&\, \neg\psi) \to \neg\varphi$$

which has (6) as a particular case.

(*ii*) One has as a particular case of axiom schema $\mathsf{Ax}^*_{\mathsf{ML}}1$ the derivability of the wff

$$(\varphi \wedge \psi \to \psi \wedge \varphi) \to ((\psi \wedge \varphi \to \psi) \to (\varphi \wedge \psi \to \psi))$$

within the logical calculus $\mathbb{K}_{\mathsf{ML}}$. From this wff two applications of the rule of detachment, using $\mathsf{Ax}^*_{\mathsf{ML}}6, \mathsf{Ax}^*_{\mathsf{ML}}7$, give

$$\vdash_{\mathsf{ML}} \varphi \wedge \psi \to \psi .$$

On the other hand one has

$$(\varphi \wedge \psi \to \psi) \to ((\varphi \wedge \psi \to \varphi) \to (\varphi \wedge \psi \to \psi \wedge \varphi))$$

as a particular case of axiom schema $\mathsf{Ax}^*_{\mathsf{ML}}8$. And from this wff one gets $\mathsf{Ax}^*_{\mathsf{ML}}7$ by two applications of the rule of detachment, using (6) and $\mathsf{Ax}^*_{\mathsf{ML}}6$.

(*iii*) One first has the derivability of each wff

$$(\varphi \to \psi) \to (\varphi \,\&\, \chi \to \psi \,\&\, \chi) \tag{9}$$

because one gets the wffs

$$\varphi \,\&\, (\varphi \to \psi) \to \psi , \qquad \psi \to (\chi \to \psi \,\&\, \chi)$$

via importation/exportation $\mathsf{Ax}^*_{\mathsf{ML}}4, \mathsf{Ax}^*_{\mathsf{ML}}5$ from (6). By chaining $\mathsf{Ax}^*_{\mathsf{ML}}1$ one derives

$$\varphi \mathbin{\&} (\varphi \to \psi) \to (\chi \to \psi \mathbin{\&} \chi),$$

and from this wff again via importation/ exportation successively

$$\varphi \to ((\varphi \to \psi) \to (\chi \to \psi \mathbin{\&} \chi)),$$
$$\varphi \to (\chi \to ((\varphi \to \psi) \to \psi \mathbin{\&} \chi)),$$
$$\varphi \mathbin{\&} \chi \to ((\varphi \to \psi) \to \psi \mathbin{\&} \chi).$$

Now an application of (5) finally gives (9). Thus one gets from the schema $\varphi \mathbin{\&} (\varphi \to \psi) \to \psi$ the further schema

$$\varphi \mathbin{\&} (\varphi \to \psi) \mathbin{\&} (\psi \to \chi) \to \psi \mathbin{\&} (\psi \to \chi),$$

which gives via $\mathsf{Ax}^*_{\mathsf{ML}}8$ and chaining $\mathsf{Ax}^*_{\mathsf{ML}}1$ all the wffs

$$\varphi \mathbin{\&} (\varphi \to \psi) \mathbin{\&} (\psi \to \chi) \to \psi \wedge \chi.$$

Now it is a routine matter to derive ($\mathsf{Ax}_{\mathsf{ML}}12$) via importation/exportation.

On the other hand one gets from ($\mathsf{Ax}_{\mathsf{ML}}12$) immediately

$$(\varphi \mathbin{\&} (\varphi \to \psi) \to \varphi) \to$$
$$((\varphi \mathbin{\&} (\varphi \to \psi) \to \psi) \to (\varphi \mathbin{\&} (\varphi \to \psi) \to \varphi \wedge \psi)),$$

and thus via $\mathsf{Ax}^*_{\mathsf{ML}}2$ and (7) also $\mathsf{Ax}^*_{\mathsf{ML}}8$.

(*iv*) From $\mathsf{Ax}^*_{\mathsf{ML}}11$ together with (6) one gets $\varphi \mathbin{\&} (\varphi \to 0) \to 0$ and hence $\mathsf{Ax}_{\mathsf{ML}}13$ via $\mathsf{Ax}^*_{\mathsf{ML}}12$ and chaining. □

And now we also have to prove that the axiom schemata of $\mathsf{Ax}^*_{\mathsf{ML}}$ which are missing in $\mathsf{Ax}_{\mathsf{ML}}$, are derivable in $\mathbb{K}_{\mathsf{ML}}$. To reach this goal we extend $\mathbb{K}_{\mathsf{ML}}$ with the definition

$$0 =_{\mathrm{def}} p' \mathbin{\&} \neg p' \tag{10}$$

for some propositional variable p'.

Proposition 7 *In the logical calculus $\mathbb{K}_{\mathsf{ML}}$ one can derive the formulas*

($\mathsf{Ax}^*_{\mathsf{ML}}10$) $\varphi \wedge \psi \to \psi \wedge \varphi$,
($\mathsf{Ax}^*_{\mathsf{ML}}11$) $\varphi \mathbin{\&} (\varphi \to \psi) \to \varphi \wedge \psi$,
($\mathsf{Ax}^*_{\mathsf{ML}}12$) $0 \to \varphi$.

Proof. From (4) one immediately gets via (9), which both are derivable also in $\mathbb{K}_{\mathsf{ML}}$, the formula

$$\varphi \mathbin{\&} \psi \to \varphi \mathbin{\&} (\varphi \to \psi),$$

and therefore $\mathsf{Ax}^*_{\mathsf{ML}}10$ by chaining from $\mathsf{Ax}_{\mathsf{ML}}8$.

That one can derive the schema $\mathsf{Ax}^*_{\mathsf{ML}}11$ in $\mathbb{K}_{\mathsf{ML}}$ follows from the last proof: the derivation of (7) works in $\mathbb{K}_{\mathsf{ML}}$ as in $\mathbb{K}^*_{\mathsf{ML}}$.

Finally, by definition (10) schema $\mathsf{Ax}^*_{\mathsf{ML}}12$ becomes a particular case of schema $\mathsf{Ax}_{\mathsf{ML}}13$. □

5 Concluding remarks

The reformulation of the original axiomatization of monoidal logic, which was presented here, fits well with some more recent axiomatizations of classes of t-norm related algebraic structures.

The first restriction which shall be mentioned here is to restrict the class of residuated lattices, characteristic for the monoidal logic, to those ones which additionally satisfy the pre-linearity condition $x \rightarrowtail y \vee x \rightarrowtail y = 1$. This *monoidal t-norm logic*, discussed in [3] and first called QBL logic in [2], can adequately be axiomatized by extending the list of axiom schemata of $\mathbb{K}^*_{\mathsf{ML}}$ by the schema

$$((\varphi \to \psi) \to \chi) \to (((\psi \to \varphi) \to \chi) \to \chi) \,.$$

And a second restriction is to consider the class of all pre-linear residuated lattices which additionally satisfy the condition

$$a \cap b = a * (a \rightarrowtail b)$$

of divisibility. This leads to the ***basic t-norm logic*** of [7,8].

In the situation of the monoidal t-norm logic the disjunction connective $\vee$ becomes definable. So the corresponding axiom schemata can be deleted, and the system simplified.

In the case of the basic t-norm logic the addition of the further axiom schemata

$$\varphi \,\&\, (\varphi \to \psi) \to \varphi \wedge \psi \,,$$
$$\varphi \wedge \psi \to \varphi \,\&\, (\varphi \to \psi) \,,$$

which express divisibility, give an adequate axiomatization. However in basic t-norm logic even the conjunction connective $\wedge$ becomes definable. Therefore a further deletion of axiom schemata is possible, cf. e.g. [8]. More details can also be found in [5,4].

Additionally it should be mentioned that the basic t-norm logic is a logical system, which may also be characterized by the (much more restricted) class of all t-norm structures $\langle [0,1], \min, \max, \boldsymbol{t}, \rightarrowtail, 0, 1\rangle$ determined by a continuous t-norm $\boldsymbol{t}$, as shown in [1,7,8].

And if one considers the even more specific situation that the negation defined in (3) is characterized by an involutive operation $-x = x \rightarrowtail 0$ one recognizes that the basic importance of the adjointness condition (1) relativizes: in this case the two axiom schemata ($\mathsf{Ax_{ML}}4$) and ($\mathsf{Ax_{ML}}5$) for importation and exportation can essentially be replaced by the "rotation" schemata

$$(\varphi \,\&\, \psi \to \chi) \to (\psi \,\&\, \neg\chi \to \neg\varphi) \,,$$
$$(\psi \,\&\, \neg\chi \to \neg\varphi) \to (\varphi \,\&\, \psi \to \chi) \,,$$

as discussed in [6].

References

1. CIGNOLI, R. – ESTEVA, F. – GODO, L. – TORRENS, A. (2000): Basic Fuzzy Logic is the logic of continuous t-norms and their residua, *Soft Computing* **4**, 106–112.
2. ESTEVA, F. – GODO, L. (1999): QBL: towards a logic for left-continuous t-norms, in: European Soc. Fuzzy Logic and Technol.: *Eusflat-Estylf Joint Conference, Palma (Mallorca), 1999,* Proceedings, Univ. de les Illes Balears, 35–37.
3. ESTEVA, F. – GODO, L. (200x): Monoidal t-norm based logic: towards a logic for left-continuous t-norms, *Fuzzy Sets Systems* (to appear).
4. GOTTWALD, S. (2000): Axiomatizations of t-Norm Based Logics – A Survey. *Soft Computing* **4**, 63–67.
5. GOTTWALD, S. (2001): *A Treatise on Many-Valued Logics.* Research Studies Press, Baldock/Hertfordshire.
6. GOTTWALD, S. – JENEI, S. (200x): A new axiomatization for involutive monoidal t-norm-based logic, *Fuzzy Sets Systems* (to appear).
7. HÁJEK, P. (1998): Basic fuzzy logic and BL-algebras, *Soft Computing* **2**, 124–128.
8. HÁJEK, P. (1998): *Metamathematics of Fuzzy Logic.* Kluwer Acad. Publ., Dordrecht.
9. HÖHLE, U. (1994): Monoidal logic, in: R. Kruse/J. Gebhardt/R. Palm (eds.), *Fuzzy Systems in Computer Science,* Vieweg, Wiesbaden, 233–243.
10. HÖHLE, U. (1995): Commutative, residuated l-monoids. In: U. Höhle/E.P. Klement eds., *Non-Classical Logics and Their Applications to Fuzzy Subsets,* Kluwer Acad. Publ., Dordrecht, 53–106.
11. HÖHLE, U. (1995): Presheaves over GL-monoids. In: U. Höhle/E.P. Klement eds., *Non-Classical Logics and Their Applications to Fuzzy Subsets,* Kluwer Acad. Publ., Dordrecht, 127–157.
12. HÖHLE, U. (1996): On the fundamentals of fuzzy set theory; *J. Math. Anal. Appl.* **201**, 786–826.
13. ROSSER, J.B. – TURQUETTE, A.R. (1952): *Many-Valued Logics.* North-Holland Publ. Comp., Amsterdam.

Logical Measure – Structure of Logical Formula

Dragan Radojević

Mihajlo Pupin Institute, Volgina 15, 11000 Beograd, Serbia, Yugoslavia
e-mail: draganr@L100.imp.bg.ac.yu

Abstract. The structure of logical and/or pseudo-logical formula is introduced. The structure of logical formula is its characteristic invariant to its functional realization ({0,1}-valued, many-valued and/or [0,1]-valued logical function). The Boolean algebra is defined on the set of all n-ary logical structures. The fundamental principle of structural functionality is introduced. A logical discrete Choquet integral is defined as [0,1]-valued logical and pseudo-logical function for AND operator defined as min function.

Keywords: Logical structure, structural function of logical formula, structural vector of logical formula, the principle of structural functionality, Logical discrete Choquet integral

1 Introduction and motivation

Many-valued logics [5], [3], and, accordingly, fuzzy sets theory, rely on the principle of truth functionality. The principle is the assumption that the truth value of a compound sentence depends only on the truth values of the components. The following considerations may confirm that it, in a general case, it is not justified to treat this property as a fundamental one in case of many-valued generalizations:

Fuzzy sets theory and fuzzy logic are intended for the treatment of uncertainty that is more general than probability. Therefore, the results of probability theory should be obtained as a special case. However, the truth functionality principle, for example, does not offer the possibility of distinguishing between the following two elementary problems: When a coin is thrown and the probability of obtaining tails is p, the following two questions can arise: (a) what is the probability of the obtaining simultaneously tails, (p), and non-tails, $(1-p)$ when coin is thrown once, and (b) what is the probability of obtaining tails and non-tails when the coin is thrown twice?

Evidently, the truth functionality principle does not make any difference between these two essentially different problems!

To permit a natural extension of classical logic by many-valued and/or [0,1]-valued logics, in this paper we introduce a new notion - the structure of a logical formula. The structure of a logical formula is determined by a set function and represents its unique characteristic invariant to its truth realizations - {0,1}-valued, many-valued and/or [0,1]-valued logical function.

[0,1]-valued logic that is completely compatible with classical logic and based on the structure of logical n-ary formulae is presented in [10].

In this paper we introduce the principle of structural functionality which means that the structure of a compound logical formula is determined only on the basis of the structures of the formulae of the components. Because of the coincidence of the structure of a logical formula and the {0,1}-valued realization of its logical function given by a truth table, it follows that truth functionality is a naturally inherited property, but in the {0,1}-valued realization. Any attempt of treating the principle of truth functionality as a fundamental property in case of many-valued logics entails many problems, constraints and, even, incorrectness.

In this paper we define a logical discrete Choquet integral as a consistent general [0,1]-valued logical function realized for the case when the AND operator is defined as a *min* function. The value of logical Choquet integral depends on the values of elementary logical variables, given in the list of arguments, and on the structure of logical formula or pseudological formula of {0,1}-valued and [0,1]-valued generalized measure [9] [7], respectively.

2 The structure of logical formula

In this paper we consider the finite universe $\Omega = \{a_1, ..., a_n\}$ of n [0,1]-valued logical variables (atomic symbols) and n-ary logic formulae.

A logical formula is defined, as in classical logic, inductively as follows: (i) a logical variable $a_i \in \Omega$ is a formula (ii) If $\Diamond$ is an n-ary connective and $\varphi_1, \varphi_2, ..., \varphi_n$ are logical formulae, then

$$\Diamond\,(\varphi_1, \varphi_2, ..., \varphi_n)$$

is a logical formula.

The structure is a fundamental characteristic of a logical formula. In this section we define the structure of logic formula by a structural function and/or a structural vector of logical formula. A structural function and structural vector of n-ary logical and/or pseudo-logical formula are defined in [8] as a general measure - set function and general measure vector, respectively.

A structural function of logic formula is invariant to the possible number of truth values of a corresponding logical function of logical formula and truth values themselves of logical variables - atomic symbols. A structural vector of logical formula is defined on the basis of a structural function. The set of all structural vectors of n-ary logical formulae is the Boolean algebra.

Every pseudo-logical formula can be represented as a linear convex combination of corresponding logical formulae. As a consequence, a structural function and/or structural vector of pseudo-logical formulae can be represented as a linear convex combination of structural functions and/or vectors of corresponding logical formulae.

2.1 Structural function and structural vector of logical formula

A structural function of n-ary logical formula φ is $\{0,1\}$-valued set function. A structural function of a logical variable $a_i \in \Omega$ is given by the following definition:

Definition 1. A structural function of a logical variable $a_i \in \Omega$ is a set function $\mu_{a_i} : \mathcal{P}(\Omega) \to \{0,1\}$ defined by:

$$\mu_{a_i}(A) = \begin{cases} 1 & a_i \in A \\ 0 & a_i \notin A \end{cases}; \quad A \in \mathcal{P}(\Omega).$$

For defining a [0,1]-valued logical function, its valuable to define a structural vector of logical variable.

Definition 2. A structural vector $\vec{\mu}_{a_i}$ of logical variable $a_i \in \Omega$ has components equal to the values of structural function of logical variable a_i in a given order (lexicographic or modified lexicographic, for example).

Definition 3. A modified lexicographic order of elements of a power set means that elements $A, B \in \mathcal{P}(\Omega)$ are ordered in the following way: $A \prec B$ if and only if $|A| < |B|$ or $|A| = |B| = s$ and A is before B in the lexicographic order between s-ary sets ordered by an increasing index.

A Boolean, $\{0,1\}$-valued, n-ary logical function $e\varphi(a_1, ..., a_n)$, where $e\varphi : \{0,1\}^n \to \{0,1\}$; in classical logic is defined by a truth-table. A generalization of Boolean function is [0,1]-valued logical function
$L\mu_\varphi(a_1, ..., a_n)$ where $L\mu_\varphi : [0,1]^n \to [0,1]$; which have equivalent values to a corresponding Boolean function for $\Omega \subset \{0,1\}^n$.

A logical (0-1) structural function μ_φ of a logical formula φ is given by the following definition:

Definition 4. A structural function of an n-ary logical formula φ, is a set function $\mu_{L\varphi} : \mathcal{P}(\Omega) \to \{0,1\}$, such that for every $A \in \mathcal{P}(\Omega)$

$$\mu_\varphi(A) = e\varphi(e_A),$$

where: $e_A = ((e_A)_i) \subset \{0,1\}^{|\Omega|}$ is the characteristic vector of $A \in \mathcal{P}(\Omega)$ and components $(e_A)_i = 1$ if and only if $a_i \in A$ and $e\varphi$ is $\{0,1\}$-valued function of logical formula φ.

For defining a [0,1]-valued logical function, its valuable to define a structural vector of logical formula.

Definition 5. A structural vector $\vec{\mu}_\varphi$ of a logical formula φ, has components equal to the values of structural function of that logical formula in a given order (lexicographic or modified lexicographic, for example).

A structural vector of logical formula corresponds to the column of that formula in a classical - Boolean truth-table. A very important property of a structural vector, which follows from the definition of a structural function of a logical formula, is given in the following corollary:

Corollary 1. *All n-ary logical functions $L\mu_\varphi$ ([0,1]-valued, many-valued and /or {0,1}-valued) which map*

$$L\mu_\varphi : \{0,1\}^n \rightarrow \{0,1\}$$

in the same way, have the same structural function and as a consequence structural vector.

Example 1. A structural vector of a binary logical function $L_{a_1 \odot a_2}(a_1, a_2)$ can be represented in the following way:

$$\begin{aligned} \vec{\mu}_{a_1 \odot a_2} &= \left[L_{a_1 \odot a_2}(0,0), L_{a_1 \odot a_2}(1,0), L_{a_1 \odot a_2}(0,1), L_{a_1 \odot a_2}(1,1)\right]^T \\ &= \left[\mu_{a_1 \odot a_2}(\emptyset), \mu_{a_1 \odot a_2}(\{a_1\}), \mu_{a_1 \odot a_2}(\{a_2\}), \mu_{a_1 \odot a_2}(\{a_1, a_2\})\right]^T \end{aligned}$$

Example 2. logical structural "vectors" (scalars) for nullary logical (Boolean constants) are:

	$\vec{\mu}_{\mathbf{0}}$	$\vec{\mu}_{\mathbf{1}}$
μ_0	0	1

.

Example 3. logical structural vectors for unary logical formulae $\varphi \in \{\mathbf{0}, a, \bar{a}, \mathbf{1}\}$, are

	$\vec{\mu}_{\mathbf{0}}$	$\vec{\mu}_a$	$\vec{\mu}_{\bar{a}}$	$\vec{\mu}_{\mathbf{1}}$
μ_0	0	0	1	1
μ_a	0	1	0	1

.

Example 4. logical structural vectors for binary logical formulae:

$$\begin{aligned} \varphi \in \{&\mathbf{0}, a_2 \Mapsto a_1, a_1 \Mapsto a_2, a_1 \veebar a_2, a_1 \wedge a_2, a_1, a_2, a_1 \vee a_2\} \cup \\ &\{\mathbf{1}, a_1 \Rightarrow a_2, a_2 \Rightarrow a_1, a_1 \Leftrightarrow a_2, a_1 \barwedge a_2, \bar{a}_1, \bar{a}_2, a_1 \overline{\nabla} a_2\} \end{aligned}$$

are given in the following table:

	$\vec{\mu}_\otimes$							
$\otimes$	$\mathbf{0}$	$a_1 \nabla a_2$	$a_2 \Mapsto a_1$	$a_1 \Mapsto a_2$	$a_1 \wedge a_2$	$\bar{a}_2$	$\bar{a}_1$	$a_1 \Leftrightarrow a_2$
μ_0	0	1	0	0	0	1	1	1
μ_1	0	0	1	0	0	1	0	0
μ_2	0	0	0	1	0	0	1	0
$\mu_{1,2}$	0	0	0	0	1	0	0	1

	$\vec{\mu}_\otimes$							
$\otimes$	$a_1 \veebar a_2$	a_1	a_2	$a_1 \barwedge a_2$	$a_2 \Rightarrow a_1$	$a_1 \Rightarrow a_2$	$a_1 \vee a_2$	$\mathbf{1}$
μ_0	0	0	0	1	1	1	0	1
μ_1	1	1	0	1	1	0	1	1
μ_2	1	0	1	1	0	1	1	1
$\mu_{1,2}$	0	1	1	0	1	1	1	1

The values of {0,1}-valued (Boolean), n-ary logical function $e\varphi(a_1, ..., a_n)$ of a logical formula φ

$$e\varphi : \{0,1\}^n \rightarrow \{0,1\}$$

and its generalization many-valued and/or [0,1]-valued logical function $L\mu_\varphi(a_1, ..., a_n)$

$$L\mu_\varphi : [0,1]^n \rightarrow [0,1]$$

are equal for $\{0,1\}$-valued logical variables (atomic symbols)

$$e\varphi(a_1, ..., a_n) = L\mu_\varphi(a_1, ..., a_n); \quad a_i \in \{0,1\}$$

¿From the definition of a structural vector of logical formula it follows that every extension of Boolean function (many-valued and/or [0,1]-valued) has the same structural function and/or structural vector as the original Boolean formula.

Nullary logical formulae - logical constants, have trivial structural vectors:

$$\mu_1(A) = 1; \quad A \in \mathcal{P}(\Omega),$$
$$\mu_0(A) = 0; \quad A \in \mathcal{P}(\Omega),$$

or

$$\vec{\mu}_1 = \mathbf{1},$$
$$\vec{\mu}_0 = \mathbf{0}.$$

An unary logical operation on a structural vector:
(a) A structural vector of the negation of a logical formula φ:

$$\vec{\mu}_{\bar{\varphi}} = \overline{\vec{\mu}}_\varphi = \vec{\mu}(\mathbf{1}) - \vec{\mu}_\varphi,$$

or the components of a structural vector of the negation of a logical formula:

$$\overline{\mu}_\varphi(A) = 1 - \mu_\varphi(A); \quad A \in \mathcal{P}(\Omega).$$

A structural vector of the negation of a logical formula is equal to the negation of a structural vector of that logical formula.

A structural vector $\vec{\mu}_{\varphi_1 \odot \varphi_2}$ of a binary operation on two logical formulae φ_1 and φ_2 is equal to a binary logical operation on these two structural vectors $\vec{\mu}_{\varphi_1}$ and $\vec{\mu}_{\varphi_2}$:

$$\vec{\mu}_{\varphi_1 \odot \varphi_2} = \vec{\mu}_{\varphi_1} \odot \vec{\mu}_{\varphi_2},$$

or in scalar form:

$$\mu_{\varphi_1 \odot \varphi_2}(A) = \mu_{\varphi_1}(A) \odot \mu_{\varphi_2}(A), \quad A \in \mathcal{P}(\Omega),$$

where: $\odot \in \{\Leftarrow\!\!\!\mid, \mapsto, \veebar, \wedge, \vee, \Rightarrow, \Leftarrow, \Leftrightarrow, \overline{\wedge}, \overline{\vee}\}.$

Definition 6. The principle of structural functionality - means that the structure (structural function and/or structural vector) of compound logical formula $\Diamond(\varphi_1, ..., \varphi_n)$depends only on the structures of the components $\varphi_1, ..., \varphi_n$.

$$\mu_{\Diamond(\varphi_1,...,\varphi_n)}(A) = \Diamond\left(\mu_{\varphi_1}(A), ..., \mu_{\varphi_n}(A)\right), \quad A \in \mathcal{P}(\Omega),$$

or in vector form:

$$\vec{\mu}_{\Diamond(\varphi_1,...,\varphi_n)} = \Diamond\left(\vec{\mu}_{\varphi_1}, ..., \vec{\mu}_{\varphi_n}\right).$$

The structures of elementary variables are determined by definition of structural function of elementary variables.

Since truth values of {0,1}-valued logical function (classical logic) are determined by truth table and structure of corresponding logical formula coincides follows as a consequence the famous principle of classical logic truth functionality. Truth functionality is not fundamental property in general case (theory of probability for example).

Definition 7. $\vec{\mu}(n)$ is a set of structural vectors of all n-ary logical formulae $\varphi(n)$:

$$\vec{\mu}(n) = \left\{\vec{\mu}_{\varphi_i} \mid \varphi_i \in \varphi(n)\right\}; \quad n \in N_0.$$

The dimension of a structural vector of n-ary logical function is 2^n, and the number of n-ary 0-1 structural vectors is 2^{2^n}.

Boolean algebra $\mathcal{B}_\mu$ on a set $\vec{\mu}(n)$ of all 0-1 structural vectors of n-ary logical formulae is defined as the quadruple:

$$\mathcal{B}_\mu = \langle \vec{\mu}(n), \vee, \wedge, - \rangle$$

where $\vee, \wedge$ are binary operations and $-$ is an unary operation on $\vec{\mu}(n)$ for which the following properties are satisfied.

(B1)	$\vec{\mu}_{\varphi} \vee \vec{\mu}_{\varphi} = \vec{\mu}_{\varphi}$
	$\vec{\mu}_{\varphi} \wedge \vec{\mu}_{\varphi} = \vec{\mu}_{\varphi}$
(B2)	$\vec{\mu}_{\varphi_1} \vee \vec{\mu}_{\varphi_2} = \vec{\mu}_{\varphi_2} \vee \vec{\mu}_{\varphi_1}$
	$\vec{\mu}_{\varphi_1} \wedge \vec{\mu}_{\varphi_2} = \vec{\mu}_{\varphi_2} \wedge \vec{\mu}_{\varphi_1}$
(B3)	$(\vec{\mu}_{\varphi_1} \vee \vec{\mu}_{\varphi_2}) \vee \vec{\mu}_{\varphi_3} = \vec{\mu}_{\varphi_1} \vee (\vec{\mu}_{\varphi_2} \vee \vec{\mu}_{\varphi_3})$
	$(\vec{\mu}_{\varphi_1} \wedge \vec{\mu}_{\varphi_2}) \wedge \vec{\mu}_{\varphi_3} = \vec{\mu}_{\varphi_1} \wedge (\vec{\mu}_{\varphi_2} \wedge \vec{\mu}_{\varphi_3})$
(B4)	$\vec{\mu}_{\varphi_1} \vee (\vec{\mu}_{\varphi_1} \wedge \vec{\mu}_{\varphi_2}) = \vec{\mu}_{\varphi_1}$
	$\vec{\mu}_{\varphi_1} \wedge (\vec{\mu}_{\varphi_1} \vee \vec{\mu}_{\varphi_2}) = \vec{\mu}_{\varphi_1}$
(B5)	$\vec{\mu}_{\varphi_1} \wedge (\vec{\mu}_{\varphi_2} \vee \vec{\mu}_{\varphi_3}) = (\vec{\mu}_{\varphi_1} \wedge \vec{\mu}_{\varphi_2}) \vee (\vec{\mu}_{\varphi_1} \wedge \vec{\mu}_{\varphi_3})$
	$\vec{\mu}_{\varphi_1} \vee (\vec{\mu}_{\varphi_2} \wedge \vec{\mu}_{\varphi_3}) = (\vec{\mu}_{\varphi_1} \vee \vec{\mu}_{\varphi_2}) \wedge (\vec{\mu}_{\varphi_1} \vee \vec{\mu}_{\varphi_3})$
(B6)	$\vec{\mu}_{\varphi} \vee \vec{\mu}_{\mathbf{0}} = \vec{\mu}_{\varphi}; \quad \vec{\mu}_{\varphi} \vee \vec{\mu}_{\mathbf{1}} = \vec{\mu}_{\mathbf{1}}$
	$\vec{\mu}_{\varphi} \wedge \vec{\mu}_{\mathbf{1}} = \vec{\mu}_{\varphi}; \quad \vec{\mu}_{\varphi} \wedge \vec{\mu}_{\mathbf{0}} = \vec{\mu}_{\mathbf{0}}$
(B7)	$\vec{\mu}_{\varphi} \vee \vec{\mu}_{\overline{\varphi}} = \vec{\mu}_{\mathbf{1}}$; or $\vec{\mu}_{\varphi} \vee \overline{\vec{\mu}}_{\varphi} = \vec{\mu}_{\mathbf{1}}$
	$\vec{\mu}_{\varphi} \wedge \vec{\mu}_{\overline{\varphi}} = \vec{\mu}_{\mathbf{0}}$; or $\vec{\mu}_{\varphi} \wedge \overline{\vec{\mu}}_{\varphi} = \vec{\mu}_{\mathbf{0}}$
	$\vec{\mu}_{\overline{\mathbf{1}}} = \vec{\mu}_{\mathbf{0}}$; or $\overline{\vec{\mu}}_{\mathbf{1}} = \vec{\mu}_{\mathbf{0}}$
(B8)	$\vec{\mu}_{\overline{\overline{\varphi}}} = \vec{\mu}_{\varphi}$; or $\overline{\overline{\vec{\mu}}}_{\varphi} = \vec{\mu}_{\varphi}$
(B9)	$\overline{\vec{\mu}_{\varphi_1} \vee \vec{\mu}_{\varphi_2}} = \vec{\mu}_{\overline{\varphi_1}} \wedge \vec{\mu}_{\overline{\varphi_2}}$ $\quad \overline{\vec{\mu}_{\varphi_1} \vee \vec{\mu}_{\varphi_2}} = \overline{\vec{\mu}}_{\varphi_1} \wedge \overline{\vec{\mu}}_{\varphi_2}$
	$\overline{\vec{\mu}_{\varphi_1} \wedge \vec{\mu}_{\varphi_2}} = \vec{\mu}_{\overline{\varphi_1}} \vee \vec{\mu}_{\overline{\varphi_2}}$; or $\overline{\vec{\mu}_{\varphi_1} \wedge \vec{\mu}_{\varphi_2}} = \overline{\vec{\mu}}_{\varphi_1} \vee \overline{\vec{\mu}}_{\varphi_2}$

(B1) Idempotence, (B2) Commutativity, (B3) Associativity, (B4) Absorption, (B5) Distributivity, (B6) Universal bounds, (B7) Complementarity, (B8) Involution and (B9) Dualization.

Corollary 2. *All properties (B1)-(B9) are valid for 0-1 structural functions as components of structural vectors.*

Properties (B1)-(B4) are common to all lattices. Boolean algebras are therefore lattices that are distributive (B5), bounded (B6), and complemented (B7)-(B9).

¿From classical Boolean logic it follows that a structural vector $\vec{\mu}_{\varphi}$ of any n-ary logical formula φ can be represented by structural vectors $\vec{\mu}_{a_i}$ of atomic symbols $i = 1, ..., n$; or their negation in normal forms:

(a) Disjunctive normal form of structural vector:

$$\vec{\mu}_{\varphi} = \bigvee_{A \in \mathcal{P}(\Omega)} \mu_{\varphi}(A) \bigwedge_{a_i \in A} \vec{\mu}_{a_i} \bigwedge_{a_j \in A^c} \vec{\mu}_{\overline{a}_j}$$

(b) Conjunctive normal form of structural vector:

$$\vec{\mu}_{\varphi} = \overline{\bigwedge_{A \in \mathcal{P}(\Omega)} \mu_{\varphi}(A) \bigvee_{a_i \in A} \vec{\mu}_{\overline{a_i}} \bigvee_{a_j \in A^c} \vec{\mu}_{a_j}}.$$

Every conjunctive normal form is dual to a corresponding disjunctive normal form:

$$\bigvee_{A\in\mathcal{P}(\Omega)} \mu_\varphi(A) \bigwedge_{a_i\in A} \vec{\mu}_{a_i} \bigwedge_{a_j\in A^c} \vec{\mu}_{\bar{a}_j} = \overline{\bigwedge_{A\in\mathcal{P}(\Omega)} \mu_\varphi(A) \bigvee_{a_i\in A} \vec{\mu}_{\overline{a_i}} \bigvee_{a_j\in A^c} \vec{\mu}_{a_j}}.$$

Every structural vector is equivalent to a corresponding conjunctive or disjunctive normal form, and can be reduced to those.

2.2 Structural function and structural vector of pseudo-logical formula

A pseudo-Boolean formula $\sigma\varphi$ is linear convex combination of logical formulae. Here we present a structural function of a n-ary pseudo-Boolean logical formula. A pseudo-Boolean logical n-ary function $e\sigma\varphi : \{0,1\}^n \to [0,1]$, of pseudo-logical formula $\sigma\varphi$, is defined as:

$$e\sigma\varphi(a_1,...,a_n) = \sum_{A\in\mathcal{P}(\Omega)} e\sigma\varphi(e_A) \prod_{a_i\in A} a_i \prod_{a_j\in A^c} \bar{a}_j.$$

$$\Omega = \{a_1,...,a_n\} \subset \{0,1\}^n$$

$$e\sigma\varphi(e_A) \in [0,1]; \quad A \in \mathcal{P}(\Omega).$$

Every pseudo-Boolean n-ary function $e\sigma\varphi(a_1,...,a_n)$ can be represented as a linear convex combination of n-ary logical functions $e\varphi_i(a_1,...,a_n)$.

A structural function of a pseudo-Boolean formula and its generalization is determined by the truth-values of a pseudo-Boolean function for characteristic vectors.

Definition 8. A structural function of pseudo-logical formula $\sigma\varphi$ is a set function $\mu_{\sigma\varphi} : \mathcal{P}(\Omega) \to [0,1]$; such that for every $A \in \mathcal{P}(\Omega)$

$$\mu_{\sigma\varphi}(A) = e\sigma\varphi(e_A),$$

where: $e_A = ((e_A)_i) \subset \{0,1\}^{|\Omega|}$ is the characteristic vector of $A \in \mathcal{P}(\Omega)$ and components $(e_A)_i = 1$ if and only if $a_i \in A$ and $e\sigma\varphi$ is [0,1]-valued function of pseudo-logical (pseudo-Boolean) formula.

For defining a [0,1]-valued logical function, it is valuable to define a structural vector of pseudo-logical formula.

Definition 9. A structural vector $\vec{\mu}_{\sigma\varphi}$ of a pseudo-Boolean formula $\sigma\varphi$, has components equal to the values of pseudo-structural function of that pseudo-logical formula in a given order (lexicographic or modified lexicographic, for example).

Every structural vector of pseudo-logical formula $\sigma\varphi = \sum \lambda_i \varphi_i$; $\sum_i \lambda_i = 1, \quad \lambda_i \geq 0$ can be represented as a linear convex combination of logical (0-1) structural vectors:

$$\vec{\mu}_{\sigma\varphi} = \sum_i \lambda_i \vec{\mu}_{\varphi_i}$$

$$\sum_i \lambda_i = 1, \quad \lambda_i \geq 0.$$

In a general case a component in a linear convex combination can be a null-vector too.

Geometrically the structural vectors of logical formulae are the $2^{2^{|\Omega|}}$ vertices of structural hyper-cube $[0,1]^{2^{|\Omega|}}$ which is a structural vector space. All other vectors of structural hyper-cube are structural vectors of pseudo-logical formulae.

Unary logical operations on a structural vector of pseudo-logical formula: a structural vector of negation:

$$\vec{\mu}_{\overline{\sigma\varphi}} = \overline{\vec{\mu}}_{\sigma\varphi} = \vec{\mu}(\mathbf{1}) - \vec{\mu}_{\sigma\varphi},$$

or components of a structural vector of negation of pseudo-logical function:

$$\overline{\mu}_{\sigma\varphi}(A) = (1 - \mu_{\sigma\varphi}(A)) \in [0,1]; \quad A \in \mathcal{P}(\Omega).$$

Binary logical operations $\odot \in \{\Leftarrow\!\!\!|, |\!\!\!\Rightarrow, \veebar, \wedge, \vee, \Rightarrow, \Leftarrow, \Leftrightarrow, \overline{\wedge}, \overline{\vee}\}$ on structural vectors:

(a) A structural vector of binary logical operation on a logical structural vector $\vec{\mu}_{\sigma\varphi}$ of pseudo-logical formula $\sigma\varphi$ and 0-1 structural vector $\vec{\mu}_{\varphi}$ of logical formula φ :

$$\begin{aligned} \vec{\mu}_{\sigma\varphi\odot\varphi} &= \vec{\mu}_{\sigma\varphi} \odot \vec{\mu}_{\varphi} \\ &= \sum_i \lambda_i \vec{\mu}_{\varphi_i} \odot \vec{\mu}_{\varphi} \\ &= \sum_i \lambda_i \vec{\mu}_{\varphi_i \odot \varphi} \end{aligned}$$

$$\sum_i \lambda_i = 1, \quad \lambda_i \geq 0.$$

(b) A pseudo-structural vector of binary logical operation of two pseudo-logical formulae

$$\begin{aligned} \vec{\mu}_{\sigma\varphi_1 \odot \sigma\varphi_2} &= \vec{\mu}_{\sigma\varphi_1} \odot \vec{\mu}_{\sigma\varphi_2} \\ &= \sum_i \lambda_i \vec{\mu}_{\varphi_{1,i}} \odot \sum_j \lambda_j \vec{\mu}_{\varphi_{2,j}} \\ &= \sum_i \sum_j \lambda_i \lambda_j \vec{\mu}_{\varphi_{1,i}} \odot \vec{\mu}_{\varphi_{2,j}} \end{aligned}$$

$$= \sum_i \sum_j \lambda_i \lambda_j \vec{\mu}_{\varphi_{1,i} \odot \varphi_{2,j}};$$

$$\sum_i \lambda_i = 1, \quad \sum_j \lambda_j = 1, \quad \lambda_i, \lambda_j \geq 0.$$

[0,1]-valued logics based on logical structures completely compatible to classical $\{0,1\}$-valued logic are given in [10]. An important class of [0,1]-valued logical functions based on logical structure is a logical Choquet integral.

3 Logical Choquet integral

The known definition of a discrete Choquet integral [1] for a fuzzy measure [11], here is redefined for a structure of logical and/or pseudo-logical formula - a general measure.

Definition 10. Let μ_φ $(\mu_{\sigma\varphi})$be a logical structure of logic formulae φ (pseudo-logical formula $\sigma\varphi$) on $\Omega \subset [0,1]^n$. The logical discrete Choquet integral with respect to μ_φ is defined by

$$C\mu_\varphi(a_1, ..., a_n) := \sum_{i=1}^{n+1} \left(a_{(i)} - a_{(i-1)}\right) \mu_\varphi\left(A_{(i)}\right)$$

where: $\cdot_{(i)}$indicates that the indices have been permuted so that $0 \leq a_{(1)} \leq ... \leq a_{(n)}$, and
$A_{(i)} := \left\{a_{(i)}, ..., a_{(n)}\right\}$,
$A_{(n+1)} := \emptyset; \quad \Rightarrow \mu\left(A_{(n+1)}\right) = \mu(\emptyset)$, and
$a_{(0)} = 0$ and $a_{(n+1)} = 1$.

A logical representation of discrete Choquet integral for a general measure - structure of logical formula:

Proposition 1. *A logical discrete Choquet integral for a structural function μ_φ ($\mu_{\sigma\varphi}$) of logical formula φ (pseudo-logical formula $\sigma\varphi$) is equal to the corresponding logical function $L\mu_\varphi(a_1, ..., a_n)$ (pseudo-logical function $L\mu_{\sigma\varphi}(a_1, ..., a_n)$):*

$$C\mu_\varphi(a_1, ..., a_2) = L\mu_\varphi(a_1, ..., a_2)$$
$$C\mu_{\sigma\varphi}(a_1, ..., a_2) = L\mu_{\sigma\varphi}(a_1, ..., a_2)$$

Example 5. Equivalent logical representations of logical discrete Choquet integrals for the following logical structures

	$\vec{\mu}_{a_1 \wedge a_2}$	$\vec{\mu}_{a_1 \Rightarrow a_2}$	$\vec{\mu}_{a_2 \Rightarrow a_1}$	$\vec{\mu}_{\overline{a_1 \vee a_2}}$
μ_0	0	0	0	1
μ_1	0	0	1	0
μ_2	0	1	0	0
$\mu_{1,2}$	1	0	0	0

are

$$C\mu_{a_1 \wedge a_2}(a_1, a_2) = a_1 \wedge a_2$$

$$C\mu_{a_1, \Rightarrow a_2}(a_1, a_2) = a_1 \Rightarrow a_2$$

$$C\mu_{a_2, \Rightarrow a_1}(a_1, a_2) = a_2 \Rightarrow a_1$$

$$C\mu_{\overline{a_1 \vee a_2}}(a_1, a_2) = \overline{a_1 \vee a_2}$$

respectively.

Since all four binary logical formulae from the previous example have orts for structural vectors it follows that a structural vector of any binary logical and/or pseudo-logical formula can be represented as their linear combination:

$$\vec{\mu}_\varphi = \mu_\varphi(\emptyset)\,\vec{\mu}_{\overline{a_1 \vee a_2}} + \mu_\varphi(\{a_1\})\,\vec{\mu}_{a_2, \Rightarrow a_1} + \mu_\varphi(\{a_2\})\,\vec{\mu}_{a_1, \Rightarrow a_2} + \mu_\varphi(\{a_1, a_2\})\,\vec{\mu}_{a_1 \wedge a_2}$$

And as a consequence:

$$C\mu_\varphi(a_1, a_2) = \mu_\varphi(\emptyset)\,C\mu_{\overline{a_1 \vee a_2}}(a_1, a_2) + \mu_\varphi(\{a_1\})\,C\mu_{a_2, \Rightarrow a_1}(a_1, a_2) + \mu_\varphi(\{a_2\})\,C\mu_{a_1, \Rightarrow a_2}(a_1, a_2) + \mu_\varphi(\{a_1, a_2\})\,C\mu_{a_1 \wedge a_2}(a_1, a_2).$$

In the following proposition is given the logical representation of logical Choquet integral in a general case:

Proposition 2. *A logical representation of logical discrete Choquet integral of n attributes as a function of structural function - a general measure is:*

$$C\mu_\varphi(a_1, ..., a_n) = \mu_\varphi(\emptyset)\,C\mu_{\overline{\bigvee_{a_i \in \Omega} a_i}}(a_1, ..., a_n) +$$

$$+ \sum_{A \subset \Omega} \mu_\varphi(A)\,C\mu_{\left[\left(\bigvee_{a_j \in \Omega \setminus A} a_j\right) \Rightarrow \left(\bigwedge_{a_i \in A} a_i\right)\right]}(a_1, ..., a_n) +$$

$$+\mu_\varphi(\Omega)\,C\mu_{\bigwedge_{a_i \in \Omega} a_i}(a_1, ..., a_n).$$

or

$$C\mu_\varphi(a_1, ..., a_n) = \mu_\varphi(\emptyset)\,\overline{\bigvee_{a_i \in \Omega} a_i} +$$

$$+ \sum_{A \subset \Omega} \mu_\varphi(A)\left[\left(\bigvee_{a_j \in \Omega \setminus A} a_j\right) \Rightarrow \left(\bigwedge_{a_i \in A} a_i\right)\right] +$$

$$+\mu_\varphi(\Omega)\bigwedge_{a_i \in \Omega} a_i.$$

This logical representation shows clearly the meaning of a logical structure and, in a special case, a fuzzy measure [11] too.

The compound n-ary logical Choquet integral of two n-ary logical functions $C\mu_{\varphi_1}(a_1, ..., a_n)$ and $C\mu_{\varphi_2}(a_1, ..., a_n)$ by some binary logical operation $\otimes$ is:

$$C\mu_{\varphi_1 \otimes \varphi}(a_1, ..., a_n) = C\mu_{\varphi_1}(a_1, ..., a_n) \otimes C\mu_{\varphi_2}(a_1, ..., a_n).$$

Example 6. (A) The law of the excluded middle is valid in general ([0,1]-valued) case:

$$\begin{aligned} C\mu_{\varphi}(a_1, ..., a_n) \vee C\mu_{\overline{\varphi}}(a_1, ..., a_n) &= C\mu_{\varphi \vee \overline{\varphi}}(a_1, ..., a_n) \\ &= C\mu_{\mathbf{1}}(a_1, ..., a_n) \\ &\equiv 1 \end{aligned}$$

(B) The contradiction law (dual to the law of the excluded middle) is valid in general case too:

$$\begin{aligned} C\mu_{\varphi}(a_1, ..., a_n) \wedge C\mu_{\overline{\varphi}}(a_1, ..., a_n) &= C\mu_{\varphi \wedge \overline{\varphi}}(a_1, ..., a_n) \\ &= C\mu_{\mathbf{0}}(a_1, ..., a_n) \\ &\equiv 0 \end{aligned}$$

4 Conclusion

The structure - structural function and/or structural vector of logical and/or pseudo-logical formula is introduced. The structural function of n-ary logical formula is a 0-1 set function. Structural 0-1 vector of logical formula has as components the values of its structural function in a given order. The structure of logical formula is its fundamental and unique characteristic invariant to its functional realization ({0,1}-valued, many-valued and/or [0,1]-valued logical function).

The set of all n-ary logical structures (structural vectors) forms Boolean algebra. The the fundamental principle of structural functionality for {0,1}-valued, many-valued and/or [0,1]-valued logic follows as a consequence. The principle of structural functionality - means that the structure (structural function and/or structural vector) of compound logical formula depends only on the structures of the components. Since the truth values of {0,1}-valued logical function (classical logic) and the structure of corresponding logical formula coincide the principle truth functionality for classical logic follows as a consequence but not as the fundamental principle in general case.

A logical discrete Choquet integral is defined as [0,1]-valued logical and pseudo-logical function for AND operator defined as Min function. [0,1]-valued logic - compatible with classical (Boolean) logic - based on structures of logical formulae is given in [10].

The application of the logical discrete Choquet integral to MADM, analysis of similarity, data mining, reliability analyses and multi-agent systems will be the subject of a forthcoming paper.

References

1. G. Choquet, Theory of capacities, Ann. Inst. Fourier 5 (1953) 131-295.
2. D. Dubois, H. Prade, Possibility Theory, Plenum Press, New York, 1988.
3. S. Gottwald, A Treatise on Many - Valued Logic, Research Studies Press, UK, (2001)
4. G. Klir, T. Folger, Fuzzy Sets, Uncertainty, and Information, Prentice-Hall, Englewood Cliffs, NJ. 1988.
5. P.Hajek, Metamatematics of Fuzzy Logic, Kluwer, (1998)
6. T. Murofushi, M. Sugeno, An interpretation of fuzzy measure and the Choquet integral as an integral with respect to fuzzy measure, Fuzzy Sets and Systems 29 (1989) 201-227.
7. D. Radojević, Logical interpretation of discrete Choquet integral defined by general measure, International Journal of Uncertainty, Fuzzines and Knowledge-Based Systems, Vol. 7, No. 6 (1999) 577-588.
8. D. Radojević, Logical measure of continual logical function, 8th Int. Conf. IPMU - Information Processing and Management of Uncertainty in Knowledge-based Systems, Madrid, (2000) 574-581.
9. D. Radojević, The logical representation of discrete Choquet integral, JORBEL - The Belgian Journal of Operations Research, Statistics and Computer Science, Vol. 38 (2-3), (1998), 67-89.
10. D. Radojević, [0,1]-valued logic: a natural generalization of Boolean logic, YUJOR - Yugoslav Journal of Operational Research Vol 10, Number 2,(2000) 85-216,
11. M. Sugeno, Theory of fuzzy integrals and its applications, Thesis, Tokyo Institute of Technology, 1974..
12. L.A. Zadeh, Similarity Relations and Fuzzy Orderings, Information Sciences, 3 (1971) 177-200.

FSC
www.fsc.org
MIX
Papier | Fördert gute Waldnutzung
FSC® C083411

Kolibri 360 GmbH
Ferdinand-Jühlke-Straße 7
99095 Erfurt, Deutschland
produktsicherheit@kolibri360.de